D1037031

Glencoe Spanish 3

¡Buen viaje!

Conrad J. Schmitt
Protase E. Woodford

New York, New York Columbus, Ohio Chicago, Illinois Woodland Hills, California

The McGraw·Hill Companies

Send all inquiries to:
Glencoe/McGraw-Hill
8787 Orion Place
Columbus, OH 43240-4027

ISBN: 978-0-07-879142-0
MHID: 0-07-879142-1

Printed in the United States of America.

3 4 5 6 7 8 9 10 079/055 13 12 11 10 09 08

About the Authors

Conrad J. Schmitt

Conrad J. Schmitt received his B.A. degree magna cum laude from Montclair State College, Upper Montclair, NJ. He received his M.A. from Middlebury College, Middlebury, VT. He did additional graduate work at Seton Hall University and New York University. Mr. Schmitt has taught Spanish and French at the elementary, junior, and senior high school levels, as well as at the undergraduate and graduate levels. In addition, he has traveled extensively throughout Spain, Central and South America, and the Caribbean.

Protase E. Woodford

Protase "Woody" Woodford has taught Spanish at all levels from elementary through graduate school. At Educational Testing Service in Princeton, NJ, he was Director of Test Development, Director of Language Programs, Director of International Testing Programs, and Director of the Puerto Rico Office. He has served as a consultant to the United Nations Secretariat, UNESCO, the Organization of American States, the U.S. Office of Education, and many ministries of education in Asia, Latin America, and the Middle East.

For the Parent or Guardian

We are excited that your child continues to study Spanish. Foreign language study provides many benefits for students in addition to the ability to communicate in another language. Students who study another language improve their first language skills. They become more aware of the world around them and they learn to appreciate diversity.

You can help your child be successful in his or her study of Spanish even if you are not familiar with that language. Encourage your child to talk to you about the places where Spanish is spoken. Engage in conversations about current events in those places. The section of their Glencoe Spanish book called **El mundo hispanohablante** on pages xxiii–xxxv may serve as a reference for you and your child. In addition, you will find information about the geography of the Spanish-speaking world and links to foreign newspapers at **glencoe.com**.

The methodology employed in the Glencoe Spanish books is logical and leads students step by step through their study of the language. In this third level book, emphasis on reading in Spanish increases as students advance in their study of the language. Consistent instruction and practice are essential for learning a foreign language. You can help by encouraging your child to review vocabulary each day. As he or she progresses through the text, you may wish to refer to the reading skills chart on pages xxxvi–xxxix to help your child improve his or her reading skills in Spanish. If you have Internet access, encourage your child to practice using the activities, games, and practice quizzes at **glencoe.com**.

¡Buen viaje!

Contenido

Capítulo 1

Objetivos

In this chapter you will:

- learn about the geography, history, and culture of Spain
- review how to express past actions
- discuss taking a trip to Spain
- read and discuss newspaper articles about the metro in Barcelona and immigrants arriving in Spain
- learn to refer to specific things
- learn to express ownership

España

Lección 1 Cultura

Lección 2 Conversación

Lección 3 Periodismo

Literatura española

Capítulo 2

Objetivos

In this chapter you will:

- learn about the geography, history, and culture of Ecuador, Peru, and Bolivia
- review how to describe habitual past actions
- discuss a robbery
- review how to talk about past events
- read and discuss newspaper articles about a volcano eruption in Ecuador and a centenarian in Peru
- learn to express what may or may not take place
- learn to express necessity and possibility; wishes, preferences, and demands

Países andinos Ecuador, Perú, Bolivia

Lección 3 Periodismo

Literatura de los países andinos

Capítulo 

El Cono sur Chile, Argentina, Paraguay, Uruguay

Objetivos

In this chapter you will:

- learn about the geography, history, and culture of Chile, Argentina, Paraguay, and Uruguay
- review how to state location and origin; characteristics and conditions
- discuss shopping for shoes and clothes
- review how to express surprise, interest, annoyance; likes, dislikes, and needs
- review how to express affirmative and negative ideas
- read and discuss newspaper articles about "acceptable" attire at work and leaving home to go to college
- learn to express emotions, doubt, or uncertainty

Lección 3 Periodismo

Literatura de los países del Cono sur

Capítulo  La América Central

Objetivos

In this chapter you will:

- ❖ **learn about the geography, history, and cultures of the Central American countries**
- ❖ **review how to express future events; conditions**
- ❖ **discuss finances**
- ❖ **review how to refer to people and things already mentioned**
- ❖ **read and discuss social announcements and human interest articles as they appear in newspapers**
- ❖ **learn to express emotions and possibilities about past events**
- ❖ **learn to use certain time expressions such as en cuanto, hasta que**

Lección 3 Periodismo

Literatura centroamericana

Capítulo 5

Objetivos

In this chapter you will:

- ❖ learn about the geography, history, and culture of Mexico
- ❖ review how to express what you have done recently
- ❖ review how to give commands
- ❖ discuss traveling by car in Mexico
- ❖ review how to describe actions in progress
- ❖ review how to refer to people and things already mentioned
- ❖ read and discuss articles about windsurfing and Mexican families
- ❖ learn to describe actions completed prior to other actions
- ❖ learn to express what you would have done and will have done
- ❖ learn to express indefinite ideas and the known and unknown

México

Lección 1 Cultura

Lección 2 Conversación

Lección 3 Periodismo

Contenido

Capítulo 6  El Caribe Cuba, Puerto Rico, la República Dominicana

Objetivos

In this chapter you will:

- learn about the geography, history, and culture of Cuba, Puerto Rico, and the Dominican Republic
- review how to express what people do for themselves
- review how to express reciprocal actions
- discuss an experience in a restaurant
- review how to make comparisons
- read and discuss newspaper articles about sports and a special education program
- learn to express *although* and *perhaps*
- learn to express opinions and feelings about what has or had happened
- learn to discuss contrary-to-fact situations

Lección 3 Periodismo

Capítulo 7

Objetivos

In this chapter you will:

- learn about the geography, history, and culture of Venezuela and Colombia
- review shortened forms of adjectives
- review uses of articles
- discuss a museum visit and a show
- review prepositional pronouns
- read and discuss newspaper articles about teachers in Colombia and the hazards of gasoline
- learn the uses of por and para
- learn to express duration of time using hace and hacía

Venezuela y Colombia

Lección 1 Cultura

Lección 2 Conversación

Contenido

Contenido

Capítulo 8  Estados Unidos

Objetivos

In this chapter you will:

- **learn about the history and culture of Hispanics or Latinos in the United States**
- **review how to tell how actions are carried out**
- **review how to express more activities in the present and past**
- **discuss the medium of television**
- **read and discuss newspaper articles about the rise of the Hispanic or Latino population in the United States and about a storm with torrential rains and flooding**
- **learn to tell what was done or what is done in general**

Lección 3 Periodismo

Literatura hispana de Estados Unidos

Literary Companion

Handbook

Guide to Symbols

Throughout **¡Buen viaje!** you will see these symbols, or icons. They will tell you how to best use the particular part of the chapter or activity they accompany. Following is a key to help you understand these symbols.

Audio link This icon indicates material in the chapter that is recorded on CDs.

Recycling This icon indicates sections that review previously introduced material.

Paired Activity This icon indicates sections that you can practice with a partner.

Group Activity This icon indicates sections that you can practice together in groups.

Literary Companion This icon appears at the end of the chapter to let you know that there are literature selections that accompany each chapter. These selections are reflective of the geographical area you have studied in the particular chapter.

El mundo hispanohablante

El español es el idioma de más de 350 millones de personas en todo el mundo. La lengua española tuvo su origen en España. A veces se le llama cariñosamente «la lengua de Cervantes», el autor de la novela más famosa del mundo y del renombrado personaje, *Don Quijote.* Los exploradores y conquistadores españoles trajeron su idioma a las Américas en los siglos XV y XVI. El español es la lengua oficial de casi todos los países de Centro y Sudamérica. Es la lengua oficial de México y varias naciones del Caribe. El español es también la lengua de herencia de más de 40 millones de personas en Estados Unidos.

▼ España

▲ México

▲ Chile

◀ Perú

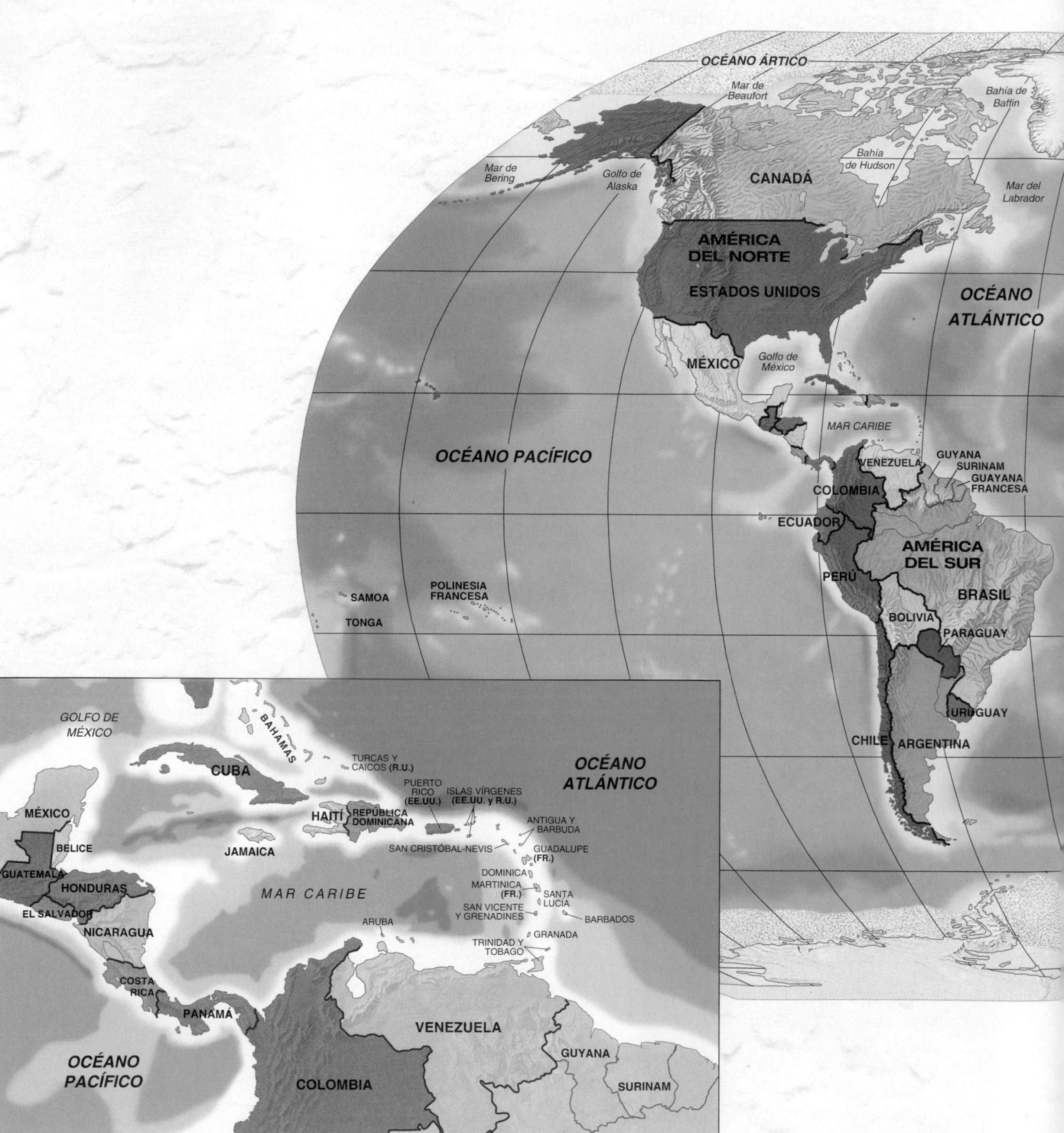

OCÉANO ÁRTICO
Mar de Beaufort
Bahía de Baffin
Mar de Bering
Golfo de Alaska
CANADÁ
Bahía de Hudson
Mar del Labrador
AMÉRICA DEL NORTE
ESTADOS UNIDOS
OCÉANO ATLÁNTICO
MÉXICO
Golfo de México
MAR CARIBE
OCÉANO PACÍFICO
VENEZUELA
GUYANA
SURINAM
GUAYANA FRANCESA
COLOMBIA
ECUADOR
AMÉRICA DEL SUR
PERÚ
BRASIL
BOLIVIA
PARAGUAY
URUGUAY
CHILE
ARGENTINA
SAMOA
TONGA
POLINESIA FRANCESA
GOLFO DE MÉXICO
BAHAMAS
TURCAS Y CAICOS (R.U.)
OCÉANO ATLÁNTICO
CUBA
PUERTO RICO (EE.UU.)
ISLAS VÍRGENES (EE.UU. y R.U.)
MÉXICO
HAITÍ
REPÚBLICA DOMINICANA
ANTIGUA Y BARBUDA
BELICE
JAMAICA
SAN CRISTÓBAL-NEVIS
GUADALUPE (FR.)
GUATEMALA
HONDURAS
DOMINICA
MARTINICA (FR.)
SANTA LUCÍA
MAR CARIBE
EL SALVADOR
SAN VICENTE Y GRENADINES
BARBADOS
NICARAGUA
ARUBA
GRANADA
TRINIDAD Y TOBAGO
COSTA RICA
PANAMÁ
VENEZUELA
GUYANA
OCÉANO PACÍFICO
COLOMBIA
SURINAM

OCÉANO ÁRTICO
Mar de Groenlandia
ISLANDIA
Mar de Noruega
Mar de Barents
Mar de Kara
Mar de Láptiev
RUSIA
ASIA
Mar del Norte
Mar de Ojotsk
EUROPA
KAZAJSTÁN
MONGOLIA
Mar Negro
GEORGIA
ARMENIA
UZBEKISTÁN
KIRGUIZISTÁN
TURKMENISTÁN
TAYIKISTÁN
TURQUÍA
CHINA
COREA DEL NORTE
Mar del Japón
JAPÓN
MELILLA
CEUTA
MARRUECOS
TÚNEZ
MAR MEDITERRÁNEO
LÍBANO
SIRIA
AZERBAIJÁN
ISRAEL
IRAK
IRÁN
AFGANISTÁN
COREA DEL SUR
JORDANIA
NEPAL
BHUTÁN
Mar de la China oriental
KUWAIT
BAHREIN
PAKISTÁN
ARGELIA
LIBIA
EGIPTO
QATAR
EMIRATOS ÁRABES UNIDOS
ARABIA SAUDITA
INDIA
OCÉANO PACÍFICO
TAIWÁN
BANGLADESH
MYANMAR
MALÍ
NÍGER
CHAD
SUDÁN
OMÁN
LAOS
Mar de la China meridional
Golfo de Bengala
ERITREA
YEMEN
TAILANDIA
FILIPINAS
MARSHALL
BURKINA FASO
NIGERIA
ÁFRICA
DJIBOUTI
VIETNAM
GHANA
BENIN
ETIOPÍA
SRI LANKA
CAMBOYA
MICRONESIA
REPÚBLICA CENTROAFRICANA
TOGO
CAMERÚN
BRUNEI
PALAU
SOMALIA
MALAYSIA
UGANDA
KENYA
MALDIVAS
KIRIBATI
GUINEA ECUATORIAL
GABÓN
RUANDA
REP. DEL CONGO
REP. DEM. DEL CONGO
SINGAPUR
NAURÚ
BURUNDI
PAPÚA-NUEVA GUINEA
SEYCHELLES
INDONESIA
SALOMÓN
TANZANIA
OCÉANO ÍNDICO
TUVALU
ISLAS COMORES
WALLIS Y FUTUNA
ANGOLA
MALAWI
ZAMBIA
MOZAMBIQUE
Mar del Coral
VANUATU
MADAGASCAR
MAURICIO
ISLAS FIJI
NAMIBIA
ZIMBABWE
REUNIÓN
BOTSWANA
AUSTRALIA
NUEVA CALEDONIA
SWAZILANDIA
SUDÁFRICA
LESOTHO
Mar de Tasmania
NUEVA ZELANDIA
ANTÁRTIDA
NORUEGA
FINLANDIA
SUECIA
ESTONIA
REINO UNIDO
IRLANDA
DINAMARCA
LETONIA
RUSIA
LITUANIA
PAÍSES BAJOS
ALEMANIA
BELARÚS
BÉLGICA
POLONIA
LUXEMBURGO
OCÉANO ATLÁNTICO
REPÚBLICA CHECA
UCRANIA
ESLOVAQUIA
FRANCIA
SUIZA
AUSTRIA
MOLDOVA
HUNGRÍA
ESLOVENIA
ANDORRA
CROACIA
RUMANIA
BOSNIA-HERZEGOVINA
PORTUGAL
ESPAÑA
MÓNACO
YUGOSLAVIA (Fed. Rep.)
Mar Negro
GEORGIA
ITALIA
BULGARIA
ALBANIA
MACEDONIA
Mar Mediterráneo
MELILLA
CEUTA
GRECIA
TURQUÍA
ÁFRICA
MALTA
CHIPRE
SIRIA
LÍBANO

El mundo hispanohablante

España

CAPITAL
Madrid

POBLACIÓN
40.217.000

NOTAS NOTABLES

Las verdes colinas de Galicia, los dorados campos de Castilla y los pueblos blancos de Andalucía tanto como las áreas industriales de Cataluña y el País Vasco pertenecen todos a la bella España. En diferentes épocas, tierra de íberos, cartagineses, romanos, celtas y moros, España es la cuna de la lengua española, lengua de naciones en los cinco continentes. Madrid, en pleno centro del país es un importante centro cultural de Europa.

México

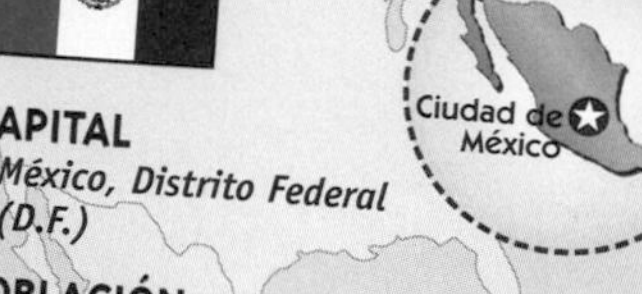

CAPITAL
México, Distrito Federal (D.F.)

POBLACIÓN
104.908.000

NOTAS NOTABLES

Precioso México comparte la frontera con Estados Unidos. Esta magnífica nación de herencia azteca, maya y española es un país de contrastes: ciudades cosmopolitas como la Ciudad de México; centros industriales como Monterrey; pintorescos pueblos como Taxco y San Miguel de Allende; famosísimas playas como Acapulco y Cancún e impresionantes vestigios de civilizaciones precolombinas en Chichén Itzá y Tulum.

Estados Unidos

CAPITAL
Washington, DC

POBLACIÓN
290.343.000

NOTAS NOTABLES

La influencia española y mexicana ha sido notable en el sudoeste de Estados Unidos desde hace generaciones. Más reciente ha sido la difusión de las culturas hispanas a todas las áreas del país. Los que han llegado recientemente del Caribe, Centro y Sudamérica traen consigo su lengua, sus tradiciones, música y cocina, agregándolas a la riquísima diversidad de este país multicultural. Hoy se oye hablar español en Nueva York, Chicago, Denver y Minneapolis igual que en Miami, El Paso, Santa Fe y Los Ángeles.

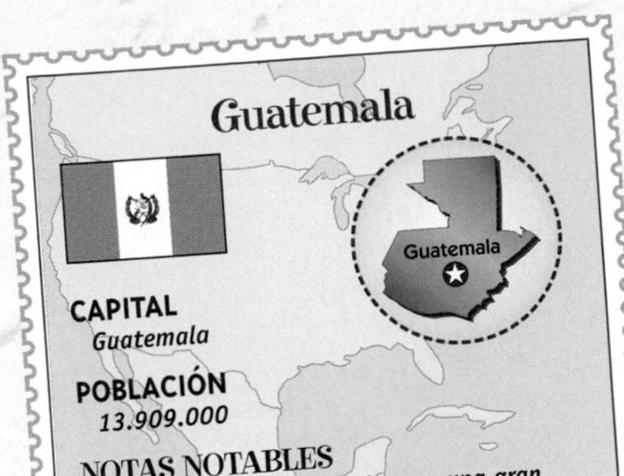

CAPITAL
Guatemala

POBLACIÓN
13.909.000

NOTAS NOTABLES
Guatemala, país de verdor con una gran población indígena—descendientes de los mayas. Las ruinas de magníficas ciudades cubiertas de hierbas nos hablan de una civilización que duró unos dos mil años y cuya decadencia todavía no se explica. Guatemala es hermosa con sus volcanes, montañas, selvas y pintorescos pueblos y aldeas como Antigua, Panajachel y Chichicastenango.

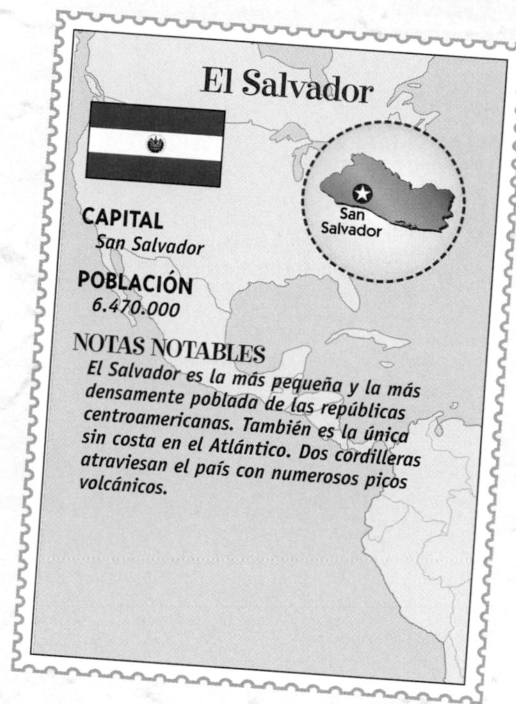

El mundo hispanohablante

Costa Rica

CAPITAL
San José

POBLACIÓN
3.896.000

NOTAS NOTABLES

Para muchos, Costa Rica es un lugar muy especial. Los «ticos» son serenos, atentos y amistosos. Costa Rica no tiene ejército y se enorgullece de tener más profesores que policías. Tiene soleadas playas en el Pacífico, selvas tropicales en la costa del Caribe, ciudades cosmopolitas como San José, montañas altas y bellos valles. Costa Rica es un paraíso para el turista y hogar para muchos expatriados norteamericanos.

Panamá

CAPITAL
Panamá

POBLACIÓN
2.961.000

NOTAS NOTABLES

Panamá es un país de variedades—variedad de razas, costumbres y bellezas naturales. Es un país de bosques tropicales, montañas, preciosas playas, excelente pesca, lagos pintorescos, ríos y dos océanos, y una maravilla de ingeniería—el Canal de Panamá. Panamá es también el mayor centro financiero de Latinoamérica. ¡Todo esto en sólo 77.432 kilómetros cuadrados!

Cuba

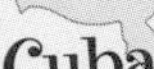

CAPITAL
La Habana

POBLACIÓN
11.263.000

NOTAS NOTABLES

La Habana, la capital de Cuba, es famosa por su bellísima arquitectura colonial. Esta exuberante isla, cerca de la Florida, es uno de los mayores productores de caña de azúcar en el mundo. El gobierno de Fidel Castro ha estado en poder desde el derrocamiento del dictador Fulgencio Batista en 1959.

La República Dominicana

CAPITAL
Santo Domingo

POBLACIÓN
8.716.000

NOTAS NOTABLES

La República Dominicana comparte la isla de La Española con Haití. La universidad más antigua de nuestro hemisferio es la Universidad de Santo Domingo, fundada en la ciudad de Santo Domingo. Los dominicanos son apasionados fanáticos del béisbol. Este relativamente pequeño país ha contribuido gran número de estrellas de las Grandes Ligas.

Puerto Rico

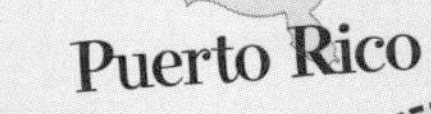

CAPITAL
San Juan

POBLACIÓN
3.886.000

NOTAS NOTABLES

Los puertorriqueños con gran afecto llaman su isla «La isla del encanto». Estado Libre Asociado de Estados Unidos, Puerto Rico es una isla de profusa vegetación tropical con playas en las costas del Atlántico y el Caribe, preciosas montañas en el interior, y bosques tropicales. Sólo en Puerto Rico vive el querido coquí—una ranita muy tímida que no deja que nadie la vea.

Venezuela

CAPITAL
Caracas

POBLACIÓN
24.655.000

NOTAS NOTABLES

Venezuela es el nombre que los exploradores españoles le dieron al país en 1499 cuando encontraron pueblos construidos sobre las aguas y donde los indígenas comerciaban en canoas. Estos canales y vías fluviales les recordaban a Venecia, Italia. Caracas es una gran ciudad cosmopolita de rascacielos rodeada de montañas y metida en un angosto valle de nueve millas de largo. El Salto del Ángel en el sur del país es el salto más alto del mundo a una altura de 3.212 pies con una caída ininterrumpida de 2.638 pies.

Colombia

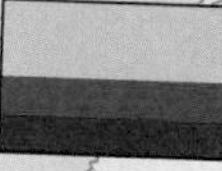

CAPITAL
Bogotá

POBLACIÓN
41.662.000

NOTAS NOTABLES

Colombia cubre un territorio de montañas, selvas y llanuras de más de 440.000 millas cuadradas. En el centro del país, en un valle andino, está Bogotá a 8.640 pies sobre el nivel del mar. En la costa caribeña en el norte hay preciosas playas; en el sur se encuentran selvas y el puerto de Leticia que queda en el río Amazonas.

Ecuador

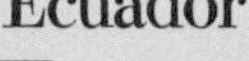

CAPITAL
Quito

POBLACIÓN
13.710.000

NOTAS NOTABLES

Ecuador deriva su nombre del ecuador, la línea ecuatorial que atraviesa el país. Pasando por el centro hay dos cordilleras andinas con magníficos volcanes. Entre las cordilleras está el valle central donde reside la mitad de la población. Y allí está la capital, Quito, bella ciudad colonial. Las islas Galápagos con su increíble fauna, pertenecen a Ecuador.

Perú

CAPITAL
Lima

POBLACIÓN
28.410.000

NOTAS NOTABLES

Perú, igual que Ecuador, se divide en tres áreas geográficas—una estrecha franja costal desértica en el Pacífico, el altiplano andino donde vive la mitad de la población y la selva amazónica al este. Lima está en la costa, y durante unos nueve meses del año está cubierta de una neblina llamada la garúa. Perú es famoso por su herencia incaica. Hay poco que se puede comparar con la vista de Machu Picchu que se le presenta al visitante. Es una ciudad inca, un impresionante complejo arquitectónico en las alturas de los Andes.

Bolivia

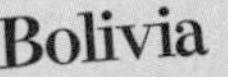

CAPITAL
La Paz

POBLACIÓN
8.568.000

NOTAS NOTABLES

Bolivia es uno de los dos países sudamericanos sin costa. Las montañas dominan su paisaje. La Paz es la ciudad de mayor altura en el mundo a unos 12.500 pies sobre el nivel del mar. En Bolivia también está el lago Titicaca rodeado de pintorescos pueblos de los indios aymara. No hay lago navegable en el mundo a mayor altura.

Chile

CAPITAL
Santiago

POBLACIÓN
15.665.000

NOTAS NOTABLES
Chile, largo y angosto, nunca con más de 111 millas de ancho, se extiende unas 2.666 millas de norte a sur a lo largo del Pacífico. Los imponentes Andes lo separan de Bolivia y Argentina. En el norte del país lo característico es el aridísimo desierto de Atacama; en el sur los inhóspitos glaciares y los fiordos de la Patagonia. Más de la tercera parte de la población reside en el área de Santiago.

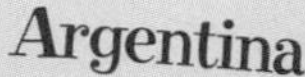

Argentina

CAPITAL
Buenos Aires

POBLACIÓN
38.741.000

NOTAS NOTABLES
Muchos consideran a Argentina la más europea de las naciones sudamericanas. Buenos Aires es una bella ciudad de parques, boutiques, restaurantes y anchas avenidas. Argentina es famosa por su carne, el bife que viene del ganado que pace en las enormes estancias de la Pampa. Más al sur en la frontera con Chile está la preciosa área de los lagos con sus pintorescos pueblos cerca de Bariloche. Al extremo sur está la Patagonia con su rocoso terreno donde pacen las ovejas de los galeses.

Paraguay

CAPITAL
Asunción

POBLACIÓN
6.037.000

NOTAS NOTABLES
Paraguay, como Bolivia, no tiene costa. Asunción, ubicada sobre siete colinas a la orilla este del río Paraguay, es donde vive la quinta parte de la población. Casi en pleno centro de Sudamérica, esta pintoresca ciudad queda casi equidistante entre el Atlántico y los Andes. Al oeste del río Paraguay se encuentra el Chaco—un área de matorrales, seca, calurosa y azotada por los vientos.

Uruguay

CAPITAL
Montevideo

POBLACIÓN
3.413.000

NOTAS NOTABLES
Uruguay es el país más pequeño de Sudamérica. Casi todo el terreno se dedica al ganado, vacuno y ovejuno. Montevideo, ubicado donde el río de la Plata desemboca en el Atlántico, es una ciudad tranquila cuyos suburbios se parecen más a bonitos balnearios. Las playas del Atlántico uruguayo, especialmente Punta del Este, atrae a muchos brasileños y argentinos.

Ceuta y Melilla
Ceuta
Melilla
POBLACIÓN
72.200
NOTAS NOTABLES
Ceuta y Melilla, en la costa norte de África, constituyen una comunidad autónoma de España. Ambas ciudades modernas son puertos libres y presentan una bella mezcla de culturas: cristiana, islámica, hebrea e hindú.

Guinea Ecuatorial
Malabo
CAPITAL
Malabo
POBLACIÓN
510.000
NOTAS NOTABLES
La República de Guinea Ecuatorial, en la costa oeste de África entre Gabón y Camerún, antes de su independencia era la Guinea Española. Ocupa 10.000 millas cuadradas en el continente y varias islas pequeñas. La capital, Malabo, está en la isla de Bioko. Su lengua oficial es el español.

Las Islas Filipinas
Manila
CAPITAL
Manila
POBLACIÓN
84.620.000
NOTAS NOTABLES
La República de las Filipinas es un archipiélago del Pacífico sur. La lengua oficial del país es el filipino, que antes se llamaba tagalo, un idioma con muchos préstamos del español. La influencia española fue enorme en los siglos XVII, XVIII y XIX cuando las Filipinas eran una colonia española. Muchos filipinos tienen nombres españoles y muchos todavía hablan español.

España

OCÉANO ATLÁNTICO
MAR CANTÁBRICO
Golfo de Vizcaya
FRANCIA
ANDORRA
La Coruña
Santiago de Compostela
Oviedo
Asturias
Santander
Cantabria
San Sebastián
Bilbao
País Vasco
Roncesvalles
LOS PIRINEOS
Pamplona
Navarra
Galicia
CORDILLERA CANTÁBRICA
León
Burgos
Rioja
Castilla y León
Río Ebro
Cataluña
Valladolid
Río Duero
Zaragoza
Barcelona
Aragón
Salamanca
Segovia
Río Tajo
Ávila
Madrid
SIERRA DE GUADARRAMA
Madrid
Menorca
Islas baleares
Palma
Mallorca
PORTUGAL
ESPAÑA
Comunidad Valenciana
Valencia
Castilla-la Mancha
Ibiza
Formentera
Lisboa
Río Guadiana
Extremadura
Alicante
Murcia
Murcia
MAR MEDITERRÁNEO
Río Guadalquivir
Córdoba
Cartagena
Sevilla
Granada
SIERRA NEVADA
Andalucía
Jerez de la Frontera
Málaga
COSTA DEL SOL
Cádiz
Marbella
Estepona
Gibraltar (R.U.)
Estrecho de Gibraltar
Ceuta (Esp.)
Tánger
Melilla (Esp.)
OCÉANO ATLÁNTICO
ARGELIA
MARRUECOS
Islas Canarias
La Palma
Santa Cruz de Tenerife
Lanzarote
Fuerteventura
Gomera
Las Palmas
Tenerife
Hierro
Gran Canaria
MARRUECOS
ÁFRICA
OCÉANO ATLÁNTICO
SAHARA OCCIDENTAL

La América del Sur

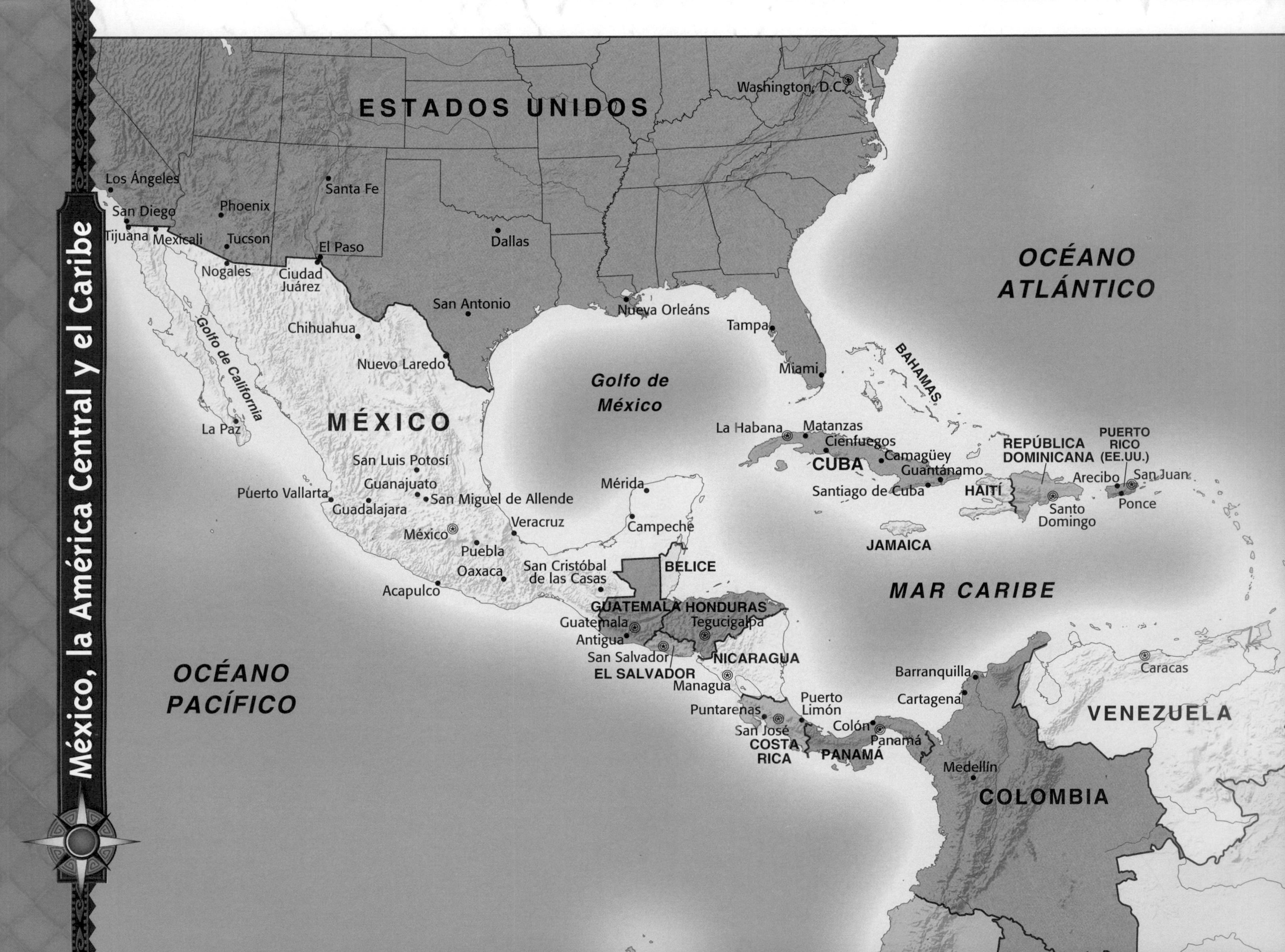

México, la América Central y el Caribe
ESTADOS UNIDOS
Washington, D.C.
Los Ángeles
Santa Fe
San Diego
Phoenix
Tijuana
Mexicali
Tucson
El Paso
Dallas
Nogales
Ciudad Juárez
San Antonio
Nueva Orleáns
Tampa
Miami
OCÉANO ATLÁNTICO
BAHAMAS
Chihuahua
Golfo de California
Nuevo Laredo
Golfo de México
La Paz
MÉXICO
La Habana
Matanzas
Cienfuegos
Camagüey
CUBA
Guantánamo
Santiago de Cuba
HAITÍ
REPÚBLICA DOMINICANA
PUERTO RICO (EE.UU.)
Arecibo
San Juan
Ponce
Santo Domingo
San Luis Potosí
Guanajuato
Puerto Vallarta
San Miguel de Allende
Guadalajara
Mérida
Veracruz
Campeche
México
Puebla
Oaxaca
San Cristóbal de las Casas
BELICE
Acapulco
JAMAICA
MAR CARIBE
GUATEMALA
HONDURAS
Guatemala
Tegucigalpa
Antigua
San Salvador
NICARAGUA
EL SALVADOR
Managua
OCÉANO PACÍFICO
Barranquilla
Caracas
Puerto Limón
Cartagena
Puntarenas
VENEZUELA
San José
Colón
COSTA RICA
Panamá
PANAMÁ
Medellín
COLOMBIA

Estados Unidos

The What, Why, and How of Reading

Reading is a learned process. You have been reading in your first language for a long time and now your challenge is to transfer what you know to enable you to read fluently in Spanish. Reading will help you improve your vocabulary, cultural knowledge, and productive skills in Spanish. The strategies in the chart are reading strategies you are probably familiar with. Review them and apply them as you continue to improve your Spanish reading skills.

Skill/Strategy

What Is It?	Why It's Important	How To Do It
Preview Previewing is looking over a selection before you read.	Previewing lets you begin to see what you already know and what you'll need to know. It helps you set a purpose for reading.	Look at the title, illustrations, headings, captions, and graphics. Look at how ideas are organized. Ask questions about the text.
Skim Skimming is looking over an entire selection quickly to get a general idea of what the piece is about.	Skimming will tell you what a selection is about. If the selection you skim isn't what you're looking for, you won't need to read the entire piece.	Read the title of the selection and quickly look over the entire piece. Read headings and captions and maybe part of the first paragraph to get a general idea of the selection's content.
Scan Scanning is glancing quickly over a selection in order to find specific information.	Scanning helps you pinpoint information quickly. It saves you time when you have a number of selections to look at.	As you move your eyes quickly over the lines of text, look for key words or phrases that will help you locate the information you're looking for.
Predict Predicting is taking an educated guess about what will happen in a selection.	Predicting gives you a reason to read. You want to find out if your prediction and the selection events match, don't you? As you read, adjust or change your prediction if it doesn't fit what you learn.	Combine what you already know about an author or subject with what you learned in your preview to guess what will be included in the text.
Summarize Summarizing is stating the main ideas of a selection in your own words and in a logical sequence.	Summarizing shows whether you've understood something. It teaches you to rethink what you've read and to separate main ideas from supporting information.	Ask yourself: What is this selection about? Answer *who, what, where, when, why,* and *how?* Put that information in a logical order.

What Is It?	Why It's Important	How To Do It
Clarify Clarifying is looking at difficult sections of text in order to clear up what is confusing.	Authors will often build ideas one on another. If you don't clear up a confusing passage, you may not understand main ideas or information that comes later.	Go back and reread a confusing section more slowly. Look up words you don't know. Ask questions about what you don't understand. Sometimes you may want to read on to see if further information helps you.
Question Questioning is asking yourself whether information in a selection is important. Questioning is also regularly asking yourself whether you've understood what you've read.	When you ask questions as you read, you're reading strategically. As you answer your questions, you're making sure that you'll get the gist of a text.	Have a running conversation with yourself as you read. Keep asking yourself: Is this idea important? Why? Do I understand what this is about? Might this information be on a test later?
Visualize Visualizing is picturing a writer's ideas or descriptions in your mind's eye.	Visualizing is one of the best ways to understand and remember information in fiction, nonfiction, and informational text.	Carefully read how a writer describes a person, place, or thing. Then ask yourself: What would this look like? Can I see how the steps in this process would work?

What Is It?	Why It's Important	How To Do It
Monitor Comprehension Monitoring your comprehension means thinking about whether you're understanding what you're reading.	The whole point of reading is to understand a piece of text. When you don't understand a selection, you're not really reading it.	Keep asking yourself questions about main ideas, characters, and events. When you can't answer a question, review, read more slowly, or ask someone to help you.
Identify Sequence Identifying sequence is finding the logical order of ideas or events.	In a work of fiction, events usually happen in chronological order. With nonfiction, understanding the logical sequence of ideas in a piece helps you follow a writer's train of thought. You'll remember ideas better when you know the logical order a writer uses.	Think about what the author is trying to do. Tell a story? Explain how something works? Present information? Look for clues or signal words that might point to time order, steps in a process, or order of importance.
Determine the Main Idea Determining an author's main idea is finding the most important thought in a paragraph or selection.	Finding main ideas gets you ready to summarize. You also discover an author's purpose for writing when you find the main ideas in a selection.	Think about what you know about the author and the topic. Look for how the author organizes ideas. Then look for the one idea that all of the sentences in a paragraph or all the paragraphs in a selection are about.
Respond Responding is telling what you like, dislike, find surprising or interesting in a selection.	When you react in a personal way to what you read, you'll enjoy a selection more and remember it better.	As you read, think about how you feel about story elements or ideas in a selection. What's your reaction to the characters in a story? What grabs your attention as you read?
Connect Connecting means linking what you read to events in your own life or to other selections you've read.	You'll "get into" your reading and recall information and ideas better by connecting events, emotions, and characters to your own life.	Ask yourself: Do I know someone like this? Have I ever felt this way? What else have I read that is like this selection?
Review Reviewing is going back over what you've read to remember what's important and to organize ideas so you'll recall them later.	Reviewing is especially important when you have new ideas and a lot of information to remember.	Filling in a graphic organizer, such as a chart or diagram, as you read helps you organize information. These study aids will help you review later.
Interpret Interpreting is using your own understanding of the world to decide what the events or ideas in a selection mean.	Every reader constructs meaning on the basis of what he or she understands about the world. Finding meaning as you read is all about interacting with the text.	Think about what you already know about yourself and the world. Ask yourself: What is the author really trying to say here? What larger idea might these events be about?

What Is It?	Why It's Important	How To Do It
Infer Inferring is using your reason and experience to guess what an author does not come right out and say.	Making inferences is a large part of finding meaning in a selection. Inferring helps you look more deeply at characters and points you toward the theme or message in a selection.	Look for clues the author provides. Notice descriptions, dialogue, events, and relationships that might tell you something the author wants you to know.
Draw Conclusions Drawing conclusions is using a number of pieces of information to make a general statement about people, places, events, and ideas.	Drawing conclusions helps you find connections between ideas and events. It's another tool to help you see the larger picture.	Notice details about characters, ideas, and events. Then make a general statement on the basis of these details. For example, a character's actions might lead you to conclude that he is kind.
Analyze Analyzing is looking at separate parts of a selection in order to understand the entire selection.	Analyzing helps you look critically at a piece of writing. When you analyze a selection, you'll discover its theme or message, and you'll learn the author's purpose for writing.	To analyze a story, think about what the author is saying through the characters, setting, and plot. To analyze nonfiction, look at the organization and main ideas. What do they suggest?
Synthesize Synthesizing is combining ideas to create something new. You may synthesize to reach a new understanding or you may actually create a new ending to a story.	Synthesizing helps you move to a higher level of thinking. Creating something new of your own goes beyond remembering what you learned from someone else.	Think about the ideas or information you've learned in a selection. Ask yourself: Do I understand something more than the main ideas here? Can I create something else from what I now know?
Evaluate Evaluating is making a judgment or forming an opinion about something you read. You can evaluate a character, an author's craft, or the value of the information in a text.	Evaluating helps you become a wise reader. For example, when you judge whether an author is qualified to speak about a topic or whether the author's points make sense, you can avoid being misled by what you read.	As you read, ask yourself questions such as: Is this character realistic and believable? Is this author qualified to write on this subject? Is this author biased? Does this author present opinions as facts?

READING IN A NEW LANGUAGE

Following are skills and strategies that can help you understand what you read as you continue to learn a language. *Reading and Succeeding* will help you build skills and strategies that will make it easier to understand what you are reading in your exciting new language.

The strategies you use frequently depend on the purpose of your reading. You do not read a textbook or standardized testing questions the same way you read a novel or a magazine article. You read a textbook for information. You read a novel or magazine article for fun.

While learning a second language your vocabulary is limited in comparison to the vast number of words you already know in English. The material presented to you to read must accommodate this reality. Your lack of fluency does not have to deter you from enjoying what you are reading. Most of what you read, however, will come from your textbook, since original novels and magazine articles are not written for people who have limited exposure to the language.

Readings

As you continue to learn Spanish and develop more proficiency in the language you will be able to increase the amount of material you can read in Spanish. In this level of **¡Buen viaje!** you will encounter three types of reading material: text material dealing with many aspects of the cultures of the Spanish-speaking world; articles taken from newspapers and magazines published in Spanish; and literary works of authors from Spain and Latin America.

The cultural readings have been carefully controlled, using only language that you have already learned. You should find these readings easy and enjoyable. These informative readings present to you the fascinating cultures of the Spanish-speaking world.

It is unrealistic to assume that you will never encounter new words or structures as you branch out and read material on your own. For this reason, the newspaper and magazine articles you will read this year appear exactly as they did in the original periodical. In order to help you read them with relative ease, each article is preceded by a vocabulary section that introduces you to key words that appear in the section but that may be unfamiliar to you.

The literary selections represent all genres: short story, novel (fragments), poetry, drama, and legend. As with the newspaper and magazine articles, the language in the literary selections is original and will therefore be the most challenging for you. In order to assist you, the introductory vocabulary section presents key words from the literary selection. In addition, less important words that you do not know but need for comprehension are sidenoted.

In this *Reading and Succeeding* section, you will learn to develop many skills that will enable you to read all types of material with relative ease. It is also important to pay particular attention to the strategies that accompany many of the reading selections.

USE *READING AND SUCCEEDING* TO HELP YOU:

- **adjust the way you read to fit the type of material you are reading**
- **identify new words and build your vocabulary**
- **use specific reading strategies to better understand what you read**
- **improve your ability to speak by developing strategies that enable you to retell orally what you have read**
- **use critical thinking strategies to think more deeply about what you read**

Identifying New Words and Building Vocabulary

What do you do when you come across a word you do not know as you read? Do you skip the word and keep reading? You might if you are reading for fun. If it hinders your ability to understand, however, you might miss something important. When you come to a word you don't know, try the following strategies to figure out what the word means.

• Reading Aloud

In the early stages of learning a second language a good strategy is to sit by yourself and read the selection aloud. This can help you understand the reading because you once again hear words that you have already practiced orally in class. Hearing them as you read them can help reinforce meaning.

• Identifying Cognates

As you read you will come across many cognates. Cognates are words that look alike in both English and Spanish. Not only do they look alike but they mean the same thing. Recognizing cognates is a great reading strategy. Examples of cognates are:

cómico	**nacionalidad**	**entra**	**popular**	**secundaria**	**clase**
cubano	**matemática**	**prepara**	**video**	**blusa**	**televisión**

• Identifying Roots and Base Words

The main part of a word is called its root. From a root, many new words can be formed. When you see a new word, identify its root. It can help you pronounce the word and figure out its meaning.

For example, if you know the word **importante,** there is no problem determining the meaning of **importancia.** The verb **importar** becomes a bit more problematic, but with some intelligent guessing you can get its meaning. You know it has something to do with importance so it means *it is important,* and by extension it can even carry the meaning *it matters.*

• Prefixes

A prefix is a word part added to the beginning of a root or base word. Spanish as well as English has prefixes. Prefixes can change, or even reverse, the meaning of a word. For example, the prefixes **in-, im-,** and **des-** mean *not.*

estable/inestable **posible/imposible** **honesto/deshonesto**

Using Syntax

Like all languages, Spanish has rules for the way words are arranged in sentences. The way a sentence is organized is called its syntax. Spanish syntax, however, is a bit more flexible than English. In a simple English sentence someone or something (its subject) does something (the predicate or verb) to or with another person or thing (the object). This word order can vary in Spanish and does not always follow the subject/verb/object order.

READING PRACTICE

English always states: *John speaks to me.*

Spanish can state: *John to me speaks.*

or *To me speaks John.*

The latter leaves the subject to the end of the sentence and emphasizes that it is John who speaks to me.

Taking into account that Spanish and English syntax vary is one of the many important reasons why, when you read, you should think in Spanish and not try to translate what you are reading into English. Reading in Spanish will then have a natural flow and follow exactly the way you learned it. Trying to translate it into English confuses the matter and serves no purpose.

Using Context Clues

This is a very important reading strategy in a second language. You can often figure out the meaning of an unfamiliar word by looking at it in context (the words and sentences that surround it). Let's look at the following example.

READING PRACTICE

The glump ate it all up and flew away.

You have no idea what a *glump* is. Right? But from the rest of the sentence you can figure out that it's a bird. Why? Because it flew away and you know that birds fly. In this way you guessed at the meaning of an unknown word using context. Although you know it is a bird, you cannot determine the specific meaning such as a robin, a wren, or a sparrow. In many cases it does not matter because that degree of specificity is not necessary for comprehension. Let's look at another example:

The glump ate it all up and phlumped.

In this case you do not know the meaning of two key words in the same sentence—*glump* and *phlumped*. This makes it impossible to guess the meaning and this is what can happen when you try to read something in a second language that is beyond your proficiency level. This makes reading a frustrating experience. For this reason all the readings in your textbook control the language to keep it within your reach. Remember, if you have studied the vocabulary in your book, this will not happen.

Understanding What You Read

Try using some of the following strategies before, during, and after reading to understand and remember what you read.

Previewing

When you preview a piece of writing, you are looking for a general idea of what to expect from it. Before you read, try the following.

- Look at the title and any illustrations that are included.
- Read the headings, subheadings, and anything in bold letters.
- Skim over the passage to see how it is organized. Is it divided into many parts? Is it a long poem or short story?
- Look at the graphics—pictures, maps, or diagrams.
- Set a purpose for your reading. Are you reading to learn something new? Are you reading to find specific information?

Using What You Know

Believe it or not, you already know quite a bit about what you are going to read. Your own knowledge and personal experience can help you create meaning in what you read. There is, however, a big difference in reading the information in your Spanish textbook. You already have some knowledge about what you are reading from a United States oriented base. What you will be reading about takes place in a Spanish-speaking environment and thus you will be adding an exciting new dimension to what you already know. Comparing and contrasting are important critical skills to put to use when reading material about a culture other than your own. This skill will be discussed later.

Visualizing

Creating pictures in your mind about what you are reading—called visualizing—will help you understand and remember what you read. With the assistance of the many accompanying photos, try to visualize the people, streets, cities, homes, etc., you are reading about.

Identifying Sequence

When you discover the logical order of events or ideas, you are identifying sequence. Look for clues and signal words that will help you find how information is organized. Some signal words are **primero, al principio, antes, después, luego, entonces, más tarde, por fin, finalmente.**

Determining the Main Idea

When you look for the main idea of a selection, you look for the most important idea. The examples, reasons, and details that further explain the main idea are called supporting details.

Reviewing

When you review in school, you go over what you learned the day before so that the information is clear in your mind. Reviewing when you read does the same thing. Take time now and then to pause and review what you have read. Think about the main ideas and organize them for yourself so you can recall them later. Filling in study aids such as graphic organizers can help you review.

Monitoring Your Comprehension

As you read, check your understanding by summarizing. Pause from time to time and state the main ideas of what you have just read. Answer the questions: **¿Quién?** *(Who?)* **¿Qué?** *(What?)* **¿Dónde?** *(Where?)* **¿Cuándo?** *(When?)* **¿Cómo?** *(How?)* **¿Por qué?** *(Why?)*. Summarizing tests your comprehension because you state key points in your own words. Remember something you read earlier: reading in Spanish empowers your ability to speak by developing strategies that enable you to retell orally what you have read.

Thinking About Your Reading

Sometimes it is important to think more deeply about what you read so you can get the most out of what the author says. These critical thinking skills will help you go beyond what the words say and understand the meaning of your reading.

Compare and Contrast

To compare and contrast shows the similarities and differences among people, things, and ideas. Your reading experience in Spanish will show you many things that are similar and many others that are different depending upon the culture groups and social mores.

As you go over these culturally oriented readings, try to visualize what you are reading. Then think about the information. Think about what you know about the topic and then determine if the information you are reading is similar, somewhat different, or very different from what you know.

Continue to think about it. In this case you may have to think about it in English. Determine if you find the similarities or the differences interesting. Would you like to experience what you are reading about? Analyzing the information in this way will most certainly help you remember what you have read.

- Signal words and phrases that indicate similarity are **similar, semejante, parecido, igual.**
- Signal words and phrases that indicate differences are **diferente, distinto, al contrario, contrariamente, sin embargo.**

Cause and Effect

Just about everything that happens in life is the cause or the effect of some other event or action. Writers use cause-and-effect structure to explore the reasons for something happening and to examine the results of previous events. This structure helps answer the question that everybody is always asking: Why? Cause-and-effect structure is about explaining things.

- Signal words and phrases are **así, porque, por consiguiente, resulta que.**

Using Reference Materials

Even in the intermediate stages of second-language learning you will not be able to use certain types of reference materials that are helpful to you in English. For example, it would still be problematic for you to look up a word in a Spanish dictionary as you would not be able to understand many of the words used in the definition.

You can, however, make use of the dictionary that appears at the end of your textbook. The dictionary at the end of **¡Buen viaje!** also includes the vocabulary you learned in the previous levels. You are provided with a Spanish-English list and an English-Spanish list. If you use a bilingual dictionary other than the one in your textbook, you should use it with caution since many entries are followed by more than one translation and it is difficult to discern the precise word you are looking for. This is not the case with the dictionary in your book.

Enjoy reading as you take **un buen viaje.**

Dear Student,

Foldables are interactive study organizers that you can make yourself. They are a wonderful resource to help you organize and retain information. Foldables have many purposes. You can use them to remember vocabulary words or to organize more in-depth information on any given topic, such as keeping track of what you know about a particular country.

You can write general information, such as titles, vocabulary words, concepts, questions, main ideas, and dates, on the front tabs of your Foldables. You view this general information every time you look at a Foldable. This helps you focus on and remember key points without the distraction of additional text. You can write specific information—supporting ideas, thoughts, answers to questions, research information, empirical data, class notes, observations, and definitions—under the tabs. Think of different ways in which Foldables can be used. Soon you will find that you can make your own Foldables for study guides and projects. Foldables with flaps or tabs create study guides that you can use to check what you know about the general information on the front of tabs. Use Foldables without tabs for projects that require information to be presented for others to view quickly. The more you make and use graphic organizers, the faster you will become able to produce them.

To store your Foldables, turn one-gallon freezer bags into student portfolios which can be collected and stored in the classroom. You can also carry your portfolios in your notebooks if you place strips of two-inch clear tape along one side and punch three holes through the taped edge. Write your name along the top of the plastic portfolio with a permanent marker and cover the writing with two-inch clear tape to keep it from wearing off. Cut the bottom corners off the bag so it won't hold air and will stack and store easily. The following figures illustrate the basic folds that are referred to throughout the following section of this book.

Good luck!

Dinah Zike

www.dinah.com

Pocket Book

La geografía Use this *pocket book* organizer in your ongoing study of all the countries in the Spanish-speaking world.

Step 1 **Fold** a sheet of paper (8½" x 11") in half like a *hamburger.*

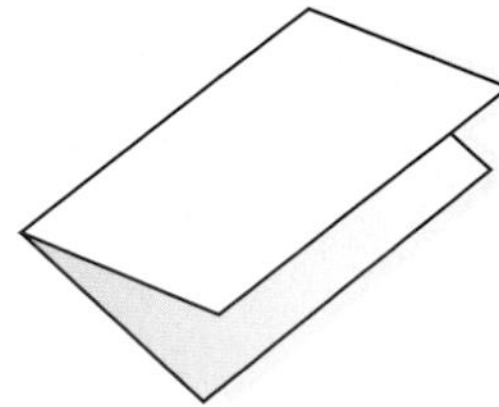

Step 2 **Open** the folded paper and fold one of the long sides up two inches to form a pocket. Refold the *hamburger* fold so that the newly formed pockets are on the inside.

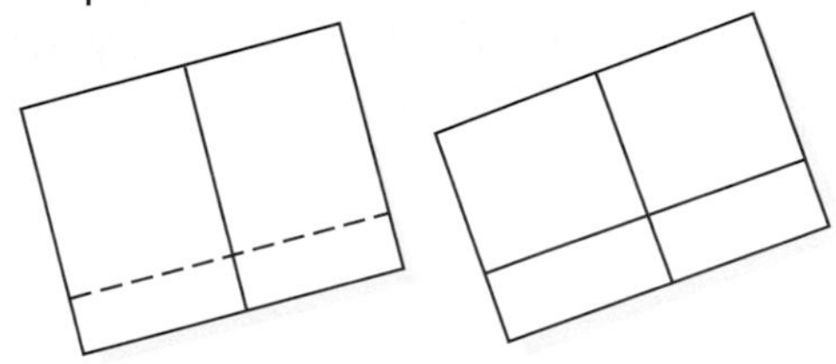

Step 3 **Glue** the outer edges of the two-inch fold with a small amount of glue.

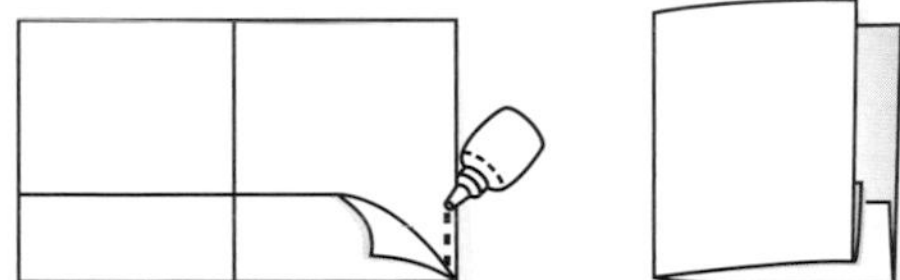

Step 4 **Make a multipaged booklet** by gluing six pockets side-by-side. Glue a cover around the multipaged *pocket book.*

Step 5 **Label** five pockets with the following geographical areas: **Europa, la América del Norte, la América del Sur, la América Central,** and **Islas del Caribe.** Use index cards inside the pockets to record information each time you learn something new about a specific country. Be sure to include the name of the country (in Spanish, of course) and its capital.

OTHER SUGGESTIONS FOR A *POCKET BOOK* FOLDABLE

You may wish to use a *pocket book* foldable to help you use different past tenses correctly. Label two pockets, one for the imperfect and the other for the **preterite.** Then write sentences using each tense on index cards and file them in the correct pocket. You may also wish to make a pocket for sentences that use both tenses correctly.

Vocabulary Book

Sinónimos y antónimos Use this *vocabulary book* to practice your vocabulary through the use of synonyms and antonyms.

Step 1 **Fold** a sheet of notebook paper in half like a *hot dog*.

Step 2 On one side, **cut** every third line. This usually results in ten tabs. Do this with two sheets of paper to make two books.

Step 3 **Label** the tops of the *vocabulary books* with the word **Sinónimos** on one and **Antónimos** on the other. As you learn new vocabulary in each unit, try to categorize words in this manner. Remember also to think of words you have previously learned to fill in your books.

Antónimos

Sinónimos

OTHER SUGGESTIONS FOR A *VOCABULARY BOOK* FOLDABLE

You can use a *vocabulary book* foldable to help remember any verb conjugation in Spanish. Write the infinitive at the top. If you know several tenses of a verb, you should also write what tense or tenses are being practiced. On the outside of the foldable, write the pronouns, and on the inside, write the corresponding verb form. You can use this as a quick study and review tool for any verb. At a more advanced level, you may wish to write many verbs down the outside and entire conjugations on the inside.

Tab Book

Preguntas Use this *tab book* to practice asking and answering questions.

Step 1 **Fold** a sheet of paper (8½" x 11") like a *hot dog* but fold it so that one side is one inch longer than the other.

Step 2 On the shorter side only, **cut** five equal tabs. On the front of each tab, **write** a question word you have learned. For example, you may wish to write the following.

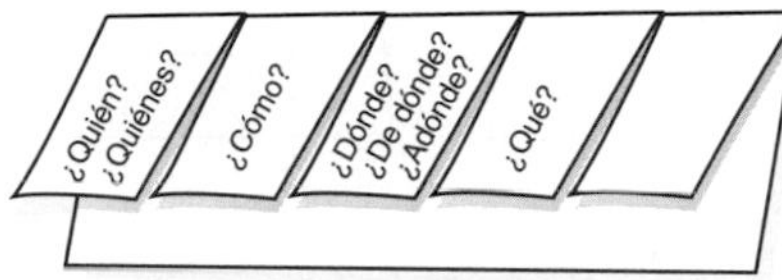

Step 3 On the bottom edge, **write** any sentence you would like.

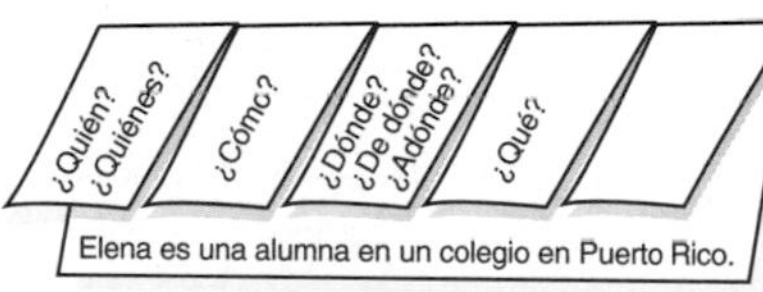

Step 4 Under each flap, **write** the word from your sentence that answers the question on the front of the flap.

OTHER SUGGESTIONS FOR A *TAB BOOK* FOLDABLE

You may also use a *tab book* foldable to practice verb conjugations. You would need to make six tabs instead of five. Write a verb and a tense on the bottom edge and write the pronouns on the front of each tab. Under each flap, write the corresponding verb form.

You may wish to use a *tab book* foldable to practice new vocabulary words. Leave extra space on the bottom edge. Choose five or six vocabulary words and write each one on a tab. You may also make multiple *tab book* foldables to practice more words. Under each flap, write a definition or translation of the word. If you can, write an original definition in Spanish. Use the bottom edge to write one or more original sentences using all of the words on the tabs.

Miniature Matchbook

Descripciones Use this *miniature matchbook* to help you communicate in an interesting and more descriptive way.

Step 1 **Fold** a sheet of paper (8½" x 11") in half like a *hot dog*.

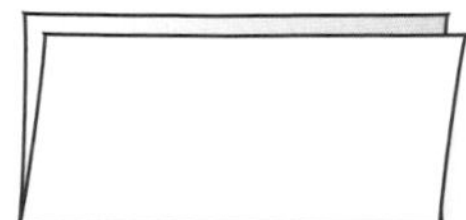

Step 2 **Cut** the sheet in half along the fold line.

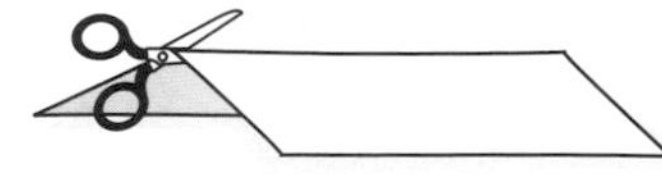

Step 3 **Fold** the two long strips in half like *hot dogs,* leaving one side ½" shorter than the other side.

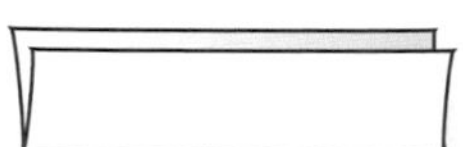

Step 4 **Fold** the ½" tab over the shorter side on each strip.

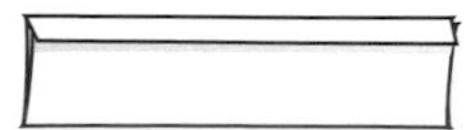

Step 5 **Cut** each of the two strips in half forming four halves. Then cut each half into thirds, making twelve miniature matchbooks.

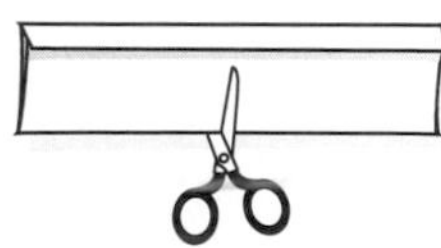

Step 6 **Glue** the twelve small matchbooks inside a *hamburger* fold (three rows of four each).

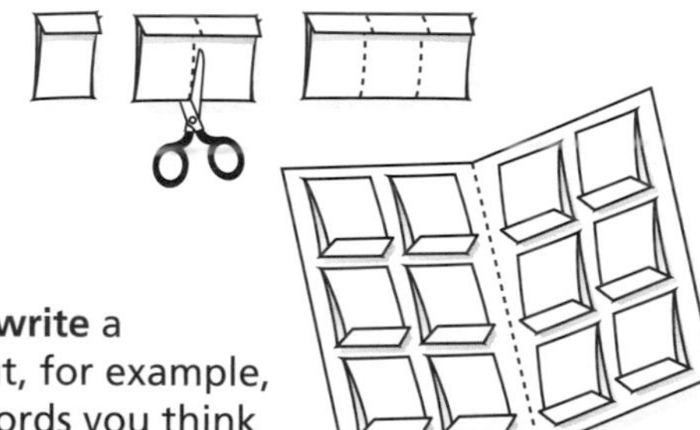

Step 7 On the front of each matchbook, **write** a subject you are going to tell or write about, for example, **la escuela**. Open up the tab and list any words you think you could use to make your discussion more interesting. You can add topics and words as you continue with your study of Spanish. If you glue several sections together, this foldable will "grow."

OTHER SUGGESTIONS FOR A *MINIATURE MATCHBOOK* FOLDABLE

You may use a *miniature matchbook* foldable to test each other on your knowledge of the vocabulary. Work in pairs with each partner making a blank *miniature matchbook* foldable. Each partner writes a topic related to the subjects you have just studied on the front of each matchbook. You may use categories of vocabulary, verbs you have recently learned to conjugate, or the subject of a reading. Your partner then writes as much as he or she can about that topic under the flap. This can alert you if you need to go back and review a topic.

A *miniature matchbook* foldable may help you organize and remember information you have read. After doing a cultural or literary reading, write down a concept presented in the reading on the front of each matchbook. Open up each tab and write down supporting details that support the idea.

Minibook

Mi autobiografía Use this *minibook* organizer to write and illustrate your autobiography. Before you begin to write, think about the many things concerning yourself that you have the ability to write about in Spanish. On the left pages, draw the events of your life in chronological order. On the right, write about your drawings.

Step 1 **Fold** a sheet of paper (8½" x 11") in half like a *hot dog*.

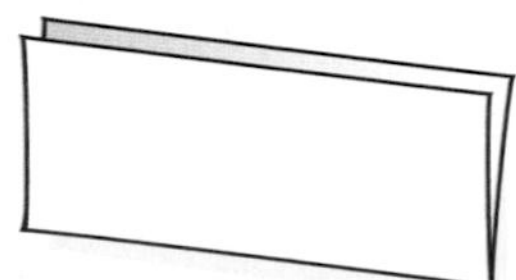

Step 2 **Fold** it in half again like a *hamburger*.

Step 3 Then **fold** in half again, forming eights.

Step 4 **Open** the fold and **cut** the eight sections apart.

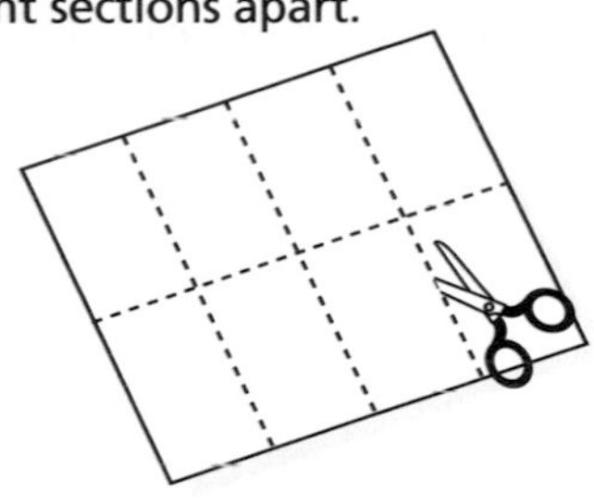

Step 5 **Place** all eight sections in a stack and fold in half like a hamburger.

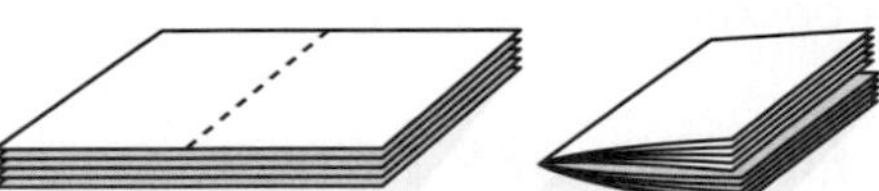

Step 6 **Staple** along the center fold line. **Glue** the front and back sheets into a construction paper cover.

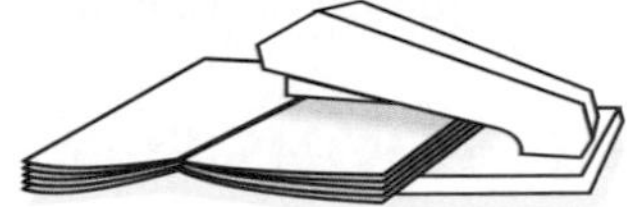

OTHER SUGGESTIONS FOR A *MINIBOOK* FOLDABLE

Work in small groups and use *minibook* foldables to practice the subjunctive. Each person writes the beginnings of sentences that take the subjunctive on the left pages. Then pass your *minibook* to the next group member, who, on the right page, completes each sentence. That group member will pass the *minibook* on to a third group member, who will write an alternate completion for each sentence under the first one. This may be repeated until all group members have written a completion for all sentences.

Paper File Folder

Las emociones Use this *paper file folder* organizer to keep track of happenings or events that cause you to feel a certain way.

Step 1 **Fold** four sheets of paper (8½" x 11") in half like a *hamburger*. Leave one side one inch longer than the other side.

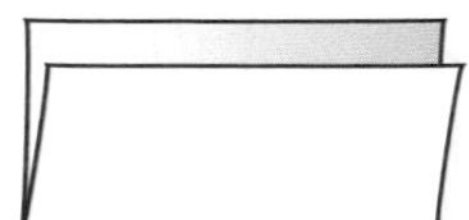

Step 2 On each sheet, **fold** the one-inch tab over the short side, forming an envelope-like fold.

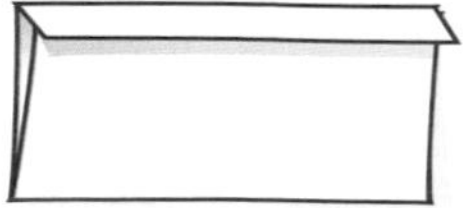

Step 3 **Place** the four sheets side-by-side, then move each fold so that the tabs are exposed.

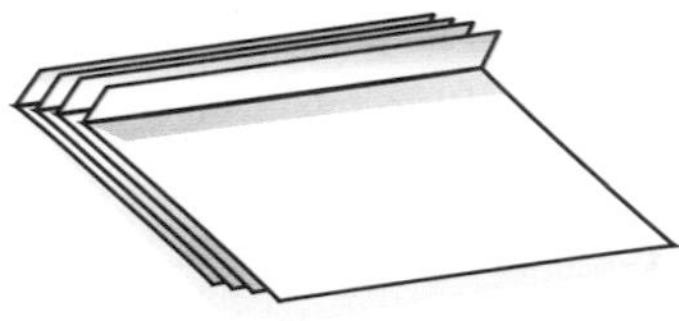

Step 4 Moving left to right, **cut** staggered tabs in each fold, 2⅛" wide. Fold the tabs upward.

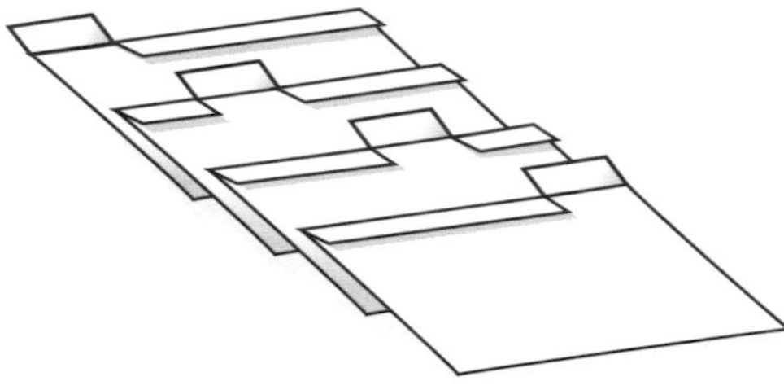

Step 5 **Glue** the ends of the folders together. On each tab, write an emotion you sometimes feel. Pay attention to when it is that you feel happy, sad, nervous, etc. Describe the situation in Spanish and file it in the correct pocket.

OTHER SUGGESTIONS FOR A *PAPER FILE FOLDER* FOLDABLE

You may use a *paper file folder* organizer to keep track of verbs and verb forms. You should make a folder for each type of regular verb and for each type of irregular verb. Write the conjugations for some important verbs in each category and file them in the *paper file folder* organizer. Add new tenses to the existing cards and new verbs as you learn them.

A *paper file folder* organizer can be useful for keeping notes on the cultural information that you will learn. You may wish to make categories for different types of cultural information and add index cards to them as you learn new facts and concepts about the target cultures.

Large Sentence Strips

El presente y el pasado Use these *large sentence strips* to help you compare and contrast activities in the past and in the present.

Step 1 Take two sheets of paper (8½" x 11") and **fold** into *hamburgers.* Cut along the fold lines, making four half sheets. (Use as many half sheets as necessary for additional pages to your book.)

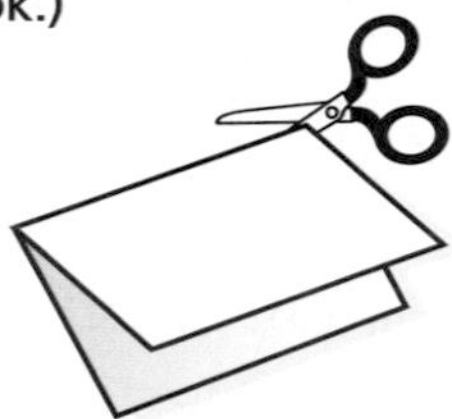

Step 2 **Fold** each half sheet in half like a *hot dog.*

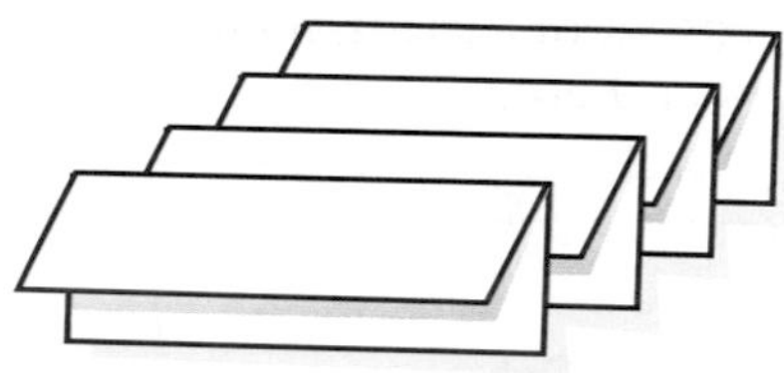

Step 3 Place the folds side-by-side and **staple** them together on the left side.

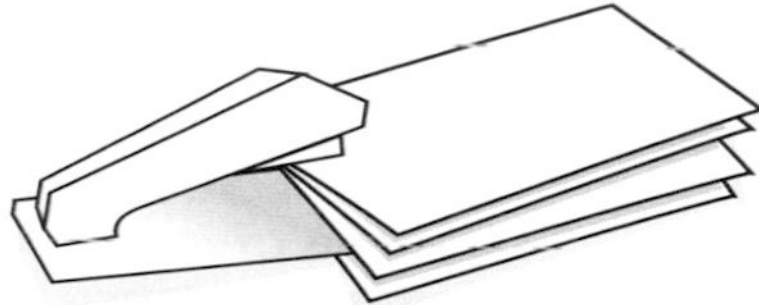

Step 4 About one inch from the stapled edge, **cut** the front page of each folded section up to the mountain top. These cuts form flaps that can be raised and lowered.

Step 5 To make a half-cover, use a sheet of construction paper one inch longer than the book. **Glue** the back of the last sheet to the construction paper strip, leaving one inch on the left side to fold over and cover the original staples. Staple this half-cover in place.

Step 6 With a friend, **write** sentences on the front of the flap, either in the present tense or in the past tense. Then switch your books of sentence strips and write the opposite tense inside under the flaps.

OTHER SUGGESTIONS FOR A *LARGE SENTENCE STRIPS* FOLDABLE

You may work in pairs to use *large sentence strips* to practice using direct and/or indirect object pronouns. On the front of each flap, write full sentences which have direct or indirect objects or both. Then trade sentence strips. You and your partner will each write sentences under the flaps replacing the direct or indirect objects with object pronouns.

You may use *large sentence strips* to practice using verbs that can be used reflexively and nonreflexively. Write a sentence using a reflexive verb on the outside of each flap. Under the flap, write a sentence using the same verb nonreflexively.

Project Board With Tabs

Diversiones favoritas Use this *project board with tabs* to display a visual about your favorite movie or video. Be sure to make it as attractive as possible to help convince others to see it.

Step 1 **Draw** a large illustration, a series of small illustrations, or write on the front of a sheet of paper.

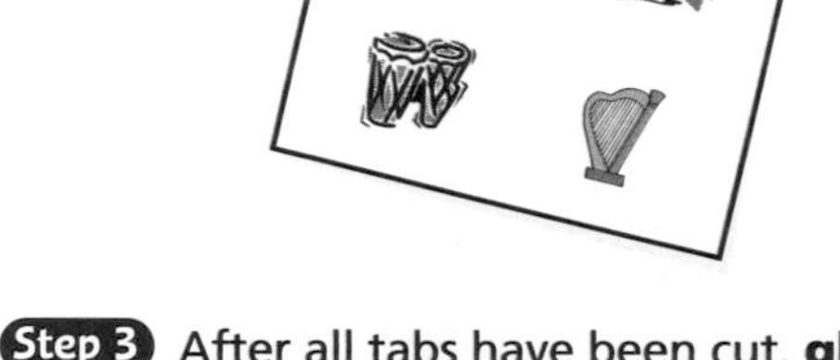

Step 2 **Pinch** and slightly fold the sheet of paper at the point where a tab is desired on the illustrated piece of paper. Cut into the paper on the fold. Cut straight in, then cut up to form an "L." When the paper is unfolded, it will form a tab with the illustration on the front.

Step 3 After all tabs have been cut, **glue** this front sheet onto a second sheet of paper. Place glue around all four edges and in the middle, away from tabs.

Step 4 **Write** or draw under the tabs. If the project is made as a bulletin board using butcher paper, tape or glue smaller sheets of paper under the tabs.

Think of favorite scenes from a movie or cultural event that you enjoyed and draw them on the front of the tabs. Underneath the tabs write a description of the scene or tell why you liked that part of the movie. It might be fun to not put a title on the project board and just hang it up and let classmates guess the name of the movie you are describing.

OTHER SUGGESTIONS FOR A *PROJECT BOARD WITH TABS* FOLDABLE

You may wish to use a *project board with tabs* to practice the use of object pronouns. Draw a series of scenes involving two or more people on the outside of the tabs. Write sentences using object pronouns describing the people's conversations or interactions under the tabs.

You can also use a *project board with tabs* to practice the future tense. Illustrate what you plan to do in college or in your career on the outside of the tabs. Under each tab, write one or more sentences in the future about your plans.

Sentence Strip Holder

Para practicar más Use this *sentence strip holder* to practice your vocabulary, your verbs, or anything else you might feel you need extra help with.

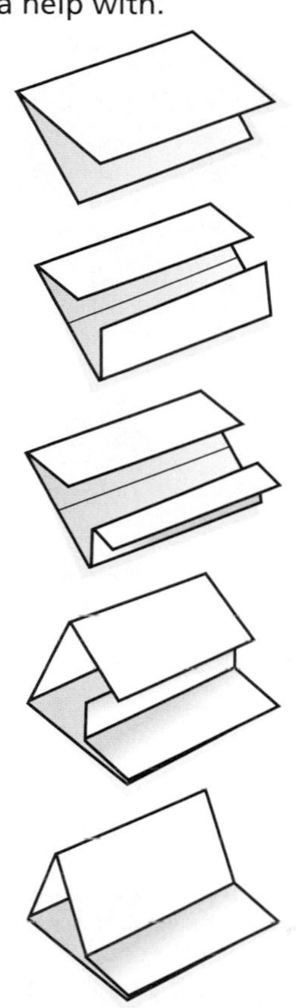

Step 1 **Fold** a sheet of paper (8½" x 11") in half like a *hamburger*.

Step 2 **Open** the *hamburger* and fold the two outer edges toward the valley. This forms a shutter fold.

Step 3 **Fold** one of the inside edges of the shutter back to the outside fold. This fold forms a floppy L.

Step 4 **Glue** the floppy L tab down to the base so that it forms a strong straight L tab.

Step 5 **Glue** the other shutter side to the front of this L tab. This forms a tent that is the backboard for the flashcards or student work to be displayed.

Step 6 **Fold** the edge of the L up ¼" to ½" to form a lip that will keep the sentence strips from slipping off the holder.

Vocabulary and spelling words can be stored inside the "tent" formed by this fold.

OTHER SUGGESTIONS FOR A *SENTENCE STRIP HOLDER* FOLDABLE

You may wish to practice new or irregular verbs using a *sentence strip holder.* Work in pairs. Make flash cards showing the infinitives of the verbs to practice in Spanish. You should each take half of the cards and take turns setting one verb on the *sentence strip holder.* One partner will then say as many sentences as possible using different forms of that verb, and the other will write down the subject and conjugated verb form (or just the verb form) for each sentence. Partners should check to make sure each verb form is spelled correctly. You can repeat this activity for each verb.

Expand your view of the Spanish-speaking world.

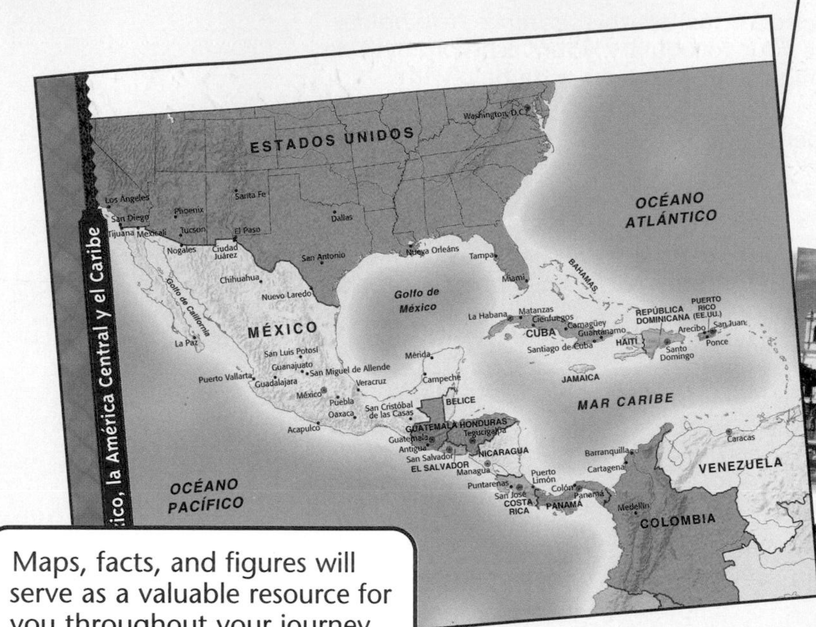

Maps, facts, and figures will serve as a valuable resource for you throughout your journey.

El mundo hispanohablante

Glencoe's **El mundo hispanohablante** will take you to the many places where you will be able to use your Spanish.

Start your journey with an introduction to each of the diverse regions of the Spanish-speaking world.

Each lesson is structured consistently to make learning easy.

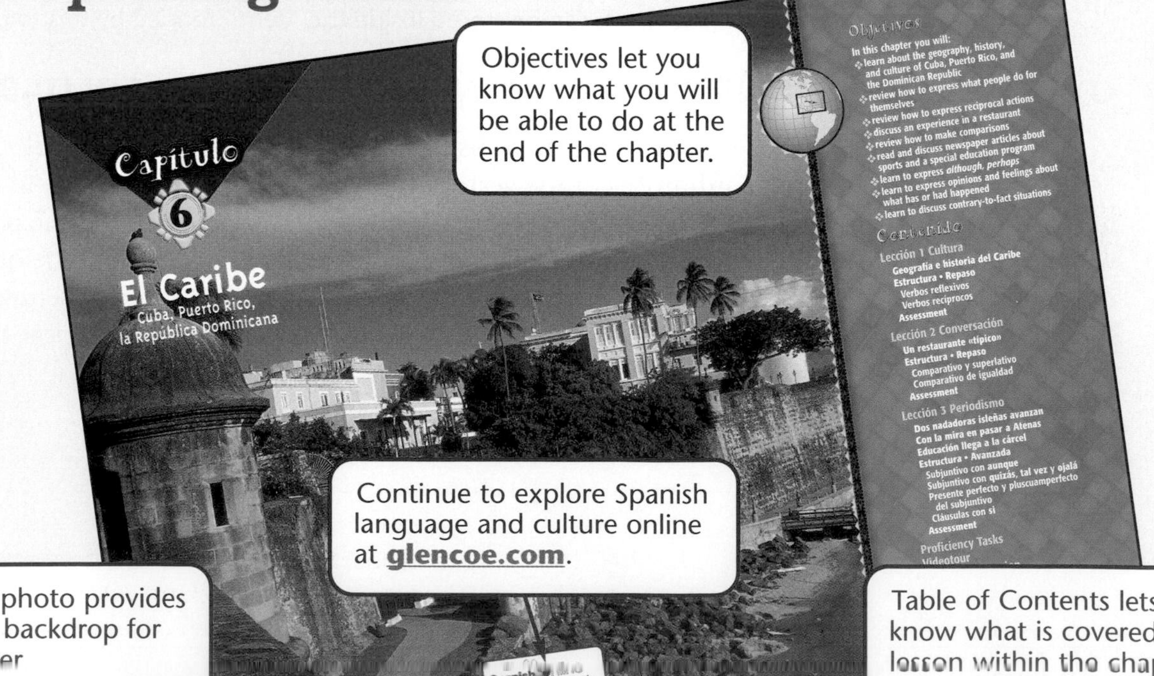

Objectives let you know what you will be able to do at the end of the chapter.

Continue to explore Spanish language and culture online at **glencoe.com**.

Opening photo provides a cultural backdrop for the chapter.

Table of Contents lets you know what is covered in each lesson within the chapter.

Talk about the Spanish-speaking world with your new vocabulary.

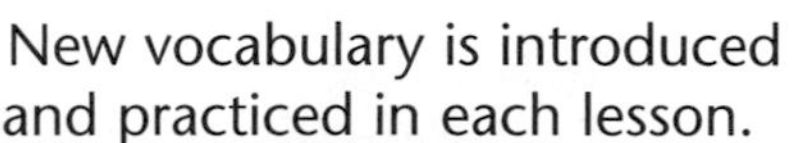

New vocabulary is introduced and practiced in each lesson.

Recorded presentation ensures proper pronunciation.

LECCIÓN I

Cultura

Vocabulario para la lectura

Use your StudentWorks Plus CD for more practice.

Los vientos del huracán castigaban el galeón.
El galeón no se hundió.
Pero por poco se hunde.

El cacique nunca se sometió a los españoles.
Nunca llevaría cadenas.

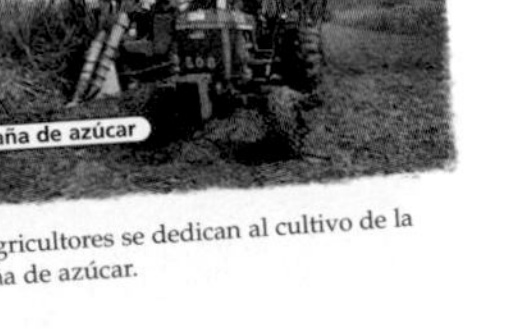

Los agricultores se dedican al cultivo de la caña de azúcar.

el lechón asado

Algunas frutas tropicales

el coco

la piña

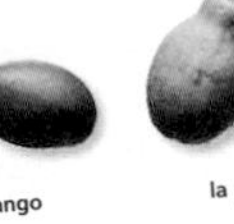

el mango

la papaya

CAPÍTULO 6

272 doscientos setenta y dos

Más vocabulario

el cacique jefe de los indígenas
el/la ciudadano(a) persona con los derechos y obligaciones de su nacionalidad
la toma acción de tomar posesión de algo como un territorio o una ciudad
apartado(a) retirado, distante, alejado
desafecto(a) opuesto, contrario, enemigo
emprender comenzar, empezar, iniciar como un viaje o aventura
rebosar abundar, contener demasiado
reposar descansar, posar sobre algo

¿Qué palabra necesito?

1 Historieta Los galeones Contesten con sí.

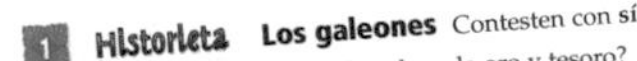
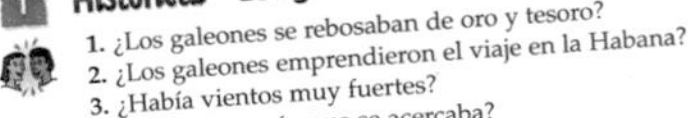

1. ¿Los galeones se rebosaban de oro y tesoro?
2. ¿Los galeones emprendieron el viaje en la Habana?
3. ¿Había vientos muy fuertes?
4. ¿Era un huracán que se acercaba?
5. ¿Los vientos castigaban el galeón?

2 ¿Cuál es la palabra? Den la palabra cuya definición sigue.

1. habitante, persona con cierta nacionalidad
2. la ocupación, la conquista
3. descansar, estar encima de otra cosa
4. separado, aparte

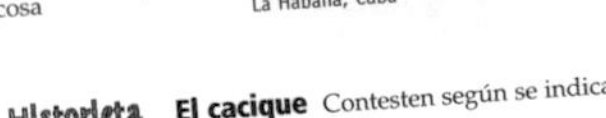

La Habana, Cuba

3 Historieta El cacique Contesten según se indica.

1. ¿Quién era el jefe indígena? (el cacique)
2. ¿Se sometió el cacique a los españoles? (no)
3. ¿Quisieron ponerlo en cadenas los españoles? (sí)
4. ¿El cacique era desafecto al gobierno español? (sí)
5. ¿Él quería hispanizarse? (no)

Pinar del Río, Cuba

4 Los agricultores Completen con una palabra apropiada.

divertirse	lechón	el mango	la piña
cultivar	la caña	el coco	frijoles

1. Los agricultores van a _____ la tierra.
2. Ellos se dedican al cultivo de _____ de azúcar.
3. _____, _____ y _____ son frutas tropicales.
4. Los muchachos están cocinando un _____ asado.
5. Lo van a servir con arroz y _____.

EL CARIBE

doscientos setenta tres 273

Photos and illustrations aid comprehension and vocabulary acquisition.

New words prepare you for the material that follows.

Access your book, the practice activities, and the audio recordings on any computer with StudentWorks.

Get an in-depth look at the culture of the region.

In Lesson 1 of each chapter, you will learn about many aspects of culture, including geography, history, politics, famous people, food, and everyday life.

LECCIÓN I

Cultura

Lectura

La geografía del Caribe

Es común hablar del «Caribe», que es un mar, cuando nos referimos a las Antillas, un archipiélago constituido por miles de islas que forman tres grupos importantes. Estas son las Grandes Antillas, las Pequeñas Antillas y las Bahamas. Las islas en las que nos enfocamos aquí son tres de las cuatro que forman las Grandes Antillas, o sea, Cuba, Puerto Rico y la Española. La cuarta, Jamaica, es una isla y un país de habla inglesa.

Using background knowledge When you are first assigned a reading, quickly look at the accompanying visuals to determine what the reading is about. Once you know what the topic is, spend a short time thinking about what you already know about it. If you do this, the reading will be easier to understand.

Santo Domingo, la República Dominicana

Cuba es la más grande de las Grandes Antillas y la que está más cerca de Norteamérica. Al este de Cuba se encuentra la Española, una isla compartida por dos repúblicas, Haití y la República Dominicana. Al este de la Española está Puerto Rico, la más pequeña del grupo. Las Grandes Antillas son mayormente montañosas y reposan sobre una cadena de montañas submarinas.

La Habana, Cub

LECCIÓN I

Cultura

Pinar del Río, Cuba

Clima

Las Grandes Antillas se encuentran en la zona tropical. No obstante, el clima es tropical en los llanos pero subtropical en las áreas montañosas. Hay dos estaciones: la seca, de noviembre a mayo, y la húmeda, de junio a octubre. Comenzando en julio y hasta octubre, los huracanes, que nacen en el océano Atlántico, veces castigan las costas de estas islas. En todas las Antillas la egetación es exuberante. El clima es especialmente apropiado ra el cultivo de la caña de azúcar, el café y el tabaco, productos portantes en las tres islas.

Un huracán, San Juan, Puerto Rico

Contesten.

1. ¿Cuál es la diferencia entre el «Caribe» y las «Antillas»?
2. ¿En cuál de las Antillas se encuentran Cuba, Puerto Rico y la Española?
3. ¿Cuál de las islas está más cerca de la América del Norte?
4. En una de las islas hay dos repúblicas. ¿Cuál es la isla?
5. ¿Sobre qué se sitúan las Grandes Antillas?
6. ¿En qué zona climática se encuentran las Grandes Antillas?

En las Grandes Antillas hay áreas con clima subtropical. ¿Dónde están?

¿Cómo se llaman las dos estaciones del año n las Antillas?

Qué fenómeno meteorológico puede causar ucho daño en el Caribe?

ómo es la vegetación d

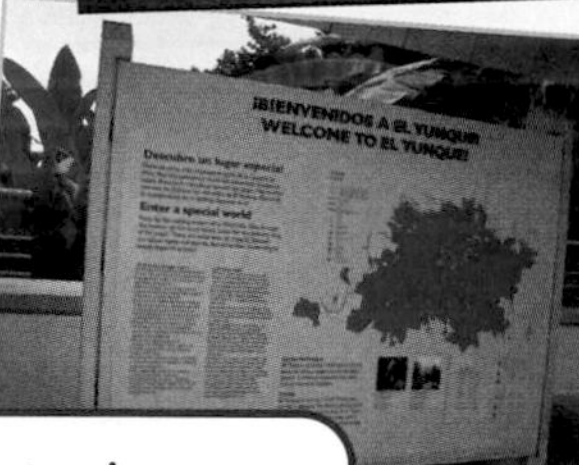

LECCIÓN I

Cultura

Reading Strategy

Using pictures and photographs Before you begin to read, look at the pictures, photographs, or any other visuals that accompany a reading. By doing this, you can often tell what the reading selection is about before you actually read it.

Lectura

La geografía

Chile

El Cono sur comprende los países de Chile, Argentina, Uruguay y Paraguay. Chile es un país largo y estrecho que tiene la forma de una habichuela verde (de un poroto). Siendo tan largo desde el norte hasta el sur, tiene un terreno extremadamente variado y variaciones climáticas extremas. El desierto de Atacama en el norte es uno de los desiertos más áridos del mundo. El centro, cerca de Santiago, la capital, disfruta de un clima templado como el del Mediterráneo. Aquí hay viñedos y huertas. La región de los bellísimos lagos goza también de un clima templado, pero un poco más hacia el sur en Puerto Montt, por ejemplo, el clima es lluvioso y borrascoso incluso en el verano. La Patagonia en el sur tiene un clima casi siempre frío y lluvioso con chaparrones frecuentes y ráfagas de viento que alcanzan una velocidad increíble. La Patagonia es famosa por sus fiordos y glaciares.

Saltos de Petrohue, Chile

Santiago, Chile

Argentina

Argentina es el segundo mayor país de Sudamérica. Se puede dividir el país en cuatro grandes regiones naturales.

Las llanuras del nordeste Se caracterizan las llanuras por vastas zonas de terreno pantanoso[1] y sabanas. Es la región de los ríos Paraná y Uruguay. Una región húmeda de fértil tierra roja, es famosa por su gran ganadería y agricultura incluyendo el cultivo de la hierba mate, de la que se hace la bebida nacional.

[1] pantanoso swampy, marshy

Río Uruguay, Argentina

Reading strategies are included to help you continue to improve your reading skills.

Photographs illustrate the readings and provide images of the region.

Engage classmates in real conversation.

Vocabulary is presented to help you understand the conversations and to help you create your own conversations.

Listen to the conversation on any computer using StudentWorks.

Expand your knowledge about the topic of the conversation with **Web Explore**.

Activities ensure that you have understood the conversations.

LECCIÓN 2

Conversación

Vocabulario para la conversación

Use your StudentWorks Plus CD for more practice.

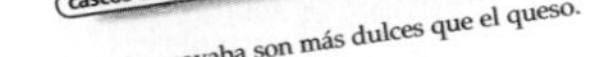

cascos de guayaba y queso blanco

Los cascos de guayaba son más dulces que el queso.

un churrasco

A mí me gusta un buen churrasco.

Más vocabulario

la carne quemada la carne bien hecha
los dueños los patronos, los jefes, los propietarios
descortés ineducado, grosero, no cortés
lento(a) contrario de «rápido»
listo(a) inteligente
rico(a) delicioso
acompañar ir con, juntarse
evitar eludir, evadir
por colmo para ser peor, para pasar el límite

2. ¿Quién te ...?
3. ¿Qué pediste? (un churrasco)
4. ¿Te gustó? (no)
5. ¿Por qué no te gustó? (estaba quemado)
6. De postre, ¿qué pidió tu amigo? (cascos de guayaba con queso blanco)
7. ¿Le gustó? (estaba muy rico)
8. ¿Y el servicio? (un poco lento)
9. ¿Evitarás volver al restaurante? (creo)

2 **¿Cuál es otra palabra?** Den un sinónimo

1. los amos o los propietarios
2. sabroso, gustoso
3. evadir, escaparse de
4. astuto, hábil
5. carne de res, biftec
6. juntarse, ir con otra persona

LECCIÓN 2

...te «típico»

Antonio ¿Adónde fueron ustedes a comer anoche?
Elena Es mejor que no me preguntes. Fue la peor comida y un servicio tan malo que no lo puedes imaginar.
Antonio ¿Y dónde fue esto? Si aquí en la capital se come muy bien, mejor que en muchas partes. Y preparan nuestros platos caribeños tan ricos como ninguno.
Elena Pues, si yo fuera tan lista como tú, habría evitado el problema. Es verdad, muy pocas ciudades tienen tantos buenos restaurantes caribeños como aquí. Pero nosotros fuimos a un restaurante «argentino». Porque dicen que el «bife» argentino es el mejor del mundo, pedimos un churrasco.
Antonio Ah. Ustedes fueron a «El Gaucho Moncho», ¿verdad?
Elena Sí. ¿Cómo lo sabías?
Antonio Yo fui allí el otro día. Fue terrible. La carne era tan dura como una piedra. Además estaba quemada y tan seca como el desierto. Y el mesero… el hombre era tan lento y descortés que no le dejamos una propina. Y por colmo, los dueños del restaurante ni son argentinos ni han visitado nunca Argentina. Allí no hay nada auténtico. Esta noche vamos a un restaurante caribeño, «La flor de las Antillas». Ellos preparan nuestros platos mejor que nadie. ¿Quieres acompañarnos?
Elena Ay, Antonio. Lechón asado, tostones, bacalaítos[1]…
Antonio Ah, y lo mejor es que todo va acompañado de arroz con frijoles.
Elena ¡Cállate, Antonio! Se me hace agua la boca[2] sólo con pensarlo. Y de postre, cascos de guayaba y queso blanco. Tengo tanta hambre como un tigre. ¿A qué hora me buscas?
Antonio La mejor hora para comer allí es a las ocho. Te buscaré a las siete y media.

[1] bacalaítos *bits of fried codfish*
[2] Se me hace agua la boca *Makes my mouth water*

Spanish Online: To learn more about restaurants in the Caribbean, do the Chapter 6 **WebQuest** activity on the Glencoe Spanish Web site at glencoe.com.

La República Dominicana

LECCIÓN 2

Conversación

¿Comprendes?

A Contesten.

1. ¿Dónde comió Elena anoche?
2. ¿Qué tipo de restaurante fue?
3. ¿Fue buena la comida?
4. ¿Qué tal el servicio?
5. ¿Comió Elena comida caribeña?
6. ¿Qué pidieron Elena y sus amigos?
7. ¿Les gustó?
8. ¿Ha comido Antonio en ese restaurante?
9. ¿Cuánto dejó de propina al mesero Antonio?
10. ¿Qué problemas tuvo con el mesero Antonio?
11. ¿Adónde va a comer Antonio esta noche?
12. ¿Qué tipo de comida sirven allí?

Spanish Online: For more information about Caribbean foods, go to **Web Explore** on the Glencoe Spanish Web site at glencoe.com.

B Expliquen y describan.

1. ¿Cómo sabía Antonio que Elena había comido en «El Gaucho Moncho»?
2. ¿Cómo era la carne que pidió Antonio en «El Gaucho Moncho»?
3. ¿Por qué dice Antonio que el lugar no es auténtico?
4. ¿Cuáles son algunos platos típicos de la comida caribeña?

C Completen.

1. La Flor de las Antillas es un ____ caribeño.
2. Los cascos de guayaba se sirven con ____.
3. ____ son pedacitos de bacalao frito en forma de panqueque.
4. Muchos platos cubanos, puertorriqueños y dominicanos vienen acompañados de ____.

Un parque en Santo Domingo

CAPÍTULO 6

You will learn about culture through journalism.

You will have the opportunity to learn about the perspectives of the people in the target culture.

LECCIÓN 3
Periodismo

EL MERCURIO
SANTIAGO DE CHILE

Cuando hay que dejar el hogar

El salir de la casa para dar comienzo a una carrera universitaria es muchas veces ingrato. A pesar de ello, las vivencias[1] de quienes así lo hacen son positivas, convirtiéndose en una opción real y creciente.

Comenzar la vida universitaria no es tarea fácil. Son muchas las opciones que se presentan y diversas las variables que se deban considerar. Una de ellas es realizar los estudios superiores fuera de la ciudad en donde crecimos, dejando amigos y la familia.

Este importante desafío[2] parte por definir la vocación, escoger la carrera, universidad y hasta la ciudad en donde empezará esta nueva etapa.

La capital siempre ha sido una de las opciones preferidas ... jóvenes que inician ... ilidad

El número de jóvenes que se va a estudiar a regiones crece cada día más, y un importante número de ellos toman esta opción por sobre el arraigo[4] y apego[5] a todos los seres queridos. Las ventajas y los ... que trae, a juicio ...

continuar en región. No quería más smog, tráfico, distancias largas, además nació en mí una fuerte necesidad de independencia y de vivir algo diferente.»

El hecho de partir, cuenta, le trajo muchos beneficios, pero también debió enfrentar la soledad que muchas veces se presenta y que puede ser la peor compañera de esta nueva vida. «Luego de la decisión vino lo más complicado. Asumir que estaba sola, sin mis padres, mis amigos. La casa es un soporte emocional muy fuerte e importante, el que muchas veces te ayuda a pasar los problemas más fácilmente. ... debía darle la cara a lo ...

También se deben combatir los obstáculos que se cruzan en este nuevo camino.

El vivir fuera de casa implica responsabilidades en términos prácticos y económicos. Ya no está la mamá o la nana para hacer la comida y lavar la ropa, no está el padre para dar más dinero si la mesada[6] se acabó, y los amigos no están al alcance[7] de una llamada telefónica para organizar una «junta».

«La independencia que se logra tiene dos caras, por un lado te sientes muy bien cuando te haces cargo de todo y resulta, pero no puedes estar con los amigos o la familia si tienes pena o simplemente quieres conversar con alguien. A pesar de todo, he madurado y crecido mucho. Soy más tolerante y me llevo mejor con mis padres, los veo menos, por lo que disfruto cada momento que comparto con ellos» reflexiona Marión.

... a compartir

comunitaria es complicado y difícil. Cuando recién llegué a Valparaíso, arrendé una casa con compañeras que no conocía. No sabía cuáles eran sus costumbres y menos el estilo de vida que llevaban, tuve más de un problema, pero finalmente logré encontrar la persona adecuada para compartir.»

Un elemento que no se debe dejar de lado al momento de tomar la decisión junto a la familia, es el factor económico. Hay que arrendar un lugar para vivir, tener el dinero necesario para asumir los costos de la carrera misma, divertirse, recrearse y considerar que cada cierto tiempo se visita el hogar.

Según José Cortés, director de asuntos estudiantiles del Campus Viña del Mar de la Universidad Nacional Andrés Bello, indica que «el elemento económico es muy importante; en algunos casos las familias hacen un gran esfuerzo para mandarlos a estudiar fuera de su casa. Los alumnos que ... en esta aventura son los ...

administrar sus recursos, el tiempo y hacerse cargo del paso académico y el estar solos haciéndose cargo de todo.»

Superar la soledad

La gran desventaja que percibe Cortés es la soledad, muchos de los alumnos sufren lejos de su casa y deciden volver antes de terminar el primer año de carrera. «La mayor desventaja es la soledad. Los padres los ubican en departamentos o pensiones, pero hay muchos que no son capaces de superar su nuevo estado. Son varios los casos en los que caen en depresión en el primer semestre, lo que les dificulta llevar el peso académico que se les exige y terminan regresando a sus casas.»

Estas situaciones, añade José Cortés, son consideradas por la mayoría de las universidades y por ello se realizan diferentes actividades para lograr que los novatos se integren y adapten. Es así como el encargado de asuntos estudiantiles explica que en la universidad «para ...

LECCIÓN 3
Periodismo

LECCIÓN 3

Vocabulario para la lectura

Dos nadadoras isleñas avanzan
Con la mira en pasar a Atenas

Use your StudentWorks Plus CD for more practice.

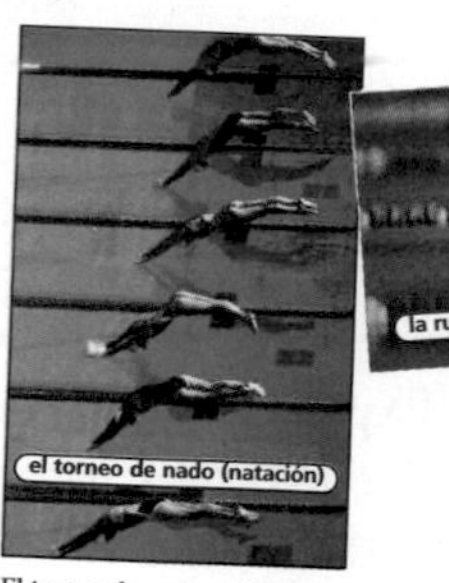

El torneo de nado está integrado por muchas atletas. ¡Ojalá que ganen el campeonato mundial!

Más vocabulario

la mira intención, idea, propósito
remozado(a) renovado, modernizado
zurdo(a) que usa la mano izquierda
encabezar ir al frente, ir a la cabeza
realizar hacer, efectuar
ubicarse colocarse, situarse

¿Qué palabra necesito?

1 Historieta El torneo de nado (natación) Contesten.

1. ¿Qué tipo de torneo es? ¿De nado?
2. ¿La nadadora realiza clavados?
3. ¿Es ella experta en clavados?
4. ¿Se realizará la rutina libre hoy?
5. ¿Se realizará la rutina libre en la piscina municipal?

2 Sóftbol femenino Completen.

1. La pítcher lanza la pelota con la mano izquierda. Ella es ____.
2. Ella es la mejor jugadora y por eso ____ el equipo.
3. La ____ del equipo es su participación en los juegos Preolímpicos.
4. El equipo está ____ por muchas atletas muy buenas.
5. El estadio estaba en malas condiciones, pero ahora está totalmente ____.

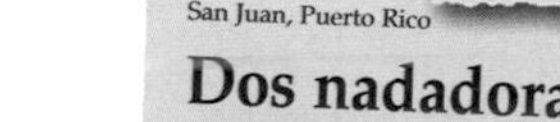

San Juan, Puerto Rico

Dos nadadoras isleñas avanzan

EL DUETO puertorriqueño integrado por Luna del Mar Aguilú y Leilani Torres se ubicó ayer en la posición 24 de entre 34 equipos al concluir con 81.000 la preliminar técnica del nado sincronizado de los Campeonatos Mundiales de Natación y Clavados que se celebrarán hasta el domingo 27 en Barcelona, España. Hoy se realizará la rutina libre.

Con la mira en pasar a Atenas

LA ESTELAR zurda Jessica van der Linden Dávila encabeza el grupo de 18 jugadoras que integrarán el Equipo Nacional que participará desde el próximo lunes 21 en el torneo Preolímpico de Sóftbol Femenino en el remozado estadio Donna Terry de Guaynabo.

¿Comprendes?

A Dos nadadoras isleñas Contesten.

1. ¿En qué deporte participan Leilani y Luna del Mar?
2. ¿Los campeonatos son de natación y qué otra cosa?
3. ¿Cuántos equipos en total estuvieron en el preliminar de nado sincronizado?
4. ¿En qué lugar se encontró el equipo puertorriqueño?
5. ¿Dónde tuvo lugar el evento?
6. ¿Qué evento se realizará hoy?

B A Atenas Contesten.

... en el equipo nacional de sóftbol?
... e encabeza el equipo?
... pelota?
... ueblo van a jugar ellas?
... dio?

Cultural selections from newspapers and magazines provide high-interest reading.

In the Structure sections, continue to improve your knowledge of how Spanish works.

LECCIÓN I
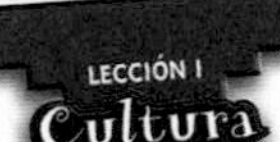
Cultura

Estructura • Repaso

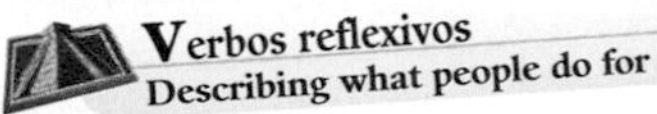

Verbos reflexivos
Describing what people do for th

Each lesson includes a Structure section. In Lessons 1 and 2, the material is review. In Lesson 3, the advanced material introduces new structures.

1. A verb is reflexive when the action is both execute by the subject.

   Me lavo. *I wash myself.*

2. Because the subject also receives the action of the verb an additional pronoun is required. This pronoun is called a reflexive pronoun.

INFINITIVE	lavarse	bañarse
yo	me lavo	me baño
tú	te lavas	te bañas
él, ella, Ud.	se lava	se baña
nosotros(as)	nos lavamos	nos bañamos
vosotros(as)	*os laváis*	*os bañáis*
ellos, ellas, Uds.	se lavan	se bañan

...have a stem change in both the present and preterite tenses.

The structure is taught and practiced within the context of and with the vocabulary of the lesson.

...subject and recipient of ...omething other than the

LECCIÓN I
Cultura

¿Cómo lo digo?

1 Historieta Algunas costumbres mías
Contesten.

1. ¿A qué hora te acuestas?
2. ¿Te duermes enseguida o pasas la noche dando vueltas en la cama?
3. ¿A qué hora te levantas?
4. ¿Te despiertas fácilmente?
5. ¿Te bañas o te duchas antes de acostarte o después de levantarte?
6. ¿Te desayunas antes de salir para la escuela?
7. ¿Te cepillas los dientes después de tomar el desayuno?
8. ¿Te pones un uniforme para ir a la escuela?
9. ¿Te vistes elegantemente para ir a la escuela?
10. ¿Te diviertes con tus amigos en la escuela?
11. ¿Te despides de tus amigos cuando sales de la escuela?

San Juan, Puerto Rico

2 Historieta En Puerto Rico Contesten.

1. ¿Te divertiste cuando estabas en Puerto Rico?
2. ¿Te sentiste en casa?
3. ¿Te vestiste de sport?
4. ¿Te pusiste el bañador para ir a la playa?
5. ¿Te pusiste una crema protectora en la playa?
6. ¿Te bronceaste?
7. ¿Te dormiste en la playa?
8. Al salir de Puerto Rico, ¿te despediste de tus nuevos amigos?

LECCIÓN 3
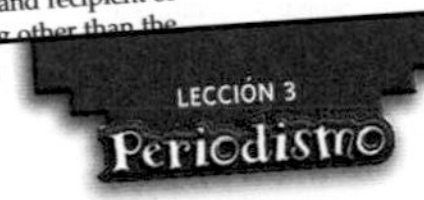
Periodismo

Estructura • Avanzada

Subjuntivo con aunque
Expressing *although*

The conjunction **aunque** *(although)* may be followed by the subjunctive or the indicative depending upon the meaning of the sentence.

Ellas nadarán aunque haga mucho frío.
Ellas nadarán aunque hace mucho frío.

In the first example, the subjunctive is used to indicate that although it may not be cold now, they will swim even if it gets very cold. In the second example, the indicative is used to indicate that it actually is very cold but they will still swim.

La República Dominicana

¿Cómo lo digo?

1 Historieta ¿Lo hacemos o no?
Contesten con **aunque**.

1. No tienes un boleto. ¿Vas al concierto?
2. No sé si el carro tiene bastante gasolina. ¿Vas a ir en el carro?
3. Podría llover. ¿Vendrá Diana con nosotros?
4. Subieron los precios de las entradas. ¿Todavía vamos?
5. Y si hay mucho tráfico, ¿qué? ¿Iremos o no?
6. No sé si Paco Mendes va a tocar. ¿Vas a ir?
7. Tito no tiene dinero. ¿Lo vas a llevar al concierto?
8. Y si la profesora nos da tarea, ¿todavía vamos a ir?

Carretera entre San Juan y Arecibo, Puerto Rico

2 Historieta Los reclusos
Escojan la forma apropiada del verbo.

1. El profesor recibe un salario. Pero le gusta tanto su trabajo, el profesor enseñará aunque no le (pagan/paguen).
2. Les dieron materiales a los reclusos. Pero tienen tantas ganas de aprender que los reclusos estudiarán aunque no (tienen/tengan) materiales.
3. Los oficiales no visitan la cárcel hoy. Pero no importa. V... hoy aunque no (vienen/vengan) los oficiales.
4. No hay duda que falta dinero. Pero siguen implement... aunque no (hay/haya) dinero.
5. El público se opone. El Secretario seguirá con el progr... público no (quiere/quiera) que siga.

Numerous activities allow you to practice what you have learned.

EL CARIBE

LECCIÓN 3
Periodismo

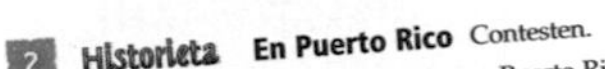

Cláusulas con si
Discussing contrary-to-fact situations

1. Si *(if)* clauses are used to express contrary-to-fact conditions. Si clauses conform to a specific sequence of tenses.

   Si tengo tiempo iré al torneo. *If I have time, I'll go to the tournament.*
   Si tuviera tiempo iría al torneo. *If I had time, I would go to the tournament.*
   Si hubiera tenido tiempo, habría ido al torneo.

2. The sequence of tenses for si clau...

MAIN CLAUSE	SI CLA...
Future	Prese...
Conditional	Impe...
Conditional perfect	Plupe...

Realia lets you see the structure used in real-life contexts.

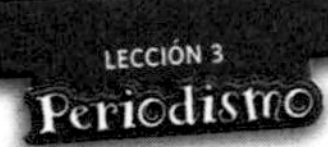
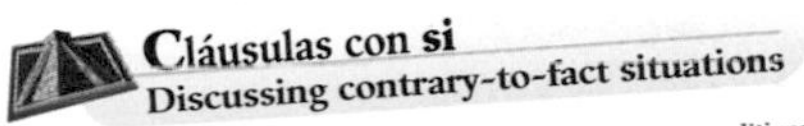

¿Cómo lo digo?

9 Yo Contesten.

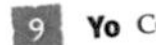

1. Si tienes el dinero, ¿irás a Puerto Rico?
2. Si tuvieras el dinero, ¿irías a Puerto Rico?
3. Si hubieras tenido el dinero, ¿habrías ido a Puerto Rico?
4. Si vas a Puerto Rico, ¿visitarás las cuevas de Camuy?
5. Si fueras a Puerto Rico, ¿visitarías las cuevas de Camuy?
6. Si hubieras ido a Puerto Rico, ¿habrías visitado las cuevas de Camuy?

El Viejo San Juan, Puerto Rico

trescientos once 311

It's your turn! Apply what you have learned.

Practice what you have learned and improve your written Spanish.

LECCIÓN I
Cultura

¡Te toca a ti!
Use what you have learned

La Habana, Cuba

1 Geografía (HABLAR)

✔ *Describe the geography of Puerto Rico, Cuba, and the Dominican Republic*

Con un(a) compañero(a) describe la geografía y el clima de las islas de las Grandes Antillas. ¿Se parecen a la geografía y al clima en donde tú vives? Haz una comparación.

2 Las vacaciones (ESCRIBIR)

✔ *Write a suggestion about when to go to the Caribe*

Recibiste un e-mail de una amiga. Ella quiere ir a la República Dominicana, pero no sabe cuál sería la mejor época para su visita. Mándale un e-mail y dale una recomendación pensando en el clima y las estaciones del año.

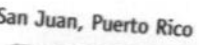

3 Las Antillas (HABLAR)

✔ *Make some comparisons between the islands of the Greater Antilles*

Describe algunas diferencias y semejanzas geográficas, históricas y políticas entre Puerto Rico, Cuba y la República Dominicana.

4 ¿De qué país hablas? (HABLAR)

✔ *Play a game and guess the country being discussed*

Tú vas a mencionar un lugar, monumento o evento en uno de los países de las Antillas. Tu compañero(a) tiene que adivinar cuál es el país. Si tu compañero(a) contesta correctamente, entonces él o ella te hará una pregunta a ti.

288 doscientos ochenta y ocho

CAPÍTULO 6

LECCIÓN I
Cultura

5 La República Dominicana y el béisbol (HABLAR)

✔ *Talk about the Dominican Republic and baseball*

Explícale como y por qué la República Dominicana es tan importante en cuanto al béisbol.

6 Tus rutinas (HABLAR, ESCRIBIR)

✔ *Compare your daily routines*

Por lo general hay una diferencia entre tu rutina de entre semana y tu rutina de fin de semana, ¿no? Dile a un(a) compañero(a) como son diferentes.

7 ¡Al Caribe! (HABLAR, ESCRIBIR)

✔ *Tell why you would like to visit the Greater Antilles*

En tus estudios de español ya has aprendido mucho sobre las islas del Caribe. En tus propias palabras explica por qué las quisieras visitar.

Villa Fundación, la República Dominicana

Guajataca, Puerto Rico

EL CARIBE

doscientos ochenta y nueve  289

Use what you have learned in cumulative, open-ended activities.

Check your progress.

Review what you have learned and prepare for your chapter test.

LECCIÓN 1

Assessment

Vocabulario

1 Completen con una palabra apropiada.

1. Lo tomaron prisionero y lo llevaron a la prisión en ____.
2. Él tenía un espíritu independiente y nunca se ____ a los invasores.
3. Nunca colaboró con ellos, fue siempre ____ al gobierno.
4. Estaba muy cansado y buscaba donde ____ su cabeza.
5. Lo tenían en un lugar muy ____, muy lejos de todo.
6. Era un jefe de los indígenas, un ____ de gran fama.
7. Quería ____ su viaje aquel día pero no pudo a causa del viento.
8. Él luchó por la independencia para que sus hijos pudieran ser ____ de una nación independiente.
9. El clima de su bella isla era benévolo salvo cuando los ____ con sus tremendos vientos castigaban la isla.

To review vocabulary, turn to page 272.

La Habana, Cuba

Lectura

2 Escojan.

10. Hay ____ islas en las Grandes Antillas.
  a. dos b. cuatro c. ocho
11. Las Grandes Antillas, las Pequeñas Antillas y las Bahamas forman ____.
  a. un archipiélago b. un istmo c. una península
12. En el Caribe hay solamente ____ estaciones.
  a. dos b. cuatro c. seis
13. Los huracanes normalmente aparecen en ____.
  a. enero b. abril c. septiembre

To review some geographical facts about the Caribbean, turn to pages 274–275.

3 Contesten.

14. ¿Cómo llamaban los españoles a la isla que los taínos llamaban «Quisqueya»?
15. ¿Qué producto agrícola introdujeron los españoles a las Antillas?
16. Cuando ya no había indígenas para trabajar, ¿en qué continente encontraron los colonizadores más mano de obra?
17. ¿Cuáles son los tres partidos políticos de Puerto Rico?
18. ¿Por qué tuvieron que fortificar a La Habana los españoles?
19. ¿Por qué salieron muchos cubanos de su país después de 1959?

To review some historical facts about the Caribbean, turn to pages 276–283.

Estructura

4 Completen con el pronombre apropiado si es necesario.

20. Yo ____ puse unos jeans para ir a la fiesta.
21. ¿A qué hora ____ acostaste anoche?
22. Hace tiempo que tú y yo ____ conocemos, ¿verdad?
23. Pero Ramón y Carolina ____ conocieron hace solamente una semana.
24. Ella ____ divirtió mucho en la fiesta.
25. Después de la fiesta nosotros ____ lavamos todos los platos y vasos.

To review reflexive verbs, turn to pages 284 and 287.

"Sticky" notes direct you to appropriate pages for review.

290 doscientos noventa CAPÍTULO 6 doscientos noventa y uno 291

Demonstrate your written and verbal skills to show your proficiency in Spanish.

Learn strategies to become a better writer.

CAPÍTULO 6

Proficiency Tasks

Composición

Cada escrito tiene un propósito. El propósito de tu primera tarea es la de informar. Vas a compartir con otros la información que has obtenido de tus propias lecturas y experiencias. Vas a escribir un artículo de crónica. En este tipo de artículo normalmente se presenta la información en un orden cronológico.

TAREA 1 **Escritura expositiva** Acabas de leer en detalle sobre la geografía, historia y cultura de tres países de habla española: Cuba, Puerto Rico y la República Dominicana. Tienes que seleccionar el tema en que vas a enfocar. Como lo que tienes que escribir es una crónica, obviamente la historia es lo indicado como tema.

Antes de escribir Primero debes releer el material de fondo. Entonces toma apuntes sobre los detalles de más importancia, siempre en orden cronológico. Si crees que necesitas más información, pregúntale a tu profesor(a) donde puedes encontrar recursos adicionales.

Bosquejo Prepara ahora un bosquejo del ... organizar tus ideas. Ahora piensa ... tu crónica. Piensa en tu ... interesarle en el tema. Por ... ue vas a escribir es una ... ón tiene el propósito de atraer ... marle a leer el artículo. Aquí ... gerencias: ... interesante ... en que indica la idea central ... ripción gráfica del lugar ... de la gente ... o que da impulso a la historia ... te principal del artículo: ... detalles vivaces, escoge adjetivos ... e los personajes importantes. ... el orden cronológico. ... e los lectores se identifiquen con ... sonajes. ... nal del artículo puedes emplear las ... strategias como para la introducción: un detalle interesante, una imagen, etc.

Presentación Escribe la crónica.

Repasar y revisar Revisa tu crónica para verificar si todo está escrito correctamente y si has incluido toda la información necesaria. Corrige cualquier error ortográfico o gramatical.

TAREA 2 **Explicación** Un propósito de muchos escritos es la explicación de un evento o condición. Por lo que has leído de otros países de Latinoamérica sabes que las poblaciones indígenas son significativas en varios, pero no en el Caribe. En un breve escrito explica como es que desaparecieron casi por completo las poblaciones indígenas del Caribe. En tu escrito debes indicar:

- donde en el Caribe existían las poblaciones indígenas
- cuáles eran las poblaciones y de donde vinieron
- las características de las poblaciones
- la causa de su desaparición

Antes de escribir Antes de comenzar a escribir, piensa en como vas a organizar tu explicación. Determina los detalles que vas a incluir. Decide también en el tono de tu escrito. ¿Será simplemente expositivo o tendrá también un matiz emotivo? Cuando tengas todo decidido, prepara un borrador.

Revisa tu borrador para ver si estás satisfecho(a) con el contenido. ¿Está completo? ¿Falta algún detalle? ¿Son vívidas las descripciones? Cuando estás satisfecho(a) con el borrador léelo de nuevo y corrige cualquier error de gramática u ortografía. Ahora prepara tu versión final, revísala para que no haya errores. Corrige los errores que encuentres.

TAREA 3 **Una biografía** Como ya sabes, una biografía es la historia de la vida de una persona real, no ficticia. Ya has escrito una biografía de una persona que tú mismo(a) has escogido. Ahora vas a limitarte a uno de los personajes que aparecen en el capítulo que acabas de leer. Para prepararte adecuadamente tendrás que hacer alguna investigación sobre la persona. Los personajes que aparecen en la lectura son: Guarionex, Cayacoa, Cristóbal Colón, «el Drake», don Juan Ponce de León, José Martí, Antonio Maceo y Fidel Castro.

Antes de ... ... de la lista de personajes algunos que tú crees serán interesantes. Después busca a ver si existe bastante información sobre estas personas para poder escribir una biografía. Ahora escoge el individuo que más te interese. Prepara una lista de detalles que vas a incluir en tu biografía, por ejemplo: descripción física de la persona, su personalidad o carácter, su importancia histórica. Puedes seguir un orden cronológico, o puedes enfocar en uno de los detalles que creas más importante, su importancia histórica, por ejemplo. Trata de dar vida al personaje empleando adjetivos y adverbios vívidos.

Discurso

El debate es similar a una competencia deportiva. Se juega para ganar y se gana obteniendo ventaja sobre el rival. Una forma de debate consiste en una proposición. Un grupo o individuo tiene que defender la proposición mientras que el otro lleva la contraria. Un ejemplo de proposición sería: *A los atletas profesionales se les paga demasiado.* Un grupo defiende la proposición y el otro se opone. Para debatir eficazmente hay que ordenar los argumentos y presentarlos enérgicamente. Algunas armas son la veracidad, el humor, el dramatismo y la emoción. En muchos debates se le otorga a cada partido una oportunidad de responder a los argumentos del rival. Por eso es importante tratar de adivinar cuales serán los argumentos que presentará el rival y poder contestar vigorosamente. El buen debatiente puede tomar cualquier posición, en pro o en contra de la proposición y defender su posición con éxito.

TAREA 4 Para nuestro debate vamos a dividirnos en grupos de dos. La proposición es la siguiente: *El único propósito de las cárceles debe ser castigar a los criminales.* Una persona en cada grupo tiene que defender la proposición y la otra argüir en contra. Después de presentar los argumentos cada uno tendrá un minuto para refutar los argumentos del otro. La clase decidirá el ganador.

In each chapter, you will learn or improve upon techniques and strategies for writing and speaking. Apply these strategies to talk about or write about what you have learned.

Improve your speaking skills.

316 trescientos dieciséis CAPÍTULO 6 trescientos diecisiete 317

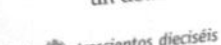

Video transports you to the Spanish-speaking world.

Visit the region you are studying.

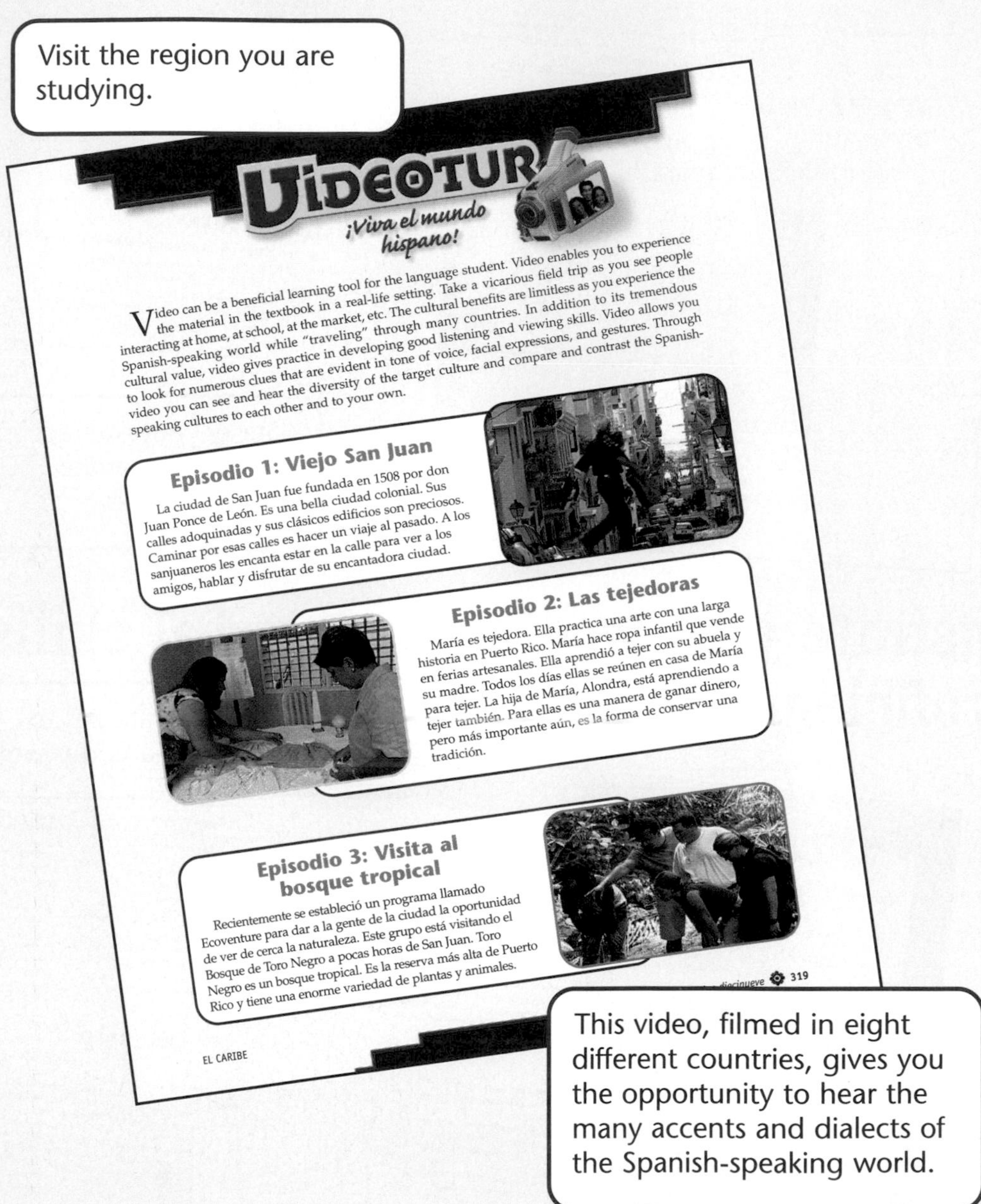

VIDEOTUR
¡Viva el mundo hispano!

Video can be a beneficial learning tool for the language student. Video enables you to experience the material in the textbook in a real-life setting. Take a vicarious field trip as you see people interacting at home, at school, at the market, etc. The cultural benefits are limitless as you experience the Spanish-speaking world while "traveling" through many countries. In addition to its tremendous cultural value, video gives practice in developing good listening and viewing skills. Video allows you to look for numerous clues that are evident in tone of voice, facial expressions, and gestures. Through video you can see and hear the diversity of the target culture and compare and contrast the Spanish-speaking cultures to each other and to your own.

Episodio 1: Viejo San Juan

La ciudad de San Juan fue fundada en 1508 por don Juan Ponce de León. Es una bella ciudad colonial. Sus calles adoquinadas y sus clásicos edificios son preciosos. Caminar por esas calles es hacer un viaje al pasado. A los sanjuaneros les encanta estar en la calle para ver a los amigos, hablar y disfrutar de su encantadora ciudad.

Episodio 2: Las tejedoras

María es tejedora. Ella practica una arte con una larga historia en Puerto Rico. María hace ropa infantil que vende en ferias artesanales. Ella aprendió a tejer con su abuela y su madre. Todos los días ellas se reúnen en casa de María para tejer. La hija de María, Alondra, está aprendiendo a tejer también. Para ellas es una manera de ganar dinero, pero más importante aún, es la forma de conservar una tradición.

Episodio 3: Visita al bosque tropical

Recientemente se estableció un programa llamado Ecoventure para dar a la gente de la ciudad la oportunidad de ver de cerca la naturaleza. Este grupo está visitando el Bosque de Toro Negro a pocas horas de San Juan. Toro Negro es un bosque tropical. Es la reserva más alta de Puerto Rico y tiene una enorme variedad de plantas y animales.

EL CARIBE

trescientos diecinueve 319

This video, filmed in eight different countries, gives you the opportunity to hear the many accents and dialects of the Spanish-speaking world.

Enhance your appreciation of literature and culture.

Literary Companion gives you yet another opportunity to apply your reading skills in Spanish.

Literary selections present another view of Hispanic culture.

Literary Companion

These literary selections develop reading and cultural skills and introduce you to Hispanic literature. They are organized to coincide with the chapters presented in the text. For example, **Literatura española** is designed to be done in conjunction with **Capítulo 1, España.**

416 cuatrocientos dieciséis

Biblioteca, Universidad de México

Literature selections written by authors from the region accompany each chapter.

Capítulo
1
España
Spanish Online
To interact with your online edition of
¡Buen viaje! go to: glencoe.com.

Objetivos

In this chapter you will:

- learn about the geography, history, and culture of Spain
- review how to express past actions
- discuss taking a trip to Spain
- read and discuss newspaper articles about the metro in Barcelona and immigrants arriving in Spain
- learn to refer to specific things
- learn to express ownership

Contenido

Cultura

Vocabulario para la lectura

Son el rey y la reina de España.
El rey estableció una monarquía constitucional.

Unas tropas extranjeras invadieron el país.
Los soldados españoles lucharon contra los invasores.
Las tres carabelas salieron del puerto.

Palabras españolas de origen árabe

una almohada

una alfombra

unas almendras

una alberca

Comida española

El cocinero rebanó la berenjena.
Cortó el jamón en trocitos.

Picó el ajo.
Peló el tomate.

Más vocabulario

la neblina nube muy baja que está en contacto con la tierra
el siglo un período de cien años
veraniego(a) del verano
huir escapar
parecerse a ser muy parecido, similar, semejante

LECCIÓN I

Cultura

¿Qué palabra necesito?

1 **Historieta** **Una guerra** Contesten.

1. ¿Reinaron Fernando e Isabel por mucho tiempo?
2. ¿Establecieron ellos una monarquía absoluta?
3. ¿Invadieron España unas tropas extranjeras?
4. ¿Fueron a la guerra los españoles?
5. ¿Lucharon por la corona?
6. ¿Tomaron parte en una batalla naval?
7. ¿Salieron victoriosos o perdieron muchas carabelas en la batalla?

2 **¿Y tú?** Contesten personalmente.

1. ¿Tienes una casa veraniega?
2. ¿Te gusta caminar o dar un paseo a lo largo de un río?
3. Donde vives, ¿hay colinas o llanuras?
4. Si hay mucha neblina, ¿puedes ver lo que hay en la distancia?
5. ¿Te gustan las almendras? ¿Comes muchas almendras o no?
6. ¿Cuántas almohadas tienes en tu cama? ¿Te gusta dormir con muchas almohadas?

Condominios veraniegos, Casares, Andalucía

3 Unos manjares españoles Completen.

1. El señor _____ el ajo. Luego puso el ajo _____ en una sopa.
2. El señor _____ el tomate. Luego puso el tomate _____ en la sopa con el ajo.
3. El señor _____ la berenjena. Luego frió las _____ de berenjena en aceite.
4. El señor _____ el jamón serrano. Lo cortó en _____.
5. El señor _____ el queso manchego en trocitos también.

Extremadura

4 ¿Cuál es la palabra? Den la palabra cuya definición sigue.

1. una serie de batallas
2. un período de cien años
3. las esmeraldas, los rubíes, los diamantes
4. una cosa sobre la cual se reclina la cabeza en la cama
5. escapar
6. un barco antiguo
7. lo que se usa para cubrir el piso de una habitación
8. ser semejante o parecido
9. donde hay muchos olivos
10. depósito artificial de agua

5 Palabras relacionadas Den una palabra relacionada.

1. el llano
2. el reinado
3. la joyería
4. el guerrero
5. cocinar
6. parecido
7. la lucha
8. el colorido
9. la oliva
10. el monarca

Lectura

La geografía

España, un país de grandes contrastes y mucha diversidad, se encuentra al sudoeste de Europa. Con su vecino Portugal, forma la península ibérica. Con excepción de Suiza, España es el país más montañoso de Europa. En el norte los Pirineos forman una frontera natural con Francia.

> **Reading Strategy**
>
> **Cognates** Words that look alike and have similar meanings in Spanish and English (**diversidad,** *diversity*) are called "cognates." Look for cognates whenever you read in Spanish. Recognizing cognates can help you figure out the meaning of many words in Spanish and will thus help you understand what you read.

El norte

A lo largo de toda la costa norte las montañas suben hacia el cielo desde las orillas del Cantábrico. Los majestuosos picos de Europa en Cantabria y Asturias alcanzan una altura de 8.600 pies. En Galicia, la pintoresca región del noroeste, hay mucha neblina y llueve mucho. El paisaje[1] gallego es muy verde y se parece mucho al paisaje de Irlanda.

Picos de Europa, Asturias

Galicia

El centro

Las llanuras interminables de color pardo naranja de Castilla y Extremadura en el centro del país contrastan mucho con las colinas verdes de Galicia. Aquí el clima es muy seco. En el invierno no cae mucha nieve pero hace un frío tremendo y los vientos fuertes son frecuentes. En el verano brilla un sol fuerte y hace mucho calor. En Madrid, la capital, hay un refrán que dice que allí hay «seis meses de invierno y seis meses de infierno[2]».

[1] paisaje *landscape*
[2] infierno *hell*

Madrid

Casares, Andalucía

El sur

En la pintoresca región de Andalucía el invierno y la primavera son benignos[3]. Pero en el verano, con la excepción de los pueblos de la Sierra Nevada y la Sierra Morena, hace un calor tremendo. Las ciudades andaluzas como Sevilla y Córdoba son un verdadero horno[4] en el verano. Andalucía es conocida por sus olivares que le dan al paisaje un color verde olivo.

Por toda la costa de España abundan playas bañadas de las cristalinas aguas del Mediterráneo en el este y en el sur y del Cantábrico en el norte.

También son partes de España las islas Baleares en el Mediterráneo, las islas Canarias al oeste de África en el Atlántico y dos ciudades en el norte de África—Ceuta y Melilla.

Antes de 1979 España se dividía en regiones pero actualmente se les llama «comunidades autónomas». Hay diecisiete comunidades autónomas que se pueden comparar más o menos con los estados de Estados Unidos. Cada una tiene su propio gobernador, congreso de diputados y elecciones.

Estepona, Andalucía

[3] benignos *mild*
[4] horno *oven*

A Contesten.

1. ¿Dónde está España?
2. ¿Cuáles son los dos países que forman la península ibérica?
3. ¿Qué tipo de país es España?
4. ¿Es montañosa la costa norte de España?
5. ¿Cómo es Galicia y qué tiempo hace allí?
6. ¿Qué color predomina en el centro del país?
7. ¿Cuáles son algunas características del tiempo en el centro del país?
8. ¿Qué tiempo hace en el sur de España?
9. ¿Por qué tiene el paisaje de Andalucía un color verde olivo?
10. ¿Dónde abundan las playas en España?
11. ¿Qué son Ceuta y Melilla?
12. ¿En cuántas comunidades autónomas está dividida España?

Ceuta, África del Norte

Una ojeada histórica

Los moros

En el año de 711 ocurrió algo muy importante en la historia de España. Los moros o musulmanes invadieron el país desde el norte de África y se quedaron en la península por ocho siglos. La enorme influencia de los moros hace que la civilización española sea muy diferente de la de los otros países europeos.

Córdoba, la capital de los moros, llegó a ser la ciudad más culta de Europa cuando el resto del continente vivía en la oscuridad de la Edad Media. A mediados del siglo X Córdoba tenía una población de más de trescientos mil habitantes. Se estableció una biblioteca que contaba con más de doscientos cincuenta mil tomos. Los moros trabajaban en armonía con los cristianos y los judíos e hicieron importantes descubrimientos en la medicina, las matemáticas y otras ciencias.

Más de cuatro mil palabras españolas son de origen árabe. Algunos ejemplos son los nombres de los productos introducidos por los moros, tales como el azúcar, la naranja y la berenjena. Casi todas las palabras que empiezan en **al-** son de origen árabe: el alcázar, la almohada y la alfombra. Muchas expresiones y costumbres de cortesía tienen sus raíces[5] en la cultura musulmana. Ejemplos son: **Esta casa es su casa**—lo que te dirá un español cuando entras en su casa; **¡Buen provecho!**—lo que se dice al pasar por una persona que está comiendo; **¡Ojalá!**—una expresión que significa «si Dios quiere».

[5] raíces *roots*

Córdoba

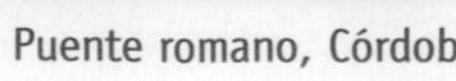
Puente romano, Córdoba

La Mezquita de Córdoba

Cuando los moros llegaron en 711 muchos cristianos huyeron a las montañas de Asturias en el norte. Nombraron rey a don Pelayo, el primer rey de la dinastía española. En 718 los españoles ganaron su primera batalla contra los moros en Covadonga. Así empezó la Reconquista—una guerra de batallas intermitentes que duró ocho siglos. Durante este período los reyes cristianos iban recuperando terreno a los árabes. Con el terreno recuperado formaban reinos independientes y desunidos resultando en una falta de unidad política que se manifiesta aun hoy en el afán independentista y separatista de varias comunidades autónomas, sobre todo el País Vasco (Euskadi) y Cataluña.

B Identifiquen y den detalles.

1. la importancia del año 711
2. Córdoba durante la Edad Media
3. palabras españolas de origen árabe
4. costumbres de cortesía que tienen raíces árabes
5. la batalla de Covadonga
6. la falta de unidad política en España

Spanish Online

For more information about Córdoba and the history and culture of Spain, go to **Web Explore** on the Glencoe Spanish Web site at glencoe.com.

Los Reyes Católicos

La «unidad» de España se realizó en 1469 con el casamiento[6] de Isabel de Castilla y Fernando de Aragón, los Reyes Católicos, quienes establecieron una monarquía absoluta. Los Reyes Católicos querían no sólo la unidad territorial y política: querían también la unidad religiosa. Bajo ellos no existía la tolerancia religiosa que había existido en la España musulmana. En 1481 establecieron el Tribunal de la Inquisición y en 1492 expulsaron a los judíos no conversos. Su expulsión fue un desastre para España porque habían contribuido en muchos campos a la prosperidad del país. Los judíos expulsados, llamados sefardíes, fueron al norte de África, a Grecia y a Turquía. Algunos de ellos siguen hablando ladino, un idioma que se parece mucho al español del siglo XV.

[6] casamiento *marriage*

The Return of Columbus de Eugène Delacroix

La antigua judería, Hervás, Extremadura

La Alhambra, Granada

En 1492 las tropas de Fernando e Isabel entraron en Granada, el último bastión de los moros en España. Tomaron la ciudad poniendo fin a la Reconquista. Se dice que Boabdil, el último rey moro, les dio las llaves de la ciudad y salió de Granada llorando la pérdida[7] de su querida Alhambra.

El año 1492 es una fecha importantísima en la historia de España. El mismo año en que fueron expulsados los moros, el navegador genovés, Cristóbal Colón, patrocinado[8] por la reina Isabel, salió del puerto de Palos en el sur de España con tres carabelas para descubrir una nueva ruta a las Indias. Pero cuando Colón puso pie en tierra el doce de octubre de 1492, no había llegado a la India sino a una isla de las que son hoy las Bahamas en las Américas. Ese día empezaron la conquista, la exploración y la colonización de las Américas en nombre de la corona española, convirtiendo a España en el Imperio más rico y más poderoso del mundo.

[7] pérdida *loss*
[8] patrocinado *sponsored*

C Completen cada frase.

1. La «unidad» de España se realizó en 1469 con…
2. Los Reyes Católicos querían la unidad territorial y política y…
3. Ellos establecieron el Tribunal de la Inquisición en…
4. Los sefardíes son…
5. El último rey moro…
6. En 1492…
7. Colón no descubrió una nueva ruta a la India. Él llegó…
8. Con la llegada de Colón a estas islas, empezaron…

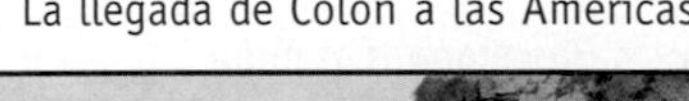
La llegada de Colón a las Américas

Visitas históricas

Si algún día vas a España, no puedes perder la oportunidad de visitar las dos grandes ciudades cosmopolitas de Madrid y Barcelona. Y tienes que visitar también algunos lugares de gran interés histórico. En Andalucía son imprescindibles las joyas arquitectónicas de los moros—el alcázar de Sevilla, la mezquita de Córdoba, la alhambra de Granada y la residencia veraniega de los reyes moros, el Generalife, con sus espléndidos jardines con numerosas fuentes y albercas.

El Generalife, Granada

Barcelona, Cataluña

Anfiteatro romano, Mérida, Extremadura

Si vas a Mérida en Extremadura, puedes ver las ruinas de muchos monumentos romanos. Los romanos invadieron España en 218 a.C. y tardaron dos siglos en someter a los celtíberos que habitaban la península en aquel entonces. Por fin los celtíberos se mezclaron con los romanos y adoptaron su lengua, sus leyes y sus costumbres. Todavía hoy siguen dando conciertos y representaciones en las ruinas del famoso teatro romano en Mérida. Si te interesa, puedes ir también a Segovia donde verás el famoso acueducto romano hecho de piedras gigantescas sin una sola gota de argamasa[9].

[9] argamasa *mortar*

¿Sí o no?

1. Los árabes fueron magníficos arquitectos.
2. Hay muchas joyas arquitectónicas de los moros en el norte de España, sobre todo en Galicia.
3. Hay muchas ruinas romanas en la ciudad de Mérida, en Extremadura.
4. Los romanos invadieron España cuando fueron expulsados los moros.
5. Los celtíberos se romanizaron. Adoptaron la lengua, las leyes y las costumbres de los romanos.
6. El famoso acueducto romano de Segovia está hecho de madera y argamasa.

Acueducto romano, Segovia

¿Te apetece algo?

Si vas a Segovia tienes que comer una de las especialidades de la región—el cochinillo asado. El cochinillo se asa durante horas en un horno de ladrillo[10] o de barro[11]. Es un plato suculento.

En Andalucía se ve la influencia de los árabes en la cocina también. Un ejemplo es el ajo blanco—una sopa que se parece al gazpacho andaluz, una sopa fría hecha de agua, pan, ajo, tomates y pimientos. Pero el ajo blanco no se hace con tomates. Se hace con almendras y se sirve con unas uvas peladas y unas rebanadas de melón.

A los españoles en todas partes del país les encanta picar o comer pequeñas raciones de comida—tapas. Las tapas incluyen trocitos de tortilla a la española, jamón serrano, aceitunas, sardinas, anchoas, o gambas entre otros manjares. Pues, ¿qué te apetece? Y, ¡buen provecho!

[10] ladrillo *brick*
[11] barro *clay*

Contesten.

1. ¿Cómo se prepara el cochinillo asado?
2. ¿Cuál es la diferencia entre el gazpacho andaluz y el ajo blanco?
3. ¿Qué son tapas? ¿Por qué les gustan tanto a los españoles?

Estructura • Repaso

Pretérito de los verbos regulares
Expressing actions in the past

Use your StudentWorks Plus™ CD for more practice.

1. The preterite is used to state actions that began and ended at a definite time in the past. To form the root for the preterite, drop the infinitive ending of the verb and add the appropriate endings to this root.

INFINITIVE	hablar	comer	vivir
root	habl-	com-	viv-
yo	hablé	comí	viví
tú	hablaste	comiste	viviste
él, ella, Ud.	habló	comió	vivió
nosotros(as)	hablamos	comimos	vivimos
vosotros(as)	*hablasteis*	*comisteis*	*vivisteis*
ellos, ellas, Uds.	hablaron	comieron	vivieron

2. Note the similarity in the preterite forms of the verbs **dar** and **ver.**

DAR	**di**	**diste**	**dio**	**dimos**	**disteis**	**dieron**
VER	**vi**	**viste**	**vio**	**vimos**	**visteis**	**vieron**

3. Remember the spelling changes with verbs that end in **-car, -gar,** and **-zar.**

busqué → buscó **jugué → jugó** **empecé → empezó**

4. Note the following frequently used time expressions that accompany past actions in the preterite.

ayer	**el año (mes) pasado**
anoche	**la semana pasada**
ayer por la tarde	**hace una semana (un año)**
ayer por la mañana	**en el siglo ocho**

Extremadura

¿Cómo lo digo?

1 Historieta España

Contesten según se indica.

1. ¿Quiénes fundaron la ciudad más antigua de España? (los fenicios)
2. ¿Cuánto tiempo tardaron los romanos en someter a los celtíberos? (dos siglos)
3. ¿Cuándo invadieron los moros a España? (en 711)
4. ¿Cuándo y dónde empezó la Reconquista? (en 718 en Covadonga)
5. ¿Cuándo y dónde terminó la Reconquista? (en 1492 en Granada)
6. ¿Quiénes invadieron España en 1808? (las tropas francesas de Napoleón)
7. ¿A quién nombró Napoleón rey de España? (a su hermano José Bonaparte)
8. ¿Lucharon los españoles contra los invasores franceses? (sí, valientemente)
9. ¿Cuándo salieron de España los franceses? (en 1814)

Covadonga, Asturias

2 Historieta La Guerra Civil española

Cambien en el pretérito.

El 17 de julio de 1936 se levanta el ejército bajo el general Francisco Franco. Con este levantamiento empieza una desastrosa guerra civil—un verdadero conflicto fratricida. El ejército, el clero y las clases altas en su mayoría dan su apoyo *(support)* a Franco. Los obreros o trabajadores, los campesinos y los intelectuales apoyan la República—el gobierno. Y queda una gran masa neutral.

La desastrosa Guerra Civil española dura casi tres años y deja un millón de muertos y otro millón de españoles en el exilio. Los españoles quedan divididos entre vencedores—los que ganan—y vencidos—los que pierden.

Después de la guerra el general Franco establece un régimen totalitario. No trata de unir a los españoles. Emprende una campaña de castigo *(punishment)* y represión contra los vencidos. La pobre España se ve completamente aislada y el pueblo sufre hambre y frustración. La represión continúa hasta la muerte de Franco en 1975.

Guernica de Pablo Picasso

3 Historieta El verano Contesten.

1. ¿Pasaste el fin de semana en una playa de Marbella?
2. ¿Nadaste?
3. ¿Esquiaste en el agua?
4. ¿Diste un paseo a lo largo de las orillas del mar?
5. ¿Almorzaste en un chiringuito?
6. ¿Comiste con unos amigos?
7. ¿Comieron ustedes mariscos o una paella?
8. ¿Quién pagó la cuenta?
9. ¿Dejaron ustedes una propina para el camarero (mesero)?
10. ¿A qué hora salieron del restaurante?
11. ¿Volvieron a la playa?

Un chiringuito, Marbella

Ricky Martin en concierto

4 Historieta Un concierto Completen con el pretérito.

—Anita, ¿tú __1__ (salir) anoche?

—Sí, __2__ (oír) cantar a Ricky Martin.

—¿Él __3__ (dar) un concierto aquí en Madrid?

—Sí, en el estadio municipal.

—¿Qué tal te __4__ (gustar)?

—Mucho. Como siempre, él __5__ (cantar) muy bien.

—¿Quién más __6__ (asistir)? ¿Maripaz?

—Maripaz, no. Pilar me __7__ (acompañar).

—¿A qué hora __8__ (empezar) el concierto?

—__9__ (Empezar) a las ocho y media y nosotras no __10__ (salir) del concierto hasta las once menos cuarto.

—¿A qué hora __11__ (volver) ustedes a casa?

—__12__ (Volver) a eso de las once y cuarto.

—Dime, ¿cuánto les __13__ (costar) las entradas?

—Treinta y cinco euros cada una.

—Yo quería ir al concierto. ¿Por qué no me __14__ (invitar)?

—Yo te __15__ (llamar) la semana pasada antes de sacar (comprar) las entradas pero no __16__ (contestar) nadie.

—Entiendo. Si me __17__ (llamar) el viernes por la noche, (yo) no __18__ (contestar) porque todos nosotros __19__ (salir) para el fin de semana.

5 Vimos a Ricky Martin. Escriban de nuevo la conversación de la Actividad 4 en forma narrativa.

6 **¿Quién jugó? Yo jugué.** Escriban el siguiente párrafo cambiando **nosotros** en **yo.**

Anoche nosotros llegamos al parque. Buscamos a unos amigos y empezamos a jugar al fútbol. Jugamos bien. Lanzamos el balón y marcamos tres tantos en quince minutos.

Casares, Andalucía

Pretérito de los verbos de cambio radical (e → i, o → u)
Expressing actions in the past

1. The verbs **sentir, preferir,** and **sugerir** have a stem change in the preterite. In the third person singular and plural forms **(él, ella, ellos, ellas),** the **e** changes to **i.** The **o** of the verbs **dormir** and **morir** changes to **u** in the third person singular and plural forms. Review the following.

INFINITIVE	preferir	dormir
yo	preferí	dormí
tú	preferiste	dormiste
él, ella, Ud.	prefirió	durmió
nosotros(as)	preferimos	dormimos
vosotros(as)	*preferisteis*	*dormisteis*
ellos, ellas, Uds.	prefirieron	durmieron

2. The stem of the verbs **pedir, servir, freír, medir, repetir, seguir,** and **sonreír** also changes from **e** to **i** in the third person singular and plural forms.

INFINITIVE	pedir	servir	seguir
yo	pedí	serví	seguí
tú	pediste	serviste	seguiste
él, ella, Ud.	pidió	sirvió	siguió
nosotros(as)	pedimos	servimos	seguimos
vosotros(as)	*pedisteis*	*servisteis*	*seguisteis*
ellos, ellas, Uds.	pidieron	sirvieron	siguieron

LECCIÓN I

Cultura

¿Cómo lo digo?

7 Historieta **Un problema en el restaurante** Completen.

—¡Oiga, camarero!

—Sí, señor.

—Perdón, pero yo ___1___ (pedir) una langosta y usted me ___2___ (servir) camarones.

—Lo siento señor. Pero la verdad es que yo le ___3___ (sugerir) la langosta y usted ___4___ (pedir) los camarones.

—De ninguna manera. Yo sé lo que ___5___ (pedir).

—Y yo también sé lo que usted ___6___ (pedir).

—Y además yo le ___7___ (pedir) un puré de patatas (papas) y usted me ___8___ (servir) arroz.

—Es imposible, señor. No tenemos puré de patatas. Yo sé exactamente lo que usted ___9___ (pedir), señor. Además, yo le ___10___ (repetir) la orden y usted no dijo nada.

—Lo siento, pero lo que usted ___11___ (repetir) no es lo que me ___12___ (servir).

—Señor, al fin y al cabo, no hay problema. Si usted quiere una langosta, se la puedo servir con mucho gusto. Pero el puré de patatas no se lo puedo servir, porque no lo tenemos. Lo siento mucho.

Puerto Banús, Marbella

 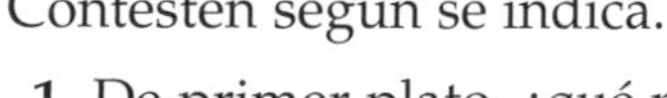

8 Historieta **En un restaurante español**

Contesten según se indica.

1. De primer plato, ¿qué pediste? (jamón serrano)
2. ¿Cuántos trocitos te sirvió el camarero (el mesero)? (a lo menos seis)
3. Y ¿qué pidió tu amigo? (gambas al ajillo)
4. ¿Le gustaron? (tanto que las repitió)
5. ¿Qué sugirió el camarero como plato principal? (el cochinillo asado)
6. ¿Lo pediste? (sí)
7. Y tu amigo, ¿qué pidió? (el pollo asado)
8. ¿Qué más sugirió el camarero? (una ración de berenjenas)
9. ¿Las pidieron ustedes? (sí)
10. De todo lo que pidieron, ¿qué prefirieron? (yo, el cochinillo y mi amigo, las gambas al ajillo)

9 Más hechos históricos Completen con el pretérito.

1. La hija de los Reyes Católicos, Juana la Loca, ____ con Felipe el Hermoso de la familia de los Hapsburgos de Austria. (casarse)
2. Su esposo ____ muy joven. (morir)
3. El hijo de Juana, Carlos V de Austria y Carlos I de España, ____ mucho territorio. (heredar)
4. Carlos V ____ contra los protestantes de Alemania, Francia e Inglaterra. (luchar)
5. Carlos V ____ la política imperialista y religiosa de sus abuelos, los Reyes Católicos. (seguir)
6. Bajo Felipe II, el hijo de Carlos V, las guerras religiosas ____ y el gran Imperio español ____ a decaer. (continuar, empezar)
7. España se ____ en un país de segundo orden. (convertir)
8. El rey Carlos II ____ sin sucesión y las familias reales ____ por ganar la corona de España. (morir, luchar)
9. Luis XIV de Francia ____ y él ____ a su nieto rey de España con el nombre de Felipe V. Así la corona española ____ de los Hapsburgos a los Borbones (de Francia). (ganar, nombrar, pasar)
10. Bajo el mando de los tres primeros Borbones la decadencia ____. En 1808 Napoleón ____ «prisionero» a Carlos IV y ____ a su hermano José Bonaparte rey de España. Hombres y mujeres ____ contra los invasores franceses con cuchillos y aceite hirviente. Fue la primera guerra de guerrilleros. (continuar, tomar, proclamar, luchar)

Palacio Real, Madrid

¡Te toca a ti!

Use what you have learned

Galicia

1 La geografía de España

✓ Describe the geography of Spain and compare it to the geography where you live

En tus propias palabras describe la geografía y el clima de España. Luego describe la geografía de la región donde tú vives. ¿Se parece mucho a la geografía de una región de España o no? Y, ¿el clima?

2 La historia de España

✓ Discuss some historical facts about Spain

Trabajen en grupos de cuatro. Hablen de todo lo que aprendieron sobre la historia de España.

3 Un personaje histórico

✓ Describe the life of an important figure in Spanish history

Escoge a uno de los personajes siguientes y da algunos informes sobre su vida.

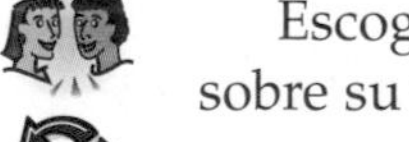

Carlos V (I de España)

Fernando VII

Francisco Franco

Juan Carlos I, el rey actual de España

4 La comida española

✔ *Discuss some Spanish dishes and role-play a scene in a restaurant*

Trabajen en pequeños grupos. Preparen una lista de todos los platos españoles que conocen. Luego preparen una conversación en un restaurante español y preséntenla a la clase.

5 Ayer

Di todo lo que hizo Sandra ayer. Depués, di todo lo que hiciste tú ayer. ¿Lo pasaste bien o no?

6 Un fin de semana fabuloso

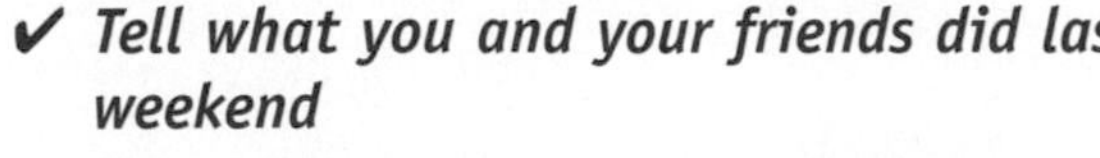

Tú y varios amigos pasaron un fin de semana fabuloso. Se divirtieron mucho. Di todo lo que hicieron.

7 ¡Qué experiencia más mala!

✔ *Tell about a restaurant experience that did not go well for you*

Fuiste a un restaurante y ¡qué experiencia más horrible! Todo salió muy mal. Describe todo lo que pasó. Explica también como reaccionaste a esta situación.

Vocabulario

1 Completen con una palabra apropiada.

To review vocabulary, turn to pages 2–3.

1–3. El _____ o la reina lleva una _____ que tiene _____ preciosas como diamantes, rubíes y esmeraldas.

4–5. Durante una _____ hay muchas batallas y las _____ luchan valientemente.

6–7. Las montañas bajan a las _____ del mar pero hoy no se pueden ver porque hay mucha _____.

8–9. Él nos sirvió unos _____ de jamón serrano en la terraza de su casa _____.

10. Un _____ es un período de cien años.

Lectura

2 ¿Sí o no?

To review some geographical facts about Spain, turn to pages 6–7.

11. Hay grandes extensiones de llanuras por todo lo largo de la costa norte de España.

12. En el verano hace muchísimo calor en las ciudades de Andalucía.

13. El paisaje del centro de España se parece mucho al paisaje de Irlanda. Llueve mucho y es muy verde.

14. El Mediterráneo está al este y al sur de España y el Cantábrico está al norte.

Ibiza, Islas Baleares

3 Contesten.

15. ¿Por qué es la civilización española muy diferente de la de los otros países europeos?
16. ¿Cuál fue la ciudad más culta de Europa durante la Edad Media?
17. ¿Cuándo empezó y cuándo terminó la Reconquista?
18. Hay dos eventos históricos muy importantes que ocurrieron en el año 1492. ¿Cuáles son?

To review some historical and cultural facts about Spain, turn to pages 8–13.

4 Completen.

19. _____ y _____ son dos ejemplos de las joyas arquitectónicas de los moros en España.
20. Hay muchas ruinas de monumentos _____ en Extremadura.
21. Si entras en la casa de un español, él te dice _____.
22. Pequeñas raciones de comida como trocitos de jamón y anchoas se llaman _____.

Plaza de España, Sevilla

Estructura

5 Completen con el pretérito.

23. Los moros _____ España en 711. (invadir)
24. Yo _____ en el mar Mediterráneo. (nadar)
25. Y yo _____ en un chiringuito. (comer)

26–27. En el restaurante yo _____ una tortilla a la española y mi amiga _____ una sopa de ajo. (pedir, pedir)

28. ¿Tú _____ el teatro romano o no? (ver)
29. El soldado _____ valientemente. (luchar)
30. Yo _____ la cuenta. (pagar)

To review verbs in the preterite, turn to pages 14 and 17.

LECCIÓN 2

Conversación

Vocabulario para la conversación

Use your StudentWorks™ Plus CD for more practice.

Hubo un embotellamiento en la autopista. Pero no importa. Los conductores tuvieron que pagar el peaje.

VUELO	DESTINO	SALIDA	OBSERVACIONES
143	BARCELONA	17:30	DEMORA SALIDA ACTUAL 18:45
159	VALENCIA	17:55	CANCELADO

Hubo una demora (un retraso).
El vuelo salió tarde.
Otro vuelo fue anulado.
No salió.

Los pasajeros estuvieron en el aeropuerto.
No pudieron salir ni en taxi ni en autocar.
Los conductores estuvieron en huelga.

Son hoteles del gobierno español. Son paradores.

Más vocabulario

el puente aéreo servicio aéreo frecuente que enlaza dos ciudades
una venta un hotel, un hostal, un albergue
enlazar unir, empalmar
recorrer atravesar un lugar en toda su extensión

Conversación

¿Qué palabra necesito?

1 Historieta En la autopista

Contesten.

1. ¿Tiene muchos carriles en cada sentido (dirección) una autopista?
2. En España, ¿hay que pagar peaje para usar la autopista?
3. En este momento, ¿hay muchos coches, autocares y taxis en la autopista?
4. ¿Hay un embotellamiento?

Autopista del Mediterráneo, Andalucía

Cáceres, Extremadura

2 ¿Qué palabra? Completen.

1. En el taxi el pasajero debe pagar lo que indica _____; es decir el _____ indicado en el _____.
2. No llegamos a tiempo. Hubo _____.
3. Y el otro vuelo no salió. Fue _____.
4. _____ es un servicio aéreo frecuente entre dos ciudades.
5. Este servicio _____ una ciudad con otra—Madrid con Barcelona, por ejemplo.
6. _____ es un hotel del gobierno.
7. Otras palabras que significan «hotel» son _____.
8. Vamos a ir desde Málaga en el sur hasta San Sebastián en el norte. Vamos a _____ todo el país.

3 Historieta Un problema Contesten.

1. ¿Estuvieron delante del aeropuerto los pasajeros?
2. ¿Hicieron cola para esperar el autocar?
3. ¿No vino el autocar?
4. ¿No pudieron salir del aeropuerto los pasajeros?
5. ¿Por qué? ¿Qué hubo?
6. ¿Quiénes estuvieron en huelga?

Un viaje a España

Marta Elena, pienso pasar el verano en España y alguien me dijo que tú fuiste el verano pasado.

Elena Sí, y no te puedo decir cuánto me gustó. Me divertí mucho.

Marta ¿Lo encontraste difícil viajar de un lugar a otro?

Elena De ninguna manera y recorrimos casi todo el país. Me acuerdo que una vez íbamos al aeropuerto de Barajas en Madrid. Hubo un embotellamiento horrible en la autopista y cuando llegamos al aeropuerto ya había salido nuestro vuelo. Pero ningún problema. Entre Madrid y Barcelona hay un puente aéreo. Hay un vuelo cada hora.

Marta ¿No había demoras ni vuelos anulados como aquí?

Elena Pues, en un vuelo a Palma de Mallorca llegamos con una demora de una hora. Y esto no es nada. Pero tuvimos una experiencia en Palma. Los conductores de los autocares que enlazan el aeropuerto con el centro de la ciudad estaban en huelga.

Marta Y, ¿qué hicieron ustedes?

Elena Tomamos un taxi. Resultó un poco más caro, pero—¡qué va!

Marta Y, ¿no les clavó[1] el taxista?

Elena No, no—fue un tipo muy amable. Nos cobró el monto que indicó el taxímetro.

[1] clavó *nailed (overcharged)*

Conversación

Marta Dime, ¿tomaste el AVE, el tren de alta velocidad?

Elena Ah, sí. De Madrid a Sevilla. Va tan rápido que en menos de tres horas estuvimos en Sevilla. Hay que pagar un suplemento, pero vale.

Marta ¿Fueron a Galicia? Quiero ir a Santiago de Compostela.

Elena Te lo aconsejo. Es una maravilla. Tomé el tren de noche (nocturno) de Madrid a La Coruña—o como dicen en gallego—el idioma autónomo—A Coruña.

Marta ¿No pudiste tomar el AVE?

Elena No, no. El AVE no va a Galicia. Si puedes, debes tratar de pasar una noche en el Hostal de los Reyes Católicos. Es bastante caro pero te aseguro que es una experiencia inolvidable.

Marta Sí, leí que Fernando e Isabel lo establecieron en 1501 como una venta y hospital para los peregrinos[2]. Hoy es un parador del gobierno, ¿no?

Elena Sí, y los paradores del gobierno son excelentes—bastante elegantes pero, ¡cuidado!, no son económicos.

[2] peregrinos *pilgrims*

Santiago de Compostela, Galicia

¿Comprendes?

Contesten.

1. ¿Adónde fue Elena el verano pasado?
2. ¿Le gustó? ¿Se divirtió?
3. ¿Lo encontró fácil o difícil viajar de un lugar a otro?
4. ¿Por qué perdió su vuelo de Madrid a Barcelona?
5. ¿Encontró ella muchas demoras o vuelos anulados?
6. ¿Qué pasó en Palma de Mallorca?
7. ¿Qué le dio al taxista?
8. ¿Cómo fue de Madrid a Sevilla?
9. ¿Dónde pasó Elena una noche en Santiago de Compostela?
10. ¿Qué dijo del hostal?

Aeropuerto de Barajas, Madrid

Den más informes.

1. Barajas
2. el puente aéreo
3. el AVE
4. A Coruña
5. los paradores españoles

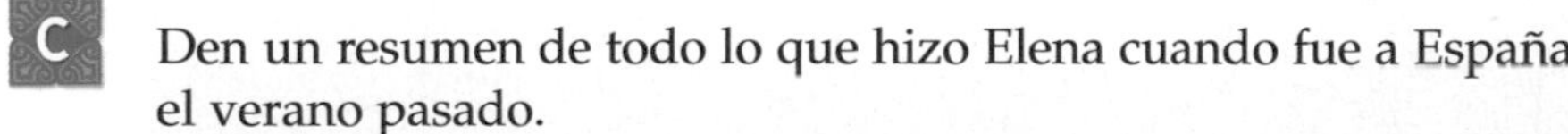

C Den un resumen de todo lo que hizo Elena cuando fue a España el verano pasado.

Hostal de los Reyes Católicos, Santiago de Compostela

Estructura • Repaso

Pretérito de los verbos irregulares
Expressing more actions in the past

A number of frequently used verbs are irregular in the preterite. Many of these verbs can be grouped together because they have common irregularities. Review the following forms.

ANDAR	TENER	ESTAR	PONER	PODER	SABER
anduve	**tuve**	**estuve**	**puse**	**pude**	**supe**
anduviste	**tuviste**	**estuviste**	**pusiste**	**pudiste**	**supiste**
anduvo	**tuvo**	**estuvo**	**puso**	**pudo**	**supo**
anduvimos	**tuvimos**	**estuvimos**	**pusimos**	**pudimos**	**supimos**
anduvisteis	***tuvisteis***	***estuvisteis***	***pusisteis***	***pudisteis***	***supisteis***
anduvieron	**tuvieron**	**estuvieron**	**pusieron**	**pudieron**	**supieron**

QUERER	VENIR	DECIR	TRAER	CONDUCIR
quise	**vine**	**dije**	**traje**	**conduje**
quisiste	**viniste**	**dijiste**	**trajiste**	**condujiste**
quiso	**vino**	**dijo**	**trajo**	**condujo**
quisimos	**vinimos**	**dijimos**	**trajimos**	**condujimos**
quisisteis	***vinisteis***	***dijisteis***	***trajisteis***	***condujisteis***
quisieron	**vinieron**	**dijeron**	**trajeron**	**condujeron**

HACER	IR, SER
hice	**fui**
hiciste	**fuiste**
hizo	**fue**
hicimos	**fuimos**
hicisteis	***fuisteis***
hicieron	**fueron**

¿Cómo lo digo?

1 **Historieta** **Un viaje** Contesten con **sí**.

1. ¿Hiciste un viaje el año pasado?
2. ¿Fuiste a España?
3. ¿Fuiste con algunos amigos?
4. ¿Alquilaron un coche en España?
5. ¿Condujiste tú o condujeron todos?
6. ¿Pusieron sus maletas en el baúl del coche?
7. ¿Trajeron mucho equipaje?
8. ¿Estuvieron en España por unos quince días?

2 **Historieta** **Al Rastro** Cambien en el pretérito.

1. El domingo voy al Rastro, un mercado antiguo en el viejo Madrid.
2. En el Rastro veo mucha chatarra *(junk)*.
3. No puedo comprar mucho.
4. En el mercado veo a algunos amigos.
5. Vamos de un puesto a otro.
6. Andamos por todo el mercado.
7. Como digo—no puedo comprar mucho.
8. Pero Antonio, él hace muchas compras.
9. Pone toda la chatarra que compra en el baúl de su coche y vuelve a casa.

El Rastro, Madrid

3 **Historieta** **Extremadura** Completen con el pretérito.

Extremadura __1__ (ser) una región bastante pobre. Pero durante la época de la colonización de Latinoamérica __2__ (llegar) a ser más conocida. Se conoce como «la cuna *(cradle)* de los conquistadores». Francisco Pizarro, el conquistador de Perú, __3__ (nacer) en Trujillo en 1475. Su hermano __4__ (hacer) construir un palacio fabuloso en esta ciudad. Se dice que Cervantes, el autor del famoso Quijote, __5__ (pasar) tiempo en este palacio. Otro palacio de interés en Trujillo es la casa de los Toledo–Moctezuma, donde __6__ (hacer) su residencia los descendientes del conquistador Juan Cano y la hija de Moctezuma, el emperador de los aztecas.

En Guadalupe, el rey Alfonso XI __7__ (hacer) construir un monasterio en el lugar donde un pastor __8__ (descubrir) una estatua milagrosa de la Virgen. __9__ (Ser) en este monasterio donde se __10__ (firmar) los documentos que __11__ (dar) la autorización para el primer viaje de Colón.

Los primeros indígenas americanos que se __12__ (convertir) al cristianismo __13__ (venir) a este monasterio donde __14__ (ser) bautizados. Hasta dos sirvientes personales de Colón __15__ (ser) bautizados en la fuente en la plazuela delante del monasterio. Hoy la Virgen de Guadalupe es la patrona de muchos pueblos latinoamericanos.

Cuando Carlos V __16__ (abdicar) el trono en 1556, __17__ (ir) a vivir en el monasterio de Yuste en Extremadura donde __18__ (morir) dos años después de su abdicación.

Trujillo, Extremadura

Monasterio de Santa María de Guadalupe, Extremadura

¡Te toca a ti!

Use what you have learned

1 De viaje a Madrid

✔ Talk about activities at an airport airline counter

Vas de Nueva York a Madrid. Estás en el mostrador de la línea aérea. Trabaja con un(a) compañero(a). Uno(a) va a ser el/la pasajero(a) y el/la otro(a) va a ser el/la agente. Preparen ustedes una conversación. Aquí tienen algunas palabras que ya han aprendido y querrán utilizar.

el billete (el boleto), el billete (el boleto) electrónico, la tarjeta de embarque, el talón, el equipaje de mano, el número del asiento, el pasaporte, el destino, la puerta de salida, el equipaje, facturar, una demora, anular

2 A Sevilla en tren

✔ Talk about activities at a train station ticket window

Vas de Madrid a Sevilla. Estás en la estación de ferrocarril. Prepara una conversación entre tú y el/la agente que trabaja en la ventanilla. Aquí tienen algunas palabras que querrán utilizar.

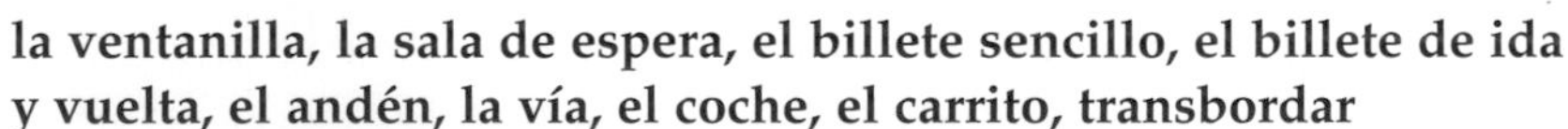

la ventanilla, la sala de espera, el billete sencillo, el billete de ida y vuelta, el andén, la vía, el coche, el carrito, transbordar

Estación Atocha, Madrid

3 El hotel en Zafra

✔ *Talk about checking into a hotel*

Has llegado a un hotel en Zafra. Trabaja con un(a) compañero(a). Uno(a) va a ser el/la cliente y el/la otro(a) va a ser el/la recepcionista. Preparen ustedes una conversación. Aquí tienen algunas palabras que querrán utilizar.

la ficha, la llave, una habitación sencilla (doble), la caja, la cuenta, el monto, los gastos, la ducha, el baño, el balcón, el aire acondicionado, el televisor

Hotel, Zafra, Extremadura

Carretera nacional

4 Un viaje por España

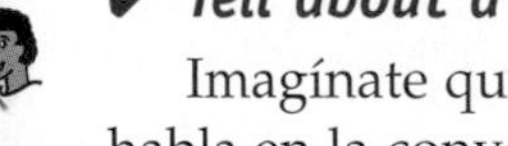

✔ *Tell about a recent trip to Spain*

Imagínate que eres Marta, la persona que habla en la conversación. Di adonde fuiste y todo lo que viste e hiciste en España.

5 Un vuelo anulado

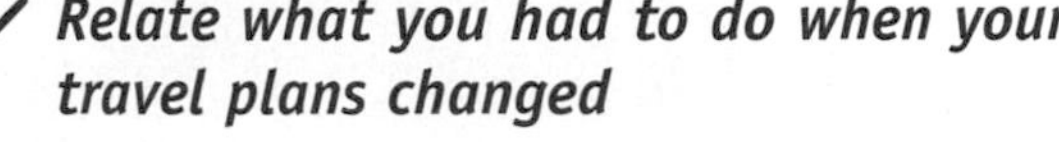

✔ *Relate what you had to do when your travel plans changed*

Imagínate que ayer tu vuelo de Madrid a Málaga fue anulado. Mándale un e-mail a un(a) amigo(a) diciéndole todo lo que tuviste que hacer para llegar a Málaga.

Vocabulario

1 Completen con una palabra apropiada.

1. Hubo un _____ en la carretera. Hubo una fila larga de coches que no pudieron mover.
2. Es necesario pagar el _____ en la autopista.
3. El vuelo no salió. Fue _____ y los pasajeros tuvieron que tomar otro vuelo.
4. La carretera _____ el aeropuerto con el centro de la ciudad.

To review vocabulary, turn to pages 24–25.

2 Den otra palabra.

5. un tapón
6. un servicio aéreo frecuente
7. un hotel, un hostal
8. un retraso
9. un hotel del gobierno español

Catedral, Santiago de Compostela

Parador San Francisco, Granada

Conversación

3 Contesten según la conversación.

10. ¿Adónde fue Marta el verano pasado?
11. ¿Qué le pasó una vez en Madrid?
12. ¿Quiénes estuvieron en huelga en el aeropuerto de Palma de Mallorca?
13. ¿Qué les cobró el conductor del taxi?
14. ¿Cómo fue Marta de Madrid a Santiago de Compostela?
15. ¿Qué es el AVE y adónde va?

To review the conversation, turn to pages 27–28.

Estructura

4 Completen con el pretérito.

16. Ella _____ un viaje. (hacer)
17. Tú _____ mucho equipaje, ¿no? (traer)
18. Nosotros _____ juntos. (ir)
19. Yo no _____ mover. (poder)
20. Ellos _____ que esperar el próximo vuelo. (tener)

To review irregular verbs in the preterite, turn to page 30.

5 Cambien en el pretérito.

21. No lo sé.
22. Él me lo dice.
23. Yo voy en avión.
24. Ponemos el equipaje en el baúl del coche.
25. ¿Andas por todo el país?

Vocabulario para la lectura

Trenes que no necesitan conductor

Es un mapa del sistema de metro de Barcelona.
El sistema de metro sirve a toda el área metropolitana.

Maripaz y Antonio hablan del mapa.
Ella dice que el mapa que tiene es suyo.
No es el de Antonio.

Más vocabulario

un pedido un encargo a un vendedor indicando lo que quiere comprar el cliente

el usuario el que utiliza o se sirve de algo

¿Qué palabra necesito?

1 Historieta El metro Contesten.

1. ¿Tienen muchas ciudades grandes un sistema de metro—un sistema de transporte subterráneo?
2. ¿Quién maneja o conduce el tren?
3. ¿A qué sirve el sistema de metro?
4. ¿Tienen los coches un pasillo estrecho o amplio?
5. ¿Tiene muchos usuarios el metro?
6. ¿Hay una barra de sujeción para las personas de movilidad reducida, para los minusválidos?
7. El mapa del sistema de metro, ¿es de Maripaz o de Antonio?
8. ¿Dónde está el de Antonio?

2 ¿Cuál es la palabra? Completen.

1. Los que se sirven de un sistema de transporte o cualquier otro servicio son sus _____.
2. El vendedor entrega las mercancías al comprador después de recibir un _____ y el pago.
3. _____ es un tren subterráneo. En muchos países de Latinoamérica se llama el subte.
4. El _____ indica la ruta que sigue cada línea del metro.

Plaza del Callao, Madrid

ABC

Trenes que no necesitan conductor

EFE, Barcelona

Los trenes de la futura línea 9 del metro de Barcelona serán los más avanzados del mundo. El grupo francés Alstom diseñará y fabricará para esta línea el llamado modelo Metrópolis, que tiene la posibilidad de funcionar sin conductor. Los trenes incorporarán tecnología punta[1], funcionarán con bajo coste energético, y su control será automático. Podrán viajar sentados hasta 154 usuarios y un máximo de 1.065 viajeros de pie.

Las unidades estarán dotadas de[2] espacios reservados para las personas de movilidad reducida, con la inclusión de un cinturón de seguridad, una barra de sujeción y la dotación de amplios pasillos.

Los trenes se construirán en la planta de Alstom en Barcelona, que ve garantizado su funcionamiento con este importante pedido. Esta factoría, situada en la localidad de Santa Perpetua de Mogoda (Valles Occidental), ya ha fabricado con anterioridad distintos modelos de trenes para su circulación en diferentes ciudades: Madrid, Londres, la capital polaca, Varsovia, y recientemente en la ciudad china de Shanghai y en la capital estadounidense, Washington.

[1] punta *latest*
[2] dotadas de *equipped with*

¿Comprendes?

A Contesten.

1. ¿Qué ciudad va a tener los trenes de metro más avanzados del mundo?
2. ¿Qué posibilidad tienen?
3. ¿Van a tener un alto coste energético?
4. ¿Cuántos pasajeros o usuarios pueden ir sentados?
5. ¿Cuántos pueden ir de pie?
6. ¿Qué van a tener los trenes para la comodidad de las personas de movilidad reducida?
7. ¿Dónde está la factoría o fábrica donde van a construir los trenes?
8. ¿En qué otras ciudades están circulando estos trenes?

Vocabulario para la lectura

Mueren cinco inmigrantes

La patera chocó contra una roca.
Chocó contra una roca en el área de Tarifa.
La patera naufragó.
Una patrulla rescató a las víctimas.

Más vocabulario

el suceso el evento
magrebí relativo a tres países del norte de África: Marruecos, Argelia y Tunicia
huir escapar
solicitar pedir

Tarifa, Costa de la Luz

¿Qué palabra necesito?

1 Un naufragio Contesten con **sí.**

1. ¿Había inmigrantes ilegales a bordo de la patera?
2. ¿Chocó la patera contra unas rocas en la costa en el área de Tarifa?
3. ¿Naufragó la embarcación?
4. ¿Llegó una patrulla para tratar de rescatar a las víctimas del naufragio?
5. ¿Rescataron a algunas?
6. ¿Se produjo ayer el suceso?

2 Otra palabra Expresen de otra manera.

1. Llegó *una patera* al puerto de Tarifa en el sur de España.
2. *El evento* tuvo lugar ayer.
3. Nadie pudo *escapar.*
4. Los políticos locales le *pidieron* ayuda al gobierno central.

Diario *de* Mallorca

Mueren cinco inmigrantes al naufragar en Tarifa la patera en la que viajaban

Cinco inmigrantes murieron ayer al naufragar la patera en la que viajaban frente a las costas de Tarifa. En la embarcación iban otras treinta y cinco personas, cuatro de las cuales son mujeres.

En la embarcación iban otras 35 personas, cuatro de ellas mujeres

OTR/PRESS-MADRID • El suceso se produjo a primera hora de la mañana, cuando la embarcación en la que viajaban se cree que en torno a cuarenta inmigrantes chocó contra una zona rocosa y varios de sus ocupantes cayeron al agua.

Los inmigrantes fueron rescatados porque las autoridades habían avistado[1] la patera una hora y media antes y se dio aviso al Servicio Marítimo y a las patrullas territoriales, que iniciaron las labores para interceptar la embarcación.

Las autoridades encontraron en el lugar del naufragio los cadáveres de cinco inmigrantes, y rescataron a otros treinta y cinco con vida; aunque ocho consiguieron huir cuando llegaron a tierra. Aunque no ha sido determinada la nacionalidad

[1] avistado *sighted*

de los inmigrantes, se cree que en su mayoría son magrebíes, saharianos y también algunos asiáticos.

Implicación

Tras este suceso, el ministro de Administraciones Públicas, Javier Arenas, lamentó la muerte de los inmigrantes y solicitó a Marruecos una mayor implicación en la lucha contra las mafias de inmigración ilegal. Arenas explicó que aunque últimamente Marruecos está colaborando en esta materia, espera que «se acentúe más», afirmó.

¿Comprendes?

A Contesten.

1. ¿Cuándo se produjo el suceso?
2. ¿Contra qué chocó la patera? ¿Dónde?
3. ¿Cuántas personas murieron? ¿Cuántas fueron rescatadas?
4. ¿Eran inmigrantes ilegales los pasajeros de la patera?
5. ¿Cuántos huyeron cuando llegaron a tierra?
6. ¿Qué se cree sobre la nacionalidad de los inmigrantes?
7. ¿Qué solicitó al gobierno de Marruecos Javier Arenas, el ministro de Administraciones Públicas?

B **Analicen.** La llegada de miles de inmigrantes ilegales a España es un problema serio para el país. Casi a diario uno lee en los periódicos españoles de catástrofes como esta. En el artículo, ¿qué indica que este suceso no es un caso aislado?

Go to World News online at glencoe.com to look for articles about this social issue in Spanish-language newspapers. Discuss this issue of illegal immigration in Spain with classmates and compare it to similar situations in this country.

Estructura • Avanzada

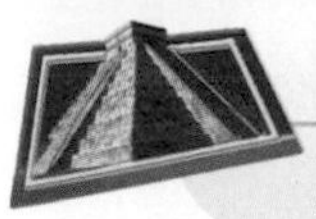

Sustantivos femeninos en a, ha inicial
Identifying items

Feminine nouns that begin with a stressed **a** or the silent **h** followed by a stressed **a** take the masculine definite article **el** or the indefinite article **un.** The reason such nouns take the articles **el** and **un** is that it would be difficult to pronounce the two vowels—**la a, una a**—together. Since the nouns are feminine, the plural articles **las** and **unas** are used and any adjective modifying the noun is in the feminine form.

el agua	**las aguas**	*water*
el (un) águila	**las águilas**	*eagle*
el (un) área	**las áreas**	*area*
el (un) arma	**las armas**	*weapon*
el (un) hacha	**las hachas**	*ax*
el (un) ala	**las alas**	*wing*
el hambre		*hunger*

El agua es potable.
Las aguas turbulentas del mar pueden ser peligrosas.

¿Cómo lo digo?

1 Historieta Un naufragio Escojan.

1. El suceso se produjo en (un/una) área (rocoso/rocosa) de la costa española cerca de Tarifa.
2. En el verano (los/las) aguas del Mediterráneo no son muy (turbulentos/turbulentas).
3. Algunas víctimas del naufragio de la patera cayeron (al/a la) agua.
4. No se puede imaginar (el/la) hambre que tenían los inmigrantes por no haber tenido comida.
5. Alguien dijo que (un/una) águila con (un/una) ala (roto/rota) voló sobre la escena del naufragio pero no lo creo.
6. (Un/Una) hacha puede ser (un/una) arma (peligroso/peligrosa).

Mazarrón, Costa de la Luz

Sustantivos irregulares que terminan en a
Identifying more items

There are several nouns in Spanish that end in **a** but are masculine. These are nouns derived from Greek roots. They take the definite article **el** and the indefinite article **un.**

el clima	**el poema**
el día	**el programa**
el drama	**el sistema**
el mapa	**el telegrama**
el planeta	**el tema**

Note that the noun **la mano** is irregular. Even though **la mano** ends in **o,** it is feminine—**la mano. La foto** is also used as a shortened version of **la fotografía.** The noun **radio** can be either **la radio** or **el radio.** The gender varies according to the region.

¿Cómo lo digo?

2 Historieta En la clase de español

Contesten.

1. ¿Estudias el mapa de España en la clase de español?
2. ¿Hablan del clima del país?
3. ¿Explica el profesor el sistema de gobierno español?
4. ¿Van ustedes a leer los poemas de Espronceda?
5. ¿Van a leer los dramas de Lope de Vega?
6. ¿Van a aprender algo sobre los idiomas autónomos como el gallego, el catalán y el euskera?

3 Historieta El metro Completen.

1. _____ sistema de transporte subterráneo de Barcelona es muy buen_____.
2. _____ mapa indica las rutas de todas las líneas.
3. _____ tema de este artículo son los nuevos trenes que podrán funcionar sin conductor.
4. Van a inaugurar los nuevos trenes _____ día 20.
5. En el metro no es necesario abrir el portón con _____ mano porque todos los portones son automáticos.
6. Es imposible escuchar _____ radio en el metro.

Pronombres demostrativos
Pointing out people and things

1. You have already learned the demonstrative adjectives *(this, that).* The forms for the demonstrative pronouns *(this one, that one)* in Spanish are the same as those for the demonstrative adjectives. The demonstrative pronouns used to be distinguished by an accent mark. Although one may still see accents on demonstrative pronouns, they are no longer required. Note the forms below.

este	esta	estos	estas
ese	esa	esos	esas
aquel	aquella	aquellos	aquellas

2. Remember that **ese** and **aquel** can both mean *that* or *that one.* **Ese** refers to something near the person spoken to. **Aquel** refers to something far away—*that one over there* **(allá).**

Este tren aquí y ese que está llegando ahora son muy modernos.
Pero creo que este (aquí) tiene pasillos más amplios que ese (allí).
Este tren aquí no sigue la misma ruta que aquel (allá en la otra vía).

Sitges, Cataluña

¿Cómo lo digo?

¿Cuál? Sigan el modelo.

El metro aquí en Madrid es más viejo que el metro allá en Barcelona. →
Este es más viejo que aquel.

1. El mapa aquí es más reciente que el mapa allá.
2. La señora aquí es de Córdoba y la señora allá es sevillana.
3. El sistema de metro aquí en Madrid es más viejo que el sistema de metro allá en Barcelona.
4. Los mapas que tú tienes son de España y los mapas que están allá en la mesa son de Francia.
5. Los pasajeros que están sentados aquí están más cómodos que los pasajeros allí que están de pie.
6. El asiento aquí está ocupado pero el asiento allí a tu lado está libre.

Pronombres posesivos
Expressing ownership

1. A possessive pronoun replaces a noun that is modified by a possessive adjective. Like any other pronoun, the possessive pronoun must agree in gender and number with the noun it replaces. Note that the possessive pronoun is accompanied by a definite article.

POSSESSIVE ADJECTIVE	POSSESSIVE PRONOUN
mi, mis	el mío, la mía, los míos, las mías
tu, tus	el tuyo, la tuya, los tuyos, las tuyas
su, sus	el suyo, la suya, los suyos, las suyas
nuestro, nuestra, nuestros, nuestras	el nuestro, la nuestra, los nuestros, las nuestras
vuestro, vuestra, vuestros, vuestras	*el vuestro, la vuestra, los vuestros, las vuestras*

Todos tenemos nuestros billetes.
Yo tengo el mío, tú tienes el tuyo y Sandra tiene el suyo.

2. Just as the adjective **su** can refer to many different people so can the pronouns **el suyo, la suya, los suyos,** and **las suyas.** Whenever it is unclear to whom the possessive pronoun refers, a prepositional phrase is used for clarification.

el suyo	**la suya**	**los suyos**	**las suyas**
el de él	**la de él**	**los de él**	**las de él**
el de ella	**la de ella**	**los de ella**	**las de ella**
el de Ud.	**la de Ud.**	**los de Ud.**	**las de Ud.**
el de ellos	**la de ellos**	**los de ellos**	**las de ellos**
el de ellas	**la de ellas**	**los de ellas**	**las de ellas**
el de Uds.	**la de Uds.**	**los de Uds.**	**las de Uds.**

¿Está llevando Elena su suéter?
No, no está llevando el suyo. Está llevando el de él.

3. Note that the definite article is often omitted after the verb **ser.**

Estos libros son de Marta. Son suyos.
No son míos.

However, the article can be used to emphasize whose they are.

Estos son los míos y aquellos son los tuyos.

¿Cómo lo digo?

5 En la estación de ferrocarril Sigan el modelo.

María, ¿tienes tu billete? →
Sí, sí. Tengo el mío.

1. María, ¿tienes tu billete?
2. María, ¿tienes mi billete también?
3. María, ¿tienes el billete de Elena?
4. María, ¿tienes todos nuestros billetes?

Málaga, Costa del Sol

6 En el aeropuerto Sigan el modelo.

¿Las revistas? →
Tengo las mías pero no sé dónde están las tuyas.

1. ¿El pasaporte?
2. ¿La tarjeta de embarque?
3. ¿Las mochilas?
4. ¿El talón para el equipaje?

7 ¿De quiénes? Usen el pronombre posesivo.

1. Yo estoy buscando mi periódico.
2. Y Elena está buscando su periódico.
3. Ellos están mirando nuestro coche (carro).
4. Y nosotros estamos mirando su coche (carro).
5. Carlos, ¿son mis fotos o son tus fotos?
6. ¿Quién tiene mis fotos?
7. Susana, esta es mi cámara y esa es tu cámara.
8. ¿Tiene Andrés su cámara?

Madrid

8 Él tiene la suya. Sigan los modelos.

Ramón tiene su entrada. →
Ramón tiene la suya.

Ramón tiene la entrada de Elena. →
Ramón tiene la de ella.

1. Ramón está en su asiento.
2. Él está guardando el asiento de Elena.
3. Ahora, ella tiene su entrada.
4. Los amigos buscan sus asientos.
5. Ellos tienen el programa de Elena y el de Ramón.
6. Y Ramón no tiene su programa.

¡Te toca a ti!

Use what you have learned

HABLAR 1

Un sistema de metro

✔ Talk about a subway system

¿Hay un sistema de metro donde vives? ¿Es bueno o malo el sistema? Si no hay metro, ¿en qué ciudad cercana hay un sistema de metro?

Gran Vía, Madrid

HABLAR 2 ESCRIBIR

Un área de España

✔ Describe your favorite area of Spain

Dibuja un mapa de un área de España que te gusta o que te interesa. Describe el área y su clima. ¿Quieres pasar algunos días allí? ¿Cuándo?

La migración

✔ ***Discuss migration in today's world***

Con algunos compañeros discute por qué en muchas áreas del planeta «Tierra» hay tanta hambre y miseria que la gente lo encuentra necesario emigrar hasta de una manera ilegal y peligrosa.

Un drama

✔ ***Write a newspaper article about a disastrous event***

Un suceso horrible tuvo lugar en las aguas turbulentas en el área de Tarifa. Escribe un artículo para un periódico español describiendo todo lo que pasó.

Tarifa, Costa de la Luz

Assessment

Vocabulario

1 Escriban con otra palabra.

1. Tiene un pasillo *ancho.*
2. Ellos quieren *escapar.*
3. Van a *pedir* ayuda.
4. *El evento* tuvo lugar ayer.

To review vocabulary, turn to pages 36 and 39.

2 Completen.

5. Un _____ indica la ruta de cada línea del metro.
6. Los _____ del metro lo toman casi todos los días para ir a su trabajo.
7. La patera naufragó. _____ contra una roca.
8. Una patrulla rescató a las _____ del naufragio. Las salvó.

Lectura

3 Contesten.

To review the newspaper article on the metro, turn to page 38.

9. ¿Por qué van a ser los trenes de la futura línea del metro de Barcelona los más avanzados del mundo?
10. ¿De qué van a estar dotados?

Parque Güell, Barcelona

To review the newspaper article on immigrants in Tarifa, turn to pages 40–41.

4 ¿Sí o no?

11. Murieron cinco inmigrantes cuando su patera naufragó en Tarifa.
12. No se sabe de qué nacionalidad son los inmigrantes.
13. Hubo sólo hombres en la embarcación.

Estructura

5 Completen.

14–15. La patera chocó en _____ área de Tarifa en _____ aguas del Mediterráneo.

16. _____ sistema de metro es muy buen___.

17. Es _____ mapa del norte de España.

To review some irregular nouns, turn to pages 42–43.

Tarifa

For more Chapter 1 test preparation, go to the Chapter 1 **Self-Check Quiz** on the Glencoe Spanish Web site at glencoe.com.

6 Escojan.

18. Esta foto es más bonita que _____ allá en la mesa.
    a. esta **b.** esa **c.** aquella
19. Esta foto es más bonita que _____ que tienes en la mano.
    a. esta **b.** esa **c.** aquella
20. _____ trenes que están aquí en la estación son todos muy modernos.
    a. Estos **b.** Esos **c.** Aquellos

To review the demonstratives, turn to page 44.

7 Escriban con un pronombre.

21. ¿Tienes *tu libro?*
22. María está mirando *sus billetes.*
23. Juan quiere usar *mi coche (carro).*
24. *Tu cámara* no está en la mochila.
25. Es *mi bolígrafo.*

To review the possessive pronouns, turn to pages 45–46.

Composición

Para escribir bien hay algunas técnicas que puedes utilizar. Una técnica muy importante es la de «visualizar». Puedes cerrar los ojos y visualizar o pintar una imagen mental sobre el contenido de tu escrito; sobre todo un escrito descriptivo. En un escrito descriptivo vas a describir algo.

TAREA 1

La geografía de España En este capítulo has leído sobre la geografía de España. Con ojos cerrados o abiertos piensa en todo lo que recuerdas sobre el clima y el paisaje de España. Al hacer tu imagen mental piensa en los colores típicos de varias regiones; piensa en palabras tales como calor/frío que puedes usar para describir las diferentes regiones. Toma una hoja de papel o tu «procesador» y escribe una lista de las palabras o expresiones que te vienen a la mente. Escribe el nombre de algunas regiones o simplemente direcciones cardinales: norte, sur, etc. Coloca tus palabras o expresiones con el área apropiada.

Ahora vas a empezar a escribir tu primer borrador. Pero antes de poner palabras en el papel, establece el orden que quieres seguir. Puede ser:

- **direccional** el norte hasta el sur
- **categórico** paisaje, clima
- **características** verde, marrón, frío, calor

Luego empieza a escribir. Dale libre albedrío a tu bolígrafo, lapicero o teclado. Escribe todo lo que te viene a la mente en el orden establecido. Puedes corregir tu primer borrador más tarde.

TAREA 2

Vas a continuar con tu escrito. Antes puedes corregir y revisar tu primer borrador de la Tarea 1 o si quieres puedes esperar hasta terminar todo el escrito.

Ahora vas a contar algo que has hecho. Pero en este caso será necesario usar la imaginación si no has visitado España. Pero no va a ser difícil porque ya has aprendido mucho sobre España en tus estudios de español.

Puedes escribir esta parte de tu escrito como una carta personal, como si contaras o relataras tu viaje a un(a) amigo(a). Puedes decirle lo que hiciste y viste durante tu estadía en España. Si quieres puedes dar algunas opiniones sobre lo que te gustó o no te gustó, lo que te interesó, etc.

Al escribir algo personal, «deja fluir tu bolígrafo». Escribe rápido todo lo que te viene a la mente. Puedes reorganizar y clarificar tus ideas más tarde.

Ahora vas a empezar.

- Escribe todo lo que viste e hiciste en España. (¿Te gustó o no? ¿Qué te interesó?, etc.)
- Lee lo que escribiste. Si es necesario, revísalo para darle mejor organización y para aclararlo.
- Antes de seguir puedes corregir en este primer borrador cualquier error que te sale (ves).

TAREA 3 **La España de hoy** El objeto de muchos escritos expositivos es el de explicar algo. Ahora vas a dar una explicación escrita de un problema que enfrenta la España actual, la España de hoy. Puedes escoger el afán independentista de algunos estados autónomos o la inmigración ilegal. En tu escrito tienes que:

- identificar el problema
- explicar lo que causa el problema
- dar algunas consecuencias del problema.

Antes de empezar a escribir una explicación de algo, debes sentarte tranquilamente sin bolígrafo en la mano y reflexionar sobre lo que vas a escribir. Debes determinar como vas a organizar y presentar tu explicación para que sea lo más clara posible.

Fin: Ahora tienes el borrador de tu escrito o composición entera. Tienes que leer cada parte con mucho cuidado. Lo tienes que revisar y corregir.

Revisar Lee el borrador para averiguar o determinar si te gusta la organización o si quieres cambiar la organización de algunas ideas. Ahora que estás leyendo tu escrito en su totalidad es posible que tengas que añadir una frase al principio de cada parte para unirla a la parte anterior.

Corregir Lee el borrador una vez más buscando errores de ortografía y gramática. Es muy importante verificar:

- la concordancia de los adjetivos
- la concordancia del verbo con el sujeto, la terminación verbal

Después de revisar y corregir tu borrador, escribe de nuevo tu composición en forma final.

Discurso

Cada día de nuestra vida pasamos mucho tiempo hablando. Hablamos de muchas cosas diferentes y por muchos motivos diferentes. Frecuentemente hablamos o entablamos una conversación para buscar información. Necesitamos saber como hacer algo, por ejemplo.

En cualquier conversación el/la que habla es el/la hablante y el/la que escucha es el/la oyente o el/la interlocutor(a). Cuando hablamos para tratar de conseguir información es necesario hacer preguntas. Debemos organizar nuestras preguntas de tal manera que nuestro interlocutor las pueda conseguir fácilmente para ayudarle a darnos la información que buscamos. No debemos saltar de un tema o tópico a otro.

TAREA 4 **En la agenica de viajes** Van a trabajar en grupos de dos. La conversación va a tener lugar en una agencia de viajes. Uno(a) va a ser el/la cliente con las preguntas y el/la otro(a) va a ser el/la agente de viajes. El/La cliente va a hacer un viaje a España y como es la primera vez que hace tal viaje necesita un montón de información y tiene muchas preguntas.

Antes de hablar con el/la agente, el/la que va a ser el/la cliente debe pensar en lo que quiere saber y organizar lógicamente las preguntas que tiene para recibir la información que necesita. Debe poner sus preguntas en orden, por ejemplo. El/La cliente necesita información sobre:

los hoteles
el viaje a España
el transporte dentro de España
el aeropuerto
el viaje de vuelta
el costo de las comidas
las ciudades o lugares que debe visitar en España

Después de empezar a hablar con el/la agente, el/la cliente debe poner estos tópicos en un orden lógico y luego pensar en las preguntas que tiene sobre cada uno.

Ustedes van a repetir la conversación dos veces para darle a cada uno la oportunidad de ser el/la cliente.

CAPÍTULO 1

Vocabulario

Lección 1 Cultura

Geografía
la colina
la llanura
la neblina
la orilla
el país
el puerto
a lo largo
de color pardo
parecerse a

Historia
la carabela
la corona
la guerra
el/la invasor(a)
la joya
la monarquía
el rey
la reina
el siglo
el soldado
la tropa
establecer
huir
invadir
luchar
reinar

Comida
el ajo
la almendra
la berenjena
el/la cocinero(a)
el jamón serrano
el olivar
la rebanada
el trocito
veraniego(a)
rebanar
cortar
pelar
picar

Influencia árabe
la alberca
la alfombra
la almendra
la almohada

Lección 2 Conversación

el aeropuerto
el autocar
la autopista
el/la conductor(a)
la demora, el retraso
el embotellamiento,
  el tapón
el mapa
la mochila
el parador (del gobierno)
el/la pasajero(a)
el peaje
el puente aéreo
el taxi
el taxímetro
el monto
la venta
el vuelo
anulado(a)
en huelga
enlazar
pagar
recorrer

Lección 3 Periodismo

Trenes que no necesitan conductor
la barra de sujeción
el metro
el pasillo
el pedido
el usuario
amplio(a)

Mueren cinco inmigrantes
la patera, la embarcación
la patrulla
la roca
el suceso
magrebí
chocar
huir
naufragar
rescatar
solicitar

LITERARY COMPANION *See pages 418–429 for literary selections related to Chapter 1. The activities for these readings will help you continue to practice your reading comprehension skills.*

VIDEOTUR

¡Viva el mundo hispano!

Video can be a beneficial learning tool for the language student. Video enables you to experience the material in the textbook in a real-life setting. Take a vicarious field trip as you see people interacting at home, at school, at the market, etc. The cultural benefits are limitless as you experience the Spanish-speaking world while "traveling" through many countries. In addition to its tremendous cultural value, video gives practice in developing good listening and viewing skills. Video allows you to look for numerous clues that are evident in tone of voice, facial expressions, and gestures. Through video you can see and hear the diversity of the target culture and compare and contrast the Spanish-speaking cultures to each other and to your own.

Episodio 1: Visita al Viejo Madrid

La Puerta del Sol está en pleno centro del viejo Madrid. Es el corazón de la ciudad. Aquí hay una placa que indica el centro preciso de España que también está en la Puerta del Sol. Muchos eventos históricos ocurrieron aquí. En 1808 los madrileños lucharon contra los soldados de Napoleón en la Guerra de la Independencia. Es un lugar muy vivo e impresionante.

Episodio 2: Invierno en verano

Este lugar se llama Madrid Xanadu. Es un lugar para esquiar, pero no está en una montaña, está en la ciudad. No solamente está en la ciudad, está en un edificio. Allí se puede esquiar día y noche, en invierno o en verano. Hay pistas para principiantes y para expertos. Es uno de los sitios más populares de Madrid para la gente joven.

Episodio 3: La tradición del café

El café es una institución en España. Es un centro social. Allí la gente no solamente toma café, allí se habla, se lee el periódico, se encuentra con los amigos. En este café de Madrid el camarero les sirve a los señores que, sin duda, son clientes habituales, clientes que van al mismo café todos los días a la misma hora.

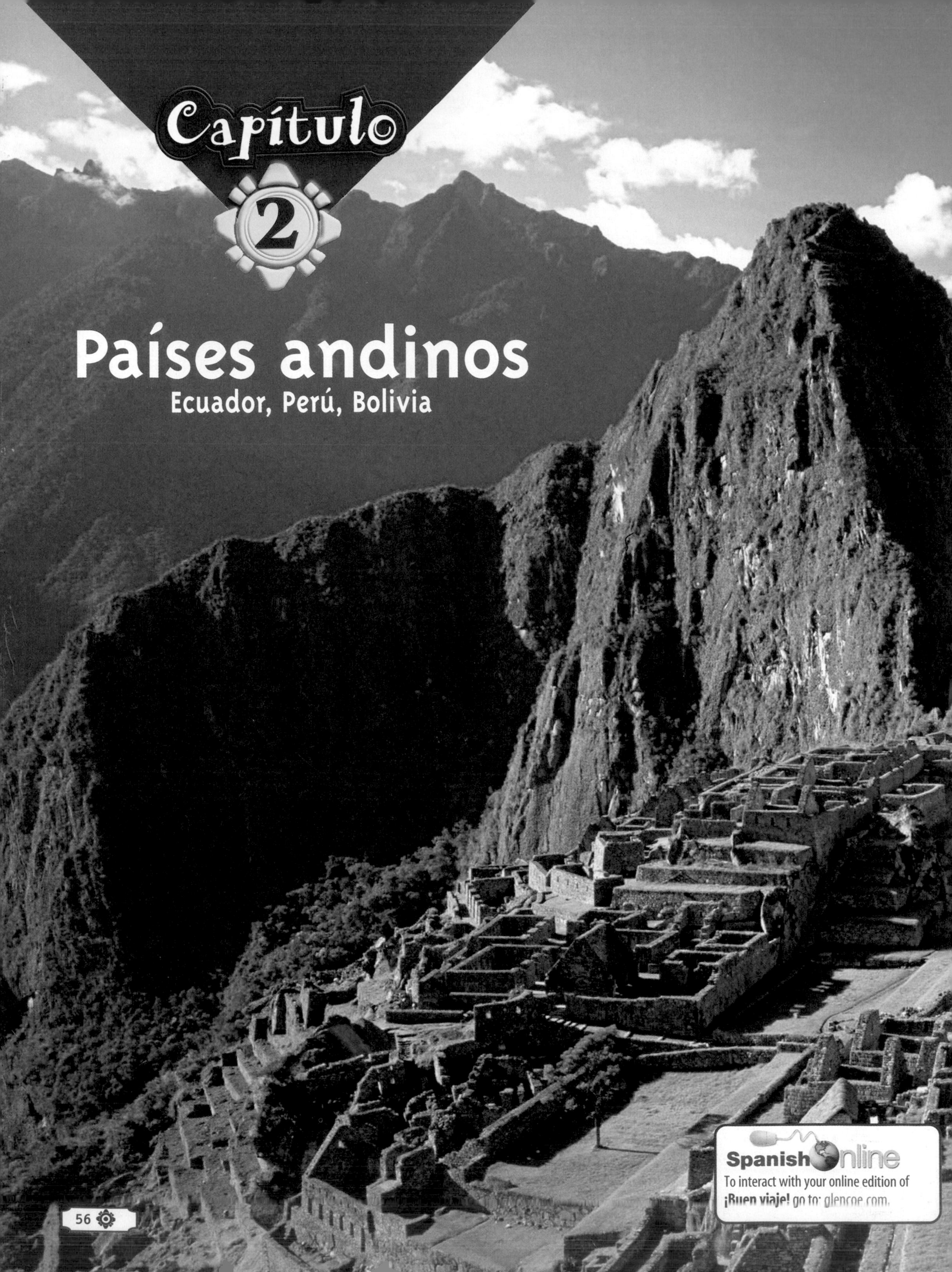

Capítulo 2

Países andinos

Ecuador, Perú, Bolivia

Spanish Online
To interact with your online edition of **¡Buen viaje!** go to: glencoe.com.

Objetivos

In this chapter you will:

- learn about the geography, history, and culture of Ecuador, Peru, and Bolivia
- review how to describe habitual past actions
- discuss a robbery
- review how to talk about past events
- read and discuss newspaper articles about a volcano eruption in Ecuador and a centenarian in Peru
- learn to express what may or may not take place
- learn to express necessity and possibility; wishes, preferences, and demands

Contenido

Vocabulario para la lectura

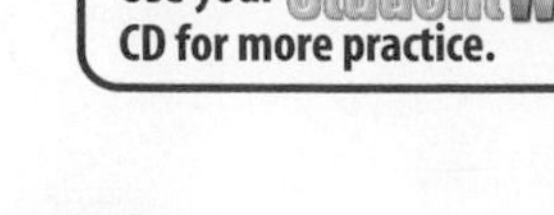

La materia prima

la madera

el oro

la plata

el choclo, el maíz

la papa

Las señoras tejían unos tejidos muy bonitos.

La indígena cultivaba la papa.

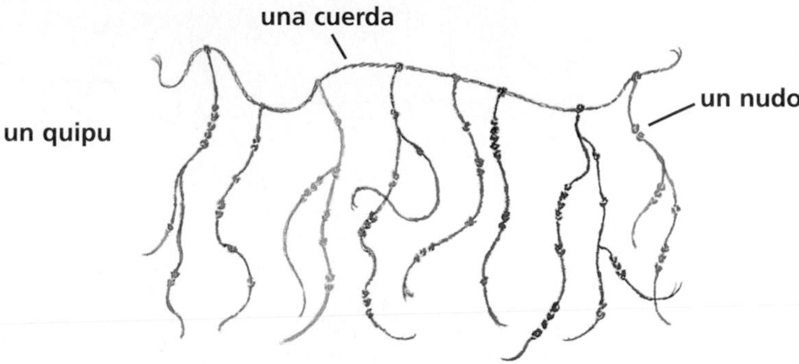

Los indígenas usaban el quipu para contar.
Los quipus tenían varios nudos.

Durante la época colonial:

Las casas más elegantes se situaban en la plaza o cerca de la plaza central.
Las casas solían tener sólo dos pisos.
Tenían balcones de madera.

Más vocabulario

un(a) criollo(a) una persona de origen español nacida en las Américas
la precipitación la lluvia
acomodado(a) bastante rico; no pobre
agrio(a) lo contrario de dulce, amargo
bello(a) bonito, hermoso, lindo
caluroso(a) donde hace mucho calor
escaso(a) poco, insuficiente
lluvioso(a) donde llueve mucho, donde hay mucha lluvia
nevado(a) cubierto de nieve
apoyar ayudar, favorecer, sostener
subyugar someter a alguien de manera violenta

LECCIÓN I

Cultura

¿Qué palabra necesito?

MONASTERIO D SANTA CATALINA
(UNICO EN EL MUNDO CON CIUDADELA)
AREQUIPA — PERÚ
www.santacatalina.org.pe
R.U.C. Nº 20134786605
Nº Reg. MICTI 9800255

ENTRADA GENERAL

S/. 2500 Nº 010456

SERVICIOS:
1.- Oficina de Informaciones.
2.- Servicio de Guías, no incluido en el boleto de ingreso.
3.- Tienda de Artesanías
4.- Botiquín de Primeros Auxilios.
5.- Servicios Higiénicos al ingreso y a mitad del recorrido.
6.- Cafetería.

ADVERTENCIA.- La empresa no se responsabiliza por accidentes. Camínese con cuidado Obserbando los desniveles del piso. Y algunas entradas muy bajas. No se permite llevar en el recorrido, radios y/o equipos.

VISITE: www.arequipa-tourism.com

1 Historieta El pasado Contesten.

1. En la época precolombina, ¿cultivaban los indígenas el maíz o el choclo?
2. ¿Qué más cultivaban?
3. ¿Usaban el quipu para contar?
4. ¿Tenía el quipu nudos?
5. En la época colonial, ¿dónde se situaban las casas más elegantes?
6. ¿Cuántos pisos solían tener?
7. ¿Tenían balcones?
8. ¿De qué eran los balcones?
9. ¿Tejían las señoras indígenas tejidos bonitos?

2 ¿Es verdad? ¿Sí o no?

1. El oro y la plata son metales preciosos.
2. La madera, como la esmeralda o el diamante, es una joya.
3. Los productos manufacturados son materia prima.
4. Se puede hacer nudos con una cuerda.
5. Nieva mucho en una región lluviosa.
6. Casi siempre hace calor en una zona calurosa.
7. El limón es una fruta bastante agria.
8. Un indígena inca es un criollo.

Calle Amazonas, Quito, Ecuador

3 ¿Cuál es la palabra?

Expresen de otra manera.

1. Estos tejidos son muy *bellos.*
2. La materia prima es *insuficiente.*
3. Donde viven ellos no hay mucha *lluvia.*
4. Las casas más elegantes *se encontraban* en la plaza.
5. Él *sometió* a su hermano.
6. Ellos *favorecieron y ayudaron* a su hermano en la batalla.

Lectura

La geografía

Pensar en Ecuador o Perú es pensar en bellos paisajes andinos. Pero la verdad es que Ecuador y Perú se dividen en tres zonas geográficas muy diferentes: en el oeste la costa, llamada el litoral en Perú; en el centro la sierra o la cordillera; y en el este la zona amazónica, llamada el Oriente en Ecuador y la selva en Perú. Estas inmensas selvas tropicales de la cuenca[1] amazónica cubren la mayor parte del territorio de los dos países. Pero debido al calor, a la vegetación densa y a la inaccesibilidad, es aquí donde vive el menor número de habitantes. Más del 50 por ciento de la población de cada país vive en la sierra.

A pesar de la proximidad de la línea ecuatorial, el clima de la costa de Ecuador y Perú no es ni muy caluroso ni muy lluvioso. ¿Por qué? Pues, una corriente fría llamada la corriente del Pacífico o la corriente Humboldt baña la costa y baja la temperatura y la precipitación. Muchas partes del litoral peruano son tan áridas que son zonas desérticas.

Bolivia no tiene costa. Perdió su acceso al mar en la guerra con Chile llamada también la guerra del Pacífico (1878–1884). En Bolivia los Andes se dividen en dos cordilleras—la oriental y la occidental—separadas por un altiplano de vientos fuertes y una vegetación muy escasa. En el este, Bolivia, como sus vecinos, tiene una inmensa área de selvas tropicales.

[1] cuenca *basin*

Reading Strategy

Using titles and subtitles Look at titles and subtitles before you begin to read. They will usually help you know what a reading selection will be about. Having an idea of what a reading will be about will help you understand better as you read.

Volcán Illimani, La Paz, Bolivia

Entre Pisco e Ica, Perú

A Identifiquen.

1. tres países andinos
2. el número de zonas geográficas que tienen Perú y Ecuador
3. el nombre que se le da a la costa de Perú
4. el nombre que se le da a la selva de Ecuador
5. donde vive la mayoría de las poblaciones ecuatoriana y peruana
6. la corriente que baja la temperatura y la precipitación a lo largo de la costa del Pacífico en Perú y Ecuador
7. cuando Bolivia perdió su acceso a la costa
8. lo que cubre la parte oriental de Bolivia

Una ojeada histórica

Estela boliviana

La época precolombina

Desde los tiempos más remotos han poblado estas regiones andinas muchos grupos indígenas. Durante unos siglos los incas los iban subyugando, llegando a formar en el siglo XV un Imperio que iba desde el sur de Colombia hasta el norte de Chile y desde los nevados picos andinos hasta las orillas del Pacífico. El Imperio cubría un área de 900.000 kilómetros cuadrados.

El jefe supremo de los incas fue el Inca, un hombre-dios que llevaba el título «Hijo del Sol». La base de la sociedad la constituía la familia o el ayllu, una comunidad formada por un conjunto de familias.

Los incas creían en un dios creador, Viracocha. Viracocha creó el mundo y los seres que lo habitaban. Luego desapareció en el mar. Otros dioses tenían más importancia que Viracocha en los ritos y en los asuntos diarios. Entre los más importantes fueron Inti, el Sol, y Pachamama, la Tierra. Los incas creían en un cielo y un infierno, un lugar asociado al frío y al hambre. El destino que esperaba a los muertos dependía de sus actos en vida y de su condición social.

Machu Picchu, Perú

Los incas hablaban quechua, un idioma que sus descendientes siguen hablando hoy. No conocían la escritura pero para contar tenían un sistema ingenioso. Usaban los quipus—series de cuerdas con nudos de varios tipos. Según el color de los cordeles[2] y la posición de los nudos, los quipus servían de registro numérico siguiendo un sistema decimal.

Los incas eran excelentes arquitectos. Construían casas, templos, fortalezas y ciudades. De estas la más famosa y la más intacta es Machu Picchu.

También era excelente el sistema de caminos que tenían. El trazado de las carreteras era sencillo. Una vía corría a lo largo de los Andes y la otra a lo largo de la zona costera. Había numerosos tambos o posadas[3] a distancias variables. En los tambos se encontraban chasquis u hombres correos que corrían a gran velocidad de un tambo a otro llevando mensajes.

[2] cordeles *cord, twine*
[3] posadas *inns*

La base del sustento de los incas era la agricultura. En las regiones más altas el único cultivo practicable era la papa. Exponiendo la papa sucesivamente a las heladas nocturnas del altiplano y al radiante sol del día, deshidrataban la papa convirtiéndola en chuño. Se podía transportar el chuño fácilmente y se conservaba por mucho tiempo. Cultivaban también el choclo y la quinua[4] que se empleaba como cereal. El ganado domesticado, llamas y alpacas, les daba lana, pieles[5] y carne. Cortaban la carne de estos animales en tiras[6] finas que secaban al sol para hacer charqui que se podía conservar por mucho tiempo.

[4] quinua *type of seed*
[5] pieles *skins*
[6] tiras *strips*

Llamas en Ingapirca, Ecuador

Baños, Ecuador

To learn more about archaeological sites in the Andean countries, go to **Web Explore** on the Glencoe Spanish Web site at glencoe.com.

 Contesten.

1. ¿Qué grupo indígena iba formando un imperio grande desde el sur de Colombia hasta el norte de Chile?
2. ¿Qué constituía la base de la sociedad inca?
3. ¿Quién era el dios creador de los incas?
4. ¿Quiénes eran dos dioses que tenían mucha importancia en su vida diaria?
5. ¿De qué dependía el destino final de los incas?
6. ¿Qué lengua hablaban?
7. ¿Conocían la escritura?
8. ¿Qué usaban para contar?
9. ¿Qué construían los incas?
10. ¿Quiénes eran los chasquis y qué hacían?
11. ¿Qué comían los incas?
12. ¿Para qué usaban las llamas y las alpacas?

La conquista

El Inca Huayna Capac murió en 1525. Con su muerte el gran Imperio fue dividido entre sus dos hijos—Huáscar, el legítimo, y Atahualpa, el ilegítimo. Atahualpa recibió el norte (Quito) y Huáscar recibió el sur (Cuzco). Enseguida Atahualpa se sublevó contra su hermano. Lo venció y lo tomó prisionero. En este momento entra Francisco Pizarro con entre 130 y 250 hombres y veinticinco a ochenta caballos, a Tumbes, cerca de Cuzco. Pizarro y sus hombres encontraron muy poca resistencia ya que los habitantes de la región habían apoyado al hermano muerto de Atahualpa. La conquista fue rápida y en noviembre de 1532 los españoles hicieron prisionero a Atahualpa en Cajamarca (hoy parte de Ecuador). Poco después lo ejecutaron. En noviembre de 1533 Pizarro entró en Cuzco y dos años después fundó la magnífica ciudad de los Reyes, Lima.

Los conquistadores tenían afán de hacerse famosos realizando hazañas[7] y obteniendo riquezas de oro y plata para la Corona española. Además se consideraban los portadores de la verdadera fe y querían convertir a los indígenas. Los conquistadores querían servir a Dios y a su Rey.

Atahualpa

[7] hazañas *deeds*

Francisco Pizarro

Lima, Perú

Como en la Edad Media europea el señor tenía vasallos, los conquistadores y los primeros pobladores de las Américas también tenían la ambición de convertirse en «señores de vasallos». Esa ambición resultó en la institución de la encomienda. Consistía en encomendar cierto grupo de indígenas a un español, al encomendero. El encomendero tenía el derecho de cobrar tributos[8] a los indígenas. En los primeros tiempos de la colonización no hubo control sobre las exigencias de los encomenderos quienes cometieron todo tipo de abusos contra los indígenas, sobre todo en el trabajo en las minas. Es difícil imaginar el trauma que sufrieron los incas tras la llegada de los españoles. La población indígena empezó a bajar dramáticamente debido a las epidemias de enfermedades que trajeron los españoles, los maltratos sufridos a causa de las exigencias laborales de los encomenderos y el colapso de su forma de vivir, de sus costumbres y de su religión. El rápido descenso poblacional indígena resultó en otro gran horror, el tráfico[9] de africanos, de gente esclavizada.

[8] tributos *taxes*
[9] tráfico *trade*

C Completen.

El Inca Huayna Capac murió en 1525. Después de su muerte el Imperio de los incas fue dividido en dos partes entre sus dos __1__. __2__ recibió el sur y __3__ recibió el norte. Enseguida __4__ sublevó contra su hermano, __5__. Lo venció y lo tomó __6__. Muy poco después llegó Francisco Pizarro, el conquistador español. Sus hombres no encontraban mucha __7__ de los incas porque ya habían apoyado al hermano muerto de Atahualpa. La conquista fue rápida y los españoles capturaron a __8__ en Cajamarca y poco después lo __9__.

Plaza de Armas, Trujillo, Perú

D ¿Sí o no?

1. Los conquistadores y los colonizadores encomendaban a un grupo de indígenas a un español. Los indígenas tenían que trabajar por el español a quien fueron encomendados.
2. El español fue el encomendado y el indígena el encomendero.
3. Los españoles nunca abusaban de los indígenas.
4. Los españoles les exigían mucho trabajo duro a los indígenas.
5. La población de los indígenas empezó a bajar dramáticamente.
6. Los indígenas fueron reemplazados por los negros esclavizados importados de África.

Cultura

La colonización

Durante la primera parte del período colonial (siglos XVI y XVII) el Virreinato de Perú se extendía desde el estrecho de Magallanes hasta Ecuador. Lima fue la capital.

Durante la época colonial los españoles establecieron muchas ciudades. Las ciudades se parecían a las de España. Las calles se cruzaban formando una red[10] octagonal. En el centro había un espacio abierto—la plaza—generalmente llamada la Plaza de Armas. La plaza servía de eje[11] a la vida urbana. Aquí se situaban los principales edificios administrativos y religiosos. El que más cerca de la plaza vivía más importancia social tenía. Sus casas solían contar con dos pisos y tenían balcones de madera. Por su parte las clases más humildes vivían en casas de un solo piso que en algunas zonas se pintaban de colores alegres. En las afueras del centro urbano se situaban los barrios o pueblos indios. La sociedad colonial se dividía en estratos bien diferenciados. En primer lugar venían los hidalgos[12] y los descendientes de los conquistadores que en siguientes generaciones constituían la nobleza criolla, hijos de españoles nacidos en América. Luego venían los mestizos, los negros y los indígenas.

Plaza de Armas, Quito, Ecuador

[10] red *network*
[11] eje *axis*
[12] hidalgos *nobles*

Calle la Ronda, Casco antiguo, Quito, Ecuador

E Contesten.

1. ¿Se parecían las ciudades que establecían los españoles a las ciudades de España?
2. ¿Qué había en el centro de la ciudad?
3. ¿Qué nombre le daban los españoles a este espacio?
4. ¿Qué edificios se situaban en la plaza?
5. ¿Dónde vivía la gente que más importancia social tenía?
6. ¿Cómo solían ser sus casas?
7. ¿Cómo eran las casas en las que vivían las clases más humildes?
8. ¿Qué había en las afueras del centro urbano?

Desde la independencia hasta hoy

Después de tres siglos de dominación española, los colonos querían su independencia. La minoría culta, la mayoría de ellos criollos, pedían reformas. Una de sus quejas[13] fue contra la política intervencionalista y de control económico que practicaba la monarquía española. La Corona no permitía el comercio con ningún otro país, sólo con España. Les compraba la materia prima a los colonos a precios muy bajos y les vendía los productos manufacturados a precios muy altos. Otro problema fue la debilidad de la monarquía española que culminó en la invasión francesa de España en 1808 cuando Napoleón nombró a su hermano José Bonaparte rey de España.

Las rebeliones independentistas empezaron a principios del siglo XIX. Simón Bolívar luchó en el norte, en Venezuela y Colombia. El general José de San Martín luchó en Argentina y Chile y siguió la costa hasta Lima. Los dos se reunieron en Guayaquil en 1822 pero no pudieron ponerse de acuerdo sobre una política de posguerra. San Martín se retiró a Francia y Bolívar continuó la lucha. Bajo Bolívar y el mariscal Sucre el dominio español en la América del Sur terminó con las victorias de Junín y Ayacucho en 1824.

[13] quejas *complaints*

Plaza de Armas, Trujillo, Perú

Hotel Gran Bolívar, Lima, Perú

Cultura

Aun antes de la independencia empezaron a surgir intereses regionalistas y separatistas. En vez de formar una gran entidad política, el sueño de Bolívar, los virreinatos se dividieron en muchas naciones diferentes. Desde la independencia las naciones andinas de Ecuador, Perú y Bolivia han tenido una historia política bastante turbulenta con enfrentamientos[14] entre conservadores y liberales, militaristas y civilistas. Cada país ha tenido gobiernos democráticos y dictaduras. Y cada uno ha gozado de períodos estables y ha sufrido de períodos inestables.

Son Ecuador, Perú y Bolivia los países que han conservado la mayor población indígena de todos los países sudamericanos. Las poblaciones indígena y mestiza alcanzan aproximadamente el 70 por ciento de la población total de cada nación. Hoy hay un fuerte renacimiento de interés en todo lo «indígena» y esta población está pidiendo una voz más fuerte en el gobierno y en el liderazgo[15] de cada país donde por lo general la élite criolla sigue ejerciendo mayor poder.

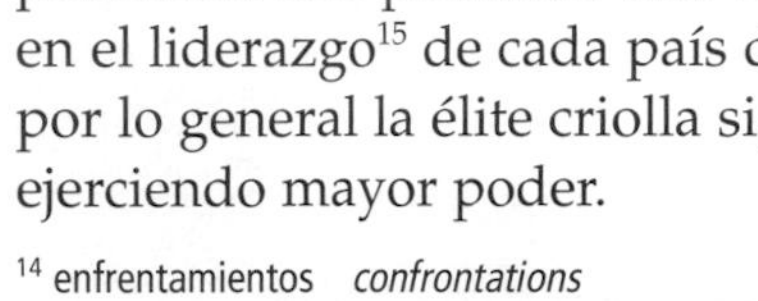

[14] enfrentamientos *confrontations*
[15] liderazgo *leadership*

F Expliquen.

1. dos razones económicas por las cuales los colonos querían su independencia de España
2. una razón política por la cual querían su independencia
3. donde luchó Simón Bolívar
4. donde luchó San Martín
5. el gran sueño de Simón Bolívar
6. la situación política y económica de Ecuador, Perú y Bolivia desde la independencia

Visitas históricas

Al visitar no importa cual de estos tres países, vas a ver unos paisajes inolvidables. Y por todas partes vas a sentir o experimentar las ricas herencias indígena y española.

La ciudad más intacta de los incas es Machu Picchu. Se discute si servía de fortaleza, de santuario religioso o de escuela para la nobleza incaica.

En 1300 la ciudad de Chan Chan de los Mochica en la costa norte de Perú fue más grande en tamaño y población que cualquier ciudad europea de la época. Sus magníficas ruinas dan testimonio de su grandeza.

Una visita al mercado de Otavalo al norte de Quito en Ecuador es una experiencia inolvidable. Aquí se puede comprar de todo. A muchos les interesan los tejidos porque los tejedores otavaleños gozan de fama mundial y sus tejidos son muy apreciados.

Chan Chan, Perú

Ejemplos de la herencia española son las bellas plazas de Lima, Quito y Sucre, todas de estilo colonial. El convento de Santa Catalina en Arequipa es una joya arquitectónica. Es todo un pueblo cerca de la Plaza de Armas que hasta recientemente sirvió de residencia a las señoritas acomodadas que decidieron dedicarse a la vida religiosa.

Plaza de Armas, Arequipa, Perú

Convento de Santa Catalina, Arequipa, Perú

Cocina

Si tienes hambre durante tu visita tienes que probar una de las muchas especialidades regionales. Hay muchas opciones pero aquí tienes una posibilidad para cada país. Vas a notar la influencia indígena en la cocina con el uso de la papa y del choclo.

Bolivia — **empanadas salteñas:** empanadas con carne picada, huevos, aceitunas, papas, cebollas y pimientos

Perú — **ceviche:** corvina u otro pescado, adobado[16] durante tres o cuatro horas en una salsa de limón y naranja agria

Ecuador — **locro:** una sopa de papa o choclo con queso a veces acompañado de palta (aguacate)

¡Buen provecho y buen viaje!

[16] adobado *marinated*

Ceviche

Contesten.

Si puedes ir a uno o más de estos tres países andinos, ¿adónde quieres ir? ¿Qué quieres ver? ¿Qué vas a comer?

Otavalo, Ecuador

Estructura • Repaso

Imperfecto
Talking about habitual, recurring past actions

1. The imperfect tense is, after the preterite, the most frequently used tense to express past actions. Review the forms of the imperfect. Note that the same endings are used for both **-er** and **-ir** verbs.

INFINITIVE	hablar	leer	escribir
root	habl-	le-	escrib-
yo	hablaba	leía	escribía
tú	hablabas	leías	escribías
él, ella, Ud.	hablaba	leía	escribía
nosotros(as)	hablábamos	leíamos	escribíamos
vosotros(as)	*hablabais*	*leíais*	*escribíais*
ellos, ellas, Uds.	hablaban	leían	escribían

2. Note that verbs that have a stem change in either the present or the preterite do not have a stem change in the imperfect.

querer	sentir	pedir
quería	sentía	pedía
querías	sentías	pedías
quería	sentía	pedía
queríamos	sentíamos	pedíamos
queríais	*sentíais*	*pedíais*
querían	sentían	pedían

Convento de Santa Catalina, Arequipa, Perú

3. The following verbs are the only irregular verbs in the imperfect tense.

ir	ser	ver
iba	era	veía
ibas	eras	veías
iba	era	veía
íbamos	éramos	veíamos
ibais	*erais*	*veíais*
iban	eran	veían

4. The imperfect tense is used to express habitual or repeated actions in the past. When the event actually began or ended is not important. Some time expressions that accompany the imperfect are:

siempre, a menudo, con frecuencia, muchas veces, cada día, cada viernes, cada semana, cada año, en la época precolombina, durante el Renacimiento

En la época precolombina, los incas hablaban quechua.
Su base de sustento era la agricultura.
Comían muchas papas y choclo.

La profesora de español siempre nos hablaba en español en clase.
De vez en cuando ella nos leía una poesía o un refrán.
A veces nos enseñaba un baile.
Y los lunes, siempre nos daba un examen.

¿Lo sabes?

The imperfect of **hay** is **había.**

Había mucha gente.
Había miles de personas.

5. The imperfect is used to describe persons, places, and things in the past.

APARIENCIA	**El general era alto, fuerte y valiente.**
EDAD	**Tenía solamente veinticinco años.**
ACTITUD Y DESEO	**Él siempre quería salir victorioso.**
ESTADO EMOCIONAL	**Él estaba contento cuando ganaba.**
TIEMPO	**Era invierno, y hacía frío.**
COLOCACIÓN	**Era en la sierra donde luchaba el general.**
HORA	**Eran las cuatro de la mañana.**
CONDICIÓN	**Él tenía mucho frío y estaba cansado.**

Altiplano, Ecuador

¿Cómo lo digo?

1 Historieta De pequeño(a) Contesten.

1. Cuando eras pequeño(a), ¿a qué hora te levantabas por la mañana?
2. ¿A qué escuela asistías?
3. ¿Te gustaba ir a la escuela?
4. ¿Te acuerdas? ¿Quién era tu maestro(a) en el quinto grado?
5. ¿Cómo se llamaba? ¿Qué edad tenía, más o menos? ¿Cómo era?
6. ¿Daba muchos exámenes?
7. ¿Recibías buenas notas en su clase?
8. ¿Tomabas el almuerzo en la escuela o volvías a casa para almorzar?
9. ¿A qué hora terminaban las clases?
10. ¿A qué hora salías de la escuela?

2 Historieta Los incas Completen con el imperfecto.

Durante siglos los incas __1__ (ir) subyugando a muchos grupos indígenas incluyendo a los chimú que __2__ (vivir) en la maravillosa ciudad de adobe, Chan Chan. Los incas __3__ (llamar) a su imperio Tahuantinsuyo que __4__ (significar) las cuatro regiones de la tierra. Su lengua oficial __5__ (tener) el nombre de runasimi o quechua. La base de su estructura social __6__ (ser) el ayllu o sea un grupo de familias que __7__ (cultivar) la tierra, __8__ (dividir) el trabajo y __9__ (hacer) labores en común. La base de su sustento __10__ (ser) la agricultura. Parte de la cosecha __11__ (ser) para el inca y otra parte se __12__ (repartir) entre las familias del ayllu.

Chan Chan, Perú

Cuzco, Perú

3 Historieta El papel de la mujer

Cambien en el imperfecto.

En la familia indígena de la época precolombina, la mujer es considerada inferior al hombre. Ella tiene un montón de ocupaciones. Ella recoge el combustible, prepara la comida, cuida de los niños y de los animales, cultiva la huerta y teje la ropa. Cuando tiene que ir de un lugar a otro y si tiene un hijo que todavía no puede caminar, lo lleva en la espalda en un repliegue *(pleat, fold)* de su capa. Si el viaje dura más de medio día, carga también el alimento de la familia y la leña para el fuego.

¡Te toca a ti!

Use what you have learned

Altiplano, Ecuador

HABLAR 1

La geografía de los países andinos

✔ Describe the geography of Ecuador, Peru, and Bolivia

Muchos norteamericanos al pensar en la América del Sur piensan en un clima y paisaje tropicales. Pero es una idea errónea que tienen. Explícale a un(a) amigo(a) como es el clima en Ecuador, Perú y Bolivia. Descríbele también el paisaje.

HABLAR 2

La vida en la época de los incas

✔ Describe the lifestyle of the Incas

Has aprendido mucho sobre la vida de los incas. En tus propias palabras, describe algunos aspectos de su vida diaria. Puedes incluir sus creencias religiosas, como escribían, contaban o enviaban mensajes y lo que comían.

ESCRIBIR 3

Un rebelde

✔ Discuss some events that led to the Conquest

Escribe un artículo para un periódico describiendo los eventos que siguieron la muerte del inca Huayna Capac. Explica como y por qué fue tan rápida la conquista.

La Paz, Bolivia

Los países andinos

✔ ***Discuss what you know about Andean countries***

Trabajen en grupos de cuatro. Compartan sus opiniones. Cada uno(a) dirá lo que para él o ella era lo más interesante de todo lo que aprendió sobre los países andinos. Luego, un miembro de su grupo va a compartir las opiniones de todos con la clase.

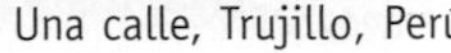

Una calle, Trujillo, Perú

Una ciudad de la época colonial

✔ ***Describe a typical colonial city***

Descríbele a un(a) amigo(a) como era una típica ciudad colonial latinoamericana. Incluye el eje central, quienes vivían donde, y como eran sus casas.

Subtanjalla, Perú

Cuando yo era niño(a)

✔ ***Describe some events from your childhood***

En tus propias palabras describe todo lo que tú recuerdas de tu niñez. Dile donde vivías, lo que hacías y con quien jugabas.

Como vivían mis abuelos

✔ ***Describe some events in the lives of your grandparents***

Trabajen en grupos de cuatro. Hablen de como vivían sus abuelos cuando ellos eran muy jóvenes. ¿Tenían televisores a color? ¿Computadoras? ¿E-mail o correo electrónico? ¿Había jets? ¿Cómo existían sin estas comodidades? ¿Qué hacían?

Assessment

Vocabulario

To review vocabulary, turn to pages 58–59.

1 Den la palabra cuya definición sigue.

1. favorecer y ayudar a alguien
2. un metal precioso
3. insuficiente
4. lo que son el petróleo, la madera, etc.
5. lo que se puede hacer con una cuerda

Lectura

To review some geographical facts about the Andean countries, turn to page 61.

2 ¿Qué país es?

6. su costa occidental se llama el litoral
7. el Oriente se refiere a las selvas tropicales del este
8. muchas partes de su costa son tan áridas que son zonas desérticas
9. no tiene costa
10. los Andes se dividen en dos cordilleras separadas por un altiplano

Playa, Huanchaco, Perú

3 Pareen.

11. el Inca — a. el Hijo del Sol
12. el ayllu — b. cuerdas con nudos que usaban los incas para contar
13. quechua — c. comunidad formada de familias
14. los quipus — d. mensajeros de los incas
15. los chasquis — e. el idioma de los incas

4 ¿Sí o no?

16. La conquista de los incas fue muy larga y dura porque el Inca Huayna Capac era un líder muy fuerte.
17. Los encomenderos españoles les trataban muy bien a los indígenas.
18. En los siglos XVI y XVII el Virreinato de Perú se extendía de México a Chile.
19. Las clases más humildes siempre vivían en las plazas del centro de una ciudad colonial.
20. Son Ecuador, Perú y Bolivia los países que hoy tienen la mayor población indígena de todos los países sudamericanos.

To review some historical and cultural facts about the Andean countries, turn to pages 62–70.

Estructura

5 Completen con el imperfecto.

21–22. Yo ____ ceviche cuando ____ en Perú. (comer, estar)

23. En Bolivia, (ellos) ____ las empanadas salteñas con carne picada, huevos, papas y otros ingredientes. (preparar)

24–25. Las señoras que ____ en el convento de Santa Catalina en Arequipa se ____ a la vida religiosa. (vivir, dedicar)

26–27. Yo te ____ algo pero no entendiste porque (tú) no me ____ caso. (decir, hacer)

28–30. Nosotros no ____ que no ____ mucho calor en la costa y que una gran parte de la región ____ desértica. (saber, hacer, ser)

To review verbs in the imperfect, turn to pages 71–72.

Conversación

Vocabulario para la conversación

El carterista empujó al señor.
Otro le quitó la cartera del bolsillo.
Mientras uno lo empujaba, el otro lo robaba.

La víctima fue a la comisaría.
Le dio al policía una descripción del carterista.
Hizo una denuncia.

Más vocabulario

la comisaría oficina de la policía

1 **Historieta** **Un crimen** Contesten.

1. ¿Estaba el señor de pie en la esquina?
2. ¿Había mucha gente?
3. ¿Lo empujó alguien?
4. Mientras uno lo empujaba, ¿le quitaba el otro su cartera?
5. ¿Tenía el señor su cartera en su bolsillo?
6. ¿Le quitó la cartera del bolsillo el carterista?
7. ¿Fue el señor a la comisaría?
8. ¿Hizo una denuncia?

Un robo

Elena ¿Oíste lo que me pasó el otro día?

José No. Dime.

Elena Pues, estaba en el casco antiguo. Visitaba la iglesia de la Merced.

José Sí, la conozco. Es una iglesia preciosa, bastante pequeña.

Elena Precisamente. Pues, había mucha gente como siempre y yo estaba para salir. Un señor que entraba me empujó un poco y creí que quería avanzar.

José Y… ¡te robó!

Elena Sí. ¿Cómo sabías? Unos momentos después me di cuenta de que no tenía mi cartera. Pero no sé si fue él quien me robó.

José Probablemente no. Es un truco de los carteristas. Casi siempre trabajan en pares. Uno te empuja o hace algo para distraerte mientras el otro abre el bolso y te quita la cartera. ¿Llevabas mucha plata?

Elena No. Unos veinte dólares en efectivo.

José ¿Él llevaba algún arma?

Elena No, no lo creo. No me pareció un tipo peligroso.

José Una vez me pasó igual en Madrid. Estaba de pie en el andén del metro y un joven de mi edad me pidió la hora. Miré el reloj, le di la hora, llegó el tren y subí abordo.

Elena Otro truco. Mientras tú le dabas la hora, otro te robaba.

José Exactamente. Me quitó la cartera del bolsillo. Y como yo podía dar una descripción del carterista, fui a la comisaría para hacer una denuncia. El agente de policía tomó todos los detalles, pero…

Elena Pues, la verdad es que hay que tener mucho cuidado no importa donde, sobre todo cuando hay un montón de gente. Es allí donde hacen su trabajo los carteristas.

LECCIÓN 2

Conversación

¿Comprendes?

Contesten.

1. ¿Sabía José lo que le pasó a Elena?
2. ¿En qué parte de Quito estaba ella?
3. ¿Qué visitaba?
4. ¿Quería salir?
5. ¿Había mucha gente a la salida?
6. ¿Había gente que salía y entraba?
7. ¿Entraba un señor?
8. El señor que entraba, ¿empujó a Elena?
9. Unos momentos después, ¿de qué se dio cuenta Elena?
10. ¿Cuánto dinero llevaba ella?

Quito, Ecuador

Expliquen.

En tus propias palabras, describe como trabajan en pares los carteristas.

Corrijan las oraciones falsas.

1. Alguien le robó a José también.
2. Él estaba de pie en una calle de Madrid.
3. Un joven le pidió su reloj.
4. José le dio la hora y subió al metro.
5. Mientras José le daba la hora, su compañero le robaba su reloj.
6. José no hizo ninguna denuncia.

Estructura • Repaso

Imperfecto y pretérito
Talking about past events

1. You use the preterite to express actions or events that began and ended at a specific time in the past.

   Los carteristas robaron a dos víctimas ayer.
   Alguien me quitó la cartera.
   Yo fui a la comisaría esta mañana.
   Hice una denuncia.

2. You use the imperfect to talk about a continuous, habitual, or repeated past action. The exact moment when the action began or ended is not important. Compare the following sentences.

COMPLETE ACTION	REPEATED, HABITUAL ACTIONS
Él fue al cine el viernes.	**Ella iba al cine todos los viernes.**
Vio un filme policíaco.	**Siempre veía filmes policíacos.**
Le gustó el filme.	**Le gustaban todos los filmes.**

Miraflores, Perú

3. You most often use the imperfect with verbs such as **querer, saber, pensar, preferir, desear, sentir, poder,** and **creer,** that describe a state of mind or a feeling.

Él sabía donde estaba la iglesia.
La quería visitar.
Sentía mucho no poder verla.

¿Cómo lo digo?

 **Yo** Contesten personalmente.

1. ¿Leíste el periódico esta mañana?
2. ¿Viste el artículo sobre el robo en el metro?
3. ¿Lo leíste?
4. ¿Te interesó el artículo?
5. ¿Leías el periódico cada día?
6. ¿Veías artículos sobre robos en la ciudad?
7. ¿Siempre los leías?
8. ¿Te interesaban estos artículos o no?

Un quiosco, Quito, Ecuador

2 **Historieta** **Yo** Contesten.

1. ¿A qué hora te levantaste esta mañana?
2. ¿A qué hora te levantabas cuando tenías seis años?
3. ¿Cómo viniste a la escuela esta mañana?
4. ¿Cómo ibas a la escuela cuando estabas en el primer grado?
5. ¿Dónde tomaste el almuerzo hoy?
6. ¿Dónde tomabas el almuerzo cuando estabas en la escuela elemental?
7. ¿Qué comiste hoy en el desayuno?
8. ¿Qué comías en el desayuno cuando eras niño(a)?

Quito, Ecuador

3 **Historieta** **Cada sábado, no. El sábado pasado, sí.**
Hagan los cambios necesarios.

Cada sábado yo me levantaba temprano. Me lavaba y me vestía rápido. Tomaba un chocolate caliente y corría a tomar el bus al centro. Cada sábado nuestra tienda de departamentos ofrecía gangas tremendas. Yo compraba mucho y pagaba poco. Volvía a casa por la tarde con un montón de paquetes. Yo recibía buen valor por el dinero que gastaba.

El sábado pasado...

Dos acciones en la misma oración
Expressing two past events in the same sentence

A sentence in the past will frequently have two verbs. Both may be in the same tense or each one in a different tense.

Look at the following time line. Any verbs that you can place in the wavy area describe what was going on. They describe the background or scenery and are in the imperfect. Any verbs that you can place in the slash indicate what happened, what took place. They tell the action and are in the preterite.

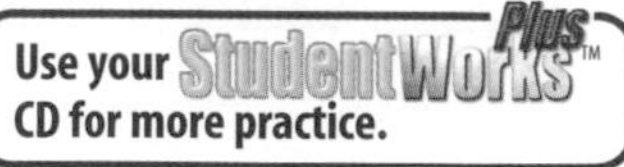

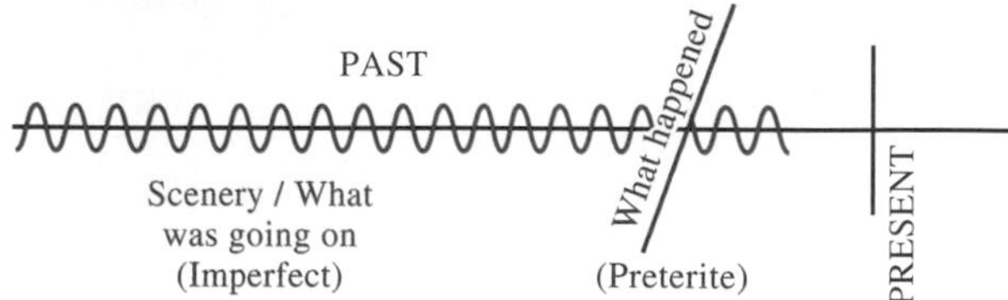

Decide where each of the following verbs belongs.

1. **Él me pidió la hora y yo le di la hora.**
   Both verbs in the preterite go on the slash because they indicate two completed actions or events.
2. **Mientras yo le daba la hora, el otro me robaba.**
   Both of these imperfect verbs go in the wavy area because they describe what was going on. They set the scene.
3. **El agente de policía me hacía preguntas cuando sonó el teléfono.**
   The verb in the imperfect, **hacía,** goes in the wavy area because it describes what was going on, the scenery or background. The verb in the preterite, **sonó,** expresses an action or event that intervened and interrupted what was going on.

Restaurante, Arequipa, Perú

¿Cómo lo digo?

4 Historieta ¿Qué pasaba cuando... ? Contesten.

1. ¿Miraba Juan la televisión cuando sonó el teléfono? ¿Contestó el teléfono?
2. ¿Leía su madre el periódico cuando Juan la llamó al teléfono? ¿Fue su madre al teléfono?
3. ¿Hablaba su madre por teléfono cuando Juan salió? ¿Fue Juan a un restaurante?
4. ¿Caminaba Juan al restaurante cuando vio a su amiga Lola? ¿Fueron juntos al restaurante?
5. En el restaurante, ¿hablaban Juan y Lola cuando llegaron dos amigos más?
6. ¿Hablaban los amigos cuando el mesero vino a la mesa?

5 Historieta Anoche Completen.

Anoche yo __1__ (hacer) mis tareas cuando __2__ (sonar) el teléfono. Yo __3__ (levantarse) y __4__ (ir) a contestar el teléfono. Yo __5__ (hablar) por teléfono cuando __6__ (llegar) mi amigo Carlos. Carlos __7__ (sentarse) en la sala. Mientras yo __8__ (hablar) por teléfono, él __9__ (leer) el periódico. Cuando yo __10__ (terminar) de hablar por teléfono Carlos __11__ (empezar) a hablar. Él me __12__ (decir) que alguien le __13__ (robar). Él me __14__ (describir) lo que __15__ (pasar). Él __16__ (estar) en la estación del metro cuando alguien lo __17__ (empujar) para distraerlo. Mientras uno lo __18__ (empujar), otro carterista lo __19__ (robar). Él le __20__ (quitar) la cartera del bolsillo. Afortunadamente, Carlos no __21__ (tener) mucho dinero en su cartera.

Arequipa, Perú

¡Te toca a ti!

Use what you have learned

En el casco antiguo

✔ ***Describe a past event***

En tus propias palabras explica a un(a) amigo(a) todo lo que le pasó a Elena cuando estaba para salir de la iglesia de la Merced.

En el metro

✔ ***Describe a past event***

En tus propias palabras explica a un(a) amigo(a) lo que le pasó una vez a José en una estación de metro en Madrid. Compara los trucos de los carteristas en cada episodio.

¿Yo, la víctima?

✔ ***Role play a victim reporting a crime to the police***

Imagínate la víctima de un robo. Vas a la comisaría para hacer una denuncia. Trabaja con un(a) compañero(a). Uno(a) de ustedes va a ser la víctima. Preparen la conversación que tiene lugar en la comisaría y preséntenla a la clase.

Policías, Arequipa, Perú

Parque de atracciones para niños, Tingo, Perú

4 Para el periódico

✔ ***Describe a robbery***

Escribe un artículo para un periódico ecuatoriano describiendo un robo sobre el cual tú leíste en tu periódico local.

5 En aquel entonces y recientemente

✔ ***Describe and state past events***

Habla con un(a) amigo(a). Dile todo lo que tú hacías cuando tenías unos seis o siete años. Luego compara lo que hacías a los seis o siete años con lo que hiciste ayer. ¿Ha cambiado mucho la vida?

Vocabulario

1 Identifiquen.

To review vocabulary, turn to page 78.

Conversación

To review the conversation, turn to page 79.

2 Contesten según la conversación.

5. ¿Qué visitaba Elena?
6. ¿Qué hizo un señor que entraba en la iglesia?
7. ¿Fue este el señor quien la robó?
8. ¿Cómo trabajan los carteristas?
9. ¿Cuál es un truco de ellos?
10. ¿Llevaba mucho dinero Elena?

Estructura

3 Completen.

11–12. Alguien me ____ ayer. Me ____ la cartera del bolsillo. (robar, quitar)

13–14. Mientras uno me ____, el otro me ____. (robar, distraer)

15–16. Yo ____ a la comisaría porque ____ hacer una denuncia. (ir, querer)

17–19. El señor que me ____, ____ en la iglesia mientras yo ____. (empujar, entrar, salir)

20–22. Cuando el carterista me ____, él no ____ ningún arma y yo no ____ mucho dinero. (robar, llevar, llevar)

23–25. Yo siempre lo ____ cuando ____ unos cinco años pero te aseguro que no lo ____ ayer. (hacer, tener, hacer)

26–27. Nosotros ____ cada viernes pero no ____ el viernes pasado. (salir, salir)

28–29. Yo ____ por teléfono cuando tú ____ a la puerta. (hablar, llegar)

30. Mis padres siempre nos ____ a la playa en el verano. (llevar)

To review the use of the preterite and the imperfect, turn to pages 80–82.

Península Paracas, Perú

Periodismo

Vocabulario para la lectura

Nuevas explosiones en volcán Tungurahua

el volcán

la ceniza

el hongo

Es probable que haya una erupción volcánica.
Los habitantes de la zona esperan que no sea muy violenta.
No quieren que su pueblo esté cubierto de ceniza volcánica.
Es posible que la erupción cause mucha destrucción.

Más vocabulario

la tregua la cesación de hostilidad, el cese, la pausa
alcanzar llegar a un punto determinado
desvanecer disipar o evaporarse hasta desaparecer completamente
reubicar mover, trasladar
ubicar encontrarse o situarse en un lugar determinado

¿Qué palabra necesito?

1 **Historieta** **Una erupción** Contesten.

1. ¿Es posible que una erupción volcánica resulte en una catástrofe?
2. Cuando hay una erupción, ¿sale un hongo de vapor y ceniza del cráter del volcán?
3. ¿Esperan los habitantes que la erupción no sea muy violenta?
4. ¿Quieren que sus pueblos estén cubiertos de ceniza volcánica?
5. ¿Esperan que el hongo desvanezca rápido?
6. Si hay una erupción violenta, ¿es posible que los residentes tengan que reubicarse?

2 **La lengua es rica.** Expresen de otra manera.

1. *La cesación de hostilidad* va a durar seis meses.
2. ¡Qué bonito es el cielo *sin nubes!*
3. Ellos van a tener que *mover* el ganado *a otro lugar.*
4. Yo sé que el hongo va a *disipar* antes de causar mucha destrucción.
5. Me parece que el hongo *llega hasta* el cielo.

EL UNIVERSO

Nuevas explosiones en volcán Tungurahua provocan temor entre los pobladores

Riobamba, Ecuador
Victor Hugo Cevallos

La mañana del pasado martes el volcán Mama Tungurahua rompió la tregua que mantenía con las poblaciones de Tungurahua y Chimborazo, al registrar una fuerte explosión cuyo hongo alcanzó los cinco kilómetros de altura.

Residentes y turistas que por fin de año visitan Riobamba, conocida como la Sultana de los Andes, observaron un hermoso espectáculo natural que ofreció el volcán Tungurahua en un día despejado y caluroso. Luego de la erupción y de la desaparición del hongo, la Mama Tungurahua se mantenía tranquila.

Geovanny Heredia Fuenmayor, de la Facultad de Geología de la Escuela Politécnica Nacional, dijo que se trató de una erupción freática[1] con columnas de vapor y ceniza.

Aseguró que el volcán Tungurahua está en permanente control a través de varias estaciones ubicadas alrededor de este y que incluso se ha instalado un Observatorio Vulcanológico del Tungurahua (UVT); como no ha variado la actividad volcánica, se mantiene la alerta naranja.

Una vez que se desvaneció el hongo la nube de ceniza afectó a las

poblaciones de Penipe, El Manzano, Yuyibug, Chontapamba, que debieron reubicar al ganado.

Los lahares[2] y las lluvias mantienen interrumpida la vía Penipe-Baños. Los habitantes de la zona esperan que el gobierno de Lucio Gutiérrez que se posesiona[3] en los próximos días inicie su reconstrucción.

[1] fréatica *subsurface*
[2] lahares *volcanic ashslides*
[3] se posesiona *be installed*

¿Comprendes?

Contesten.

1. ¿Es la primera erupción del volcán Tungurahua?
2. ¿Rompió el volcán la tregua que tenía con las poblaciones cercanas? ¿Qué significa esto?
3. ¿Era fuerte la explosión?
4. ¿Cuántos kilómetros alcanzó el hongo que salió del volcán?
5. ¿Qué ciudad visitaban los turistas?
6. ¿Qué observaron los turistas y residentes?
7. ¿Qué tipo de día era?
8. ¿Duró mucho tiempo la erupción?
9. ¿Por qué no tienen que estar nerviosos los residentes cercanos?
10. ¿Qué quieren los residentes que el gobierno haga con la carretera entre Penipe y Baños?

Región de Riobamba, Ecuador

Vocabulario para la lectura

Ayacuchana cumplió 110 años

La viuda es una señora mayor.
Tiene una sonrisa agradable.
Ella nos da algunos consejos.

Más vocabulario

la viuda una señora cuyo marido (esposo) está muerto

acogedor(a) agradable, placentero, caluroso

donar dar como un regalo sin recibir pago

renegar (ie) negar (no) hacer lo que uno debe hacer

1 **Historieta** **La viuda** Contesten según se indica.

1. ¿Es una señora joven la viuda? (no, una señora mayor)
2. ¿Cuándo murió su esposo? (hace poco)
3. ¿Qué tipo de sonrisa tiene la señora? (agradable)
4. ¿Qué tiene para nosotros? (unos consejos)
5. Según ella, ¿es importante que trabajemos mucho? (sí)
6. ¿Es necesario que respetemos a los otros? (sí)

2 **¿Cuál es la palabra?** Completen.

1. Tiene una casa muy ____. Todo el mundo la quiere visitar.
2. Ella nunca ____ cumplir con sus responsabilidades.
3. Ella siempre tiene una ____ agradable.
4. Ella no vendió su casa. La ____ a una organización caritativa.

La República

Ayacuchana cumplió 110 años

Lima, Perú

Su secreto es comer mucho, no renegar y trabajar bastante

Doña Silveria Pomarino Cueva, viuda de Ubargüen, acaba de cumplir este 1 de enero la edad de 110 años. Ella no es de muchas palabras, prefiere guardar discreción, pero de todos modos le arrancamos[1] su secreto de la longevidad:

«Para vivir tantos años hay que comer mucho, no renegar y trabajar bastante,» nos dice con tono suave y confidencial y nos obsequia[2] una leve sonrisa. La familia de doña Silveria, madre de cuatro hijos, seis nietos y un bisnieto, considerada la mujer de mayor edad del país, recibió ayer a **La República** en su acogedora vivienda de Pueblo Libre.

En su hogar y en el barrio todos la llaman cariñosamente «la abuelita».

Su hijo Sindulfo Javier Ubargüen de 76 años de edad, reconocido periodista y odontólogo[3], reveló orgullosamente[4] un poco de la vida de su longeva madre.

«Mi madre siempre fue una mujer batalladora y alegre. Toda nuestra familia está orgullosa de tenerla con nosotros. Es un privilegio,» manifestó. Refirió que doña Silveria tuvo gran fortaleza moral y física para sacar a la familia adelante a pesar de que quedó viuda muy joven.

La familia de doña Silveria realizó ayer un almuerzo familiar en su honor. Su nieta Cecilia manifestó que tenerla con ellos es como «contar con un ángel de la guardia que siempre está con la familia para cuidarlos y protegerlos.»

Por su avanzada edad ya adolece[5] de eventuales lagunas mentales, por lo que está recibiendo tratamiento geriátrico.

«No siempre se puede conversar con ella, pero por momentos recupera totalmente su lucidez y entonces empieza a recordar sus mejores años,» refirió don Sindulfo.

Doña Silveria nació en Parapausa, Parinacochas, Ayacucho, y hace unos años donó a su pueblo un extenso terreno para que se construya una escuela de educación superior.

«Es un sueño que siempre tuvo,» manifestaron sus familiares, tras señalar que hizo esa donación ya que ella no pudo realizar estudios superiores.

[1] arrancamos *we obtained, got*
[2] obsequia *she gives*
[3] odontólogo *dentist*
[4] orgullosamente *proudly*
[5] adolece *she suffers from*

¿Comprendes?

Corrijan las oraciones falsas.

1. La señora acaba de cumplir cien años.
2. Su cumpleaños es el diez de diciembre.
3. Según ella, para vivir tantos años no se puede comer mucho.
4. Hay que trabajar poco.
5. La señora tiene seis hijos.
6. Tiene cuatro nietos y un bisnieto.
7. Todo el mundo en su barrio la llama «mamacita».
8. Su hijo tiene dieciséis años.
9. La señora quedó viuda cuando tenía noventa y cinco años.
10. La señora nació en Quito.
11. Ella vendió a su pueblo un extenso terreno para construir una escuela.
12. Ella recibió su doctorado de la universidad.

Pisac, Perú

Ayacucho, Perú

¿Cómo se expresa en el artículo?

1. Doña Silveria no habla mucho.
2. Prefiere ser discreta.
3. Doña Silveria tiene cuatro hijos.
4. Ella perdió a su esposo muy joven.
5. Ya no se acuerda de todo; pierde la memoria.
6. Ella no pudo asistir a la escuela secundaria.

To explore more newspaper articles in Spanish, do the Chapter 2 **WebQuest** activity on the Glencoe Spanish Web site at glencoe.com.

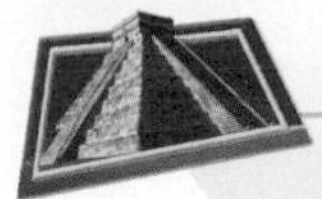

Estructura • Avanzada

Subjuntivo
Discussing what may or may not take place

1. The subjunctive mood is used frequently in Spanish to express an action that is desired or hoped for but that is not necessarily real. The indicative mood is used to indicate or express actions that definitely are taking place, did take place, or will take place. Analyze the following sentences.

Cristina trabaja mucho y paga sus gastos personales.
Abuelita quiere que su nieta Cristina trabaje mucho y que pague sus gastos personales.

The first sentence is an independent statement of fact—*Cristina works a lot and pays her personal expenses.* The second sentence contains a dependent clause—*that Cristina work a lot and pay her personal expenses.* The actions expressed in this dependent clause are actions desired but not necessarily real. They are dependent upon, and subordinate to, the verb in the main clause "want." What Cristina's grandmother wants may or may not occur. Since it may or may not occur, the verbs in the dependent clause must be in the subjunctive mood.

2. To form the present subjunctive, drop the **o** ending of the first person singular of the present indicative.

hablo	vendo	recibo	pongo	salgo	conozco
habl-	vend-	recib-	pong-	salg-	conozc-

Then add to this root the endings for the present subjunctive. The vowel of the subjunctive endings is the opposite of the vowel used for the present indicative. Verbs ending in **-ar** take the vowel **e,** and verbs ending in **-er** and **-ir** take the vowel **a.**

INFINITIVE	hablar	vender	recibir	poner	salir	conocer
yo	hable	venda	reciba	ponga	salga	conozca
tú	hables	vendas	recibas	pongas	salgas	conozcas
él, ella, Ud.	hable	venda	reciba	ponga	salga	conozca
nosotros(as)	hablemos	vendamos	recibamos	pongamos	salgamos	conozcamos
vosotros(as)	*habléis*	*vendáis*	*recibáis*	*pongáis*	*salgáis*	*conozcáis*
ellos, ellas, Uds.	hablen	vendan	reciban	pongan	salgan	conozcan

3. The verbs **dar, estar, ir, saber,** and **ser** are the only verbs that do not follow the normal pattern for the formation of the present subjunctive.

dar	estar	ser	ir	saber
dé	esté	sea	vaya	sepa
des	estés	seas	vayas	sepas
dé	esté	sea	vaya	sepa
demos	estemos	seamos	vayamos	sepamos
deis	*estéis*	*seáis*	*vayáis*	*sepáis*
den	estén	sean	vayan	sepan

4. The subjunctive form of **hay** is **haya.**

Selva, Tambopata, Perú

LECCIÓN 3

Periodismo

¿Cómo lo digo?

Una señora de Cuzco

1 **La abuela de Cecilia** La abuela de Cecilia quiere que ella haga muchas cosas. Es probable que ella las haga, pero es también posible que ella no las haga. No sabemos. Por consiguiente, es necesario usar el subjuntivo. Sigan el modelo.

estudiar →
La abuela de Cecilia quiere que ella estudie.

1. estudiar mucho
2. tomar cinco cursos
3. trabajar duro
4. aprender mucho
5. leer mucho
6. comer bien
7. vivir con sus padres
8. recibir buenas notas
9. asistir a la universidad
10. tener éxito
11. salir bien en los exámenes
12. decir siempre la verdad
13. tener buenos modales
14. ser cortés
15. conducir el carro con cuidado
16. hacerse rica

Volcán Lincancabur y Laguna Blanca, Potosí, Bolivia

2 **Historieta** **Una erupción** Contesten.

1. ¿Es posible que haya una erupción volcánica?
2. ¿Es posible que las explosiones sean violentas?
3. ¿Es posible que la erupción cause mucha destrucción?
4. ¿Es posible que haga mucho daño?
5. ¿Es posible que destruya las vías y las carreteras?
6. ¿Es posible que los residentes sufran?
7. ¿Es posible que ellos tengan que reubicarse?

Subjuntivo con expresiones impersonales
Expressing necessity and possibility

1. Note that the following stem-changing verbs have the same stem change in the subjunctive as in the indicative.

INFINITIVE	pensar	contar	perder	volver
yo	piense	cuente	pierda	vuelva
tú	pienses	cuentes	pierdas	vuelvas
él, ella, Ud.	piense	cuente	pierda	vuelva
nosotros(as)	pensemos	contemos	perdamos	volvamos
vosotros(as)	*penséis*	*contéis*	*perdáis*	*volváis*
ellos, ellas, Uds.	piensen	cuenten	pierdan	vuelvan

2. Note the stem changes in verbs such as **pedir, servir, preferir,** and **dormir.**

INFINITIVE	pedir	servir	preferir	dormir
yo	pida	sirva	prefiera	duerma
tú	pidas	sirvas	prefieras	duermas
él, ella, Ud.	pida	sirva	prefiera	duerma
nosotros(as)	pidamos	sirvamos	prefiramos	durmamos
vosotros(as)	*pidáis*	*sirváis*	*prefiráis*	*durmáis*
ellos, ellas, Uds.	pidan	sirvan	prefieran	duerman

3. The following expressions are followed by the subjunctive since it is not definite that the action in the dependent clause that follows each expression will be a reality. It may or may not take place.

Es posible	**Es bueno**
Es imposible	**Es mejor**
Es probable	**Es fácil**
Es improbable	**Es difícil**
Es importante	**Es necesario**

Es posible que ellos vayan a Miraflores.
Es imposible que lleguen a tiempo.
Es probable que haya mucho tráfico porque hay un desvío en la carretera.
A causa del desvío, es fácil que se pierdan.

Expreso, Miraflores, Perú

¿Cómo lo digo?

Historieta **Posibilidades** Contesten.

1. ¿Es posible que ellos pasen sus vacaciones en Ecuador?
2. ¿Es probable que ellos viajen de una ciudad a otra en avión?
3. ¿Es importante que vean el valle de los volcanes?
4. ¿Es probable que ellos quieran pasar unos días en una playa de Manta?
5. ¿Es mejor que vayan a las Galápagos en barco?

Playa, Manta, Ecuador

Historieta **Es probable.**
Sigan el modelo.

ir a Perú →
Es probable que yo vaya a Perú.

1. hacer el viaje en avión
2. no perder mi vuelo
3. pasar unos días en la capital
4. comprar unos regalos en una tienda de artesanía
5. hacer una excursión a Chan Chan
6. divertirme en la playa de Huanchaco
7. ir al sur
8. sobrevolar las líneas de Nazca

Líneas de Nazca, Perú

Te voy a decir una cosa.
Sigan el modelo.

tener mis documentos →
Te digo. Es necesario que tengas tus documentos.

1. llegar a La Paz temprano
2. acostumbrarte a la altura
3. tener una reservación en el hotel
4. descansar al llegar al hotel
5. dormir un poco
6. ir al lago Titicaca
7. visitar los pueblos de los aymara

Lago Titicaca, Bolivia

6 Conversación El hotel

Completen.

—¿Es posible que el hotel en Arequipa __1__ (estar) completo?

—Sí, puede ser.

—Luego es mejor que yo __2__ (hacer) una reservación, ¿no?

—Sí, sí. A mi parecer es importante que (tú) __3__ (tener) la reservación ya hecha.

—¿Es necesario que yo les __4__ (enviar) un correo electrónico o es mejor que tú les __5__ (dar) una llamada telefónica?

Hostal del puente, Arequipa, Perú

—No es necesario que yo les __6__ (hablar) por teléfono. Es probable que ellos __7__ (contestar) enseguida tu correo electrónico.

—¿Qué opinas? ¿Vamos a conducir o es mejor que (nosotros) __8__ (ir) en avión?

—Ni hablar. Es casi imposible que (nosotros) __9__ (conducir). Es un viaje bastante largo y en algunas partes la vía no es muy buena. Te aseguro que es mejor que nosotros __10__ (tomar) el avión. Y el aeropuerto de Arequipa no está muy lejos de la ciudad.

Aeropuerto, Arequipa, Perú

LECCIÓN 3

Periodismo

Subjuntivo en cláusulas nominales
Expressing wishes, preferences, and demands

The subjunctive is also used after the following verbs.

desear	*to desire*
esperar	*to hope*
preferir	*to prefer*
mandar	*to order*
insistir en	*to insist*

Note that the use of the subjunctive is extremely logical in Spanish. Whether one desires, hopes, prefers, demands, or insists that another person do something, one can never be sure that the person will in fact do it. Therefore, the action of the verb in the dependent clause is not necessarily real and the subjunctive must be used.

Él quiere que yo lo ayude. — **Y yo quiero que él me ayude.**
Yo prefiero que tú lo hagas. — **Y tú prefieres que yo lo haga.**
Ustedes insisten en que (nosotros) se lo pidamos. — **Y nosotros insistimos en que ustedes se lo pidan.**

¡Así es la vida!

Quito, Ecuador

Lima, Perú

¿Cómo lo digo?

7 ¿Hacerlo? Sigan el modelo.

¿Venderlo? →
Tú quieres que yo lo venda.
Y yo quiero que tú lo vendas.

1. ¿Comprarlo?
2. ¿Pagarlo?
3. ¿Aprenderlo?
4. ¿Recibirlo?
5. ¿Devolverlo?
6. ¿Servirlo?
7. ¿Conocerlo?
8. ¿Hacerlo?
9. ¿Traerlo?
10. ¿Decirlo?

8 Historieta ¿Qué quieres? Escriban las frases empezando con **Yo quiero que.**

Ustedes compran pan para la cena. →
Yo quiero que ustedes compren pan para la cena.

1. Ustedes me esperan.
2. Ustedes salen conmigo.
3. Todos nosotros vamos juntos a la tienda.
4. Ustedes me ayudan a buscar un regalo para Cristina.
5. Ustedes no le dicen nada a Cristina.

9 Historieta ¿En qué insiste mamá?

Escriban las frases empezando con **Mamá insiste en que.**

Lavamos los platos. →
Mamá insiste en que lavemos los platos.

1. Nos levantamos temprano.
2. Tomamos un buen desayuno.
3. Salimos a tiempo.
4. No llegamos tarde a la escuela.
5. Estudiamos y aprendemos.
6. Somos diligentes.

10 Historieta ¿Qué prefiere él?

Escriban las frases empezando con **Él prefiere que.**

Yo escribo los detalles. →
Él prefiere que yo escriba los detalles.

1. Yo hablo del robo.
2. Yo describo lo que pasó.
3. Yo voy a la comisaría.
4. Yo hago la denuncia.
5. Yo doy la descripción del carterista.

Miraflores, Perú

Máscara Chimú, Museo del Oro, Lima, Perú

11 Historieta Al museo Contesten.

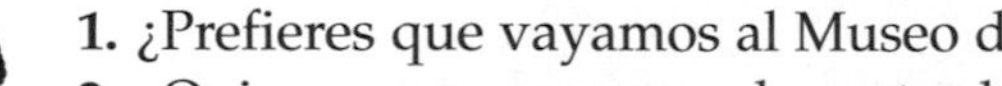

1. ¿Prefieres que vayamos al Museo del Oro?
2. ¿Quieres que yo compre las entradas?
3. ¿Esperas que no haya mucha gente en el museo?
4. ¿Quieres que yo invite a Sandra a acompañarnos?
5. Al salir del museo, ¿quieres que vayamos a un restaurante a comer o prefieres que volvamos a casa?
6. ¿Va a insistir Sandra en que comamos en un restaurante?
7. ¿Prefieres que Sandra nos encuentre en el museo o que la vayamos a buscar?

¡Te toca a ti!

Use what you have learned

1 Un desastre natural

✔ ***Describe a natural disaster that sometimes occurs where you live***

Cada día leemos en el periódico noticias de desastres naturales tales como una erupción volcánica, un terremoto, un huracán o un tornado. En los países de la región andina hay muchas erupciones volcánicas. En Estados Unidos no hay muchos volcanes pero es posible que haya otro tipo de desastre natural. ¿Qué posibilidades existen donde tú vives? Describe lo que pasa y lo que hace la gente para protegerse.

Volcán Tungurahua, Ecuador

Mujer peruana

2 La tercera edad o la vejez

✔ ***Describe ways to maintain a long, healthy life***

Hoy en día la longevidad es bastante común. ¿Qué están haciendo muchos en la vida diaria para que lleguen a disfrutar de más años y una vejez placentera? ¿Qué hizo la señora Silveria Pomarino Cueva para vivir hasta cumplir los ciento diez años?

3 Una biografía

✔ ***Describe a family member or friend who has enjoyed a long life***

Piensa en un(a) pariente tal como un(a) abuelo(a) o bisabuelo(a) o un(a) amigo(a) de la familia que ha llegado a una edad bastante avanzada. Describe a esta persona.

¿Sí o no?

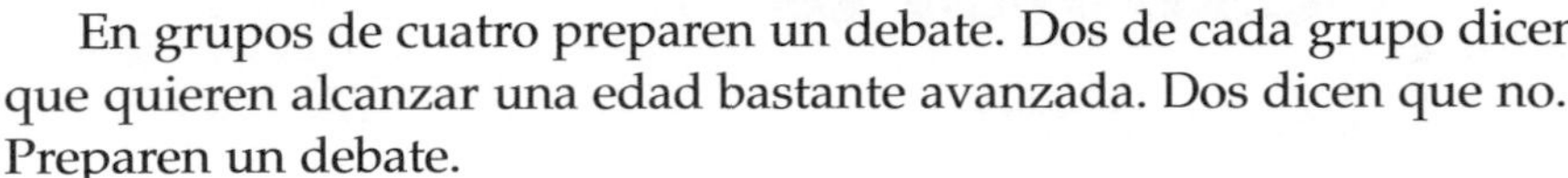

✔ Discuss benefits and drawbacks of living a long life

En grupos de cuatro preparen un debate. Dos de cada grupo dicen que quieren alcanzar una edad bastante avanzada. Dos dicen que no. Preparen un debate.

Todo lo que espero de ti

✔ Describe things you want from someone else

Imagina que tienes un(a) novio(a) a quien quieres mucho. Escríbele una carta describiendo todo lo que esperas que él o ella haga para hacerte feliz.

¡Exigentes!

✔ Describe what family and friends want from you

Hay personas en tu vida que exigen, demandan, piden y quieren mucho de ti. Pueden ser tus padres u otros parientes, profesores o aún amigos. Hay cosas que quieren que hagas. Hay otras cosas que prefieren que hagas. Y hay cosas que absolutamente insisten en que hagas. Da el nombre de la persona o personas. Di todo lo que quiere(n), prefiere(n) e insiste(n) en que tú hagas. Luego decide y explica si ocurren o suceden o si van a ocurrir o suceder todos sus deseos, preferencias y exigencias. ¿Se van a realizar o no?

Vocabulario

1 Den la palabra.

1. mover, trasladar
2. sin nubes
3. lo que sale de un volcán en erupción
4. llegar a un punto determinado

2 Completen.

5. La ____ perdió su esposo cuando era bastante joven.
6. Ella siempre está contenta y tiene una ____ agradable.
7. Ella no lo vendió. Lo ____. No recibió ningún dinero.
8. Me gusta mucho este hotel. Tiene un ambiente muy ____.

To review vocabulary, turn to pages 88 and 91.

Hotel, Manta, Ecuador

Lectura

To review the newspaper article on the volcano, turn to page 89.

3 Contesten.

9. ¿Dónde está el volcán Tungurahua?
10. ¿Desvaneció el hongo bastante rápido?
11. ¿Causó mucha destrucción la erupción de Tungurahua?

4 ¿Sí o no?

12. Doña Silveria era de Arequipa.
13. Ella cumplió cien años.
14. Ella siempre sacaba a su familia adelante aunque quedó viuda muy joven.
15. Ella hizo estudios secundarios y universitarios.
16. Ella donó el terreno para hacer construir una escuela superior.

To review the newspaper article on Doña Silveria, turn to page 92.

Estructura

5 Sigan el modelo.

Es imposible / saber →
Es imposible que él lo sepa.

17. Es imposible / comprar
18. Es imposible / vender
19. Es imposible / tener
20. Es imposible / conocer
21. Es imposible / perder
22. Es imposible / decir

To review the subjunctive, turn to pages 94–95, 97, and 100.

6 Completen.

23. Es probable que ____ ellos. (ser)
24. Yo quiero que tú lo ____. (hacer)
25. Ellos quieren que el gobierno ____ la reconstrucción de la vía Penipe-Baños. (iniciar)
26. Ellos insisten en que nosotros ____ a la fiesta. (ir)
27. Yo sé que ella espera que yo ____ mucha suerte. (tener)
28. Prefiero que ella no se lo ____. (pedir)
29. Es necesario que ustedes ____ allí. (estar)
30. Es importante que tú ____ algo antes de salir. (decir)

For more Chapter 2 test preparation, go to the Chapter 2 **Self-Check Quiz** on the Glencoe Spanish Web site at glencoe.com.

Composición

Mucho de lo que tienes que escribir para tus cursos escolares son escritos expositivos. El propósito de muchos escritos expositivos es el de dar información.

TAREA 1

Un asunto histórico Vas a escribir sobre un aspecto o una época en la historia de los países andinos. Para escribir sobre un asunto histórico tienes que usar información que ya has aprendido. Y tienes que asegurar que tus hechos son correctos. Si no recuerdas todos los detalles que has aprendido será necesario leer de nuevo los textos que has estudiado—en este capítulo sobre la historia de la región andina. Al leer, toma apuntes sobre los detalles que quieres incluir en tu escrito.

Al escribir algo expositivo, en este caso histórico, trata de escribir de una manera sencilla, directa y clara. Tus frases no tienen que ser muy largas. En cada frase presenta un hecho o evento. En la oración siguiente descríbelo o indica la razón por la cual tiene importancia. Siempre ten en mente que quieres que tus lectores comprendan sin dificultad lo que estás escribiendo.

TAREA 2

Un artículo para el periódico Ahora vas a escribir un artículo para un periódico. Puedes escoger cualquier sujeto que te interese. Algunas posibilidades son: la delincuencia, un robo, un incendio, un desastre natural, un accidente, una crisis internacional, un evento deportivo, un proyecto escolar. En cuanto hayas escogido tu sujeto o tópico, empieza a explorarlo. Escribe todo lo que te viene a la mente en cuanto a tu tópico. Entonces lee todo lo que has escrito y agrupa todos los hechos e ideas que van juntos.

Comienza a escribir tu artículo. La primera frase de cada párrafo debe anunciar la idea principal. Continúa con las frases que sostienen o apoyan la idea principal. Puedes sacar muchas de ellas de la lista que ya has hecho.

Como estás escribiendo un artículo para un periódico, utiliza frases cortas: sujeto, verbo, complemento. Contesta las preguntas *quién, qué, dónde, cómo.* Trata de estar objetivo(a) sin dar opiniones personales. Los que leen el artículo pueden llegar a sus propias opiniones y conclusiones.

TAREA 3

Una biografía En una biografía el autor cuenta la historia de la vida de una persona. La historia es siempre verdadera, nunca ficticia.

¿Qué te parece escribir una biografía? Pero, ¿de quién? Te toca a ti. Puedes escoger un miembro de la familia, un(a) buen(a) amigo(a), un(a) profesor(a), un actor, una actriz, un personaje histórico. Antes de empezar a escribir la biografía es posible que sea necesario hacer algunas investigaciones o hacer una entrevista para aprender más sobre la vida de la persona. Trata de escoger una persona que haya tenido una vida interesante o excepcional. Eso te ayudará a escribir una biografía interesante.

Al contar la vida de la persona, escribe todo lo que ha hecho de manera que le des vida en el papel. Describe su apariencia física, su personalidad y sus actitudes. Utiliza detalles vivos y un lenguaje preciso para describir tus impresiones.

Organiza tu biografía de una manera clara. Puedes presentarla en orden cronológico desde el nacimiento hasta hoy. Si la persona ha hecho algo extraordinario, puedes comenzar con este acontecimiento y volver a explicar lo que lo hizo posible.

Muchos poemas hablan del amor, del tiempo que pasa, de los sentimientos y en la poesía latinoamericana de la belleza del pasaje autóctono. El lenguaje de un poema es artístico y musical. Se dice que hay que tener un talento especial para crear poesía y puede ser verdad. Pero ahora vas a escribir un poema corto. No es necesario que el poema tenga rima.

Puedes escoger cualquier tema: el amor, una persona, un paisaje, el mar.

Para escribir tu poema, vas a:

- escribir un sustantivo
- escribir dos adjetivos que describen el sustantivo
- escribir una frase de sólo tres palabras
- escribir un sinónimo del primer sustantivo, del que aparece en el primer verso

Y ahora, lee tu poema a la clase.

Discurso

Una entrevista es una reunión o una conversación entre dos personas. El/La que da (hace) la entrevista le hace preguntas a la segunda persona para obtener información. La entrevista puede ser también un artículo o reportaje escrito sobre esta conversación.

La entrevista puede tener varias metas. Se puede entrevistar a alguien para informarse de las últimas noticias, para investigar un acto criminal, para conseguir información sobre una persona interesante o famosa o sencillamente para solicitar un trabajo.

Vas a entrevistar a una persona que acaba de volver de la región andina. Con un colega decide quién será el/la entrevistador(a) y quién contestará las preguntas. Antes de empezar el/la entrevistador(a) tiene que preparar todas las preguntas que va a hacer. Organiza las preguntas en categorías como clima, paisaje, ciudades, gente, sucesos.

Un(a) buen(a) entrevistador(a) quiere que su primera pregunta les pique el interés a los que le escuchan. Así, podrías empezar tu entrevista con: «Pues, ___, acaba de volver de (Perú, Ecuador, Bolivia). ¿Nos puede decir algo que le sorprendió o fascinó al visitar este país?»

Entonces puedes continuar con preguntas que te permiten obtener detalles precisos. Las primeras preguntas de un(a) entrevistador(a) o reportero(a) comienzan con: *qué, quién, cuándo, dónde.* Entonces introduce preguntas más abiertas con *cómo* y *por qué* que le permiten a la persona contestar de manera más libre o más amplia. La última pregunta que va a llevar la entrevista a una conclusión debe ser muy general, «Pues ___, ¿hay algo más que usted les quisiera decir a nuestros oyentes?»

Vocabulario

Lección 1 Cultura

el choclo, el maíz
la papa
la precipitación

Geografía
agrio(a)
caluroso(a)
escaso(a)
lluvioso(a)
nevado(a)
cultivar

Historia
el balcón
el criollo
la cuerda
la época
el/la indígena
la madera
la materia prima
el nudo
el oro
el piso
la plata
la plaza
el quipu
el tejedor
el tejido
acomodado(a)
bello(a)
colonial
apoyar
contar (ue)
situarse
soler (ue)
subyugar
tejer

Lección 2 Conversación

el bolsillo
la cartera
el/la carterista
la comisaría
el crimen
la denuncia
el/la policía
el robo
la víctima
empujar
quitar
robar
mientras

Lección 3 Periodismo

Nuevas explosiones en volcán Tungurahua
la ceniza
el cielo
la destrucción
la erupción
el/la habitante
el hongo
el pueblo
la tregua
el volcán
cubierto(a)
despejado(a)
violento(a)
volcánico(a)
alcanzar
causar
desvanecer
esperar
reubicar
ubicar

Ayacuchana cumplió 110 años
el consejo
la sonrisa
la viuda
acogedor
agradable
mayor
donar
renegar (ie)
respetar

Literary Companion *See pages 430–439 for literary selections related to Chapter 2.* *The activities for these readings will help you continue to practice your reading comprehension skills.*

VIDEOTUR

¡Viva el mundo hispano!

Video can be a beneficial learning tool for the language student. Video enables you to experience the material in the textbook in a real-life setting. Take a vicarious field trip as you see people interacting at home, at school, at the market, etc. The cultural benefits are limitless as you experience the Spanish-speaking world while "traveling" through many countries. In addition to its tremendous cultural value, video gives practice in developing good listening and viewing skills. Video allows you to look for numerous clues that are evident in tone of voice, facial expressions, and gestures. Through video you can see and hear the diversity of the target culture and compare and contrast the Spanish-speaking cultures to each other and to your own.

Episodio 1: Los fardos funerales

José Luis es profesor en una pequeña escuela del pueblo de Puruchuco, cerca de Lima. Está enseñándole una momia a uno de sus alumnos. Debajo del patio de esta escuela está un antiguo cementerio inca donde enterraban a sus muertos entre 1465 y 1540. Las momias se encuentran en grupos que se llaman «fardos funerales». Los arqueólogos que estudian las momias dicen que están aprendiendo mucho sobre como vivían, lo que ellos apreciaban y como murieron.

Episodio 2: Un viaje por tren

Este tren cubre el trayecto Cuzco-Machu Picchu. Machu Picchu, antigua ciudad de los incas estuvo escondida durante siglos. Ni los conquistadores españoles sabían donde estaba. En 1911 un campesino se lo enseñó a un explorador norteamericano, Hiram Bingham. Por mucho tiempo la única manera de llegar a Machu Picchu era a pie o en tren. Las vistas y el paisaje que se ven desde el tren son maravillosos.

Episodio 3: Alfarería andina

Pablo Seminario es ceramista. Ha estudiado la alfarería precolombina por mucho tiempo. Él quiere conservar la cultura y las artes del pasado. Su esposa, Marilú, trabaja con él. Los dos crean preciosas tazas y vasijas y diferentes obras de arte. Sus obras son tan populares que ahora tienen todo un equipo de artesanos que les ayudan con su cerámica.

Capítulo 3

El Cono sur

Chile, Argentina, Paraguay, Uruguay

Spanish Online

To interact with your online edition of **¡Buen viaje!** go to: glencoe.com.

Objetivos

In this chapter you will:

- learn about the geography, history, and culture of Chile, Argentina, Paraguay, and Uruguay
- review how to state location and origin; characteristics and conditions
- discuss shopping for shoes and clothes
- review how to express surprise, interest, annoyance; likes, dislikes, and needs
- review how to express affirmative and negative ideas
- read and discuss newspaper articles about "acceptable" attire at work and leaving home to go to college
- learn to express emotions, doubt, or uncertainty

Contenido

Vocabulario para la lectura

En el norte de Argentina hay huertas de sandía.
Las huertas de sandía están en el norte.
Las sandías son muy dulces.

El tiempo está muy borrascoso hoy.

El ganado pace en las llanuras.
Come mucha hierba.

Los cerros no son muy altos.
No son tan altos como un monte.

La indumentaria del gaucho

Animales marinos

Más vocabulario

una huerta un jardín bastante grande
el odio la antipatía, la aversión, la repulsión, el rencor
una ráfaga un viento que aumenta de velocidad rápidamente pero por poco tiempo
el peonaje grupo de peones o labradores
austral del sur
belicoso(a) guerrero, agresivo
pacífico(a) calmo, tranquilo, contrario de belicoso

¿Qué palabra necesito?

Información Contesten según se indica.

1. ¿Qué es un chaparrón? (una tempestad o una tormenta)
2. ¿Cómo está el tiempo cuando hay un chaparrón? (borrascoso)
3. ¿Qué cultivan en un viñedo? (uvas)
4. ¿Dónde cultivan vegetales y frutas? (en una huerta)
5. ¿Cómo son las sandías del norte de Argentina? (muy dulces)
6. ¿Dónde pace el ganado? (en las llanuras o en las sabanas)
7. ¿Hay muchos árboles en una sabana? (no, ningún)
8. ¿Qué come el ganado? (hierba)
9. ¿Qué dan las ovejas? (lana)
10. ¿Es muy alto un cerro? (no)

2 **La indumentaria del gaucho** Identifiquen.

Ushuaia, Argentina

3 **Minucia** Completen.

1. _____ es un animal marino mamífero muy grande. Nada por la superficie del agua pero puede permanecer debajo del agua una media hora. Al emerger del agua, exhala un aire saturado de vapor de agua.
2. _____ tiene una cara blanca y negra.
3. _____ es un grupo de peones.
4. _____ es el cuchillo que lleva el gaucho.
5. Las ovejas se quedan en _____.
6. _____ es un viento veloz y rápido.
7. Ushuaia es la ciudad más _____ del hemisferio.
8. Es mejor el amor que _____.
9. Los elefantes marinos machos son muy _____. Tienen muchas peleas o luchas.
10. _____ es una acumulación de nieve transformada en hielo.

Lectura

La geografía

> **Reading Strategy**
>
> **Using pictures and photographs** Before you begin to read, look at the pictures, photographs, or any other visuals that accompany a reading. By doing this, you can often tell what the reading selection is about before you actually read it.

Chile

El Cono sur comprende los países de Chile, Argentina, Uruguay y Paraguay. Chile es un país largo y estrecho que tiene la forma de una habichuela verde (de un poroto). Siendo tan largo desde el norte hasta el sur, tiene un terreno extremadamente variado y variaciones climáticas extremas. El desierto de Atacama en el norte es uno de los desiertos más áridos del mundo. El centro, cerca de Santiago, la capital, disfruta de un clima templado como el del Mediterráneo. Aquí hay viñedos y huertas. La región de los bellísimos lagos goza también de un clima templado, pero un poco más hacia el sur en Puerto Montt, por ejemplo, el clima es lluvioso y borrascoso incluso en el verano. La Patagonia en el sur tiene un clima casi siempre frío y lluvioso con chaparrones frecuentes y ráfagas de viento que alcanzan una velocidad increíble. La Patagonia es famosa por sus fiordos y glaciares.

Saltos de Petrohue, Chile

Santiago, Chile

Río Uruguay, Argentina

Argentina

Argentina es el segundo mayor país de Sudamérica. Se puede dividir el país en cuatro grandes regiones naturales.

Las llanuras del nordeste Se caracterizan las llanuras por vastas zonas de terreno pantanoso[1] y sabanas. Es la región de los ríos Paraná y Uruguay. Una región húmeda de fértil tierra roja, es famosa por su gran ganadería y agricultura incluyendo el cultivo de la hierba mate, de la que se hace la bebida nacional.

[1] pantanoso *swampy, marshy*

Cultura

El Aconcagua, Argentina

Los Andes del Noroeste Es aquí donde se encuentra el Aconcagua, la cumbre más alta de América (6.959 metros). Es una región de volcanes nevados, altiplanos y desiertos. La mayoría de la población argentina es de ascendencia europea, pero en el noroeste hay una gran población indígena.

La Pampa La Pampa es una inmensa llanura de hierba verde que cubre el 25 por ciento del territorio argentino. Es el centro económico del país e incluye los centros urbanos de Buenos Aires. Las ciudades de Rosario y Santa Fe tienen pocos habitantes pero en sus alrededores hay millones de bovinos y carneros. Es la región de los famosos bifes argentinos.

Patagonia, Argentina

La Patagonia y Tierra del Fuego Es la región más extensa y menos poblada del país. El estrecho de Magallanes separa la Tierra del Fuego del continente. Es una región de llanuras inmensas de suelo rocoso batidas de vientos secos y fríos.

Tierra del Fuego, Argentina

Montevideo, Uruguay

Uruguay

Uruguay es el país más pequeño de la América del Sur. Un país tranquilo y placentero, la mitad de la población vive en la capital, Montevideo. La mayor parte del país comprende terrenos llanos y algunos cerros poco elevados. La tierra y el clima moderados son muy propicios para la agricultura y la ganadería. Los llanos uruguayos son muy conocidos por sus estancias grandes.

Paraguay

Paraguay, como su vecino Bolivia, no tiene costa. En gran parte del país hace mucho calor. En el este hay un área de bosque tropical húmedo y en el oeste está el Chaco, una zona árida donde es importante la explotación de madera.

Reserva Mbaracayu, Paraguay

Corrijan las oraciones falsas.

1. Chile es un país largo y ancho que tiene la forma de una papa.
2. El desierto de Atacama en el sur de Chile es uno de los desiertos más áridos del mundo.
3. En la región de Puerto Montt, al sur de los lagos chilenos, el clima es caluroso y húmedo.
4. El nordeste de Argentina es una región de terreno pantanoso y seco de tierra infértil.
5. El noroeste de Argentina es una región de llanuras y sabanas y la mayoría de la población es europea.
6. La Pampa es una inmensa llanura de hierba verde donde hay mucho ganado.
7. Uruguay es el país más grande de la América del Sur y una gran parte del país comprende terrenos llanos con algunos cerros no muy altos.
8. Gran parte de Paraguay es un bosque tropical húmedo y el Chaco es una zona muy árida.

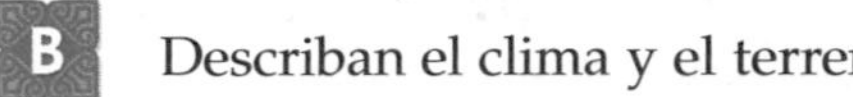

Desierto de Atacama, Arica, Chile

LECCIÓN I

Cultura

Una ojeada histórica

Las civilizaciones precolombinas

En la costa del Pacífico al norte de Chile y en Centroamérica y México los españoles encontraron civilizaciones indígenas muy avanzadas. Pero la situación fue diferente en los países del Cono sur. En Argentina había varios grupos indígenas pero en su mayoría no se establecieron en un lugar fijo y tenían una cultura bastante primitiva basada en la recolección y la caza. En Uruguay vivían los charrúas, un grupo muy belicoso. Los araucanos que poblaban una gran parte del centro de Chile eran feroces guerreros que nunca aceptaron someterse a la espada castellana. Ellos condujeron una larga y sangrienta guerra contra los conquistadores.

Los guaraníes

En Paraguay vivían los guaraníes, un grupo muy pacífico, quienes dieron la bienvenida a los españoles, sobre todo a los jesuitas. Muchos fueron a vivir en sus reducciones o misiones. Hay quienes dicen que los jesuitas realizaban una verdadera obra civilizadora entre los guaraníes. Los defendían de la esclavitud y la muerte a manos de los bandeirantes[2] de Brasil. Dicen otros que los guaraníes perdieron su independencia y sus derechos fundamentales al aceptar las enseñanzas[3] de los jesuitas.

Actualmente una gran parte de la población paraguaya tiene sangre española y guaraní. La moneda de Paraguay es el guaraní y las dos lenguas oficiales de Paraguay son el español y el guaraní. Se dice que el español es la lengua del comercio y el guaraní, una lengua melodiosa, la lengua del amor. Las canciones guaraníes son muy placenteras. Algunas de sus canciones con el acompañamiento del arpa imitan la voz del ave, la caída de la lluvia y otros sonidos agradables de la naturaleza.

[2] bandeirantes *Brazilian gauchos*
[3] enseñanzas *teachings*

Un guaraní, Paraguay

Misión jesuita, Paraguay

C Comparen.

En pocas palabras comparen los indígenas que encontraron los españoles en la costa del Pacífico al norte de Chile con los que encontraron en los países del Cono sur.

Asunción, Paraguay

D Contesten.

1. ¿Dónde vivían los guaraníes?
2. ¿Cómo eran?
3. ¿Cómo aceptaron a los españoles?
4. ¿Adónde fueron a vivir muchos de ellos?
5. ¿Cómo los trataban los jesuitas?
6. Actualmente, ¿qué tiene una gran parte de la población paraguaya?
7. ¿Cuál es la moneda de Paraguay?
8. ¿Cuáles son los dos idiomas oficiales de Paraguay?
9. ¿Cómo son las canciones guaraníes?

El gaucho y las pampas

El mito del gaucho de la pampa argentina o uruguaya continúa todavía hoy. El gaucho es el símbolo del hombre libre, de el que se burla de[4] las normas o convenciones sociales. El gaucho apareció en el siglo XVIII por las necesidades de la explotación de la ganadería. Hacía falta un peonaje diestro en el manejo[5] del lazo y las boleadoras.

Una familia de gauchos

En su origen los gauchos eran hijos de indias y españoles. Con su poncho, sus bombachas, su ancho cinturón adornado de monedas de plata, su facón (cuchillo) y su lazo y boleadoras, ellos eran los guardianes del ganado. Y eran ellos los que reinaban sobre las vastas extensiones de la Pampa. Trabajaban a sueldo en las estancias. No conocían ni leyes ni frontera. Tenían un espíritu independiente y un carácter revolucionario. El primer gran dictador argentino, Manuel de Rosas, era gaucho.

Al igual que ocurrió en Estados Unidos con los *cowboys* o vaqueros del oeste, los auténticos gauchos han desaparecido. Ya sólo quedan unos peones que guardan rebaños sueltos. Pero el mito del verdadero gaucho no ha desaparecido.

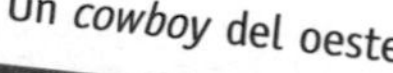
Un *cowboy* del oeste

[4] se burla de *mocks*
[5] manejo *handling*

E Expliquen.

1. la razón por la aparición del gaucho
2. la indumentaria del gaucho
3. el trabajo de los gauchos
4. el espíritu y el carácter de los gauchos

Evita Duarte de Perón y su marido

Evita, la persona tan querida de tantas almas argentinas, nació Eva Perón en 1919. Era la hija de una costurera[6] y de un obrero. De sus raíces humildes le venía su odio a los ricos. De joven ella trabajó de actriz de cine de segunda fila. También trabajó en la radio y se hizo conocer por sus emisiones en las que denunciaba ardientemente la injusticia y la miseria.

Eva conoció a Juan Perón, un joven oficial ambicioso. Se casaron en 1945 y un poco más tarde Perón fue elegido presidente de la República Argentina. Los aristócratas de Buenos Aires nunca le perdonaron a Evita sus raíces pobres pero ella se hizo la matrona de los descamisados—los que no tenían camisa—los pobres. Perón le dio a Evita el cargo de directora de la Fundación Social, lo que le dio la oportunidad de visitar fábricas, hospitales y barrios populares donde pronunciaba discursos a la gloria de su marido, el presidente Perón. Ella se presentó como candidata a la vicepresidencia en las elecciones de 1951 pero el ejército intervino y le puso el veto. Eva anunció en la radio que quería someterse a la voluntad del pueblo. Pero Evita sabía algo que no sabía el pueblo. Le quedaban muy pocos meses de vida porque padecía de un cáncer mortal. Murió el 27 de julio de 1952 a los 33 años.

Tal fue su don de hacerse amar que millones lloraron su muerte. Su figura inspiró una comedia, o mejor dicho tragedia, musical—Evita—la cual se ha presentado en muchos países del mundo. Además se produjo un filme del mismo título que ha sido estrenado mundialmente.

A pesar de que Perón dejó al país en una situación económica desastrosa, todavía hoy el peronismo sigue marcando de manera profunda la vida política argentina y sigue viviendo en el corazón de muchos argentinos el mito de su querida Evita.

[6] costurera *seamstress*

Eva y Juan Perón

La tumba de Eva Perón, La Recoleta, Buenos Aires

Casa Rosada, Buenos Aires

Contesten.

1. ¿Cuándo nació Eva Perón?
2. ¿Qué eran sus padres?
3. ¿Por qué odiaba Evita a los ricos?
4. ¿Cómo trabajó ella?
5. ¿A quién conoció? ¿Qué fue elegido él?
6. ¿Quiénes eran los descamisados?
7. ¿Qué tipo de discursos pronunciaba Evita?
8. ¿A qué edad murió Evita? ¿De qué?

La Patagonia y Tierra del Fuego

La Patagonia y Tierra del Fuego cubren el área más austral del continente sudamericano y se encuentran en Argentina y Chile. Muchos llaman este territorio el fin del mundo. Es una región batida de frecuentes vientos de increíble violencia, un clima tempestuoso y frío y un cielo frecuentemente nublado. La costa patagónica chilena (Pacífico) está dotada de numerosos fiordos, glaciares y cumbres nevadas. En las aguas de la costa patagónica argentina (Atlántico) viven elefantes marinos, lobos marinos, ballenas francas y pingüinos de Magallanes.

Tierra del Fuego, Argentina

En el interior del sur de Patagonia hay grandes estancias donde los descendientes de inmigrantes ingleses y galeses[7] guardan rebaños de ovejas que pacen en la tierra rocosa. Es interesante notar que son los galeses[7] quienes les dieron su nombre a los pingüinos. «Pengywn» en galés significa «cabeza blanca».

Se le atribuye el origen de los nombres de Patagonia y Tierra del Fuego al explorador Fernando de Magallanes. Se dice que al llegar a lo que es hoy Patagonia gritó «Ah, Patagón» al ver la medida de los mocasines y el tamaño de los pies de los fuertes indígenas tehuelches. En el año 1520 cuando franqueaba[8] el estrecho que hoy lleva su nombre, el estrecho de Magallanes, vio los fuegos de los campamentos indios y llamó a este lugar Tierra del Humo. Pero al oír una descripción de las hazañas de Magallanes el rey Carlos V pensó que no puede haber humo si no hay fuego y rebautizó la isla Tierra del Fuego. La Tierra del Fuego es un verdadero archipiélago prácticamente deshabitado separado del resto de Sudamérica por el estrecho de Magallanes.

Ushuaia, la ciudad más austral del mundo, es la capital de la provincia argentina de Tierra del Fuego. A pesar del clima duro la vida en Ushuaia es muy apacible. Sus casas de colores pastel son muy pintorescas.

Ushuaia, Argentina

[7] galeses *Welsh*
[8] franqueaba *passing through*

G Expliquen.

1. la diferencia entre la costa patagónica chilena y la argentina
2. como recibió Patagonia su nombre
3. como recibió su nombre Tierra del Fuego
4. lo que separa la Tierra del Fuego del resto del continente

Visitas históricas

Si visitas los países del Cono sur hay muchos lugares que tienes que ver. Vamos a empezar con las grandes capitales, Santiago de Chile y Buenos Aires. Estas dos ciudades muy cosmopolitas ofrecen de todo: cine, teatro, museos, estadios, parques, cafés y buenos restaurantes. Montevideo, la capital uruguaya, es más pequeña que las otras pero muy bonita e interesante. Si te gusta nadar o tomar el sol, hay muchas playas en la ciudad misma.

Montevideo

Caminito, Buenos Aires

Valle del Elqui, Chile

Si la naturaleza te atrae, no hay nada más bonito que los lagos en la frontera entre Chile y Argentina o los fiordos y glaciares chilenos. El gran número de animales marinos les da un carácter inolvidable a lugares como la Península de Valdés, Punta Loma y Punta Tombo en la costa del Atlántico en Argentina.

La lista de posibilidades es sin límite. ¡Buen viaje!

Comidas

En Argentina y Uruguay con tanta ganadería hay que comer la carne de vaca o el bife—una carne tierna y sabrosa asada a la parrilla. Pero, ¡cuidado! Como al gaucho le gustaba quemar su carne en la pampa, los argentinos siguen sirviéndola bien hecha o como dicen «quemada». Si no te gusta así hay que pedirla «vuelta y vuelta» o «cruda».

En Chile con tanta costa, claro que la especialidad es el pescado y los mariscos. El chupe de mariscos es un tipo de sopa o puchero[9] lleno de camarones, langostinos, jaibas[10] y almejas con trozos de papa y choclo.

Paraguay tiene su comida nacional—so'o yosopy en guaraní. Es una rica sopa de carne. ¡Buen provecho!

[9] puchero *stew*
[10] jaibas *land crabs*

Contesten personalmente.

1. Si puedes visitar unos países del Cono sur, ¿adónde querrás ir?
2. ¿Qué vas a comer?

To explore recipes from the Southern Cone countries, do the Chapter 3 **WebQuest** activity on the Glencoe Spanish Web site at glencoe.com.

Arica, Chile

Use your StudentWorks Plus™ CD for more practice.

Estructura • Repaso

Colocación y origen ¿Ser o estar?
Contrasting location and origin

1. There are two verbs to express *to be* in Spanish. They are **ser** and **estar.** Each of these verbs has specific uses. They are not interchangeable. The verb **estar** is always used to express location, both temporary and permanent.

PERMANENT	TEMPORARY
Buenos Aires está en Argentina.	**Mis primos uruguayos no están en casa ahora.**
Martínez está en los suburbios de Buenos Aires.	**Están aquí en Martínez.**
Nuestra casa está en Martínez.	**Están con nosotros.**

2. The verb **ser** is used to express origin, where someone or something is from.

Yo soy de Estados Unidos.
Pero mi abuelo es de Uruguay.
El pescado es de Chile y el bife es de Argentina.

3. Note that the following sentence illustrates both origin and location.

El señor Salas es de Paraguay pero ahora está en Chile.

4. Ser de is also used to express ownership and what something is made from.

Esta casa es de los Amaral. Es de piedra.

Valparaíso, Chile

¿Cómo lo digo?

¿Dónde está? Contesten personalmente.

1. ¿Dónde estás ahora?
2. ¿Dónde está tu casa?
3. Y tu escuela, ¿dónde está?
4. ¿Dónde están tus padres?
5. Y tus amigos, ¿dónde están?
6. ¿Dónde está tu profesor(a) de español?

¿De qué país es? Contesten según el modelo

¿Es chileno el señor Suárez? →
Sí, sí. Es de Chile.

1. ¿Son argentinos los Martini?
2. ¿Son paraguayos los amigos de Felipe?
3. ¿Es chileno este pescado?
4. ¿Es uruguayo el pintor Iturria?
5. ¿Es chilena la autora Isabel Allende?

3 Historieta La Recoleta

Completen con **ser** o **estar.**

1. Francisco y Julia ____ de Buenos Aires.
2. Su departamento ____ en la avenida Callao.
3. La avenida Callao ____ en el barrio la Recoleta.
4. La avenida Callao no ____ muy lejos del cementerio de la Recoleta.
5. La tumba de Evita Perón ____ en este cementerio.
6. Los turistas que vienen a visitar su tumba ____ de todas partes del mundo.

Cementerio de la Recoleta

Sacramento, Uruguay

4 Historieta La casa de los Amaral Completen.

Aquí tenemos una foto de una casa. La casa __1__ muy bonita. La casa __2__ de la familia Amaral. La casa no __3__ de madera. __4__ de piedra. __5__ en un barrio residencial en la costa de Uruguay.

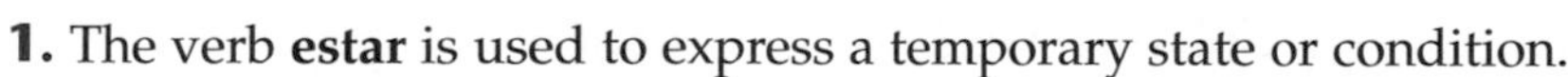

Característica y condición ¿Ser o estar?
Expressing characteristics and conditions

1. The verb **estar** is used to express a temporary state or condition.

El agua está muy fría.
Y el té está muy caliente.
No sé por qué estoy tan cansado.

2. The verb **ser,** however, is used to express an inherent quality or characteristic.

El hermano de Juan es muy simpático.
Y él es guapo.
Y además es muy sincero.

5 Yo Contesten personalmente.

1. ¿Eres alto(a) o bajo(a)?
2. ¿Eres fuerte o débil?
3. ¿De qué nacionalidad eres?
4. ¿Eres simpático(a) o antipático(a)?
5. ¿Cómo estás hoy?
6. ¿Estás de buen humor o estás de mal humor?
7. ¿Estás bien o estás enfermo(a)?
8. ¿Estás contento(a) o triste?
9. ¿Estás cansado(a)?

6 Historieta La capital de Uruguay

Completen con **ser** o **estar.**

1. La ciudad de Montevideo ____ en Uruguay.
2. Montevideo ____ la capital de Uruguay.
3. La capital ____ muy bonita.
4. La ciudad de Montevideo no ____ muy grande.
5. Algunas calles en el centro de la ciudad ____ bastante anchas.
6. En el casco antiguo las calles suelen ____ estrechas.
7. El casco antiguo ____ cerca del puerto.
8. Algunas calles del casco antiguo ____ en malas condiciones porque ____ muy viejas.
9. Los barrios residenciales que ____ dentro de la ciudad ____ muy bonitos.
10. Los barrios residenciales ____ muy cerca de la playa y en el verano cuando hace mucho calor las playas ____ llenas de gente.

Plaza Independencia, Montevideo

Usos especiales de ser y estar
More about ser and estar

1. As you have already learned, the verb **ser** is used to express origin, a characteristic, or an inherent quality. The verb **estar** is used to express a permanent or temporary location, a temporary state, or a condition. The speaker often chooses the verb **ser** or **estar** depending upon the meaning he or she wishes to convey. Observe and analyze the following.

El tiempo en la Patagonia es muy borrascoso.
Hoy el tiempo aquí está muy borrascoso.

The first sentence uses **ser** because the meaning conveyed is that the weather is characteristically stormy and nasty in Patagonia. In the second sentence it's not a characteristic of the weather in that locale. It's an isolated, temporary condition.

2. Note the difference in meaning in the following pairs of sentences.

Carlos es guapo.	*Charles is handsome (a handsome person).*
Carlos está muy guapo hoy.	*Charles looks very handsome today.*
La sopa es buena.	*Soup is (inherently) good (healthful).*
La sopa está buena.	*The soup tastes good.*

3. Many words actually change meaning when used with **ser** or with **estar.** Study the following.

	WITH **SER**	WITH **ESTAR**
aburrido	*boring*	*bored*
cansado	*tiresome*	*tired*
divertido	*amusing, funny*	*amused*
enfermo	*sickly*	*sick, ill*
listo	*bright, clever, smart, shrewd*	*ready*
triste	*dull*	*sad*
vivo	*lively, alert*	*alive*

Note that the verb **estar** with **vivo** means *to be alive.* The verb **estar** is also used with **muerto** to mean *to be dead,* even though death is permanent.

Su abuelo está muerto.

Teatro Solís, Montevideo

4. The verb **ser** is used whenever the verb *to be* has the meaning of *to take place.*

El concierto tendrá lugar mañana.	**El concierto será mañana.**
Tendrá lugar en el teatro.	**Será en el teatro.**

¿Cómo lo digo?

Mercado, Puerto Montt, Chile

7 ¿Ser o estar? Completen.

1. Tienes que comer más verduras. Las verduras tienen muchas vitaminas y _____ muy buenas para la salud.
2. ¡Qué deliciosas! ¿Dónde compraste estas verduras? _____ muy buenas.
3. No sé lo que le pasa a la pobre Marta. Tiene que estar enferma porque _____ muy pálida.
4. No, no está enferma. Es su color. Ella _____ muy pálida.
5. Él _____ tan aburrido que cada vez que empieza a hablar, todo el mundo se duerme.
6. ¡Elena! Me encanta el vestido que llevas hoy. ¡Qué bonita _____!
7. El pobre Juanito _____ tan cansado que sólo quiere volver a casa para dormir un poco.
8. ¿_____ listos todos? Vamos a salir en cinco minutos.
9. Ella _____ muy lista. Sabe exactamente lo que está haciendo.
10. Él _____ muy vivo y divertido. Me gusta mucho estar con él.
11. No, no se murió el padre de Josefina. Él _____ vivo.

8 ¿Cuándo y dónde será? Contesten según se indica.

1. ¿Dónde será el concierto? (en el parque central)
2. ¿Cuándo es la fiesta? (el domingo por la tarde)
3. ¿Cuándo será la exposición? (del 5 al 12 de este mes)
4. ¿A qué hora es la película? (a las ocho de la noche)

LECCIÓN I

Cultura

¡Te toca a ti!

Use what you have learned

La geografía de los países del Cono sur

✔ ***Describe the geography of one of the countries of the Southern Cone and compare it to the geography where you live***

Escoge uno de los cuatro países del Cono sur y describe su geografía y clima. Compáralos con la geografía y el clima donde tú vives.

Saltos de Petrohue, Chile

Influencias indígenas

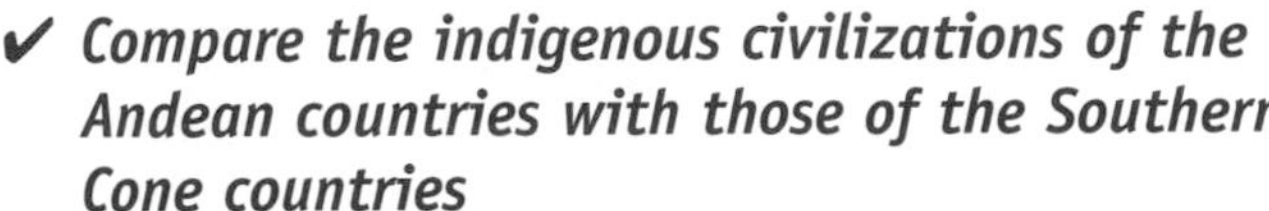

✔ ***Compare the indigenous civilizations of the Andean countries with those of the Southern Cone countries***

Ya sabes que en los países andinos hay ruinas fabulosas de templos, fortalezas y ciudades indígenas. ¿Qué piensas? ¿Hay tales ruinas en Argentina o Chile, por ejemplo? Explica por qué o por qué no.

Una estancia argentina

El gaucho

✔ ***Describe a gaucho and his life***

En tus propias palabras, describe al gaucho y su vida. ¿Te interesa el mito del gaucho o no? ¿Con quién lo puedes comparar? Aunque ha desaparecido el gaucho del mito, ¿te interesa visitar una gran estancia de la pampa argentina? ¿Qué esperas o piensas ver al visitar una estancia?

Evita Perón

✓ Speak and write about the life of Evita Perón

Escucha el CD del espectáculo de Broadway *Evita.* ¿Te parece que la letra corresponde mucho a la vida de Evita? Si te interesan los temas de Evita y del peronismo, haz más investigaciones. Escribe una biografía corta sobre ella.

La Patagonia, ¿sí, sí o nunca?

✓ Discuss if Patagonia is a spot for you

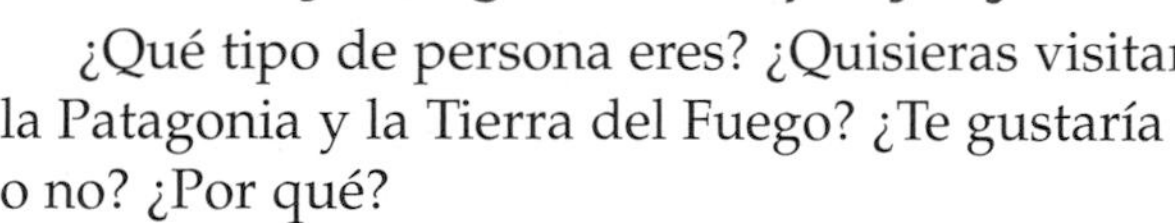

¿Qué tipo de persona eres? ¿Quisieras visitar la Patagonia y la Tierra del Fuego? ¿Te gustaría o no? ¿Por qué?

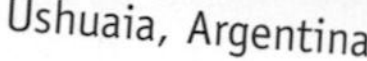

Ushuaia, Argentina

Ushuaia, Argentina

Yo

✓ Talk about yourself

No eres egoísta pero ahora tienes la oportunidad de hablar de ti mismo(a). Toma el micrófono. Queremos saber quien eres, de donde eres, el tipo de persona que eres, el tipo de gente que te interesa, con quien o quienes quieres estar. Anda—te toca a ti o como dicen en el Cono sur—queremos saber de vos—hablá, andá.

Assessment

Vocabulario

1 Completen.

1. Un _____ es una tormenta o tempestad.
2. Durante una tormenta el tiempo está bastante _____.
3. Una _____ produce vegetales o frutas.
4. El ganado pace en las llanuras y come _____.
5. Las llanuras o _____ no tienen muchos cerros ni colinas.
6. Los indígenas de Chile no eran pacíficos. Eran muy _____.

7–8. _____ y _____ son dos animales marinos.

To review vocabulary, turn to pages 112–113.

2 Den otra palabra.

9. del sur
10. la antipatía, el rencor
11. un viento veloz de corta duración
12. una acumulación de nieve transformada en hielo

Lectura

To review some geographical facts, turn to pages 115–117.

3 Identifiquen.

13. el segundo país más grande de la América del Sur
14. el país más pequeño de la América del Sur
15. el país más largo y más estrecho de la América del Sur
16. uno de los dos países sudamericanos que no tienen costa

To review some historical and cultural facts, turn to pages 118–123.

4 ¿Sí o no?

17. Las civilizaciones indígenas a lo largo del Pacífico al norte de Chile eran más belicosos que los indígenas chilenos.
18. Los araucanos eran muy belicosos.
19. Los guaraníes vivían en Uruguay.
20. Los guaraníes eran muy pacíficos y su lengua es bonita y melodiosa.

5 Identifiquen.

21. el gaucho
22. Evita Perón
23. los descamisados

To review some historical and cultural facts, turn to pages 118–123.

Estructura

6 Completen con ser o estar.

24–25. Montevideo _____ muy bonita. _____ en Uruguay.
26. Yo _____ triste porque no puedo hacer el viaje.
27. El clima de la Patagonia _____ muy borrascoso.
28–29. Las sandías del norte de Argentina _____ muy dulces. No sé por qué pero esta que estoy comiendo ahora _____ agria.
30. La carne _____ quemada pero me gusta casi cruda.
31. En Chile muchas casas _____ de madera.
32–33. Sus abuelos _____ de Uruguay pero ahora _____ en Chile.
34–35. Su casa _____ nueva. _____ en la calle O'Higgins.

To review **ser** and **estar**, turn to pages 124, 126–127.

Frutillar, Chile

Conversación

Vocabulario para la conversación

La zapatería

Una zapatería es también una tienda de calzado.
El cordón es también un pasador.

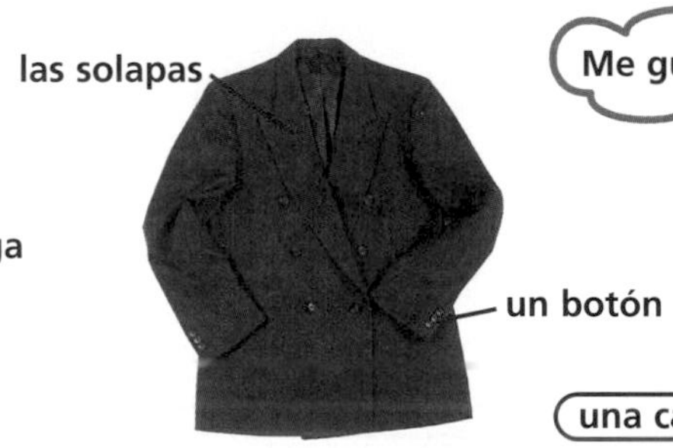

las solapas
un botón
el saco cruzado

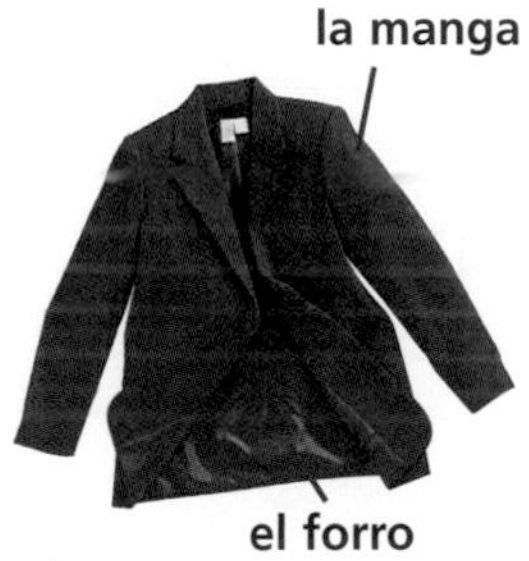

la manga
el forro
la chaqueta, el saco

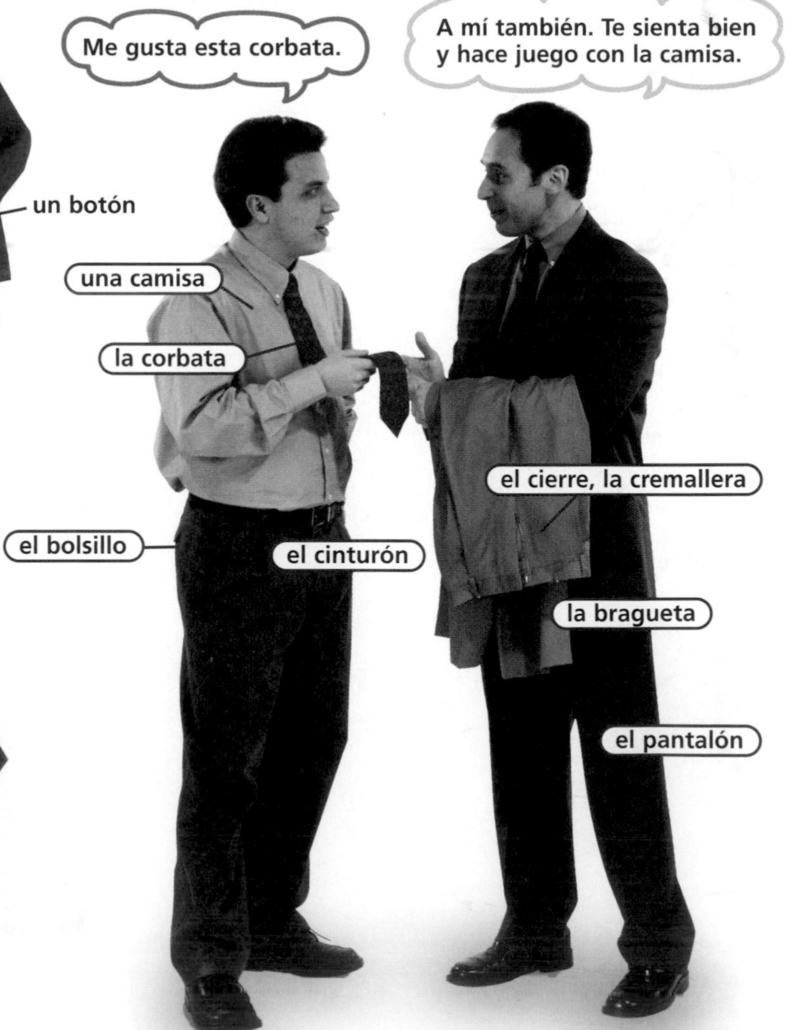

Me gusta esta corbata.
A mí también. Te sienta bien y hace juego con la camisa.

una camisa
la corbata
el bolsillo
el cinturón
el cierre, la cremallera
la bragueta
el pantalón

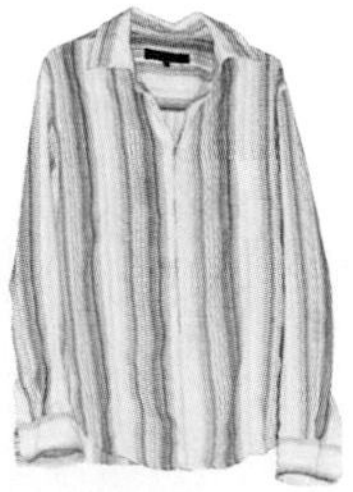

una blusa rayada (de rayas)

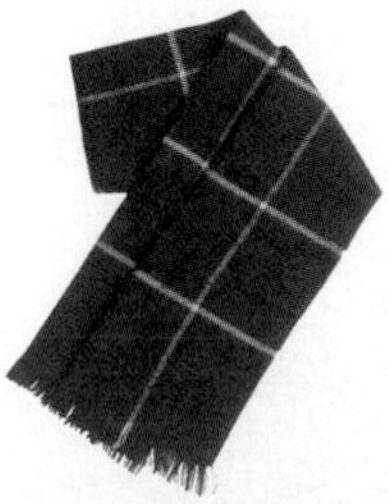

una bufanda de cuadros

Las telas

tela de lana

tela de algodón

tela de punto

tela de dénim

tela de ante, gamuza

tela de cuero

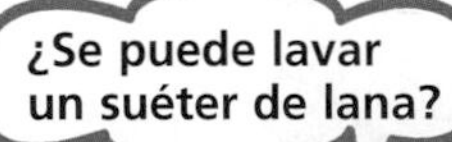

se arruga

A mí me gusta el poliéster porque no se arruga.

¡¡El poliéster!! No me gusta nada.

¿Por qué no? ¿A ti te gusta planchar?

LECCIÓN 2

Conversación

¿Qué palabra necesito?

1 Historieta En la tienda de calzado

Contesten personalmente.

1. ¿Quieres comprar un par de zapatos?
2. ¿Vas a la tienda de calzado?
3. ¿Qué número usas?
4. ¿Prefieres una suela de goma o de cuero?
5. ¿Quieres zapatos con cordones o no?
6. Estos zapatos marrón, ¿te gustan? ¿Te sientan bien?
7. Si te aprietan, ¿qué necesitas?

Santiago, Chile

2 Un pantalón y una camisa Describan.

1. ¿Es un pantalón largo o corto?
2. ¿Tiene la bragueta un cierre o botones?
3. ¿Cuántos bolsillos tiene el pantalón?
4. ¿De qué color es la camisa?
5. ¿Qué talla es?
6. ¿Tiene mangas largas o cortas?
7. ¿Te gusta la camisa?
8. ¿Hace juego con el pantalón?

Calle Florida, Buenos Aires, Argentina

3 Prendas ¿Sí o no?

1. Una camisa rayada juega bien con una corbata de cuadros.
2. Muchas chaquetas tienen forro.
3. Si algo no te sienta bien necesitas una talla mayor o una talla menor.
4. Muchos suéteres de punto son de lana y se encogen fácilmente.
5. Las prendas de algodón no se arrugan pero las prendas de poliéster se arrugan fácilmente.
6. Un cinturón puede ser de cuero, de ante o de una materia sintética.

De compras

En una tienda de calzado

Dependiente Sí, señor. ¿En qué puedo servirle?
Roberto Mientras estoy aquí en Argentina quiero comprarme un par de botas de cuero.
Dependiente Muy buena idea. Como sabe usted nuestra calidad es excelente. ¿Qué número usa usted?
Roberto Cuarenta.
Dependiente ¿Prefiere usted un tacón bastante alto?
Roberto No, mediano, por favor.
Dependiente Aquí tiene usted una bota de muy buena calidad en su número. ¿La quiere probar?
Roberto Sí, ¿cómo no?
Dependiente Fíjese también en la calidad de la cremallera. ¿Le sientan bien las botas?
Roberto Un poco apretadas aquí.
Dependiente No hay problema. Le traigo un número mayor.
Roberto Ah, sí. Perfecto. ¿Cuánto es?
Dependiente A ver. Trescientos pesos.
Roberto De acuerdo.

En la tienda de ropa

Dependienta Sí, señorita. ¿En qué puedo servirle?
Madela Quisiera una chaqueta y una falda, de estilo deportivo, por favor.
Dependienta Sí, señorita. Aquí tengo una falda gris acero que llega justo a encima de la rodilla.
Madela El gris acero es un color muy neutro que me gusta mucho. La voy a probar.

(Un poco después)
Dependienta ¡Qué elegante se ve usted! Y aquí tengo una chaqueta azul oscuro con solapas anchas y botones dorados. Combina estupendamente bien con la falda. ¿No le parece?
Madela Sí, sí. La verdad es que me gusta mucho. Me encanta.
Dependienta Y esta bufanda le da al conjunto el toque «extra».

Conversación

¿Comprendes?

A Corrijan las oraciones falsas.

1. Roberto está en una tienda de ropa.
2. Quiere comprarse un par de zapatos de ante.
3. Él no sabe el número que usa.
4. A él le gusta más un tacón muy alto.
5. Las botas tienen botones y cordones.
6. Las botas le sientan muy bien. Necesita un número menor.

Punta Arenas, Chile

B **Historieta** Contesten.

1. ¿Qué quiere comprar Madela?
2. ¿De qué color es la falda que la dependienta le muestra?
3. ¿Hasta dónde llega la falda?
4. ¿Cómo se ve Madela en esta falda?
5. ¿De qué color es la chaqueta que le sugiere la dependienta?
6. ¿Qué tiene la chaqueta?
7. ¿Son anchas o estrechas las solapas?
8. ¿De qué color son los botones?
9. ¿Qué le da al conjunto la bufanda?

C Descripciones.

1. Da una descripción completa de las botas que compra Roberto.
2. Da una descripción completa de la falda que compra Madela.
3. Da una descripción completa de la chaqueta que compra Madela.

For more information about shopping in the Southern Cone countries, go to **Web Explore** on the Glencoe Spanish Web site at glencoe.com.

Estructura • Repaso

Verbos especiales con complemento indirecto
Expressing surprise, interest, and annoyance

The following verbs function the same in Spanish and English.

aburrir	*to bore*	**fascinar**	*to fascinate*
asustar	*to scare*	**importar**	*to matter*
encantar	*to enchant, to delight*	**interesar**	*to interest*
enfurecer	*to infuriate, to anger*	**molestar**	*to bother*
enojar	*to annoy*	**sorprender**	*to surprise*

These verbs take an indirect object pronoun in both Spanish and English. Note too that the subject of the sentence often comes after the verb.

Me sorprende que a ti no te importe nada la moda.
A mí me interesa mucho.
A ella le encantan los nuevos estilos. Le fascinan.
Pero a mí me enojan los colores tan llamativos que están de moda. Me molestan.

Calle Florida, Buenos Aires

¿Cómo lo digo?

1 Historieta El Cono sur Contesten.

1. ¿Te interesó leer sobre la cultura de los países del Cono sur?
2. ¿Te sorprendió aprender que los indígenas eran tan feroces?
3. ¿Te interesa o te aburre el mito de los gauchos?
4. ¿Te interesaron o te aburrieron los detalles sobre la vida de Evita Perón?
5. A Evita, ¿le enojaron los ricos?
6. Y a los ricos, ¿les molestó Evita?
7. ¿Les enfurecieron sus ideas políticas?
8. A los descamisados, ¿les fascinó su querida Evita?

2 Historieta La indumentaria Completen.

1. A mí no _____ interes___ nada como se visten los otros pero, sí, _____ interes___ lo que llevo yo.
2. A mi amiga Elena _____ fascin___ las últimas modas.
3. A mí no _____ aburr___ las modas pero no _____ fascin___ tampoco.
4. ¿_____ enoj___ cuando alguien te dice que te ves muy elegante?
5. A mí no _____ molest___ cuando alguien me dice eso pero _____ sorprend___.
6. ¿_____ sorprend___? ¿Por qué?
7. Pues _____ sorprend___ porque tú me conoces. No _____ import___ lo que llevo (tengo puesto).

Gustar y faltar
Expressing likes and needs

1. The verb **gustar** in Spanish functions the same as verbs like **interesar** and **aburrir. Gustar** conveys the meaning *to like,* but its literal meaning is *to please.* The Spanish equivalent of *I like that shirt* is *That shirt pleases me.* The same is true of **faltar** which conveys the meaning *to need* but whose literal meaning is *to lack.*

Me gusta aquella camisa.
Estos pantalones, ¿a ti te gustan?
¿Te gustan los deportes?
Mucho. Me gusta jugar fútbol y baloncesto.
Desgraciadamente me falta tiempo para practicarlos.

Poconchile, Chile

3 Gustos Sigan el modelo.

pantalones con un cierre o con botones →
—¿Te gustan más pantalones con un cierre o con botones?
—Me gustan más ____.

1. una camisa de manga larga o de manga corta
2. botas de tacón alto o tacón bajo
3. zapatos de cuero o de ante
4. zapatos con cordones o sin cordones
5. una blusa rayada o de cuadros
6. una camisa con corbata o sin corbata
7. un saco con forro o sin forro

Una calle peatonal, Montevideo

4 ¿Te gusta o no te gusta? Sigan el modelo.

el bife quemado →
A mí me gusta el bife quemado pero a mi hermano no le gusta. /
A mí no me gusta el bife quemado pero a mi hermano le gusta.

1. el chupe de mariscos
2. las empanadas
3. las tapas
4. el queso manchego
5. el ceviche
6. el locro
7. las berenjenas fritas
8. las gambas al ajillo

5 ¿Qué no tienes? Contesten según el modelo.

¿No tienes papel? →
No, me falta papel.

1. ¿No tienes un bloc?
2. ¿No tienes una pluma?
3. ¿No tienes un lápiz?
4. ¿No tienes libros?

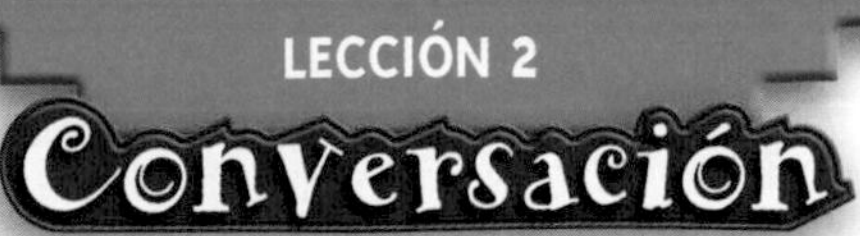

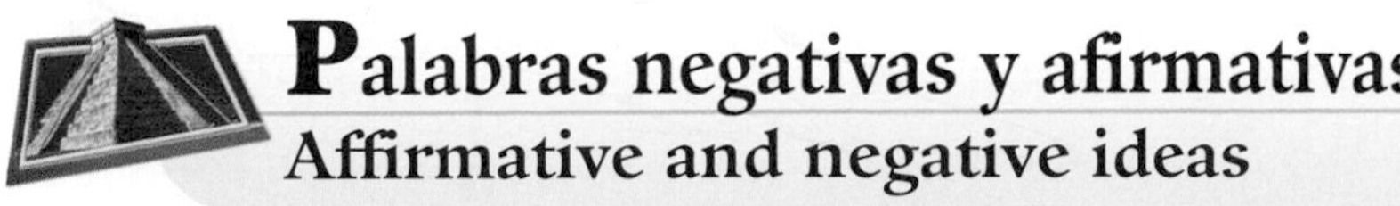

Palabras negativas y afirmativas
Affirmative and negative ideas

1. The most frequently used negative words in Spanish are:

nada	**ni... ni**
nadie	**ninguno (ningún)**
nunca	

2. Review and contrast the following affirmative and negative sentences.

AFFIRMATIVE	NEGATIVE
Yo sé que él tiene algo.	**Yo sé que él no tiene nada.**
Yo sé que alguien está allí.	**Yo sé que nadie está allí.**
Yo sé que él ve a alguien.	**Yo sé que él no ve a nadie.**
Yo sé que él siempre está.	**Yo sé que él nunca está.**
Yo sé que él tiene un perro o un gato.	**Yo sé que él no tiene ni un perro ni un gato.**
Yo sé que él tiene algún dinero.	**Yo sé que él no tiene ningún dinero.**

Note that **alguno** and **ninguno** shorten to **algún** and **ningún** before a masculine singular noun and carry a written accent.

3. In Spanish the placement of the negative words can vary and, unlike English, more than one negative word can be used in the same sentence.

Él nunca va allá.
Nadie está.
Él nunca dice nada a nadie.
Él no va allá nunca.
No está nadie.

4. Note that the personal **a** must be used with **alguien** or **nadie** when either of these words is the direct object of the sentence.

Él vio a alguien.
Él no vio a nadie.

5. **Tampoco** is the negative word that replaces **también.**

Él lo sabe también.
Él no lo sabe. (Ni) yo tampoco.
A mí no me gusta.
Ni a mí tampoco.

Buenos Aires

LECCIÓN 2

Conversación

¿Cómo lo digo?

6 **Historieta** **Yo** Contesten negativamente.

1. ¿Vas siempre a aquella tienda?
2. ¿Quieres hablar con un dependiente?
3. ¿Quieres comprar algo?
4. ¿Quieres comprar un par de zapatos o botas?
5. ¿Vas a comprar un regalo?
6. ¿Viste a alguien en la tienda?
7. ¿Y alguien te vio a ti?

7 **El pobre bebé** Den la forma negativa.

1. El bebé tiene algo en la boca.
2. El bebé está con alguien.
3. El bebé está jugando con el gato o con el perro.
4. El bebé tiene miedo de algo.
5. El bebé ve a alguien.
6. El bebé siempre quiere algo de alguien.
7. Alguien está con el bebé.

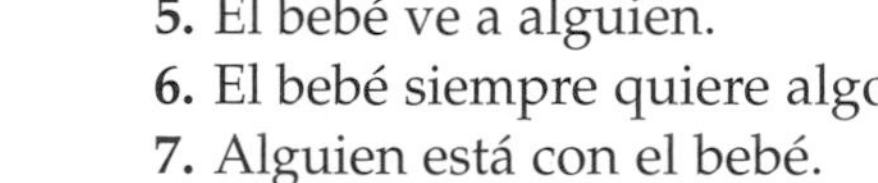

8 **Ni los otros tampoco**
Den la forma negativa.

1. Él lo sabe y yo lo sé también.
2. Ella quiere ir a Chile y yo quiero ir también.
3. A él le gusta y a mí me gusta también.
4. Yo voy a ir y ellos van también.
5. Ustedes lo van a hacer y nosotros también.
6. A mí me gusta y a él también.

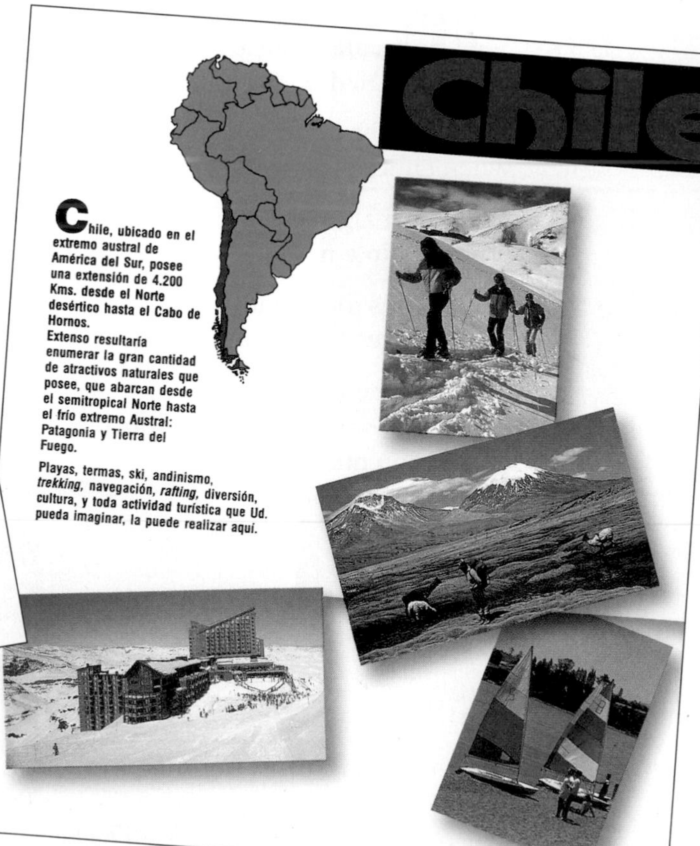

¡Te toca a ti!

Use what you have learned

Arica, Chile

Lo que voy a comprar

✔ ***Make a list of the clothing you will need for a trip to Chile***

Vas a hacer un viaje a Chile y piensas recorrer todo el país desde el norte hasta el sur. Prepara una lista de toda la ropa que vas a necesitar y decide lo que tienes que comprar.

Volcán Osorno, Chile

En una tienda de ropa

✔ ***Role play a customer and salesperson in a clothing store***

Alguien te ha invitado a una fiesta que va a ser un poco especial. A ti no te gusta mucho vestirte de una manera elegante pero te falta algo especial para esta fiesta especial. Trabaja con un(a) compañero(a). Uno va a ser el/la cliente y el/la otro(a) el/la dependiente(a). El/La cliente tiene que comprar todo nuevo para la fiesta. Preparen la conversación que tiene lugar en la tienda.

CALZADOS

SENSO UNICO - AV. SANTA FE 1929 / 2158 / 3237 AV. SANTA FE ESQ. PUEYRREDON - 4826-3343.

Se inspira en los diseños italianos, franceses, ingleses y alemanes para desarrollar sus productos en el más fino cuero.

Un anuncio

✔ ***Create an advertisement for clothing***

Prepara un anuncio para una revista de moda juvenil. Sé lo más original posible. Tu anuncio puede ser serio o cómico.

Compañeros de cuarto

✔ ***Discuss and compare your likes and dislikes with a group of classmates***

Divídanse en grupos de tres. Imagínense que ustedes no se conocen bien. Sin embargo, el año próximo tienen que compartir un apartamento en la universidad. Para evitar problemas, han decidido abrir un diálogo entre sí. Descríbanse a sí mismos(as) y comenten sobre sus gustos, intereses, antipatías, enojos, etc.

Buenos Aires

Vocabulario

1 Identifiquen.

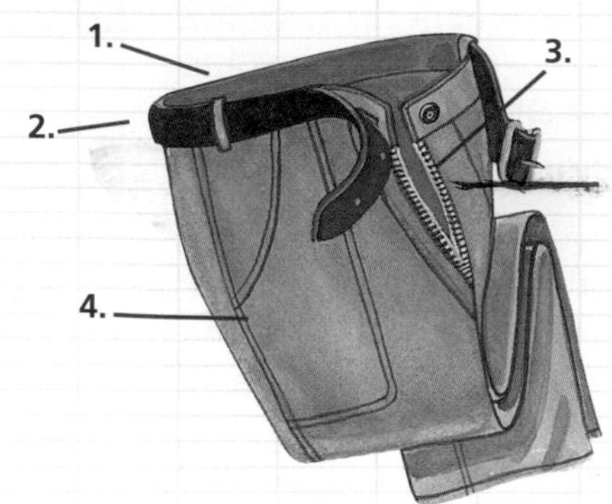

To review vocabulary, turn to pages 132–133.

2 Completen.

5. ¿Te gusta llevar botas o zapatos de ____ alto?
6. Me gustan camisas y blusas de ____ cortas o largas.
7. Un suéter de lana ____ en la lavadora.
8–9. El algodón ____ pero el nilón no ____.

Conversación

3 ¿Correcto o absurdo?

10. —Estos zapatos te aprietan.
—Sí, me sientan bien.
11. —¿Te sientan bien?
—Sí, necesito una talla mayor.
12. —¡Qué feo este conjunto! ¿No?
—Sí, sí. Hace juego.
13. —¿Puedo lavar este suéter de lana?
—Siempre. Se encoge enseguida.

To review the conversation, turn to page 135.

Estructura

4 Completen.

14–17. A mí ____ gust__ vestirme muy de moda pero a mi hermano ____ enfurec__ tener que llevar chaqueta y corbata.

18–19. ¿A ti ____ gust__ más los zapatos con cordones o los zapatos sin cordones—de estilo mocasines?

20–21. ¿A ellos ____ interes__ más dar o recibir regalos?

22–25. No ____ qued__ una hoja de papel y ____ falt__ porque tengo que escribir una carta.

To review these verbs, turn to pages 137–138.

5 Escriban en la forma negativa.

26. A mí me gusta y a él también.
27. Yo voy siempre de compras.
28. Siempre necesito algo.
29. Alguien me ayuda a buscar lo que necesito.
30. ¿Tienes algún dinero?

To review affirmative and negative ideas, turn to page 139.

Avenida 9 de Julio, Buenos Aires

Vocabulario para la lectura

Ejecutivos en manga corta

Estoy contenta que lleves un traje.

Me sorprende que te guste que yo lleve traje.

¿Sí? ¿Por qué?

Porque sabes que a mí no me gusta nada. No aguanto llevar traje.

un traje

un botón desabrochado

la espalda

un botón abrochado

estampada

un pliegue

Más vocabulario

la lapicera otra palabra por el bolígrafo, la pluma o el lapicero
cursi se dice de una persona que se considera fina y elegante sin serlo
llamativo(a) que llama mucho la atención, de colores muy brillantes, vivos
pecar cometer un pecado; faltar a una regla moral o a un deber social

¿Qué palabra necesito?

Use your StudentWorks Plus™ CD for more practice.

1 Gustos Contesten personalmente.

1. ¿Te gusta llevar (un) traje?
2. ¿Te parece cursi llevar traje?
3. ¿Prefieres que el botón superior de la camisa esté abrochado o desabrochado?
4. ¿Te gusta más una camisa sin diseño o una camisa estampada?
5. ¿Prefieres los colores discretos o llamativos?
6. ¿Pones una lapicera en el bolsillo de tu camisa o blusa?

2 Palabras relacionadas Emparejen.

1. el lápiz	a. el pliegue
2. plegar	b. el pecado, el pecador
3. llamar	c. la lapicera
4. pecar	d. llamativo

Clarín

Buenos Aires

Moda hombre: camisas

Ejecutivos en manga corta

Verano agobiante[1] en el asfalto y ellos también buscan atajos[2] para estar elegantes y más cómodos. Las camisas de manga corta se presentan como una alternativa válida. Pero hay que llevarlas sin perder estilo ni autoridad.

Unos las consideran «cursis»; otros, juveniles y cómodas. Lo cierto es que cuando la temperatura es insoportable, se convierten en la prenda favorita e indispensable. He aquí el decálogo para no pecar a la hora de usarlas:

No se llevan con trajes.

De acuerdo con el corte, se pueden combinar con saco y pantalón sport, pero jamás de noche.

Omitir la camiseta «musculosa» debajo de la camisa. Siempre se ve y da la apariencia de friolento[3] a quien la lleva.

Los dos botones superiores van desabrochados.

Pueden usarse fuera o dentro del pantalón sport.

Para los excedidos en peso, evitar las rayas pronunciadas, sean horizontales o verticales, los colores estridentes o estampados llamativos. Aumentan el tamaño de la figura.

Hay modelos con uno o dos bolsillos grandes al frente, que son puramente decorativos. Evite parecerse a un

cobrador[4]. No lleve lapiceras visibles en ellos así como tampoco anteojos o celulares.

Es aconsejable comprar la camisa que tiene un amplio pliegue en la espalda porque permite mayor comodidad de movimientos.

Sea precavido[5]: antes de usar una camisa, verifique que su cuello no esté desgastado[6], las costuras descosidas[7] y otros detalles similares que tan poco dicen en favor de quien los consiente.

Si su barriga[8] lo supera, renueve sus camisas. Es desagradable ver a un supuesto caballero con los botones de la camisa a punto de estallar, dando la impresión de que se la ha prestado su amigo al que le llaman «Flaco».

por Sylvia Albisu

[1] agobiante *stifling*
[2] atajos *shortcuts*
[3] friolento *susceptible to colds*
[4] cobrador *conductor*
[5] precavido *careful*
[6] desgastado *frayed*
[7] costuras descosidas *undone stitches*
[8] barriga *belly*

¿Comprendes?

 Contesten.

1. ¿Cuándo es cierto que una camisa de manga corta se convierte en una prenda favorita?
2. ¿Les aconseja la autora a los hombres llevar una camisa de manga corta con un traje?
3. ¿Cuándo se puede combinar una camisa de manga corta con un saco?
4. ¿Prefiere la autora que el señor omita la camiseta debajo de la camisa?
5. ¿Qué botones pueden ir desabrochados?
6. ¿Se puede usar la camisa fuera o dentro del pantalón sport?
7. ¿Quiénes deben evitar los colores o estampados llamativos?
8. ¿Cuáles son tres cosas que no se deben llevar en el bolsillo de la camisa?
9. ¿Por qué es aconsejable comprar la camisa que tiene un amplio pliegue en la espalda?

02 CAMISA DE LINO, $134,

03 CAMISA CUADRILLÉ, $134,

04 CAMISA DE ALGODÓN, $50 Y CORBATA RAYADA, $192,

B ¿Cómo se expresa en el artículo?

1. un verano en que hace muchísimo calor
2. buscar medios rápidos o convenientes
3. se convierten en una prenda absolutamente necesaria
4. pero nunca de noche
5. fuera o dentro del pantalón deportivo

C En el artículo, ¿han encontrado algunos elementos sarcásticos? ¿Cuáles son?

Vocabulario para la lectura
Cuando hay que dejar el hogar

el/la egresado(a) graduado de un colegio
el hogar la casa familiar
la meta el objetivo, el gol
adecuado(a) apropiado, suficiente
a juicio de en la opinión de
compartir tener en común
crecer aumentar
fracasar no tener éxito, no realizar el resultado deseado

¿Qué palabra necesito?

De otra manera Expresen de otra manera.

1. *El objetivo* de cada individuo es recibir una formación o educación *apropiada.*
2. *Los graduados* van a seguir con su carrera.
3. A veces es triste dejar *la casa familiar.*
4. Pero *en la opinión de* muchos, estudiar en otra ciudad, estado, provincia o país tiene muchas ventajas.
5. El número de jóvenes que dejan *la casa familiar* para hacer estudios superiores está *aumentando.*
6. Muchos estudiantes tienen que *tener en común* un departamento porque muchas universidades no tienen residencias estudiantiles.
7. Afortunadamente muy pocos estudiantes *no tienen éxito.*

Valparaíso, Chile

EL MERCURIO
SANTIAGO DE CHILE

Cuando hay que dejar el hogar

El salir de la casa para dar comienzo a una carrera universitaria es muchas veces ingrato. A pesar de ello, las vivencias[1] de quienes así lo hacen son positivas, convirtiéndose en una opción real y creciente.

Comenzar la vida universitaria no es tarea fácil. Son muchas las opciones que se presentan y diversas las variables que se deban considerar. Una de ellas es realizar los estudios superiores fuera de la ciudad en donde crecimos, dejando amigos y la familia.

Este importante desafío[2] parte por definir la vocación, escoger la carrera, universidad y hasta la ciudad en donde empezará esta nueva etapa.

La capital siempre ha sido una de las opciones preferidas de los jóvenes que inician sus estudios y la posibilidad de hacerlo en regiones está creciendo lentamente.

En el país existen 61 universidades, de las cuales más de la mitad son regionales, o bien de Santiago, con una o varias sedes[3] fuera.

Por esto es que estudiantes del extremo sur del país terminan en Arica o La Serena y los capitalinos, en Temuco o en Valparaíso.

Aparte de la oferta en el centro del país, las ciudades que ofrecen mayores alternativas son Valparaíso y Viña del Mar, luego Concepción, Talcahuano y Temuco.

Un cambio adecuado

La vida fuera del hogar es más que sólo una nueva experiencia para cualquier egresado.

El número de jóvenes que se va a estudiar a regiones crece cada día más, y un importante número de ellos toman esta opción por sobre el arraigo[4] y apego[5] a todos los seres queridos. Las ventajas y los beneficios que trae, a juicio de los que han vivido la experiencia, son múltiples.

Por una parte se mejora la calidad de vida, ya que para algunos el vivir en ciudades más pequeñas y en un entorno más natural es positivo.

Por lo general los aranceles son más bajos, al igual que los puntajes, existe excelencia académica y la infraestructura que ofrecen no tiene nada que envidiarles a las de la capital.

La experiencia que nos cuenta Marión Silva, estudiante de cuarto año de Servicio Social de la Universidad Católica de Valparaíso, confirma estas afirmaciones. «Santiago me tenía saturada. Comencé mis estudios en la capital, pero al cabo de un par de años tomé la opción de continuar en región. No quería más smog, tráfico, distancias largas, además nació en mí una fuerte necesidad de independencia y de vivir algo diferente.»

El hecho de partir, cuenta, le trajo muchos beneficios, pero también debió enfrentar la soledad que muchas veces se presenta y que puede ser la peor compañera de esta nueva vida. «Luego de la decisión vino lo más complicado. Asumir que estaba sola, sin mis padres, mis amigos. La casa es un soporte emocional muy fuerte e importante, el que muchas veces te ayuda a pasar los problemas más fácilmente. Ahora debía darle la cara a lo bueno y lo malo, desenvolverme y enfrentar todo tipo de cosas.»

A pesar de la ingrata realidad que debió asumir en un comienzo, evalúa su decisión como positiva y provechosa para su vida, ya que «en Valparaíso se respira aire limpio, veo el mar todos los días, mi costo de vida es menor, camino mucho y todo me queda cerca. Las distancias son más cortas, tengo las mismas comodidades que en Santiago y todo lo necesario para vivir bien, en el fondo hay menos factores de stress» afirma.

Pero no todo es tan simple y fácil.

[1] vivencias *personal experiences*
[2] desafío *challenge*
[3] sedes *branches*
[4] arraigo *roots, rootedness*
[5] apego *fondness, attachment*

También se deben combatir los obstáculos que se cruzan en este nuevo camino.

El vivir fuera de casa implica responsabilidades en términos prácticos y económicos. Ya no está la mamá o la nana para hacer la comida y lavar la ropa, no está el padre para dar más dinero si la mesada[6] se acabó, y los amigos no están al alcance[7] de una llamada telefónica para organizar una «junta».

«La independencia que se logra tiene dos caras, por un lado te sientes muy bien cuando te haces cargo de todo y resulta, pero no puedes estar con los amigos o la familia si tienes pena o simplemente quieres conversar con alguien. A pesar de todo, he madurado y crecido mucho. Soy más tolerante y me llevo mejor con mis padres, los veo menos, por lo que disfruto cada momento que comparto con ellos» reflexiona Marión.

Aprender a compartir

Un desafío importante, para los que pretenden vivir en residenciales o compartir departamento, es aprender a tolerar a las personas extrañas y de diferentes costumbres.

Sobre este último punto, la estudiante de Servicio Social indica que «aprender a vivir con otras personas y ceder en la vida comunitaria es complicado y difícil. Cuando recién llegué a Valparaíso, arrendé una casa con compañeras que no conocía. No sabía cuáles eran sus costumbres y menos el estilo de vida que llevaban, tuve más de un problema, pero finalmente logré encontrar la persona adecuada para compartir.»

Un elemento que no se debe dejar de lado al momento de tomar la decisión junto a la familia, es el factor económico. Hay que arrendar un lugar para vivir, tener el dinero necesario para asumir los costos de la carrera misma, divertirse, recrearse y considerar que cada cierto tiempo se visita el hogar.

Según José Cortés, director de asuntos estudiantiles del Campus Viña del Mar de la Universidad Nacional Andrés Bello, indica que «el elemento económico es muy importante; en algunos casos las familias hacen un gran esfuerzo para mandarlos a estudiar fuera de su casa. Los alumnos que fracasan en esta aventura son los que destinan sus recursos a otras cosas, como pasarlo bien y olvidarse a lo que vinieron, pero son los menos. El ochenta por ciento de nuestros alumnos de fuera logra sus metas académicas.»

La experiencia de José Cortés indica que esta alternativa es muy importante y fuerte para sus vidas.

«Para los que recién egresan, el tomar esta decisión es muy complicado, maduran rápidamente, ya que deben asumir responsabilidades domésticas, administrar sus recursos, el tiempo y hacerse cargo del paso académico y el estar solos haciéndose cargo de todo.»

Superar la soledad

La gran desventaja que percibe Cortés es la soledad, muchos de los alumnos sufren lejos de su casa y deciden volver antes de terminar el primer año de carrera. «La mayor desventaja es la soledad. Los padres los ubican en departamentos o pensiones, pero hay muchos que no son capaces de superar su nuevo estado. Son varios los casos en los que caen en depresión en el primer semestre, lo que les dificulta llevar el peso académico que se les exige y terminan regresando a sus casas.»

Estas situaciones, añade José Cortés, son consideradas por la mayoría de las universidades y por ello se realizan diferentes actividades para lograr que los novatos se integren y adapten. Es así como el encargado de asuntos estudiantiles explica que en la universidad «para lograr que los estudiantes se integren realizamos actividades deportivas y recreativas. Tenemos todo tipo de instalaciones para que realicen actividades en conjunto, multicanchas, espacios verdes, además del apoyo sicológico que entregamos si el alumno lo necesita. Nuestro campus es pequeño, por lo tanto, podemos conocer mejor al alumno que en universidades más grandes, así es más fácil ayudarlos y tratar de buscar la salida necesaria.»

[6] mesada *monthly allowance*
[7] alcance *within reach*

LECCIÓN 3

Periodismo

¿Comprendes?

Contesten.

1. ¿Cuál es una opción que tienen los estudiantes chilenos al comenzar sus estudios universitarios?
2. ¿Dónde han hecho siempre la mayoría de los estudiantes chilenos sus estudios universitarios?
3. ¿Cuántas universidades hay en el país y cuántas se encuentran en la región de Santiago?
4. ¿Qué otras ciudades ofrecen mayores alternativas?
5. ¿Está aumentando el número de estudiantes que dejan el hogar para ir a estudiar en otra ciudad?
6. Desde el punto de vista académico, ¿son tan buenas las universidades regionales como las de la capital?
7. ¿Qué son más bajos?

Valparaíso, Chile

Viña del Mar, Chile

Den la siguiente información.

1. de donde es Marión
2. lo que estudia y donde
3. lo que dice de la vida en Santiago
4. lo que debió enfrentar al dejar a la familia
5. algunas ventajas de estar en Valparaíso
6. algunos obstáculos que hay que enfrentar

C

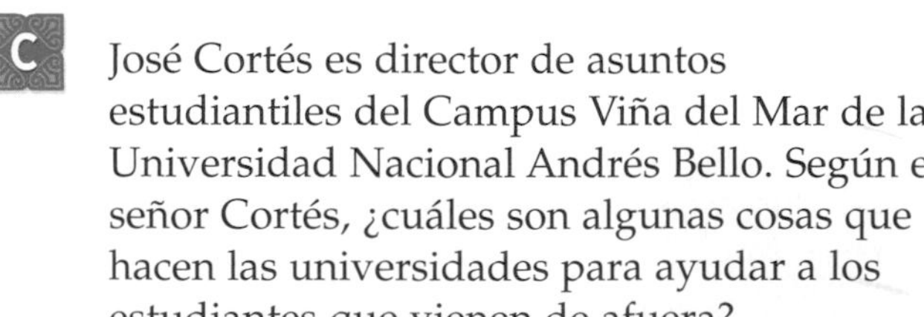

José Cortés es director de asuntos estudiantiles del Campus Viña del Mar de la Universidad Nacional Andrés Bello. Según el señor Cortés, ¿cuáles son algunas cosas que hacen las universidades para ayudar a los estudiantes que vienen de afuera?

Estructura • Avanzada

Subjuntivo con expresiones de emoción
Expressing emotions

1. The subjunctive is also used in a clause that modifies a verb or expression conveying any kind of emotion. Some verbs or expressions of emotion are:

alegrarse de	*to be happy about*	**gustar**	*to like*
estar contento(a)	*to be glad*	**es una lástima**	*it's a pity*
estar triste	*to be sad*	**temer**	*to fear*
sorprender	*to surprise*	**tener miedo de**	*to be afraid*

2. Unlike the other expressions that take the subjunctive, the information in a clause following a verb or expression of emotion can be factual. If the information in the clause is real, why is the subjunctive used? Observe and analyze the following sentences.

Me alegro de que Teresa esté con nosotros.
¿Estás contento de que Teresa esté aquí?
Creo que es una lástima que esté con nosotros.

In the sentences above, Teresa's presence is a fact, but the subjunctive is used because the clause is introduced by an expression of feeling. As illustrated by the examples, feelings can be positive or negative and vary from person to person.

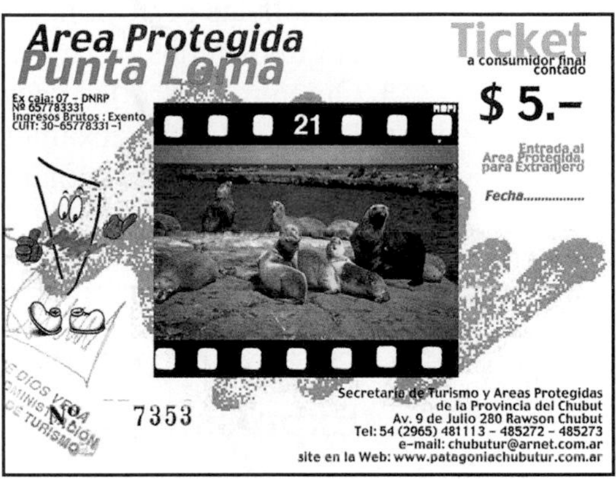

¿Cómo lo digo?

Historieta **Mis padres** Contesten.

1. ¿Están contentos tus padres que quieras hacer estudios universitarios?
2. ¿Están tristes que vayas a dejar el hogar?
3. ¿Es una lástima que no haya una universidad más cercana?
4. ¿Se alegran ellos de que sepas a qué universidad quieres asistir?
5. ¿Tienes miedo de que te sea difícil adaptarte a la vida universitaria?
6. ¿Te sorprende que la universidad cueste tanto?

2 Historieta ¿Cómo te sientes? Sigan el modelo.

Ganamos el partido. (Me alegro) →
Me alegro de que ganemos el partido.

1. Paco viene con nosotros a Ushuaia. (Me sorprende)
2. Nadie quiere estar con él. (Siento)
3. Paco se comporta mejor ahora. (Me alegro de)
4. Marta lo invita a la fiesta. (Estoy contento[a])
5. Paco se va el jueves. (Es una lástima)
6. Roberto vuelve hoy. (Me gusta)

3 ¿Qué emoción sientes? Contesten con frases completas.

1. La economía está mucho mejor.
2. Muchas personas no tienen hogar.
3. Los atletas profesionales ganan millones de dólares.
4. Algunos niños pasan mucha hambre.
5. Quieren reducir las vacaciones.
6. Piensan dar más exámenes.
7. Te dan veinte mil dólares.

Subjuntivo con expresiones de duda
Expressing doubt or uncertainity

1. When a clause is introduced by a statement of doubt, the subjunctive is used in the dependent clause since it is not known if the action will in fact take place. However, if the introductory statement conveys certainty, the indicative is used.

SUBJUNCTIVE	INDICATIVE
dudar	**no dudar**
es dudoso	**no es dudoso (no hay duda)**
no estar seguro	**estar seguro**
no creer	**creer**
no es cierto	**es cierto**

Dudo que ellos lleguen mañana de Punta del Este.
Creo que ellos van a llegar hoy.

2. When asking a question the speaker can use the indicative when he or she thinks the answer is *yes*, and the subjunctive when he or she thinks the answer is *no*.

¿Crees que él venga? Yo, no.
¿Crees que él viene? Yo, sí.

Punta del Este, Uruguay

¿Cómo lo digo?

4 ¿Lo crees o lo dudas? Sigan el modelo.

Lourdes cree que comenzar la vida universitaria va a ser tarea fácil. →
Yo dudo que comenzar la vida universitaria sea tarea fácil.

1. Lourdes cree que su hermana va a dejar el hogar para ir a estudiar.
2. Lourdes cree que su hermana va a adaptarse fácilmente.
3. Lourdes cree que su hermana va a estar muy contenta.
4. Lourdes cree que su hermana va a tener muchos amigos.
5. Lourdes cree que su hermana va a tener bastante dinero para vivir fuera de casa.
6. Lourdes cree que va a encontrar un lugar para vivir sin problema.
7. Lourdes cree que su hermana puede darle cara a lo bueno y a lo malo sin ningún problema.
8. Lourdes cree que su hermana va a divertirse mucho.

Universidad de Santiago, Chile

5 ¿Cree que sí, o lo duda? Escojan.

1. Pedro: «¿Crees que ellos irán a Chile?»
   - **a.** Pedro cree que ellos van a ir a Chile.
   - **b.** Pedro duda que ellos vayan a Chile.
2. Carolina: «¿Crees que ellos tengan bastante dinero para el viaje?»
   - **a.** Carolina cree que ellos tienen el dinero.
   - **b.** Carolina duda que ellos tengan el dinero.
3. Pedro: «¿Crees que sus padres les den el dinero?»
   - **a.** Pedro cree que sus padres les darán el dinero.
   - **b.** Pedro duda que sus padres les den el dinero.
4. Carolina: «¿Crees que ellos puedan trabajar en Chile?»
   - **a.** Carolina cree que ellos podrán trabajar.
   - **b.** Carolina duda que ellos consigan trabajo.

Spanish Online
For more information about the Southern Cone countries, go to **Web Explore** on the Glencoe Spanish Web site at glencoe.com.

Subjuntivo en cláusulas adverbiales
Subjunctive after certain conjunctions

The subjunctive is used after the following conjunctions because the information that follows is not necessarily real.

para que	*so that*	**con tal de que**	*provided that*
de modo que	*so that, in such a way that*	**sin que**	*unless, without*
de manera que	*so that, in such a way that*	**a menos que**	*unless*

Marta no irá a menos que tú la acompañes.
Ellos harán el viaje con tal de que vayamos en tren.
El profesor te lo explica de manera que comprendas.

6 **Los estudiantes** Contesten.

1. ¿Estudian mucho los estudiantes para que salgan bien en sus exámenes?
2. ¿Ahorran dinero para que puedan ir a estudiar en otro país?
3. ¿Es posible que Sandra asista a esa universidad sin que le den una beca?
4. ¿Dejará Ana el hogar familiar sin que sus padres consientan?
5. ¿No irá Roberto a estudiar en Valparaíso a menos que vaya su hermano también?

7 **La profesora** Completen.

1. La doctora Ramírez siempre presenta la lección de modo que todos nosotros ____. (comprender)
2. Nadie entiende a menos que ella la ____ claramente. (presentar)
3. Ella siempre nos explica todo de manera que ____ bien claro. (estar)
4. Ella nos enseña de manera que (nosotros) ____ aprender más. (querer)
5. Ella ayudará a sus alumnos con tal de que le ____ atención. (prestar)
6. Ella te ayudará a menos que no ____. (estudiar)

Universidad Concepción, Chile

¡Te toca a ti!

Use what you have learned

Mis opiniones

✔ ***Discuss clothing styles in the workplace***

No importa si eres varón o hembra. ¿Qué opiniones tienes de los consejos que da la señora Albisu sobre el uso de camisas de manga corta? ¿Estás de acuerdo con ella o no?

Un código de vestir

✔ ***Discuss the advantages and disadvantages of school dress codes***

Hasta recientemente muchas compañías y escuelas han tenido un código de vestir. ¿Tiene tu escuela un código? ¿Estás a favor o en contra de un código de vestir?

Alumnas chilenas

Un debate

✔ ***Discuss the advantages and disadvantages of going to college far from home***

Trabajen en grupos de cuatro. Dos están a favor de dejar el hogar e ir a estudiar no muy cerca de donde viven. Dos están en contra. Prefieren quedarse en casa y estudiar en una universidad cercana. Preparen un debate.

En mi vida

✔ ***Describe what may or may not happen in your future***

Habla de cosas que crees que van a pasar en tu vida y de cosas que dudas que ocurran en tu vida.

Emociones

✔ ***Compare feelings about college with a classmate***

Trabaja con un(a) compañero(a). Hablen de las emociones que tienen en cuanto a sus estudios universitarios. ¿Hay algunas emociones que tienen en común? Compárenlas usando expresiones tales como **me alegro de que, siento que, estoy contento(a) que, estoy triste que, tengo miedo de que.**

Assessment

Vocabulario

1 Completeten.

1. Ella es muy ____. Tiene muchas pretensiones.
2. No me gustan nada los colores ____. Prefiero los colores más suaves.
3. ¿Me permite usar tu ____? Tengo que escribir algo.
4. La camisa tiene un ____ bastante amplio en la espalda.

To review vocabulary, turn to pages 144 and 147.

2 Den la palabra.

5. no salir bien
6. el objetivo
7. tener en común
8. en la opinión de

Lectura

3 ¿Sí o no?

To review the newspaper article on clothing at the work place, turn to page 145.

9. La señora dice que nunca es apropiado llevar una camisa de manga corta.
10. Ella dice que se puede combinar una camisa de manga larga con un saco y un pantalón sport.
11. Si el señor quiere, puede poner su lapicera en el bolsillo de la camisa.
12. Todos los botones de la camisa deben estar abrochados.
13. Les sugiere a los señores llevar una camiseta debajo de la camisa.

4 Contesten.

To review the newspaper article on going away to college, turn to pages 148–150.

14. ¿Dónde han hecho sus estudios universitarios la mayoría de los estudiantes chilenos hasta recientemente?
15. ¿Qué están haciendo muchos estudiantes ahora?
16. ¿Cuáles son algunas ventajas de estudiar en una ciudad más lejana?
17. ¿Cuáles son algunos obstáculos que hay que enfrentar?

Estructura

5 Completen.

18. Me alegro que tú ____ en qué universidad quieres estudiar. (saber)
19. Dudo mucho que él____ el hogar. (dejar)
20. Ella habla de manera que sus alumnos ____ atención. (prestar)
21. Yo sé que ellos no irán a menos que ____ ustedes. (ir)
22. Yo te lo digo para que ____ lo que está pasando. (saber)
23. Estoy triste que ellos no nos ____. (acompañar)
24. Yo creo que todo ____ listo. (estar)
25. Me sorprende que Paco te ____ tal cosa. (decir)

To review the subjunctive, turn to pages 151–152, 154.

Universidad de Magallanes, Punta Arenas, Chile

For more Chapter 3 test preparation, go to the Chapter 3 **Self-Check Quiz** on the Glencoe Spanish Web site at glencoe.com.

Composición

Cuando tienes una opinión muy fuerte sobre algo, es posible que la quieras compartir con otros. Es posible que les quisieras convencer o persuadir de aceptar tu opinión.

TAREA 1 Ahora vas a escribir un editorial para un periódico. En un editorial puedes dar tus opiniones sobre el sujeto. Pero hay algo muy importante. Tienes que poder justificar tus opiniones con la ayuda de hechos e información fiables que la apoyen.

Puedes escribir tu editorial sobre cualquier sujeto que te interese. Un tópico posible sería «La popularidad de Evita Perón entre los argentinos». Antes de empezar a escribir tu editorial es posible que sea necesario hacer algunas investigaciones.

TAREA 2 Es casi siempre necesario hacer investigaciones antes de empezar a escribir un escrito expositivo, sobre todo cuando se trata de un sujeto histórico o técnico. Antes los alumnos iban a la biblioteca donde consultaban libros y enciclopedias para hacer sus investigaciones. Hoy en día hay muchos más recursos disponibles y a la biblioteca de hoy se le llama Centro de recursos o Centro de medias. En el centro se encuentran libros, periódicos, diarios, revistas semanales o mensuales, boletines, enciclopedias, diccionarios, CD-ROM, DVD y computadoras.

Cuando haces investigaciones, usas computadora, ¿no? Pero mientras navegas la red para buscar nuevos sitios Web, hay que saber que quienquiera que sea puede crear un sitio Web. Esto significa que no puedes tener confianza en la fiabilidad de los datos del sitio. No es cierto que sean exactos.

Los libros, periódicos, revistas, etc., de calidad son revisados cuidadosamente por editores profesionales pero no es así con Internet. No existen normas ni reglamentos obligatorios que tienen que seguir los individuos u organizaciones que ponen información en el Internet. Por eso tú tienes la responsabilidad de determinar si los datos y la información son fiables.

Antes de determinar si la información que encuentras en un sitio es fiable hay que hacerte unas preguntas.

¿Qué persona o sociedad se responsabiliza por este sitio Web?

¿Cuándo ha sido puesto al día el sitio?

¿Cómo pueden ser verificados sus datos?

En el sitio, ¿has encontrado errores de ortografía o de gramática? ¿Hay muchos errores tipográficos? Si así es el caso, no debes confiar en el sitio.

Escribe algunos párrafos en los cuales describes como haces tus investigaciones al preparar una tarea escolar. ¿Qué medias prefieres y por qué? ¿Cuáles consideras las más prácticas y fiables? ¿Qué haces para verificar si los sitios que utilizas son en realidad fiables? ¿Tienes algunos sitios favoritos? ¿Cuáles? ¿Te gusta utilizar libros para hacer investigaciones o no? ¿Por qué razones?

TAREA 3 No importa donde mires, vas a ver anuncios publicitarios. Los anuncios publicitarios tratan de vender productos, localidades, candidatos e ideas. Las agencias de publicidad o propaganda y los departamentos (servicios) de *marketing* utilizan muchas tácticas y técnicas para tratar de persuadir a su público.

Un anuncio publicitario no se dirige a un público universal. Se dirige al mercado para el producto específico. El departamento de *marketing* ya ha informado al que escribe el anuncio sobre los deseos, las necesidades y los recursos de los compradores potenciales. Una vez que el público esté identificado, se empieza a escribir. Crear un anuncio publicitario exige una imaginación viva y un talento para usar bien la lengua. Hay que transmitir el mensaje en muy pocas palabras. El/La que escribe publicidad nunca puede olvidar que tiene la obligación de atraer atención, captar interés y crear un deseo.

Imagínete trabajando en el departamento de *marketing*. Tú jefe(a) quiere que tú escribas un anuncio publicitario en español porque quiere captar el interés de la población hispana. Vas a escribir un anuncio publicitario para promover un blue jean, botas de cuero fino o lo que sea. Tú puedes escoger el producto. En pocas palabras tienes que describir tu producto y convencer a tus lectores que no pueden vivir sin él.

Si quieres, puedes buscar un anuncio publicitario en un periódico o en una revista que consideras persuasivo. Puedes usarlo como un modelo. ¡A ver si puedes captivar a muchos clientes!

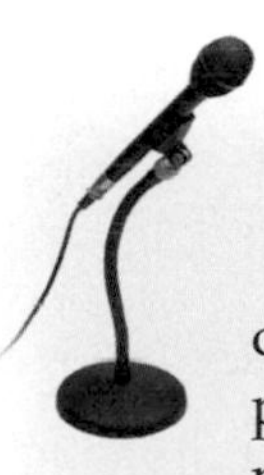

Discurso

Se puede decir que un debate es «una batalla entre ideas.» Eso significa que cuando dos personas no están de acuerdo y cada uno presenta su idea tratando de probar su superioridad sobre la del otro—es un debate—un debate informal. Se puede decir que estamos casi siempre involucrados en un debate. Es una forma de comunicación interpersonal.

TAREA 4 Ahora van a trabajar en grupos de cuatro. Van a discutir el tema siguiente, «¿Es mejor dejar el hogar familiar para hacer estudios universitarios o quedarse en casa?» Para formar su grupo hay que escoger personas que tienen opiniones opuestas. Dos creen que se debe dejar el hogar y dos creen que no. Cada uno tendrá sus propios argumentos. Al presentar sus argumentos, cada grupo tratará de dominar o superar al otro. Dentro de poco los argumentos de un grupo o sea de un lado empezarán a superar los del otro lado y habrá «un ganador». ¡Quizás tendrán una disputa! Pero no es nada malo. Hay muchos tipos de disputas: disputas amables, animadas, serias, hasta divertidas. Todas estas disputas son en un sentido debates—o sea batallas entre ideas opuestas. ¡Buena suerte!

Vocabulario

Lección 1 Cultura

la ballena
el cerro
el chaparrón
el elefante marino
el glaciar
la llanura
el lobo marino
el monte
la oveja
el pingüino
la ráfaga
la sabana
la sandía
el viñedo

alto(a)
austral
belicoso(a)
borrascoso(a)
dulce
marino(a)
pacífico(a)

la ganadería
el ganado
el gaucho
la hierba
la huerta
la indumentaria
el odio
el rebaño
pacer

Lección 2 Conversación

el algodón
el ante, la gamuza
la blusa
el bolsillo
la bota
el botón
la bragueta
la bufanda
el calzado
la camisa
la chaqueta, el saco

el cierre, la cremallera
el cinturón
la corbata
el cordón, el pasador
el cuero
el dénim
el forro
la goma
la lana
la manga
el nilón

el pantalón
el poliéster
el punto
el saco cruzado
la solapa
la suela
el suéter
el tacón
la tela
la zapatería
el zapato

de cuadros
mayor
rayada (de rayas)
apretar (ie)
arrugarse
encogerse
hacer falta
hacer juego
planchar
sentar (ie)

Lección 3 Periodismo

Ejecutivos en manga corta

el botón
la espalda
la lapicera
el pliegue
el traje
abrochado(a)
contento(a)
cursi
desabrochado(a)
estampado(a)
llamativo(a)
pecar

Cuando hay que dejar el hogar

el/la egresado(a)
el hogar
la meta
adecuado(a)
compartir
crecer
fracasar
a juicio de

Literary Companion *See pages 440–455 for literary selections related to Chapter 3. The activities for these readings will help you continue to practice your reading comprehension skills.*

VIDEOTUR

¡Viva el mundo hispano!

Video can be a beneficial learning tool for the language student. Video enables you to experience the material in the textbook in a real-life setting. Take a vicarious field trip as you see people interacting at home, at school, at the market, etc. The cultural benefits are limitless as you experience the Spanish-speaking world while "traveling" through many countries. In addition to its tremendous cultural value, video gives practice in developing good listening and viewing skills. Video allows you to look for numerous clues that are evident in tone of voice, facial expressions, and gestures. Through video you can see and hear the diversity of the target culture and compare and contrast the Spanish-speaking cultures to each other and to your own.

Episodio 1: Teatro de la comunidad

Estos actores forman parte del grupo *Teatro Catalinas Sur.* Ellos trabajan en La Boca, un barrio de Buenos Aires cerca del puerto. El espectáculo que presentan se llama *El fulgor argentino* en el que representan cien años de la historia de Argentina. Emplean ciento veinte actores, un coro y una orquesta y títeres gigantes. Es un teatro de la comunidad para la comunidad.

Episodio 2: Fiebre de fútbol

Esta es la sala de la casa de Flavio Nardini en Buenos Aires. Flavio es fanático o hincha del Racing, un equipo de fútbol. Los argentinos toman el fútbol muy en serio. Hay cinco equipos nacionales en el país y muchísimos equipos pequeños. Flavio lleva los colores del Racing, azul y blanco. A su lado está la estatua de un antiguo entrenador del Racing que ocupa un lugar de honor en su sala.

Episodio 3: Tango en Buenos Aires

Esta pareja está bailando el tango. El tango se creó en Buenos Aires a fines del siglo XIX. Los inmigrantes italianos, españoles, franceses y africanos expresaban su pasión, su tristeza, su desesperación en esta música y baile. Empezó con los pobres pero después fue adoptado por los ricos. La pareja que está bailando probablemente recibirá propinas de los espectadores.

Capítulo 4

La América Central

Spanish Online
To interact with your online edition of **¡Buen viaje!** go to: glencoe.com.

Objetivos

In this chapter you will:

- learn about the geography, history, and cultures of the Central American countries
- review how to express future events; conditions
- discuss finances
- review how to refer to people and things already mentioned
- read and discuss social announcements and human interest articles as they appear in newspapers
- learn to express emotions and possibilities about past events
- learn to use certain time expressions such as **en cuanto, hasta que**

Contenido

Vocabulario para la lectura

Use your StudentWorks™ Plus CD for more practice.

Se dice que habrá un terremoto.
Un terremoto fuerte podría causar mucha destrucción.

Si ustedes van a Copán, verán muchas estelas y animales tallados de los mayas.

Los bohíos suelen ser de paja.

La hamaca cuelga del techo del bohío.

Una mola es una blusa que llevan las indígenas de San Blas.

Más vocabulario

picante que tiene un sabor fuerte de especias que pican

soler (ue) tener la costumbre, hacer normalmente

trasladar mover de un lugar a otro, cambiar de lugar; reubicar

¿Qué palabra necesito?

1 Historieta Un viaje a Centroamérica
Contesten con **sí**.

1. ¿Hará Carlos mucho durante su viaje a Centroamérica?
2. ¿Andará por las pintorescas callejuelas de adoquines en Antigua, Guatemala?
3. ¿Admirará las estelas mayas con animales tallados en Copán, Honduras?
4. ¿Verá los rascacielos modernos de la ciudad de Panamá?
5. ¿Comprará una mola en las islas de San Blas?
6. ¿Irá a unos restaurantes típicos?
7. ¿Pedirá a lo menos un plato picante?
8. ¿Qué piensas? ¿Le gustará?

Antigua, Guatemala

Tegucigalpa, Honduras

2 ¿Cuál es la palabra? Completen.

1. Un ____ es un edificio muy alto de muchos pisos (muchas plantas).
2. No me gustaría estar en un rascacielos durante un ____. Me daría mucho miedo.
3. Los bohíos ____ ser de paja.
4. Se puede dormir cómodamente en una ____.
5. La hamaca ____ del techo.
6. Otra palabra que significa «bohío» es ____.
7. A los niños les gusta ____ la pelota pero es un poco difícil en una antigua callejuela de adoquines.
8. Van a reubicarse. Van a ____ el negocio de Tegucigalpa a San Pedro Sula.

Lectura

La geografía

El istmo de Centroamérica comprende todos los países entre Guatemala y Panamá. Cubre un área de 196.000 millas cuadradas o sea el tamaño de una cuarta parte de México. En algunos lugares el istmo tiene un ancho de sólo cincuenta millas. Una cordillera que une las Rocosas con los Andes va desde el norte hasta el sur. Esta cordillera domina casi todos los países menos Panamá. Algunos picos alcanzan 14.000 pies de altura.

Centroamérica es una región de muchos volcanes. Más de veinte son activos. Sus erupciones son peligrosas y año tras año han causado mucho daño. Sin embargo, es la ceniza volcánica la que hace la tierra tan fértil para la agricultura.

Como el istmo es tan largo hay una gran variedad de terreno y clima. En la Mosquitia en la costa nordeste de Honduras y en el Darién en la costa oriental de Panamá hay selvas tropicales, muchas partes de las cuales no han sido exploradas. Los Chocó, un grupo indígena del Darién, siguen viviendo aún hoy como vivían sus ancestros hace ya miles de años. Su sociedad primitiva se basa en la recolección[1] y la caza.

[1] recolección *harvest, gathering*

Reading Strategy

Making comparisons while reading If you read a passage that discusses a topic from different points of view, you can make comparisons while reading. Noting such similarities and differences will help make the ideas clearer and you will probably remember more of what you read. You can make these comparisons in your head or write them down as you read.

Lago Atitlán, Guatemala

Una selva tropical, Honduras

Darién, Panamá

LECCIÓN I

Cultura

Isla de las Perlas, Panamá

Panamá y muchas regiones de la costa de Centroamérica tienen un clima tropical. Las costas son calurosas y húmedas. En la cordillera se dice que la primavera es eterna aunque las noches pueden ser frías en la estación seca. Hay sólo dos estaciones—la estación seca más o menos de noviembre a abril y la estación lluviosa y más cálida de mayo a octubre.

Se le da el nombre de invierno a la estación lluviosa y verano a la estación seca. La costa del Caribe es mucho más lluviosa que la costa del Pacífico con sus playas de ceniza volcánica negra.

A Completen.

1. Centroamérica es un _____ que comprende todos los países entre _____ en el norte y _____ en el sur.
2. Una _____ va desde el norte hasta el sur.
3. En Centroamérica hay muchos _____, de los cuales más de veinte son _____.
4. Es la _____ de los volcanes que hace la tierra tan fértil.
5. _____ y _____ son dos regiones de selvas tropicales.
6. Los _____ viven en el Darién como vivían sus ancestros hace ya miles de años.
7. Las costas de Centroamérica son _____ y _____.
8. Hay dos estaciones: la _____ y la _____.

Una selva tropical, Costa Rica

Civilización precolombina—Los mayas

Copán, Honduras

El territorio ocupado por los mayas, en el que se han descubierto más de cincuenta ciudades importantes, se extendía por zonas de México; y en Centroamérica en Guatemala, Belice y gran parte de Honduras y El Salvador. La teoría más probable es que sus ancestros vinieron de Asia, habiendo cruzado el estrecho de Bering, hace unos dieciocho mil años.

Los mayas desarrollaron su civilización durante dos períodos. El más importante es el Viejo Imperio de los siglos IV a IX d.C. Durante este período los mayas habitaron Guatemala y Honduras y se unieron a[2] los quichés, procedentes de las alturas de Guatemala.

Los progresos que hicieron los mayas entre 300 y 900 d.C. son increíbles. Su calendario fue más perfecto que el de los cristianos de la época y se dice que fue aún más preciso que el nuestro. Los mayas tenían un tipo de escritura jeroglífica muy parecida a la egipcia. Sus reyes solían mandar grabar en estelas jeroglíficos que representaban todos los acontecimientos que ocurrían durante su reinado.

Los mayas eran expertos en arquitectura. Construyeron palacios y templos que adornaron con enormes esculturas. Tenían cuchillos, vasijas y piezas de cerámica adornadas con jeroglíficos. Los quichés tenían su libro sagrado, el Popol Vuh, que relata el origen del ser humano.

Tikal, Guatemala

Desgraciadamente este desarrollo formidable terminó de forma inexplicable poco antes del año 900 d.C. Nuevos descubrimientos arqueológicos indican que existe la posibilidad de que los mayas quisieron lograr una gran expansión territorial y que las confrontaciones bélicas que acompañaban esa expansión fueran la causa más importante de la decadencia del Imperio maya.

Actualmente en Guatemala, el país de mayor población indígena de Centroamérica, se hablan veintiuna lenguas de origen maya. Sesenta por ciento de los guatemaltecos tienen una lengua materna que no es el español. La lengua más extendida es el quiché que tiene 1.900.000 hablantes.

[2] se unieron a *merged with*

 Identifiquen.

1. donde vivían los mayas
2. las fechas del Viejo Imperio
3. el calendario maya
4. la escritura maya
5. instrumentos y utensilios que tenían los mayas
6. el Popol Vuh
7. una posible razón por la rápida decadencia del Imperio maya
8. el quiché

Cerámica maya, Tikal, Guatemala

Capitales centroamericanas

Algunas capitales centroamericanas no han sido siempre la capital de su país. Por una variedad de razones la capital ha sido cambiada de una ciudad a otra.

La Ciudad de Guatemala

Ciudad de Guatemala

Hoy la Ciudad de Guatemala es la capital del país del mismo nombre. Es una ciudad de mucho movimiento, y de todas las ciudades centroamericanas es la que tiene la mayor población. La mayor parte de la ciudad es moderna porque sufrió un terremoto en 1917 que causó mucha destrucción.

De 1543 a 1773 Antigua fue la capital. Cuando fue fundada llevaba el nombre de «Muy Noble y Muy Leal Ciudad de Santiago de los Caballeros de Goathemala». Goathemala en aquel entonces comprendía Chiapas en México y todos los países de Centroamérica menos Panamá. La capital fue trasladada a Guatemala en 1773 cuando un terremoto destruyó Antigua.

A pesar de esta destrucción Antigua ha conservado su belleza. No hay duda que se ven ruinas de magníficas iglesias, conventos y otros edificios coloniales. Pero es una ciudad placentera con callejuelas de adoquines y bonitas mansiones de colores vivos que también datan de la época colonial.

Antigua, Guatemala

Tegucigalpa, Honduras

Tegucigalpa, Honduras

Tegucigalpa

El nombre de la capital de Honduras, Tegucigalpa, tiene su orígen en dos palabras indígenas—*teguz* que significa **colina** y *galpa* que significa **plata.** Durante años fue un centro minero de plata. La ciudad actual no ha perdido su cualidad de pequeña ciudad colonial con calles estrechas y casas de colores vivos. Actualmente el 70 por ciento de la población hondureña vive en el área metropolitana de Tegucigalpa.

Antes de 1880 Comayagua fue la capital. Pero fue destruida en una guerra civil en 1873 y siete años después se decidió restablecer la capital en Tegucigalpa.

Managua

Managua, la capital de Nicaragua, es otra capital cuyo nombre tiene origen en una lengua autóctona[3], el náhuatl. Significa «donde hay una extensión de agua». Es un nombre apropiado porque aquí se encuentran el lago Managua, la laguna Tiscapa y otras lagunas de origen volcánico que rodean el área urbana. Managua es una de las pocas ciudades que tiene grandes espacios abiertos.

Hay dos ciudades nicaragüenses conocidas por su belleza. Son León y Granada. Durante doscientos años León fue la capital del país. Pero León, de índole liberal y Granada, de índole conservadora, siempre rivalizaban por el liderazgo del país. Por consiguiente en 1851 la cabeza del país pasó a Managua, una ciudad equidistante o a medio camino de estas dos urbes rivales.

[3] autóctona *indigenous*

Managua, Nicaragua

San José

San José, la capital de Costa Rica, y sus suburbios ocupan una gran parte de la sección central del país. Aquí vive más del cincuenta por ciento de la población costarricense. San José tiene la reputación de ser una ciudad muy «manejable». Hay algunos rascacielos pero la mayoría de sus edificios son de sólo tres o cuatro plantas (pisos).

La antigua capital, Cartago, se encuentra a sólo 25 kilómetros de San José. En 1821 Costa Rica ganó su independencia de España de forma pacífica. Como la ciudad de San José ya llevaba el liderazgo económico, se resolvió en 1823 trasladar la capital a esta ciudad para accederle también el liderazgo político. En aquel entonces la población total de Costa Rica era de cincuenta y siete mil habitantes. Hoy sólo la capital y sus alrededores tienen una población de ochocientos mil.

San José, Costa Rica

Cartago, Costa Rica

C

Den el nombre de la capital actual y la capital antigua de cada país. Expliquen por qué fue trasladada cada capital de una ciudad a otra.

1. Guatemala
2. Honduras
3. Nicaragua
4. Costa Rica

Tikal, Guatemala

Visitas históricas

Un viaje a Centroamérica requiere una visita a las famosas ciudades mayas de Tikal en Guatemala y Copán en Honduras.

Tikal

Tikal se encuentra en el Petén, una zona selvática calurosa, bastante llana, en el norte de Guatemala. El entorno natural de Tikal es fantástico, si no místico. Unas macizas[4] pirámides emergen sobre el techo de la vegetación de la impenetrable selva. Un ruido ensordecedor de los monos y las chicharras[5] sale de los árboles.

La Gran Plaza de Tikal es uno de los sitios más impresionantes de todo el mundo maya. El Templo I llamado también el Templo del Gran Jaguar accede a la Plaza. Es una pirámide que alcanza cuarenta y cinco metros de altura. En su interior se halla la tumba de Ah Cacao, el principal soberano de Tikal. El templo, formado de tres cuartos, está en la parte superior de la pirámide.

La Gran Pirámide es el más antiguo de los grandes edificios destapados[6] en Tikal. Se cree que la Gran Pirámide fue usada para observaciones astronómicas en vez de ritos ceremoniales.

[4] macizas *solid*
[5] chicharras *cicadas*
[6] destapados *unearthed*

Gran Plaza, Tikal, Guatemala

Estela, Copán, Honduras

Copán

La historia de Copán en Honduras no parece empezar hasta 435 d.C. pero hay arqueólogos que creen que estaba habitada mucho antes. Alcanzó su apogeo entre 650 y 750.

La Gran Plaza de Copán es impresionante por sus estelas con figuras humanas y altares con animales tallados. Estas estelas tenían para los mayas un significado profundo. A través de ellas se rendía culto a los árboles que sustentaban el cielo. Y servían de puerta hacia el Xibalba o mundo subterráneo y místico.

No muy lejos de la Gran Plaza está la cancha de pelota. Los jugadores tenían que rebotar la pelota, una pelota grande y pesada hecha de goma, haciéndola subir la pared hasta tocar una de las metas talladas en piedra en la parte superior de la pared. Los jugadores no podían usar las manos, los brazos ni los pies. Fue un juego duro, una combinación de soccer, fútbol americano y balonmano.

Una cancha de pelota, Copán, Honduras

Islas de San Blas, Panamá

Si estás en Panamá y no quieres pasar todo tu tiempo en una de sus magníficas playas, tendrás que visitar el archipiélago de San Blas formado de 365 islotes. Es aquí donde viven los famosos kunas. Sus casas son bohíos o sea chozas de paja y caña. En el interior del bohío cuelgan las hamacas. La mayoría de los kunas viven de la recolección de productos marinos y de la pesca. Algunos que viven en tierra firme son agricultores.

Las mujeres kunas llevan molas. Una mola es una blusa hecha de telas de distintos colores. La mola tiene también motivos geométricos y mitológicos. Las molas de las kunas son tan apreciadas que se consideran objetos de arte.

Una mujer kuna, Islas de San Blas, Panamá

Isla Acuatupu, Islas de San Blas, Panamá

Contesten.

1. ¿Dónde está Tikal?
2. ¿Qué se ve en Tikal?
3. ¿Para qué servía la Gran Pirámide en Tikal?
4. Según los arqueólogos, ¿desde cuándo fue habitada Copán?
5. ¿Cómo es la Gran Plaza de Copán y qué tiene?
6. ¿Cómo jugaban pelota en Copán?
7. ¿Dónde viven los kunas?
8. ¿Cómo son sus casas?
9. ¿Qué es una mola? Descríbela.

Copán, Honduras

Comida

Cuando tienes hambre y decides comer algo creerás estar en México. No hay duda que la cocina centroamericana tiene mucho parentesco con la cocina mexicana, sobre todo por el empleo del maíz en forma de tortillas y frijoles o como dicen aquí en muchas partes de Centroamérica alubias negras refritas con arroz. Igual que a los mexicanos, a la mayoría de los centroamericanos les gustan las salsas picantes.

En Guatemala los chiles rellenos son populares. En Honduras puedes comer enchiladas o tamales.

¿Quieres probar un desayuno favorito de los nicaragüenses, los nicas, y de los costarricenses, los ticos? Se llama «gallopinto». Es una mezcla de arroz y frijoles acompañada de huevos.

A los salvadoreños les gustan el pescado y los mariscos. Sirven el ceviche igual que en Perú. La mariscada, una sopa que lleva almejas, camarones y cangrejos, es otro plato favorito.

Y el plato nacional de Panamá es el sancocho. El sancocho lleva pollo, cebolla, maíz y papas.

Como a los españoles les gusta comer pequeñas raciones de comida, a los centroamericanos también les gusta comer raciones pequeñas, pero no se llaman «tapas». En Nicaragua y Costa Rica son «bocas», y en Guatemala «boquitas». Una boquita favorita guatemalteca es el pan con ajo—rebanadas de pan frito frotadas[7] con ajo. Una de las bocas nicaragüenses muy buena y un poco exótica son los huevos de tortuga[8].

[7] frotadas *rubbed*
[8] tortuga *turtle*

Identifiquen.

1. alubias negras
2. el gallopinto
3. el ceviche
4. el sancocho
5. las bocas
6. las boquitas
7. los habitantes de Nicaragua
8. los habitantes de Costa Rica

For more information about foods in Central America, go to **Web Explore** on the Glencoe Spanish Web site at glencoe.com.

Sancocho

Estructura • Repaso

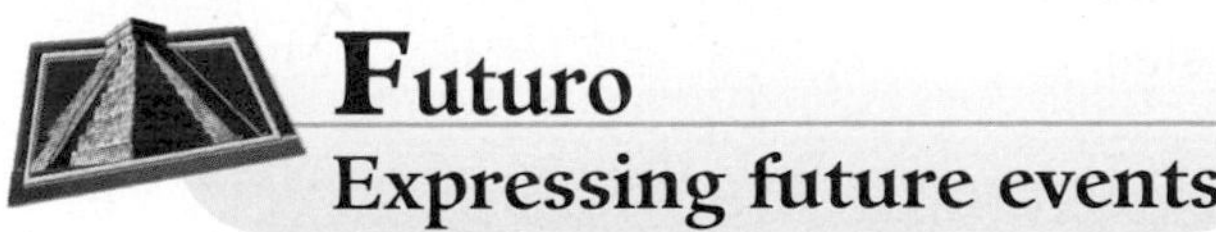

Futuro
Expressing future events

1. The future tense of regular verbs is formed by adding the personal endings to the entire infinitive.

INFINITIVE	estudiar	comer	vivir
yo	estudiaré	comeré	viviré
tú	estudiarás	comerás	vivirás
él, ella, Ud.	estudiará	comerá	vivirá
nosotros(as)	estudiaremos	comeremos	viviremos
vosotros(as)	*estudiaréis*	*comeréis*	*viviréis*
ellos, ellas, Uds.	estudiarán	comerán	vivirán

2. The following verbs have an irregular root for the future tense. All the endings, however, are the same as those of a regular verb.

hacer	har-	**venir**	vendr-
decir	dir-	**poner**	pondr-
querer	querr-	**salir**	saldr-
saber	sabr-	**tener**	tendr-
poder	podr-	**valer**	valdr-

INFINITIVE	decir	poder	salir
yo	diré	podré	saldré
tú	dirás	podrás	saldrás
él, ella, Ud.	dirá	podrá	saldrá
nosotros(as)	diremos	podremos	saldremos
vosotros(as)	*diréis*	*podréis*	*saldréis*
ellos, ellas, Uds.	dirán	podrán	saldrán

3. The future is used in Spanish as in English to express a future event.

Ellos llegarán a Panamá mañana.
Nosotros los veremos el sábado que viene.
José tendrá muchas noticias.

4. Note that the future is often expressed with **ir a** + the infinitive or the present tense.

Ellos van a salir la semana próxima.
Y yo voy mañana.

Puente de las Américas, Panamá

¿Cómo lo digo?

1 Historieta **Un viaje a Centroamérica** Contesten.

1. ¿Irás algún día a Centroamérica?
2. ¿Qué países visitarás?
3. ¿Querrás ver algunas ruinas mayas?
4. ¿Irás a Tikal o a Copán?
5. Para el desayuno, ¿comerás un gallopinto?
6. ¿Qué crees? ¿Te gustará?
7. Después de subir muchas pirámides, tendrás mucha hambre, ¿no?
8. Para el almuerzo, ¿pedirás enchiladas con alubias refritas y arroz?

2 **Hoy, sí. Mañana, no.** Sigan el modelo.

Hoy estudio, _____. →
Hoy estudio, pero mañana no estudiaré.

1. Hoy me levanto temprano, _____.
2. Hoy tomo el desayuno en casa, _____.
3. Hoy mamá nos lleva a la escuela, _____.
4. Hoy nos dan un examen en español, _____.
5. Hoy jugamos (al) baloncesto, _____.
6. Hoy recibimos uniformes, _____.
7. Hoy las clases terminan a las dos, _____.
8. Hoy cenamos en un restaurante, _____.
9. Hoy leo después de comer, _____.

Tegucigalpa, Honduras

3 Historieta **Hay que ser positivos.**

Contesten con **sí** y el futuro.

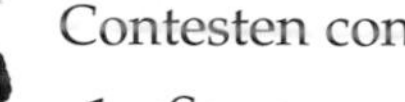

1. ¿Se va a poner el uniforme el jugador?
2. ¿Va a estar en forma?
3. ¿Va a poder jugar?
4. ¿Todos van a venir al estadio?
5. ¿Van a tener entradas para todos?
6. ¿Le van a enseñar a jugar?
7. ¿Él va a hacer todo lo necesario?
8. ¿Va a ganar?
9. Y tú, ¿vas a estar contento(a)?

4 Historieta **¿Qué hará el campeón?**

Cambien en el futuro.

1. Él nunca dice nada.
2. Pero puede jugar.
3. El problema es que no quiere.
4. Tenemos que rogarle.
5. Le decimos que no ganamos sin él.
6. Y que todo el mundo viene a verlo jugar.
7. Vale la pena intentarlo.
8. Si no, nunca sabemos.

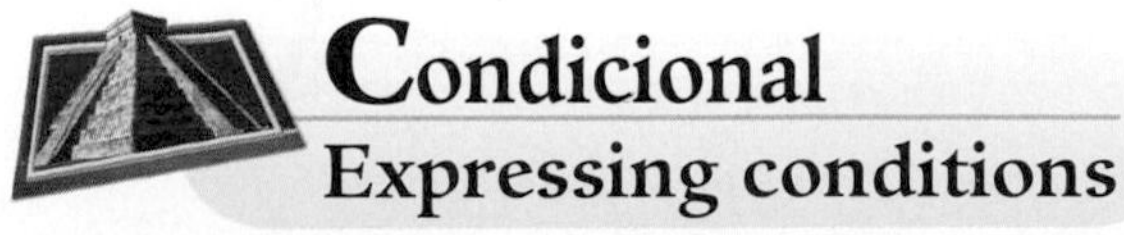

Condicional
Expressing conditions

1. The conditional, like the future, is formed by adding the personal endings to the entire infinitive. Note that the conditional endings are the same as the imperfect endings of **-er** and **-ir** verbs.

INFINITIVE	estudiar	beber	escribir
yo	estudiaría	bebería	escribiría
tú	estudiarías	beberías	escribirías
él, ella, Ud.	estudiaría	bebería	escribiría
nosotros(as)	estudiaríamos	beberíamos	escribiríamos
vosotros(as)	*estudiaríais*	*beberíais*	*escribiríais*
ellos, ellas, Uds.	estudiarían	beberían	escribirían

2. Verbs with an irregular root in the future tense have the same irregular root in the conditional.

hacer	haría	**poder**	podría	**salir**	saldría
decir	diría	**venir**	vendría	**tener**	tendría
querer	querría	**poner**	pondría	**valer**	valdría
saber	sabría				

3. The conditional is used in Spanish as it is in English, to express what would or would not happen under certain circumstances or "conditions." The conditional in English is usually expressed by "would."

Yo lo llamaría, pero no tengo tiempo. *I would call him, but I don't have time.*

¿Cómo lo digo?

5 Historieta ¡A Guatemala, ya! Contesten.

1. ¿Te gustaría hacer un viaje a Guatemala?
2. ¿Irías al Petén? ¿Visitarías Tikal?
3. ¿Te interesarían las fabulosas ruinas mayas?
4. ¿Pasarías algunos días en Antigua?
5. ¿Darías un paseo por sus callejuelas de adoquines?
6. ¿Irías también a Panajachel?
7. ¿Rentarías un barquito? ¿Remarías por el lago Atitlán?
8. No perderías la oportunidad de visitar el mercado de Chichicastenango, ¿verdad?

Mercado de Chichicastenango, Guatemala

6 La ropa Contesten.

1. ¿Llevarían tus amigos camisas o camisetas de manga corta?
2. Estos mismos amigos, ¿se pondrían jeans amarillos?
3. ¿Les gustaría llevar una mola?
4. Y tú, ¿llevarías una mola?
5. ¿Qué preferirías llevar?

¡Te toca a ti!

Use what you have learned

El clima

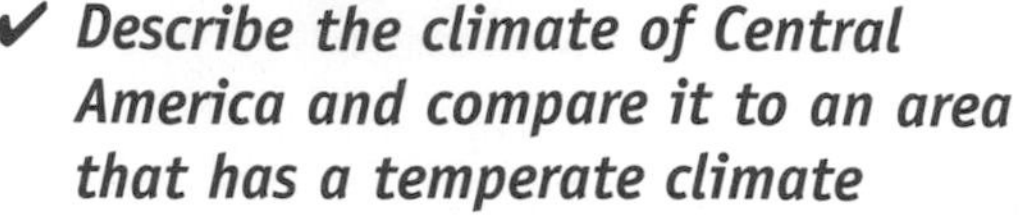

✔ ***Describe the climate of Central America and compare it to an area that has a temperate climate***

Compara el clima de Centroamérica con el clima de una región templada donde hay cuatro estaciones. En Centroamérica, ¿hay variaciones entre el clima de la sierra y el de la costa? ¿Cuáles son?

Parque Nacional Corcovado, Costa Rica

Las civilizaciones precolombinas

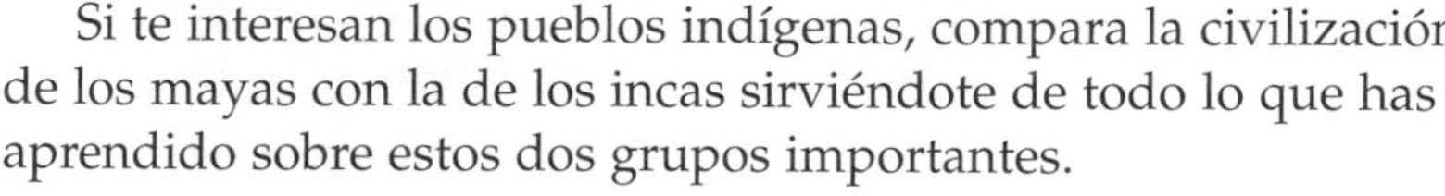

✔ ***Compare the Maya civilization to the Inca civilization***

Si te interesan los pueblos indígenas, compara la civilización de los mayas con la de los incas sirviéndote de todo lo que has aprendido sobre estos dos grupos importantes.

To learn more about the Mayan civilization, go to **Web Explore** on the Glencoe Spanish Web site at glencoe.com.

Cerámica inca

Cerámica maya

Un terremoto

✔ ***Research the life of the famous baseball player Roberto Clemente***

Dos días antes de Navidad en 1972 un terremoto destruyó desastrosamente la ciudad de Managua. El gobierno de Nicaragua le pidió ayuda al mundo entero y el gran beisbolista puertorriqueño Roberto Clemente decidió ayudar. Haz alguna investigación y prepara una biografía sobre este héroe universal humano—Roberto Clemente.

Roberto Clemente

Lo que ocurrirá

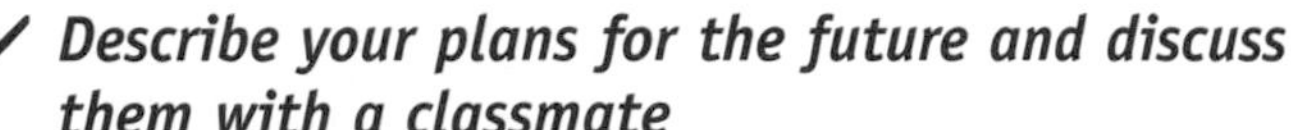

✔ ***Describe your plans for the future and discuss them with a classmate***

Habla con un(a) compañero(a). Según tus propios planes, dile lo que ocurrirá o sucederá en tu vida. Luego tu compañero(a) te dirá lo que pasará en su vida. Comparen sus ideas o planes. Hablen de como les ayudará el español en sus carreras.

Con un millón de dólares

✔ ***Describe what you would do with a million dollars***

Di todo lo que harías con un millón de dólares. Y tu hermano o tu hermana, ¿haría lo mismo con su millón de dólares? ¿Qué haría (él, ella) que no harías tú?

Assessment

Vocabulario

To review vocabulary, turn to pages 164–165.

1 Pareen.

1. una hamaca
2. una mola
3. una choza
4. paja
5. un rascacielos
6. un terremoto

a. un desastre natural
b. materia de la que se hacen casitas en una zona tropical
c. algo de tejido fuerte que sirve para dormir
d. un edificio de muchos pisos
e. una blusa con diseños bonitos
f. un bohío

Lectura

To review some geographical facts about Central America, turn to pages 167–168.

2 ¿Sí o no?

7. Centroamérica es un istmo muy ancho que comprende tres países.
8. Una gran parte de Centroamérica es montañosa.
9. La ceniza volcánica es muy mala para la agricultura.
10. El clima en las costas es más caluroso y húmedo que en la cordillera.
11. En Centroamérica hay cuatro estaciones pero no hace mucho frío en el invierno.

To review some historical and cultural facts about Central America, turn to pages 169–171.

3 Contesten.

12. ¿Qué países habitaron los mayas durante el período del Viejo Imperio?
13. ¿Cómo fue el calendario maya?
14. ¿Qué instrumentos y utensilios tenían los mayas?
15. ¿Cuál es el país de mayor población indígena de Centroamérica?

4 Identifiquen.

16. la antigua capital de Guatemala
17. la capital de Honduras
18. lo que significa «Managua» en náhuatl
19. como es la ciudad de San José

5 **Describan.**

20. Tikal
21. Copán
22. Islas de San Blas
23. gallopinto

To review some places of interest and foods from Central America, turn to pages 172–174.

Estructura

6 **Completen con el futuro.**

24. Nosotros ____ el viaje. (hacer)
25. Ellos nos ____. (acompañar)

26–27. Yo ____ a Guatemala pero tú ____ a Honduras, ¿no? (ir)

28. Yo ____ que comprarme una mola en San Blas. (tener)
29. Sandra ____ a sus primos que viven en El Salvador. (ver)

To review verbs in the future tense, turn to page 175.

7 **Completen con el condicional.**

30. Nosotros ____ el viaje. (hacer)
31. Ellos nos ____. (acompañar)

32–33. Yo ____ a Guatemala pero tú ____ a Honduras, ¿no? (ir)

34. Yo ____ que comprarme una mola en San Blas. (tener)
35. Sandra ____ a sus primos que viven en El Salvador. (ver)

To review verbs in the conditional, turn to page 177.

Lago Atitlán, Guatemala

Conversación

Vocabulario para la conversación

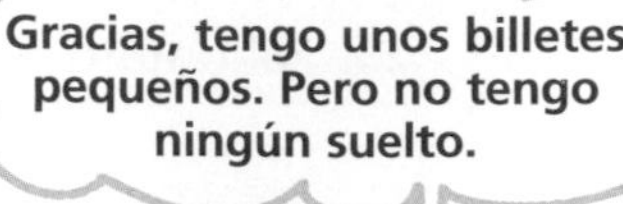

el dinero en efectivo

billetes pequeños

suelto

monedas

billetes grandes

una chequera, un talonario

una cuenta corriente

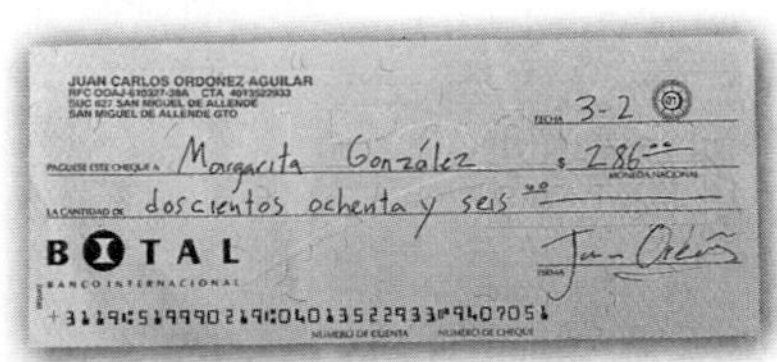

un cheque

el cajero automático

Tienes que introducir tu tarjeta (bancaria).
Te salen las instrucciones en la pantalla.
Pulsas (Oprimes) unos botones para entrar tu pin o código.

Más vocabulario

un cargo un pago que se debe hacer
una hipoteca un préstamo a largo plazo para comprar una casa
el monto el total
un préstamo el recibo de una cantidad de dinero que se devolverá en una fecha futura
- **a largo plazo** un préstamo por unos quince a veinticinco años
- **a corto plazo** un préstamo por unos tres años o menos
- **la tasa de interés** para un préstamo a corto plazo es más alta que la de un préstamo a largo plazo

cobrar recibir una cantidad de dinero como pago de algo
pagar al contado comprar algo y pagarlo todo enseguida
pagar a cuotas (a plazos) comprar algo haciendo pagos mensuales después de hacer un pago inicial (un pie, un pronto, un depósito, un enganche)

Conversación

¿Qué palabra necesito?

1 Historieta Las finanzas de José

Contesten según se indica.

1. ¿Lleva José mucho dinero en efectivo? (no)
2. ¿Le gusta tener mucho suelto en su bolsillo? (no, le molesta)
3. ¿Cómo prefiere pagar sus gastos? (con una tarjeta de crédito)
4. ¿Tiene José una cuenta corriente? (no)
5. ¿Quién tiene una? (sus padres)
6. ¿Qué pagan ellos con cheque? (sus facturas)
7. ¿Es importante mantener un saldo en la cuenta corriente? (sí)

Banco de Costa Rica, San José, Costa Rica

2 Historieta El cajero automático

Completen.

Para usar el ___1___ automático hay que introducir tu ___2___. Todas las instrucciones que necesitas salen en la ___3___. Tienes que ___4___ un botón para entrar tu pin o ___5___. Luego puedes ___6___ unos ___7___ más para indicar el monto de dinero que quieres retirar.

3 Al contado o a cuotas ¿Sí o no?

1. Al comprar un televisor, hay gente que lo paga al contado y hay otros que lo pagan a cuotas.
2. Si lo vas a pagar a cuotas, tienes que pagar un pronto.
3. A veces hay muchos cargos en una factura.
4. La tasa de interés de un préstamo es siempre muy baja.
5. La hipoteca es un ejemplo de un préstamo a corto plazo.
6. El tipo de cambio de una moneda puede cambiar de un día a otro.

Asuntos financieros

Sr. Rubén ¿Vas a pasar el año en Panamá?
Sandra Sí, voy a tomar cursos en la Universidad del Istmo.
Sr. Rubén ¿Sabes que Panamá es el centro financiero de todo Latinoamérica?
Sandra Sí, lo sé. Pero no me importa porque no voy a tener mucha plata. Me pregunto si debo comprar cheques de viajero.
Sr. Rubén No, no. No te harán falta. Tendrás una tarjeta bancaria, ¿no?
Sandra Sí.
Sr. Rubén Pues, puedes hacer todo en el cajero automático. Introduces la tarjeta, pulsas unos botones para entrar tu pin o código y la cantidad de dinero que quieres. En unos momentos te sale el monto que has pedido—en efectivo.
Sandra Y, ¿de dónde se saca el dinero?
Sr. Rubén Pues, se retira enseguida de tu cuenta corriente. Es necesario que tengas una cuenta corriente en tu banco y que tu saldo sea suficiente para cobrar la cantidad que retiras.
Sandra ¿Me da el dinero en dólares o en la moneda local?
Sr. Rubén Pues, en Panamá la moneda es el dólar estadounidense. El balboa es sólo una moneda de veinticinco centavos. Pero si vas a Costa Rica, por ejemplo, te lo dará en colones—y a un tipo de cambio bastante favorable y con un cargo mínimo.
Sandra Entonces no tengo que ir a una casa de cambio.
Sr. Rubén No. Y por lo general ellos te cobran (clavan) una comisión bastante alta. Te conviene más el cajero automático. El único problema puede ser que te dé sólo billetes grandes y la máquina no te los puede cambiar en billetes más pequeños ni en suelto.

LECCIÓN 2

Conversación

Sandra Pero si compro algo la mayoría de los negocios aceptan tarjetas de crédito, ¿no?

Sr. Rubén ¡Por supuesto! Pero, ¡cuidado! No debes hacer cargos que no puedes pagar en cuanto recibas la factura o el estado de la tarjeta de crédito. Sencillamente dicho, el saldo que no pagas se convierte en un préstamo y la tasa de interés es muy alta.

Sandra No, no quiero hacer ningún préstamo. Tengo una filosofía—si no tengo los recursos necesarios, no lo compro.

Sr. Rubén Es una filosofía muy buena. Cuando seas mayor y necesites un préstamo a corto plazo para comprarte un carro o una hipoteca para comprarte una casa, es otra cosa. En ese caso un préstamo es indispensable. Pero como regla general es aconsejable comprar muy poco a cuotas porque una vez más la tasa de interés es muy alta. Una regla de oro es: comprar todo lo posible al contado.

Sandra ¡Ya! Y todo eso es para el futuro. Ahora todo lo que necesito es lo suficiente para permitirme un año en Panamá.

Sr. Rubén Sí, Sandra. Te deseo muy buena suerte y que lo pases bien en Panamá. Será una experiencia inolvidable.

Barrio Charrillo, Panamá

¿Comprendes?

A Contesten.

1. ¿Dónde va a pasar el año Sandra?
2. ¿Qué es la Ciudad de Panamá?
3. ¿Va a tener mucho dinero Sandra?
4. ¿Ella debe comprar cheques de viajero?
5. Si tiene una tarjeta bancaria, ¿qué puede usar?
6. ¿Qué tiene que introducir en el cajero automático?
7. ¿Cómo entra su pin o código?
8. En unos momentos, ¿qué le sale?
9. ¿Qué tiene que tener Sandra para usar el cajero automático?

Spanish Online

To learn more about the economies of Central America, do the Chapter 4 **WebQuest** activity on the Glencoe Spanish Web site at glencoe.com.

B Corrijan las oraciones falsas.

1. La moneda oficial de Panamá es el dólar estadounidense.
2. La moneda de Costa Rica es el dólar también.
3. El cajero automático te da dinero en la moneda nacional.
4. El cajero automático te puede cambiar billetes grandes en billetes pequeños.
5. Te puede dar suelto también.
6. Uno debe tener un saldo alto en su tarjeta de crédito y pagarlo a cuotas.
7. La tasa de interés de una tarjeta de crédito es muy baja.
8. Una hipoteca es un préstamo a largo plazo que se usa para comprar una casa.

Estructura • Repaso

Pronombres de complemento
Referring to people and things already mentioned

1. The pronouns **me, te, nos** in Spanish can be either a direct or an indirect object.

DIRECT	INDIRECT
¿Él te conoce?	**¿Él te debe dinero?**
Sí, me conoce.	**No, no me debe nada.**

2. The pronouns **lo, la, los,** and **las** are direct object pronouns. They can refer to persons or things.

Tengo el cheque.	**Lo tengo.**
Tengo la tarjeta de crédito.	**La tengo.**
Quiero ver los cargos.	**Los quiero ver.**
Quiero ver las facturas.	**Las quiero ver.**
Invité a Juan.	**Lo invité.**
Invité a sus amigas también.	**Las invité también.**

3. **Le** and **les** are indirect object pronouns. They can replace both masculine and feminine nouns. Since they can refer to different people, they are often clarified by a prepositional phrase.

Le hablé { **a él. / a ella. / a usted.** }

Les hablé { **a ellos. / a ellas. / a ustedes.** }

Avenida Balboa, Ciudad de Panamá, Panamá

Conversación

¿Cómo lo digo?

1 Historieta El señor Salas Contesten.

1. ¿Te vio el señor Salas?
2. ¿Te habló de tus finanzas?
3. ¿Te dijo que es fácil usar el cajero automático?
4. ¿Te preguntó si tienes una tarjeta bancaria?

2 Historieta En la fiesta Completen.

Teresa __1__ llamó a Luis y a mí. Ella __2__ invitó a la fiesta. Ella __3__ llamó a ti también, y __4__ invitó, ¿no? Perdón, ahora tengo que tocar el piano, porque Teresa __5__ lo pidió. A mí __6__ gusta mucho la música latina. ¿Y a ti __7__ gusta también?

3 Historieta Al cajero automático

Contesten con pronombres.

1. ¿Quién necesita el dinero? ¿Sandra?
2. ¿Tiene ella su tarjeta bancaria?
3. ¿Introduce la tarjeta en el cajero automático?
4. ¿Ella lee las instrucciones en la pantalla?
5. ¿Ella comprende las instrucciones?
6. ¿Ella pulsa los botones?
7. ¿Entra su código?
8. ¿Cuenta el dinero que sale?
9. ¿Pone el dinero en su cartera?
10. ¿Pone su cartera en su bolso?

Canal de Panamá, Panamá

4 Historieta Sandra salió para Panamá. Completen.

Sandra llegó al mostrador de la línea aérea en el aeropuerto. Ella __1__ habló al agente. Ella __2__ habló en español. Sandra __3__ dio las maletas al agente y el agente __4__ puso en la báscula y __5__ pesó. El agente __6__ dijo a Sandra cuanto pesaban. La pasajera __7__ dio su boleto al agente. El agente __8__ miró. Facturó el equipaje, y __9__ dio el boleto y los talones a Sandra. El agente __10__ dio las gracias a la pasajera y __11__ deseó un feliz viaje.

Dos complementos en la misma oración
Referring to people and things already mentioned

1. Very often both a direct and an indirect object pronoun appear in the same sentence. When they do, the indirect object comes before the direct object.

Él me dio el dinero.	**Él me lo dio.**
Ella te devolvió la chequera.	**Ella te la devolvió.**

2. The indirect object pronoun **le** and **les** change to **se** when used with **lo, la, los,** or **las.**

¿La factura? Yo se la di	**a él.** **a ella.** **a usted.** **a ellos.** **a ellas.** **a ustedes.**	**¿Los cheques de viajero? Yo se los di**	**a él.** **a ella.** **a usted.** **a ellos.** **a ellas.** **a ustedes.**

Canal de Tortuguero, cerca de Puerto Limón, Costa Rica

¿Cómo lo digo?

5 **¿Quién te lo compró?** Sigan el modelo.

la hamaca →
—¿Quién te la compró?
—Mi hermano me la compró cuando estaba en Centroamérica.

1. la mola
2. la estatua
3. los animales tallados
4. el calendario
5. la figura del jaguar
6. las vasijas
7. las piezas de cerámica
8. la pirámide

¿Te gusta? Sigan el modelo.

—¿Te gusta el traje?
—Sí, mucho. ¿Quién te lo dio?
—Nadie me lo dio. Me lo compré.

1. ¿Te gustan las botas?
2. ¿Te gusta el saco?
3. ¿Te gusta la camisa?
4. ¿Te gusta el pantalón?
5. ¿Te gustan los mocasines?
6. ¿Te gustan las corbatas?

Sololá, Guatemala

Finanzas Contesten según el modelo.

—¿Le diste el código a Elena?
—No, se lo di a Tomás.
—¿Se lo diste a él? ¿Por qué?

1. ¿Le diste la tarjeta a Elena?
2. ¿Le diste el talonario a Elena?
3. ¿Le enviaste los billetes a Elena?
4. ¿Le diste las monedas a Elena?
5. ¿Le diste el cheque a Elena?

8 **Historieta Una carta a la abuela**

Contesten con pronombres.

1. ¿Le escribiste una carta a abuelita?
2. ¿Le mandaste un cheque?
3. ¿Les enviaste tus saludos a sus hermanos?
4. ¿Le mandaste las fotos de la familia?
5. ¿Le dijiste que se las mostrara a sus hermanos?
6. ¿Crees que abuelita te contestará la carta enseguida?

¡Te toca a ti!

Use what you have learned

¿Qué tipo eres?

✔ ***Describe your personal financial habits***

En cuanto a tus finanzas personales, ¿qué tipo de persona eres? ¿Compras sólo lo que puedes pagar al contado? Si no tienes los recursos necesarios, ¿compras algo que quieres o no? ¿Usas mucho una tarjeta de crédito? ¿Pagas el saldo total o no? ¿Te molesta comprar a cuotas y tener que hacer pagos mensuales? ¿Te gusta gastar tu dinero fácilmente o prefieres ahorrar dinero?

Un peligro

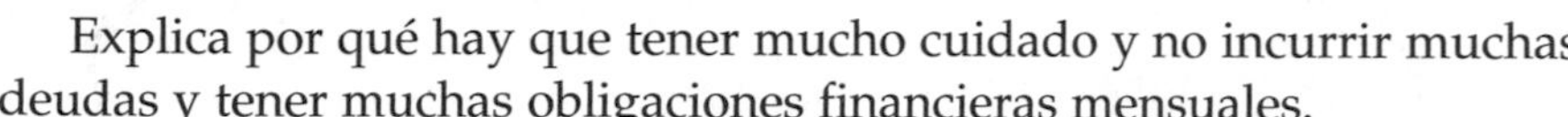

✔ ***Discuss the possible pitfalls of increasing your spending habits***

Explica por qué hay que tener mucho cuidado y no incurrir muchas deudas y tener muchas obligaciones financieras mensuales.

Una beca

✔ ***Discuss options for student loans and financial aid for college***

Muchas veces es necesario recibir una beca para pagar o a lo menos ayudar a pagar los gastos universitarios. Y a veces es necesario pedir un préstamo estudiantil. En este momento, ¿qué condiciones están en vigencia? ¿Cuál es la tasa de interés? ¿Puedes tener el préstamo por un plazo de cuánto tiempo? ¿Cuándo tendrás que empezar a hacer pagos?

Universidad de San Carlos de Borromeo, Guatemala

El cajero automático

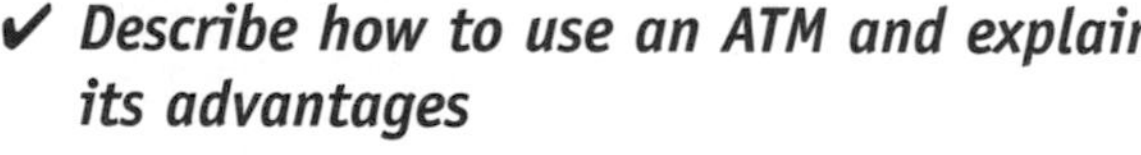

✔ ***Describe how to use an ATM and explain its advantages***

Explica a alguien como usar el cajero automático. Explícale las ventajas de usarlo en un país extranjero.

Al contado o no

✔ ***Describe financial payment options***

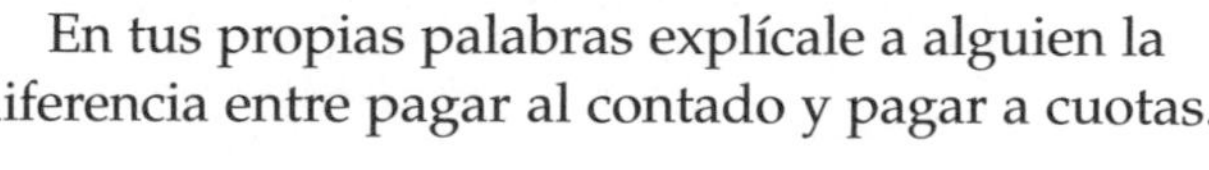

En tus propias palabras explícale a alguien la diferencia entre pagar al contado y pagar a cuotas.

Assessment

Vocabulario

1 Completen.

1–2. Para escribir cheques es necesario tener una ____ en el banco y los gastos no pueden exceder el ____ que tienes en la cuenta.

3–6. Si vas a usar el ____, tienes que seguir las instrucciones en la ____; introducir tu ____, y pulsar unos botones para entrar tu pin o ____.

7. Cuando recibes una ____, la tienes que pagar.

8–9. Una hipoteca es ejemplo de un ____ a largo ____.

10. Si no puedes pagar al contado, lo puedes pagar ____ después de hacer un pago inicial.

11–12. La ____ es más alta para un préstamo a largo plazo que para un préstamo a ____ plazo.

To review vocabulary, turn to pages 182–183.

Conversación

2 Contesten.

13. ¿Qué ciudad es el centro financiero de todo Latinoamérica?

14. ¿Cuál es la moneda oficial de Panamá?

15. ¿Por qué no va a necesitar Sandra cheques de viajero?

16. Cuando uno retira dinero del cajero automático, ¿de dónde se saca?

17. ¿Qué acepta la mayoría de los negocios? ¿Con qué puedes pagar?

18. ¿Cuándo es necesario pedir un préstamo?

19. ¿Qué significa comprar algo a cuotas?

20. Y, ¿pagar al contado?

To review the conversation, turn to pages 185–186.

Estructura

3 Completen.

21–26. —Roberto, ¿quién ____ regaló los anteojos para el sol?
—Pues, mi hermana ____ ____ regaló. ¿____ gustan?
—Sí, ____ gustan mucho. ____ voy a comprar unos parecidos.

27–33. —Antonia, ¿____ diste la tarjeta a Enrique?
—Sí, ____ ____ di ayer.
—¿Cuándo ____ ____ va a devolver?
—____ ____ va a devolver mañana. Y no estoy preocupada porque Enrique es un tipo muy serio.

34–40. —Anita, ¿a cuánto ____ salieron las molas?
—¿Cuáles, Elena, las que ____ mostré anoche?
—No, ____ ____ mostraste esta mañana, no anoche.
—Ah, esas. ____ salió en unos veinticinco cada una.
—Pero, ¿cuántas molas compraste?
—Compré a lo menos cinco. ____ encantan. Yo ____ considero verdaderas obras de arte.

To review object pronouns, turn to pages 187 and 189.

Avenida Balboa, Ciudad de Panamá, Panamá

Periodismo

Vocabulario para la lectura

Anuncios sociales

Use your StudentWorks Plus™ CD for more practice.

La pareja quería que se efectuara su matrimonio en la iglesia parroquial.
Ellos deseaban que todos sus familiares estuvieran presentes.

Más vocabulario

el deceso la muerte, el fallecimiento
el/la difunto(a) una persona muerta
la esquela el obituario
el velorio acción de velar el cadáver de un difunto; el velatorio
culminar dar fin a una cosa, terminar, acabar
debutar realizar un debut
efectuarse tener lugar, realizarse, llevar a cabo
fallecer morir
felicitar expresar buenos deseos a una persona
festejar celebrar

¿Qué palabra necesito?

1 **Eventos de la vida** Contesten.

1. ¿Querían sus padres que él culminara su carrera universitaria?
2. ¿Se graduó cuando culminó la carrera?
3. ¿Se casó la pareja?
4. ¿Querían que su matrimonio se efectuara en la iglesia parroquial?
5. ¿Querían que sus familiares estuvieran presentes?
6. ¿Les felicitaron sus familiares después de la ceremonia?

2 **Otra palabra, por favor.** Expresen de otra manera.

1. Ellas *realizaron su debut* en una gala en el Club Náutico.
2. Todos los familiares y amigos asistieron *a la boda.*
3. Todos sus amigos le *expresaron sus buenos deseos* al graduado.
4. Después de la ceremonia todos *festejaron* por la felicidad de los graduados.
5. El señor *murió* ayer.
6. *El obituario* salió en el periódico.
7. *El velatorio* será en Funerales Ortiz.
8. *El sepelio* se efectuará en el cementerio municipal.

Iglesia de San José, Panamá

Anuncios sociales

Se suelen marcar los pasajes de la vida con una ceremonia. Y por lo general se quiere informar a todas las personas que pudieran tener interés en el evento. Una manera eficaz de informar a un amplio público es por medio del periódico donde se anuncian las galas, los cumpleaños, las bodas y las muertes. Aquí tenemos algunos de estos anuncios que aparecieron en el periódico *La Prensa* en Panamá.

Sociales

La Prensa

Noche de alegría, lujo y esplendor

La noche del viernes pasado estuvo llena de belleza y alegría, al debutar cuarenta jóvenes en la sociedad en el 48.° festival de debutantes organizado por las Damas Guadalupanas. El evento se celebró en la Terraza Mar del Sur del Club Unión y contó con la presencia de familiares, amigos e invitados de las jóvenes que debutaron.

Graduación

La Universidad del Istmo felicita a Gabriel Velásquez por culminar con éxito un ciclo más de enseñanza en el departamento de postgrados y maestrías de la universidad.

Boda Guerra-Miranda

El altar de la Iglesia San Juan Bautista de Boquete fue escogido por la pareja formada por la señorita Danitza Miranda y Antonio Guerra para unir sus vidas en santo matrimonio. Los nuevos esposos son hijos de Honorio Gil y Nora Quiel de Miranda y de Antonio Guerra y Melva Pinto de Guerra. Luego de la ceremonia religiosa, los padres de los novios ofrecerán una elegante recepción que tendrá lugar en el salón Arco Iris de la Feria de las Flores y el Café, donde se festejará por la felicidad de Danitza y Antonio.

Primer añito

Hoy cumple su primer añito el encantador bebé Fernando F. Castro; que el niño Jesús lo proteja y lo guíe por el mejor camino, son los deseos de sus queridos abuelitos, tíos, primitos, y sus padres Luis Castro y Lizbeth de Castro.

Obituarios

Fallece padre de Jorge

En la madrugada del sábado, murió el padre del futbolista salvadoreño Jorge «Mágico» González.

Luego de padecer una grave enfermedad, falleció en el hospital Médico Quirúrgico, el señor Óscar González, padre de toda una generación de futbolistas como Efraín, conocido como «Pachín González»; Jesús, llamado «Chud González»; y de «Mágico González», considerado el mejor futbolista que ha dado El Salvador.

Los restos del señor González están siendo velados en Funerales Modernos, de esta capital, y está previsto que su entierro se efectuará para la tarde del domingo.

Al momento del deceso, Jorge González estaba fuera del país, integrando una selección de Estrellas en Estados Unidos.

de *El Diario de Hoy*
San Salvador

Funerales Reforma, lamenta el sensible fallecimiento de
José Luis Portillo Amaya
Falleció el día 6 de julio.
Descanse en paz.
El cortejo fúnebre sale el 7 de julio a las 15:00 de las capillas de: Funerales Reforma, Zona 9, hacia Santa Lucía Cotzumalguapa.
Guatemala, 7 de julio

de la *Prensa Libre*
Ciudad de Guatemala

¿Comprendes?

A Sociales Contesten.

1. ¿Dónde se celebró la gala de las debutantes?
2. ¿Cuántas jóvenes debutaron?
3. ¿Quiénes asistieron a la gala?
4. ¿Dónde culminó un ciclo más el joven?
5. ¿En qué iglesia se efectuó el matrimonio de la pareja?
6. ¿Qué ofrecerán los padres de los novios?
7. ¿Dónde tendrá lugar?
8. ¿Cuántos años cumple el niño?

Catedral Santiago, Managua, Nicaragua

B Obituarios Contesten.

1. ¿Dónde y cuándo falleció el padre del futbolista Jorge González?
2. ¿Para cuándo está previsto el entierro?
3. ¿Murió el padre antes de que volviera su hijo de Estados Unidos?
4. ¿Cuándo falleció José Luis Portillo Amaya?
5. ¿De dónde y cuándo saldrá el cortejo fúnebre?
6. ¿Dónde se efectuará el sepelio?

LECCIÓN 3

Periodismo

Vocabulario para la lectura

Amigos con «cédula»

La mascota se extravió.
Los dueños no sabían dónde estaba.
La buscaban por todas partes.
Le rogaban a quien encontrara su mascota que se la devolviera.

Más vocabulario

la cédula tarjeta de identidad, documento
el extravío acción de tomar un camino equivocado
las siglas OTAN, AAA, OEA son siglas
devolver (ue) restituir (dar) una cosa a la persona que la poseía
rechazar resistir, lo contrario de «aceptar»

¿Qué palabra necesito?

1 **Historieta** **Su mascota** Contesten.

1. ¿Estaban desesperados los Gómez?
2. ¿No podían encontrar su perro?
3. ¿Temían que él se extraviara?
4. ¿Tenían miedo de que alguien lo robara?
5. ¿Le rogaban a quien encontrara su mascota que se la devolviera?

2 **¿Cuál es la palabra?** Completen.

1. Mucha gente adora a su _____. No hay nada más adorable que un perrito o un gatito.
2. En muchos países los ciudadanos tienen que llevar siempre una _____ de identidad.
3. Él tiene mi lápiz. Yo lo necesito y él no me lo quiere _____.
4. No lo va a _____. Lo va a aceptar.
5. OEA son las _____ de la Organización de Estados Americanos.

Darién, Panamá

Al Día

San José, Costa Rica

Amigos con «cédula»

«Chip» se implanta en animales para poder identificarlos.

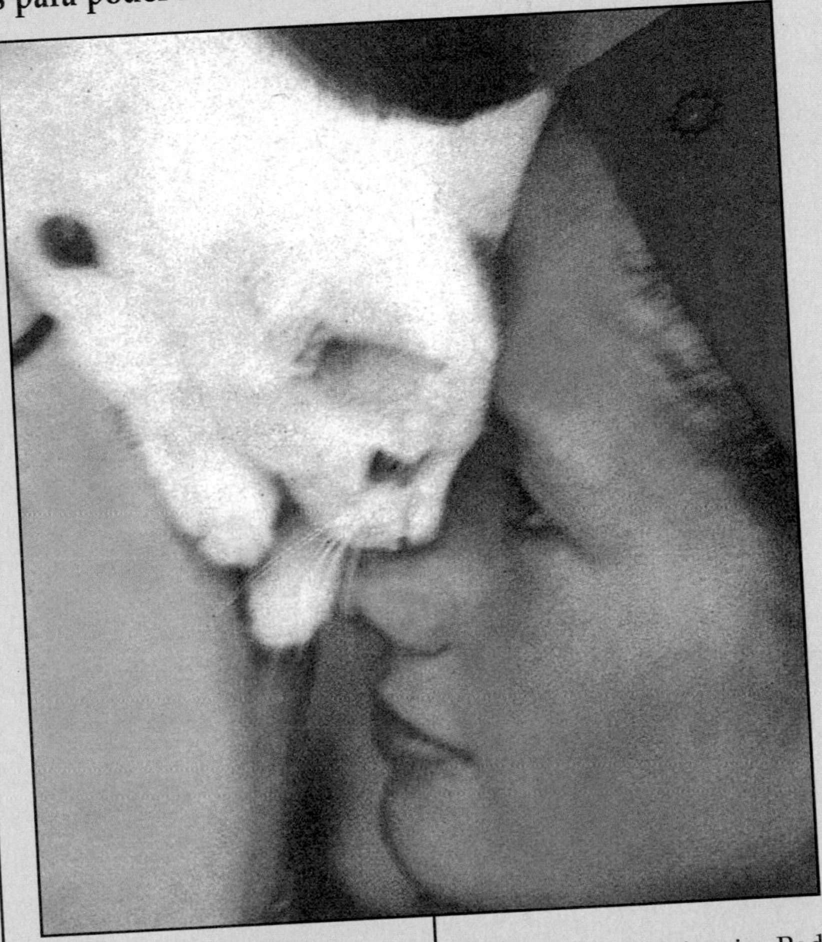

A veces, ver abierta la puerta de la casa que da a la calle es una mala señal. Puede significar que el perro salió y anda vagando por el barrio. A menudo hay que preguntar a los vecinos o salir a «patrullar» las calles para dar con la mascota.

La angustia y la preocupación que invade a los dueños es fuerte. Sin embargo, esas sensaciones podrían ser cosa del pasado.

Para que «los mejores amigos del hombre» puedan ser identificados y devueltos a casa se creó un microchip que se les coloca en el cuerpo y reúne toda su información. Esta pequeña pieza, aunque parezca ciencia-ficción, es lo último en tecnología.

Aunque ya tiene algunos años en el mercado aún no es muy difundido en el país y se llama AVID, (siglas en inglés para *American Veterinarian Identification Device*) y en Costa Rica se usa desde hace un año y medio.

Al servicio

«Este sistema fue ideado por una compañía estadounidense para proporcionar una identificación individual de todas las mascotas y así poder localizarlas mediante el servicio ID Animal (como una cédula), en caso de extravío,» explicó el veterinario Oldemar Echandi, de la veterinaria Doctores Echandi.

El AVID es un pequeñísimo circuito de computadora, recubierto con una proteína biocompatible (que el cuerpo del animal no rechaza) y almacena[1] el número de identificación de cada mascota.

«Es como la punta de un lápiz, se inyecta bajo la piel y es inalterable e irremovible,» aseguró el veterinario Pedro Villalobos, de la Veterinaria Lutz.

Ambas veterinarias, Dr. Echandi y Lutz, implantan el AVID en el país y dan el servicio de identificación con un costo de ¢7.000 y ¢8.000 respectivamente.

«Si un animal se pierde o es robado, el dueño puede comprobar que es suyo con sólo revisar el chip,» comentó Villalobos.

[1] almacena *stores*

¿Cómo se implanta?

Este dispositivo se aplica mediante una sencilla inyección, con un aparato especial mediante la cual el microchip es colocado bajo la piel del animal, específicamente en la región cruz (lomo). La aplicación no significa ninguna molestia para las mascotas.

Aunque el dispositivo sólo se coloca en perros y caballos, es posible usarlo en cualquier otro animal, incluso en aves.

«Antes nosotros lo implantábamos en animales salvajes, pero luego se exportó a los domésticos,» aseguró Echandi.

Además, el chip se puede colocar en animales de cualquier edad pues no causa efectos secundarios negativos.

«Una vez inyectado la capa que recubre al microchip evita su migración del sitio donde se puso y garantiza la permanencia y durabilidad por el resto de la vida del animal,» explicó Echandi.

Este chip no funciona con baterías, ni requiere mantenimiento. La memoria computarizada del mismo contiene un código individual e irrepetible, por lo que es imposible que existan dos iguales.

Para leer el código se utiliza un lector[2] especial, el cual al ser activado registra el número en una pantalla de cristal líquido.

«Una vez identificada la serie, ésta se mete en la computadora, la cual indica el nombre del propietario, su dirección y cédula, así como las características del animal ya sea raza, color y edad,» comentó Echandi.

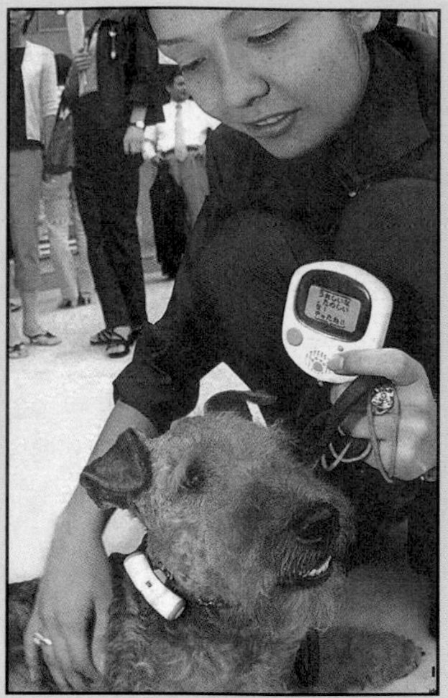

Este código no sólo funciona en Costa Rica (se aplica en más de veinticinco veterinarias en San José, Cartago, Heredia y Alajuela), pues también en Estados Unidos, Canadá, Europa y todo Latinoamérica.

[2] lector *scanner*

¿Comprendes?

A **Protección** Contesten.

1. ¿Por qué puede ser una puerta abierta que da a la calle una mala señal?
2. ¿Quiénes son «los mejores amigos del hombre»?
3. ¿Qué se ha creado?
4. ¿Dónde se coloca el microchip?
5. ¿Qué es el AVID? Descríbelo.

B **El microchip** Expliquen.

1. como se implanta
2. por cuanto tiempo dura el chip
3. como funciona
4. lo que se usa para leer el código
5. la información que da el código
6. donde funciona el código

Estructura • Avanzada

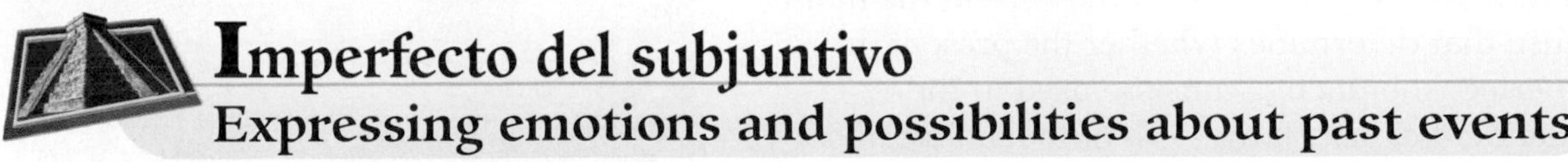

Imperfecto del subjuntivo
Expressing emotions and possibilities about past events

1. The imperfect subjunctive of all verbs is formed by dropping the **-on** ending of the third person plural, **ellos(as),** form of the preterite tense of the verb.

PRETERITE	hablaron	comieron	pidieron	tuvieron	dijeron
STEM	hablar-	comier-	pidier-	tuvier-	dijer-

2. To this stem, you add the following endings: **-a, -as, -a, -amos, *-ais*, -an.**

INFINITIVE	hablar	comer	pedir	tener	decir
yo	hablara	comiera	pidiera	tuviera	dijera
tú	hablaras	comieras	pidieras	tuvieras	dijeras
él, ella, Ud.	hablara	comiera	pidiera	tuviera	dijera
nosotros(as)	habláramos	comiéramos	pidiéramos	tuviéramos	dijéramos
vosotros(as)	*hablarais*	*comierais*	*pidierais*	*tuvierais*	*dijerais*
ellos, ellas, Uds.	hablaran	comieran	pidieran	tuvieran	dijeran

IRREGULAR VERBS			
andar	anduvieron	anduvier-	anduviera
estar	estuvieron	estuvier-	estuviera
tener	tuvieron	tuvier-	tuviera
poder	pudieron	pudier-	pudiera
poner	pusieron	pusier-	pusiera
saber	supieron	supier-	supiera
querer	quisieron	quisier-	quisiera
venir	vinieron	vinier-	viniera
hacer	hicieron	hicier-	hiciera
leer	leyeron	leyer-	leyera
oír	oyeron	oyer-	oyera
decir	dijeron	dijer-	dijera
conducir	condujeron	condujer-	condujera
traer	trajeron	trajer-	trajera
ir	fueron	fuer-	fuera
ser	fueron	fuer-	fuera
dar			dieras

3. The same rules that govern the use of the present subjunctive govern the use of the imperfect subjunctive. It is the tense of the verb in the main clause that determines whether the present or imperfect subjunctive must be used in the dependent clause. If the verb of the main clause is in the present or future tense, the present subjunctive is used in the dependent clause.

   Quiero que ellos me digan donde se casarán.
   Será necesario que lo sepamos pronto.

4. When the verb of the main clause is in the preterite, imperfect, or conditional, the imperfect subjunctive must be used in the dependent clause.

   Él habló así para que comprendiéramos.
   Quería que ellos me representaran.
   Sería absolutamente imposible que yo asistiera.

Puerto Limón, Costa Rica

5. The following is the sequence of tenses for using the present and imperfect subjunctive.

Main clause	Dependent clause	Main clause	Dependent clause
Present **Future**	**Present Subjunctive**	**Preterite** **Imperfect** **Conditional**	**Imperfect Subjunctive**

¿Cómo lo digo?

Él lo quería. Sigan el modelo.

invitarlo →
Él quería que yo lo invitara.

1. mirarlo
2. pagarlo
3. comerlo
4. devolverlo
5. escribirlo
6. servirlo
7. tenerlo
8. saberlo
9. hacerlo
10. leerlo
11. decirlo
12. ponerlo

2 Historieta Los padres de Alejandra Contesten.

1. ¿Querían los padres de Alejandra que ella asistiera a la universidad?
2. ¿Insistieron en que ella culminara su carrera?
3. ¿Se alegraban de que ella se graduara con honores?
4. ¿Quería Alejandra que ellos pusieran un anuncio en el periódico?

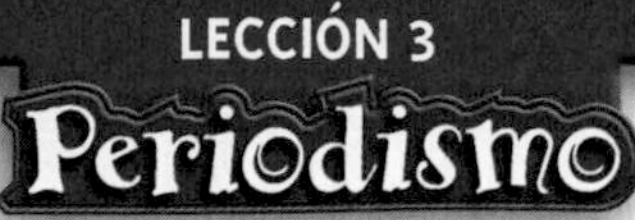

Historieta Una mascota extraviada Contesten.

1. ¿Tenían miedo tus vecinos mayores que su perro se extraviara?
2. ¿Te rogaron que lo buscaras?
3. ¿Sería necesario que tú anduvieras por todo el barrio buscándolo?
4. ¿Estaban contentos con que tú quisieras y pudieras ayudarlos?
5. ¿Querías que ellos pusieran un anuncio en el periódico?

Nuestro profesor exigente Sigan el modelo.

hablarle en español →
Nuestro profesor insistió en que le habláramos en español.

1. hablar mucho
2. pronunciar bien
3. llegar a clase a tiempo
4. aprender la gramática
5. escribir composiciones
6. leer novelas
7. trabajar mucho
8. hacer nuestras tareas

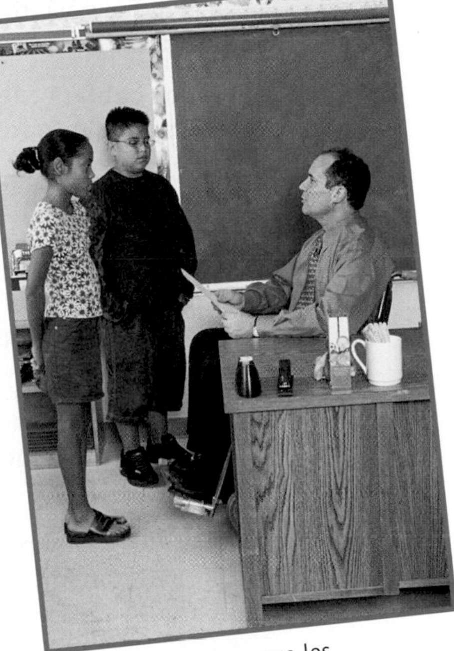

El profesor insiste en que los alumnos escuchen.

Historieta Un viaje Sigan el modelo.

¿Él hace un viaje? →
¿Sería posible que él hiciera un viaje?

1. ¿Él va a Centroamérica?
2. ¿Tú lo acompañas?
3. ¿Visitan Panamá?
4. ¿Toman el tren de Colón a Balboa?
5. ¿Hacen una excursión a las islas San Blas?

Tren de Balboa a Colón, Panamá

Las finanzas Completen.

1. Ella quiere que yo cambie dinero.
   Ella quería que yo _____ dinero.
2. Ella espera que hables con el cajero.
   Ella esperaba que _____ con el cajero.
3. Ella exige que yo traiga cheques de viajero.
   Ella me dijo que sería importante que yo _____ cheques de viajero.
4. Ella insiste en que el banco le haga cambio.
   Ella insistió en que el banco le _____ cambio.
5. Ella quiere que ellos pongan su dinero en el banco.
   Ella quería que ellos _____ su dinero en el banco.

¿Iría o no? Completen.

1. Él irá con tal de que _____ ustedes. (ir)
2. Él iría con tal de que _____ ustedes. (ir)
3. Ellos no harán el viaje a menos que _____ bastante dinero. (tener)
4. Ellos no harían el viaje a menos que _____ bastante dinero. (tener)
5. Tu padre te dará el dinero para que tú _____ hacer el viaje. (poder)
6. Tu padre te daría el dinero para que tú _____ hacer el viaje. (poder)

Subjuntivo con conjunciones de tiempo
Using time expressions

Use your StudentWorks Plus™ CD for more practice.

1. The subjunctive is used with adverbial conjunctions of time when the verb of the main clause is in the future, since it is uncertain if the action in the adverbial clause will really take place. When the verb in the main clause is in the past, the indicative is used since the action of the clause has already been realized.

   Ella nos hablará cuando lleguemos.
   Ella nos habló cuando llegamos.

2. Some frequently used adverbial conjunctions of time that follow the same pattern are:

cuando	*when*	**hasta que**	*until*
en cuanto	*as soon as*	**después de que**	*after*
tan pronto como	*as soon as*		

3. The conjunction **antes de que,** *before,* is an exception. **Antes de que** is always followed by the subjunctive. The imperfect subjunctive is used after **antes de que** when the verb of the main clause is in the past or in the conditional.

   Ellos saldrán antes de que nosotros lleguemos.
   Ellos salieron antes de que nosotros llegáramos.
   Ellos saldrían antes de que nosotros llegáramos.

¿Cómo lo digo?

8 **Yo** Contesten personalmente.

1. ¿Qué piensas hacer en cuanto te gradúes?
2. ¿Qué piensas hacer cuando tengas tu diploma universitario?
3. Cuando seas mayor, ¿vas a tener tu propia tarjeta de crédito?
4. Cuando pagues tus facturas, ¿vas a escribir cheques o vas a pagar todo *online?*
5. Cuando tengas tu propia familia, ¿necesitarás una hipoteca para comprarte una casa?
6. Cuando compres un carro, ¿lo vas a pagar a cuotas?

9 **Historieta** **¿Cuándo sea o cuándo fue?** Completen.

1. Ellos quieren casarse en cuanto ____. (poder)
2. Van a casarse cuando el novio ____ del ejército. (volver)
3. Luego tendrán que esperar hasta que se ____ todos los planes. (hacer)
4. Ellos se casaron en cuanto ____. (poder)
5. Se casaron cuando él ____ del ejército. (volver)
6. Esperaron hasta que se ____ todos los planes. (hacer)

¡Te toca a ti!

Use what you have learned

En nuestro periódico

✔ ***Discuss your local newspaper's social announcements***

¿Qué tipo de anuncios sociales salen en tu periódico? ¿Son parecidos a los que salen en un periódico hispano? ¿Te interesan o no? ¿Los lees?

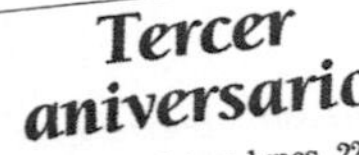

Tercer aniversario

El próximo lunes, 22 de diciembre, a las siete de la noche, se ofrecerá una misa de recordación de quien fuera distinguida dama, doctora Carmita Olavarrieta, al cumplirse el tercer año de su triste fallecimiento. La doctora Olavarrieta, durante muchos años, fue miembro destacada de distintas organizaciones cívicas, culturales y sociales, y muy especialmente de UNICEF. Piadoso acto al que invita su viudo, el doctor José Luis Olavarrieta.

Un anuncio social

✔ ***Create your own wedding announcement***

Escribe un anuncio sobre el matrimonio de unos amigos tuyos. Puede ser ficticio.

Mi mascota

✔ ***Describe your family pet***

¿Tienes una mascota? Descríbela. ¿La adoras? ¿Cuáles son algunas cosas «adorables» que hace? ¿Saldrá si dejas una puerta abierta? ¿Se extravía de vez en cuando o regresa (vuelve) enseguida?

Amigos con «cédula»

✔ ***Discuss the article about inserting a chip in your pet***

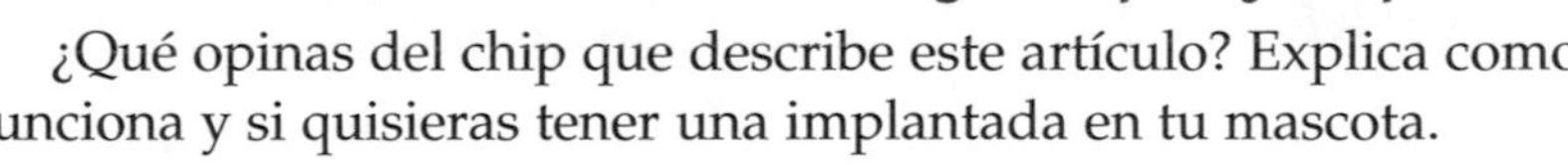

¿Qué opinas del chip que describe este artículo? Explica como funciona y si quisieras tener una implantada en tu mascota.

Niña con su mascota, Portobello, Panamá

Mi adorable familia

✔ ***Discuss with a classmate all the things your family would like to have you do***

Habla con un(a) compañero(a). Dile todo lo que tu adorada familia quisiera que tú hicieras. A tu parecer, ¿son muy exigentes o no? Tu compañero(a), ¿quisiera su familia que él/ella hiciera más o menos las mismas cosas?

En el futuro

✔ ***Describe your plans for the future***

Habla de todo.

- lo que quieres hacer en cuanto termines con la escuela secundaria
- lo que esperas hacer cuando seas adulto(a)
- lo que quieres hacer antes de que cumplas los veintiún años

Vocabulario

1 Completen.

1. La ____ se casará en junio.
2. Su matrimonio ____ en la iglesia parroquial.
3. Todos sus amigos ____ a los nuevos casados.
4. Unas cuarenta muchachas lindas ____ en una gran gala en el Club Náutico de la ciudad.

To review vocabulary, turn to pages 194 and 198.

2 Den otra palabra.

5. terminar, acabar
6. una persona muerta
7. morir
8. la muerte
9. conjunto de personas
10. festejar

Lectura

3 Contesten.

To review these social announcements, turn to page 196.

11. La noche del viernes pasado estuvo llena de belleza y alegría. ¿Qué pasó en la terraza del Club Unión?
12. ¿Por qué felicitó la Universidad del Istmo a Gabriel Velásquez?
13. ¿Qué ofrecieron los padres de los nuevos esposos después de la ceremonia religiosa?
14. ¿Cuántos años cumplió el encantador bebé?

4 Lean y contesten.

Funerales Reforma, lamenta el sensible fallecimiento de
José Luis Portillo Amaya
Falleció el día 6 de julio.
Descanse en paz.
El cortejo fúnebre sale el 7 de julio a las 15:00 de las capillas de: Funerales Reforma Zona 9, hacia Santa Lucía Cotzumalguapa.
Guatemala, 7 de julio

de la *Prensa Libre*
Ciudad de Guatemala

For more Chapter 4 test preparation, go to the Chapter 4 **Self-Check Quiz** on the Glencoe Spanish Web site at glencoe.com.

15. ¿Quién murió?
16. ¿Cuándo?
17. ¿De dónde saldrá el cortejo fúnebre?
18. ¿En qué cementerio se efectuará el sepelio?

Estructura

5 Sigan el modelo.

saberlo →
Fue necesario que él lo supiera.

19. comprarlo
20. recibirlo
21. leerlo
22. hacerlo
23. pedirlo
24. decirlo
25. ponerlo
26. pagarlo

To review the imperfect subjunctive, turn to pages 201–202.

6 Completen.

27. Él estaba viajando cuando ____ su padre. (morir)
28. Él volverá en cuanto ____ de su muerte. (saber)
29. ¿Podrán esperar hasta que él ____? (regresar)
30. No, el sepelio se efectuó antes de que él ____. (llegar)

To review the subjunctive with expressions of time, turn to page 204.

Proficiency Tasks

Composición

Al escribir algo expositivo, puede ser necesario tomar algunos apuntes sobre el tema o tópico expositivo que quieres desarrollar. Tomando apuntes te ayuda a organizar tu escrito y evitar la posibilidad de introducir información errónea.

TAREA 1

Durante tus estudios de español has aprendido mucho sobre las costumbres y tradiciones de los habitantes de los países latinoamericanos. Ahora vas a escribir un escrito expositivo sobre estas costumbres y tradiciones. Antes de empezar a escribir piensa en todo lo que has aprendido sobre este sujeto. Escribe rápido algunas notas sobre los hechos, datos e ideas que recuerdas. Si sólo puedes escribir tres o cuatro notas tendrás que leer de nuevo la lectura cultural de este capítulo y las de los Capítulos 2 y 3. Al leer, toma apuntes.

Luego escoge los hechos que has encontrado interesantes. Al escribir tu escrito expositivo recuerda que es necesario que tus lectores puedan seguir fácilmente tus ideas. Por consiguiente hay que escribir de una manera muy clara.

El buen escritor quiere también captar el interés de los que leen su escrito. Para que tu escrito sea más vivo da algunos ejemplos de las actividades que ilustran las costumbres y tradiciones que estás describiendo.

Antes de empezar a escribir haz una lista de los sujetos sobre los cuales quieres escribir. Algunos ejemplos son:

las lenguas
las prácticas religiosas
la vida en la selva
la vida en el altiplano
la comida
el transporte

Luego escribe algunos datos o ideas que quieres desarrollar en tu escrito.

Ahora puedes empezar a escribir tu primer borrador. Toma tus notas, organizándolas en párrafos.

Al terminar tu escrito, no olvides de revisarlo.

TAREA 2

Has aprendido mucho sobre las diferentes civilizaciones precolombinas igual que grupos indígenas de hoy. Vas a escribir un ensayo en el cual vas a comparar y contrastar estas civilizaciones. Cuando comparas dos cosas, tienes que explicar como son similares (semejantes). Cuando las contrastas tienes que explicar como son diferentes. Al comparar y contrastar hay que analizar. Antes de empezar a escribir tienes que identificar las semejanzas y las diferencias entre las diferentes civilizaciones. Un diagrama tal como el siguiente te puede ayudar.

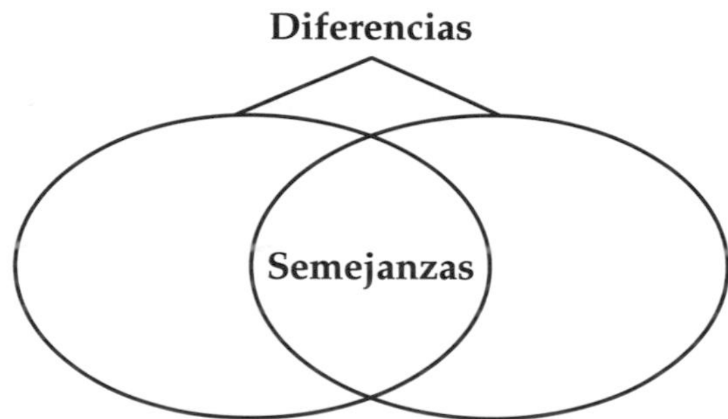

Hay que decidir como vas a organizar tu ensayo. Puedes escoger el sujeto como los mayas, por ejemplo, y escribir todo lo que tienes que decir sobre ellos. O puedes organizar tu ensayo por tema o tópico, tal como la arquitectura. Si organizas tu ensayo por tema, tienes que aplicar este tema a los varios sujetos al mismo tiempo.

Una narración o un escrito narrativo cuenta algo. Puede contar la vida de una persona, un acontecimiento, un evento, una película, una emisión televisiva. Muchos escritores de narración inventan los personajes o lugares de sus cuentos. En este caso sólo tienen que consultar su imaginación antes de empezar a escribir. A veces escogen una figura histórica y tienen que buscar hechos y eventos.

Ahora vas a escribir una narración sobre tu mascota, si tienes mascota. Describe a tu mascota—su apariencia y personalidad, sus acciones y comportamientos. ¿Es tu mascota tu mejor amigo(a)? ¿Por qué?

Si no tienes mascota tendrás que usar tu imaginación. ¿Qué tipo de mascota quisieras tener? ¿Qué harías con tu mascota? Si prefieres no tener mascota, explica por qué. ¿La encuentras una molestia?

Muchas veces tenemos que escribir algo que le dé instrucciones a una persona—como hacer algo o como reparar algo, por ejemplo. Al escribir unas instrucciones hay que dar detalles muy precisos para que el lector sepa exactamente lo que tiene que hacer. Si la receta para un plato no está bien escrita, al seguirla el cocinero puede estropear el plato completamente.

Tienes un(a) amigo(a) que no tiene muy buena memoria para los detalles y no sabe usar el cajero automático. Escríbele las instrucciones paso a paso.

Discurso

Cuando hablas, la gente que te escucha pone más atención a lo que dices si hablas con entusiasmo. Como se dice en inglés *Get fired up!*—es decir, «¡dale tu máximo!» Aún si hablas a una sola persona, pero sobre todo si te diriges la palabra a un grupo, hay que tener entusiasmo y energía. Nadie quiere escuchar una estatua sin vida. Al pronunciar un discurso hay que ser una fuente de inspiración para los que te escuchan. Algo bastante ordinario puede ser interesante y hasta divertido si lo presentas con entusiasmo y energía.

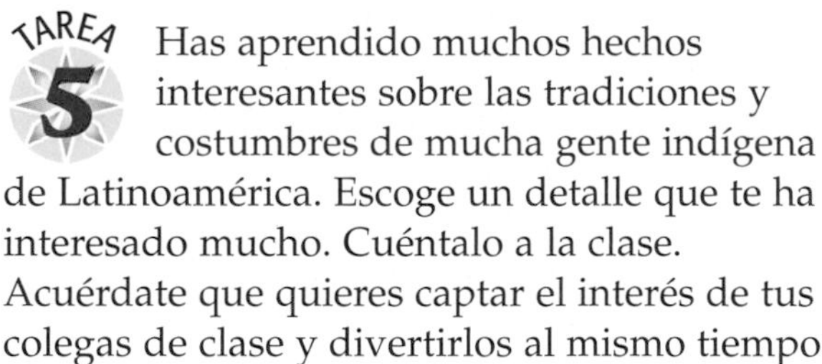

Has aprendido muchos hechos interesantes sobre las tradiciones y costumbres de mucha gente indígena de Latinoamérica. Escoge un detalle que te ha interesado mucho. Cuéntalo a la clase. Acuérdate que quieres captar el interés de tus colegas de clase y divertirlos al mismo tiempo.

Vocabulario

Lección 1 Cultura

el animal tallado
el bohío, una choza de paja
la callejuela de adoquines
la destrucción
la estela
la hamaca
la mola
la pelota
el rascacielos
el techo
el terremoto
fuerte
picante
botar
causar
colgar (ue)
soler (ue)
trasladar

Lección 2 Conversación

el billete
el botón
el cajero automático
el cargo
la casa de cambio
el cheque
la chequera, el talonario
el código
la cuenta corriente
el dinero
el dólar
la factura
la hipoteca
la moneda
el monto
la pantalla
el pin
el préstamo
el saldo
el suelto
la tarjeta
el tipo de cambio
a corto plazo
a largo plazo
bancario(a)
en efectivo
cambiar
cobrar
introducir
oprimir
pagar a cuotas (a plazos)
pagar al contado
pulsar

Lección 3 Periodismo

Anuncios sociales

el cortejo
la debutante
el deceso
el/la difunto(a)
el entierro, el sepelio
la esquela
el familiar
la iglesia
el matrimonio, la boda
la pareja
el velorio
parroquial
culminar
debutar
desear
efectuarse
fallecer
felicitar
festejar

Amigos con «cédula»

la cédula
el/la dueño(a)
el extravío
el lomo
la mascota
la sigla
devolver (ue)
encontrar (ue)
extraviarse
rechazar
rogar (ue)

LITERARY COMPANION *See pages 456–463 for literary selections related to Chapter 4. The activities for these readings will help you continue to practice your reading comprehension skills.*

VIDEOTUR

¡Viva el mundo hispano!

Video can be a beneficial learning tool for the language student. Video enables you to experience the material in the textbook in a real-life setting. Take a vicarious field trip as you see people interacting at home, at school, at the market, etc. The cultural benefits are limitless as you experience the Spanish-speaking world while "traveling" through many countries. In addition to its tremendous cultural value, video gives practice in developing good listening and viewing skills. Video allows you to look for numerous clues that are evident in tone of voice, facial expressions, and gestures. Through video you can see and hear the diversity of the target culture and compare and contrast the Spanish-speaking cultures to each other and to your own.

Episodio 1: Una artesanía costarricense

Los agricultores costarricences hoy usan tractores. Pero hace un siglo usaban carretas tiradas por bueyes. La gente entonces empezó a decorar sus carretas. Las pintaban de colores vivos y brillantes y diseños complicados. Hoy las carretas son parte del folclore de Costa Rica. Los artesanos pintan estas carretas para exhibirlas.

Episodio 2: Soñadores y malabaristas

Hace muchos siglos que acróbatas, malabaristas y payasos presentan sus espectáculos en las calles y plazas de todo el mundo. Estos jóvenes son miembros del grupo *Magos del tiempo* en San José, Costa Rica. El grupo se estableció en 2002. Aquí uno de ellos está enseñándoles a los compañeros como hacer malabarismo.

Episodio 3: Una finca de mariposas

En esta finca no crían vacas ni ovejas. Lo que crían son mariposas. María Fernanda guía a un grupo de visitantes por la finca. La mariposa comienza como un huevecito. Luego se convierte en larva y después en crisálida. La Finca de Mariposas envía crisálidas a todo el mundo. Una visita a la Finca de Mariposas es una experiencia inolvidable.

Capítulo 5

México

Spanish Online
To interact with your online edition of ¡Buen viaje! go to: glencoe.com.

Objetivos

In this chapter you will:

- learn about the geography, history, and culture of Mexico
- review how to express what you have done recently
- review how to give commands
- discuss traveling by car in Mexico
- review how to describe actions in progress
- review how to refer to people and things already mentioned
- read and discuss articles about windsurfing and Mexican families
- learn to describe actions completed prior to other actions
- learn to express what you would have done and will have done
- learn to express indefinite ideas and the known and unknown

Contenido

LECCIÓN I

Cultura

Vocabulario para la lectura

El desierto es árido.
Ha llovido poco.
En los desiertos áridos vemos cactos y flores silvestres.

En la bandera mexicana un águila devora una serpiente que tiene en sus garras.

En la selva tropical hay muchos animales y pájaros.
Estos animales han vivido en la selva por generaciones.
Pero, ha llegado la influencia del hombre a la selva.
La deforestación y la caza hacen desaparecer la fauna.
Han desaparecido árboles y animales.

Más vocabulario

el ajuste el arreglo, la modificación
el/la aliado(a) colaborador, miembro de una alianza
el centauro criatura mítica que es medio hombre y medio caballo
los restos vestigios, residuos
Mesoamérica México, Centroamérica y las Antillas
adelantado(a) desarrollado, progresivo
aterrador(a) que causa terror, muchísimo miedo
temible espantoso, aterrador, terrorífico
juntarse unirse

¿Qué palabra necesito?

Sonora

1 Historieta La naturaleza Contesten.

1. ¿Ha llovido poco en el desierto?
2. ¿Hemos visto cactos y flores allí?
3. En la selva, ¿ha desaparecido mucha fauna?
4. ¿Han deforestado la selva los hombres?
5. ¿Los animales han perdido su hábitat?
6. ¿Se han juntado algunos ecologistas para proteger la fauna y flora?

2 ¿Cuál es la palabra?

Den la palabra cuya definición sigue.

1. el que es un colaborador o camarada
2. una modificación que se hace para hacer algo más preciso
3. que causa mucho miedo o terror
4. una criatura mítica, medio hombre, medio caballo
5. un ave que aparece en la bandera mexicana
6. lo que queda de una civilización antigua
7. bien desarrollado
8. México, Centroamérica y las Antillas

El Castillo, Chichén Itzá

Lectura

> **Reading Strategy**
>
> **Guessing meaning from context** It's easy to understand words you have already studied. There are also ways to understand words you are not familiar with. One way is to use the context—the way these words are used in the sentence—to help you guess the meaning of those words you do not know.

La geografía

México con Canadá y Estados Unidos forma el continente norteamericano. Al sur de México están Guatemala y Belice donde comienza la América Central. El territorio mexicano es extenso. Es cuatro veces más grande que España.

Las costas

Las aguas del golfo de México y del mar Caribe bañan las costas orientales de la república y las del océano Pacífico las costas occidentales. México goza de magníficas playas al este y al oeste. Cancún, Cozumel e Isla Mujeres en el Caribe tienen playas muy bonitas. Puerto Vallarta, Acapulco e Ixtapa son destinos populares en el Pacífico. Todas estas playas atraen[1] turistas de todo el mundo.

Cancún

Puebla

La meseta y las sierras

Una enorme meseta cubre gran parte del país. De norte a sur se extienden las dos grandes sierras, la Sierra Madre Occidental y la Sierra Madre Oriental. Estas sierras forman un cuadro[2] que rodea la meseta. Las dos sierras se juntan en el sur por medio de la cordillera neovolcánica donde se encuentran tres altísimos e impresionantes volcanes—el pico de Orizaba, Popocatépetl e Iztaccíhuatl.

[1] atraen *attract*
[2] cuadro *square, frame*

Desiertos y selvas

Gran parte del norte del país es árido. En los desiertos de Sonora y Chihuahua, a pesar de[3] que durante años ha llovido muy poco hay preciosos cactos y flores silvestres. En contraste con el clima desértico de mucho del norte, en el sureste encontramos selvas tropicales. En el estado de Chiapas, está la selva Lacandona. En esta selva hay fauna típica de Centroamérica; armadillos y tapires, guacamayos y quetzales y hasta jaguares que, lamentablemente, casi han desaparecido a causa de la caza y de la pérdida de hábitat por deforestación.

Clima

Como hemos visto, el clima de México es de una gran variedad; un árido norte, un tórrido sur tropical y una gran meseta con un clima templado de bruscas diferencias de temperatura y grandes cambios entre el día y la noche.

[3] a pesar de *in spite of*

Selva Lacandona

Paseo de la Reforma en la Ciudad de México

A Contesten.

1. ¿Cuáles son los países que forman el continente de Norteamérica?
2. ¿Qué países están al sur de México?
3. ¿Cuál de los dos países es más grande, México o España?
4. ¿Qué océano está al oeste de México?
5. ¿Adónde van muchos turistas que visitan a México?
6. ¿Cuáles son dos volcanes mexicanos?
7. ¿Dónde se encuentran estos volcanes?
8. ¿Qué parte de México es mayormente árido, el norte o el sur?
9. ¿Qué flora se ve en los desiertos de Sonora y Chihuahua?
10. ¿Qué hay en el sureste de México, desiertos o selvas?
11. ¿Dónde se encuentra la selva Lacandona?
12. ¿Cuáles son algunos animales de la selva mexicana?
13. ¿Cuáles son algunas causas de la desaparición de ciertos animales?
14. ¿Cómo se llama el tipo de clima de la meseta?

La historia

El México de nuestros días se ha creado de una fusión de culturas que ha resultado del encuentro de los españoles con las adelantadas civilizaciones de Mesoamérica. Ésta fusión comenzó cuando llegó Hernán Cortés en 1520. Pero la historia de esta gran república se remonta[4] a muchos siglos antes de esa fecha.

Las épocas precolombinas

Sus primeros habitantes llegaron a México desde el norte durante la «Edad de Piedra». Al principio fueron cazadores-recolectores[5]. Más tarde aprendieron el cultivo del maíz.

Los olmecas

Los adelantos en la agricultura permitieron la fundación de grandes comunidades y la oportunidad de dedicarse la gente a más que la mera supervivencia[6]. En esta época aparece la primera importante cultura, la de los olmecas. Ellos levantaron centros ceremoniales y pirámides. También nos han dejado colosales cabezas y otras masivas figuras talladas en basalto, una piedra volcánica. Los antropólogos consideran esta la «cultura madre» de la civilización en Mesoamérica.

Los olmecas han desaparecido pero han dejado su influencia en las culturas que la han seguido como las de los mayas, los toltecas y los aztecas.

Cabeza colosal, La Venta

Calendario maya

Los mayas

Ya se ha dicho que los mayas eran excelentes matemáticos y astrónomos y que su calendario fue uno de los más exactos que nos vienen de tiempos antiguos. Se llamaba el Haab. Este calendario dividía el año en 365 días, como el nuestro, pero los 365 días se dividían en 18 períodos o meses de 20 días cada uno con un período de 5 días al final. Los mayas sabían compensar las fracciones de horas y segundos por día causadas por las variaciones en la rotación e inclinación de la tierra. Agregaban[7] días enteros después de cierto número de años, lo que hacemos hoy con los años bisiestos[8] en los calendarios modernos. Todo esto lo hicieron sin la tecnología ni los instrumentos que tenemos hoy. Lo hicieron a base de observación e infinita paciencia.

[4] se remonta *goes back*
[5] cazadores-recolectores *hunters/gatherers*
[6] supervivencia *survival*
[7] Agregaban *They added*
[8] años bisiestos *leap years*

Los toltecas

Los toltecas se establecieron en el valle de México donde levantaron la ciudad de Tula con una población de quizás cuarenta mil. Eran buenos comerciantes y feroces guerreros.

Los aztecas

El último gran imperio de Mesoamérica fue el de los aztecas. Los aztecas fueron temibles guerreros. Su principal dios era Huitzilopochtli, el dios de la guerra. Según la tradición, Huitzilopochtli les mandó a los aztecas salir de su tierra en el norte y buscar un lugar mejor. Les dijo que el sitio sería donde vieran a un águila sobre un cacto (nopal) devorando una serpiente que tenía entre sus garras. La vieron en una isla de un lago. Allí se establecieron en lo que llegaría a ser Tenochtitlán, el sitio donde hoy en día se encuentra la Ciudad de México. El águila y la serpiente están conmemoradas para siempre en la bandera mexicana.

Tula, México

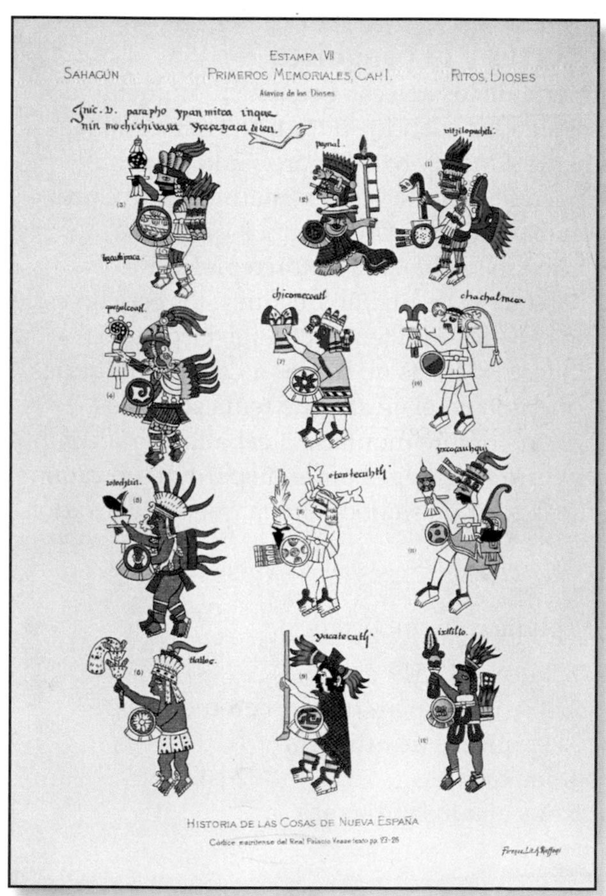

Dioses aztecas

 ¿Sí o no?

1. Los primeros habitantes de México vinieron del sur durante la «Edad de Piedra».
2. Al principio no eran agricultores, eran cazadores-recolectores.
3. La «cultura madre» de Mesoamérica es la de los mayas.
4. El calendario de los aztecas era el *Haab.*
5. La causa de las fracciones de horas y segundos son las variaciones en la rotación e inclinación de la tierra.
6. Los mayas no sabían compensar las fracciones de horas y segundos.
7. El calendario dividía el año en doce meses de veinte días.
8. El año maya era de 365 días.

C ¿Qué será un «año bisiesto»? ¿Para qué sirve el año bisiesto? ¿Con qué frecuencia hay años bisiestos? Expliquen, por favor.

D Completen.

1. Los _____ construyeron la ciudad de Tula.
2. Tula estaba en el _____.
3. El imperio _____ fue el último gran imperio de Mesoamérica.
4. El dios de los aztecas, Huitzilopochtli, era el dios de la _____.
5. Los aztecas se establecieron donde vieron un águila con una _____ en sus garras.
6. La imagen del águila y la serpiente está en la _____ mexicana.

Ruinas de Tenochtitlán, Ciudad de México

Hernán Cortés y la conquista

El imperio de los aztecas gozaba su momento de máximo esplendor cuando su mundo iba a cambiar drásticamente. Once barcos llegaron a la península de Yucatán en febrero de 1519. Vinieron desde Cuba. Abordo estaban Hernán Cortés, unos quinientos hombres, dieciséis caballos y catorce piezas de artillería. Poco más de un año después, los españoles, con muchos aliados indígenas, conquistaron a los aztecas. En las Américas no había ni caballos ni armas de fuego. Piensen en el efecto que tenía sobre los aztecas ver un hombre montado a caballo. Sería como ver un centauro. Y después oír el disparo de un cañón y ver el fuego salir de su boca. Tenía que ser aterrador.

Hernán Cortés

E Expliquen su importancia.

1. Yucatán, 1519
2. los once barcos que vinieron de Cuba
3. las piezas de artillería
4. los caballos
5. los aliados indígenas

Si haces una visita...

Si un día decides visitar a México tienes que ir primero a la capital. Vete al Zócalo, o la plaza mayor, en el centro histórico de la Ciudad de México. Fue construido sobre las ruinas de Tenochtitlán. Allí verás la Catedral Metropolitana, los restos del Templo Mayor de los aztecas y el Palacio Nacional con magníficas murallas de Diego Rivera. Después, visita el Museo Nacional de Antropología para ver los artefactos que representan las culturas tolteca, maya y azteca, incluso la piedra calendario de los aztecas, similar al calendario maya, y las cabezas colosales de los olmecas.

Si tienes hambre busca donde comer unos tamales, tostadas, quesadillas o tacos, todos a base de tortilla de maíz, tortilla hecha a mano y no unas tortillas de fábrica. El maíz es la base de toda una cultura y el tema de varios murales del gran artista Diego Rivera. Rivera es sólo uno de los grandes muralistas mexicanos. José Clemente Orozco y David Alfaro Siqueiros, contemporáneos de Rivera, junto con él revolucionaron el arte muralista. También contemporánea de los famosos muralistas fue Frida Kahlo, gran pintora mexicana y esposa de Diego Rivera.

Catedral Metropolitana, Ciudad de México

Museo Nacional de Antropología Ciudad de México

Preparando tortillas de Diego Rivera

Cultura

Después de comer, descansa un rato paseando por el Bosque de Chapultepec. En este bello parque hay museos de arte y un castillo del siglo XVIII. Aquí está el monumento a los «Niños Héroes», jóvenes cadetes que murieron defendiendo el castillo contra tropas norteamericanas en 1847.

Después de visitar la capital, tienes que decidir adonde ir después. ¿A las playas? ¿A los pueblos coloniales como San Miguel de Allende o Guanajuato? ¿Te interesa la arqueología? Pues, anda a ver las pirámides de Teotihuacán o los templos de Chichén Itzá.

En este maravilloso país hay de todo y para todos los gustos.

Monumento a los Niños Héroes, Ciudad de México

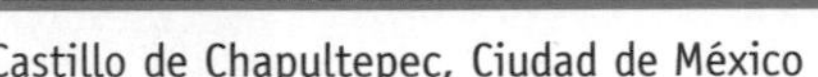

Castillo de Chapultepec, Ciudad de México

San Miguel de Allende

Teotihuacán

Contesten.

1. ¿Qué es el Zócalo?
2. ¿Sobre qué construyeron el Zócalo?
3. ¿Qué hay hoy día en el Zócalo?
4. ¿Por qué es famoso Diego Rivera?
5. ¿Cuál es el tema de varios de sus murales?
6. ¿Que podemos ver en el Museo Nacional de Antropología?
7. ¿Cuáles son algunos platos que se preparan con tortillas?
8. ¿Cómo se llama el parque donde hay un castillo del siglo XVIII?
9. ¿Quiénes eran los «Niños Héroes»?
10. ¿Cuáles son algunos lugares de interés arqueológico en México?

Estructura • Repaso

Presente perfecto
Telling what you have done recently

Use your StudentWorks™ Plus CD for more practice.

1. The present perfect tense is formed by using the present tense of the helping (auxiliary) verb **haber** and the past participle. Study the following forms of the present tense of the verb **haber.**

yo	he
tú	has
él, ella, Ud.	ha
nosotros(as)	hemos
vosotros(as)	*habéis*
ellos, ellas, Uds.	han

2. To form the past participle of regular verbs, drop the infinitive ending **-ar, -er, -ir** and add **-ado** to **-ar** verbs and **-ido** to both **-er** and **-ir** verbs.

hablar	comer	vivir
habl-	com-	viv-
hablado	comido	vivido

3. The following verbs have irregular past participles.

abrir	abierto
cubrir	cubierto
descubrir	descubierto
morir	muerto
volver	vuelto
poner	puesto
escribir	escrito
freír	frito
romper	roto
ver	visto
hacer	hecho
decir	dicho

Teatro Juárez, Guanajuato

4. Following are the forms of some regular and irregular verbs in the present perfect tense.

INFINITIVE	descansar	salir
yo	he descansado	he salido
tú	has descansado	has salido
él, ella, Ud.	ha descansado	ha salido
nosotros(as)	hemos descansado	hemos salido
vosotros(as)	*habéis descansado*	*habéis salido*
ellos, ellas, Uds.	han descansado	han salido

INFINITIVE	volver	escribir
yo	he vuelto	he escrito
tú	has vuelto	has escrito
él, ella, Ud.	ha vuelto	ha escrito
nosotros(as)	hemos vuelto	hemos escrito
vosotros(as)	*habéis vuelto*	*habéis escrito*
ellos, ellas, Uds.	han vuelto	han escrito

5. The present perfect tense is used to express a past action without reference to a particular time. It usually denotes an occurrence that continues into the present or relates closely to the present. Study the following.

Su madre ha estado enferma. *His mother has been ill.*

6. The adverb **ya** *(already)* is often used with the present perfect tense.

Ellos ya han visto el mural. *They have already seen the mural.*

Mosaico de David Alfaro Siqueiros, Universidad Nacional Autónoma de México

¿Cómo lo digo?

Historieta Civilizaciones precolombinas

Contesten según se indica.

1. ¿Desde dónde han llegado los primeros pobladores de México? (el norte)
2. ¿Ellos han sido agricultores? (no, cazadores-recolectores)
3. ¿Cuál de las culturas se ha llamado «la cultura madre»? (la olmeca)
4. ¿Qué nos han dejado los olmecas? (grandes figuras de basalto)
5. ¿Dónde hemos visto las figuras? (en el Museo de Antropología)
6. ¿Quiénes han sabido mucho de astronomía? (los mayas)
7. ¿Qué han descubierto los arqueólogos? (muchos artefactos)
8. ¿Han desaparecido los olmecas y los toltecas? (sí)

He estado en la playa recientemente.

Contesten.

1. ¿Has viajado a la playa recientemente?
2. ¿Has comido mariscos recientemente?
3. ¿Has nadado en el mar recientemente?
4. ¿Han sacado ustedes muchas fotos recientemente?
5. ¿Han escrito tarjetas postales a sus amigos recientemente?

Acapulco

Tulum

Historieta México Contesten personalmente.

1. ¿Has aprendido algo de la historia de México?
2. ¿Tu profesor o profesora ha hablado mucho de México?
3. ¿Tu profesor o profesora ha estado en México alguna vez?
4. ¿Han viajado a México tú y tu familia?
5. ¿Han visto ustedes los museos de la Ciudad de México?
6. ¿Han ido tú y tu familia a Tulum?
7. ¿Tus padres han aprendido un poco de español?
8. ¿Ha leído tu padre o tu madre una guía turística sobre México?

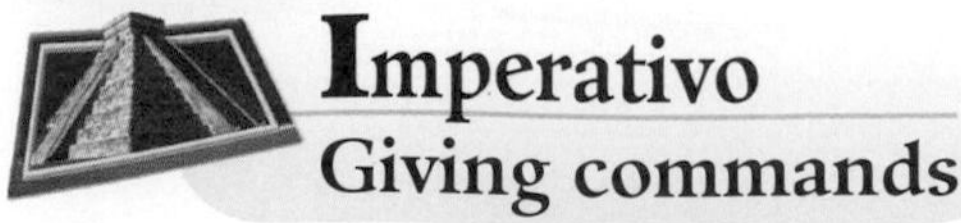

Imperativo
Giving commands

1. Most commands are expressed by using the subjunctive. Review the following.

	usted	ustedes	tú
hablar	(no) hable Ud.	(no) hablen Uds.	no hables
comer	(no) coma Ud.	(no) coman Uds.	no comas
subir	(no) suba Ud.	(no) suban Uds.	no subas
volver	(no) vuelva Ud.	(no) vuelvan Uds.	no vuelvas
pedir	(no) pida Ud.	(no) pidan Uds.	no pidas
salir	(no) salga Ud.	(no) salgan Uds.	no salgas
hacer	(no) haga Ud.	(no) hagan Uds.	no hagas
conducir	(no) conduzca Ud.	(no) conduzcan Uds.	no conduzcas
ir	(no) vaya Ud.	(no) vayan Uds.	no vayas

2. The affirmative **tú** command is not expressed by the subjunctive. The affirmative **tú** command of regular verbs is the same as the **usted** form of the present indicative.

hablar	habla
comer	come
subir	sube
volver	vuelve
pedir	pide

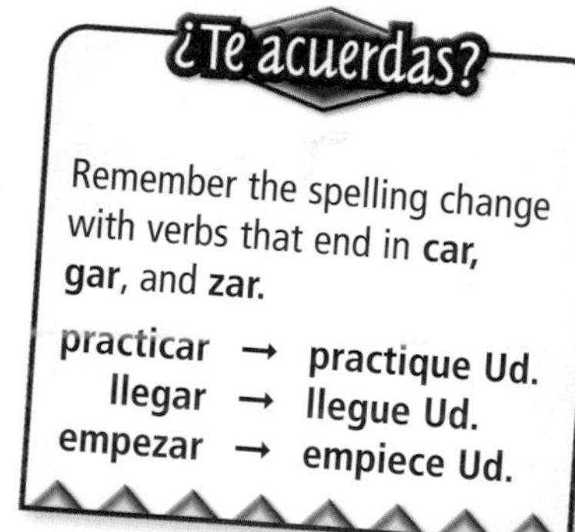

¿Te acuerdas?

Remember the spelling change with verbs that end in **car, gar,** and **zar.**

practicar → **practique Ud.**
llegar → **llegue Ud.**
empezar → **empiece Ud.**

3. The following verbs have irregular forms in the affirmative **tú** command.

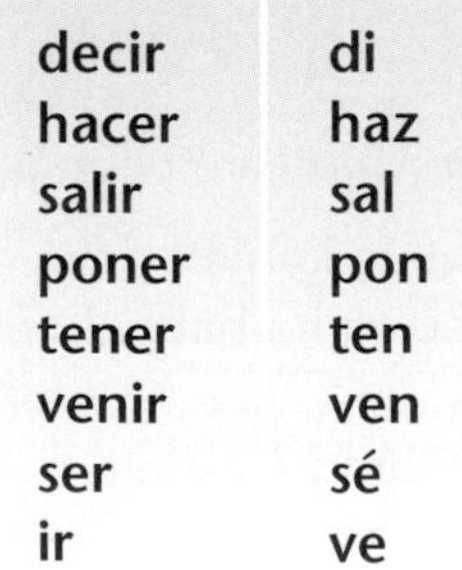

decir	di
hacer	haz
salir	sal
poner	pon
tener	ten
venir	ven
ser	sé
ir	ve

PRIMEROS AUXILIOS PARA ASFIXIAS POR INMERSION

- Mantenga la calma.
- Elimine cuerpos extraños de la boca (arena, comida, prótesis).
- Elimine el agua de los pulmones. Para ello, ponga de lado a la víctima y comprímale el abdomen.
- Al sacar a una persona accidentada desde aguas profundas, debe iniciarse la respiración boca a boca en cuanto pise firmemente o disponga de un bote o algún elemento que sirva de apoyo.
- Inicie respiración boca a boca y masaje (cinco masajes cardíacos alternadamente con una respiración).
- Abrigue al afectado.
- Mientras lo traslada a un centro asistencial, no suspenda las maniobras de resucitación.

¡Aprendamos a disfrutar del Agua!

¿Cómo lo digo?

4 ¿Qué debo hacer?

Contesten según el modelo.

—¿Debo volver a México?
—Sí, vuelva usted a México.

1. ¿Debo viajar a México?
2. ¿Debo esperar hasta el verano?
3. ¿Debo hablar con un agente de viajes?
4. ¿Debo leer la historia primero?
5. ¿Debo escribir a la oficina de turismo?
6. ¿Debo pedir información sobre el país?
7. ¿Debo ir a la selva tropical?
8. ¿Debo buscar flores silvestres?
9. ¿Debo visitar los museos?
10. ¿Debo volver a México en el invierno?
11. ¿Debo hacer compras antes de ir?

Palacio de Bellas Artes, Ciudad de México

For more information about Mexico, go to **Web Explore** on the Glencoe Spanish Web site at glencoe.com.

Veracruz

5 Quiero ir a Veracruz. ¿Me puede dar direcciones desde aquí en la capital?

Completen con el imperativo formal.

Sí, con mucho gusto. __1__ (Tomar) esta calle, Fray Servando Teresa de Mier por unas 2 millas. Entonces __2__ (virar) a la izquierda en dirección norte. Es el bulevar Puerto Aéreo. Enseguida __3__ (doblar) a la derecha y __4__ (entrar) en Ignacio Zaragoza. __5__ (Seguir) en Zaragoza unas 7 millas. __6__ (Continuar) en esta carretera que cambia su nombre a Autopista a Puebla. No __7__ (salir) de la carretera aunque cambia de nombre varias veces. __8__ (Tener) dinero a mano para pagar peaje. __9__ (Pasar) la ciudad de Puebla. Después de Puebla, __10__ (descansar) usted un rato porque quedan 160 millas para Veracruz. Y __11__ (conducir) con mucho cuidado. Son un total de 240 millas y 4 horas y media de viaje. ¡Buena suerte!

6 ¿Cómo se prepara un taco? Una receta

Completen con el imperativo formal.

San Miguel de Allende

__1__ (Calentar) el horno a temperatura moderada. En una sartén, __2__ (calentar) el aceite a fuego moderado. __3__ (Añadir) la cebolla y el ajo, __4__ (freír) hasta que la cebolla se dore y esté transparente. __5__ (Añadir) la salsa de tomate y __6__ (dejar) hervir. __7__ (Bajar) la temperatura y __8__ (cocinar) a fuego lento por cinco minutos. __9__ (Añadir) la carne y el cilantro y __10__ (mezclar) todo. __11__ (Cocinar) hasta que la mezcla esté caliente. __12__ (Retirar) de la hornilla. En una sartén, __13__ (calentar) 1/4 taza de aceite vegetal a fuego mediano-alto. __14__ (Freír) las tortillas rápidamente una a una, varios segundos por ambos lados. __15__ (Dividir) el relleno entre las tortillas y __16__ (enrollar) las tortillas. __17__ (Añadir) 1/2 taza adicional de aceite vegetal a la sartén y __18__ (calentar) aceite a fuego mediano-alto. __19__ (Freír) los tacos por grupos. __20__ (Voltear) los tacos una o dos veces hasta que estén dorados por todos los lados. __21__ (Poner) los tacos en papel toalla. __22__ (Adornar) los tacos a su gusto.

7 ¿Qué hago? Sigan el modelo.

Necesito hacer unos cálculos complicados. (usar la calculadora) →
Usa la calculadora.

1. Tengo sed. (tomar agua)
2. Tengo hambre. (comer el almuerzo)
3. Tengo un examen mañana. (estudiar ahora)
4. Quiero jugar baloncesto. (practicar con tus amigos)
5. Necesito escribir algo. (buscar un bolígrafo)
6. Quiero ver una película. (ir al cine)

8 Si quieres, hazlo. Contesten con sí y el imperativo familiar.

1. ¿Debo ir a un restaurante mexicano?
2. ¿Debo comer temprano?
3. ¿Debo reservar una mesa?
4. ¿Debo leer el menú?
5. ¿Debo pedir enchiladas?
6. ¿Debo probar chiles picantes?
7. ¿Debo dejar una propina?

Guanajuato

9 **No, no debes.** Contesten las preguntas de la Actividad 8 con **no** y el imperativo familiar **negativo.** Sigan el modelo.

—¿Debo ir a un restaurante mexicano?
—No, no vayas a un restaurante mexicano.

Guanajuato

10 **Pues, haz lo que tienes que hacer.** Completen con el imperativo familiar. Sigan el modelo.

Tengo que escribir sobre los aztecas. →
Pues, escribe sobre los aztecas.

1. Tengo que ir a clase.
2. Tengo que dar un informe.
3. Tengo que escribir sobre los aztecas.
4. Tengo que tener fotos.
5. Tengo que hacer un bosquejo *(outline)* primero.
6. Tengo que poner todos los acentos.
7. Tengo que decir algo sobre Cortés.
8. Tengo que ser interesante.

11 **Tú, sí. Ellos, no.** Sigan el modelo.

comer →
Tú, come. Pero no coman ustedes.

1. viajar a Puebla
2. leer el mapa
3. escribir postales
4. visitar los museos
5. subir las pirámides
6. pedir direcciones
7. volver tarde

Puebla

¡Te toca a ti!

Use what you have learned

Cañón del Cobre, Chihuahua

1 La geografía de México

HABLAR / ESCRIBIR

✔ ***Describe the geography of Mexico and compare it to Spain***

Has leído que México es cuatro veces más grande que España. En tus propias palabras describe como son similares México y España y cuales son algunos importantes contrastes. Piensa en el clima y la topografía. Luego, dibuja un mapa de México que demuestra su topografía. Consulta a tu profesor(a) si necesitas ayuda.

2 La historia de México

HABLAR

✔ ***Discuss some events and famous figures in the history of Mexico***

En un grupo de cuatro, hablen de todo lo que aprendieron sobre la historia de México. Mencionen algunos personajes famosos y expliquen su importancia. Algunas personas o figuras que podrán describir son: Hernán Cortés, Diego Rivera, Huitzilopochtli, Maximiliano de Austria, el padre Hidalgo, Benito Juárez, los Niños Héroes.

Fiestas y Celebraciones

Natalicio del General Ignacio Allende y Unzaga: (21 de enero) Celebración con actos cívicos y un desfile militar en honor al Insurgente Ignacio Allende.

Semana Santa: (marzo o abril) Comienza con el concurso de altares a la virgen de los Dolores y culmina con el Viernes Santo en una solemne procesión del Santo Entierro.

Fiesta de San Antonio de Padua: (13 de junio) Tradicional y popular desfile de "Los Locos" donde la gente participa disfrazada y con máscaras por las principales calles de la ciudad. Desfile con carros alegóricos, bandas musicales y mucha alegría.

Festival de Música de Cámara. (1-15 de agosto) Evento cultural que se realiza en el Teatro Angela Peralta bajo los auspicios del INBA.

Sanmiguelada. (Tercer sábado de septiembre) Encierro de toros estilo Pamplona. Se lleva a cabo en el Jardín Principal.

Fiesta de San Miguel Arcángel: (29 de septiembre) Celebración del Santo Patrono de la ciudad, se llevan a cabo eventos sociales, artísticos, deportivos, culturales además de sus famosas corridas de toros.

Feria Nacional de la Lana y el Latón: (segunda quincena de noviembre): Exposición en la que participan artesanos nacionales y extranjeros.

Festival Internacional de Jazz: (última semana de noviembre) Semana dedicada a presentaciones de bandas y solistas nacionales e internacionales en este genero musical.

Fiesta de Navidad: (segunda quincena de diciembre): Comienza el día 16 con las tradicionales posadas publicas. Se realizan pastorelas, música, cánticos, carros alegóricos, entre otros festejos populares.

3 El guía

ESCRIBIR

✔ ***Create a travel brochure***

Prepara unos párrafos en forma de propaganda turística para informar a la gente sobre lo que pueden ver en un viaje a México. Puedes buscar ejemplos de propaganda turística en español en el Internet o en una agencia de viajes en tu comunidad.

4 Algún día

HABLAR

✔ ***Describe what you want to do some day but have yet to do***

Hay tantas cosas que nos gustaría hacer algún día que hasta ahora no hemos hecho. Trabaja con un(a) compañero(a). Hablen de las cosas que quieren hacer algún día pero que hasta ahora no han hecho nunca. Expliquen por qué no las han hecho.

¡Come los vegetales!

✔ *Tell someone what they have to and do not have to do*

Imagínate que eres padre o madre de un niño muy travieso (*mischievous*). Dile las cosas que debe hacer y las que no debe hacer.

Del colegio al restaurante

✔ *Give directions*

Tu clase de español va a hacer una celebración en un restaurante mexicano cerca del colegio. Pero, ¡muchos no saben dónde está el restaurante! Con un(a) compañero(a) escriban las instrucciones para ir del colegio al restaurante. Indiquen las calles importantes y donde doblar. Escriban las instrucciones para tus compañeros. Palabras útiles:

doblar, virar, tomar, seguir, continuar, la calle, la avenida, la cuadra

Autorretrato con trenza de Frida Kahlo

Para pensar

✔ *Discuss the implications of Cortés' arrival in Mexico*

Cortés llegó a México con sólo quinientos soldados. ¿Cómo pudo conquistar el gran Imperio azteca? Con tu grupo de cuatro discutan los factores que contribuyeron a la derrota de los aztecas.

Las artes

✔ *Describe some well-known artists in Mexico*

México tiene una gran tradición artística. Busca un ejemplo de la obra de uno de los siguientes artistas, tráelo a clase y descríbelo a la clase. Habla un poco sobre el artista.

Clemente Orozco	Diego Rivera
David Alfaro Siqueiros	Frida Kahlo

Zapatistas de José Clemente Orozco

Assessment

Vocabulario

1 Completen con una palabra apropiada.

To review vocabulary, turn to page 214.

1. En el desierto hay _____ y flores silvestres.
2. El _____ es un ave que se encuentra en la selva tropical de México.
3. Los animales han perdido hábitat a causa de la caza y la _____.
4. Las civilizaciones de Mesoamérica no eran primitivas sino muy _____.
5. Los arqueólogos han encontrado los centros ceremoniales de antiguas civilizaciones, y han descubierto _____ como las de Egipto.

Lectura

2 Contesten.

To review some geographical facts about Mexico, turn to pages 216–217.

6. ¿Qué forman Estados Unidos, Canadá y México?
7. ¿Cómo se compara la extensión de México con la de España?
8. ¿En qué parte de México se encuentran las regiones más áridas?
9. ¿Qué son Popocatépetl, Iztaccíhuatl y Orizaba?
10. ¿Qué aguas bañan las diferentes costas de México?

3 Completen.

To review some historical and cultural facts about Mexico, turn to pages 218–222.

11. La «cultura madre» de México fue la de los _____.
12. Los _____ tenían excelentes matemáticos y astrónomos.
13. Los aztecas fundaron Tenochtitlán donde vieron un _____ devorando una serpiente.

4 Contesten.

14. En el Museo Nacional de Antropología hay enormes cabezas de basalto. ¿Quiénes las hicieron?
15. ¿Quiénes son dos famosos muralistas mexicanos?
16. ¿Cuáles son algunos platos que se hacen a base de la tortilla?
17. Se dividía en dieciocho períodos de veinte días con cinco días al final. ¿Qué era?

Estructura

5 Completen con el presente perfecto.

18. Muchos animales de la selva _____. (desaparecer)
19. Los aztecas nos _____ templos y pirámides. (dejar)
20. Nosotros _____ muchos artefactos en el museo. (ver)
21. Yo _____ a México con mi familila. (viajar)
22. Y tú, ¿_____ alguna vez a México? (ir)

To review the present perfect, turn to pages 223–224.

6 Completen con el imperativo apropiado.

23. Usted, _____ un momento. (esperar)
24. Tú, ¡_____ a tus padres! (escribir)
25. Y ustedes, ¡no _____ nada! (decir)
26. Usted, ¡_____ con nosotros! (venir)
27. Y tú, ¡no _____ muy tarde! (volver)
28. _____ ustedes un viaje a México. (hacer)
29. Tú, _____ ahora mismo. (ir)
30. Ustedes, no _____ tanto. (hablar)

To review commands, turn to page 226.

Coyoacán, México

LECCIÓN 2

Conversación

Vocabulario para la conversación

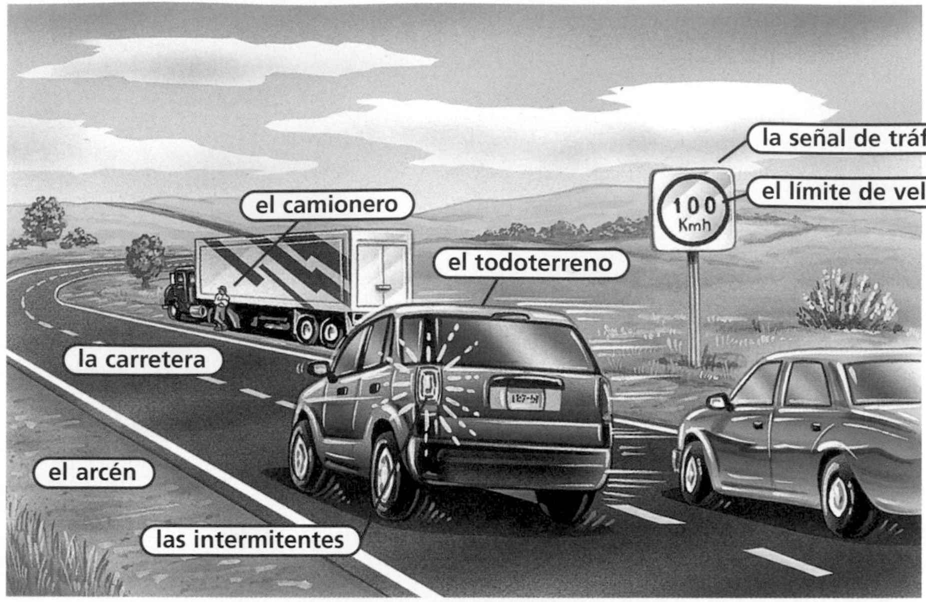

El todoterreno está rebasando un carro. Está rebasándolo con cuidado.
Hay un camión en el arcén derecho de la carretera. El camionero está descansando.
El límite de velocidad es de 100 kilómetros por hora.

la licencia de conductor

la tarjeta de crédito

el cinturón de seguridad

Ella se abrocha el cinturón de seguridad.

Más vocabulario

el cargo lo que uno tiene que pagar
el contrato papel legal que representa una obligación comercial
el kilometraje ilimitado kilómetros sin límite que el cliente puede recorrer
el seguro contrato que protege contra accidentes, daños, etc.
el semáforo la luz roja
el riesgo el peligro, la contingencia, la posibilidad de daño
firmar escribir su nombre
retroceder ir en marcha atrás, ir en reversa

¿Qué palabra necesito?

1 ¿Cuál es la palabra? Completen.

1. Hay que parar el carro cuando el ____ está en rojo.
2. Nunca debes exceder el ____ de ____.
3. Cuando vas a virar o doblar debes poner las ____.
4. Si tienes un problema puedes parar en el ____ de la derecha.
5. El semáforo es solamente una de las ____ de tráfico.
6. El camión es muy grande y el ____ tiene que ser buen conductor.
7. Siempre debemos ponernos el ____ cuando estamos en el carro.

Avenida de la Reforma, Ciudad de México

Baja California Sur

2 Historieta El todoterreno Contesten.

1. ¿Qué tipo de vehículo tiene tracción a cuatro ruedas?
2. ¿Necesitas una licencia para conducir un todoterreno?
3. ¿Se le permite al todoterreno rebasar por la derecha?
4. Cuando conduces un todoterreno, ¿debes tener cuidado al retroceder?

3 Historieta En la agencia de alquiler de carros Contesten con **sí**.

1. ¿Está alquilando un todoterreno el cliente?
2. ¿Va a pagarlo con tarjeta de crédito?
3. ¿El agente está añadiéndole cargos adicionales?
4. ¿También está vendiéndole un seguro?
5. ¿Va a dárselo contra todo riesgo?
6. ¿El agente está recomendando un contrato de kilometraje ilimitado?
7. ¿Está firmando el contrato el cliente?

LECCIÓN 2

Conversación

En la agencia de alquiler de carros

Cliente Buenos días.

Agente Buenos días, joven. ¿En qué puedo servirle?

Cliente Mis padres y yo estamos visitando parientes aquí en México. Yo estaba considerando alquilar un vehículo para recorrer el país.

Agente Excelente idea. Hoy estamos ofreciendo unos precios muy atractivos. ¿Qué tipo de vehículo le interesa y por cuánto tiempo va a quererlo?

Cliente Estaremos viajando por áreas rurales donde las carreteras no son muy buenas. Estábamos pensando en un todoterreno con tracción a cuatro ruedas. Se lo devolveremos en quince días.

Agente Muy bien. Podemos ofrecerle varios contratos. Tenemos uno con kilometraje ilimitado. Se lo recomiendo porque va a recorrer muchos kilómetros en quince días. El seguro contra todo riesgo está incluido.

Cliente Me parece muy bien. Aquí tiene mi licencia de conductor. Es la primera vez que estaré conduciendo en México. ¿Qué consejos me puede dar?

Agente Bueno, los normales. Lleve siempre el cinturón de seguridad. No exceda los límites de velocidad y obedezca todas las señales de tráfico y los semáforos. Y tenga mucho cuidado al retroceder y al rebasar.

Cliente ¿Rebasar? ¿Quiere decir adelantar o pasar?

Agente Precisamente. Ah, y dos cosas que hacemos aquí en México, sobre todo en las áreas rurales. Cuando un camionero pone la intermitente izquierda no es que va a virar. Está indicándole al que está detrás que puede rebasar.

Cliente Y si uno de veras quiere virar a la izquierda, ¿cómo puede hacerlo?

Agente Pues, nosotros nos ponemos en el arcén de la derecha y allí esperamos un claro en el tráfico para entonces virar.

Cliente Muchas gracias. Se lo agradezco mucho. Dígame, por favor, cuáles son los cargos y si puedo pagarlos con tarjeta de crédito.

Agente Claro que sí. Espéreme un momentito y le preparo el contrato. Se lo tendré listo enseguida. Su tarjeta y su licencia, por favor. Y, ¿dónde estarán hospedándose?

Cliente Aquí las tiene. Estaremos quedándonos con unos primos en Oaxaca. Este es su número de teléfono.

Oaxaca

¿Comprendes?

A Contesten.

1. ¿Dónde está el joven?
2. ¿Con quiénes está viajando el joven?
3. ¿A quiénes están visitando ellos?
4. ¿Qué está pensando alquilar el joven?
5. ¿Por dónde estarán viajando?
6. ¿Por cuánto tiempo estarán recorriendo el país?
7. ¿Qué están ofreciendo hoy en la agencia?
8. ¿Qué puede el agente ofrecerles?
9. ¿Qué está recomendándole el agente?
10. ¿Cómo estará pagando el cliente?

To learn more about the process of renting a car in a Spanish-speaking country, do the Chapter 5 **WebQuest** activity on the Glencoe Spanish Web site at glencoe.com.

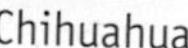

Chihuahua

B Expliquen.

1. un seguro contra todo riesgo
2. para lo que ponen la intermitente izquierda los camioneros
3. lo que hacen para virar a la izquierda en las áreas rurales de México
4. la ventaja del kilometraje ilimitado
5. tracción a cuatro ruedas

C Comenten sobre los consejos que da el agente al joven.

D Resuman y escriban la conversación en forma narrativa.

For more information about travel in Mexico, go to **Web Explore** on the Glencoe Spanish Web site at glencoe.com.

Estructura • Repaso

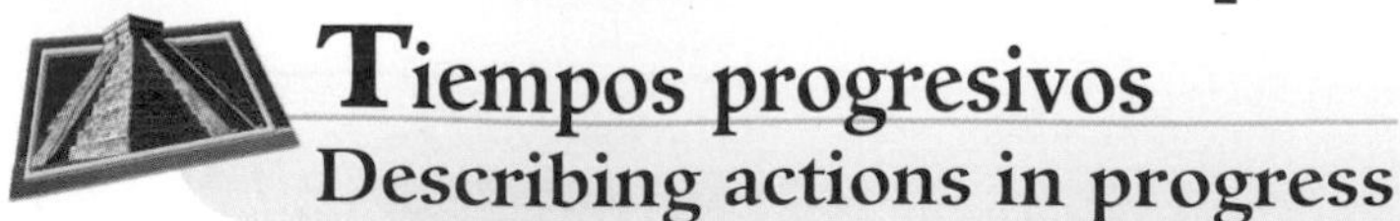

Tiempos progresivos
Describing actions in progress

1. The progressive tenses are used to express actions going on, actions viewed as in progress in the past, present or future. The progressive tenses are all formed with the appropriate tense of the verb **estar** and the present participle—*speaking, writing, etc.* To form the present participle of **-ar** verbs, drop the infinitive **-ar** ending and add **-ando.** For **-er** and **-ir** verbs drop the infinitive ending and add **-iendo.**

INFINITIVE	hablar	llegar	comer	hacer	salir
STEM	habl-	lleg-	com-	hac-	sal-
PARTICIPLE	hablando	llegando	comiendo	haciendo	saliendo

Note that the verbs **leer, traer,** and **construir** have a **y** in the present participle.

leyendo **trayendo** **construyendo**

2. Look at these examples of the progressive tenses.

Estoy mirando el mapa.
(present progressive)
Luisa estaba conduciendo.
(imperfect or past progressive)
Estaremos llegando pronto.
(future progressive)

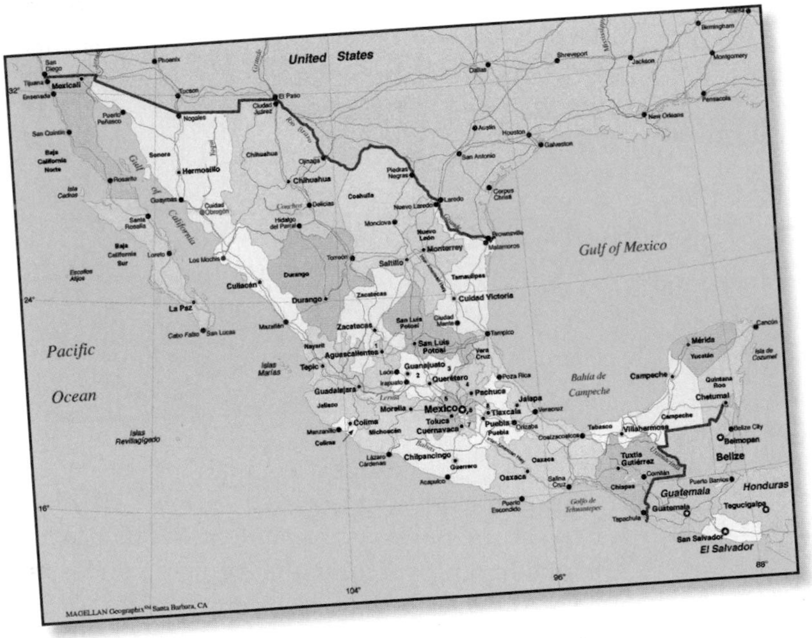

¿Cómo lo digo?

Historieta En clase

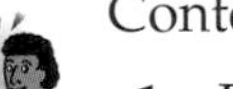

Contesten personalmente.

1. ¿Estás haciendo la tarea ahora?
2. ¿Estás escribiendo las respuestas?
3. ¿Estás estudiando mucho?
4. ¿Estás practicando el español?
5. ¿Estás escuchando al (a la) profesor(a)?
6. ¿Estás tomando apuntes?

2 Historieta ¿Estás conduciendo?

Contesten según se indica.

1. ¿Quién está conduciendo? (yo)
2. ¿Quiénes están llevando un cinturón de seguridad? (todos nosotros)
3. ¿Adónde están viajando ustedes? (a Chiapas)
4. ¿Está controlando el tráfico el policía? (sí)
5. ¿Quién está leyendo el mapa? (Roberto)
6. ¿Quiénes están escuchando la radio? (nosotros)

San Cristóbal de las Casas, Chiapas

3 Historieta Dentro de poco...

Completen con el futuro progresivo.

1. Dentro de poco nosotros _____ al aeropuerto. (llegar)
2. Dentro de poco toda la familia nos _____. (esperar)
3. Dentro de poco el asistente de vuelo _____ las tarjetas de turismo. (distribuir)
4. Dentro de poco el avión _____. (aterrizar)
5. Dentro de poco tú _____ México por primera vez. (ver)

4 No hace tantas horas que...

Completen la Actividad 3 con el imperfecto progresivo.

Colocación de los pronombres de complemento
Referring to people and things already mentioned

1. As you know, direct and indirect object pronouns precede a conjugated verb.

   Él me dio el mapa.
   Ellos nos regalaron las entradas.

2. Often both a direct and an indirect object pronoun can appear in the same sentence.

   Él me lo dio.
   Ellos nos las regalaron.

3. However, when a direct or indirect object pronoun is used with an infinitive **(-ar, -er, -ir)** or a present participle **(-ando, -iendo),** the pronoun or pronouns may either be attached to the infinitive or participle or precede the auxiliary verb that accompanies the infinitive or participle.

With the infinitive
Él quiere explicarte el problema. → **Él te quiere explicar el problema.**
Él quiere explicártelo. → **Él te lo quiere explicar.**
Él va a explicártelo. → **Él te lo va a explicar.**

With the present participle
Él estaba explicándole el problema. → **Él le estaba explicando el problema.**
Él estaba explicándoselo. → **Él se lo estaba explicando.**

4. Note that when two pronouns are attached to the infinitive, the infinitive carries a written accent to maintain the same stress. The present participle carries a written accent when either one or two pronouns is attached.

¿Cómo lo digo?

5 Historieta En el restaurante

Contesten con **sí.** Sigan el modelo.

—¿Estás comiendo el pescado?
—Sí, estoy comiéndolo.

1. ¿Estás leyendo el menú?
2. ¿Estás hablando al mesero?
3. ¿El mesero le está recomendando la especialidad de la casa?
4. ¿Estás pidiendo el pescado a la veracruzana?
5. ¿Tu amiga está pidiendo el plato combinado que lleva tacos, enchiladas y chiles rellenos?
6. ¿Están comiendo los frijoles refritos?
7. ¿Estás pidiendo la cuenta?
8. ¿Estás pagando la cuenta?

Un tamal
Una quesadilla

Una tostada

6 Historieta En la agencia de alquiler

Sigan el modelo.

Ella está hablando *al agente.* →
Ella le está hablando. Ella está hablándole.

1. El agente está atendiendo *a la cliente.*
2. La cliente está hablando *al agente.*
3. Ellos están discutiendo *el contrato.*
4. Ella quiere firmar *el contrato* ahora.
5. El agente está recomendando *el seguro a la cliente.*
6. La cliente va *a darle la tarjeta de crédito al agente.*
7. El agente le está dando *las llaves del todoterreno.*
8. Ella va a comprarle *el seguro al agente.*

Pronombres de complemento con el imperativo
Using commands

1. The direct and indirect object pronouns are always attached to affirmative commands. The pronouns precede negative commands.

FORMAL	
Hábleme usted.	**No me hable usted.**
Dígamelo en español.	**No me lo diga en español.**
Cómprenselo ustedes.	**No se lo compren ustedes.**

INFORMAL	
Háblame.	**No me hables.**
Dímelo en español.	**No me lo digas en español.**

2. Note that the command form carries a written accent when a pronoun is added.

¿Cómo lo digo?

7 **Venden un todoterreno.** Cambien del negativo en el afirmativo.

1. No nos lo demuestre usted.
2. No me lo describa usted.
3. No se lo compre usted.
4. No lo conduzca usted.

8 **Historieta En un restaurante mexicano**
Contesten según el modelo.

—**Voy a llamar *al cocinero.***
—**¡Buena idea! Llámalo.**

1. Voy a escoger *el restaurante.*
2. Voy a invitarlos *a ustedes.*
3. Voy a invitarlos *a Conrado y Susana* también.
4. Voy a probar *los tamales.*
5. Voy a pedirle *la cuenta al mesero.*
6. Voy a dejarle *una propina al mesero.*

San Miguel de Allende

9 **No, no.** Contesten las preguntas de la Actividad 8 con **¡Mala idea!** y el negativo.

—**Voy a llamar *al cocinero.***
—**¡Mala idea! No lo llames.**

10 **Regalos para todos** Sigan el modelo.

—**¿Compro los zapatos para mi amiga?**
—**Sí, cómpraselos.**

1. ¿Compro la corbata para mi padre?
2. ¿Compro los aretes para mi hermana?
3. ¿Compro la camisa para mi hermano?
4. ¿Compro el pantalón para mi madre?
5. ¿Compro las botas para mí?
6. ¿Compro el reloj para ti?

¡Te toca a ti!

Use what you have learned

Alquilando un vehículo

✔ Role play a conversation in a car rental agency

Estás en una agencia de alquiler de autos en México D.F. Quieres recorrer el país y necesitas un vehículo. Tu compañero(a) es el o la agente. Preparen ustedes una conversación.

Unos consejos para conductores

✔ Give advice about driving in Mexico

Tu amigo(a) piensa conducir en México. Como tú ya has conducido allí y conoces las condiciones, contesta sus preguntas y dale buenos consejos. Después, tu amigo(a) te va a repetir los consejos que le diste.

Isla Mujeres

Mazatlán

Lo que tenemos y lo que quiero

✔ Tell what you have and what you like

Con tu compañero(a) hablen de los vehículos que tienen o que sus familias tienen. Descríbanlos e indiquen si les gustan o no. ¡Buenas noticias! Ustedes acaban de ganar la lotería. Pregúntenle a su profesor(a) cuánto dinero ganaron ustedes. Ahora, hablen de los nuevos vehículos que quieren comprar.

Viajando en carro

✔ Describe a car trip in Mexico

El joven de la **Conversación** en la página 236 estaba viajando por México con su familia. Imagina un viaje que estás haciendo ahora en carro. Cuenta los lugares que estás visitando y lo que estás viendo.

Gasolinera, Tepoztlán, Morelos

En la gasolinera

✔ ***Explain what you want someone to do***

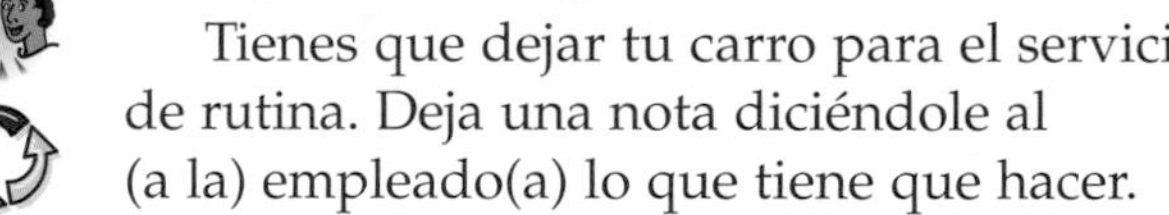

Tienes que dejar tu carro para el servicio de rutina. Deja una nota diciéndole al (a la) empleado(a) lo que tiene que hacer.

Carro de segunda mano

✔ ***Describe a car you are trying to sell***

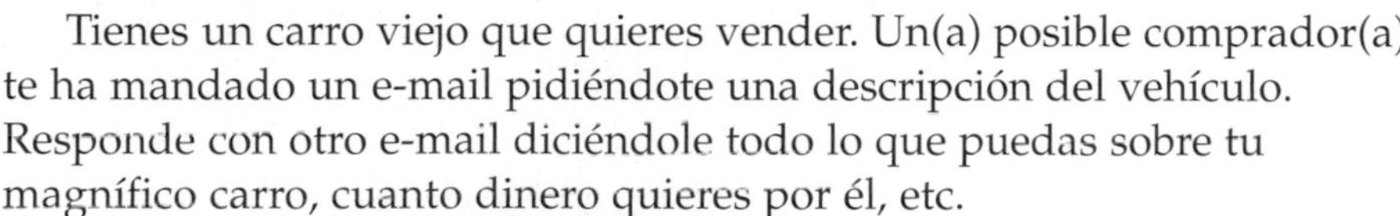

Tienes un carro viejo que quieres vender. Un(a) posible comprador(a) te ha mandado un e-mail pidiéndote una descripción del vehículo. Responde con otro e-mail diciéndole todo lo que puedas sobre tu magnífico carro, cuanto dinero quieres por él, etc.

Real del Monte

¡Véndemelo!

✔ ***Tell what you want and don't want***

Tú y tu compañero(a) mencionan cada artículo de ropa que el otro o la otra lleva y dile que te la venda. Usa el imperativo familiar. Por ejemplo: **Tu camisa, ¡véndemela!—No, no te la vendo.**

Vocabulario

1 Completen con una palabra apropiada.

1. Hay que parar cuando el _____ está en rojo.
2. Hay que respetar todas las _____ de tráfico.
3. Cien kilómetros por hora es el _____.
4. Cuando vamos a virar a la izquierda o a la derecha usamos las _____.

To review vocabulary, turn to page 234.

2 Den un sinónimo o equivalente.

5. adelantar
6. el permiso de conducir
7. el peligro, la contingencia
8. ir en reversa
9. escribir su nombre
10. área al lado u orilla de la carretera

Mazatlán

Conversación

3 Contesten según la conversación.

11. ¿Qué está buscando el joven?
12. ¿Qué están ofreciendo hoy en la agencia?
13. ¿Por dónde estarán viajando el joven y su familia?
14. ¿Qué tipo de seguro está recomendando el agente?
15. ¿Por qué está pensando en un todoterreno el cliente?
16. ¿Cómo va a pagar los cargos el cliente?

To review the conversation, turn to page 236.

Estructura

4 Cambien en el imperfecto progresivo.

17. Yo visitaba la agencia de alquiler de coches.
18. Mis padres alquilaban un todoterreno.
19. El agente explicaba las condiciones.
20. Nosotros mirábamos los vehículos.

To review the progressive, turn to page 238.

5 Completen en el presente progresivo.

21. Nosotros ____ un todoterreno. (alquilar)
22. Yo no ____ un todoterreno. (conducir)
23. ¿Tú lo ____? (ver)
24. El agente me ____ todo lo que debo hacer. (decir)

6 Completen con los pronombres apropiados.

25. Ella quiere comprar____. (el carro / a mí)
26. El agente está vendiendo____. (el seguro / a la señora)
27. El todoterreno está rebasando____. (el camión)
28. El camionero está leyendo____. (la señal de tráfico)
29. Yo no quiero dar____. (la tarjeta de crédito / al agente)
30. Y tú, ¡da____! (las llaves / a mí)

To review pronoun placement, turn to pages 239–240 and 241.

Vocabulario para la lectura
Wind surf: agua, aire y ¡diversión!

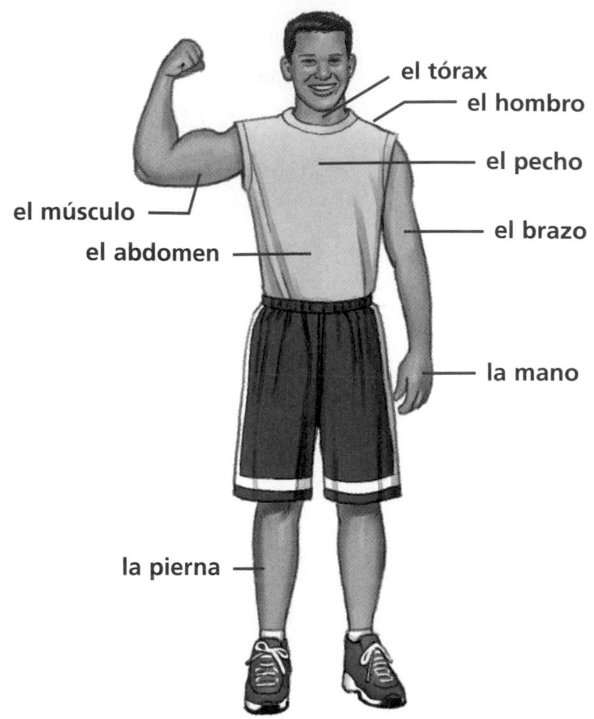

Están haciendo ejercicios.
Están haciendo calentamiento.

El joven se resbaló.
La tabla dio unos brincos.
Se volteó.

Más vocabulario

los ligeros los que no pesan mucho, los que pesan pocos kilos
los pesados los que tienen mucho peso, lo contrario de «ligeros»
los novatos los principiantes, lo contrario de «expertos»
ejercitar darle ejercicio a
lastimar hacerle daño, dañar, herir

¿Qué palabra necesito?

¿Qué es? Identifiquen.

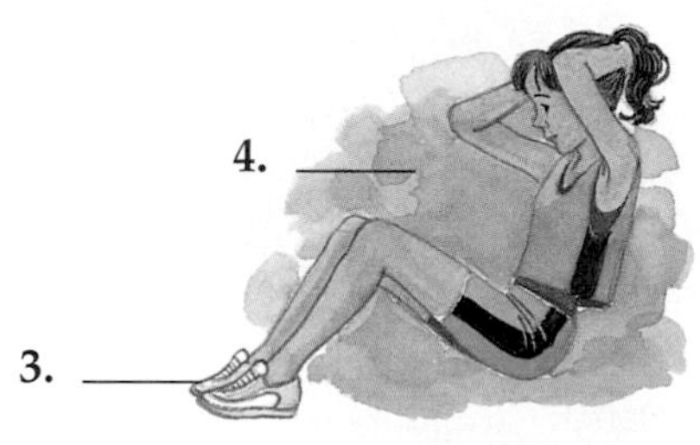

2 **Historieta ¿Qué habrá pasado?**
Contesten según se indica.

1. ¿Qué tenía la tabla? (una vela)
2. ¿Qué había saltado el joven? (la onda)
3. ¿Por qué se habrá caído de la tabla? (se habrá resbalado)
4. ¿Se había volteado? (sí)
5. ¿Por qué se había volteado? (había dado unos brincos fuertes)
6. ¿Por qué habrá llevado guantes para el wind surf? (para no lastimarse las manos)
7. ¿Qué ejercicios había hecho como calentamiento? (sentadillas y estiramientos)

3 **Palabras emparentadas** Den una palabra relacionada.

1. estirar
2. pesar
3. sentar
4. brincar
5. calentar
6. resbaladizo

Wind surf: agua, aire ¡y diversión!

Para ti que te encanta pasártela súper con tus cuates[1] cerca del mar o de algún lago, haciendo deporte, ésta es una de las opciones con la que además de que te vas a sentir de maravilla, te vas a poner… ¡guauuuu!

Por Jorge Barajas Rocha

El wind surf es un deporte que no sólo es divertidísimo, sino que en él ejercitas muchísimas partes del cuerpo, además de que como se tiene que practicar en el agua, puedes echarte unas asoleadas[2] y nadadas, ¡otra onda!

Poco a poco ha ido agarrando[3] más fuerza en México, y desde hace unos años existe un equipo profesional de wind surf que, por cierto, hizo un excelente papel en los Juegos Centroamericanos; últimamente se ha estado poniendo muy de moda en Valle de Bravo, Presa Escondida, Cancún y Puerto Vallarta porque son lugares que se prestan[4] muchísimo para que puedas practicarlo y volverte un verdadero campeón en este rollo[5].

Realmente, no necesitas de muchas cosas para poder hacer wind surf, sólo te hace falta una tabla con vela y, ¡listo! (Nada más

no se te olvide el lago, ¿eh?) Eso sí, es básico estar protegido para que no te vayas a lastimar a las primeras de cambio[6], ¿no? Así, te conviene usar wetsuit, que son trajes color neón para que no te confundas con el agua (además de que guardan el calor de tu cuerpo), guantes especiales para que no te lastimes las manos, cinturón o arnés[7] (si es en forma de calzón, ¡mucho mejor!), chaleco salvavidas y tenis ligeros de suela blanda para que no te resbales.

Pero, ¿en qué consiste este deporte? El wind surf viene siendo algo así como una especialización del famosísimo "surfing", sólo que aquí tienes muchas más cosas de las que tienes que estar al pendiente porque a cada rato[8] andas en el aire dando unos brincos como para dejar a todo el mundo con el ojo cuadrado[9]. Lo fundamental del wind surf es aprender a controlar la vela para que el viento te lleve hacia donde tú quieras, así como aprovechar la fuerza del viento para tomar velocidad; obvio que también hay que saber manejar la tabla y mover tu cuerpo para que le hagas contrapeso[10] a la

PARA PRACTICARLO

Cerca del D.F.
Presa Escondida, Hgo.
Valle de Bravo, Edo. de Méx.
Atlangatepec, Tlax.

En la costa del Pacífico
Puerto Vallarta, Jal.
Puerto Escondido, Oax.
Puerto Ángel, Oax.
Huatulco, Oax.
Ensenada, B.C.
Cabo San Lucas, B.C.
La Paz, B.C.
Bahía Negra, B.C.
Acapulco, Gro.

En el Golfo de México
Cancún, Q. Roo

[1] cuates *amigos (México)*
[2] echarte unas asoleadas *broncearte*
[3] agarrando *grabbing*
[4] se prestan *lend themselves*
[5] en este rollo *este deporte*
[6] primeras de cambio *primera vez*
[7] arnés *harness*
[8] a cada rato *a cada momento*
[9] con el ojo cuadrado *amazed*
[10] contrapeso *counterbalance*

vela y así evitar que te voltees a cada rato. Aunque al principio te la pasas en el agua, el chiste es que no te desesperes y vayas mejorando[11] poco a poco. Acuérdate que nadie nace siendo un campeón en ningún deporte, sino que se va aprendiendo con el tiempo y la experiencia.

Lo prendidísimo[12] es que cada fin de semana se organizan competencias en las que hay que recorrer un circuito en plan de carreras, así que además de ponerse súper listo para la onda de los saltos, también hay que tener rapidez para ganar.

La edad para practicarlo no tiene que ser una en específico, sólo que mientras más chico[13] empieces, vas adquiriendo más elasticidad, coordinación, control de la vela y sentido del equilibrio. De todos modos, no tengas miedo de hacer osos[14] si estás empezando y mejor concéntrate en este rollo; sólo hay que tener mucha disciplina. Además, la verdad, no es tan complicado como parece y, eso sí, es divertidísimo.

De cualquier forma, tienes que prepararte muy bien: primero, hay que tener una condición física excelente y, segundo, muchísima fuerza en tus piernas, brazos y abdomen, que es lo que más ejercitas. Para eso, antes de entrar al agua, es muy conveniente que hagas un poco de calentamiento para que no vayas a tener problemas con tus músculos, que sólo así estarán listos para ponerlos a prueba; puedes hacer sentadillas, abdominales, lagartijas[15], estiramientos y torsiones de tronco.

TIPS BÁSICOS

- **Mantén el equilibrio en base a la velocidad y a la intensidad del viento.**
- **Conserva la ruta de la línea del viento.**
- **No luches contra el viento, sino ayúdate de él para ir en la dirección que quieras.**
- **Si no puedes pararte porque hay mucho viento, espérate a que baje un poco.**
- **Sé muy constante.**

En México, hay varias asociaciones en las que puedes meterte para practicarlo más seguido dentro de diferentes categorías, por lo que igual encuentras un equipo de cuates que van desde los doce años hasta uno de gente mayor a los treinta años, además de que hay grupos de ligeros, pesados, masters y novatos. Como quien dice, ¡hay de todo para todos! Otra cosa de lo más padre[16] es que estás en pleno contacto con la naturaleza porque siempre vas a estar rodeado de viento, agua, sol y con unos paisajes a tu alrededor que de plano ¡no te los acabas[17]!, además de que el ambiente es de lo más sano porque hay un buen de gente que le está entrando[18] al wind surf y a la que también le encanta todo ese rollo, así es que siempre vas a conocer gente muy prendida[19].

Sobre las partes del cuerpo que ejercitas, te sirve muchísimo para los brazos, piernas y tórax, aunque igual te fortalece los hombros, el pecho y las pompas[20]. Como quien dice, ¡todo!

Así que ya lo sabes, para pasarte unos fines de semana ¡otro rollo! en medio de un súper ambiente, haciendo ejercicio y agarrando un color envidiable, el wind surf es… ¡la mejor opción!

[11] mejorando *improving*
[12] Lo prendidísimo *Más importante*
[13] chico *joven, pequeño*
[14] hacer osos *cometer errores*
[15] lagartijas *push-ups*
[16] padre *nice (Mexico)*
[17] no te los acabas *increíble*
[18] entrando *practicando*
[19] prendida *interesante*
[20] pompas *buttocks*

¿Comprendes?

A Contesten.

1. ¿Existe un equipo profesional de wind surf en México?
2. ¿Necesitas de muchas cosas para hacer el wind surf?
3. ¿Hay que pensar en más cosas cuando uno hace el wind surf que cuando uno hace surfing (tabla)?
4. ¿Hay una edad específica para practicar el wind surf?

Baja California

B Contesten.

1. ¿Cuáles son algunas ventajas del wind surf?
2. ¿Cuáles son algunas cosas esenciales para hacer el wind surf?
3. ¿Por qué le conviene a uno llevar un wetsuit?
4. ¿Qué dice el artículo sobre la gente que practica el wind surf?

Vocabulario para la lectura

¿Mis padres no me gustan?

Los padres y los hijos platican.
La madre le muestra mucho cariño a la hija.

Los niños están involucrados en una pelea.
Habrían tenido una disputa.

Más vocabulario

el acuerdo resolución mutua, convenio
el arete adorno que se lleva en la oreja
la confianza seguridad en el buen carácter y honestad de uno
la muestra señal, indicio, indicación
abundar ser abundante, ser muchos
bastar ser bastante, suficiente
llevar a cabo acabar, llevar a una conclusión
suceder ocurrir, pasar

¿Qué palabra necesito?

San Miguel de Allende

1 Los padres Contesten según se indica.

1. ¿Qué les muestran a los hijos los padres? (mucho cariño)
2. ¿Con quiénes platican los padres? (con los hijos)
3. ¿Cuál es una muestra de cariño? (un beso)
4. ¿En qué tienen confianza los padres? (los amigos de los hijos)
5. ¿Qué le molesta a la madre? (el arete grande en la oreja de su hija)

2 ¿Cuál es la palabra? Completen.

1. Hay que tener ____ en tus amigos.
2. Un beso es una ____ de cariño.
3. ¡____, ya! No quiero oír más de esta disputa. Ya estoy harto.
4. Ellos están involucrados en una pelea y va a ____ algo malo si no llegan a un ____ para poner fin a su disputa.
5. Desgraciadamente ____ ejemplos de malos conductores. Hay muchos en las carreteras.
6. Un ____ es una joya.
7. Tiene que ____ lo que ha empezado.

el mexicano

Tijuana, México

¿Mis padres no me gustan?

Cada persona es un mundo y cada familia es un universo distinto. Las familias de tus amigos también son diferentes: padres que discuten, que no te entienden o que son un dilema andando. Los padres suelen ser todo lo que menos esperas y hasta deseas tener la familia de alguno de tus amigos. Sin embargo, recuerda que no los conoces en realidad, si no, ¿por qué tu amiga quiere tener tus padres y no los de ella?

Distintos tipos de padres

1. Controla-todo

Temen que sucedan catástrofes cuando los hijos salen de casa, incluso acompañados por amigos de confianza. No es para menos: las noticias están llenas de problemas como asaltos y secuestros[1]; además, las tentaciones (piensan ellos) abundan en las fiestas de adolescentes; por ejemplo las drogas y el alcohol; entre otros. ¿Solución? En general basta con hacerles sentir confianza por las personas con quienes sales. Además, es posible negociar con ellos la hora de llegada a casa, personas con quienes estás, lugares a donde te diviertes. Lo más importante es hacerles sentir que vas con gente que te cuidan y que no vas a cometer locuras[2]. Aprende a controlarte y cumple con los acuerdos a los que lleguen.

2. Indiferentes

Contrarios a los anteriores, parece que no les importa si sales, entras o no llegas a casa. Pero tampoco dan muchas muestras de afecto, lo que seguramente también es frustrante para todos. Algunos lo hacen porque asumen que la libertad te da más criterio para decidir por ti mismo, mientras otros simplemente no saben cómo mostrarte cariño. Cualquiera que sea el caso, acércate a ellos y platica sobre los temas que quieras tratar. Explícales que de vez en cuando es necesario que te expresen cuanto te quieren; que aún esperas la guía de personas con experiencia que te ayuden a decidir el mejor camino en la vida. Si aún así no reaccionan ante tu ánimo por convivir más con ellos, encuentra tutores en amigos, familiares y profesores, otros guías que con gusto te ayudan.

[1] secuestros *kidnappings*
[2] cometer locuras *do silly things*

3. Censura total

Simplemente nada les gusta: tu pelo, tu ropa, tus amigos, en fin, no les convence como eres. Estos detalles que a ti te parecen normales como tu forma de ser, no son los correctos desde el punto de vista de tus papás. Lo peor que puedes hacer es comenzar una pelea; es inútil porque son tan diferentes que esperan que estés de acuerdo con lo que piensan, mientras tú quieres seguir en desacuerdo con ellos y no ceder en sus exigencias. Así no llegan a ninguna parte. Lo más razonable es preguntar qué les molesta exactamente. En muchos casos se trata de cuestiones superficiales y sin mayor importancia, como el estilo de peinado, el color de la ropa o que te pongas un arete en el ombligo[3]. Recuérdales que ellos también fueron jóvenes, les gustaba la moda y querían ser especiales. Seguro recuerdan las críticas de tus abuelos y pueden llegar a alguna resolución.

4. Perfectos a morir

Te ponen expectativas tan altas que no crees alcanzarlas. Esperan que seas el mejor de la clase, que ganes los premios escolares, que entres a las mejores escuelas, que tengas un buen trabajo y que tengas tiempo para ellos el fin de semana—¡todo al mismo tiempo! Aclárales lo que esperas de tu vida y como piensas llevarlo a cabo. Si ellos quieren ayudarte, está bien, pero sólo tú puedes encontrar tu camino.

5. Padres solteros

Ser padre y madre a la vez no es cosa fácil: sacar adelante la familia así como tratar de arreglar la situación personal. Es comprensible que tenga poco tiempo para platicar contigo o que no tenga paciencia como antes. En este caso la situación familiar sigue un proceso más complicado, sólo te queda ser tolerante y cooperar en lo que puedas. Ayuda a hacer la comida, ordena tu cuarto, gasta lo menos posible y trata de no involucrarte en problemas. Como ves, el universo de padres es enorme y cada uno es diferente y tiene sus propias complicaciones. Las familias ideales no existen; la cuestión es saber sobrellevar[4] las situaciones de la mejor manera.

[3] ombligo *belly button*
[4] sobrellevar *to put up with*

LECCIÓN 3

Periodismo

¿Comprendes?

A **Los padres controla-todo** Contesten.

1. ¿De qué tienen miedo estos padres?
2. ¿De qué están llenas las noticias?
3. ¿Cuáles son las tentaciones que estos padres piensan que abundan en las fiestas?
4. ¿En quiénes debes hacer que tus padres sienten confianza?
5. ¿Cuáles son algunas cosas que puedes negociar con los padres?

B **Los padres indiferentes** Completen.

1. Estos padres generalmente no muestran mucho ____.
2. Ellos creen que la libertad te permite ____ mejor por ti mismo.
3. Tú debes acercarte a ellos y ____ sobre lo que te es importante.
4. Diles que esperas la ____ de personas con experiencia.

Una familia mexicana

C **¿Qué tipo de padre es?** Identifiquen: **censura total, perfectos a morir** o **soltero.**

1. Tiene que ser padre y madre a la vez.
2. No le gusta tu pelo, ni tu ropa, ni tus amigos.
3. Es razonable preguntarles lo que les molesta exactamente.
4. Quieren que entres en las mejores escuelas y muchas cosas más, todas al mismo tiempo.
5. Es buena idea recordarles que ellos también fueron jóvenes.
6. Es probable que no tengan tiempo para platicar contigo o que no tengan la paciencia de antes.

D **Opiniones** ¿Cuál de los tipos de padres consideras los más difíciles para los hijos, los que menos te gustarían tener? ¿Por qué?

Estructura • Avanzada

Use your StudentWorks Plus CD for more practice.

Pluscuamperfecto
Describing actions completed prior to other actions

1. The pluperfect tense is formed by using the imperfect tense of the auxiliary verb **haber** and the past participle.

INFINITIVE	llegar	cumplir
yo	había llegado	había cumplido
tú	habías llegado	habías cumplido
él, ella, Ud.	había llegado	había cumplido
nosotros(as)	habíamos llegado	habíamos cumplido
vosotros(as)	*habíais llegado*	*habíais cumplido*
ellos, ellas, Uds.	habían llegado	habían cumplido

2. The pluperfect tense is used in the same way in Spanish as it is in English. The pluperfect describes a past action completed before another past action.

   El partido ya había empezado cuando llegaron algunos de los jugadores.
   The game had already begun when some of the players arrived.

3. Note that both actions in the sentence above took place in the past. The action that took place first, *the game had already begun* is in the pluperfect. The action that followed it, *the players arrived,* is in the preterite.

Santa Clara del Cobre

¿Cómo lo digo?

1 Historieta En la playa Cambien del presente perfecto en el pluscuamperfecto.

1. Ellos han ido a la playa.
2. Ha hecho mucho viento.
3. Alicia no ha querido hacer el wind surf.
4. Pero los amigos la han convencido.
5. Desgraciadamente, la plancha ha volteado.
6. Y Alicia se ha lastimado.
7. Pero se ha recuperado enseguida.
8. Y se ha subido a la plancha otra vez.

Baja California Sur

2 Ya lo habían hecho

Contesten según el modelo.

¿Hacer los ejercicios? →
Pero ya los habían hecho.

1. ¿Prepararse?
2. ¿Hacer las sentadillas?
3. ¿Ejercitar los músculos?
4. ¿Comprar una tabla nueva?
5. ¿Ponerse el chaleco salvavidas?
6. ¿Saltar las ondas?

Acapulco, México

3 Y yo después...

Formen oraciones según el modelo.

Ellos salieron. Yo salí después. →
Ellos ya habían salido cuando yo salí.

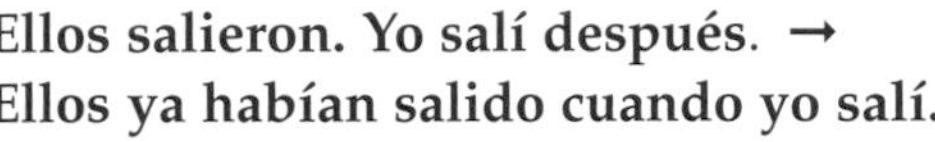

1. Ellos compraron unos guantes. Yo compré unos guantes después.
2. Ellos llegaron a la playa. Yo llegué después.
3. Ellos hicieron calentamiento. Yo hice calentamiento después.
4. Ellos cayeron de la plancha. Yo caí de la plancha después.
5. Ellos se lastimaron. Yo me lastimé después.
6. Ellos volvieron a casa. Yo volví a casa después.

El Arco, Cabo San Lucas

4 Historieta Andrés en Cabo San Lucas

Completen con el pluscuamperfecto.

Roberto __1__ (estar) en Cabo San Lucas antes de ir a Acapulco. Él __2__ (conocer) esa playa antes de conocer la otra. Él __3__ (aprender) el surfing antes de hacer el wind surf. Roberto __4__ (practicar) otros deportes antes que estos. Pero ninguno le __5__ (gustar) tanto como el wind surf.

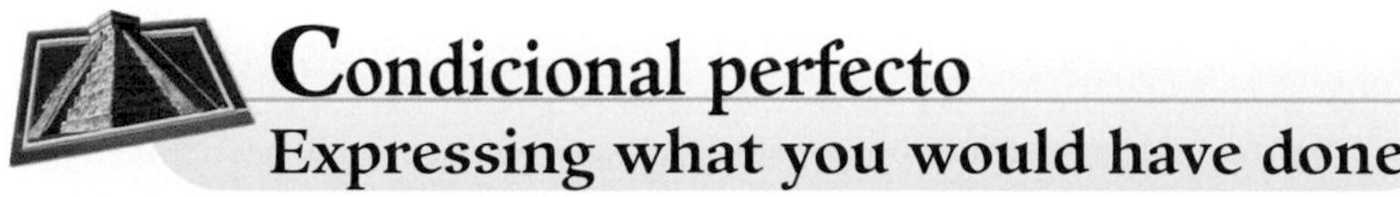

Condicional perfecto
Expressing what you would have done

1. The conditional perfect is formed by using the conditional of the auxiliary verb **haber** and the past participle.

INFINITIVE	platicar	aprender
yo	habría platicado	habría aprendido
tú	habrías platicado	habrías aprendido
él, ella, Ud.	habría platicado	habría aprendido
nosotros(as)	habríamos platicado	habríamos aprendido
vosotros(as)	*habríais platicado*	*habríais aprendido*
ellos, ellas, Uds.	habrían platicado	habrían aprendido

2. The conditional perfect is used in Spanish, as it is in English, to state what would have taken place had something else not interfered or made it impossible.

Yo habría hablado con mi padre pero él estaba muy ocupado.
I would have talked to my father but he was very busy.

Ella habría limpiado el cuarto pero tenía mucha tarea.
She would have cleaned her room but she had a lot of homework.

¿Cómo lo digo?

5 **Historieta** **Paz en la familia** Contesten personalmente.

1. ¿Habrías platicado con tus padres?
2. ¿Habrías escuchado sus consejos?
3. ¿Les habrías presentado tus amigos a tus padres?
4. ¿Habrías ayudado en la casa?
5. ¿Habrías regresado temprano de las fiestas?
6. ¿Les habrías mostrado mucho cariño?

6 **Ella lo habría hecho pero...** Completen.

1. Ella ____ pero estaba ocupada. (estudiar)
2. Ella ____ a su madre pero no encontraba teléfono. (llamar)
3. Ella ____ un arete en la nariz pero sus padres le dijeron que no. (ponerse)
4. Ella ____ algo a su madre pero no la encontraba. (decir)
5. Ella ____ con el acuerdo pero se le olvidó. (cumplir)

7 **Ellos también** Completen la Actividad 6 cambiando **ella** en **ellos.**

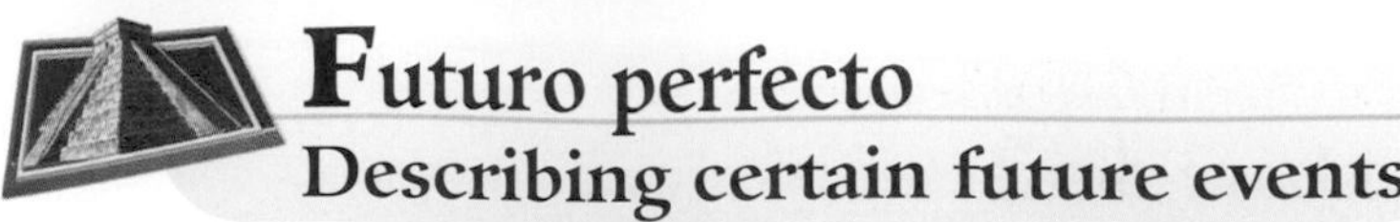

Futuro perfecto
Describing certain future events

1. The future perfect tense is formed by using the future tense of the auxiliary verb **haber** and the past participle.

INFINITIVE	terminar	comer
yo	habré terminado	habré comido
tú	habrás terminado	habrás comido
él, ella, Ud.	habrá terminado	habrá comido
nosotros(as)	habremos terminado	habremos comido
vosotros(as)	*habréis terminado*	*habréis comido*
ellos, ellas, Uds.	habrán terminado	habrán comido

2. The future perfect tense is used to express a future action that will be completed prior to another future action. Look at the example.

Pablo y Luisa no estarán en la playa. Habrán vuelto a la ciudad antes de llegar nosotros.

3. Note that Pablo and Luisa will not be present at some time in the future. They will have already left before our arrival. Both actions are in the future but one precedes the other.

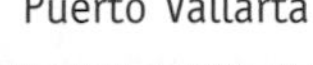
Puerto Vallarta

Los amigos habrán terminado el trabajo.

¿Cómo lo digo?

8 **Historieta** **Antes de verme...** Contesten.

1. Antes de verme, ¿habrás hablado con tu amigo?
2. Antes de verme, ¿le habrás dicho algo?
3. Antes de verme, ¿le habrás explicado la situación?
4. Antes de verme, ¿te habrás calmado?
5. Antes de verme, ¿habrás pensado en todo?

Subjuntivo con expresiones indefinidas
Expressing indefinite ideas

A number of words are made indefinite by adding **-quiera.** Note that with some words **quiera** is attached, while with others it is not.

quienquiera *whoever*	**cualquiera** *whatever*
dondequiera *wherever*	**como quiera** *however*
adondequiera *(to) wherever*	**cuando quiera** *whenever*

The subjunctive is used after indefinite expressions when uncertainty is implied.

Quienquiera que seas, adondequiera que vayas y cuando quiera que salgas, como quiera que vayas y dondequiera que estés, espero que tengas suerte y que te diviertas.

Whoever you may be, wherever you may go and whenever you may leave, however you may go and wherever you may be, I wish you luck and hope you enjoy yourself.

Un grupo mariachi, Xochimilco, México

¿Cómo lo digo?

9 Dondequiera que vayas Completen.

1. Quienquiera que lo _____, nos lo debe decir. (saber)
2. Tú sabes que yo te ayudaré con cualquier problema que _____. (tener)
3. Dondequiera que tú _____, estaré a tu lado. (estar)
4. Cuando quiera que tú _____ mi ayuda, llámame. (necesitar)

Subjuntivo en cláusulas relativas
Expressing the known and the unknown

1. A relative clause modifies or describes a noun. If the noun refers to a definite person or thing, the indicative is used in the relative clause. If the noun refers to an indefinite person or thing, the subjunctive is used in the relative clause.

Tenemos un guía que conoce México muy bien.
Queremos un guía que conozca México muy bien.

Conozco a una persona que visita México con frecuencia.
Estoy buscando una persona que visite México con frecuencia.

Note that the **a personal** is omitted when the noun is indefinite or follows **tener.**

2. The subjunctive is used in a relative clause that modifies a superlative statement or a negative expression.

Es el templo más impresionante que exista en el mundo.
No hay nadie que pinte como ella.

Kohunlich, Quintana Roo

¿Cómo lo digo?

10 **Historieta** **El chofer** Sigan el modelo.

conducir bien →
Buscamos un hombre que conduzca bien.
Conozco a un hombre que conduce bien.

1. conocer las carreteras
2. poseer una licencia profesional
3. ser honesto
4. poder trabajar los fines de semana
5. tener mucha experiencia

Ciudad de México

Opiniones Contesten.

1. ¿Son las playas de México las más bellas que haya en el mundo?
2. ¿Es el Museo Antropológico el mejor que exista?
3. ¿Es verdad que no hay ningún otro que sea tan interesante?
4. ¿No hay ninguna capital que sea tan bella como la Ciudad de México?
5. ¿Es verdad que no hay otra ciudad que valga la pena (de) visitar?

Bosque de Chapultepec, Ciudad de México

¡Te toca a ti!

Use what you have learned

1 Un deporte nuevo

✓ Tell what sport you would have liked to play

¿Qué deporte que nunca habías practicado te habría gustado practicar? ¿Por qué? Escribe un e-mail a un(a) deportista hispano(a) que practica ese deporte. Pregúntale todo lo que habrías querido saber del deporte.

Parque Alameda, Ciudad de México

2 Lugares para wind surf

✓ Tell where windsurfing might be popular

Un amigo quiere hacer wind surf en México. Mándale un e-mail con los nombres de algunos lugares que puedes recomendar.

3 Tipos de padres

✓ Talk about your parents and tell your experiences

Con tus compañeros, consideren los diferentes tipos de padres que describe el artículo y comenten según sus propias experiencias.

Los padres perfectos

✔ Tell what you would like from "perfect" parents

Los padres siempre dicen lo que esperan de sus hijos. ¿Qué esperan los hijos de los padres? En unos párrafos describe las características que tendrían unos padres perfectos.

De compras

✔ Talk about what you would have done

En un viaje a México, ¿qué habrías comprado en este mercado al aire libre? Piensa en todos los productos mexicanos que conoces y contesta con el condicional perfecto.

Guadalajara

Principiante

✔ Talk about what you will have done

Un amigo ha decidido empezar a hacer wind surf. Se fue a comprar el equipo necesario. ¿Qué habrá comprado? Prepara una lista.

E-mail al grupo

✔ Discuss joining a sports team

Quieres meterte en un grupo de aficionados de tu deporte favorito. Prepara un e-mail diciéndoles que quieres entrar en el grupo, el equipo que tienes, y hazles preguntas sobre donde practican el deporte, cuantos miembros hay y cualquier otra cosa importante. Haz algunas investigaciones en el Internet para encontrar a unos aficionados en un país hispano. Mándales tu e-mail.

For more information about leisure-time activities in Mexico, go to **Web Explore** on the Glencoe Spanish Web site at glencoe.com.

Assessment

Vocabulario

1 ¿Cuál es la palabra?

1. Los ejercicios como las sentadillas y los estiramientos que debes hacer antes de practicar un deporte.
2. Lo que uno debe llevar en caso de caerse al agua.
3. El que no es experto ni experimentado; el que es nuevo.
4. Hacerse daño, recibir una herida.

To review vocabulary, turn to pages 246 and 251.

2 Completen.

5. La madre le muestra mucho _____ al niño, lo besa y lo abraza.
6. Va a _____ algo desagradable si ellos no ponen fin a su disputa.
7. Ya es suficiente. _____.
8. Su hijo siempre hace lo que debe hacer. Sus padres tienen mucha _____ en él.
9. El beso y el abrazo son _____ de cariño y afecto.

Lectura

To review the article about windsurfing, turn to pages 248–249.

3 Contesten.

10. ¿Cuáles son las tres partes del cuerpo que más ejercitas en el wind surf?
11. ¿Qué usas para protegerte las manos y los pies?

To review the newspaper article about parents, turn to pages 252–253.

4 ¿Sí o no?

12. El estilo del peinado o el color de la ropa son cuestiones superficiales.
13. Para los padres solteros, ser madre y padre a la vez no es muy difícil.
14. Los padres «indiferentes» a veces simplemente no saben mostrar afecto.

Estructura

5 Completen con el pluscuamperfecto (pasado perfecto).

15. Yo nunca lo _____ antes. (ver)
16. Porque yo nunca _____ el wind surf. (hacer)
17. Nadie me _____. (enseñar)
18. Mis amigos sí que lo _____. (practicar)
19. Y tú no lo _____ antes tampoco. (conocer)

To review the pluperfect, turn to page 255.

6 Contesten con el condicional perfecto según el modelo.

Él habló. (yo) →
Pues yo no habría hablado.

20. Ella llevó guantes. (tú)
21. Nosotros resbalamos. (ella)
22. Yo compré unos tenis nuevos. (él)
23. Tú hiciste calentamiento. (ellos)

To review the conditional perfect, turn to page 257.

7 Escriban en el futuro perfecto.

24. Hablarás.
25. Sucederá.
26. Saldrán.

To review the future perfect, turn to page 258.

8 Completen.

27. Quienquiera que _____ a México estará contento. (visitar)
28. Y adondequiera que _____ verá bellezas. (viajar)
29. Cuando yo vaya, buscaré un guía que _____ el país. (conocer)
30. Mi hermano conoce a un guía que lo _____ muy bien. (conocer)

To review indefinite ideas and expressing the known and unknown, turn to pages 259 and 260.

Cabo San Lucas

Spanish Online
For more Chapter 5 test preparation, go to the Chapter 5 **Self-Check Quiz** on the Glencoe Spanish Web site at glencoe.com.

Proficiency Tasks

Composición

Una de las técnicas que emplean los buenos escritores es la de resumir. Durante tu carrera académica tendrás que leer cantidades de escritos para sacar la información que necesitas. Luego tendrás que presentar esa información de forma abreviada pero sin omitir los datos de mayor importancia.

TAREA 1 **Resumir** Has leído en este capítulo sobre la historia de México desde la prehistoria hasta la conquista. En esta tarea vas a resumir en un par de párrafos lo que aprendiste. Aquí tienes unos pasos a seguir.

Antes de escribir

- Repasa lo que leíste sobre la historia de México.
- Apunta los datos de mayor importancia, por ejemplo: orígenes, civilizaciones, restos… etc.
- Ordena los apuntes en un orden lógico.

Bosquejo Prepara un bosquejo de tu resumen. Escribe el resumen.

Repasar y revisar Repasa el resumen para asegurarte que la información es precisa y que no hay faltas gramaticales.

Corregir Corrige cualquier falta gramatical u ortográfica.

TAREA 2 **Descripción** Hay escritos formales e informales. Un escrito informal tradicional es la carta personal.

Obviamente, hay cartas formales también; cartas que se escriben a entidades del gobierno, cartas de condolescencia, etc. Pero ahora lo que vas a hacer es escribir una carta a un amigo o amiga. El tema será imaginario—a no ser que hayas visitado México y puedas escribir basado en tu propia experiencia—el tema es un viaje por México en automóvil. Para esta tarea puedes valerte de información de distintas partes del capítulo que acabas de leer. En particular debes releer: La geografía; Visitas históricas; Conversación; Periodismo *Wind surf.*

De estas lecturas puedes sacar algunas ideas para tu carta. Debes, otra vez, hacer apuntes de la información que creas más interesante para incluir en tu viaje de fantasía. Apunta también los adjetivos que van a dar vida a las descripciones de lugares y eventos.

Piensa en la persona a quien vas a escribir. ¿Es un amigo o amiga, un pariente, una persona mayor? Tienes que pensar en lo que le va a interesar a esa persona. Todas las cartas, formales e informales, siguen un mismo patrón. Hay tres partes de la carta:

- el encabezamiento—que contiene tu dirección y la fecha
- el cuerpo de la carta
- la conclusión

El saludo informal es algo como: **Querido Pablo; Querida Elena; Muy querida madre mía.** La conclusión o final de la carta tiene dos partes, la despedida y la firma.

Algunas conclusiones informales son: **Un abrazo de tu amiga que te quiere; Sinceramente; Afectuosamente.** La firma tiene que ser en tinta.

Ahora, escribe tu carta. Cuando termines, léela de nuevo y haz cualquier corrección necesaria.

TAREA 3 **Escritura persuasiva** Ahora que has tenido alguna práctica con escribir cartas, tu próxima tarea será también una carta, pero esta vez una carta más formal con un propósito más importante. Leíste sobre los problemas ecológicos que están afectando negativamente las selvas de México y Centroamérica. El efecto dañino de la caza indiscriminada de animales y la deforestación. Hay muchos organismos nacionales e internacionales que se interesan en el tema. Vas a escribir una carta general exponiendo tus preocupaciones y tus sugerencias sobre como confrontar el problema. Vas a exponer tu opinión. Verifica que tu información es precisa. Emplea un tono razonable pero firme. Organiza tu exposición de esta manera.

- Descripción del problema, citando datos y fuentes de información
- Lo que tú crees que se debe hacer

Sigue el formato para una carta formal.

- Prepara tu bosquejo
- Repasa y revisa el bosquejo
- Corrige cualquier falta de ortografía o gramática

El saludo para este tipo de carta es: **Muy señores míos** (si es a una organización), o **Muy estimada señora Rodríguéz; Estimado Dr. López,** etc.

La despedida es: **Respetuosamente; Muy atentatmente, Atentamente.**

TAREA 4 **Pidiendo información** Hoy día la carta formal o informal está cediendo el paso al e-mail para todos los propósitos excepto los más formales u oficiales. La gran ventaja del e-mail es que es instantáneo. La desventaja es que muchas veces los escribimos sin fijarnos bien si está completo y correcto. Lo primero que tienes que hacer con tu e-mail es llenar el título que le dice a quien lo recibe de qué se trata. El e-mail que vas a preparar se dirige a la oficina de turismo de México. En tu e-mail vas a pedir información sobre: lugares de interés turistico, documentos necesarios, seguros, transporte y seguridad. No te olvides de indicar adonde deben enviarte panfletos u otros materiales. Y al final de tu e-mail, dales las gracias anticipadas.

Discurso

El buen orador es uno que sabe entusiasmar a su público. Primero tiene que comprender quien es su público, sus intereses y gustos. El buen orador trata de convencer a su público a aceptar su punto de vista. El buen orador sabe usar su voz, sabe cuando levantar la voz y cuando bajarla para tener el efecto deseado en sus oyentes. Sabe emplear el gesto de forma apropiada. Y es muy importante mirarles a los ojos a los que escuchan.

TAREA 5 **Discurso persuasivo** Leíste el artículo sobre el windsurf. Sin duda tú tienes un deporte o pasatiempo favorito. Convence a tus compañeros de clase a participar en esa actividad. Explícales lo que es, como se juega y por qué a ti te gusta tanto.

CAPÍTULO 5

Vocabulario

Lección 1 Cultura

el cacto
el desierto
la flor silvestre
el guacamayo
el jaguar
la caza
la deforestación
la fauna
la selva
el águila
el ajuste
el aliado
la bandera mexicana
el centauro
Mesoamérica
el resto
la serpiente
árido(a)
adelantado(a)
aterrador(a)
temible
desaparecer
devorar
juntarse

Lección 2 Conversación

el arcén
el camión
el camionero
el cargo
la carretera
el cinturón de seguridad
el contrato
las intermitentes
el kilometraje ilimitado
la licencia de conductor
el límite de velocidad
el riesgo
el seguro
el semáforo
la señal de tráfico
la tarjeta de crédito
el todoterreno
abrochar
descansar
firmar
rebasar
retroceder

Lección 3 Periodismo

Wind surf: agua, aire y ¡diversión!

el abdomen
el brazo
el hombro
la mano
el músculo
el pecho
la pierna
el tórax
el brinco
el calzón
el chaleco salvavidas
la onda, la ola
el salto
la tabla
la vela
el calentamiento
el ejercicio
los estiramientos
los ligeros
los novatos
los pesados
las sentadillas
las suelas
los tenis
resbalar(se)
voltear(se)
ejercitar
lastimar(se)

¿Mis padres no me gustan?

el acuerdo
el arete
el cariño
la confianza
la muestra
la pelea
involucrado(a)
abundar
bastar
llevar a cabo
mostrar (ue)
platicar
suceder

LITERARY COMPANION *See pages 464–475* *for literary selections related to Chapter 5. The activities for these readings will help you continue to practice your reading comprehension skills.*

VIDEOTUR

¡Viva el mundo hispano!

Video can be a beneficial learning tool for the language student. Video enables you to experience the material in the textbook in a real-life setting. Take a vicarious field trip as you see people interacting at home, at school, at the market, etc. The cultural benefits are limitless as you experience the Spanish-speaking world while "traveling" through many countries. In addition to its tremendous cultural value, video gives practice in developing good listening and viewing skills. Video allows you to look for numerous clues that are evident in tone of voice, facial expressions, and gestures. Through video you can see and hear the diversity of the target culture and compare and contrast the Spanish-speaking cultures to each other and to your own.

Episodio 1: La vida del Zócalo

Los bailarines son **concheros.** Su música y baile son de origen nahua y sus trajes fueron inspirados por los aztecas. Están enfrente del Palacio Nacional en el Zócalo, la plaza principal de la Ciudad de México. Aquí los españoles levantaron sus edificios sobre las ruinas de un templo azteca. Los aztecas gobernaron aquí hasta el siglo XV y los españoles desde el siglo XVI hasta el XIX.

Episodio 2: Un carro y sus admiradores

Luis es taxista. Él lleva veinticuatro años como taxista, siempre manejando su carro favorito, su Vocho. Puedes ver Vochos en toda la Ciudad de México, en las grandes avenidas y en las pequeñas calles. El 70 por ciento de los taxis de la ciudad son Vochos. El primero fue construido en México en 1956 y el último en julio de 2003. Para muchos taxistas su Vocho no es sólo un carro, es un amigo y compañero.

Episodio 3: La historia de Teotihuacán

Estas son las ruinas de una gran ciudad de 150.000 habitantes. Es Teotihuacán. Hace mil setecientos años allí construyeron templos y pirámides a sus dioses. Teotihuacán está a 30 millas al norte de la Ciudad de Mexico. Los arqueólogos descubren cada día artefactos de la gente que habitaba la ciudad. Pero, ¿qué les pasó? ¿Por qué desaparecieron? Todavía no sabemos.

Capítulo 6

El Caribe

Cuba, Puerto Rico, la República Dominicana

Objetivos

In this chapter you will:

- learn about the geography, history, and culture of Cuba, Puerto Rico, and the Dominican Republic
- review how to express what people do for themselves
- review how to express reciprocal actions
- discuss an experience in a restaurant
- review how to make comparisons
- read and discuss newspaper articles about sports and a special education program
- learn to express *although, perhaps*
- learn to express opinions and feelings about what has or had happened
- learn to discuss contrary-to-fact situations

Contenido

LECCIÓN I

Cultura

Vocabulario para la lectura

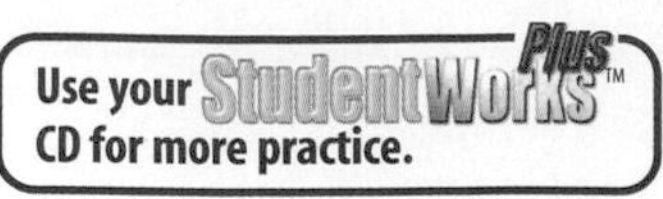

Los vientos del huracán castigaban el galeón.
El galeón no se hundió.
Pero por poco se hunde.

El cacique nunca se sometió a los españoles.
Nunca llevaría cadenas.

Los agricultores se dedican al cultivo de la caña de azúcar.

Algunas frutas tropicales

el coco

la piña

el mango

la papaya

Más vocabulario

el cacique jefe de los indígenas
el/la ciudadano(a) persona con los derechos y obligaciones de su nacionalidad
la toma acción de tomar posesión de algo como un territorio o una ciudad
apartado(a) retirado, distante, alejado
desafecto(a) opuesto, contrario, enemigo
emprender comenzar, empezar, iniciar como un viaje o aventura
rebosar abundar, contener demasiado
reposar descansar, posar sobre algo

¿Qué palabra necesito?

La Habana, Cuba

1 **Historieta** **Los galeones** Contesten con **sí.**

1. ¿Los galeones se rebosaban de oro y tesoro?
2. ¿Los galeones emprendieron el viaje en la Habana?
3. ¿Había vientos muy fuertes?
4. ¿Era un huracán que se acercaba?
5. ¿Los vientos castigaban el galeón?

2 **¿Cuál es la palabra?** Den la palabra cuya definición sigue.

1. habitante, persona con cierta nacionalidad
2. la ocupación, la conquista
3. descansar, estar encima de otra cosa
4. separado, aparte

Pinar del Río, Cuba

3 **Historieta** **El cacique** Contesten según se indica.

1. ¿Quién era el jefe indígena? (el cacique)
2. ¿Se sometió el cacique a los españoles? (no)
3. ¿Quisieron ponerlo en cadenas los españoles? (sí)
4. ¿El cacique era desafecto al gobierno español? (sí)
5. ¿Él quería hispanizarse? (no)

4 **Los agricultores** Completen con una palabra apropiada.

divertirse	**lechón**	**el mango**	**la piña**
cultivar	**la caña**	**el coco**	**frijoles**

1. Los agricultores van a _____ la tierra.
2. Ellos se dedican al cultivo de _____ de azúcar.
3. _____, _____ y _____ son frutas tropicales.
4. Los muchachos están cocinando un _____ asado.
5. Lo van a servir con arroz y _____.

Lectura

La geografía del Caribe

Es común hablar del «Caribe», que es un mar, cuando nos referimos a las Antillas, un archipiélago constituido por miles de islas que forman tres grupos importantes. Estas son las Grandes Antillas, las Pequeñas Antillas y las Bahamas. Las islas en las que nos enfocamos aquí son tres de las cuatro que forman las Grandes Antillas, o sea, Cuba, Puerto Rico y la Española. La cuarta, Jamaica, es una isla y un país de habla inglesa.

Reading Strategy

Using background knowledge When you are first assigned a reading, quickly look at the accompanying visuals to determine what the reading is about. Once you know what the topic is, spend a short time thinking about what you already know about it. If you do this, the reading will be easier to understand.

Santo Domingo, la República Dominicana

Cuba es la más grande de las Grandes Antillas y la que está más cerca de Norteamérica. Al este de Cuba se encuentra la Española, una isla compartida por dos repúblicas, Haití y la República Dominicana. Al este de la Española está Puerto Rico, la más pequeña del grupo. Las Grandes Antillas son mayormente montañosas y reposan sobre una cadena de montañas submarinas.

Una vista de Puerto Rico

La Habana, Cuba

Pinar del Río, Cuba

Clima

Las Grandes Antillas se encuentran en la zona tropical. No obstante, el clima es tropical en los llanos pero subtropical en las áreas montañosas. Hay dos estaciones: la seca, de noviembre a mayo, y la húmeda, de junio a octubre. Comenzando en julio y hasta octubre, los huracanes, que nacen en el océano Atlántico, a veces castigan las costas de estas islas. En todas las Antillas la vegetación es exuberante. El clima es especialmente apropiado para el cultivo de la caña de azúcar, el café y el tabaco, productos importantes en las tres islas.

Un huracán, San Juan, Puerto Rico

 Contesten.

1. ¿Cuál es la diferencia entre el «Caribe» y las «Antillas»?
2. ¿En cuál de las Antillas se encuentran Cuba, Puerto Rico y la Española?
3. ¿Cuál de las islas está más cerca de la América del Norte?
4. En una de las islas hay dos repúblicas. ¿Cuál es la isla?
5. ¿Sobre qué se sitúan las Grandes Antillas?
6. ¿En qué zona climática se encuentran las Grandes Antillas?
7. En las Grandes Antillas hay áreas con clima subtropical. ¿Dónde están?
8. ¿Cómo se llaman las dos estaciones del año en las Antillas?
9. ¿Qué fenómeno meteorológico puede causar mucho daño en el Caribe?
10. ¿Cómo es la vegetación de la zona?

Historia

La Española y la República Dominicana

Haití ocupa la parte occidental de la isla de la Española y la República Dominicana la oriental. Casi las dos terceras partes de la isla corresponden a la República Dominicana. En Haití se habla francés y en la República Dominicana se habla español.

En su primer viaje a las Américas en 1492 Cristóbal Colón llegó a la isla que los indígenas llamaban «Quisqueya» que quiere decir «Madre de todas las tierras». Él la llamó «La Española», y allí se estableció la primera colonia española en América.

Santo Domingo, la República Dominicana

Durante unos tres mil años hasta la llegada de Colón, venía gente de Sudamérica a las Antillas en canoa. El nombre que ellos se dieron a sí mismos era «taínos» que significaba «los buenos». Crearon una cultura basada en la agricultura. Los taínos de Quisqueya desaparecieron bajo el dominio de los españoles. Pero antes de someterse a los españoles muchos lucharon valientemente bajo el mando de ilustres caciques—nombre que se daba a gobernadores indígenas—como Guarionex y Cayacoa. En poco tiempo la isla se hispanizó totalmente.

La introducción del azúcar tuvo un tremendo impacto. Las plantaciones de caña necesitaban mucha mano de obra. Ya no había indígenas para hacer el trabajo y para sustituirlos, esclavizaron a africanos y los trajeron a las Antillas.

Durante casi dos siglos esta isla se vio sometida a ataques de piratas y corsarios[1] como «el Drake» y a disputas y acuerdos diplomáticos entre españoles, ingleses y franceses. La República Dominicana se independizó por fin en 1865.

[1] corsarios *corsairs, privateers*

Estelas taínas

 Contesten.

1. ¿En qué parte de la isla se encuentra la República Dominicana, este u oeste?
2. ¿Cuál ocupa más territorio, Haití o la República Dominicana?
3. ¿Qué quiere decir «Quisqueya»?
4. ¿Qué transporte emplearon los primeros habitantes para llegar a La Española?
5. ¿En qué se basaba la cultura de los taínos?
6. ¿Qué cultivo introdujeron los españoles a la isla?
7. ¿Quiénes sustituyeron a los indígenas en el trabajo forzado?
8. ¿Quién era «el Drake» y qué hicieron él y otros como él?
9. ¿Quiénes mantuvieron disputas sobre la isla durante muchos años?
10. ¿Qué significa el año 1865 en la historia de la República Dominicana?

La República Dominicana

 Identifiquen.

1. Guarionex y Cayacoa
2. El Drake

 Discutan.

Los taínos y otros indígenas de las Grandes Antillas casi desaparecieron. ¿Por qué?

Calle El Conde, Santo Domingo

Viejo San Juan, Puerto Rico

Puerto Rico

Puerto Rico, USA. Así dicen los anuncios turísticos. Puerto Rico es un Estado Libre Asociado de EE.UU. Los puertorriqueños son ciudadanos de EE.UU. como consecuencia de la guerra contra España en 1898.

Ponce de León

Igual que en la Española, los taínos se establecieron en Puerto Rico, isla que ellos llamaban Borinquén—«Tierra del altivo señor». Los españoles llegaron durante el segundo viaje de Colón a las Américas. Uno de los colonizadores de La Española, un soldado que había luchado contra los moros en la toma de Granada, don Juan Ponce de León, se vio nombrado primer gobernador de la isla que los españoles llamaban Isla de San Juan Bautista. Con el correr del tiempo San Juan pasó a ser el nombre de la capital y Puerto Rico el de la isla. Igual que en La Española, la población indígena se fue disminuyendo a causa de batallas, maltratos y enfermedades.

En Puerto Rico, como en sus otras colonias, los españoles, a diferencia de otros colonizadores, no se mantienen apartados de los indígenas. En 1514 el Rey da permiso oficial para que los españoles se casen con indígenas y más tarde se celebran matrimonios entre españoles y africanas. La mezcla de blancos, taínos y negros es la base de la población actual no sólo de Puerto Rico, sino de Cuba y la República Dominicana también.

Ponce, Puerto Rico

Casa Blanca, Viejo San Juan, Puerto Rico

Cancha de pelota de los taínos, Puerto Rico

Al terminar la Guerra de Cuba de 1898 entre España y Estados Unidos, Puerto Rico se convierte en colonia estadounidense. Medio siglo después Puerto Rico se establece como Estado Libre Asociado[2] de Estados Unidos adquiriendo un alto grado de gobierno propio y conservando la ciudadanía norteamericana. Hoy día en Puerto Rico la gente se divide en tres grupos políticos: los independentistas, que quieren independizarse de Estados Unidos, los «populares», que quieren mantener el Estado Libre Asociado y los estadistas, que quieren que Puerto Rico se haga un estado de Estados Unidos.

[2] Estado Libre Asociado *Commonwealth*

El Morro, San Juan, Puerto Rico

San Juan, Puerto Rico

Completen.

1. Puerto Rico es un _____ de Estados Unidos.
2. Los puertorriqueños son _____ de Estados Unidos.
3. En 1898 hubo una guerra entre Estados Unidos y _____.
4. En tiempos de los taínos, la isla se llamaba _____.
5. Al principio los españoles llamaban a Puerto Rico, Isla de _____.
6. El resultado de la Guerra de Cuba para Puerto Rico fue que se convirtió en _____ de Estados Unidos.
7. Con el Estado Libre Asociado, los puertorriqueños mantienen su ciudadanía estadounidense y también tienen un alto grado de _____.

Universidad de Puerto Rico

Identifiquen.

1. Cristóbal Colón
2. Don Juan Ponce de León

Cuba

Cuba, la Perla de las Antillas, fue la más importante de las colonias españolas en el Caribe. Colón la descubrió en su primer viaje pero pasaron veinte años antes de que los españoles tomaran posesión de la isla. Durante la primera mitad del siglo XIX cuando la mayoría de las colonias españolas se independizaron, Cuba se mantuvo fiel a la metrópoli[3]. Pero comenzando en 1868 y durante los siguientes treinta años los cubanos lucharon contra la dominación española hasta que ganaron su independencia después de la intervención de Estados Unidos en 1898. Los héroes de la independencia, José Martí y Antonio Maceo, perdieron la vida en esa lucha.

En 1959 Fidel Castro, a la cabeza de un grupo revolucionario, derrocó al gobierno corrupto del dictador Fulgencio Batista y estableció el primer gobierno comunista en las Américas. Miles de cubanos, desafectos al gobierno castrista, salieron de Cuba para establecerse en Estados Unidos, Puerto Rico y España.

[3] metrópoli *estado en relación con sus colonias*

José Martí

Fidel Castro

Teatro García Lorca, La Habana, Cuba

¿Sí o no?

1. De las colonias españolas del Caribe, Cuba fue la más importante.
2. Cuba se llamaba la Perla del Caribe.
3. Colón llegó a Cuba en su segundo viaje a las Américas.
4. Cuba se independizó al mismo tiempo que las otras colonias españolas.
5. Durante unos treinta años, los cubanos lucharon por su independencia.
6. En 1859 fue derrocado el gobierno de Batista.
7. Muchos cubanos desafectos al gobierno comunista salieron del país.

Identifiquen.

1. José Martí y Antonio Maceo
2. Fulgencio Batista
3. Fidel Castro

Visitas históricas

Cuba

Tienes que ver una de las ciudades más bellas de las Américas, San Cristóbal de La Habana, hoy simplemente, La Habana. Fundada en 1519, fue donde los galeones rebosando tesoro se reunían para emprender el viaje a España. Los españoles se dedicaron a hacer de La Habana la ciudad más fortificada de las Américas para protegerla de los ataques de ingleses y holandeses. La Habana colonial fue un centro de comercio, arte y cultura durante los siglos XVIII y XIX luciendo magníficas iglesias, residencias y otros edificios como la Catedral, el Castillo del Morro y el Castillo de la Real Fuerza, el edificio más antiguo de Cuba. Por su belleza y su enorme importancia histórica, la UNESCO ha declarado La Habana «Patrimonio de la Humanidad».

Santiago, Cuba

La Habana, Cuba

El Faro a Colón, Santo Domingo, la República Dominicana

La República Dominicana

Tienes que visitar la ciudad más antigua de las Américas, Santo Domingo, con sus muchos monumentos coloniales. Pero al oeste de la ciudad verás un monumento moderno, el Faro a Colón. Este monumento se abrió al público en octubre de 1992 para celebrar el quinto centenario del primer viaje de Cristóbal Colón a las Américas. Es un faro grande en forma de cruz. De noche 157 luces se proyectan verticalmente y reflejan la cruz en el cielo. Durante más de un siglo, según los dominicanos, los restos de Colón reposaban en la Catedral de Santo Domingo (aunque los españoles dicen que están en la Catedral de Sevilla). En 1992 se trasladaron al Faro y más de un millón de personas lo han visitado. A pesar de lo impresionante que es el monumento, es también tema de controversia. Lo construyeron en medio de un barrio pobre de casas muy humildes. En un país donde el 40 por ciento de la población carece de electricidad se cuestiona el gasto de millones para iluminar el cielo con miles de vatios.

Puerto Rico

Puerto Rico también tiene su preciosa capital colonial, San Juan. El Viejo San Juan es una verdadera joya. Pero si quieres visitar un monumento creado por la naturaleza, debes ir a ver las Cuevas de Camuy, no muy lejos de San Juan. En el Parque del Río Camuy existe un sistema de cavernas subterráneas, el tercero más grande del mundo. Allí, hasta la fecha, han descubierto dieciséis entradas y unos 11 kilómetros de pasajes subterráneos. Una de las cuevas, la Cueva Clara es más grande que un campo de fútbol. El río Camuy ha ido formando estas cavernas durante un millón de años. Un pequeño tranvía te llevará al Sumidero[4] Tres Pueblos donde puedes observar caer las aguas del río cientos de pies hasta el fondo del sumidero.

[4] Sumidero *Sinkhole*

I Cuba ¿Sí o no?

1. Los galeones se reunían en La Habana para comenzar su viaje a España.
2. Los españoles fortificaron La Habana contra ataques de los indígenas.
3. En La Habana colonial el comercio, las artes y la cultura florecieron.
4. La Catedral es el edificio más antiguo de La Habana.
5. La UNESCO declaró a La Habana «Patrimonio de la Humanidad».

Calle de las Damas, Santo Domingo, la República Dominicana

J La República Dominicana Contesten.

1. ¿Cuál es un monumento moderno en la República Dominicana?
2. ¿Cuál es la ciudad más antigua de las Américas?
3. ¿Qué forma tiene el Faro a Colón?
4. ¿Cuándo se inauguró el Faro?
5. ¿Cuál es la controversia sobre los restos de Cristóbal Colón?

K Puerto Rico Completen.

1. Las Cuevas de Camuy fueron creadas por la ____.
2. Allí hay 11 kilómetros de ____.
3. La Cueva Clara es más grande que un ____.
4. Puedes tomar un ____ para llegar al Sumidero Tres Pueblos.
5. El sistema de cavernas de Camuy es el ____ más extenso del mundo.

Comida

Claro está que cada país tiene sus especialidades de cocina, pero hay algunos platos que se encuentran en los tres países. En los tres se prepara el arroz con frijoles, en Cuba se llaman «moros y cristianos», en Puerto Rico «arroz con habichuelas», y para los dominicanos es, sencillamente, «arroz con frijoles». También a todos les encanta el lechón asado. Y en los tres países uno puede comer deliciosas frutas tropicales como la papaya, el mango, la piña, el coco y la banana. No te sorprendas si encuentras que las frutas a veces cambian de nombre de un país a otro, como es el caso de la banana, que también se llama guineo, plátano y otros nombres. Ah, y para beber, no hay nada como un vasito de guarapo frío, guarapo, el jugo de la caña de azúcar, tan dulce como el azúcar mismo.

Ponce, Puerto Rico

 De todos los alimentos del Caribe que se han mencionado, ¿cuál crees que te gustaría más, y por qué?

Beisbolista dominicano Danny Bautista

Anecdotario histórico-cultural

Criadero de beisbolistas En las últimas décadas del siglo XIX se empezó a jugar béisbol en la República Dominicana. Los dueños de las azucareras promovían partidos entre empleados de los distintos ingenios[5]. Hoy es el deporte nacional. Desde muy pequeños los niños aprenden a jugar. La pequeña ciudad de San Pedro de Macorís, en particular, ha mandado muchos jugadores a las Grandes Ligas, jugadores como Sammy Sosa de los Cachorros de Chicago, Alfonso Soriano de los Yankees y Pedro Martínez de Boston. Y no es nada nuevo, de allí han venido estrellas del pasado como Juan Marichal y los hermanos Alou; Matty, Felipe y Jesús. Hoy día veintinueve equipos de las Grandes Ligas mantienen «academias» para jugadores jóvenes en la República Dominicana. Hay setenta y cuatro dominicanos en las Grandes Ligas y ciento cincuenta en las Ligas Menores. ¡Increíble para un país con una población de sólo ocho y medio millones!

[5] ingenios *lugares donde se convierte la caña en azúcar*

 Contesten.

1. ¿Cuál es el deporte nacional de la República Dominicana?
2. ¿Cómo llegó a ser el deporte nacional?
3. ¿Qué fama tiene San Pedro de Macorís?
4. ¿Qué mantienen en la República Dominicana las Grandes Ligas?

Estructura • Repaso

Use your StudentWorks Plus CD for more practice.

Verbos reflexivos
Describing what people do for themselves

1. A verb is reflexive when the action is both executed and received by the subject.

Me lavo. *I wash myself.*

2. Because the subject also receives the action of the verb an additional pronoun is required. This pronoun is called a reflexive pronoun.

INFINITIVE	lavarse	bañarse
yo	me lavo	me baño
tú	te lavas	te bañas
él, ella, Ud.	se lava	se baña
nosotros(as)	nos lavamos	nos bañamos
vosotros(as)	*os laváis*	*os bañáis*
ellos, ellas, Uds.	se lavan	se bañan

3. These verbs have a stem change in both the present and preterite tenses.

despedirse (i, i)
vestirse (i, i)
divertirse (ie, i)
sentirse (ie, i)
dormirse (ue, u)

4. The reflexive pronoun is required only when the subject and recipient of the action are one and the same. If someone or something other than the subject receives the action of the verb, no reflexive pronoun is used.

María se lava.

María lava el carro.

Papá se acuesta.

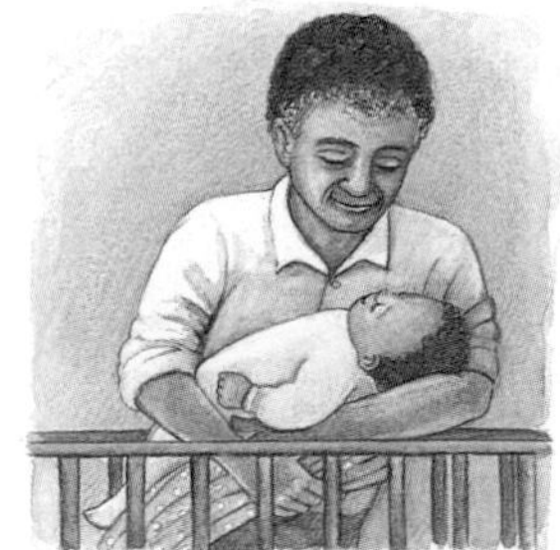
Papá acuesta al bebé.

¿Cómo lo digo?

1 Historieta Algunas costumbres mías

Contesten.

1. ¿A qué hora te acuestas?
2. ¿Te duermes enseguida o pasas la noche dando vueltas en la cama?
3. ¿A qué hora te levantas?
4. ¿Te despiertas fácilmente?
5. ¿Te bañas o te duchas antes de acostarte o después de levantarte?
6. ¿Te desayunas antes de salir para la escuela?
7. ¿Te cepillas los dientes después de tomar el desayuno?
8. ¿Te pones un uniforme para ir a la escuela?
9. ¿Te vistes elegantemente para ir a la escuela?
10. ¿Te diviertes con tus amigos en la escuela?
11. ¿Te despides de tus amigos cuando sales de la escuela?

San Juan, Puerto Rico

2 Historieta En Puerto Rico Contesten.

1. ¿Te divertiste cuando estabas en Puerto Rico?
2. ¿Te sentiste en casa?
3. ¿Te vestiste de sport?
4. ¿Te pusiste el bañador para ir a la playa?
5. ¿Te pusiste una crema protectora en la playa?
6. ¿Te bronceaste?
7. ¿Te dormiste en la playa?
8. Al salir de Puerto Rico, ¿te despediste de tus nuevos amigos?

3 Historieta El coronel

Completen con el presente.

El coronel __1__ (levantarse) y __2__ (vestirse) rápidamente. En estos días de guerra él __3__ (acostarse) muy tarde y __4__ (despertarse) pocas horas después. El coronel __5__ (ponerse) el uniforme. Hace tiempo que no __6__ (bañarse) ni __7__ (desayunarse) porque no hay tiempo ni posibilidad. Esta mañana él __8__ (entrevistarse) con el general. Los dos __9__ (sentarse). Después de una hora el general __10__ (ponerse) de pie y __11__ (despedirse) del coronel. La guerra no __12__ (detenerse).

4 No me dormí.

Escriban las oraciones en el pretérito.

1. Juan se acuesta a las diez y media.
2. Se duerme enseguida.
3. Desgraciadamente, yo no me duermo enseguida.
4. ¿A qué hora se acuestan ustedes?
5. ¿Y a qué hora se levantan?
6. Nosotros nos desayunamos en casa.
7. ¿Te desayunas en casa o en la escuela?
8. Juan se despide de sus padres antes de salir para la escuela.
9. Juan y sus amigos se divierten mucho en la escuela.

Santurce, Puerto Rico

5 Historieta ¿Reflexivo o no?

Completen con el pronombre si es necesario.

1. La señora _____ levanta temprano.
2. Después ella _____ despierta a su hijo.
3. Los dos _____ lavan el carro.
4. El hijo también _____ lava al perro.
5. Y después él _____ baña.
6. Los dos entran a la cocina y _____ desayunan.

Verbos recíprocos
Reciprocal actions

The subject of a reciprocal verb will always be two or more persons or things that simultaneously act upon each other. For this reason all reciprocal verbs are conjugated only in the plural, never in the singular.

Rosa y yo nos conocemos.	*Rose and I know one another.*
Ellos se vieron pero no se hablaron.	*They saw one another but they didn't speak to each other.*

In English the concept of reciprocity is often expressed by *each other* or *one another.*

¿Cómo lo digo?

6 **Se conocieron en la fiesta.** Completen.

1. Él me vio y yo lo vi. Nosotros _____ en la tienda por departamentos.
2. Ella me conoció y yo la conocí. Nosotros _____ en la fiesta de Alejandro.
3. Ella le escribió a él y él le escribió a ella. Ellos _____ la semana pasada.
4. Él la quiere y ella lo quiere. Ellos _____.
5. El niño ayuda a la niña y la niña ayuda al niño. Los niños _____ mucho.
6. Carlos encontró a María y María encontró a Carlos. Ellos _____ por casualidad en la esquina de Sol y Mayor.

7 **Historieta** **Se conocieron en San Pedro**
Completen.

Los dos jugadores, Roberto y Pepe __1__ (conocer) en San Pedro de Macorís. Pasaron años en qué no __2__ (ver). Pero sí que __3__ (escribir). Por fin __4__ (encontrar) en Nueva York con los Mets. Ellos __5__ (saludar) calurosamente. Son buenos amigos y __6__ (ayudar). Roberto dice: Pepe y yo __7__ (querer) como hermanos.

Los amigos no se hablan.
Ellos leen. San Juan

¡Te toca a ti!
Use what you have learned

La Habana, Cuba

1 Geografía

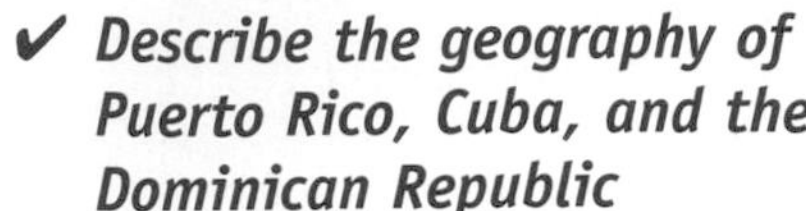

✔ ***Describe the geography of Puerto Rico, Cuba, and the Dominican Republic***

Con un(a) compañero(a) describe la geografía y el clima de las islas de las Grandes Antillas. ¿Se parecen a la geografía y al clima en donde tú vives? Haz una comparación.

2 Las vacaciones

✔ ***Write a suggestion about when to go to the Caribe***

Recibiste un e-mail de una amiga. Ella quiere ir a la República Dominicana, pero no sabe cuál sería la mejor época para su visita. Mándale un e-mail y dale una recomendación pensando en el clima y las estaciones del año.

San Juan, Puerto Rico

3 Las Antillas

✔ ***Make some comparisons between the islands of the Greater Antilles***

Describe algunas diferencias y semejanzas geográficas, históricas y políticas entre Puerto Rico, Cuba y la República Dominicana.

4 ¿De qué país hablas?

✔ ***Play a game and guess the country being discussed***

Tú vas a mencionar un lugar, monumento o evento en uno de los países de las Antillas. Tu compañero(a) tiene que adivinar cuál es el país. Si tu compañero(a) contesta correctamente, entonces él o ella te hará una pregunta a ti.

La República Dominicana y el béisbol

✔ ***Talk about the Dominican Republic and baseball***

Explícale como y por qué la República Dominicana es tan importante en cuanto al béisbol.

Tus rutinas

✔ ***Compare your daily routines***

Por lo general hay una diferencia entre tu rutina de entre semana y tu rutina de fin de semana, ¿no? Dile a un(a) compañero(a) como son diferentes.

¡Al Caribe!

✔ ***Tell why you would like to visit the Greater Antilles***

En tus estudios de español ya has aprendido mucho sobre las islas del Caribe. En tus propias palabras explica por qué las quisieras visitar.

Villa Fundación, la República Dominicana

Guajataca, Puerto Rico

Assessment

Vocabulario

1 Completen con una palabra apropiada.

1. Lo tomaron prisionero y lo llevaron a la prisión en _____.
2. Él tenía un espíritu independiente y nunca se _____ a los invasores.
3. Nunca colaboró con ellos, fue siempre _____ al gobierno.
4. Estaba muy cansado y buscaba donde _____ su cabeza.
5. Lo tenían en un lugar muy _____, muy lejos de todo.
6. Era un jefe de los indígenas, un _____ de gran fama.
7. Quería _____ su viaje aquel día pero no pudo a causa del viento.
8. Él luchó por la independencia para que sus hijos pudieran ser _____ de una nación independiente.
9. El clima de su bella isla era benévolo salvo cuando los _____ con sus tremendos vientos castigaban la isla.

To review vocabulary, turn to page 272.

La Habana, Cuba

Lectura

2 Escojan.

10. Hay ____ islas en las Grandes Antillas.
    a. dos b. cuatro c. ocho
11. Las Grandes Antillas, las Pequeñas Antillas y las Bahamas forman ____.
    a. un archipiélago b. un istmo c. una península
12. En el Caribe hay solamente ____ estaciones.
    a. dos b. cuatro c. seis
13. Los huracanes normalmente aparecen en ____.
    a. enero b. abril c. septiembre

To review some geographical facts about the Caribbean, turn to pages 274–275.

3 Contesten.

14. ¿Cómo llamaban los españoles a la isla que los taínos llamaban «Quisqueya»?
15. ¿Qué producto agrícola introdujeron los españoles a las Antillas?
16. Cuando ya no había indígenas para trabajar, ¿en qué continente encontraron los colonizadores más mano de obra?
17. ¿Cuáles son los tres partidos políticos de Puerto Rico?
18. ¿Por qué tuvieron que fortificar a La Habana los españoles?
19. ¿Por qué salieron muchos cubanos de su país después de 1959?

To review some historical facts about the Caribbean, turn to pages 276–283.

Estructura

4 Completen con el pronombre apropiado si es necesario.

20. Yo ____ puse unos jeans para ir a la fiesta.
21. ¿A qué hora ____ acostaste anoche?
22. Hace tiempo que tú y yo ____ conocemos, ¿verdad?
23. Pero Ramón y Carolina ____ conocieron hace solamente una semana.
24. Ella ____ divirtió mucho en la fiesta.
25. Después de la fiesta nosotros ____ lavamos todos los platos y vasos.

To review reflexive verbs, turn to pages 284 and 287.

Conversación

Vocabulario para la conversación

cascos de guayaba y queso blanco

Los cascos de guayaba son más dulces que el queso.

un churrasco

A mí me gusta un buen churrasco.

Más vocabulario

la carne quemada la carne bien hecha
los dueños los patronos, los jefes, los propietarios
descortés ineducado, grosero, no cortés
lento(a) contrario de «rápido»
listo(a) inteligente
rico(a) delicioso
acompañar ir con, juntarse
evitar eludir, evadir
por colmo para ser peor, para pasar el límite

¿Qué palabra necesito?

1 Historieta Al restaurante

Contesten según se indica.

1. ¿Adónde fuiste anoche? (a un restaurante)
2. ¿Quién te acompañó? (un buen amigo)
3. ¿Qué pediste? (un churrasco)
4. ¿Te gustó? (no)
5. ¿Por qué no te gustó? (estaba quemado)
6. De postre, ¿qué pidió tu amigo? (cascos de guayaba con queso blanco)
7. ¿Le gustó? (estaba muy rico)
8. ¿Y el servicio? (un poco lento)
9. ¿Evitarás volver al restaurante? (creo)

San Juan, Puerto Rico

2 ¿Cuál es otra palabra? Den un sinónimo.

1. los amos o los propietarios
2. sabroso, gustoso
3. evadir, escaparse de
4. astuto, hábil
5. carne de res, biftec
6. juntarse, ir con otra persona

Un restaurante «típico»

Antonio ¿Adónde fueron ustedes a comer anoche?

Elena Es mejor que no me preguntes. Fue la peor comida y un servicio tan malo que no lo puedes imaginar.

Antonio ¿Y dónde fue esto? Si aquí en la capital se come muy bien, mejor que en muchas partes. Y preparan nuestros platos caribeños tan ricos como ninguno.

Elena Pues, si yo fuera tan lista como tú, habría evitado el problema. Es verdad, muy pocas ciudades tienen tantos buenos restaurantes caribeños como aquí. Pero nosotros fuimos a un restaurante «argentino». Porque dicen que el «bife» argentino es el mejor del mundo, pedimos un churrasco.

Antonio Ah. Ustedes fueron a «El Gaucho Moncho», ¿verdad?

Elena Sí. ¿Cómo lo sabías?

Antonio Yo fui allí el otro día. Fue terrible. La carne era tan dura como una piedra. Además estaba quemada y tan seca como el desierto. Y el mesero… el hombre era tan lento y descortés que no le dejamos una propina. Y por colmo, los dueños del restaurante ni son argentinos ni han visitado nunca Argentina. Allí no hay nada auténtico. Esta noche vamos a un restaurante caribeño, «La flor de las Antillas». Ellos preparan nuestros platos mejor que nadie. ¿Quieres acompañarnos?

Elena Ay, Antonio. Lechón asado, tostones, bacalaítos[1]…

Antonio Ah, y lo mejor es que todo va acompañado de arroz con frijoles.

Elena ¡Cállate, Antonio! Se me hace agua la boca[2] sólo con pensarlo. Y de postre, cascos de guayaba y queso blanco. Tengo tanta hambre como un tigre. ¿A qué hora me buscas?

Antonio La mejor hora para comer allí es a las ocho. Te buscaré a las siete y media.

[1] bacalaítos *bits of fried codfish*
[2] Se me hace agua la boca *Makes my mouth water*

La República Dominicana

Spanish Online
To learn more about restaurants in the Caribbean, do the Chapter 6 **WebQuest** activity on the Glencoe Spanish Web site at glencoe.com.

LECCIÓN 2

Conversación

¿Comprendes?

Contesten.

1. ¿Dónde comió Elena anoche?
2. ¿Qué tipo de restaurante fue?
3. ¿Fue buena la comida?
4. ¿Qué tal el servicio?
5. ¿Comió Elena comida caribeña?
6. ¿Qué pidieron Elena y sus amigos?
7. ¿Les gustó?
8. ¿Ha comido Antonio en ese restaurante?
9. ¿Cuánto dejó de propina al mesero Antonio?
10. ¿Qué problemas tuvo con el mesero Antonio?
11. ¿Adónde va a comer Antonio esta noche?
12. ¿Qué tipo de comida sirven allí?

For more information about Caribbean foods, go to **Web Explore** on the Glencoe Spanish Web site at glencoe.com.

Expliquen y describan.

1. ¿Cómo sabía Antonio que Elena había comido en «El Gaucho Moncho»?
2. ¿Cómo era la carne que pidió Antonio en «El Gaucho Moncho»?
3. ¿Por qué dice Antonio que el lugar no es auténtico?
4. ¿Cuáles son algunos platos típicos de la comida caribeña?

Completen.

1. La Flor de las Antillas es un _____ caribeño.
2. Los cascos de guayaba se sirven con _____.
3. _____ son pedacitos de bacalao frito en forma de panqueque.
4. Muchos platos cubanos, puertorriqueños y dominicanos vienen acompañados de _____.

Un parque en Santo Domingo

Estructura • Repaso

Comparativo y superlativo—formas regulares
Making comparisons

1. The comparative construction is used to compare one item with another. In English you add *-er* to short adjectives and the word *more* in front of longer adjectives. To form the comparative in Spanish, you place the word **más** before the adjective and **que** after the adjective.

Elena es más lista que Antonio.
Ella come fuera más que yo.
Ella conoce más restaurantes que nadie.

2. When a pronoun follows the comparative construction, either the subject pronoun **(yo, tú, él, ella, usted, nosotros(as), ellos, ellas, ustedes)** or a negative word **(nadie)** is used.

Él dice que come más que yo.
La verdad es que come más que nadie.

3. The superlative expresses that which is the *most.* In English the suffix *-est* is added to short adjectives and *most* in front of longer adjectives. To form the superlative in Spanish, you use the definite article **(el, la, los, las)** plus **más** before the adjective. The adjective is usually followed by **de.**

La piña es la (fruta) más rica de todas.
El helado de coco es el más sabroso de todos.

The opposite of **más** is **menos** *(less),* **el menos** *(least).*

El pescado tiene menos grasa que la carne.
Para mí, el helado de vainilla es el menos interesante de todos.

San Juan, Puerto Rico

LECCIÓN 2

Conversación

¿Cómo lo digo?

1 **Tu familia** **Preguntas personales** Contesten.

1. En tu familia, ¿quién es más alto(a) que tú?
2. ¿Quién come más que tú?
3. ¿Quién es más listo(a) que tú?
4. ¿Quién es menos listo(a) que tú?
5. ¿Quién es el (la) más listo(a) de la familia?
6. ¿Quién es el (la) más descortés de la familia?

2 **El Caribe** Formen oraciones con el superlativo.

1. Cuba / isla / grande / Antillas
2. La Española /colonia /antigua / Américas
3. lechón /comida / típica / región
4. caña / producto / importante / país
5. taínos / indígenas / numerosos / Caribe

3 **Comidas** Sigan el modelo.

guayaba / manzana / naranja (rico) →
La guayaba es rica, la manzana es más rica que la guayaba, pero la naranja es la más rica de todas.

1. el bife / el pollo / el pescado (delicioso)
2. el helado / la fruta / el flan (dulce)
3. el jamón / el chorizo / el marisco (caro)
4. los plátanos / las guayabas / los melones (fresco)
5. el arroz / las papas / el maíz (sabroso)

Una vista de la costa cubana

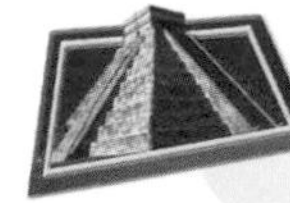

Comparativo y superlativo—formas irregulares
Making comparisons

1. The following adjectives have irregular comparative and superlative forms.

bueno	**mejor**	**el / la mejor**	**malo**	**peor**	**el / la peor**
grande	**mayor**	**el / la mayor**	**pequeño**	**menor**	**el / la menor**

Menor and **mayor** refer to age and quantity. For size, use **más grande** or **más pequeño.**

Ella es mayor que su hermano. (Tiene más años.)
Ella es más grande que su hermano. (Es más alta, etc.)

2. Mejor and **peor** are also used as adverbs.

bien	**mejor**	**el mejor**	**mal**	**peor**	**el peor**

José cocina mejor que yo.
De todos es él que cocina el mejor.

¿Cómo lo digo?

4 **Tu clase de español** Contesten.

1. ¿Quién es el/la mejor estudiante de la clase?
2. ¿Quién recibe las mejores notas?
3. ¿Recibes tú las mejores notas?
4. ¿Quién es el/la mayor de la clase? ¿Cuántos años tiene?
5. ¿Quién es el/la menor de la clase y cuántos años tiene?

Villa Fundación, la República Dominicana

5 **Los pacientes** Completen con un adverbio apropiado.

1. Don Ramón está _____ ahora; ya no está enfermo.
2. Doña Elena sigue enferma pero está _____ ahora; ya no le duele tanto.
3. Pero el señor Álvarez está _____ y los médicos están preocupados.
4. Y la señora Rosas se siente _____, pero no es nada grave.

6 **Patricia perfecta** Escojan.

1. Patricia juega béisbol mejor que _____.
   a. ti **b.** tú
2. Y ella juega mejor que _____ también.
   a. mi **b.** yo
3. La verdad es que ella juega mejor que _____.
   a. nadie **b.** alguien
4. Ella prefiere jugar béisbol más que _____.
   a. nada **b.** algo

Comparativo de igualdad
Stating like qualities

1. Very often we compare two items that have the same characteristics. Such a comparison is called the comparison of equality. In English we use the expression *as . . . as*. In Spanish **tan... como** is used with either an adjective or an adverb.

   José es tan deportista como su hermana.
   Él juega tan bien como ella.

2. The comparison of equality can also be used with nouns. In English we use *as much as, as many as*. In Spanish the expression **tanto... como** is used with nouns. **Tanto** must agree with the noun it modifies.

   Ella tiene tanta fuerza como él.
   Ella ha ganado tantos campeonatos como él.

¿Cómo lo digo?

7 Historieta **Al restaurante** Contesten.

1. ¿Ella tiene tanto dinero como tú?
2. ¿Ella es tan rica como tú?
3. ¿Ella va con tanta frecuencia al restaurante como tú?
4. ¿Ella va a tantos restaurantes como tú?
5. ¿Ella es tan aficionada a la cocina antillana como tú?

8 Historieta **Los cocineros** Completen con expresiones de igualdad.

1. Él prepara ____ platos ____ ella.
2. Él ha cocinado para ____ personas ____ ella.
3. Ella usa ____ ingredientes ____ él.
4. Su restaurante es ____ popular ____ el de él.
5. Ella tiene ____ clientes ____ él.
6. Sus postres son ____ ricos ____ sus quesos.

9 Historieta **Las Grandes Antillas**
Completen con expresiones de igualdad.

1. Puerto Rico es ____ montañosa ____ la República Dominicana.
2. Cuba tiene ____ playas ____ Puerto Rico.
3. En Santo Domingo hace ____ calor ____ en San Juan.
4. En Cuba se juega ____ béisbol ____ en Puerto Rico.
5. La República Dominicana cultiva ____ frutas ____ Puerto Rico.

San Juan, Puerto Rico

¡Te toca a ti!
Use what you have learned

En el peor de los restaurantes

✔ ***Describe a horrendous restaurant experience***

Con un(a) compañero(a), vas a preparar la siguiente conversación. Acabas de comer quizás la peor comida de tu vida. No había nada bueno y el servicio era peor. Llama al dueño(a) (tu compañero[a]) para contarle todo lo que pasó. Tu compañero(a) dará tantas explicaciones como pueda.

Este restaurante me gustó.

✔ ***Write about a good restaurant experience***

Anoche fuiste a un restaurante «auténtico» que te gustó muchísimo. Prepara un e-mail a un amigo diciéndole qué tipo de restaurante era. Describe el restaurante y dile lo que comiste y por qué te gustó tanto. Dile si tienes planes para volver en el futuro.

El menú

✔ ***Write a menu for a Caribbean restaurant***

En tus estudios de español has aprendido los nombres de muchos platos típicos de la región caribeña. Con un(a) compañero(a), preparen un menú para un restaurante caribeño. No se olviden de los postres.

Una reservación

✔ ***Make a restaurant reservation on the telephone***

Tú eres el/la cliente y tu compañero(a) trabaja en un restaurante caribeño. Llama por teléfono. Quieres hacer una reservación. Tienes que decirle para cuando, para cuantas personas, la hora, lo que prefieren comer, etc. Después cambien de rol.

Assessment

Vocabulario

1 Completen con una palabra apropiada.

1. La comida estuvo muy ____ , realmente sabrosa.
2. ¿La carne? Comimos un ____ argentino.
3. Me gusta la carne a término medio pero me la sirvieron ____. La habían cocinado demasiado.

4–5. De postre pedimos cascos de ____ con ____ blanco.

To review vocabulary, turn to page 292.

2 Escriban la palabra cuya definición sigue.

6. hacerle compañía a una persona, ir con él o ella
7. grosero o ineducado, desatento
8. para hacerlo aún peor
9. lo contrario de «rápido», que toma tiempo en funcionar
10. personas que son amos o propietarios de propiedades, tiendas, etc.

Conversación

3 Contesten según la conversación.

To review the conversation, turn to page 293.

11. En la ciudad donde están Antonio y Elena, ¿qué tipo de comida preparan muy bien?
12. ¿A qué tipo de restaurante fue Elena anoche?
13. Cuando Antonio fue al restaurante, ¿qué problema había con la carne?
14. ¿Por qué no le dejó Antonio una propina al mesero?
15. ¿Por qué cree Antonio que «El Gaucho Moncho» no es auténtico?
16. ¿Qué postres servirán esta noche en «La Flor de las Antillas»?
17. ¿Con qué sirven arroz con frijoles?
18. ¿A qué hora irá Antonio a buscar a Elena?

Estructura

4 Completen con el comparativo o superlativo.

To review comparative and superlative, turn to pages 295 and 296.

19–20. Este restaurante es _____ caro _____ el otro. El otro es económico.

21–22. Hay más meseros aquí porque el restaurante es _____ grande _____ el otro.

23–24. El postre _____ delicioso _____ todos es el flan.

5 Completen con el comparativo de igualdad.

To review comparisons of equality, turn to page 298.

25–26. Puerto Rico es _____ montañoso _____ la República Dominicana.

27–28. Cuba tiene _____ vegetación tropical _____ Puerto Rico.

29–30. Ponce no tiene _____ habitantes _____ San Juan.

San Juan, Puerto Rico

Periodismo

Vocabulario para la lectura

Dos nadadoras isleñas avanzan
Con la mira en pasar a Atenas

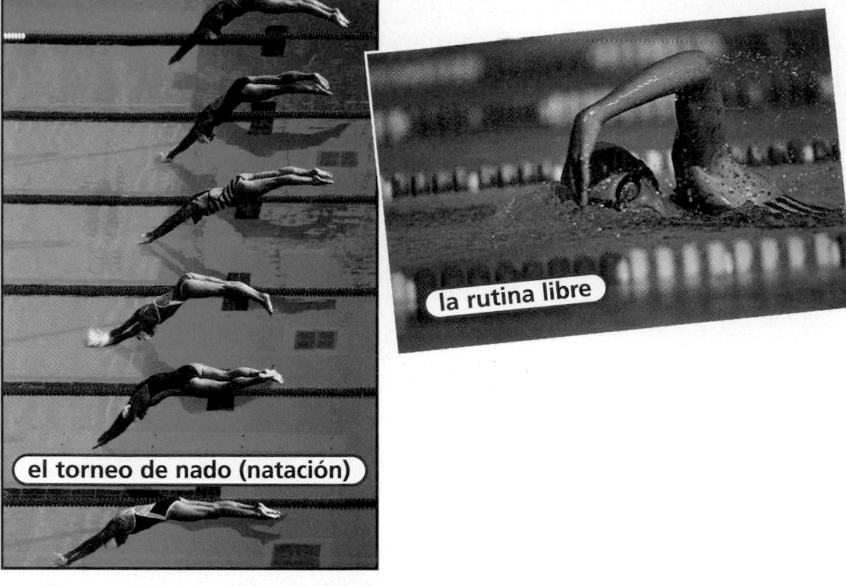

El torneo de nado está integrado por muchas atletas. ¡Ojalá que ganen el campeonato mundial!

Más vocabulario

la mira intención, idea, propósito
remozado(a) renovado, modernizado
zurdo(a) que usa la mano izquierda
encabezar ir al frente, ir a la cabeza
realizar hacer, efectuar
ubicarse colocarse, situarse

¿Qué palabra necesito?

1 Historieta **El torneo de nado (natación)** Contesten.

1. ¿Qué tipo de torneo es? ¿De nado?
2. ¿La nadadora realiza clavados?
3. ¿Es ella experta en clavados?
4. ¿Se realizará la rutina libre hoy?
5. ¿Se realizará la rutina libre en la piscina municipal?

2 **Sóftbol femenino** Completen.

1. La pítcher lanza la pelota con la mano izquierda. Ella es ____.
2. Ella es la mejor jugadora y por eso ____ el equipo.
3. La ____ del equipo es su participación en los juegos Preolímpicos.
4. El equipo está ____ por muchas atletas muy buenas.
5. El estadio estaba en malas condiciones, pero ahora está totalmente ____.

San Juan, Puerto Rico

Dos nadadoras isleñas avanzan

EL DUETO puertorriqueño integrado por Luna del Mar Aguilú y Leilani Torres se ubicó ayer en la posición 24 de entre 34 equipos al concluir con 81.000 la preliminar técnica del nado sincronizado de los Campeonatos Mundiales de Natación y Clavados que se celebrarán hasta el domingo 27 en Barcelona, España. Hoy se realizará la rutina libre.

Con la mira en pasar a Atenas

LA ESTELAR zurda Jessica van der Linden Dávila encabeza el grupo de 18 jugadoras que integrarán el Equipo Nacional que participará desde el próximo lunes 21 en el torneo Preolímpico de Sóftbol Femenino en el remozado estadio Donna Terry de Guaynabo.

¿Comprendes?

Dos nadadoras isleñas Contesten.

1. ¿En qué deporte participan Leilani y Luna del Mar?
2. ¿Los campeonatos son de natación y qué otra cosa?
3. ¿Cuántos equipos en total estuvieron en el preliminar de nado sincronizado?
4. ¿En qué lugar se encontró el equipo puertorriqueño?
5. ¿Dónde tuvo lugar el evento?
6. ¿Qué evento se realizará hoy?

A Atenas Contesten.

1. ¿Cuántas jugadoras integran el equipo nacional de sóftbol?
2. ¿Cómo se llama la joven que encabeza el equipo?
3. ¿Con qué mano tira ella la pelota?
4. ¿En qué estadio y en qué pueblo van a jugar ellas?
5. ¿Qué han hecho con el estadio?

Vocabulario para la lectura
Educación llega a la cárcel

Los reclusos están en la cárcel.
Aunque están en la cárcel, pueden seguir con sus estudios.

Más vocabulario

el/la analfabeto(a) el que no sabe leer ni escribir
el conocimiento entendimiento, lo que uno sabe o entiende
la marginalidad estado de separación de la sociedad
conductual respecto a la conducta
imprescindible esencial, indispensable, absolutamente necesario
mediante por medio de
proclive con tendencia o inclinación
requerible necesario
manejar usar, utilizar

¿Qué palabra necesito?

1 **Las clases** Contesten.

1. Están en la cárcel. ¿Qué son?
2. No saben leer ni escribir. ¿Qué son?
3. Aunque son reclusos, ¿con qué pueden seguir?
4. Tu lápiz no tiene punta. ¿Qué necesitas?

2 **Los reclusos** Contesten.

1. Son ____ porque cometieron un crimen.
2. Están en la ____ con los otros prisioneros.
3. Algunos son muy ____ a la violencia.
4. Tenemos muchos problemas ____ con ellos. Su conducta es a veces peligrosa.
5. Es ____ mantener la disciplina y el orden.
6. Como no han tenido mucha instrucción, tienen un nivel de ____ muy bajo.
7. Queremos integrar a los reclusos a la sociedad porque ahora sufren de la ____.

3 **Sinónimos** Expresen de otra manera.

1. Es *indispensable* mantener la disciplina estricta.
2. Ellos tienen problemas *de conducta.*
3. Pueden mejorar su vida *por medio de* la educación.
4. Yo sé que él lo sabrá *utilizar.*
5. Tienen todos los materiales *necesarios.*

Listín Diario

Educación llega a la cárcel de San Fco. de Macorís y Salcedo

Voz escrita de San Francisco y el Nordeste, No. 365, Edición 1, Rep. Dom.
—Por Francisco Taveras Ortíz

Con la firme convicción de que sólo mediante el recurso de la educación se reducen los niveles de pobreza y marginalidad social, se han implementado en la cárcel pública de esta ciudad de San Francisco de Macorís cinco grupos de estudiantes adultos (reclusos) cuyo nivel de conocimiento o son analfabetos o no han cursado el tercer ciclo (8vo.), lo mismo ha ocurrido en la cárcel para mujeres de Salcedo.

Se han integrado de acuerdo a sus niveles de conocimiento y han recibido todo el material requerible para que asistan al grupo con el material didáctico imprescindible, tales como módulos, tiza, lápices, sacapuntas, pizarras y los maestros facilitadores recibieron los entrenamientos necesarios para manejar con un mínimo de error los diferentes procesos que tienen que manejar, incluyendo situaciones conductuales.

Los reclusos que prestan servicio como facilitadores recibirán incentivos económicos y de otra naturaleza, a fin de motivarlos para garantizar el éxito de estos cursos. Para la implementación de los cursos se cuenta con la colaboración del Ayuntamiento Municipal y la Gobernación Provincial. Se organiza también un curso de inglés para una cantidad de 27 reclusos que lo solicitaron, lo que suma una matrícula estudiantil de reclusos y reclusas a un total de 151 educandos.

Se aprecia que al salir de las cárceles, estos reclusos podrán insertarse a la sociedad con un mejor nivel de conciencia, mayor nivel cultural y social, que les permitirá insertarse a la vida productiva y familiar con mayor capacidad y una actitud positiva hacia la vida. Podrían manejar con más ecuanimidad[1] los diferentes conflictos con los que encuentran en la vida.

De igual manera puede crearse un mejor clima de tranquilidad y sosiego[2] entre presidiarios[3] y presidiarias, servirle de ocupación y hasta de entretenimiento mientras estén allí y los puede convertir en hombres y mujeres de bien, y al volver a las calles podrían exhibir más entusiasmo y esperanza para la vida y sus familiares.

Es interés de la vicepresidente y secretaria de Estado de Educación, doctora Milagros Ortíz Bosch, combatir la pobreza y la marginalidad social a través de la educación, que es el único y más eficaz medio para lograrlo, en el entendido que a menor nivel de conocimiento son más críticos los niveles de pobreza y a mayor nivel de conocimiento mayores serán los niveles de riquezas tanto individual como para el país.

La vida sedentaria que llevan estos seres humanos, les hace proclives a delinquir, tanto dentro de las cárceles como cuando salen, pero al tenerlos ocupados, tienen menos tiempo para la holgazanería[4] y expresar actitudes negativas donde los más vulnerables resultan siempre ser los más débiles.

[1] ecuanimidad *composure, calmness*
[2] sosiego *tranquility*
[3] presidiarios *inmates, convicts*
[4] holgazanería *laziness*

¿Comprendes?

A **Historieta** **Educación en la cárcel** Contesten.

1. ¿En qué cárcel han implementado el programa?
2. ¿Cuántos grupos de estudiantes hay en San Francisco de Macorís?
3. ¿Cuál es el nivel de conocimiento de los estudiantes?
4. ¿Quiénes son los estudiantes?
5. ¿Qué recibieron los maestros entrenadores?
6. ¿Qué han usado para motivar a los reclusos que sirven de facilitadores?
7. ¿Qué organismos oficiales han colaborado en la implementación de los cursos?
8. Veintisiete reclusos solicitaron un curso. ¿Cuál es el curso?
9. ¿Cuál es el total de reclusos que participan en el programa?
10. Según el artículo, ¿qué les hace a los reclusos proclives a delinquir?

La cárcel más antigua de Puerto Rico, Arecibo

B **Expliquen** En sus propias palabras expliquen lo que quiere decir…

1. sólo mediante el recurso de la educación se reducen los niveles de pobreza y marginalidad social.
2. lo que suma una matrícula estudiantil de reclusos y reclusas a un total de 151 educandos.
3. al volver a las calles podrían exhibir más entusiasmo y esperanza para la vida y sus familiares.

C **Síntesis** La doctora Ortíz Bosch y el licenciado Taveras Ortíz creen que el programa tendrá un efecto muy importante para el país. ¿Cuál es? En pocas palabras describe lo que ellos esperan del programa.

Estructura • Avanzada

Subjuntivo con aunque
Expressing *although*

La República Dominicana

The conjunction **aunque** *(although)* may be followed by the subjunctive or the indicative depending upon the meaning of the sentence.

Ellas nadarán aunque haga mucho frío.
Ellas nadarán aunque hace mucho frío.

In the first example, the subjunctive is used to indicate that although it may not be cold now, they will swim even if it gets very cold. In the second example, the indicative is used to indicate that it actually is very cold but they will still swim.

¿Cómo lo digo?

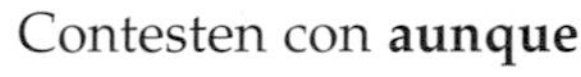

1 Historieta ¿Lo hacemos o no?

Contesten con **aunque.**

1. No tienes un boleto. ¿Vas al concierto?
2. No sé si el carro tiene bastante gasolina. ¿Vas a ir en el carro?
3. Podría llover. ¿Vendrá Diana con nosotros?
4. Subieron los precios de las entradas. ¿Todavía vamos?
5. Y si hay mucho tráfico, ¿qué? ¿Iremos o no?
6. No sé si Paco Mendes va a tocar. ¿Vas a ir?
7. Tito no tiene dinero. ¿Lo vas a llevar al concierto?
8. Y si la profesora nos da tarea, ¿todavía vamos a ir?

Carretera entre San Juan y Arecibo, Puerto Rico

2 Historieta Los reclusos

Escojan la forma apropiada del verbo.

1. El profesor recibe un salario. Pero le gusta tanto su trabajo, el profesor enseñará aunque no le (pagan/paguen).
2. Les dieron materiales a los reclusos. Pero tienen tantas ganas de aprender que los reclusos estudiarán aunque no (tienen/tengan) materiales.
3. Los oficiales no visitan la cárcel hoy. Pero no importa. Van a dar clases hoy aunque no (vienen/vengan) los oficiales.
4. No hay duda que falta dinero. Pero siguen implementando los cursos aunque no (hay/haya) dinero.
5. El público se opone. El Secretario seguirá con el programa aunque el público no (quiere/quiera) que siga.

Subjuntivo con **quizás, tal vez** y **ojalá**
Statements with *perhaps* or *maybe*

1. The adverbs **quizá(s)**, *perhaps*, and **ojalá,** *I wish, would that*, are always followed by the subjunctive. Note that **ojalá** can be followed by either the present or the imperfect subjunctive.

    Quizás jueguen hoy.
    Ojalá (que) ganen el partido.
    Ojalá (que) ganaran.

2. The expression **tal vez,** *perhaps*, can be followed by either the subjunctive or the future indicative.

    Tal vez pierdan hoy. **Tal vez perderán.**

¿Cómo lo digo?

3 Historieta Las atletas Contesten según el modelo.

¿El torneo comenzará hoy? →
No sé. Quizás comience hoy.

1. ¿El torneo comenzará hoy?
2. ¿Tus hermanas participarán?
3. ¿Tu hermana mayor encabezará el equipo?
4. ¿Ellas ganarán el campeonato de clavados?
5. ¿Recibirán un trofeo?
6. ¿El entrenador estará contento?
7. ¿Irás tú a verlas?

San Juan, Puerto Rico

Santo Domingo, la República Dominicana

4 Tal vez... Contesten con **tal vez.**

1. ¿Los reclusos van a estudiar inglés?
2. ¿Van a pagar a los profesores?
3. ¿Los facilitadores van a recibir incentivos?
4. ¿Los reclusos van a aprender mucho?
5. ¿El gobierno les va a ayudar?
6. ¿El programa va a tener éxito?

For more information about these Caribbean countries, go to **Web Explore** on the Glencoe Spanish Web site at glencoe.com.

Presente perfecto y pluscuamperfecto del subjuntivo
Expressing opinions and feelings about what has or had happened

1. The present perfect subjunctive is formed by using the present subjunctive of the auxiliary verb **haber** and the past participle. Study the following forms of the present perfect subjunctive.

INFINITIVE	hablar	comer	vivir
yo	haya hablado	haya comido	haya vivido
tú	hayas hablado	hayas comido	hayas vivido
él, ella, Ud.	haya hablado	haya comido	haya vivido
nosotros(as)	hayamos hablado	hayamos comido	hayamos vivido
vosotros(as)	*hayáis hablado*	*hayáis comido*	*hayáis vivido*
ellos, ellas, Uds.	hayan hablado	hayan comido	hayan vivido

2. The present perfect subjunctive is used when the action in the dependent clause occurred before the action in the main clause.

Me alegro mucho de que tú hayas venido. *I'm very glad that you have come.*
Dudo que ellos lo hayan visto. *I doubt that they have seen it.*

Varadero, Cuba

3. The pluperfect subjunctive is formed with the imperfect subjunctive of the auxiliary verb **haber** and the past participle. Study the forms of the pluperfect subjunctive.

INFINITIVE	hablar	comer	vivir
yo	hubiera hablado	hubiera comido	hubiera vivido
tú	hubieras hablado	hubieras comido	hubieras vivido
él, ella, Ud.	hubiera hablado	hubiera comido	hubiera vivido
nosotros(as)	hubiéramos hablado	hubiéramos comido	hubiéramos vivido
vosotros(as)	*hubierais hablado*	*hubierais comido*	*hubierais vivido*
ellos, ellas, Uds.	hubieran hablado	hubieran comido	hubieran vivido

4. The pluperfect subjunctive is used after a verb in a past tense that requires the subjunctive, when the action of the verb in the subjunctive occurred prior to the action of the verb in the main clause.

Me sorprendió que ellos hubieran hecho tal cosa. *It surprised me that they had (would have) done such a thing.*

¿Cómo lo digo?

5 Historieta Cursos en la cárcel Contesten.

1. ¿Te sorprende que hayan establecido cursos en la cárcel?
2. ¿Te alegras de que hayan comprado materiales didácticos para los reclusos?
3. ¿Te sorprende que tantos reclusos hayan tomado el curso de inglés?
4. ¿Están contentos los profesores de estos cursos que la mayoría de los estudiantes hayan salido muy bien y que hayan recibido notas altas?

6 Confusión Completen en el pasado.

1. Yo dudo que él lo ____. (hacer)
2. Y él duda que yo lo ____. (hacer)
3. ¿Es posible que nadie le ____ que yo lo he terminado? (decir)
4. Sí, es posible, porque nosotros dudamos que tú lo ____. (terminar)
5. Pues, me molesta que ustedes no ____ el trabajo que yo he hecho. (ver)

San Juan, Puerto Rico

7 Me sorprendió Sigan el modelo.

Me sorprende que tú hayas hecho tal cosa. →

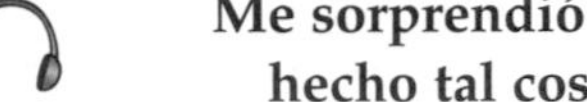

Me sorprendió que tú hubieras hecho tal cosa.

1. Me sorprende que él haya participado en el evento.
2. Me sorprende que tú hayas nadado en el torneo.
3. Me sorprende que ellos no hayan ganado el trofeo.
4. Me sorprende que no hayan ido al campeonato mundial.
5. Me sorprende que eso te haya sido una sorpresa.

8 Historieta La Guardia Civil Completen con el pluscuamperfecto del subjuntivo.

1. Temíamos que ellos ____. (volver)
2. Pero nos alegramos de que la Guardia Civil ____. (venir)
3. Yo dudaba que ellos ____ regresar a casa. (poder)
4. Nadie creía que los guardias civiles ____ a los ladrones. (arrestar)
5. Era increíble que ellos ____ a todos. (encontrar)

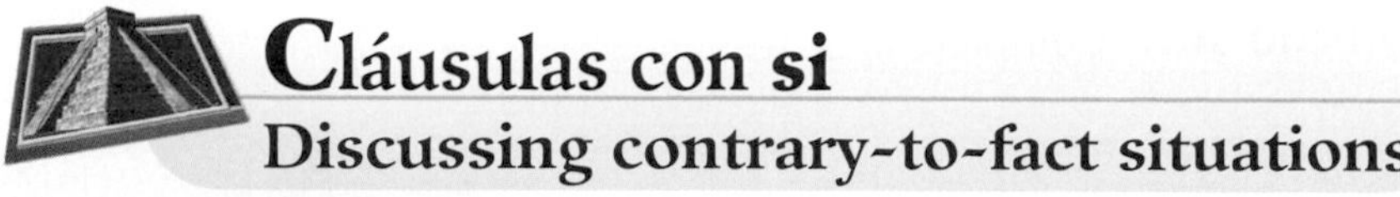

Cláusulas con si
Discussing contrary-to-fact situations

1. **Si** *(if)* clauses are used to express contrary-to-fact conditions. **Si** clauses conform to a specific sequence of tenses.

Si tengo tiempo iré al torneo.	*If I have time, I'll go to the tournament.*
Si tuviera tiempo iría al torneo.	*If I had time, I would go to the tournament.*
Si hubiera tenido tiempo, habría ido al torneo.	*If I had had time, I would have gone to the tournament.*

2. The sequence of tenses for **si** clauses is as follows:

MAIN CLAUSE	**SI** CLAUSE
Future	Present indicative
Conditional	Imperfect subjunctive
Conditional perfect	Pluperfect subjunctive

¿Cómo lo digo?

Yo Contesten.

1. Si tienes el dinero, ¿irás a Puerto Rico?
2. Si tuvieras el dinero, ¿irías a Puerto Rico?
3. Si hubieras tenido el dinero, ¿habrías ido a Puerto Rico?
4. Si vas a Puerto Rico, ¿visitarás las cuevas de Camuy?
5. Si fueras a Puerto Rico, ¿visitarías las cuevas de Camuy?
6. Si hubieras ido a Puerto Rico, ¿habrías visitado las cuevas de Camuy?

ESTADO LIBRE ASOCIADO DE PUERTO RICO
COMPAÑÍA DE
PARQUES NACIONALES
029032

PARQUE DE LAS CAVERNAS
DEL RÍO CAMUY, PUERTO RICO

Admisión para **Adultos:** $10.00

EXCURSIÓN A CUEVAS CLARAS

El Viejo San Juan, Puerto Rico

10 Lo que haré, haría o habría hecho si... Completen.

1. **invitar**
   Yo jugaré con el equipo si ellos me ____.
   Juana también jugaría si la ____.
   Y el sábado pasado, tú habrías jugado si te ____.
2. **permitir**
   Yo iré a los campeonatos si la profesora me ____.
   Ignacio también iría si la profesora le ____.
   Y ayer todos nosotros habríamos ido si la profesora nos ____.
3. **tener**
   Yo compraré las entradas si ____ bastante dinero.
   Ella también compraría las entradas si ____ bastante dinero.
   Y ustedes habrían comprado las entradas si ____ bastante dinero.
4. **dar**
   Yo asistiré si tú me ____ una entrada.
   Sé que tú asistirías si yo te ____ una entrada.
   Y mis amigos habrían asistido si alguien les ____ una entrada.
5. **jugar**
   Nosotros ganaremos si Teresa ____.
   Ellos ganarían si las hermanas Sánchez ____.
   Si Teresa ____ nosotros habríamos ganado ayer.

Santo Domingo

Palacio Nacional, Santo Domingo, la República Dominicana

11 ¿Qué harías? Preguntas personales Contesten.

1. Si cierran la escuela la semana que viene, ¿qué harás?
2. Si te dieran un carro nuevo, ¿adónde irías?
3. Si tú fueras un(a) gran atleta, ¿con qué equipo jugarías?
4. Si tú no hubieras decidido estudiar el español, ¿qué otra asignatura habrías escogido?
5. Si cualquier persona aceptara tu invitación a un baile, ¿a quién invitarías?
6. Si encuentras un millón de dólares en la calle, ¿qué harás?

¡Te toca a ti!

Use what you have learned

Las atletas

✔ Discuss female athletics in your school

En tu escuela, ¿hay muchos equipos femeninos? ¿En qué deportes participan las muchachas? A los deportes para las muchachas, ¿se les da bastante énfasis, poco énfasis, demasiado énfasis? Con tu grupo discutan y digan sus opiniones. Den un breve resumen de sus opiniones a la clase.

Los reclusos ¿Rehabilitación o castigo?

✔ Discuss your opinions on the purpose of incarceration

Algunas personas creen que las cárceles o penitenciarías deben ser para castigar a los reclusos por sus crímenes. Otros creen que el sistema debe enfocar en rehabilitar a los reclusos para reinsertarlos en la sociedad. Con tu grupo discutan los dos puntos de vista y expresen sus opiniones.

Una conversación

✔ Talk about your favorite sports

En tus estudios de español has aprendido mucho sobre varios deportes. Con un(a) compañero(a) discutan sus deportes favoritos. ¿Son ustedes aficionados a los mismos deportes o no?

Plaza las Américas, San Juan, Puerto Rico

Un millón de dólares

✔ Tell what you would do

Di todo lo que harías si tuvieras un millón de dólares.

Les he sorprendido.

✔ Tell some things you've done that surprised your friends

¿Hay algunas cosas que haces o que te interesan que les sorprende a tus padres, parientes o amigos? Di lo que les sorprende o sorprendió.

Assessment

Vocabulario

1 Completen.

1. La pítcher no tira con la mano derecha porque es ____.
2. El equipo está ____ por quince jugadoras.
3. Laura es la capitán del equipo. Ella ____ el grupo.
4. Después de ganar todos los partidos ellos se ____ en la primera división.

To review vocabulary, turn to pages 302 and 304.

2 Den otra palabra.

5. Su participación es *indispensable* para que todo salga bien.
6. Ramón sabe *utilizar* los materiales muy bien.
7. Él tiene gran *entendimiento* de asuntos técnicos.
8. No obstante, él *no sabe leer ni escribir.*

Lectura

To review the newspaper articles about sports, turn to page 303.

3 Contesten.

9. ¿Por qué fueron a Barcelona Luna del Mar Aguilú y Leilani Torres?
10. ¿Qué ha pasado con el estadio Donna Terry?

To review the newspaper article about education in jail, turn to page 305.

4 ¿Sí o no?

11. El programa en Salcedo es sólo para mujeres.
12. Un grupo de reclusos ha solicitado un curso de francés.
13. El propósito del programa es ayudar a reintegrar a los reclusos a la sociedad.

Estructura

5 Escojan.

14. La temperatura está bajo cero.
    a. Ellos irán aunque hace mucho frío.
    b. Ellos irán aunque haga mucho frío.
15. No hay duda que Sandra va a jugar.
    a. No importa. Perderán aunque juega Sandra.
    b. No importa. Perderán aunque juegue Sandra.

To review **aunque**, turn to page 307.

6 Completen con la forma apropiada del verbo.

16. ¡Ojalá los reclusos _____ a leer! (aprender)
17. Quizás _____ escribir a sus familiares. (poder)
18. Tal vez el programa _____ éxito. (tener)

To review expressions with **quizás** and **tal vez**, turn to page 308.

7 Completen en el pasado.

19. Ellos están contentos que nosotros _____ a tiempo. (llegar)
20. Me sorprendió que tú _____ tal cosa. (hacer)
21. Él te lo dijo. Francamente yo dudaba que él te lo _____. (decir)
22. ¿Te sorprende que ellos _____ tal programa? (empezar)

To review the present perfect and pluperfect subjunctive, turn to page 309.

8 Escojan.

23. Nosotros iremos si ellos nos _____.
    a. acompañan b. acompañaran c. hubieran acompañado
24. Pero Eloísa habría ido solamente si Paco la _____.
    a. acompaña b. acompañara c. hubiera acompañado
25. Y tú, ¿volverías temprano si yo _____ contigo?
    a. vuelvo b. volviera c. hubiera vuelto

To review **si** clauses, turn to page 311.

San Juan, Puerto Rico

For more Chapter 6 test preparation, go to the Chapter 6 **Self-Check Quiz** on the Glencoe Spanish Web site at glencoe.com.

Proficiency Tasks

Composición

Cada escrito tiene un propósito. El propósito de tu primera tarea es la de informar. Vas a compartir con otros la información que has obtenido de tus propias lecturas y experiencias. Vas a escribir un artículo de crónica. En este tipo de artículo normalmente se presenta la información en un orden cronológico.

TAREA 1 **Escritura expositiva** Acabas de leer en detalle sobre la geografía, historia y cultura de tres países de habla española: Cuba, Puerto Rico y la República Dominicana. Tienes que seleccionar el tema en que vas a enfocar. Como lo que tienes que escribir es una crónica, obviamente la historia es lo indicado como tema.

Antes de escribir Primero debes releer el material de fondo. Entonces toma apuntes sobre los detalles de más importancia, siempre en orden cronológico. Si crees que necesitas más información, pregúntale a tu profesor(a) donde puedes encontrar recursos adicionales.

Bosquejo Prepara ahora un bosquejo del artículo para organizar tus ideas. Ahora piensa en el formato de tu crónica. Piensa en tu público. Quieres interesarle en el tema. Por eso lo primero que vas a escribir es una introducción.

La introducción tiene el propósito de atraer al público, a animarle a leer el artículo. Aquí hay algunas sugerencias:

- un detalle interesante
- una imagen que indica la idea central
- una descripción gráfica del lugar
- un retrato de la gente
- un evento que da impulso a la historia

Para la parte principal del artículo:

- Emplea detalles vivaces, escoge adjetivos fuertes.
- Describe los personajes importantes.
- Mantén el orden cronológico.
- Haz que los lectores se identifiquen con los personajes.

Para el final del artículo puedes emplear las mismas estrategias como para la introducción: un detalle interesante, una imagen, etc.

Presentación Escribe la crónica.

Repasar y revisar Revisa tu crónica para verificar si todo está escrito correctamente y si has incluido toda la información necesaria. Corrige cualquier error ortográfico o gramatical.

TAREA 2 **Explicación** Un propósito de muchos escritos es la explicación de un evento o condición. Por lo que has leído de otros países de Latinoamérica sabes que las poblaciones indígenas son significativas en varios, pero no en el Caribe. En un breve escrito explica como es que desaparecieron casi por completo las poblaciones indígenas del Caribe. En tu escrito debes indicar:

- donde en el Caribe existían las poblaciones indígenas
- cuáles eran las poblaciones y de donde vinieron
- las características de las poblaciones
- la causa de su desaparición

Antes de escribir Antes de comenzar a escribir, piensa en como vas a organizar tu explicación. Determina los detalles que vas a incluir. Decide también en el tono de tu escrito. ¿Será simplemente expositivo o tendrá también un matiz emotivo? Cuando tengas todo decidido, prepara un borrador.

Revisa tu borrador para ver si estás satisfecho(a) con el contenido. ¿Está completo? ¿Falta algún detalle? ¿Son vívidas las descripciones? Cuando estás satisfecho(a) con el borrador léelo de nuevo y corrige cualquier error de gramática u ortografía. Ahora prepara tu versión final, revísala para que no haya errores. Corrige los errores que encuentres.

TAREA 3 **Una biografía** Como ya sabes, una biografía es la historia de la vida de una persona real, no ficticia. Ya has escrito una biografía de una persona que tú mismo(a) has escogido. Ahora vas a limitarte a uno de los personajes que aparecen en el capítulo que acabas de leer. Para prepararte adecuadamente tendrás que hacer alguna investigación sobre la persona. Los personajes que aparecen en la lectura son: Guarionex, Cayacoa, Cristóbal Colón, «el Drake», don Juan Ponce de León, José Martí, Antonio Maceo y Fidel Castro.

Antes de escribir Escoge de la lista de personajes algunos que tú crees serán interesantes. Después busca a ver si existe bastante información sobre estas personas para poder escribir una biografía. Ahora escoge el individuo que más te interese. Prepara una lista de detalles que vas a incluir en tu biografía, por ejemplo: descripción física de la persona, su personalidad o carácter, su importancia histórica. Puedes seguir un orden cronológico, o puedes enfocar en uno de los detalles que creas más importante, su importancia histórica, por ejemplo. Trata de dar vida al personaje empleando adjetivos y adverbios vívidos.

Discurso

El debate es similar a una competencia deportiva. Se juega para ganar y se gana obteniendo ventaja sobre el rival. Una forma de debate consiste en una proposición. Un grupo o individuo tiene que defender la proposición mientras que el otro lleva la contraria. Un ejemplo de proposición sería: *A los atletas profesionales se les paga demasiado.* Un grupo defiende la proposición y el otro se opone. Para debatir eficazmente hay que ordenar los argumentos y presentarlos enérgicamente. Algunas armas son la veracidad, el humor, el dramatismo y la emoción. En muchos debates se le otorga a cada partido una oportunidad de responder a los argumentos del rival. Por eso es importante tratar de adivinar cuales serán los argumentos que presentará el rival y poder contestar vigorosamente. El buen debatiente puede tomar cualquier posición, en pro o en contra de la proposición y defender su posición con éxito.

TAREA 4 Para nuestro debate vamos a dividirnos en grupos de dos. La proposición es la siguiente: *El único propósito de las cárceles debe ser castigar a los criminales.* Una persona en cada grupo tiene que defender la proposición y la otra argüir en contra. Después de presentar los argumentos cada uno tendrá un minuto para refutar los argumentos del otro. La clase decidirá el ganador.

Vocabulario

Lección 1 Cultura

Geografía
la caña de azúcar
el cultivo
el huracán
castigar

Historia
el cacique
la cadena
el/la ciudadano(a)
el galeón
la toma
apartado(a)
desafecto(a)
dedicarse
emprender
hundirse
rebosar
reposar
someterse
por poco

Comidas
el arroz con frijoles (habichuelas)
el coco
el lechón asado
el mango
la papaya
la piña

Lección 2 Conversación

el casco de guayaba
el churrasco
el/la dueño(a)
el queso blanco

descortés
bien hecho(a)
lento(a)

listo(a)
quemado(a)
rico(a)

acompañar
evitar
por colmo

Lección 3 Periodismo

Deportes
el campeonato
el clavado
la mira
el/la nadador(a)
el nado, la natación
la rutina libre
el torneo
mundial
remozado(a)
zurdo(a)
encabezar
integrar
realizar
ubicarse
ojalá

Educación llega a la cárcel
el/la analfabeto(a)
la cárcel
el conocimiento
la marginalidad
la pizarra
el recluso
el sacapuntas
conductual
imprescindible
mediante
proclive
requerible
manejar

LITERARY COMPANION *See pages 476–487 for literary selections related to Chapter 6. The activities for these readings will help you continue to practice your reading comprehension skills.*

VIDEOTUR

¡Viva el mundo hispano!

Video can be a beneficial learning tool for the language student. Video enables you to experience the material in the textbook in a real-life setting. Take a vicarious field trip as you see people interacting at home, at school, at the market, etc. The cultural benefits are limitless as you experience the Spanish-speaking world while "traveling" through many countries. In addition to its tremendous cultural value, video gives practice in developing good listening and viewing skills. Video allows you to look for numerous clues that are evident in tone of voice, facial expressions, and gestures. Through video you can see and hear the diversity of the target culture and compare and contrast the Spanish-speaking cultures to each other and to your own.

Episodio 1: Viejo San Juan

La ciudad de San Juan fue fundada en 1508 por don Juan Ponce de León. Es una bella ciudad colonial. Sus calles adoquinadas y sus clásicos edificios son preciosos. Caminar por esas calles es hacer un viaje al pasado. A los sanjuaneros les encanta estar en la calle para ver a los amigos, hablar y disfrutar de su encantadora ciudad.

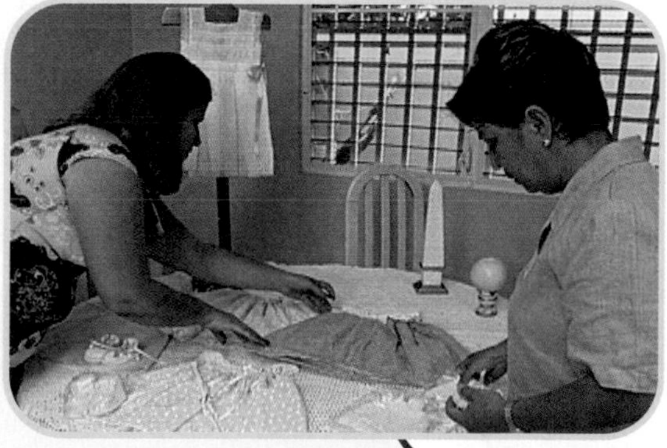

Episodio 2: Las tejedoras

María es tejedora. Ella practica una arte con una larga historia en Puerto Rico. María hace ropa infantil que vende en ferias artesanales. Ella aprendió a tejer con su abuela y su madre. Todos los días ellas se reúnen en casa de María para tejer. La hija de María, Alondra, está aprendiendo a tejer también. Para ellas es una manera de ganar dinero, pero más importante aún, es la forma de conservar una tradición.

Episodio 3: Visita al bosque tropical

Recientemente se estableció un programa llamado Ecoventure para dar a la gente de la ciudad la oportunidad de ver de cerca la naturaleza. Este grupo está visitando el Bosque de Toro Negro a pocas horas de San Juan. Toro Negro es un bosque tropical. Es la reserva más alta de Puerto Rico y tiene una enorme variedad de plantas y animales.

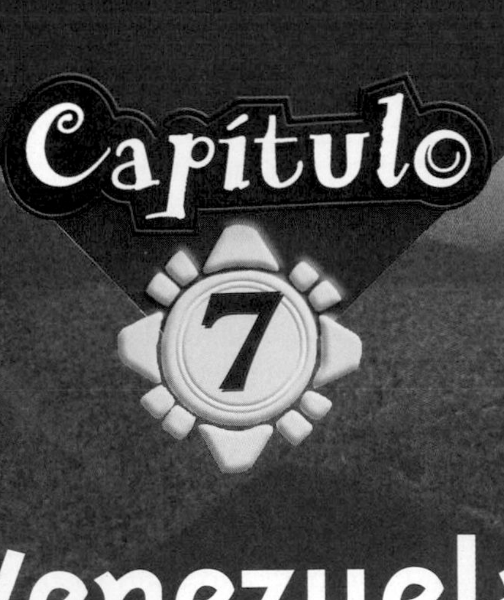

Capítulo 7

Venezuela y Colombia

Spanish Online

To interact with your online edition of **¡Buen viaje!** go to: glencoe.com.

Objetivos

In this chapter you will:

- learn about the geography, history, and culture of Venezuela and Colombia
- review shortened forms of adjectives
- review uses of articles
- discuss a museum visit and a show
- review prepositional pronouns
- read and discuss newspaper articles about teachers in Colombia and the hazards of gasoline
- learn the uses of **por** and **para**
- learn to express duration of time using **hace** and **hacía**

Contenido

Cultura

Vocabulario para la lectura

Un bohío lacustre está construido sobre pilotes.

La desembocadura es donde el río entra en el mar.

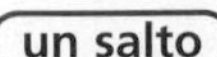

Se cultiva el café en las laderas de la montaña. El café es un producto importante de Colombia.

Más vocabulario

la deuda dinero que se debe a alguien
la empresa acción de dar principio a una obra
la sequía falta de lluvia durante largos períodos de tiempo
cálido(a) caluroso, muy caliente
espeso(a) que tiene mucha densidad; cosas muy próximas (cercanas) unas de otras
fluvial de un río
imperante que domina, que tiene el poder
inolvidable que no se puede olvidar
lacustre que vive en los bordes o en las aguas de un río
asemejarse a ser similar o semejante
enriquecerse hacerse uno rico, prosperar
oprimir someter por la violencia, poniendo uno debajo de la autoridad o dominio de otro
sellar llevar a una conclusión
surgir salir, aparecer, alcanzar algo cierta altura relativo a lo que le rodea

¿Qué palabra necesito?

A orillas del Orinoco, Venezuela

1 Cositas Contesten.

1. ¿Es un bohío una casa elegante o humilde?
2. ¿Está en el desierto una casa lacustre?
3. ¿Sobre qué está construida una casa lacustre?
4. ¿Es una caleta o una ensenada una gran extensión de agua?
5. ¿Dónde entra el río en el mar?
6. ¿Cuál es el nombre que se le da a una ciudad alrededor de la cual hay murallas?
7. ¿Dónde crece el café?
8. ¿Tiene el salto una caída larga?
9. ¿Llueve mucho durante una sequía?
10. ¿De qué color es una mazorca de maíz?

2 Definiciones Empareen.

1. cálido	a. tiranizar
2. la deuda	b. prosperar
3. imperante	c. dominante
4. sellar	d. caluroso
5. oprimir	e. dinero debido
6. enriquecerse	f. concluir

Bogotá, Colombia

3 ¿Cuál es la palabra? Completen.

1. Un bohío lacustre está construido sobre _____ en un _____.
2. El río Magdalena es navegable hasta Bogotá. Un barco _____ hace el viaje de Barranquilla a Bogotá.
3. Para él es una _____ nueva. ¡Ojalá que tenga éxito!
4. ¡Ojalá que se haga rico! Todos sabemos que tiene muchas ganas de _____.
5. Ella va a tomar una decisión para _____ el proyecto.
6. Son muy similares. El uno _____ mucho al otro.
7. La vegetación de una selva tropical es muy densa. Es muy _____.
8. El dictador _____ a sus súbditos.

Lectura

La geografía

Venezuela

Venezuela en el nordeste del continente sudamericano es un país de grandes contrastes geográficos. Dos veces más grande que California es el único país sudamericano cuya costa se encuentra totalmente en el Caribe.

El río Orinoco y sus tributarios forman el sistema fluvial más importante de Sudamérica después de el del Amazonas. Una región de temperaturas cálidas la cuenca del Orinoco se encuentra bajo agua por unos seis meses del año y durante los otros seis sufre de una sequía severa sin una gotita de lluvia.

El Orinoco divide a Venezuela en dos partes iguales. Al sur está la Sierra de la Guayana, una vasta región remota de bellísimas mesetas de arenisca[1] que surgen de la verde selva tropical que cubre la mitad del país. Al norte del río se encuentran las grandes sabanas o llanos donde viven los llaneros cuya vida ganadera es muy similar a la de los gauchos argentinos. Más al norte hacia la costa está la región andina con sus ciudades donde vive la mayoría de la población venezolana.

No muy lejos de la capital, Caracas, está el lago Maracaibo, un lago rico en oro negro o sea petróleo. Venezuela es uno de los más importantes productores de petróleo del mundo.

Fue la región de Maracaibo adonde llegaron los primeros exploradores españoles. Encontraron a muchos indígenas que vivían en bohíos lacustres y que iban de un lugar a otro en canoas. Les hizo pensar en la ciudad italiana de canales, Venecia, y le dieron al territorio el nombre de «Venezuela» o «Venecia pequeña».

[1] arenisca *sandstone*

Sierra de la Guayana, Venezuela

Yacimiento de petróleo en Trujillo, Venezuela

Caracas, Venezuela

Colombia

Se puede dividir Colombia en cuatro regiones geográficas, la costa, la sierra andina, los llanos al sureste del país y la selva tropical bañada por los afluentes de los ríos Orinoco y Amazonas. En los llanos viven los llaneros cuya vida se asemeja mucho a la de los gauchos de la Pampa argentina. Como su vecino, Venezuela, casi la mitad del país es selva tropical.

Barranquilla en la desembocadura del río Magdalena en la costa del Caribe es el puerto más importante del país. El Magdalena es uno de los ríos más largos del mundo y es navegable hasta la capital andina, Bogotá, a unos 8640 pies sobre el nivel del mar. El viaje en barco fluvial tarda nueve días.

Desde el punto de vista cultural y comercial la región andina se considera la más importante del país. Bogotá es el centro político e intelectual. Medellín, la capital de la región de Antioquia es una ciudad industrial que compite con Bogotá desde el punto de vista de importancia económica. Medellín goza de un clima ideal. Se le llama «la ciudad de las flores, la amistad y la primavera eterna». Es la capital del mundo en el cultivo de orquídeas. Y en las laderas de las montañas antioqueñas se cultiva el famoso café colombiano.

Río Magdalena, Colombia

Medellín, Colombia

A Venezuela Contesten.

1. ¿Dónde está Venezuela?
2. ¿Dónde tiene costa?
3. ¿Qué forman el Orinoco y sus tributarios?
4. ¿En qué divide el Orinoco a Venezuela?
5. ¿Qué es la Sierra de la Guayana?
6. ¿Qué cubre la mitad de Venezuela?
7. ¿Quiénes viven en las grandes sabanas o llanos?
8. ¿Dónde está la mayoría de las ciudades venezolanas?
9. ¿Qué hay en el lago Maracaibo?
10. ¿Cómo recibió su nombre Venezuela?

B El clima Describan.

Describan el clima en la cuenca del Orinoco.

C Colombia Identifiquen.

1. las cuatro regiones geográficas de Colombia
2. los llaneros
3. Barranquilla
4. el río Magdalena
5. Bogotá
6. Medellín
7. el nombre que se le da a Medellín

Medellín, Colombia

Historia

Unas anécdotas

Históricamente es Colombia el país que dio vida a la famosa leyenda de *El Dorado.* En el siglo XVI los españoles habían oído del rito de los muiscas, un grupo de los chibchas, en el cual cubrían el cuerpo de su jefe en polvo de oro. Este mito les entusiasmó a los españoles a explorar esta región. Con su afán de encontrar oro creían que aquí se enriquecerían grandiosamente.

El rey de España Carlos I, Carlos V de Austria, era soberano también de Alemania. Debía grandes cantidades de dinero a unos banqueros alemanes, los Welser. A causa de sus deudas, les concedió la conquista de Venezuela. Los Welser nombraron a Ambrosio Alfinger gobernador de Venezuela. Este fundó la ciudad de Maracaibo en 1530. Alfinger tenía la reputación de ser muy cruel y siguió explorando hasta que llegó a territorio que no le correspondía—territorio colombiano. Cayó mortalmente herido en 1533 en un encuentro con unos indígenas pero hay quienes creen que lo hirió uno de sus propios soldados. Un año más tarde llegó a Venezuela otra expedición alemana bajo el mando de Nicolás de Federman. Federman pasó tres años explorando nuevos territorios hasta llegar a la meseta de Bogotá. ¡Allí le esperaba una gran sorpresa!

Carlos I

Alonso de Ojeda fue el primer español (1530) que llegó a lo que hoy es Colombia cuando entró en Cartagena, pero enseguida fue expulsado por los indígenas. Otro explorador, Jiménez de Quesada salió del puerto de Santa Marta en 1536 para seguir el curso del río Magdalena y explorar el interior de Colombia. Subiendo montañas y cruzando torrentes Quesada encontró oro y esmeraldas y en 1537 fundó la ciudad de Santafé de Bogotá. ¡Al año siguiente recibió una sorpresa!

Alonso de Ojeda

Taganga, Magdalena, Colombia

Terminada la conquista de Perú salieron varias expediciones españolas a diferentes regiones. Un teniente de Pizarro, Sebastián de Benalcázar, fue a Quito y continuó hacia el norte donde fundó la ciudad de Popayán en Colombia y avanzó hasta la meseta de Bogotá. ¡Qué sorpresa! Allí encontró a Gonzalo Jiménez de Quesada, el fundador de Bogotá y al alemán Nicolás de Federman.

Gonzalo Jiménez de Quesada fue abogado de profesión y convenció a Benalcázar y a Federman de dejarle a él la empresa de completar la colonización de lo que sería la Nueva Granada. Y así fue.

En 1546 Carlos V suspendió los privilegios de los banqueros alemanes y nombró a Juan Pérez de Tolosa gobernador de Venezuela.

Playa Guacuco, Isla Margarita, Venezuela

D Anécdotas históricas ¿Sí o no?

1. Los muiscas eran indígenas de Colombia que cubrían el cuerpo de su jefe de joyas preciosas.
2. El rey de España permitió a unos alemanes a conquistar Venezuela.
3. El rey era un buen amigo de estos alemanes.
4. Un «explorador» alemán llegó hasta Bogotá.
5. Jiménez de Quesada es el primer español que llegó a lo que hoy es Colombia.
6. Jiménez de Quesada navegó el río Magdalena de la costa al altiplano donde fundó la ciudad de Santafé de Bogotá.
7. Terminada la conquista de Perú, todos los hombres de Pizarro volvieron a España.

E Personajes históricos Identifiquen.

1. Carlos I o Carlos V
2. Ambrosio Alfinger
3. Alonso de Ojeda
4. Gonzalo Jiménez de Quesada
5. Sebastián de Benalcázar

La independencia

Simón Bolívar nació en Venezuela en 1783 de una familia noble y adinerada. Uno de los profesores del joven Simón tenía mucha influencia en su vida. Le explicaba que el rey de España gozaba de poder absoluto y que oprimía a sus súbditos. Le enseñaba las ideas liberales imperantes en Francia y EE.UU. A su tío no le gustaba que su sobrino aprendiera tales ideas y lo envió a estudiar en España. Pero Bolívar nunca se olvidó de lo que le había enseñado su antiguo profesor, Simón Rodríguez.

Bolívar volvió a Venezuela en 1810 para tomar parte en la rebelión contra los españoles. Fue nombrado coronel del ejército y para 1812 ya era general. En 1813 entró triunfante en Caracas donde derrotó a los españoles y recibió el título de «el Libertador».

Plaza Simón Bolívar, Caracas, Venezuela

Boyacá, Colombia

Pero pronto llegaron refuerzos españoles y Bolívar tuvo que refugiarse en Santo Domingo. Allí organizó un nuevo ejército y desembarcó una vez más en Venezuela donde fue proclamado presidente de la República. Siguió la lucha por la independencia y en 1819, con mucha dificultad, atravesó los imponentes Andes. Derrotó a las fuerzas españolas y fundó la República de la Gran Colombia que hoy comprende Colombia, Venezuela y Ecuador. Aceptó la presidencia de la nueva república. Luego pasó a Perú donde selló la independencia sudamericana ganando las batallas de Junín y Ayacucho en 1824.

Después de su triunfo en Perú, el Libertador volvió a Colombia con su gran sueño de ver unido el continente sudamericano en una sola confederación que rivalizara con EE.UU. Pero al llegar a Colombia se dio cuenta de que había muchas disensiones políticas. Existían diferencias insolubles entre las distintas regiones. Bolívar tomó poderes dictatoriales para tratar de preservar la integridad de la Gran Colombia pero fue inútil. Se dividió en varias repúblicas y Bolívar murió en Santa Marta en la pobreza a los cuarenta y siete años de edad (1830), desilusionado de no haber realizado su sueño de ver al continente sudamericano convertido en una sola nación.

Después de la independencia

Tanto en Colombia como en Venezuela los años después de la independencia son muy conflictivos. Hubo intrigas políticas, épocas de mal gobierno, pronunciamientos[1] militares, guerras civiles e intervenciones extranjeras.

Si el siglo XIX fue conflictivo para las hermanas repúblicas, igual de conflictivo ha sido el siglo XX. Colombia ha tenido más de treinta y cinco cambios de gobierno y Venezuela más de veinticinco. Aunque ha habido algunos períodos cortos de relativa calma, ambos países han sufrido dictaduras militares, golpes de estado[2] y terrible violencia en el transcurso del siglo XX.

Las dos repúblicas latinoamericanas son países de jóvenes. La edad promedio[3] de Venezuela es de 22.6 años y la de Colombia es de 23.7 años. El futuro está en sus manos. Es para ellos sacar adelante a sus patrias y asegurar que las riquezas materiales y espirituales sean patrimonio de todos los que habitan estas bellas y vibrantes tierras.

Fuente de Oro, Colombia

[1] pronunciamientos *uprisings*
[2] golpes de estado *coups d'etat*
[3] promedio *average*

Simón Bolívar Den la siguiente información.

1. donde y en qué ambiente nació Bolívar
2. lo que aprendía de su profesor favorito
3. adonde lo mandó su tío a estudiar
4. lo que hizo al volver a Venezuela en 1810
5. el título que le dieron
6. por qué tuvo que refugiarse en Santo Domingo
7. lo que hizo en Santo Domingo
8. por donde siguió la lucha por la independencia al regresar de Santo Domingo
9. lo que era el gran sueño de Bolívar
10. donde murió y como

Después de la independencia Den una lista de los problemas políticos con los cuales Colombia y Venezuela han enfrentado desde su independencia.

Visitas históricas

No puedes ir a Colombia sin visitar la bonita ciudad de Cartagena. La vieja ciudad colonial amurallada ha cambiado muy poco a través de los siglos. Tan bonita es la ciudad que UNESCO la ha declarado Patrimonio de la Humanidad. Si quieres descansar puedes ir a pasar un rato en las playas de Boca Chica. O puedes volar a la isla de San Andrés donde puedes disfrutar de playas de arena blanca fina bordeadas de palmeras bajo un cielo azul caribeño. Se dice que en una cueva de una caleta de San Andrés el pirata Henry Morgan enterró un tesoro de oro que vale un billón de dólares. Los turistas siguen buscándolo.

Cartagena, Colombia

San Andrés, Colombia

Tampoco puedes perder las dos capitales, Bogotá y Caracas. Cada una tiene avenidas anchas con rascacielos modernos y grandes centros comerciales. Y cada una tiene su pintoresco casco antiguo llamado «La Candelaria» en Bogotá.

Algo inolvidable en Venezuela es el Salto Ángel que toma su nombre del piloto norteamericano que en 1935 buscaba una montaña de oro cuando chocó su avioneta. Se dice que es él que descubrió el salto más alto del mundo con una altura total de más de 3.000 pies y una caída ininterrumpida de 2.648 pies—quince veces más alto que las cataratas del Niagara.

Caracas, Venezuela

Salto Ángel, Bolívar, Venezuela

Comida

Una arepa

Si durante tus visitas tienes hambre... ¡a comer arepas! Tanto en Colombia como en Venezuela encontrarás arepas en todas partes. Son riquísimas tortas de maíz rellenas de jamón, queso, chorizo, pollo, frijoles y carne mechada.

En Colombia hay que probar un sancocho cuya preparación varía de una región a otra. Un buen sancocho es el sancocho paisa de Antioquia. Es una sopa espesa de carne de res y cerdo, yuca, papas, plátanos, mazorca y cilantro.

Y para tomar, jugo de frutas tropicales; jugo de guanábana, guayaba, papaya, mango, piña y melón. O una taza del famoso café colombiano. ¡Qué ricos!

Mérida, Venezuela

H **Lugares interesantes** Describan.

1. Cartagena
2. San Andrés
3. Bogotá y Caracas
4. Salto Ángel

I **Platos típicos** Expliquen.

Expliquen la diferencia entre «arepas» que se comen en Colombia y Venezuela y «sancocho», un plato popular en Colombia.

Sancocho

Estructura • Repaso

Adjetivos apocopados
Shortened forms of adjectives

Iglesia San Pedro Claver, Cartagena, Colombia

1. Several adjectives in Spanish have a shortened form when they precede a masculine singular noun. The **o** of the ending is dropped.

bueno	**La expedición tenía un buen jefe.**
malo	**Esa zona tenía muy mal aspecto.**
primero	**Pero allí establecieron el primer pueblo.**
tercero	**Fue el tercer intento de establecer un pueblo.**

2. The adjective **grande** becomes **gran** when it precedes a singular masculine or feminine noun. The form **gran** conveys the idea of *great* or *famous* rather than *big* or *large.*

una gran mujer	*a great woman*
una mujer grande	*a big woman*
un gran hombre	*a great man*
un hombre grande	*a big man*

3. **Alguno** and **ninguno** also drop the **o** before a masculine singular noun.

Algún día serán independientes. Ningún dictador tendrá poder.

4. The number **ciento** is shortened to **cien** before a masculine or feminine noun.

El rascacielos tiene más de cien pisos.
Y más de cien compañías tienen oficinas allí.

5. The word **Santo** becomes **San** before a masculine saint's name unless the name begins with **To-** or **Do-**.

San Pedro	**Santo Domingo**	**Santa Marta**
San Diego	**Santo Tomás**	**Santa Teresa**

¿Cómo lo digo?

1 La guerra y la independencia Completen.

1. Bolívar no es sólo un _____ general, es también un _____ héroe. (bueno, grande)
2. Pero el _____ héroe de la Independencia es Francisco de Miranda. (primero)
3. La Revolución francesa fue la _____ revolución del siglo. (primero)
4. Entre sus tropas había _____ traidor. (alguno)
5. Pero no tuvo _____ oportunidad para hacer daño. (ninguno)
6. En el _____ día de la batalla lo descubrieron. (tercero)
7. Y aunque fue un hombre _____ y fuerte, lo tomaron preso. (grande)
8. Lo llevaron a _____ Fernando. (Santo)
9. Él era un _____ hombre y tuvo muy _____ suerte. (malo, malo)
10. Lástima, porque él era de una familia _____. (bueno)

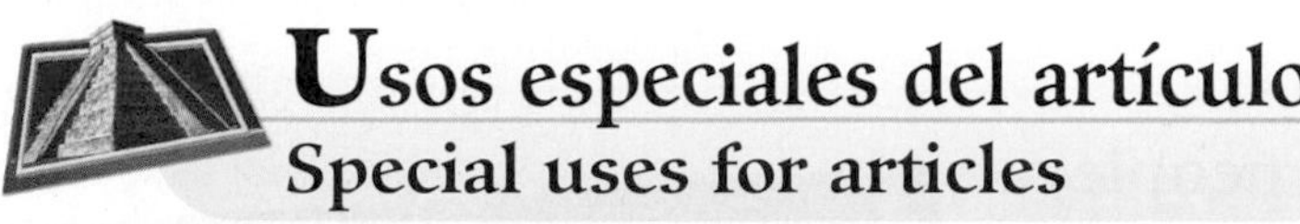

Usos especiales del artículo
Special uses for articles

In English an article is not used with an abstract noun or a noun used in a generic or general sense. In Spanish, however, the definite article is required before nouns used in a general sense and before abstract nouns. Compare the following sentences.

Me gusta el café. *I like coffee.*
El café es un producto importante de Colombia. *Coffee is an important product of Colombia.*
El valor es una virtud. *Bravery is a virtue.*

¿Cómo lo digo?

2 **Un poco de geografía** Contesten.

1. ¿Son secos los desiertos?
2. ¿Tienen agua salada o agua dulce los océanos?
3. ¿Tienen agua salada o dulce los lagos?
4. ¿Tienen una vegetación densa y espesa las selvas tropicales?
5. ¿Son hispanohablantes los colombianos y venezolanos?

3 **Las clases de ciencias** Completen.

En __1__ clases de ciencias aprendemos mucho. En __2__ clase de biología, por ejemplo, estudiamos __3__ amebas y __4__ paramecios. En la clase de química aprendemos algo sobre __5__ sustancias químicas y como afectan a __6__ seres humanos. __7__ hidrógeno y __8__ oxígeno son necesarios para la vida humana. En la clase de física estudiamos __9__ materia y __10__ energía.

Artículo definido
Addressing and referring to people

1. The definite article must be used with titles in Spanish when speaking about someone.

   El general Santander ganó las elecciones.
   La doctora Antúñez perdió.

2. The article is not used with a person´s title when addressing the person.

   —Buenos días, señor Solís.
   —Hasta mañana, doctora Antúñez.

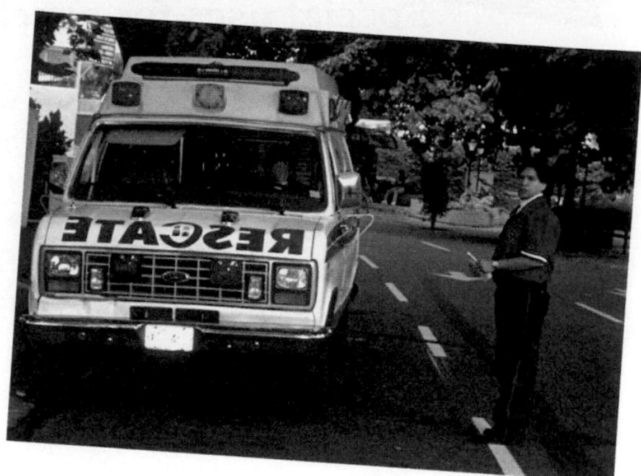

Caracas, Venezuela

¿Cómo lo digo?

4 **Historieta** **En el consultorio de la médica**
Completen con el artículo cuando sea necesario.

—Buenos días, __1__ señor Gaona.
—Buenos días, __2__ señorita Flores.
—¿Cómo se siente usted hoy?
—Bastante bien, gracias. ¿Está __3__ doctora Antúñez?
—Lo siento. En este momento __4__ doctora Antúñez no está. Tuvo que ir a la clínica para una reunión con __5__ doctor Cela.
—¿Sabe usted a qué hora va a volver?
—Por lo general, __6__ doctora Antúñez vuelve de la reunión a las dos y media. Voy a llamarla por teléfono.
—¡Aló! __7__ señorita Vélez, ¿me puede hacer un favor? Cuando salga __8__ doctora Antúñez, dígale que me llame. Ah, está. Le hablaré. Soy yo, Marta Flores, __9__ doctora Antúñez. Estoy con __10__ señor Gaona. Quiere saber cuándo usted vuelve… Bien. Se lo diré. Lo siento, __11__ señor Gaona, pero __12__ doctora Antúñez no vuelve esta tarde. Pero lo puede atender mañana a las dos.
—Entonces vuelvo mañana. Muchas gracias, __13__ señorita Flores.
—Hasta mañana, __14__ señor Gaona.

5 **¿Qué hace la doctora Antúñez?** Contesten.

1. ¿Quién busca a la doctora?
2. ¿Quién le habla al señor en el consultorio?
3. ¿Está la doctora o no?
4. ¿Dónde está la doctora?
5. ¿Con quién está ella?
6. ¿Quién llama por teléfono?
7. ¿Quién contesta el teléfono?
8. ¿Quién va a volver mañana?

Artículo con los días de la semana
Referring to the days of the week

In Spanish, the definite article is used with days of the week to convey the meaning "on."

Tengo clases los lunes.	*I have classes on Mondays.*
El domingo voy a Bogotá.	*On Sunday I'm going to Bogotá.*

¿Cómo lo digo?

¿Durante qué días? Contesten.

1. ¿Qué días tienes clase de español?
2. ¿Y qué días no tienes clases?
3. ¿Qué haces los sábados?
4. ¿Adónde vas los domingos?
5. Y esta semana, ¿qué haces el sábado?
6. Y, ¿adónde vas el domingo?
7. Algunas personas dicen que deben tener clases los sábados. Tú, ¿qué crees?

San Andrés, Colombia

Artículo con los verbos reflexivos
Clothing and parts of the body

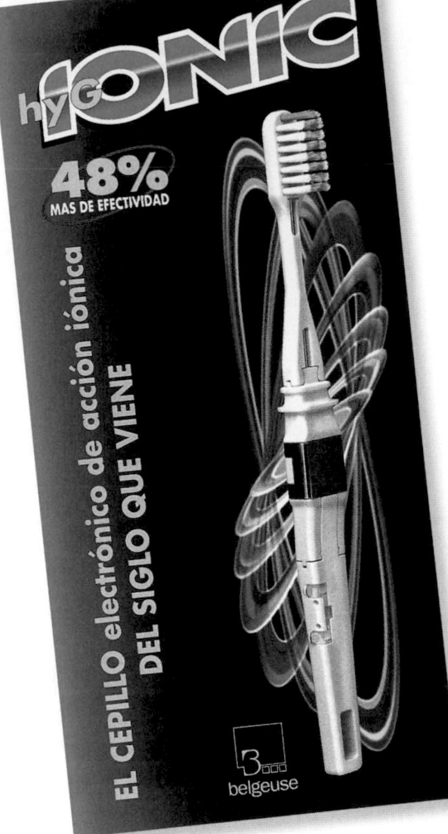

1. In Spanish when you refer to parts of the body and articles of clothing, you use the definite article with the reflexive pronoun. Observe the following examples.

Yo me lavo las manos antes de comer.	*I wash my hands before eating.*
Después de comer, me cepillo los dientes y me lavo la cara.	*After eating, I brush my teeth and wash my face.*

2. Note also that the object noun is usually in the plural in English when the subject is plural. In Spanish, the noun is in the singular. Observe the following sentences.

Nosotros nos ponemos el casco para trabajar.	*We put on our hardhats to work.*
Y nos quitamos la corbata y la gorra.	*And we take off our ties and caps.*

Since each person has only one hardhat, one tie, and one cap, the singular form is used, not the plural.

¿Cómo lo digo?

7 **Por la mañana** Completen.

1. Cuando me levanto, me lavo _____.
2. Y me cepillo _____.
3. Cuando hace frío, todos nos ponemos _____ para salir.
4. Cuando llegamos a la escuela, mi hermano y yo nos quitamos _____.
5. El profesor Pérez no ve muy bien y tiene que ponerse _____.

Amigos venezolanos

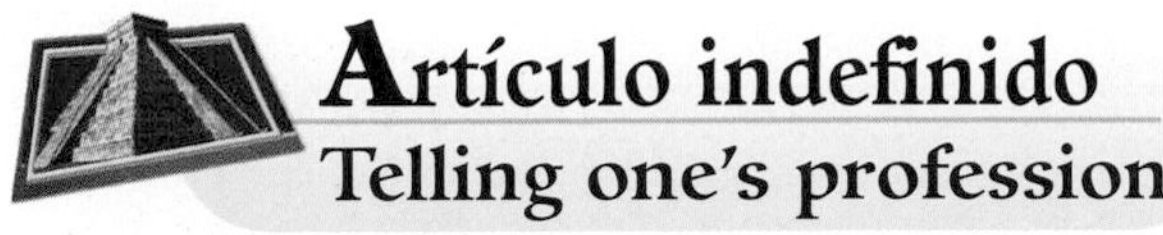

Artículo indefinido
Telling one's profession

1. The indefinite article is omitted in Spanish when the verb **ser** is followed by an unmodified noun referring to a profession. In English the indefinite article is used.

El señor Welser fue banquero.	*Mr. Welser was a banker.*
La señora Robles es pólitica.	*Mrs. Robles is a politician.*
Gonzalo Jiménez de Quesada fue abogado.	*Gonzalo Jiménez de Quesada was a lawyer.*

2. However, the indefinite article must be used whenever the noun following the verb **ser** is modified.

La doctora López es profesora.	*Doctor López is a teacher.*
La doctora López es una profesora buena.	*Doctor López is a good teacher.*

¿Cómo lo digo?

¿Qué y cómo? Sigan el modelo.

la doctora Rosas (médica) →
¿Qué es la doctora Rosas?
Es médica. Y es una médica excelente.

1. el señor Garcés (electricista)
2. la señorita Bernales (bióloga)
3. el señor Martín (contable)
4. la señora Robles (ingeniera)
5. la señorita Chávez (periodista)
6. el señor Marcos (secretario)
7. la señora Ruíz (gobernadora)
8. el señor Funes (llanero)
9. la señorita Álvarez (astronauta)

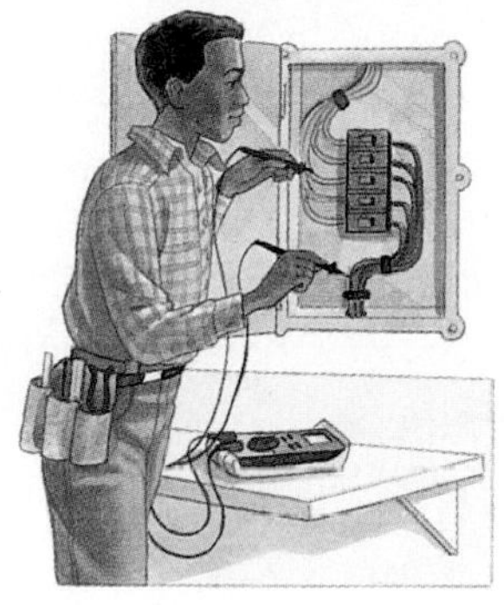

¡Te toca a ti!

La geografía de Venezuela y Colombia

✔ ***Compare the geography of Venezuela and Colombia***

Venezuela y Colombia son dos repúblicas vecinas. Describe la geografía de estos dos países e indica como se asemejan.

Parque Nacional Canaima, Venezuela

La cuenca del Orinoco

✔ ***Describe the interesting Orinoco Basin***

La cuenca del Orinoco es una región interesante. Di todo lo que sabes del río Orinoco y describe el clima de esta región. ¿Te gustaría vivir allí? ¿Por qué?

¡Qué sorpresa para los tres!

✔ ***Discuss a big surprise that took place in the history of Colombia***

Varios individuos llegaron a la meseta de Bogotá. ¿Quiénes fueron? ¿Qué es algo que no hubieran esperado al llegar a una región montañosa tan aislada en aquel entonces? Explica lo que pasó y como se resolvió el encuentro.

Un gran héroe

✔ Prepare a written and oral report about the great hero Simón Bolívar

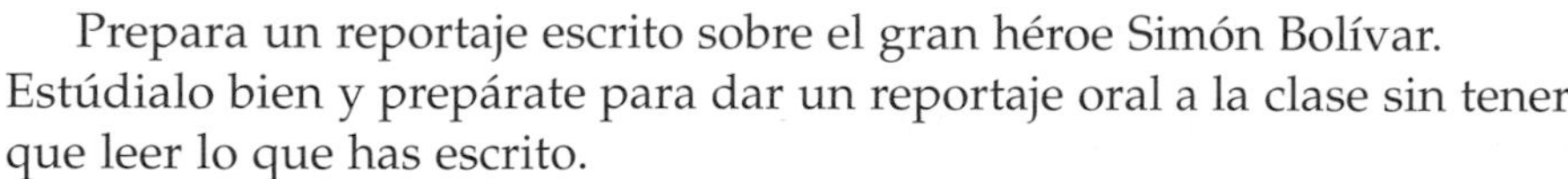

Prepara un reportaje escrito sobre el gran héroe Simón Bolívar. Estúdialo bien y prepárate para dar un reportaje oral a la clase sin tener que leer lo que has escrito.

Una visita

✔ Tell what you would like to do if you went to Colombia or Venezuela

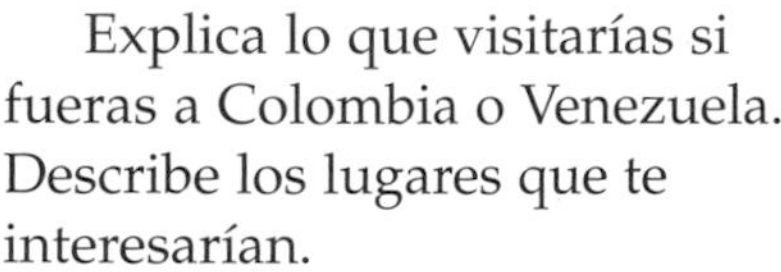

Explica lo que visitarías si fueras a Colombia o Venezuela. Describe los lugares que te interesarían.

San Andrés, Colombia

Algunas cosas históricas interesantes

✔ Write about some interesting historical events

Aprendiste algunas cosas interesantes sobre la historia de Colombia y Venezuela. Prepara un escrito sobre uno o más de los siguientes:

- la influencia alemana en la conquista de Venezuela
- el descubrimiento del Salto Ángel
- el tesoro del corsario Morgan
- la leyenda de *El Dorado*

Vocabulario

1 Completen.

1. Un _____ es una casa humilde.
2. Una casa _____ está construida sobre pilotes en un lago.
3. El café se cultiva en las _____ de la montaña.
4. La _____ es el dinero que uno le debe a otro.
5. Es una _____ horrible. No ha llovido en dos meses.
6. La _____ del río Magdalena está en Barranquilla. Allí entra en el mar.

To review vocabulary, turn to page 322.

2 Den la palabra cuya definición sigue.

7. muy caluroso
8. llevar a una conclusión
9. denso
10. someter por la violencia

Cultura

To review some geographical facts, turn to pages 324–325.

3 ¿Sí o no?

11. El río Orinoco es más largo y más importante que el Amazonas.
12. El río Magdalena en Colombia es navegable de Barranquilla a Bogotá. El viaje en barco fluvial toma nueve días.
13. Los llaneros viven solamente en Venezuela.
14. La mitad de Colombia, igual que Venezuela, es selva tropical.

To review some historical and cultural facts, turn to pages 326–329.

4 Identifiquen.

15. los Welser y Ambrosio Alfinger
16. Sebastián de Benalcázar
17. Gonzalo Jiménez de Quesada

5 Contesten.

18. ¿Qué aprendió Simón Bolívar de un profesor favorito?
19. ¿Qué hizo Bolívar al refugiarse en Santo Domingo?
20. ¿Cuál fue el gran sueño de Bolívar? ¿Lo realizó?

6 Completen.

21. Si voy a Colombia quiero visitar ____.
22. Si voy a Venezuela quiero visitar ____.
23. Si voy a Colombia quiero comer ____.

To review sights and foods of Colombia and Venezuela, turn to pages 330–331.

Estructura

7 Completen.

24. Puede ser que es una señora grande pero es una ____ señora también.

25–26. El libro tiene más de ____ páginas pero no tiene ____ capítulos.

27–29. ____ Marta, ____ Diego y ____ Domingo son los nombres de ciudades.

To review shortened forms of adjectives, turn to page 332.

8 Completen.

30. ____ petróleo es un producto muy importante de Venezuela.

31. Ustedes pueden quitarse ____ corbata si quieren.

32–33. —Hola, ____ doctor Jiménez. ¿Está ____ doctor Quesada?

34–35. Él es ____ banquero pero no sé si es ____ banquero bueno.

To review special uses of articles, turn to pages 333, 334, 335, 336, and 337.

Caracas, Venezuela

Conversación

Vocabulario para la conversación

Más vocabulario

el elenco el conjunto o grupo de actores y actrices en una obra
el intermedio el descanso entre dos actos
el vestuario la ropa que llevan los actores
agotado(a) que no queda

¿Qué palabra necesito?

1 **Historieta** **En el teatro** Contesten según se indica.

1. Para ir al teatro, ¿dónde compra el público sus entradas? (en la taquilla)
2. ¿Dónde pueden sentarse? (en el patio, en el palco de platea o en el gallinero)
3. ¿Qué entradas son más caras? (las del patio)
4. ¿Qué pasa al empezar el espectáculo? (se levanta el telón)
5. ¿Quiénes entran en escena? (los actores y las actrices)
6. Por lo general, ¿hay un intermedio o un descanso? (sí, entre el segundo y el tercer acto)
7. ¿Qué pasa al terminar el espectáculo? (cae el telón)

Teatro Metropolitano de Medellín, Colombia

2 **La palabra apropiada** Den la palabra cuya definición sigue.

1. lugar del teatro donde tiene lugar la acción de la obra o espectáculo
2. los decorados escénicos
3. todo relacionado con las luces
4. conjunto de los vestidos de los actores y actrices
5. conjunto de actores y actrices

3 **Sinónimos** Den otra palabra.

1. el alumbrado
2. el decorado
3. la boletería
4. la entrada
5. el descanso

Al museo y al teatro

En el Museo del Oro

Ramón En mi vida he visto yo tanto oro.
Sandra Es increíble, el museo, ¿no? Tiene la colección más grande de oro del mundo.
Ramón A mí me da la impresión de estar en un santuario religioso y aquí estamos en medio del bullicio y ajetreo[1] del centro de Bogotá.
Sandra A mí me da vergüenza hablar… hay tanto silencio.
Ramón Todos se quedan boquiabiertos y no pueden hablar.
Sandra ¿Te has fijado en la iluminación?
Ramón No puede haber lugar más brillante.
Sandra Todas estas máscaras, pulseras, anillos… resplandecen[2] como… pues no hay palabra para expresar lo que quiero decir.
Ramón ¡Qué artesanos eran los muisca!
Sandra Sí, y los quimbaya también.
Ramón Sandra, ¿sabes que ya son las dos y veinte y el museo se cierra a las dos y media? ¡Vamos ya!
Sandra La verdad es que no quiero salir.
(Al salir del museo)
Ramón Esta noche quisiera ver *Evita.* ¿Quieres ir conmigo?
Sandra ¿Al Teatro Colón? No creo que queden entradas. Estarán agotadas.
Ramón Pero, podemos intentar. A esta hora la taquilla estará abierta. Aun si tenemos que sentarnos en el gallinero.
Sandra Mara la vio la semana pasada y me dijo que el elenco era fabuloso—los cantantes, los actores, la orquesta…
Ramón ¿Vamos caminando hacia el teatro o quieres tomar el bus?
Sandra Vamos caminando.

[1] bullicio y ajetreo *hustle and bustle*
[2] resplandecen *they shine, glow*

(Al llegar a la taquilla)

En el teatro

Ramón ¿Tendría disponibles dos plazas para la función de esta noche?
Taquillero ¿Prefiere usted butacas de patio o de palco de platea?
Ramón ¿Quedan en el patio?
Taquillero Sí, pero solamente en las últimas filas.
Ramón Mejor luego un palco de platea.
Taquillero De acuerdo. Dos butacas en el palco de platea. Son setenta y cinco mil pesos.
Ramón ¿A qué hora se levanta el telón?
Taquillero A las veinte treinta.
Ramón Gracias. ¿Hay intermedio?
Taquillero Sí, entre el segundo y el tercer acto.
Sandra ¡Qué suerte! Tengo muchas ganas de ver *Evita.* Me encanta la canción «No llores por mí, Argentina».

To learn more about museums in Venezuela and Columbia, do the Chapter 7 **WebQuest** activity on the Glencoe Spanish Web site at glencoe.com.

¿Comprendes?

A El Museo del Oro Contesten.

1. ¿Qué tiene el Museo del Oro?
2. ¿Qué impresión le da a uno?
3. ¿Dónde está ubicado el museo?
4. ¿Por qué hablan muy poco los visitantes al museo?
5. ¿Qué tipo de joyas hay en el museo?
6. ¿De quiénes son?
7. ¿A qué hora se cierra el museo?
8. ¿Cómo pasa el tiempo en el museo?

Teatro Colón, Bogotá

B Una obra de teatro ¿Sí o no?

1. Están presentando *El fantasma de la ópera* en el Teatro Colón.
2. Sandra cree que aún a última hora habrá muchas entradas disponibles.
3. Los dos deciden ir a la taquilla o boletería aún si quedan sólo localidades de patio.
4. El elenco de la semana pasada no fue muy bueno.
5. Había plazas disponibles en el patio pero sólo en las dos primeras filas.
6. Sandra y Ramón deciden tomar butacas en un palco de platea.
7. El telón cae a las veinte treinta.
8. No hay intermedio.

Estructura • Repaso

Pronombres con preposición
Pronouns after prepositions

1. A prepositional pronoun follows a preposition, **a, de, en, con, sin,** etc. In Spanish, the prepositional pronouns are the same as the subject pronouns except for **mí** and **ti (yo** and **tú).**

SUBJECT PRONOUNS	PREPOSITIONAL PRONOUNS	SUBJECT PRONOUNS	PREPOSITIONAL PRONOUNS
yo	**mí**	**nosotros(as)**	**nosotros(as)**
tú	**ti**	*vosotros(as)*	*vosotros(as)*
él	**él**	**ellos**	**ellos**
ella	**ella**	**ellas**	**ellas**
Ud.	**Ud.**	**Uds.**	**Uds.**

Fernando vive cerca de mí.
Ellos siempre salen con nosotros.
Allí está Josefina. ¿Quién está con ella?

2. The preposition **con** together with **mí** becomes **conmigo,** and **con** together with **ti** becomes **contigo.**

Yo quería ir a la exposición contigo, pero saliste muy temprano.
¿Quieres ir conmigo mañana?

¿Cómo lo digo?

1 **Historieta En la exposición** Contesten con **sí** y el pronombre apropiado.

1. Estas entradas, ¿son para ustedes?
2. Ese cuadro, ¿es de Botero?
3. ¿Para quién es el cuadro? ¿Para ti?
4. ¿Los videos son para los niños?
5. Después de la exposición, ¿quieres cenar conmigo?
6. ¿Papi reservó una mesa para ti y para mí?
7. ¿Sara va a la exposición contigo?

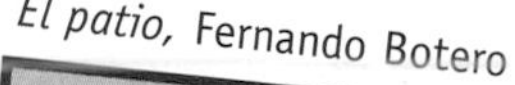

2 **Historieta El viaje** Contesten según se indica. Usen pronombres.

1. ¿Quién va a Caracas con usted? (la Sra. Ramírez)
2. ¿El carro es de la Sra. Ramírez? (sí)
3. ¿Los asientos de atrás son para los niños? (no)
4. ¿No? Entonces, ¿son para Tere y para mí? (sí)
5. Y tú, ¿quieres ir con nosotros? (no sé)
6. Pues, ¿quién va contigo? (Andrés)

¡Te toca a ti!

Use what you have learned

Avenida Abraham Lincoln, Caracas, Venezuela

Una visita al Museo del Oro

✔ Discuss a wonderful experience in a museum

La visita que hicieron Ramón y Sandra al Museo del Oro en Bogotá les entusiasmó mucho. En tus propias palabras, expresa lo que se sentían al visitar este museo y por qué.

Al teatro

✔ Talk about getting theater tickets

Estás en la taquilla de un teatro y quieres entradas para ti y algunos amigos. Ten una conversación con el/la taquillero(a), [tu compañero(a)].

Una visita personal

✔ Tell about any visit you have made to a museum

Es posible que alguna vez hayas visitado un museo. Describe tu visita —lo que viste, si te gustó, etc. Si no has visitado nunca un museo, trata de buscar información sobre un museo que no esté muy lejos de donde vives.

Venezuela

Una obra teatral o una película

✔ Tell about a night at the theater or movies

Describe una experiencia que tuviste alguna vez o en un teatro o en un cine.

Un cartel para nuestro club dramático

✔ Prepare a poster for your school's drama club

El club dramático de tu escuela va a presentar una obra. La van a presentar dos veces—un viernes por la noche y un sábado por la noche. Prepara un cartel anunciando el evento e incluye toda la información necesaria.

Assessment

Vocabulario

1 Den la palabra.

1. la localidad
2. la boletería
3. la iluminación
4. los trajes de los actores
5. que no queda
6. el conjunto de actores en una obra

To review vocabulary, turn to page 342.

2 Completen.

7. No quedan entradas. Están _____.
8. No me gusta sentarme en el gallinero. Prefiero el _____ de butacas.
9. Hay un _____ corto entre los actos.
10. Al terminar el espectáculo el _____ cae.
11. Los señores compran sus entradas en la _____.

To review the conversation, turn to pages 344–345.

Conversación

3 Contesten.

12. ¿Dónde está el Museo del Oro?
13. ¿Qué impresión le da a uno estar en este museo?
14. ¿Qué objetos de oro hay en el museo?
15. ¿Cuál es un grupo indígena de Colombia?

4 ¿Sí o no?

16. Después de visitar el museo Ramón y Sandra fueron al cine.
17. Las entradas estaban agotadas.
18. Ellos tuvieron que sentarse en el gallinero.
19. Las entradas más caras son las de las butacas del paraíso.
20. «No llores por mí, Argentina» es una canción del espectáculo *Evita.*

To review the conversation, turn to pages 344–345.

Estructura

5 Contesten con pronombres.

21. ¿Son para *Juan* las entradas?
22. ¿Te habló de *los actores?*
23. ¿Han hablado con *ustedes?*
24. ¿Quieres ir *conmigo?*
25. ¿Es para *mí* esta máscara de «oro»?

To review prepositional pronouns, turn to page 346.

Bogotá, Colombia

Periodismo

Vocabulario para la lectura

Maestros de éste y de otros mundos

Más vocabulario

despistado(a) desorientado, confuso
detenidamente lentamente, con cuidado, sin prisa
agradecer expresar gratitud
desinflarse salir el aire de un globo, una llanta, etc.
lograr alcanzar, obtener, conseguir

¿Qué palabra necesito?

1 **Yo** Contesten personalmente.

1. ¿Te gusta mirar afiches turísticos?
2. ¿Llevas un termo a la escuela?
3. ¿Siempre escribe tu profesor(a) de español en la pizarra o usa a veces un papelógrafo?
4. Yo sé que yo les agradezco a mis amigos si hacen algo por mí. Y tú, ¿les agradeces también si hacen algo por ti?
5. ¿Logras realizar todos tus sueños?
6. ¿Puedes ser una persona despistada o siempre sabes exactamente lo que estás haciendo y por qué?
7. ¿Haces tus tareas detenidamente?

2 **Otra palabra** Den una palabra relacionada.

1. la pista
2. el papel
3. el agradecimiento
4. el logro

3 **En mi sala de clase hay...** ¿Cuál es la palabra?

1. un trípode con papel grande donde el profesor escribe y dibuja
2. un tipo de botella que mantiene los líquidos o fríos o calientes
3. un cartel o papel grande con vistas de Venezuela

EL COLOMBIANO

Medellín, Antioquia, Colombia

Maestros de éste y otros mundos

Mañana se celebrará el tradicional Día del Maestro. Esta es la oportunidad de agradecerles a tus profesores por la labor que hacen a diario y por enseñarte tantas cosas. Como sabemos que ellos son muy diversos, te traemos este test (entre lo loco y lo más normal) para que descubras de qué tipo es tu maestro.

1. Lo primero que hace tu maestro (a) al llegar al salón es:
- **a.** Dirigir unos ejercicios para despertar. Terminas saltando tanto que se te cae hasta la gomina[1].
- **b.** Simplemente mira a todos detenidamente y saluda.
- **c.** Antes de que puedas sacar tu cuaderno ya tiene el tablero sin un espacio más para escribir.

2. En el recreo él o ella:
- **a.** Encabeza un buen juego de baloncesto, fútbol o lo que sea para estar en movimiento.
- **b.** Revisa que todos coman su media mañana[2] y que todos logren abrir sus termos sin problema.
- **c.** Se sienta con un grupo a hablar de las fórmulas matemáticas que se aplican en el patio de recreo.

3. Siempre lleva con él o ella:
- **a.** Un tarro de agua, una mochila y un mapa del colegio, por si llega a perderse.
- **b.** Un maletín lleno de libros, la lista de alumnos y un texto de frases para usar en clase.
- **c.** Una caja extra de tizas de colores para evitar emergencias de último minuto.

4. Para explicar un tema como el movimiento de la Tierra, tu maestro:
- **a.** Los lleva corriendo alrededor del colegio a las 12:00 del mediodía para que sientas de cerca lo que pasa en la Tierra.
- **b.** Trae el globo terráqueo de la biblioteca que ya comenzó a desinflarse.
- **c.** Llena el salón de afiches terrestres, mapas y en un segundo pinta un completo diagrama en el papelógrafo.

5. Si le regalas una manzana:
- **a.** Se la come inmediatamente para recargar energías.
- **b.** La guarda en su maletín para comérsela luego de ser debidamente pelada y lavada.
- **c.** La usa como motivo para hacer un ejercicio en clase y pintar la manzana desde 20 ángulos diferentes.

[1] gomina *hair gel*
[2] media mañana *mid-morning snack*

6. En un paseo ecológico que hace a una montaña tu profesor(a).
   a. Planea más de 50 actividades para explorar el terreno y convertir a todos en un Róbinson.
   b. Lleva cargas de protector solar y repelente y prefiere analizar el sector desde la sombra y con la ayuda de su telescopio.
   c. Les cuenta a todos como encontró allí 678.000 especies de animales en sólo quince minutos.

Respuestas

Mayoría a:
Tu profe es de la llamada especie de los Súper Energizados. Son capaces de correr, saltar, dictar clase y aún así no pierden el entusiasmo. Aunque a veces son un poco despistados y exagerados, son capaces de contagiar a todos con su alegría. Para él o ella, su palabra clave es moverse.

Mayoría b:
Aunque creas que es un poco tradicional y serio, este tipo de profesor quiere que aprendas y que aproveches el cole[3]. Si crees que a veces sus estrategias no son las mejores, habla con él o ella y te darás cuenta que es una persona simpática y maravillosa, que quiere sólo que seas una buena persona.

Mayoría c:
Tu maestro(a) pertenece a los hiperactivos académicos que no quieren perder ni un minuto. A veces es difícil llevarles el ritmo, pero con él o ella logras conocer muchas cosas interesantes y sorprendentes. Con ellos es mejor que desayunes bien y que recargues tu cerebro.

[3] cole *escuela*

¿Comprendes?

Historieta **Los maestros** Contesten.

1. ¿Cuál es el motivo para el artículo?
2. ¿Quiénes son muy diversos, según el autor?
3. ¿Cuál es el propósito del «test»?
4. ¿De qué grados serán los maestros que describe el artículo?
5. ¿Cuántos tipos de maestros describe en total?

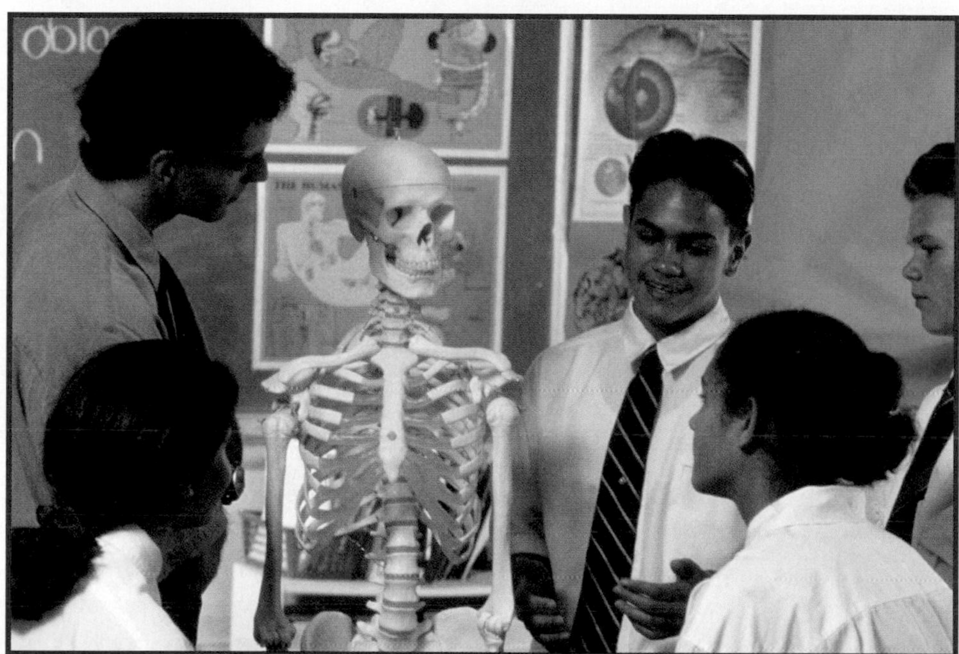

¿De qué tipo es? Escojan.

a. Súper energizado **b. Tradicional y serio** **c. Híperactivo académico**

1. Lleva un mapa de la escuela y una mochila además de un tarro de agua.
2. En el recreo dirige algún deporte para que todos se muevan.
3. Durante un paseo ecológico tiene planeadas muchas actividades de exploración.
4. Al comenzar una clase tiene el tablero lleno de apuntes.
5. Para explicar el movimiento de la Tierra hace que los estudiantes corran alrededor de la escuela al mediodía.
6. A la hora del recreo se asegura de que todos los alumnos coman y les ayuda a abrir los termos.
7. Si le das una manzana la emplea para dar una lección.

Vocabulario para la lectura

La gasolina

un envase

Más vocabulario

el combustible la gasolina o el gasoil
la escasez la insuficiencia, la falta
el riesgo el peligro
la secuela la consecuencia, el efecto, el resultado

Caracas, Venezuela

¿Qué palabra necesito?

1 **Historieta** **En la gasolinera** Completen.

1. La gasolinera vende gasolina y gasoil, dos tipos de _____.
2. Lo que pasa es que hay una _____ de gasolina, no hay bastante.
3. Los _____ de gasolina están vacíos.
4. Y la gente echa la gasolina en botellas y otros _____ inadecuados.
5. Y otros usan una _____ para sacar la gasolina de un coche para llevarla a otro.
6. Ellos corren el _____ de enfermarse o quemarse.
7. Una de las _____ de la enfermedad es la muerte.

EL COLOMBIANO

Medellín, Antioquia, Colombia

LA GASOLINA

Con la actual situación de escasez de combustible, muchas personas se han visto obligadas a manipular la gasolina de una manera inusual. Algunos la transportan libremente en envases no adecuados, otros introducen mangueras en los tanques de los carros para sacarla y traspasarla a otro automóvil. Pero, ¿sabemos realmente lo que es la gasolina? ¿Estamos conscientes de los riesgos para la salud que implica su manipulación?

La gasolina es un destilado del petróleo preparado por fraccionamiento del crudo, que contiene hidrocarburos de diferentes tipos, y que se utiliza como combustible para vehículos. La intoxicación por ingestión de gasolina se asemeja a la del alcohol etílico, produciendo incoordinación, inquietud, excitación, confusión, desorientación, delirio y, por último, coma, el cual puede durar horas o días. La inhalación de concentraciones altas de vapores de gasolina, como la que sufren los trabajadores que limpian tanques de depósito si no toman las precauciones debidas, puede causar la muerte inmediata. Los vapores mencionados sensibilizan al miocardio (el músculo del corazón), al grado en el que cantidades muy pequeñas de la adrenalina que normalmente circula en la sangre pueden desencadenar fibrilación ventricular, una arritmia de consecuencias fatales si no se revierte en segundos o pocos minutos. Las concentraciones altas de vapores de gasolina también ocasionan depresión rápida del sistema nervioso central y muerte por insuficiencia respiratoria. Si se inhalan concentraciones altas por varias horas, puede ocurrir neumonitis (inflamación del tejido pulmonar).

La intoxicación por estos hidrocarburos es consecuencia de inhalación de los vapores o de ingestión de la forma líquida. Esta última forma es la más peligrosa, porque los líquidos tienen baja tensión superficial y pueden ser broncoaspirados más facilmente en vías respiratorias por vómito o eructos[1]. La secuela más grave de la broncoaspiración es la nemonitis química complicada por neumonía bacteriana y edema pulmonar secundario. El sujeto muere por edema pulmonar hemorrágico en el término de las primeras 24 horas si no hay tratamiento.

Por último, la exposición por largo plazo a la gasolina tiene la posibilidad de causar leucemia[2], debido a que contiene cerca de 2% de benceno.

Como se puede apreciar, el manejo inadecuado de la gasolina no sólo puede producir quemaduras, sino otros trastornos potencialmente fatales, así que usémosla con el cuidado que merece[3].

[1] eructos *burps*
[2] leucemia *leukemia*
[3] merece *it deserves*

¿Comprendes?

A **La gasolina** Contesten.

1. ¿Cuál es la «situación actual» a la que se refiere el autor?
2. ¿Cuáles son algunas formas «inusuales» que emplea la gente al manipular la gasolina?
3. Según el artículo, ¿cómo se define la gasolina?
4. ¿Qué produce la intoxicación por ingestión de gasolina?
5. ¿Qué puede causar la muerte inmediata?
6. ¿De qué muere la persona que sufre la broncoaspiración de gasolina en forma de líquido?
7. Como la gasolina contiene benceno, ¿qué puede causar la exposición a ella a largo plazo?

B **Poder verbal** En el artículo busquen todas las palabras que tienen que ver con la anatomía o enfermedades serias.

C **Síntesis** ¿Cuál es el mensaje o la idea principal del artículo que escribió el Dr. Salvetti?

Estructura • Avanzada

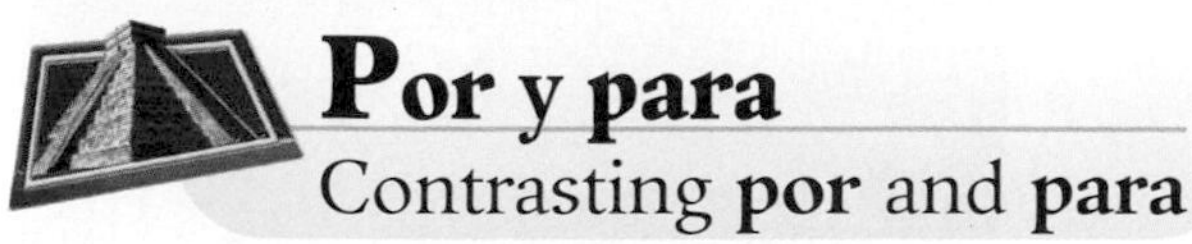

Por y para
Contrasting **por** and **para**

1. The prepositions **por** and **para** have specific uses in Spanish and are not interchangeable. They are often translated as *for.* However, **por** and **para** express many ideas in addition to *for.*

2. The preposition **para** is used to indicate destination or purpose.

El avión salió para Bogotá.	*The plane left for Bogotá.*
La manzana es para la maestra.	*The apple is for the teacher.*
Ella estudia para médica.	*She is studying to be a doctor.*

Bogotá, Colombia

3. The preposition **por,** in contrast to **para,** is less precise, conveying the idea of *through, by,* or *along,* rather than a specific destination.

Ellos viajaron por Colombia y Venezuela.	*They traveled through Colombia and Venezuela.*
El barco pasó por las costas de Panamá.	*The ship passed by the shores of Panama.*
El combustible pasó por la manguera.	*The fuel went through the hose.*

4. **Por** also can mean *on behalf of, in favor of,* and *instead of.*

Compré el afiche para mi hermano.	*I bought the poster for my brother. (I´m going to give it to him as a gift.)*
Compré el afiche por mi hermano.	*I bought the poster for my brother. (He couldn´t go out to get it, so I went for him.)*

5. The preposition **por** after the verbs **ir, mandar, volver,** and **venir** indicates purpose or intent.

El niño fue por agua.	*The boy went for water.*
Ellos mandaron por el médico.	*They sent for the doctor.*

¿Cómo lo digo?

Plaza Bolívar, Caracas, Venezuela

1 Historieta Catalina sale para Caracas.

Contesten.

1. ¿Va a salir para Caracas Catalina?
2. ¿Va a viajar por Venezuela?
3. ¿Va a estudiar para médica en Caracas?
4. ¿Va a andar por la Plaza Bolívar?
5. ¿Va a comprar regalos para sus padres?
6. Algunos amigos necesitan regalos para una boda, ¿le dieron dinero para que los comprara por ellos?

2 Historieta El mercado Completen.

1. Hoy yo salí _____ el mercado a las ocho de la mañana.
2. Marta no pudo ir, así que yo fui _____ ella.
3. Cuando salí del mercado, di un paseo _____ el centro de Bogotá.
4. Pasé _____ las elegantes tiendas del Centro Internacional.
5. Entré en una de las tiendas y compré unas esmeraldas _____ mi madre.
6. Cuando volví a casa, el hijo de Marta vino _____ las cosas que yo le había comprado.

Casco viejo, Bogotá, Colombia

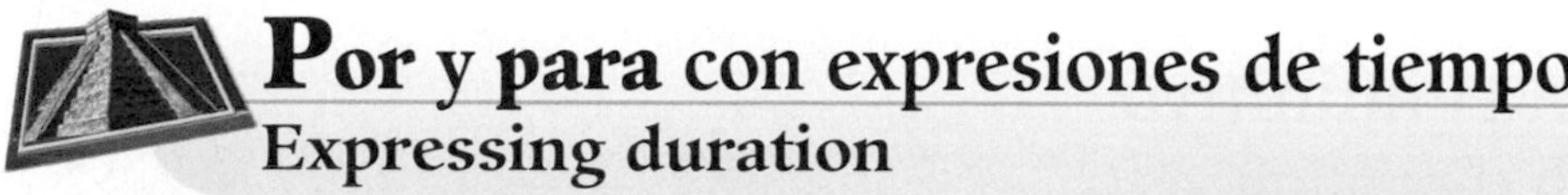

Por y para con expresiones de tiempo
Expressing duration

1. The preposition **para** is used to indicate a deadline, a specific end time.

Ellos tienen que estar en Maracaibo para el día ocho.	*They have to be in Maracaibo by the eighth.*

2. Por in contrast to **para,** is used to define a period of time.

Van a estar en Venezuela por una semana.	*They are going to be in Venezuela for a week.*

3. Por is also used to express an indefinite time.

Creo que ellos volverán por diciembre.	*I think they'll return around December.*

¿Cómo lo digo?

3 **¿Para cuándo y por cuánto tiempo?** Contesten.

1. ¿Pueden ustedes llegar para las ocho?
2. ¿Y pueden tener los resultados para mañana?
3. Cuando vienen ustedes mañana, ¿pueden quedarse aquí por una semana?
4. La última vez que vinieron, ustedes estuvieron por dos semanas, ¿no?
5. ¿Piensan ustedes volver otra vez por Navidad?

4 **Historieta Bogotá** Completen.

Los españoles salieron __1__ las Américas en el siglo XV. Gobernaron en Sudamérica __2__ cuatro siglos. Viajaron __3__ todo el continente. Por eso, si haces un viaje __4__ Sudamérica hoy, verás la influencia española __5__ todas partes. __6__ ver ejemplos de esta influencia sólo tienes que caminar __7__ las calles del casco viejo de Caracas o Bogotá.

Yo tengo que preparar un informe sobre Colombia y salgo __8__ Bogotá mañana. Estaré allí __9__ una semana. Tengo dinero que me dio mi tía __10__ comprar unas esmeraldas. Ella no puede ir a Bogotá así es que yo las compraré __11__ ella. No puedo quedarme en Bogotá __12__ más de una semana. Tengo que estar en mi pueblo __13__ el viernes que viene cuando tengo examen.

La Candelaria, Bogotá, Colombia

LECCIÓN 3
Periodismo

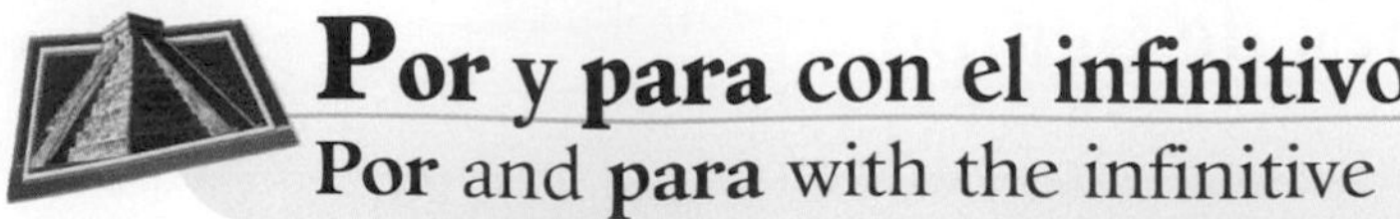

Por y para con el infinitivo
Por and para with the infinitive

Biblioteca metropolitana, Caracas, Venezuela

1. When followed by an infinitive, **para** expresses purpose and means *in order to.*

Tengo que ir a la biblioteca para hacer mis investigaciones.	*I have to go to the library (in order) to do my research.*

2. When **por** is followed by an infinitive, it expresses what remains to be done.

Me queda mucho por hacer.	*There is still a lot to do (to be done).*

3. The expression **estar para** means *to be about to* or *to be ready to.*

Ellos están para salir pero no sé lo que van a hacer porque está para llover.	*They are about (ready) to leave, but I don't know what they are going to do because it is about to rain.*

4. The expression **estar por** means *to be inclined to.* It does not mean that the action will immediately take place.

Estoy por salir porque hace buen tiempo.	*I'm in the mood to go out because the weather is nice.*

¿Cómo lo digo?

5 ¿Estás listo(a) o dispuesto(a)... ? Contesten.

1. ¿Quieres ir a tu cuarto para estudiar?
2. ¿Tienes que preparar un informe para obtener una buena nota?
3. ¿Estás para trabajar o para divertirte?
4. Para el informe, ¿te queda mucho por hacer?
5. ¿Fuiste a la biblioteca por los libros que te hacían falta?
6. Yo estoy para salir. ¿Estás para salir también?

La Candelaria, Bogotá, Colombia

6 Historieta ¿Listos? Completen.

1. Ya nos bañamos y nos vestimos y estamos listos _____ salir.
2. ¡Ay, pero mira! Está _____ llover.
3. Tendremos que subir _____ el paraguas.
4. Queremos ir a la Candelaria para comer. _____ ir allí hay que tomar un taxi porque no hay un bus que pase _____ allí ahora.
5. ¿Crees que debo llamar _____ hacer una reservación?
6. Estamos _____ divertirnos. Después de comer vamos a bailar en La Cantina.

Otros usos de por y para
Other uses of **por** and **para**

1. **Para** is used to express a comparison.

Para colombiano él habla muy bien el inglés.	*For a Colombian, he speaks English very well.*
Y para americano Roberto habla muy bien el español.	*And for an American, Robert speaks Spanish very well.*

2. **Por** is used to express means, manner, or motive.

La carta llegó por correo aéreo.	*The letter arrived by air mail.*
Bolívar y Miranda lucharon por la libertad.	*Bolívar and Miranda fought for freedom.*

3. **Por** is used to express in exchange for.

Él me pagó cien dólares por el trabajo que hice.	*He paid me a hundred dollars for the work I did.*
Él cambió pesos por dólares.	*He exchanged pesos for dollars.*

4. **Por** is also used to express an opinion or estimation.

Yo lo tomé por francés pero es español.	*I took him for French but he is Spanish.*

5. **Por** is used to indicate measure or number.

Los tomates se venden por kilo.	*They sell tomatoes by the kilo.*
Este avión vuela a 1.000 kilómetros por hora.	*This plane flies 1,000 kilometers per hour.*

Leticia, Colombia

¿Cómo lo digo?

Mérida, Venezuela

7 **Historieta** **La Sra. Sica** Completen.

1. _____ venezolana, la Sra. Sica sabe mucho de EE.UU.
2. Ella vino de Mérida en avión, un avión que volaba a 800 kilómetros _____ hora.
3. Antes de llegar aquí ella cambió sus bolívares _____ dólares.
4. Cuando conocí a la Sra. Sica por primera vez, yo la tomé _____ italiana. Ella es de ascendencia italiana pero hace años que su familia vive en Venezuela.
5. Le pedí a la Sra. Sica que me trajera unas figuras en madera y le di el dinero _____ ellas.
6. Hoy llegó un paquete _____ mí. Llegó _____ correo aéreo. Era de la Sra. Sica.

8 **Un resumen** Contesten usando **por** o **para.**

1. ¿Cuál es el destino del bus? ¿Cartagena?
2. ¿A quién vas a dar los dulces? ¿Al niño?
3. Cuando vendiste el carro, ¿te dieron mil dólares?
4. ¿Es colombiano pero habla muy bien el inglés, ¿verdad?
5. ¿Cuándo piensas venir? ¿En abril?
6. ¿Te queda mucho o poco por hacer?
7. ¿Cuándo lo terminarás? ¿Mañana?
8. Ellos pasaron mucho tiempo en La Amazonia, ¿verdad?
9. ¿Cómo mandaron el paquete que acabas de recibir? ¿Correo aéreo?

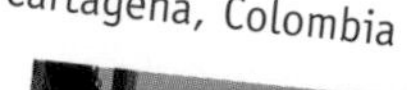

Cartagena, Colombia

9 **Un resumen** Escriban las oraciones con **por** o **para.**

1. Andan *en* el parque.
2. Mañana salen *con destino a* Maracaibo.
3. Los chicos van ahora *en la dirección de* la ciudad.
4. Tengo que estar allí *no más tarde de* las tres.
5. *A pesar de que es* viejo, viaja mucho.
6. Hay un montón de trabajo *que tengo que* terminar.
7. Papá no podía asistir, así que yo fui *en lugar de* él.
8. Los chicos corrieron *en* la calle.
9. Voy al mercado *en busca de* carne.
10. Mis padres lo pagaron *en vez de* mí.
11. *A pesar de que es* rico, no es generoso.
12. Nos gusta viajar *en* Colombia.
13. Estaremos en Cali *durante* siete días.

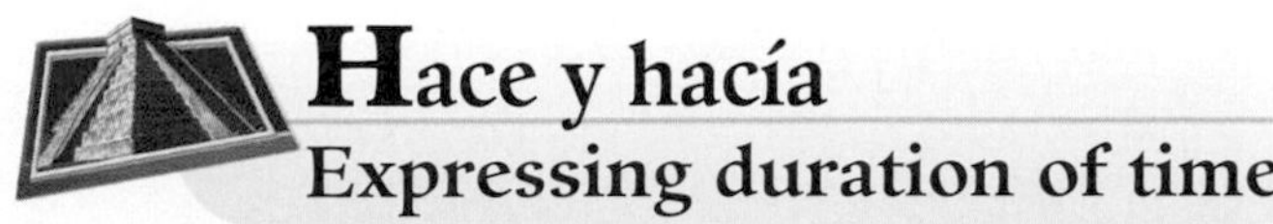

Hace y hacía
Expressing duration of time

1. The expression **hace** is used with the present tense to express an action that began sometime in the past but continues into the present.

¿Cuánto tiempo hace que estás aquí en Cali?	*How long have you been here in Cali?*
Hace un año que estoy aquí.	*I've been here for a year.*

2. Note that in English, the present perfect tense "has been" is used. But in Spanish, the present tense must be used. English uses the present perfect tense because the action began in the past. Spanish uses the present tense because the action actually continues into the present. Note too that **desde hace** as well as **hace** can be used.

Hace un año que estoy aquí.	*I've been here for a year.*
Estoy aquí desde hace un año.	*I've been here for a year.*

3. The expression **hacía** is used with the imperfect tense to express an action that had been in effect until something else interrupted it.

Hacía dos años que ellos vivían en Cali cuando se mudaron a Bogotá.
They had been living in Cali for two years when they moved to Bogotá.

Cali, Colombia

¿Cómo lo digo?

Bogotá, Colombia

10 ¿Cuánto tiempo hace? Contesten.

1. ¿Cuánto tiempo hace que usted vive en la misma casa?
2. ¿Cuánto tiempo hace que usted conoce a su mejor amigo(a)?
3. ¿Cuánto tiempo hace que usted asiste a la misma escuela?
4. ¿Cuánto tiempo hace que usted estudia español?
5. ¿Cuánto tiempo hace que usted estudia con el mismo (la misma) profesor(a) de español?

Caracas, Venezuela

11 Actividades culturales

Contesten según se indica.

1. ¿Cuánto tiempo hace que presentan la exposición? (dos semanas)
2. ¿Cuánto tiempo hace que están poniendo esa película? (sólo dos días)
3. ¿Cuánto tiempo hace que están exponiendo tus cuadros? (un mes)
4. ¿Cuánto tiempo hace que están construyendo el nuevo museo? (un año)
5. ¿Cuánto tiempo hace que no vas al cine? (mucho tiempo)

12 Historieta Mi hermano José Completen.

1. Hacía dos años que mi hermano José ____ francés cuando decidió que quería aprender el español. (estudiar)
2. Hacía mucho tiempo que él ____ que quería ir a Princeton cuando de repente decidió que quería ir a Harvard. (decir)
3. Hacía sólo dos días que él ____ de vacaciones cuando él conoció a Amalia. (estar)
4. Pero hacía un año entero que él ____ con Teresa cuando conoció a Amalia. (salir)
5. Y ahora, hace dos meses que él ____ con Amalia. (salir)
6. Hacía un mes que Teresa no le ____ cuando ella decidió que no estaba enfadada con él. (hablar)
7. Y ahora, hace un mes que Teresa ____ conmigo, el hermano mayor de Joselito. (salir)

For more information about museums and places of interest in Colombia and Venezuela, go to **Web Explore** on the Glencoe Spanish Web site at glencoe.com.

¡Te toca a ti!

Use what you have learned

1 Los tipos de maestros

✔ ***Discuss different types of teachers***

Con tus compañeros, consideren los tres tipos de maestros y piensen en cuales serán los que mejor enseñan. ¿Es posible que diferentes alumnos prefieran diferentes tipos de maestros?

Caracas, Venezuela

2 Un artículo de periódico

✔ ***Write about your favorite teacher***

Un periódico de Venezuela te pide escribir un breve artículo sobre tu maestro(a) favorito(a). Quieren una opinión de un(a) alumno(a) estadounidense y te contactaron a ti porque tú sabes hablar español. En el artículo describe a la persona y explica por qué le aprecias tanto.

3 Algo muy peligroso

✔ ***Discuss the hazards of mishandling gasoline***

Acabas de leer un artículo serio escrito por un médico sobre los potenciales peligros de la gasolina. Da un resumen de lo que aprendiste en este artículo a un(a) amigo(a) que también estudia español.

4 ¡Cuidado!

✔ ***Write an article in Spanish for your school newspaper***

El periódico de tu escuela quiere captar el interés de la población hispana en tu comunidad. Escribe un artículo para el periódico. El título de tu artículo será «¡Cuidado! La gasolina puede ser muy peligrosa».

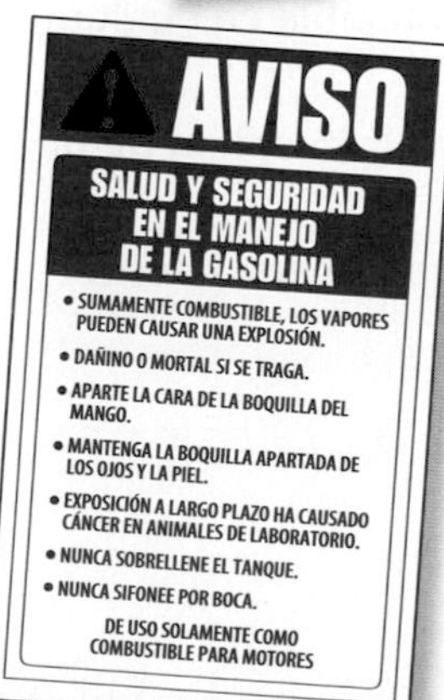

5 Ya hace mucho tiempo

✔ ***Tell what you've been doing for a long time***

Trabaja con un(a) compañero(a). Van a hablar de las cosas que ya hace mucho tiempo que cada uno de ustedes las hace. A ver si ustedes suelen hacer las mismas cosas o no.

Assessment

Vocabulario

To review vocabulary, turn to pages 350 and 354.

1 Escriban con otra palabra.

1. El profesor *consigue* que todos aprendamos.
2. Él nos explica todo *con mucho cuidado y muy lentamente.*
3. Pero él, a veces, anda un poco *desorientado.*
4. Él es un tipo sincero y yo le *expreso mi gratitud* por todo lo que hace por mí.

2 Completen.

5. Si el carro necesita _____ hay una gasolinera en la esquina.
6. Pero es difícil de conseguir porque hay una _____ de gasolina.
7. La gente lleva la gasolina en botellas y otros _____ inapropiados.
8. La _____ más grave de la enfermedad es la muerte.
9. Al manipular la gasolina siempre existe el _____ de un accidente.

Lectura

To review the article about teachers in Colombia, turn to pages 351–352.

3 Contesten.

10. En Colombia hay un día cuando se debe agradecerles a los profesores por la labor que hacen. ¿Cómo se llama este día?
11. ¿Cuál es una actividad típica del maestro súper energizado?
12. ¿Cuál es una actividad típica del maestro tradicional y serio?

To review the article about the hazards of gasoline, turn to page 355.

4 ¿Sí o no?

13. No hay ningún problema con llevar el combustible en cualquier tipo de envase.
14. Hay gente que usa una manguera para sacar la gasolina de un vehículo para meterla en otro.
15. La exposición a la gasolina por mucho tiempo puede causar leucemia y otras enfermedades graves.

For more Chapter 7 test preparation, go to the Chapter 7 **Self-Check Quiz** on the Glencoe Spanish Web site at glencoe.com.

Estructura

5 Completen con **por** o **para**.

16. Pensamos viajar _____ Colombia y Venezuela.
17. Mañana saldremos _____ Bogotá.
18. Fui a la agencia de viajes _____ los boletos.
19. Tengo los pasajes _____ mis padres, también.
20. Ellos no pudieron ir a la agencia, me dieron el dinero y yo los compré _____ ellos.
21. Tenemos que estar en Bogotá _____ el jueves, el cumpleaños de mi abuelo.
22. Y después estaremos allí _____ un par de semanas.

To review the uses of **por** and **para**, turn to pages 357, 359, 360, and 361.

6 Escojan.

23. ¿Cuánto tiempo (hace / hacía) que vives en Medellín?
24. (Hace / Hacía) un año que trabajaba allí cuando me aumentaron el sueldo.
25. (Hace / Hacía) mucho tiempo que no veo a mi familia.

To review the uses of **hace** and **hacía**, turn to page 363.

Caracas, Venezuela

Proficiency Tasks

Composición

Has leído descripciones de paisajes, ciudades y países de casi todo el mundo hispano. Cada una de las descripciones ha tenido el objetivo de hacerte ver como es el lugar. Los adjetivos han dado colorido y vida a las descripciones.

TAREA 1 **Escrito descriptivo** Ahora te toca a ti preparar una descripción de un lugar que tú conoces bien. Puede ser tu pueblo, tu escuela, tu casa o cualquier lugar que tú crees que pueda interesar a un lector. Sigue estos pasos preparativos:

- Piensa en el público que leerá tu escrito y en lo que le interesaría.
- Selecciona el lugar que vas a describir. Visualízalo en tu mente.
- Pon en orden lógico los aspectos que vas a describir: colocación, etc.
- Haz una lista de los adjetivos y adverbios que emplearás en tus descripciones.

Prepara un borrador. Cuando termines, léelo y haz cualquier cambio que creas necesario. Corrige cualquier error de gramática u ortografía. Decide si a la persona que lee tu escrito le interesará el contenido. Decide si falta algún detalle que podría hacer tu escrito más interesante para el lector o si debes eliminar algún detalle repetitivo o no interesante.

Prepara tu versión final. Una vez más revisa lo que has escrito y haz cualquier corrección de ortografía o gramática.

TAREA 2 **El diálogo** El diálogo o conversación entre personajes da vida a una historia o cuento. Cuando preparas un diálogo para una historia real, algo que tú has presenciado, trata de recordar exactamente lo que dijo cada persona. Si tu diálogo es parte de un cuento ficticio tendrás que inventar el diálogo. Imagínate que eres uno de los personajes y deja fluir tus palabras con respecto a la situación siempre desde el punto de vista del personaje. Ten en mente la edad de la persona, su historia personal y su personalidad y como estos aspectos pueden reflejarse en su forma de hablar. Acuérdate de que el diálogo debe representar el habla normal. En el habla normal la gente se interrumpe, habla en fragmentos y no presta atención a lo que dice la otra persona. Para estar seguro(a) de que tu diálogo suena natural, léelo en voz alta.

Ahora, tú vas a crear una conversación entre dos personas. Puede ser una conversación que tú has oído o en la que has participado o puede ser totalmente ficticia. Prepárate pensando en:

- la situación o el conflicto
- los personajes—limítate a solamente dos
- el lugar donde ocurre
- el tono de voz y la forma de hablar de las dos personas

Como haces con todos tus escritos, primero prepara un borrador, luego revísalo, haz las correcciones y después prepara la versión final.

TAREA 3 **La invitación** Uno de los escritos más comunes es la invitación a una celebración. Toda invitación debe contener cierta información. Debe indicar lo que se está celebrando, la fecha, la hora y el lugar de la celebración y de quien es la invitación. También se puede incluir otra información como la ropa que se debe llevar, formal o informal. Aquí tienes una lista de eventos y celebraciones: **el 5 de Mayo (México), el día de la Hispanidad 12 de Octubre (muchos países hispanos), el 4 de Julio (EE.UU.), tu cumpleaños.** Escoge uno de la lista o cualquier otro evento y prepara una invitación. Recuérdate de incluir toda la información necesaria. Recuerda también que si la persona a quien invitas es mayor tienes que usar **usted** y si es un(a) amigo(a) usas **tú**.

TAREA 4 **La investigación** En tu carrera de alumno(a) tendrás que preparar escritos de investigación. Esto quiere decir que tendrás que encontrar la información necesaria de distintas fuentes tanto primarias como secundarias. Buscarás en bibliotecas y en Internet. Podrás entrevistar a expertos. Hay distintos tipos de escritos de investigación: resumen (se prepara un resumen de las opiniones de otros investigadores), evaluativo (se presenta una opinión y lo respalda con evidencia de fuentes primarias o secundarias), original (se hacen investigaciones originales sobre el tema y se informa sobre los resultados), o combinado (una combinación de dos o más de los anteriores). Los pasos a seguir son:

- Escoger un tema, uno que te interesa o que te ha sido asignado.
- Prepara un mínimo de cinco preguntas de investigación.
- Busca información sobre el tema.
- Determina el largo de tu escrito, cuanto vas a cubrir
- Toma apuntes.
- Haz un bosquejo.
- Prepara un borrador en base a tu bosquejo y apuntes.
- Escribe la introducción y conclusión.
- Indica tus fuentes.
- Revisa y corrige.

Ahora vas a hacer tu investigación. Ya sabes que el café es uno de los productos más importantes de Colombia. Pero, ¿qué sabes del café? ¿Originó en las Américas o no? ¿Dónde, aparte de Colombia, se cultiva? Prepara las preguntas que tu investigación va a contestar y haz tu investigación sobre el café. Si es posible, entrevista a alguien de Colombia para conocer su perspectiva del tema.

Discurso

Has leído el artículo de *El Colombiano* entitulado *Maestros de éste y otros mundos.* Ahora te toca a ti a hablar de un maestro o maestra inolvidable.

TAREA 5 Antes de comenzar tu descripción piensa en los maestros que has tenido y escoge a la persona sobre la que vas a hablar. Piensa en las características que la hacen inolvidable, puede ser por su personalidad, sus conocimientos, su simpatía u otra cosa. Piensa en los adjetivos que la describen mejor y habla del efecto que la persona ha tenido en ti. Trata de crear en tus oyentes una fiel imagen de la persona a quien estás describiendo. Cada uno de ustedes presentará a la clase tu **maestro(a) inolvidable.**

CAPÍTULO 7

Vocabulario

Lección 1 Cultura

Geografía

el bohío
la caída
la caleta
la desembocadura
la ensenada
la ladera de la montaña
la mazorca de maíz
el pilote
el salto
la sequía
cálido(a)
espeso(a)
fluvial
lacustre
surgir

Historia

la deuda
la empresa
amurallado(a)
imperante
inolvidable
asemejarse a
enriquecerse
oprimir
sellar

Lección 2 Conversación

el alumbrado
la boletería
la decoración
el decorado
el descanso
el elenco
la entrada
el escenario
la escenografía
el gallinero
la iluminación
el intermedio
la localidad
el palco de platea
el paraíso
el patio de butacas
el telón
el vestuario
agotado(a)

Lección 3 Periodismo

Maestros de éste y de otros mundos

el afiche
el papelógrafo
el tarro de agua
el termo
despistado(a)
detenidamente
agradecer
desinflarse
lograr

La gasolina

el combustible
el depósito
el envase
la escasez
la manguera
el riesgo
la secuela
el tanque de gasolina

Literary Companion *See pages 488–501 for literary selections related to Chapter 7. The activities for these readings will help you continue to practice your reading comprehension skills.*

VIDEOTUR

¡Viva el mundo hispano!

Video can be a beneficial learning tool for the language student. Video enables you to experience the material in the textbook in a real-life setting. Take a vicarious field trip as you see people interacting at home, at school, at the market, etc. The cultural benefits are limitless as you experience the Spanish-speaking world while "traveling" through many countries. In addition to its tremendous cultural value, video gives practice in developing good listening and viewing skills. Video allows you to look for numerous clues that are evident in tone of voice, facial expressions, and gestures. Through video you can see and hear the diversity of the target culture and compare and contrast the Spanish-speaking cultures to each other and to your own.

Episodio 1: El Libertador

Simón Bolívar, el Libertador, el héroe de la independencia no solamente de su nativa Venezuela pero de otros países de la América del Sur. Su sueño era crear una confederación de países sudamericanos. En 1810 declaró la independencia de Venezuela y luchó contra los españoles. Hoy en casi todos los pueblos de Venezuela hay una Plaza Bolívar y hasta el dinero lleva su nombre. La moneda nacional es el «bolívar».

Episodio 2: La fábrica de chocolate

En la chocolatería San Moritz se prepara el chocolate, ricos dulces de chocolate, chocolate de excelentísima calidad. Se prepara en base de recetas europeas y de cacao venezolano. El cacao es el ingrediente más importante y no hay mejor cacao que el venezolano. En el siglo XIX el chocolate venezolano gozaba de fama mundial. Venezuela dominaba el mercado de chocolate. Se ha dicho que el chocolate hasta hace que la gente se enamore. Por algo lo llaman **comida de los dioses.**

Episodio 3: Radio Chuspa

Este joven, Romel Junior, es locutor de radio. Trabaja en la emisora Radio Chuspa, 99.9 casi 100, la estación del pueblecito de Chuspa en la costa caribeña de Venezuela. Radio Chuspa emite las veinticuatro horas del día todos los días. Es la voz del pueblo para esta comunidad de mil personas. Hay programas de música, noticias locales, programas educativos y deportes, sobre todo el béisbol que es el deporte favorito de todo Chuspa.

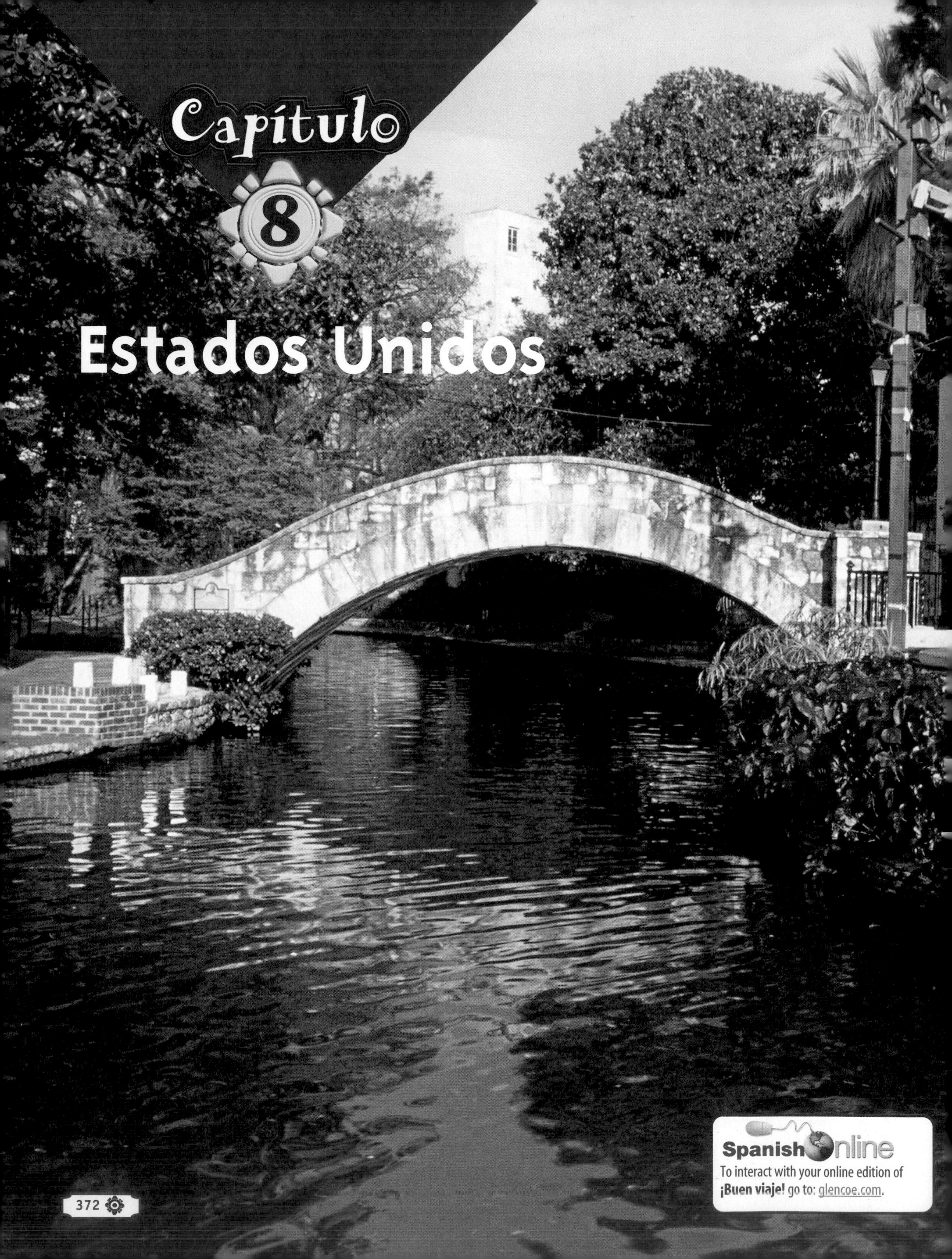

Capítulo 8

Estados Unidos

Objetivos

In this chapter you will:

- learn about the history and culture of Hispanics or Latinos in the United States
- review how to tell how actions are carried out
- review how to express more activities in the present and past
- discuss the medium of television
- read and discuss newspaper articles about the rise of the Hispanic or Latino population in the United States and about a storm in California
- learn to tell what was done or what is done in general

Contenido

Cultura

Vocabulario para la lectura

Los sefardíes son judíos.
Los sefardíes fueron expulsados de España durante la Inquisición.
Muchos sefardíes se radicaron en Nueva York.

Más vocabulario

el cese acción de cesar, suspender o acabar algo
la mano de obra trabajadores
los norteños gente del norte
el rito el ritual, la ceremonia
el vínculo la unión, el lazo, lo que une
fronterizo(a) que está en la frontera entre dos países
fundar iniciar, establecer
radicarse establecerse, echar raíces
superar exceder, pasar, sobrepasar
a escondidas en secreto, clandestinamente

¿Qué palabra necesito?

1 Historieta Los sefardíes Contesten.

1. ¿De qué religión son los sefardíes?
2. ¿De qué país fueron expulsados?
3. ¿Cuándo?
4. ¿Adónde fueron a radicarse muchos descendientes de los originales sefardíes?
5. ¿Quiénes son los norteños?

2 Otra palabra Expresen de otra manera.

1. No había *trabajadores.*
2. El *lazo* más importante que tienen es la lengua.
3. Ellos *establecieron* muchas ciudades.
4. No las establecieron *en secreto.*
5. Ellos querían *echar raíces* en un pueblo fronterizo.
6. Es *una ceremonia* religiosa tradicional.
7. Ahora que hay *una pausa o suspensión* en los conflictos, está saliendo menos gente.
8. Dentro de poco la población dominicana en la ciudad de Nueva York va a *sobrepasar* la población puertorriqueña.

La frontera entre México y Estados Unidos, Laredo, Texas

3 Palabras emparentadas Den una palabra relacionada.

1. la frontera
2. vincular
3. esconder
4. la fundación
5. cesar
6. súper
7. el ritual
8. el norte

4 Identifiquen.

1. el estado en el cual vives
2. en qué parte de EE.UU. está
3. un estado del sudeste
4. un estado del sudoeste
5. un estado del noroeste
6. un estado del nordeste
7. un estado del medio oeste

Lectura

Reading Strategy

Visualizing As you are reading, try to visualize or make a mental picture of exactly what it is you are reading. Allow your mind to freely develop an image. This will help you to remember what you read. It may also help you identify with the subject you are reading about.

Historia de los hispanos o latinos en Estados Unidos

Todo el mundo sabe que los españoles descubrieron y colonizaron la mayor parte de Centro y Sudamérica. Menos conocido es el hecho de que los españoles también exploraron y colonizaron gran parte de la América del Norte.

Fueron españoles los primeros europeos que llegaron a la Florida, Carolina del Sur, Georgia, California, Colorado, Alabama, Texas, Arizona y Nuevo México, Misisipí, Nevada, Arkansas, Luisiana, Oklahoma, Kansas y las costas de Oregon y Washington. Los ingleses se establecieron por primera vez en Jamestown, Virginia, en 1607. Los españoles ya habían fundado la ciudad más antigua de Norteamérica, San Agustín, en la Florida en 1565.

Los primeros hispanohablantes llegaron a lo que hoy es EE.UU. en 1513. Y siguen llegando. Vienen de México y Centroamérica, del Caribe y de Sudamérica y de Europa.

San Agustín, la Florida

San Agustín, la Florida

A Contesten.

1. ¿Quiénes conquistaron y colonizaron gran parte de Sudamérica?
2. ¿Quiénes fueron los conquistadores de la América Central?
3. ¿Cuál fue la primera colonia inglesa en lo que hoy es EE.UU.?
4. ¿Cuándo la establecieron?
5. ¿Cuál es la ciudad más antigua de Norteamérica?
6. ¿Cuándo llegaron los primeros españoles a Norteamérica?
7. Mayormente, ¿qué áreas de EE.UU. exploraron y colonizaron los españoles?

Las comunidades

Obviamente, las primeras comunidades fueron las que fundaron los españoles desde la Florida hasta California por todo el suroeste: San Agustín, Florida (1565), San Juan, Nuevo México (1598), Santa Fe, Nuevo México (1610). Los españoles exploraron todo el territorio del suroeste comenzando en el siglo XVI. Gran número de exploradores y colonizadores llegaron al norte desde México. Todavía hoy, en pueblos y ciudades del suroeste, los hispanos o latinos constituyen la mayoría de la población. Estos no son inmigrantes. Estos son los descendientes de los primeros pobladores de la región.

Santa Fe, Nuevo México

Los judíos

Fernando e Isabel expulsaron a los judíos de España en 1492. Los judíos españoles se llaman «sefardíes», nombre que viene de *Sefarad,* que quiere decir «España» en hebreo. Muchos sefardíes salieron de España, fueron a Holanda y, desde allí, viajaron al Caribe y a Norteamérica. En la ciudad de Nueva York hay una sinagoga sefardí que fue fundada en 1654 cuando Nueva York era New Amsterdam y pertenecía a Holanda. Recientemente se han descubierto en Nuevo México probables descendientes de judíos españoles que ni siquiera conocen su propia religión e historia pero que, a escondidas, han seguido ritos judíos heredados desde siglos atrás. Durante Pascua, por ejemplo, muchas familias sustituían tortillas de harina bien tostadas por *matzo,* el pan tradicional judío y encendían el candelabro de siete brazos, la *menorah.* Estos judíos probablemente vinieron desde México con los conquistadores después de haber salido de España. Tenían que celebrar su religión a escondidas por temor a represalias por las autoridades eclesiásticas ya que se suponía que eran conversos. Con el pasar del tiempo, sus descendientes mantuvieron las costumbres aunque olvidaron por qué las mantenían.

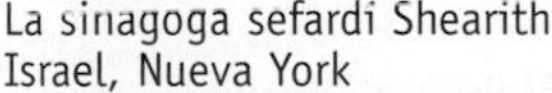

La sinagoga sefardí Shearith Israel, Nueva York

B ¿Sí o no?

1. Las primeras comunidades en lo que hoy es EE.UU. fueron fundadas por los ingleses.
2. Los españoles exploraron todo el territorio del sur comenzando en el siglo XVII.
3. Los sefardíes son judíos españoles expulsados de España durante el reinado de Fernando e Isabel.
4. Los sefardíes fueron solamente a Nueva York.

C ¿Judíos en Nuevo México?

En tus propias palabras, explica como parece que en Nuevo México hay gente de ascendencia hébrea sin saberlo.

Cultura

Los españoles

En los siglos XIX y XX venían a Norteamérica inmigrantes de España igual que de tantos otros países. Muchos españoles vinieron durante los años después de la Guerra Civil española (1936–1939), algunos porque tenían que exiliarse, otros porque España estaba devastada y había mucha hambre. Había gente de todas las clases sociales incluso académicos de gran fama que, casi inmediatamente, se colocaron en prestigiosas universidades estadounidenses.

Los mexicanos

Había mexicanos que llegaron a EE.UU. antes de que hubiera un Estados Unidos de América o un Estados Unidos Mexicanos. Vinieron a territorio que todavía pertenecía a la Corona española y se establecieron en grandes áreas del suroeste. Pero fue en los años posteriores a la Revolución mexicana (1910–1920) cuando salieron para el norte miles y miles de mexicanos, principalmente «norteños», gente del norte de México. Los primeros inmigrantes poblaron mayormente las regiones fronterizas en Texas, Arizona, Nuevo México y California.

El Paso, Texas

San Diego, California

Charro Days Fiesta, Brownsville, Texas

La frontera, Tijuana, México

Un desfile en Little Village, Chicago, Illinois

Misión San Carlos, Carmel, California

La política norteamericana con respecto a la inmigración variaba. Cuando se necesitaba mano de obra, especialmente en la agricultura, durante las dos guerras mundiales, por ejemplo, las puertas se abrían. Cuando había menos necesidad, los inmigrantes no eran bienvenidos. Hoy, inmigrantes mexicanos y los hijos de inmigrantes se encuentran en todas partes del país, de norte a sur, este a oeste, en Los Ángeles, Chicago, Nueva York, Denver, Houston y Seattle. De todos los grupos hispanos o latinos residentes en EE.UU. los mexicanos y sus descendientes forman el grupo más numeroso. De los cuarenta millones de hispanos o latinos en EE.UU. más de la mitad son de ascendencia mexicana.

D Contesten.

1. ¿Cuándo vinieron inmigrantes de España a EE.UU.?
2. ¿Por qué vinieron muchos después de la Guerra Civil?
3. ¿Hay muchos mexicanos que nacieron en territorio estadounidense antes de que fuera un Estados Unidos?
4. ¿Cuándo llegó una gran ola de mexicanos a Estados Unidos?
5. ¿De dónde salieron y dónde se establecieron?

E Describan la política norteamericana con respecto a la inmigración.

Los puertorriqueños

Con el cambio de bandera en 1898 Puerto Rico se encontró bajo la soberanía de EE.UU. Poco después, se les concedió la ciudadanía norteamericana. Antes de las décadas de 1940 y 1950 había puertorriqueños que venían al «continente» a trabajar o a estudiar, pero eran pocos. Eso cambió dramáticamente con el desarrollo de la aviación comercial. Vuelos baratos de San Juan a Nueva York trajeron miles de puertorriqueños que buscaban mejor vida en la gran ciudad. Cuando anteriormente llegaban menos de dos mil al año, ahora llegaban cuarenta y cinco mil. Aunque de nuevo son pocos los que llegan, siguen siendo el mayor grupo latino de Nueva York y el segundo mayor de EE.UU. Pero no están solamente en Nueva York sino en todo el país, mayormente en el nordeste, en ciudades como Boston, Filadelfia, Hartford y Jersey City. Muchos han salido de las ciudades para establecerse en los suburbios. Una interesante población puertorriqueña se encuentra en Hawaii. Han estado allí desde las primeras décadas del siglo XX. Se fueron allí para ayudar en establecer el cultivo de la piña. Otro dato interesante, la capital más antigua de EE.UU. es San Juan de Puerto Rico, fundada en 1521.

San Juan, Puerto Rico

El Barrio, Nueva York

El desfile puertorriqueño, Nueva York

Los cubanos

En el siglo XIX, patriotas cubanos se preparaban para su lucha contra España desde Nueva York y la Florida. Cuba, a sólo unas 90 millas de la costa de la Florida, había visto el ir y venir de la gente en ambas direcciones... hasta años recientes.

Durante las décadas de los 30, 40 y 50, los músicos cubanos eran popularísimos en todo Estados Unidos. Nuestros abuelos bailaban rumbas, congas y boleros en las elegantes salas de fiestas o en casa escuchando la radio. Los norteamericanos iban a La Habana para pasar un fin de semana gozando de baile, espectáculos, sol y playa. Pero la Revolución cubana de 1959 resultó después en el cese de relaciones diplomáticas entre EE.UU. y la Cuba de Fidel Castro. Miles y miles de cubanos, particularmente de las clases acomodadas (adineradas), salieron de Cuba para radicarse en Miami y, más tarde, en otras partes del país, como Union City y West New York en Nueva Jersey, Atlanta y Nueva Orleans. Tuvieron que abandonar sus hogares, sus familiares, sus profesiones y sus raíces para comenzar de nuevo.

Carmen Miranda

Refugiados cubanos en Miami en 1965

Calle Ocho Festival, Miami

LECCIÓN I

Cultura

Otros

Además de los grupos ya mencionados, hay muchos otros. Al nordeste han llegado gran número de dominicanos. Ellos constituyen hoy la mayor fuente de inmigrantes latinos para Nueva York. En esa ciudad sólo los puertorriqueños los superan numéricamente.

Los conflictos armados en Centroamérica resultaron en la emigración de gente que se escapaba de la violencia en El Salvador, Guatemala y Nicaragua. Muchos se fueron a California, otros a los estados del este. Se calcula que aproximadamente quinientos mil salvadoreños vinieron a EE.UU., la décima parte de la población de El Salvador. La violencia y los conflictos políticos también obligaron a colombianos, argentinos y chilenos a salir de su país para sentirse más seguros en el norte.

Sería una gran equivocación pensar que todos los hispanos o latinos son iguales. Hay diferencias raciales y culturales entre ellos. Hay quienes llevan sangre africana, europea, indígena o asiática. Cada grupo tiene sus propias costumbres y tradiciones. Hay quienes hablan solamente español o solamente inglés o ambos idiomas. Pero lo que comparten todos es una herencia común. El idioma, obviamente, es parte, aunque algunos lo hayan perdido. También los conceptos de honor y respeto, la importancia de los vínculos familiares y las relaciones personales son resultados de esta herencia.

Washington Heights, Nueva York

Columbia Road, Washington, D.C.

Unas dominicanas en Nueva York

F Identifiquen.

1. lo que pasó en 1898
2. cuando empezaron a venir miles y miles de puertorriqueños a EE.UU. y por qué
3. en qué parte de EE.UU. vivían muchos puertorriqueños
4. la influencia cubana en EE.UU. de los 30 hasta los 40 del siglo pasado
5. cuando vino la mayoría de los cubanos a EE.UU. y por qué
6. donde se establecieron
7. razones por la migración actual de muchas otras nacionalidades hispanas
8. por qué sería una gran equivocación pensar que todos los hispanos o latinos son iguales

Comida

Si visitas el barrio hispano de cualquiera de nuestras ciudades podrás disfrutar de una grata experiencia culinaria. No hace tantos años que la única comida hispana que podrías encontrar era la mexicana, y muchas veces comida mexicana poco auténtica. Eso ha cambiado radicalmente. Hoy puedes comerte un churrasco argentino, unas pupusas salvadoreñas, un pastel de choclo chileno, hasta chuño boliviano, comida heredada de los incas. Hay restaurantes en Estados Unidos donde uno puede probar especialidades de todas las repúblicas de las Américas. Y espero que te guste el arroz, porque no importa que el restaurante sea cubano, mexicano, puertorriqueño, centroamericano, colombiano, venezolano o dominicano, habrá arroz en el menú y, probablemente frijoles, aunque puede que se llamen habichuelas, fréjoles u otra cosa. ¡Moles mexicanos, asopaos caribeños, tamales, churrascos, arepas—una infinidad de sabores que nacieron en África, en Europa, en Oriente y en los pueblos indígenas de las Américas! Será una aventura para el paladar[1].

Desde hace ya medio milenio, han llegado y siguen llegando a Estados Unidos de todas partes del mundo hispánico, como de todos los rincones del planeta, gentes en busca de mejor vida, de un futuro más prometedor para sus hijos. Y todos ellos contribuyen a la prosperidad y a la grandeza de esta nación.

[1] el paladar *palate*

Mole

Una arepa

Comida cubana

Fort Myers, la Florida

Contesten.

1. Hasta recientemente, ¿cuál fue la única comida hispana que se podría encontrar en EE.UU.?
2. Pero hoy, ¿qué hay?
3. ¿Qué se sirve con muchos platos de muchos países diferentes?
4. ¿Cuáles son otros nombres para frijoles?
5. ¿De dónde son los asopaos?
6. ¿Cuáles son los origenes de muchos platos hispanos?

Estructura • Repaso

Adverbios en -mente
Telling how actions are carried out

1. An adverb modifies a verb, an adjective, or another adverb. In Spanish, many adverbs end in **-mente.** To form an adverb from an adjective that ends in **-e** or in a consonant, you simply add **-mente** to the adjective. Study the following.

ADJECTIVE		ADVERB
decente **reciente** **principal** **general**	**+ mente**	**decentemente** **recientemente** **principalmente** **generalmente**

2. To form an adverb from an adjective that ends in **-o,** add **-mente** to the feminine **-a** form of the adjective.

FEMININE ADJECTIVE		ADVERB
sincera **cariñosa**	**+ mente**	**sinceramente** **cariñosamente**

3. When more than one adverb ending in **-mente** modifies a verb, only the last adverb carries the **-mente** ending. Study the following.

Él habló lenta y claramente.
Yo se lo digo honesta y sinceramente.

Castillo de San Marcos, San Agustín, la Florida

¿Cómo lo digo?

Los adverbios

Formen adverbios de los siguientes adjetivos.

1. posible
2. necesario
3. dramático
4. numérico
5. aproximado
6. solo
7. violento
8. serio
9. individual
10. sencillo

Austin, Texas

David Farragut

Historieta Un héroe de ascendencia hispana

Contesten cambiando los adjetivos en adverbios.

1. La familia de David Farragut vino _____ de España. (original)
2. Él luchó _____ durante la Guerra Civil en Norteamérica. (valiente)
3. Ascendió _____ hasta llegar a almirante. (rápido)
4. Siempre trataba a sus marineros _____. (decente)
5. Y ellos siempre lo trataban _____. (respetuoso)
6. Los historiadores _____ consideran a Farragut un héroe ejemplar. (general)

Historieta Ramón y Laura

Contesten con adverbios.

1. ¿Cómo habla Ramón? (rápido/nervioso)
2. ¿Y cómo contesta Laura? (lento/claro)
3. ¿Cómo conduce Laura? (cuidadoso/sano)
4. Y Ramón, ¿cómo conduce él? (peligroso/loco)
5. ¿Cómo se porta Laura? (respetuoso/discreto)
6. ¿Y cómo se porta Ramón? (descortés/tonto)

¡Te toca a ti!

Use what you have learned

Dos ejecutivos latinos de Panorama City, California

1 Una entrevista

✔ *Interview a Spanish speaking student in your class*

Si en la clase de español hay un(a) alumno(a) hispanohablante, dale una entrevista. Quieres saber de donde es él o ella o sus antepasados; la lengua que hablan en casa, cuanto tiempo o cuantas generaciones viven aquí, algunas costumbres que practican y algunas de sus comidas típicas.

2 ¿Quiénes llegaron antes?

✔ *Discuss Hispanic influences in the early history of the United States*

Al estudiar la historia de Estados Unidos se pone mucho énfasis en las influencias anglosajonas. Pero la verdad es que habían estado los españoles en EE.UU. mucho antes de la llegada de los ingleses. Relata todo lo que sabes de las expediciones, exploraciones y fundaciones de los españoles.

Los mariachis, Los Ángeles, California

3 ¿Quiénes llegaron cuándo?

✔ *Discuss the migration of the various Hispanic or Latin groups of the United States*

Dentro de EE.UU. hay muchos grupos diferentes de hispanohablantes. Han llegado en épocas diferentes y por motivos diferentes. En grupos de tres o cuatro personas, hablen de los diferentes grupos hispanos. Expliquen cuando vinieron a EE.UU. y por qué.

4 Comunidades hispanohablantes

✔ *Discuss Hispanic and Latin communities near you*

Hay comunidades hispanohablantes cerca de donde tú vives. ¿De qué países son? ¿Conoces algunas de sus costumbres? ¿Cuáles?

Investigación

✔ ***Do some research on a well-known Hispanic or Latin figure***

Mira la lista de hispanos o latinos notables de EE.UU. Están agrupados en varias categorías. Escoge una persona y prepara un breve informe sobre él o ella.

Deportes Nancy López, Pancho González, Roberto Clemente, Anthony Muñoz, Mary Jo Fernández, Jennifer Rodríguez

Política/Finanzas César Chávez, Benjamín Cardozo, Antonia Coello Novello, George Santayana, Rosario Marín

Música Gloria Estefan , Jon Secada, Selena, Ricky Martin

Cine y teatro Andy García, Rita Moreno, José Ferrer, Edward James Olmos, Raquel Welch, Penelope Cruz

Andy García

Mary Jo Fernández

César Chávez

Contribuciones de los inmigrantes

✔ ***Discuss the importance of contributions made by immigrants***

Describe el significado de lo siguiente: Desde hace ya medio milenio, han llegado a Estados Unidos y siguen llegando de todas partes del mundo hispánico, como de todas las regiones del mundo entero, gente en busca de mejor vida, de un futuro más prometedor para sus hijos. Y todos ellos contribuyen a la prosperidad y a la grandeza de esta nación.

Vocabulario

1 Completen con una palabra apropiada.

To review vocabulary, turn to page 374.

1. Los españoles ____ pueblos y ciudades en las Américas.
2. Casi todas las religiones tienen sus ____ y ceremonias.
3. Ellos no podían volver a su país y tuvieron que ____ en Estados Unidos.
4. Lo que necesitamos aquí son trabajadores, mucha ____ de obra.
5. Los ____ son judíos que fueron expulsados de España durante la Inquisición.
6. A los mexicanos del norte de su país se les llama ____.
7. Hay muchos pueblos ____ de Tejas a California.
8. Todo el mundo sabía lo que estaban haciendo. No hicieron nada ____.
9. Ahora hay más calma porque ha habido un ____ en los conflictos.

Lectura

2 ¿Sí o no?

To review historical and cultural information, turn to pages 376–383.

10. Muchos inmigrantes españoles llegaron a Estados Unidos durante la Guerra Civil española.
11. Los primeros europeos en lo que es EE.UU. llegaron a Virginia.
12. San Agustín en la Florida es la ciudad más antigua de Norteamérica.
13. Los españoles exploraron gran parte del suroeste de EE.UU.
14. Los asopaos son platos típicamente mexicanos.
15. La mayoría de los cubanos que vinieron después del establecimiento del gobierno castrista eran los pobres.

La Estrella de David de un cementerio de Las Vegas, Nuevo México

3 Contesten.

16. ¿Cuándo empezaron a venir muchos puertorriqueños al «continente», o sea Estados Unidos continental?
17. ¿Cuándo vinieron miles y miles de mexicanos?
18. ¿Dónde se radicaron ellos?
19. ¿Cuál fue un motivo para la emigración de colombianos, chilenos y centroamericanos?
20. ¿Por qué vinieron muchos cubanos a EE.UU. después de 1959?

To review historical and cultural information, turn to pages 376–383.

Estructura

4 Completen con el adverbio.

21. Los inmigrantes vinieron ____ a la ciudad. (directo)
22. Algunos llegaron ____. (reciente)
23. Pero ____ ellos vivían en el campo. (antiguo)

24–25. Ahora están ____ y ____ adaptándose a la ciudad. (rápido, completo)

To review adverbs, turn to page 384.

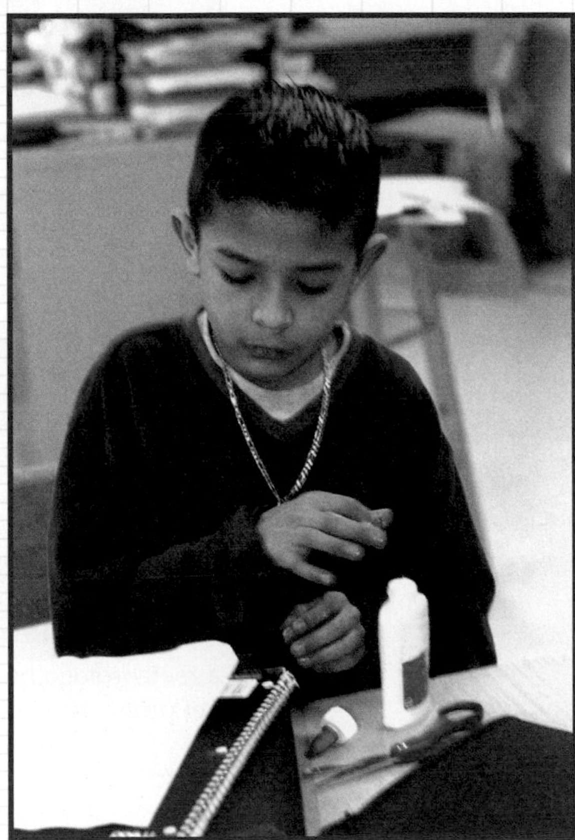

En una clase de inglés como segundo idioma, Golden Valley, Minnesota

Conversación

Vocabulario para la conversación

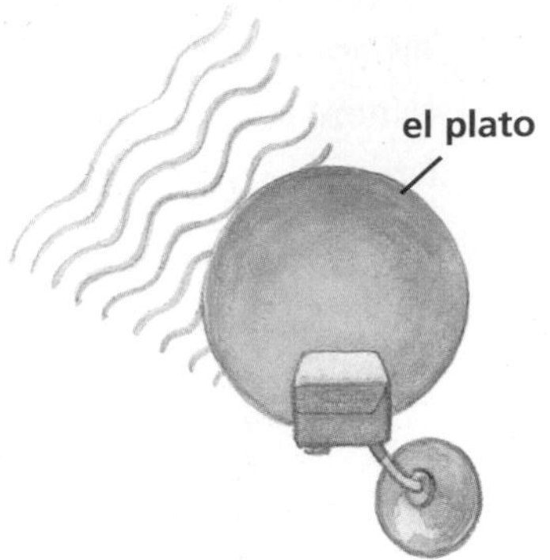

la antena parabólica

La televidente está surfeando con el control remoto.
No quiere ver los anuncios televisivos.

Con la nueva tecnología se puede grabar un programa directamente del satélite.

Son anclas de un noticiero.
Durante su programa (emisión), incluyen las noticias internacionales y nacionales.

una entrevista

Ella está haciendo una entrevista.
La están transmitiendo en vivo.

la meteoróloga

La meteoróloga presenta (da) el pronóstico del tiempo.

Más vocabulario

el payaso una persona cómica que les hace reír a todos
el/la televidente la persona que ve o mira la televisión
la telenovela una novela frecuentemente romántica, filmada y grabada para ser emitida por capítulos en la televisión

¿Cómo lo digo?

1 Historieta Contesten personalmente.

1. ¿Tienes un sistema de televisión por satélite? ¿Han instalado un plato o antena parabólica?
2. De vez en cuando, ¿grabas un programa que te gusta?
3. ¿Te gustan los anuncios televisivos?
4. ¿Surfeas los canales con tu control remoto cuando hay muchos anuncios?
5. Cada noche, ¿miras el noticiero en la televisión?
6. ¿Tienes un ancla o una mujer ancla predilecta?
7. ¿Miras la televisión para enterarte del pronóstico del tiempo?

Una emisión de Univisión, Los Ángeles, California

2 Emisiones televisivas Completen.

1. Cuando el ancla entrevista a alguien fuera del estudio tiene que usar un _____.
2. A veces transmiten la entrevista _____ pero a veces la entrevista está pregrabada.
3. Los anclas presentan las noticias _____ y _____.
4. El _____ da el pronóstico del tiempo.
5. No tengo que levantarme para cambiar de canal porque tengo un _____.
6. Hay bastante publicidad por todas partes. No aguanto los _____.
7. En la televisión hispana hay muchos programas infantiles con tiras cómicas y _____.
8. Él no se fija nunca en un solo programa. Siempre está _____ los canales.

Emisoras en español

Laura Oye, Manuel. ¿Es verdad que ustedes no tienen cable en tu casa?

Manuel No, chica. Es que donde vivo no hay cable. Por eso acabamos de instalar un sistema de televisión por satélite. Recibimos hasta doscientos canales.

Laura ¿Cómo funciona? ¿Construyen una torre o algo así para recibir los programas?

Manuel No, es muy sencillo. Sólo necesitas una antena parabólica y no tener nada que obstruya la señal de satélite.

Laura ¿Ofrecen programas en español?

Manuel Muchos. Hay telenovelas, deportes, las últimas noticias nacionales e internacionales, el pronóstico del tiempo, series policíacas y *quiz shows*. Ofrecen paquetes de programas que incluyen películas nuevas, emisoras extranjeras—de España, México y otros países. Puedes hasta sustituir un «paquete» de programas por otro si así prefieres.

Laura ¿Sabes lo que a mí me gustaría ser? Mujer ancla de un noticiero. ¡Fíjate! Allí estoy ante las cámaras. Tomo el micrófono y les digo a los televidentes: «Los criminales huyeron de la policía, pero por muy pocas horas. Aquí los ven, capturados y camino de la cárcel. Les informa Laura Santiago, ancla de tu noticiero favorito y hasta mañana, querido público.» ¿Qué te parece?

Manuel Laura, preciosa. Prendería mi grabadora DVD y te grabaría cada vez que aparecieras en la pantalla. Distribuiría los discos DVD con tu voz e imagen a todo el mundo para que los que no te pudieron ver en vivo tuvieran la oportunidad de saber lo «súper» que eres.

Laura Muy cómico. Gracias. Me voy a casa para ver unos cómicos de verdad en la tele y no un payaso como tú.

Manuel Ay, Laura, no te enojes conmigo. Estoy bromeando[1], no más. Perdóname.

Laura Perdonado. Pero verás… un día las cadenas de televisión más prestigiosas harán cualquier cosa para poder proyectar esta cara y esta voz a un público loco por verme.

Manuel ¿Loco? ¿El público o una persona a quien conozco muy bien?

Laura Manolito, si estuvieras ahora en la tele, yo tomaría el control remoto y empezaría a surfear como si estuviera tratando de evitar los anuncios. O, aún mejor, te apagaría enseguida.

[1] bromeando *joking*

¿Comprendes?

Contesten.

1. ¿Qué sistema de televisión tiene Manuel? ¿Por qué?
2. ¿Puede recibir programas en español?
3. ¿Qué tipo de programas hay?
4. ¿Qué quisiera ser Laura?
5. ¿Qué quisiera hacer?
6. ¿Qué le dirá a su público al terminar su emisión?
7. ¿Qué haría Manuel cada vez que ella aparecía en la pantalla?
8. ¿Por qué distribuiría los discos DVD?
9. ¿Por qué usa Laura la palabra «payaso»?
10. Y, ¿qué haría Laura si «Manolito» estuviera ahora mismo en la tele?

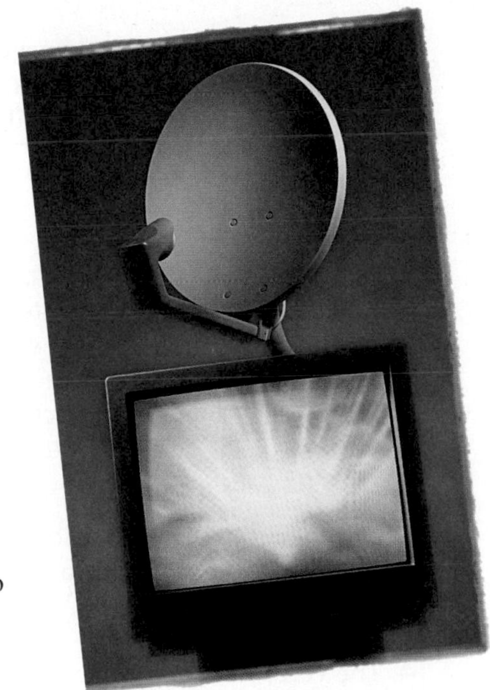

For more information about Hispanic influence in the United States, go to **Web Explore** on the Glencoe Spanish Web site at glencoe.com.

Estructura • Repaso

Verbos que terminan en -uir
Discussing activities in the present and the past

1. Verbs that end in **-uir** have a **y** in all forms of the present tense except **nosotros** and **vosotros** and in the third person singular and plural: **él, ella, usted, ellos, ellas, ustedes** of the preterite. Study these forms of the verb **construir.**

	PRESENT	PRETERITE
yo	construyo	construí
tú	construyes	construiste
él, ella, Ud.	construye	construyó
nosotros(as)	construimos	construimos
vosotros(as)	*construís*	*construisteis*
ellos, ellas, Uds.	construyen	construyeron

El señor Garcés construye casas de campo.
Él construyó la casa de los Romero.
Los señores Romero distribuyen libros de texto.

2. Other verbs ending in **-uir** are:

destruir	*to destroy*
disminuir	*to diminish, to lessen*
distribuir	*to distribute*
huir	*to flee, to escape*
incluir	*to include*
obstruir	*to obstruct*
sustituir	*to substitute*

3. Note that the verb **oír** follows the same pattern except for the **yo** form which is **oigo** in the present tense.

oír **oigo** **oyes** **oye** **oímos** ***oís*** **oyen**

4. The verbs **leer, oír,** and **caer** follow the pattern of the **-uir** verbs in the preterite tense.

LEER	**leí**	**leíste**	**leyó**	**leímos**	***leísteis***	**leyeron**
OÍR	**oí**	**oíste**	**oyó**	**oímos**	***oísteis***	**oyeron**
CAER	**caí**	**caíste**	**cayó**	**caímos**	***caísteis***	**cayeron**

Villa Viscaya, Miami, la Florida

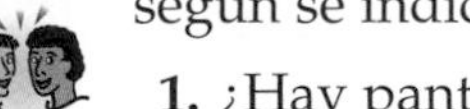

¿Cómo lo digo?

1 **Historieta** **Pantallas en el avión** Contesten según se indica.

1. ¿Hay pantallas de televisión en un avión? (sí)
2. En los aviones más viejos, ¿caen automáticamente? (sí)
3. En los aviones más modernos, ¿tiene cada pasajero su propia pantalla? (sí)
4. ¿Distribuyen los asistentes de vuelo audífonos para que los pasajeros puedan oír los programas? (sí)
5. ¿Incluyen las compañías el cargo de los audífonos en el costo del boleto (del pasaje)? (no)
6. Al escuchar los programas, ¿se disminuye el ruido del avión? (sí)
7. ¿Es posible que algunos pasajeros destruyan los audífonos? (sí)

2 **Los constructores** Completen.

1. La compañía ____ edificios para emisoras de radio. (construir)
2. El año pasado, ellos ____ solamente dos. (construir)
3. Nosotros ____ hablar de ellos con frecuencia. (oír)
4. Parece que sus ganancias ____ bastante el año pasado. (caer)
5. Una explosión ____ uno de los edificios en construcción. (destruir)
6. El responsable de la explosión ____. (huir)
7. Hoy el banco ____ los dividendos de fin de año. (distribuir)
8. Los cheques no ____ nada extra para nadie. (incluir)

3 **Historieta** **¿Qué oyes?** Completen con el presente de **oír.**

—Rosa, ¿qué __1__ tú?

—¿Yo? No __2__ nada.

—¿Que tú no __3__ nada? Pero Ramón y yo sí que __4__ algo.

—Es que ustedes __5__ algo que nadie más __6__.

—Pues todo el mundo __7__ algo, y tú no __8__ nada. Y tú tienes razón, ¿no?

4 **¿Qué oíste?** Completen la conversación de la Actividad 3 con el pretérito de **oír.**

¡Te toca a ti!

Use what you have learned

Los programas favoritos

✔ Discuss your favorite TV programs

Haz una lista de tus programas favoritos en la tele e indica si son telenovelas, música, policiales (policíacos), noticieros, etc. Después, compara tu lista con la de tu compañero(a) y determinen cuales tienen en común y cuales son diferentes.

TV NOCHE													20 DE DICIEMBRE DEL 2003
	6:00	6:30	7:00	7:30	8:00	8:30	9:00	9:30	10:00	10:30	11:00	11:30	12:00
47	La Corte del Pueblo	Noticiero Telemundo	Máximo de la Música		Ley MTV Unplugged		Película: ★★★ "El Secreto del Abismo" (1989, Ciencia Ficción) Ed Harris. Mineros investigan un submarino nuclear en el fondo del mar.				Titulares Telemundo	Sabia Usted	"Hercules-Amaz"
2	(5:00) Fútbol Americano NFL: Kansas City Chiefs en Minnesota Vikings.				Robbie-Reindr	Robbie	Hack "Gone" (N) ∩ (SS)		District "The Voice Inside" (N) (SS)		CBS 2 News 11	(:35) Sports Rap	West Wing (SS)
4	NewsChannel 4	NBC News	Access Hollywood (N) (SS)		"National Lampoon's Christmas Vacation 2: Cousin Eddie's Island"				Fear Factor "Christmas Episode"		NewsChannel 4	Saturday Night Live (N) ∩ (SS)	
5	Noticias-Fox	3rd Rock-Sun	Just Shoot Me	Seinfeld ∩ (SS)	Cops (N) (SS)	Cops (SS)	America's Most Wanted		Noticias de Fox 5 a las 10 (SS)		Mad TV "Holiday Show" (N) (SS)		Live in H-wood
7	Eyewitness	ABC Wld News	Jeopardy! (SS)	Wheel-Fortune	Merry Mickey Celebration (N) (SS)		Película: ★★★ "The Santa Clause" (1994) Tim Allen. ∩ (SS)				Eyewitness	(:35) ER ∩ (SS)	
9	King of Queens	King of Queens	Parkers ∩ (SS)	Parkers ∩ (SS)	Jets Special	Fútbol Americano NFL: New England Patriots en New York Jets. (En Vivo)						UPN 9 Noticias	That '70s Show
11	Película se Anunciará				Se Anunciará				Noticias WB11 a las Diez		Every-Raymond	Odd Couple	Taxi
13	Nature "Dive to the Abyss" ∩		New This Old House Hour ∩ (SS)		Keeping Up	Time Goes By	Película: ★★★½ "The Yearling" (1946, Drama) Gregory Peck.				(:10) Masterpiece Theatre "David Copperfield"		
21	Lawrence Welk Show (N)		World News	Antiques Rdsho	1900 House ∩ (Parte 1 de 4) (SS)		Mystery! "Touching Evil"		EastEnders ∩	EastEnders ∩	World News	This Is America	"Penny Sere."
25	Studio 3-Polish	RAI Italian News	Le Journal	Bookshow (SS)	Película: ★★★★ "Babette's Feast" (1987) Stéphane Audran.				Globe Trekker ∩ (SS)		Mountain Stage ∩ (SS)		Inner Peace
WFUT	Película: ★★★ "Disparo Mortal" (1989, Suspenso) Don Johnson, Penelope Ann Miller. Un policía de Los Ángeles investiga un asesinato.				Fútbol de la Liga Mexicana: UNL Tigres vs. Pachuca. (En Vivo)				Película: ★★★ "Las Aventuras de Jeremiah Johnson" (1972) Robert Redford, Will Geer. Solitario se hace hombre de las montañas.				Contacto Deportivo
WXTV	Noticias	Noticiero Univisión	La Familia P. Luche		Sábado Gigante Los Reyes del Corrido; la Banda los Razos de Sacramento; Reynaldo.						Noticias	Noticiero Univisión	Otro Rollo IM.
CABLE BÁSICO													
GALA	Boxeo en Esta Esquina		Al Ritmo de la Noche Jorge Ortiz presenta este programa nocturno.				Toma Libre		Sábado Musical				El Noticiero
GEMS	Fuzión	Top Ten	Chat	Jamz		Speedlogic	No Cover		Futurama ∩ (SS)	Lugar Heights	Loco Comedy Jam		NY Underground
BRV	Queer Eye for the Straight Guy		Queer Eye for the Straight Guy		Película: ★★★½ "Good Will Hunting" (1997, Drama) Matt Damon. 'R' (SS)					(:45) Película: ★★★½ "Good Will Hunting" (1997) Matt Damon. 'R'			
CUNY tv	African-Amer.	Brooklyn Coll.	Study With	Eldridge & Co.	Urban Agenda	Women-Women	Película: ★★★½ "Come and See" (1986, Drama) Alexei Kravchenko, Olga Mironova. (Subtitled-English)						Wm. Basketball
DSC	Crusades (SS)		Unsolved History		American Chopper		Monster Garage		Monster House (SS)		American Chopper		Monster Garage
E!	E! News Weekend		E! Originals Especial televisivo.		E! Originals Especial televisivo.		E! Originals Especial televisivo.		Saturday Night Live ∩ (SS)		Wild On		Howard Stern
ESPN	(5:00) Patinaje Artístico: ISU Gran Prix De Patinaje.			SportsCenter	NFL PrimeTime	Fútbol Americano NFL: New England Patriots en New York Jets. (En Vivo) (SS)						SportsCenter (En Vivo) (SS)	
ESPN2	Baloncesto Universitario Femenino			Cheerleading	Cheerleading: UCA		Cheerleading: Camp. Equipo Baile		Baloncesto Universitario: Alabama vs. Oregón. (En Vivo) (SS)				NBA Fastbreak
LIFE	"Get to the Heart-Mandrell"		Película: ★½ "Silent Victim" (1993, Drama) Michelle Greene. (SS)				Película: "Fighting for My Daughter" (1995) Lindsay Wagner. (SS)				What Should You Do? (SS)		Any Day Now
LTV	Destino X	CNN Inter.	Luz de América	Televisión Int.	Plush TV		Irie TV		Evidencias	Reconquista	Zona Impactante		Hisp. Church
MSG	Jets Journal	Rangers	Hockey NHL: New York Rangers en Ottawa Senators. Desde el Corel Centre. (En Vivo)					Un. Roughness	MSG Remix	Boomer Esiason	Giants On-Line	Mets Hot Stove	Hockey NHL
MTV	End of 2003 Countdown Final Hour		End of 2003 Countdown (N) ∩		Osbournes Christmas ∩		Viva La Bam ∩	Wild Boyz ∩	One Bad Trip ∩	Jackass ∩	Music Videos ∩		
NICK	Told by Ginger	ChalkZone (SS)	Jimmy Neutron	Oddparents	All Grown Up ∩	Romeo! ∩	All That ∩	Amanda ∩	Cosby Show ∩	Cosby Show ∩	Roseanne (SS)	Roseanne (SS)	Cosby Show ∩
SCIFI	(5:00) Película: "Prophecy II" ∩		Película: ★★ "Prophecy III" (2000) Christopher Walken. ∩ (SS)				Película: "Revelation" (2001, Terror) Jennifer Grey. Estreno. ∩ (SS)				Película: ★½ "Stigmata" (1999, Terror) ∩ (SS)		
SPCH	Thoroughbred	Baloncesto Universitario: Michigan State en UCLA. (En Vivo)				Baloncesto Universitario Femenino: Colorado en Southern California.				Best Damn Sports Show Period		Fant. Football	Beyond-Glory
TBS	Home Improve.	Friends ∩ (SS)	Película: ★ "Exit Wounds" (2001) (Aviso Paternal) Steven Seagal.				Película: ★★½ "Romeo Must Die" (2000) Jet Li, Aaliyah. (SS)				(:15) Película: ★★ "Blade" (1998) Wesley Snipes		
TNT	(5:00) Película: ★★½ "The Devil's Advocate" (1997), Al Pacino (SS)				Película: ★★★ "What's Love Got to Do With It" (1993) Angela Bassett. Estreno.					Película: ★★ "Why Do Fools Fall in Love" (1998) Halle Berry.			
TOON	(5:00) Película: "Osmosis Jones"		He-Man-Master	Yu-Gi-Oh! (SS)	Zoids Fuzors (N)	Samurai Jack	Teen Titans	Pokemon (SS)	Justice League	Justice League	Rurouni Kenshin	Yuyu Hakusho	Hack/Sign
USA	(5:00) Película: "Happy Gilmore"		Law & Order: Special Victims Unit		Law & Order: Special Victims Unit		Law & Order: Special Victims Unit		Law & Order: Special Victims Unit		Law & Order: Criminal Intent (SS)		Law & Order
CABLE PAGADO													
HBO	(:15) Película: ★★½ "The Pallbearer" (1996) David Schwimmer. ∩				Película: ★★★½ "Adaptation." (2002) Nicolas Cage. 'R' (SS)				Angels in America ∩ (Parte 6 de 6) (SS)			Película: "One Hour Photo" 'R'	
MAX	(5:30) Película: ★★★ "Ali" (2001, Biografía) Will Smith. ∩ 'R' (SS)				(:15) Película: ★½ "Showtime" (2002) Robert De Niro. 'PG-13' (SS)				"Adam Sandler's Crazy Nights"		(:15) Película: "Sapphire Girls" (2003) Mary Carey.		
SHO	(5:15) Película: ★★ "Captain Corelli's Mandolin"			Película: ★½ "Domestic Disturbance" (2001)			Free for All (SS)	Free for All (SS)	Free for All (SS)	Free for All (SS)	Free for All (SS)	Family Business	Chris Isaak (SS)

Para pensar

✔ Give some opinions about soap operas

A mi amigo le gusta ver las telenovelas, pero no quiere admitirlo. ¿Por qué? ¿Qué crees tú que será la razón?

El debate

✔ Talk about radio and TV

Hace muchos años, cuando llegó la televisión, decían que eso acabaría con la radio, que nadie escucharía la radio teniendo televisión. Todavía no ha ocurrido. Divide tu grupo en dos para debatir este tema: **Pronto morirá la radio, ¿verdad o mentira?** Presenten argumentos en pro y en contra.

Emisora puertorriqueña en un desfile, Nueva York

4 Un noticiero

HABLAR ESCRIBIR

✔ *Prepare a news broadcast*

Imagínate que eres ancla o ancla mujer para una emisora en español. Te ofrecieron el puesto porque eres bilingüe. Vas a presentar una noticia y sabes que les va a interesar mucho a tus televidentes. Primero, escribe lo que vas a presentar y luego preséntaselo a tu público—tu clase.

Emisora en español, San Antonio, Texas

5 Una entrevista

HABLAR ESCRIBIR

✔ *Interview one of your teachers in Spanish*

Vas a entrevistar a uno(a) de tus profesores(as) de español para una emisora de televisión local. Antes de comenzar la entrevista, tienes que escribir todas las preguntas que piensas hacerle a tu profesor(a). Algunas ideas son: ¿Por qué quería ser profesor(a)? ¿Le gusta? ¿Por qué sí o no?

Assessment

Vocabulario

1 Completen.

1. El televisor tiene una _____.
2–3. Los _____ pueden usar el _____ para cambiar de canal.
4. El _____ presenta las noticias nacionales e internacionales.
5–6. Ella va a entrevistar a varias personas en una calle del centro de la ciudad. Tienen que usar _____ y la emisora está transmitiendo la entrevista _____.
7. El _____ presenta el pronóstico del tiempo.
8. Mucha gente _____ los canales cuando no quieren ver los anuncios televisivos.

To review vocabulary, turn to page 390.

2 Contesten.

9. ¿Qué es una telenovela?
10. ¿Qué es un payaso?

Conversación

3 ¿Sí o no?

11. La familia de Manuel tiene cable en casa.
12. Un ancla da el pronóstico del tiempo.
13. Los payasos toman parte en los *quiz shows.*
14. Laura quiere actuar en telenovelas.
15. Laura se sirve de su control remoto cuando quiere surfear los canales para no ver los anuncios televisivos.

To review the conversation, turn to pages 392–393.

Estructura

4 Completen.

16–17. Ellos los _____ ahora porque no los _____ ayer. (distribuir)
18. Ahora yo no _____ nada. (contribuir)
19–20. Ayer, yo no lo _____ y él no lo _____ tampoco. (oír)

To review verbs ending in -uir and other similar verbs, turn to page 394.

5 Escriban en el pretérito.

21. Yo no oigo nada.
22. Teresa lee ese libro pero Pedro no lo lee.
23. Los asistentes distribuyen los papeles.
24. El vaso cae al suelo.
25. Nosotros destruimos los documentos.

Coral Gables, la Florida

LECCIÓN 3

Periodismo

Vocabulario para la lectura

Confirmado: un millón de hispanos

Use your StudentWorks™ Plus CD for more practice.

Vocabulario

la cifra el número
las divisas monedas extranjeras
el giro de dinero instrumento o documento que se usa para mandar o enviar dinero
agigantado(a) muy grande
advertir (ie, i) informar de antemano, avisar
aportar llevar, contribuir
involucrar incluir
suministrar proveer, dar

¿Qué palabra necesito?

La población latina Contesten.

1. ¿Está en aumento la cifra de hispanos o latinos en Estados Unidos?
2. ¿Están involucrados los latinos en muchos negocios diferentes?
3. ¿Han tomado pasos agigantados los latinos en la economía del país?
4. ¿Habían advertido los líderes de la comunidad latina que el gobierno no estaba reconociendo el aumento en la población latina?

Washington Heights, Nueva York

2 Otra palabra Expresen de otra manera.

1. Ellos *contribuyen* mucho al patrimonio nacional.
2. Es el gobierno que *provee* los números.
3. Yo les he *avisado* que las cifras van a cambiar.
4. Se puede enviar dinero en muchas *monedas extranjeras*.
5. La dueña está *muy metida* en su propio negocio.

Spanish Online
For more information about Hispanic influence in the United States, go to **Web Explore** on the Glencoe Spanish Web site at glencoe.com.

De aquí se envían giros, Jackson Heights, Nueva York

Hoy

Confirmado: un millón de hispanos

Néstor Cristancho

Seguimos creciendo, pero hay que hacerlo con responsabilidad. Esa frase es síntesis de la reacción de las organizaciones hispanas de Nueva Jersey a propósito de la noticia del Censo de Estados Unidos donde se reconoce que la comunidad de origen latino es la minoría más grande del país.

En Nueva Jersey hay un millón de hispanos y este es el quinto estado del país con la quinta concentración más grande de negocios latinos, de acuerdo con los datos suministrados a este diario por la Cámara de Comercio Estatal.

«No nos sorprende esta noticia. Terminado el Censo de 2000, nosotros advertimos que no se estaba reconociendo con veracidad el número de hispanos que hay en Estados Unidos. Solamente en Nueva Jersey se afirmaba que había 160.000 dominicanos, y los datos nuestros indican que hay unos 24.000», dijo la Directora del Instituto de Estudios Latinos, María Teresa Feliciano.

Lo mismo sucedía con otras comunidades en este estado, como la cubana (160.000), la colombiana (140.000) y la peruana (180.000), en las que las cifras del Censo indicaban la mitad de las cifras reales.

«El hecho de que en un país de 280 millones de personas haya 40 millones, crea una obligación a las instituciones establecidas, a los partidos políticos y a las entidades privadas. Ellos deben compartir el poder político y jurídico, el acceso a los servicios, las asignaciones[1] federales y en el respeto de los derechos[2]», subrayó Feliciano.

En economía

En donde se ha marchado a pasos agigantados es en economía. De acuerdo con Daniel Jara, presidente de la Cámara de Comercio de Nueva Jersey se estima que las ventas netas de los negocios latinos suman 750.000.000 dólares.

Esos negocios aportan 180.000 empleos. Y en un promedio general, se ha establecido que hay 45.000 empresas latinas consolidadas en el mercado de este estado.

«La mayoría de los negocios latinos eran bodegas. Pero eso ya no sucede más. Los negocios son muy diversificados. Un gran sector está involucrado en comercio internacional y otro en el área de servicios. Y todo eso nos involucra en el desarrollo de la alta tecnología como los servicios de comunicación. Además tenemos un pequeño porcentaje involucrado en la fabricación de productos», explicó Jara.

En cuanto al aporte económico que los latinos hacen desde Nueva Jersey a sus países de origen, se ha establecido que los giros de dinero constituyen un 20 por ciento de las divisas de naciones latinoamericanas.

Así están las cosas, por lo que la directora del Instituto de Estudios Latinos, María Teresa Feliciano, advirtió que «nuestro crecimiento poblacional merece que seamos responsables socialmente.»

[1] asignaciones *entitlements*
[2] derechos *rights*

¿Comprendes?

A Historieta Un millón de hispanos

Contesten.

1. ¿En qué estado hay un millón de hispanos?
2. ¿Cuál es la minoría más grande de EE.UU.?
3. ¿De dónde salió esa noticia?
4. ¿Cuántos estados tienen mayor concentración de negocios latinos que Nueva Jersey?
5. Según la Sra. Feliciano, ¿quiénes deben compartir el poder político y jurídico, el acceso a los servicios, etc.?
6. ¿Cuántos empleos aportan los negocios latinos en el estado?

West New York, Nueva Jersey

En una clase de inglés como segundo idioma, Cliffside Park, Nueva Jersey

B Más detalles Completen.

1. En el pasado, la mayoría de los negocios latinos eran _____.
2. Hoy hay unos _____ mil negocios latinos.
3. Se involucra la alta tecnología en el área de los servicios de _____.
4. Los latinos envían _____ de _____ a sus países de origen.
5. Estos giros llegan a ser el 20 por ciento de las _____ de algunos países latinoamericanos.

West New York, Nueva Jersey

C Interpretación Expliquen.

1. En donde se ha marchado a pasos agigantados es en economía.
2. … nuestro crecimiento poblacional merece que seamos responsables socialmente.
3. … no se estaba reconociendo con veracidad el número de hispanos que hay en Estados Unidos.

Vocabulario para la lectura

Inesperada tormenta en Lancaster

La tormenta fue horrenda.
Había tanta lluvia que resultó en una inundación y una ola de lodo.
Los relámpagos asustaban a todos.

Una señora fue atrapada en su carro al lado de un poste de teléfono.
Fue rescatada por un socorrista.

Los soportes del puente fueron dañados por las lluvias.
El camionero tuvo que tomar un desvío.

Más vocabulario

el desvío el acto de tener que tomar otro camino
súbito de repente, rápidamente
aflojar debilitar, hacer flojo, quitar firmeza
permanecer quedar en un lugar
reanudar continuar algo después de una interrupción

¿Qué palabra necesito?

1 Historieta La tormenta Contesten.

1. ¿A veces son súbitas las tormentas?
2. Durante las tormentas, ¿cae mucha lluvia?
3. ¿Tienes miedo de los relámpagos?
4. ¿La inundación fue causada por la lluvia?
5. ¿A veces se forma una ola de lodo?
6. ¿Puede enterrar un pueblo una ola de lodo?
7. ¿El poste de teléfono fue aflojado por el lodo?

2 Historieta El rescate Completen.

1. La señora fue ____ en su carro. No podía salir.
2. Pasaba un camión, y el ____ la vio.
3. Pronto llegó un ____ para salvarla.
4. Ella fue ____ por el socorrista.
5. La carretera fue dañada por el lodo. No se podía pasar y todos tuvieron que tomar un ____.
6. El puente estuvo en malas condiciones, los ____ fueron aflojados por el lodo.
7. Ellos tuvieron que ____ allí media hora hasta que todo estuviera seguro.
8. Luego pudieron ____ su viaje.

3 ¿Cuál es la palabra? Den la palabra cuya definición sigue.

1. una tempestad fuerte
2. el que rescata a las víctimas de un accidente o desastre natural
3. el conductor de un camión
4. un camino no previsto; no planeado
5. hacer débil
6. continuar de nuevo
7. de repente
8. lo que resulta de fuertes lluvias

La Opinión

Los Ángeles

Inesperada tormenta en Lancaster

Fuertes lluvias causan torrentes que ponen en peligro vida de automovilistas

Una tormenta eléctrica dejó caer ayer fuertes lluvias, acompañadas de frecuentes relámpagos, en un área al este de Lancaster, lo que envió torrentes de agua y lodo a través del desierto.

Los súbitos torrentes de agua dejaron atrapada en su vehículo a una conductora que eventualmente fue rescatada por la tripulación de un helicóptero. El drama se desarrolló en vivo ante las cámaras del noticiero de la estación de televisión KABC Canal 7, que documentó como las olas de lodo avanzaban en el desierto, aflojando a su paso postes de teléfono y poniendo en peligro a la mujer que por un corto tiempo se vio atrapada en un automóvil azul. El piloto del cuerpo de bomberos del condado[1] aterrizó atrás de su automóvil y un socorrista salió de la aeronave, se acercó al lado del pasajero del automóvil y ayudó a la mujer a llegar al helicóptero, para evacuarla. La densa lluvia también fue reportada por el radar del área de Bakersfield y se informó de una precipitación en el desierto bajo, cerca de Palm Springs. Mientras tanto, los camioneros del sur de California y los conductores que se dirigían a Las Vegas fueron advertidos de que la carretera interestatal 15 estaba cerrada a la altura de Barstow, debido a una inundación relámpago que dañó al menos tres soportes del puente al sur de Baker. «Cualquiera que vaya a Las Vegas no va a poder pasar de Barstow,» dijo el agente de la Patrulla de Carreteras de California (CHP), Adam Cortinas. Dijo que la única alternativa era usar el desvío de 70 millas por la Interestatal 40 Este a la U.S. 95, y de allí a Las Vegas.

[1] condado *county*

KABC Canal 7 reportó que tres de los soportes del puente de 38 años en Oat Wash sobre la I-15 están seriamente dañados y que la acumulación de autos en la ruta alterna I-40 ayer por la tarde era de unas 27 millas de largo en un punto determinado. El agente de la CHP Tim Smith dijo a la estación que en el mejor de los casos, la I-15 se reabriría cerca de las 8:00 de anoche, y con más seguridad cerca de las 2:00 A.M. Sin embargo, Caltrans dijo que podría ser que no fuera sino hasta el mediodía de hoy que se reanudaría el tráfico de nuevo en la carretera I-15.

Caltrans reportó que los aguaceros en el desierto dejaron los lechos de los ríos[2] normalmente secos, llenos con aguas corrientes que dañaron las bases del puente Oat Wash Bridge, cinco millas al sur de Baker. La oficina dijo que los conductores que no pueden pasar de Barstow a Oat Wash serán devueltos al sur en el camino Zzyzx Road.

La interestatal al norte en ese lugar permanecerá cerrada indefinidamente, pero quizás por corto tiempo, según la oficina.

[2] lechos de los ríos *riverbeds*

¿Comprendes?

A **El drama** Contesten.

1. ¿Dónde ocurrió la tormenta?
2. ¿Qué tipo de tormenta era?
3. ¿Qué le pasó a una conductora?
4. ¿Por quién fue rescatada?
5. ¿Cómo fue evacuada la señora?

B **La carretera** Completen.

1. El puente fue dañado _____ de Baker.
2. La inundación causó daño a tres o más _____.
3. Para llegar a Las Vegas tendrían que tomar un _____ de 70 millas.
4. El agente Smith indicó que la ruta I-15 no se abriría antes de las _____ de la noche.
5. Los lechos de los ríos en el desierto están normalmente _____.

Estructura • Avanzada

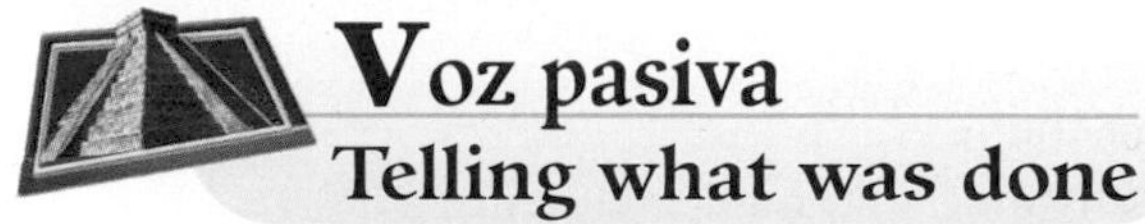

Voz pasiva
Telling what was done

1. The true passive voice is used much less in Spanish than in English. In Spanish, the active voice is usually preferred.

ACTIVE	PASSIVE
The firefighter rescued the woman.	*The woman was rescued by the firefighter.*

2. The true passive in Spanish is formed by the verb **ser** followed by the past participle.

El bombero rescató a la señora.	La señora fue rescatada por el bombero.

3. Remember that the past participle agrees with the subject. The agent, the person or thing doing the action, is introduced by the preposition **por.** Note that **por** is replaced by **de** if emotion is expressed.

Las víctimas fueron rescatadas por los socorristas.
Los socorristas son admirados de todos.

4. The true passive is often found in newspapers, often in an elliptical (shortened) form.

Puentes destruidos por olas de lodo
Camionero rescatado por socorristas

¿Cómo lo digo?

1 Historieta La tormenta

Cambien en la voz pasiva según el modelo.

El lodo destruyó el puente. →
El puente fue destruido por el lodo.

1. Las aguas atraparon al conductor.
2. El socorrista rescató al conductor.
3. Un helicóptero los llevó al pueblo.
4. La ola de lodo dañó los soportes de otro puente.
5. La policía paró el tráfico.
6. El gobierno cerró varias carreteras.
7. Un canal de televisión transmitió las noticias oficiales.
8. Todo el mundo admiró a los socorristas.

Punta Arenas, Chile

Voz pasiva con se
What is done in general

1. The passive is more often expressed in Spanish by using the reflexive pronoun **se** with the third person singular or plural of the verb, especially when the agent, the person carrying out the action, is not stated. Note that the subject often follows the verb in this construction.

Aquí se habla español.	*Spanish is spoken here.*
Se envían giros de dinero.	*Money orders are sent.*
Se reconce el aporte económico.	*The economic contribution is recognized.*

The passive **se** construction is also used when the subject is indefinite.

Se dice que las cifras son correctas.	*They say (It is said) that the figures are correct.*

Punta Arenas, Chile

El Desfile puertorriqueño, Nueva York

¿Cómo lo digo?

2 **Historieta** **El censo** Completen con **se** y el verbo.

1. _____ datos veraces y confiables. (necesitar)
2. Primero _____ personal cualificado. (buscar)
3. Después _____ les _____ una preparación intensiva. (dar)
4. _____ de casa en casa recogiendo datos. (ir)
5. Todos los datos _____ en computadoras. (entrar)
6. La información _____ a Washington. (enviar)
7. Allí _____ los datos y _____ informes. (estudiar, preparar)
8. Entonces _____ al público. (informar)
9. La información _____ por la prensa o la televisión. (recibir)

3 **Es igual.** Cambien de una forma pasiva a la otra.

1. La bodega se abrió temprano.
2. El giro fue enviado.
3. Todos los giros fueron recibidos.
4. Se vendieron muchos ese día.
5. Se estableció otro negocio cerca de la bodega.
6. La apertura fue anunciada por la radio.
7. También se reportó en la tele.
8. Pero después de unos meses las puertas fueron cerradas.
9. Bastante dinero fue perdido.

LA LOMITA DEL BARRIO GROCERY

Nueva York

¡Te toca a ti!

Use what you have learned

HABLAR

1 Hispanos o latinos en mi estado

✔ Identify the Hispanic or Latino populations in your state

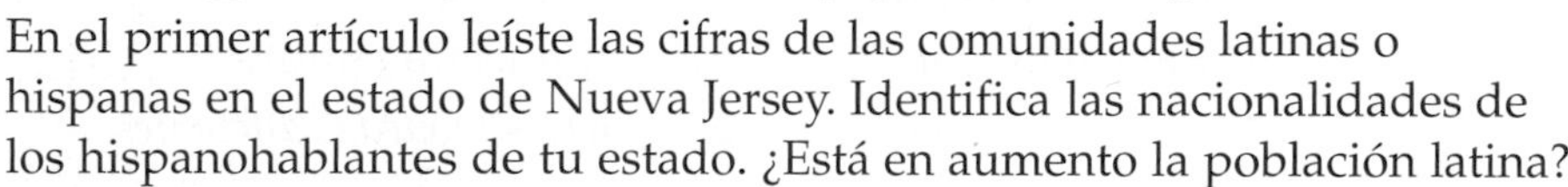

En el primer artículo leíste las cifras de las comunidades latinas o hispanas en el estado de Nueva Jersey. Identifica las nacionalidades de los hispanohablantes de tu estado. ¿Está en aumento la población latina?

Union City, Nueva Jersey

HABLAR

2 Los pequeños negocios

✔ Discuss the businesses of new arrivals in your country

Muchos inmigrantes, después de algún tiempo en EE.UU., establecen pequeños negocios que no requieren mucho capital. Con tu grupo, hablen de los tipos de negocios que han establecido inmigrantes en su comunidad, el aporte económico que llevan a la comunidad, el número de empleos que proveen, etc. Contacten a los dueños para averiguar de posibles oportunidades de empleo.

La Pequeña Habana, Miami, la Florida

San Antonio, Texas

HABLAR

3 El futuro de la población latina o hispana

✔ Discuss the future role of the Latino population in the U.S.

La población latina o hispana en EE.UU. está aumentando mucho. Según el último censo los latinos constituyen la minoría más grande del país. Esto tiene mucha importancia en la política y en la economía del país y en el poder de la comunidad latina. Discute los inevitables cambios que saldrán de este incremento poblacional.

ESCRIBIR

4 Tormentas y otros desastres naturales

✔ Write about any type of natural disaster you experienced

En un par de párrafos describe una experiencia dramática que tú o alguien en tu familia haya experimentado en una tormenta, huracán, tornado, etc. Describe especialmente el impacto emocional.

ESCRIBIR

5 Los socorristas

✔ Write a letter of thanks to the members of your community's rescue squad

Cada comunidad tiene su brigada de socorristas. Muchos de estos socorristas son voluntarios. Imagínate que en tu comunidad había un accidente horrible o un desastre natural. Como siempre acudieron los socorristas para socorrer y rescatar a las víctimas. Escríbeles una carta agradeciéndoles por todo lo que hicieron.

Assessment

Vocabulario

1 Den otra palabra.

1. Han tomado pasos *muy grandes.*

2–3. Es el gobierno que *provee los números* que nos ayudan a tomar decisiones apropiadas.

4. Ellos han *contribuido* mucho a nuestra cultura.
5. Se puede enviar giros en muchas *monedas diferentes.*

To review vocabulary, turn to pages 400 and 403.

2 Completen.

6. Las fuertes lluvias causaron una ____.
7. Una señora fue ____ en su carro y fue rescatada por los socorristas.
8. Había una ola de lodo que destruyó una parte de la carretera. La carretera fue cortada y los conductores tuvieron que tomar un ____.
9. Las aguas ____ el soporte del poste de teléfono. Por poco se cae.
10. Durante una ____ hay relámpagos, viento, truenos y fuertes lluvias.

La Florida

Lectura

3 Contesten.

11. ¿Cuál es la minoría más grande de Estados Unidos ahora?
12. ¿Cuáles son tres comunidades hispanas del estado de Nueva Jersey?
13. ¿Cuál fue la fuente de donde obtuvieron los datos para el artículo?

To review the reading **Confirmado**, turn to page 401.

4 ¿Sí o no?

14. La tormenta llegó lentamente.
15. Un hombre quedó atrapado en su automóvil.
16. La persona atrapada fue rescatada por helicóptero.
17. Los soportes de un puente fueron dañados por una ola de lodo.

To review the reading **Inesperada tormenta**, turn to pages 405–406.

Estructura

5 Cambien en la voz pasiva según el modelo.

Un relámpago causó el incendio. →
El incendio fue causado por un relámpago.

18. La ola de lodo atrapó a la víctima.
19. La policía cerró la carretera.
20. La inundación destruyó los puentes.
21. La gente respeta a los socorristas.

To review the true passive voice, turn to page 407.

6 Completen con el pasivo con **se**.

22. En esa bodega ____ periódicos. (vender)
23. Pero no ____ giros. (enviar)
24. La puerta ____ a las ocho. (abrir)
25. Y la puerta ____ a las cuatro de la tarde. (cerrar)

To review the se construction, turn to page 408.

La Pequeña Habana, Miami, la Florida

For more Chapter 8 test preparation, go to the Chapter 8 **Self-Check Quiz** on the Glencoe Spanish Web site at glencoe.com.

Composición

Uno de los tipos de escrito que se ve con frecuencia es la narrativa. La narrativa narra sucesos o acciones que cambian con el paso del tiempo: por lo general tiene personajes, escenario y trama. La narrativa puede ser ficticia o puede basarse en hechos reales.

TAREA 1

Escrito narrativo Tú vas a preparar una narrativa. Puedes inventar una ficción si quieres o igual puedes contar la historia de algo que te ha pasado a ti mismo(a). Puede ser algún viaje que hiciste con la familia, una mudanza, un evento que te ha impresionado. Una vez escogido el tema, piensa en todo lo que tiene que ver con el tema, todos los detalles que te vienen a la mente, deja correr tu imaginación. Apunta todas esas ideas. Si vas a escribir sobre algo personal expresa tus sentimientos. Ahora haz un bosquejo de tu narrativa. Piensa en **la introducción, el cuerpo** y **la conclusión.** Repasa tu bosquejo. ¿Aparece todo lo que quieres decir? ¿El orden tiene lógica? Ahora debes preparar tu borrador. Usa un lenguaje sencillo pero vivaz. Lo más importante es la claridad. Recuerda que la introducción debe agarrar al lector, hacerle querer leer tu narrativa. Cuando estés satisfecho(a) escribe tu versión final. Repásalo y corrige cualquier error de gramática u ortografía.

TAREA 2

Texto expositivo Un texto expositivo tiene la función principal de explicar algo o de hablar de algo para que otras personas lo conozcan o lo comprendan. El texto expositivo transmite información. Un texto expositivo debe presentar su información clara y ordenadamente. Las características más importantes son el orden, la objetividad y la claridad. Al preparar tu texto expositivo ten en mente el tema, la organización y el público al que te diriges.

Tu tema será: *La televisión hispana en mi comunidad.* Busca un canal que emite en español. Estudia y apunta la programación, es decir el tipo de programas que emite, como deportes, telenovelas, noticieros, etc. Escoge un tipo de programa, el noticiero, por ejemplo. Entonces mira unos cuantos noticieros y toma nota del contenido. Compara este noticiero con los noticieros emitidos en inglés. ¿Cubren las mismas noticias? ¿Hay más información sobre Latinoamérica en el noticiero hispano? ¿Informan sobre la comunidad hispana local? ¿Son similares los anclas de noticieros en inglés y en español? Apunta cualquier contrastes que notas. Cuando tienes toda la información que necesitas, prepara un bosquejo de tu informe. Repásalo y haz las correcciones necesarias.

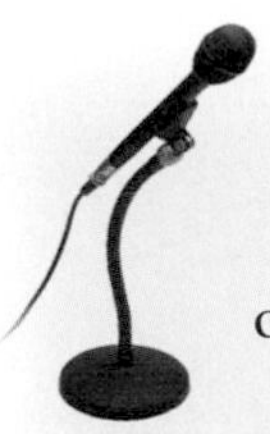

Discurso

Una entrevista es un diálogo basado en preguntas y respuestas. El propósito es obtener información para cualquiera de una variedad de fines.

TAREA 3 **Entrevista** Tú vas a entrevistar a un miembro de la comunidad hispana o latina de tu pueblo o ciudad. Lo primero que harás es pensar en lo que será de interés al público, porque tu siguiente tarea será preparar un escrito sobre la entrevista. Escoge el tema o temas que quieres cubrir en la entrevista. Después, prepara una serie de preguntas. Evita preguntas que se puedan contestar con un sencillo sí o no. Identifica y pide permiso para la entrevista a la persona con quien hablarás. Infórmale del propósito de la entrevista. Asegúrate de que cada pregunta tiene un enfoque. Algunos ejemplos de preguntas son:

- ¿De dónde es la persona y cómo llegó a EE.UU.?
- ¿Cómo era su vida en su país de origen?
- ¿Qué le sorprendió más de EE.UU.?

Al entrevistar a la persona debes mostrar gran interés en lo que dice. Toma apuntes, o igual puedes grabar la entrevista. Cuando termines, da las gracias a la persona y dile que le enviarás una copia del escrito.

TAREA 4 **Redacción de la entrevista** Tienes tus apuntes o tu grabación. Vas a preparar una versión escrita de la entrevista. Hay varios pasos a seguir. Debes tener una introducción. Primero, tienes que indicar el propósito de la entrevista e identificar a la persona entrevistada. Puedes dar una descripción de la persona, una descripción física y también de su personalidad. Si la entrevista fue grabada, debes corregir errores de pronunciación o gramática, tanto tuyos como los de la persona entrevistada. Puedes indicar la actitud de la persona durante la entrevista, por ejemplo: **Ella pensó largamente antes de contestar.** O, **Obviamente el recuerdo le puso triste.**

Como siempre, prepara un borrador del escrito. Léelo cuidadosamente y haz correcciones. Entonces prepara tu versión final. Luego preséntala a la clase.

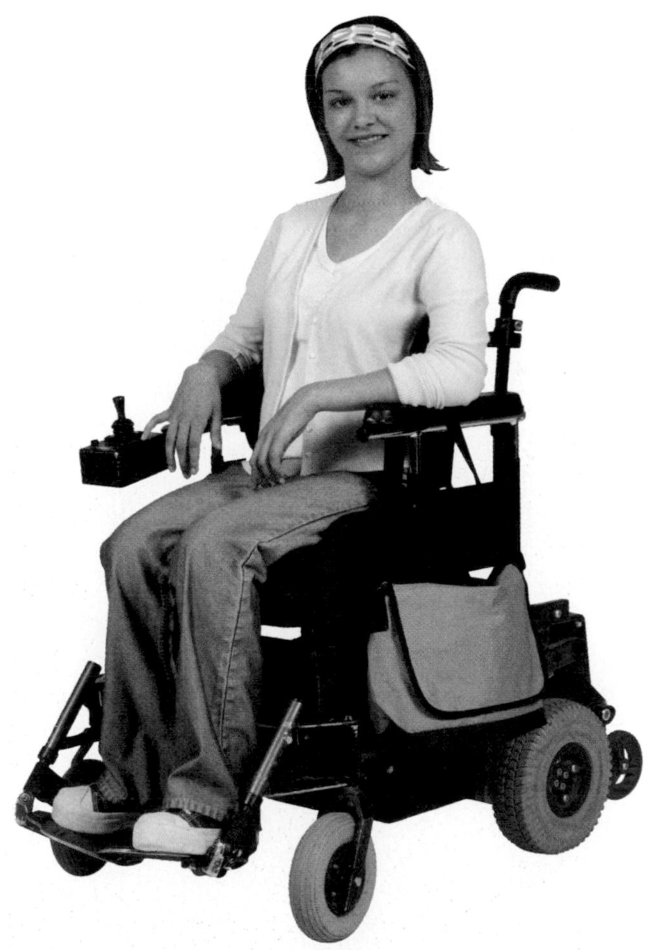

Vocabulario

Lección 1 Cultura

el cese
la Inquisición
la mano de obra
el/la norteño(a)
el rito
el sefardí
el vínculo
el medio oeste
el nordeste, el noreste
el nordoeste, el noroeste
el sudeste, el sureste
el sudoeste, el suroeste
fronterizo(a)
fundar
poblar (ue)
radicarse
superar
a escondidas

Lección 2 Conversación

el ancla
la mujer ancla
la antena parabólica
la cámara
el control remoto
la emisión
la entrevista
la grabadora DVD
el/la meteorólogo(a)
el micrófono
las noticias
el noticiero
la pantalla
el payaso
el plato
el pronóstico del tiempo
la telenovela
el/la televidente
el televisor
grabar
surfear (los canales)
transmitir
en vivo

Lección 3 Periodismo

Confirmado
la cifra
las divisas
el giro de dinero
agigantado(a)
advertir (ie, i)
aportar
involucrar
suministrar

Inesperada tormenta
el camionero
el desvío
la inundación
la ola de lodo
el poste de teléfono
el relámpago
el socorrista
el soporte
la tormenta
aflojar
asustar
atrapar
reanudar
rescatar

LITERARY COMPANION *See pages 502–517 for literary selections related to Chapter 8. The activities for these readings will help you continue to practice your reading comprehension skills.*

VIDEOTUR

¡Viva el mundo hispano!

Video can be a beneficial learning tool for the language student. Video enables you to experience the material in the textbook in a real-life setting. Take a vicarious field trip as you see people interacting at home, at school, at the market, etc. The cultural benefits are limitless as you experience the Spanish-speaking world while "traveling" through many countries. In addition to its tremendous cultural value, video gives practice in developing good listening and viewing skills. Video allows you to look for numerous clues that are evident in tone of voice, facial expressions, and gestures. Through video you can see and hear the diversity of the target culture and compare and contrast the Spanish-speaking cultures to each other and to your own.

Episodio 1: Justo Lamas en concierto

Justo Lamas es argentino. Él viaja por todo Estados Unidos dando conciertos de su música en escuelas a través del continente. Los muchachos aprenden las canciones en las clases de español. En los conciertos los chicos participan y cantan con Justo, son parte del espectáculo. Justo cree que estudiar otros idiomas es maravilloso, nos ayuda a conocer a otra gente y otras culturas.

Episodio 2: Arte e identidad

Poli da clases en *Self-help Graphics,* una organización que fomenta las artes en la comunidad en Los Ángeles Este. Ellos tienen talleres para artistas establecidos y clases para principiantes. *Self-help Graphics* se fundó en 1973 cuando sólo tenían un camión. Hoy presentan exposiciones en todo el país y hasta en Europa y Japón. Ellos creen que las artes son importantes para dar una voz a los jóvenes latinos.

Episodio 3: Espíritu salsero

Este señor es Alberto Torres. Él se crió en Puerto Rico y Nueva York. Su pasión es salsa, un tipo de música y baile que viene del Caribe, con raíces en Cuba, Puerto Rico y África. Salsa es cada día más y más popular en Estados Unidos. Hay diferentes estilos de salsa, estilo Nueva York, Los Ángeles y hasta un estilo que incorpora el *Hip Hop* y *R & B.* Pero sobre todo, ¡salsa es para bailar!

Literary Companion

These literary selections develop reading and cultural skills and introduce you to Hispanic literature. They are organized to coincide with the chapters presented in the text. For example, **Literatura española** is designed to be done in conjunction with **Capítulo 1, España.**

Capítulo 7 • Literatura de Venezuela y Colombia

Una ojeada a la poesía

Prosa

Capítulo 8 • Literatura hispana en Estados Unidos

Una ojeada a la poesía

Prosa

Biblioteca, Universidad de México

Literatura española

Una ojeada a la poesía

Vocabulario para la lectura

El señor abrazó a su mujer.
Ella lo besó.
Los dos lloraron.

El joven tomó las monedas de su bolsillo.
Las arrojó al río.

Más vocabulario

las hazañas hechos ilustres o heroicos
el mudo el que no puede hablar
la pena la tristeza, el dolor
el rumbo la dirección, el sentido
el torpe persona no muy inteligente, tonta, un poco estúpida
cotidiano(a) diario, de todos los días
filial del hijo
necio(a) tonto, estúpido
rendir (i, i) vencer, someter a alguien a su dominio, obligar a alguien a entregar algo
sujetar dominar, someter

¿Qué palabra necesito?

1 Historieta **Un día triste** Contesten.

1. ¿Desmontó el señor de su caballo?
2. ¿Fue a abrazar a su mujer?
3. ¿Su mujer lo besó?
4. ¿Estaban tristes los dos?
5. ¿Empezaron a llorar?
6. Y el joven, ¿qué tomó de su bolsillo?
7. ¿Dónde las arrojó?

2 **Otra palabra** Expresen de otra manera.

1. Él es un tipo un poco *tonto.*
2. ¡Qué *tristeza* verlos sufrir tanto!
3. No te puede contestar oralmente porque *no puede hablar.*
4. No es una parte de su rutina *diaria.*
5. No le da ningún miedo y no va a cambiar *su dirección.*
6. *Las cosas heroicas* de él le han hecho famoso.
7. *La tempestad* no le va a hacer cambiar el rumbo del *barco.*
8. Él los *dominó* en muy poco tiempo.
9. Es un río *de mucha agua.*

Sitges

El Cid

Autor anónimo[1]

Burgos

Introducción *El cantar del mío Cid* es el poema épico de la literatura española. El poema canta las hazañas del Cid, el gran héroe nacional de España. El Cid en árabe significa «Señor». El Cid es en realidad Rodrigo Díaz de Vivar. Nació en el siglo XI en el pequeño pueblo de Vivar, cerca de Burgos. Un buen hombre y padre de familia, él vivió felizmente con su mujer y sus dos hijos. Pero un día a causa de un conflicto entre él y el rey Alfonso, tuvo que dejar a su familia y abandonar la ciudad de Burgos. El Cid montó a su caballo Babieca, salió de Burgos y anduvo por los campos de Castilla donde luchó valientemente contra los árabes hasta llegar a Valencia donde conquistó a los árabes. Reunido con su familia reinó en Valencia hasta su muerte en 1099.

La escena solemne y conmovedora del trocito del poema que sigue describe la pena y tristeza del Cid cuando tiene que despedirse y separarse de su familia.

[1] anónimo *anonymous*

El Cid

El Cid a doña Jimena—íbala a abrazar;
doña Jimena al Cid—la mano va a besar
llorando de los ojos—que no sabe qué hacer.
Y él a las niñas—tornólas a mirar (catar)
«a Dios vos acomiendo—y al padre espiritual;
ahora nos partimos°—Dios sabe el ajuntar°.»
Llorando de los ojos—que no visteis atal°,
así parten unos de otros—como la uña de la carne°.

partimos *salimos*
ajuntar *when we'll be together again*
no… atal *such as you have never seen*
carne *flesh*

Valencia

El libro de buen amor

El Arcipreste de Hita

Introducción El Arcipreste de Hita, Juan Ruiz, es el autor del libro más leído de la literatura española de la Edad Media[1]. Lo que sabemos de su vida son los datos autobiográficos que puntualiza en su obra.

Nació en Alcalá de Henares hacia 1283. Fue clérigo pero por un conflicto que tuvo con el Arzobispo de Toledo, pasó mucho tiempo en la prisión. Su *libro de buen amor* es un retrato[2] de la sociedad de su tiempo. Es una «comedia humana» de la Edad Media en la cual el autor nos presenta el espectáculo de la vida cotidiana—los hábitos, caracteres y vicios de todas las clases sociales. En el trozo que sigue nos da sus ideas sobre la importancia del dinero.

[1] Edad Media *Middle Ages*
[2] retrato *portrait, description*

El libro de buen amor 

Mucho hace el dinero, mucho es de amar;
Al torpe hace bueno y hombre de prestar°,
Hace correr al cojo° y al mudo hablar;
El que no tiene manos, dinero quiere tomar.
Sea un hombre necio o rudo labrador,
El dinero le hace hidalgo° y sabidor°,
Cuanto más algo tiene,° tanto es de más valor;
El que no ha dinero, no es de sí señor.

hombre de prestar *man of means*
cojo *crippled*
hidalgo *noble person*
sabidor *wise person*
Cuanto... tiene *The more one has*

Alcalá de Henares

Coplas

Jorge Manrique

Introducción Jorge Manrique (1440–1479) fue poeta y guerrero. Como tantos caballeros de su tiempo se dedicó a las armas y a las letras.

Coplas por la muerte de su padre es su poesía más conocida. No es sólo una hermosa elegía filial. Es también una profunda y melancólica meditación sobre la vida humana.

El fragmento que sigue es una alegoría en la cual el autor compara nuestras vidas con los ríos.

Coplas

Nuestras vidas son los ríos
que van a dar en la mar,
que es el morir;
allí van los señoríos°
derechos a se acabar
y consumir;
allá los ríos caudales,
allí los otros, medianos
y más chicos;
allegados°, son iguales
los que viven por sus manos
y los ricos.

señoríos *los de la clase alta*

allegados *al llegar*

Navarra

Canción del pirata

José de Espronceda

Introducción José de Espronceda (1808–1842) nació durante un viaje que hacían sus padres de Madrid a Badajoz en Extremadura poco antes de empezar la Guerra de la Independencia contra las tropas de Napoleón. Espronceda fue un espíritu libre y su vida siguió siendo un viaje. Durante toda su vida viajó mucho y a los dieciocho años fue a Lisboa donde se dice que arrojó al río Tajo las dos pesetas que tenía en el bolsillo para no «entrar en tan gran ciudad con tan poco dinero».

Es poeta romántico y los temas esenciales de su poesía son el amor y la libertad. Al tema de la libertad se unen los de la aventura y la rebeldía como veremos en el trocito que sigue.

Río Tajo en Lisboa

Badajoz, Extremadura

Canción del pirata

—Navega, velero° mío, sin temor,
que ni enemigo navío,
ni tormenta, ni bonanza°
tu rumbo a torcer° alcanza,
ni a sujetar tu valor.
 Veinte presas°
 hemos hecho
 a despecho°
 del inglés,
 y han rendido
 sus pendones
 cien naciones
 a mis pies.
Que es mi barco mi tesoro,
que es mi Dios la libertad,
mi ley, la fuerza y el viento,
mi única patria, la mar.

velero *swift sailing vessel*
bonanza *calm sea*
torcer *turn back*
presas *prizes, captured ships*
a despecho *in spite*

Cosas del tiempo

Ramón de Campoamor

Introducción Ramón de Campoamor (1817–1901) nació en un pueblecito de Asturias en el norte de España. Estudió medicina pero su verdadera carrera eran las letras. Es un poeta que tiene el don[1] de decir mucho en muy pocas palabras.

Para los jóvenes, la juventud es eterna. A ver lo que dice Ramón de Campoamor sobre este tema. Y en muy pocas palabras.

[1] don *gift*

Asturias

Cosas del tiempo

Pasan veinte años; vuelve él,
Y al verse, exclaman él y ella:
(—¡Santo Dios! ¿Y éste es aquél?…)
(—¡Santo Dios! ¿Y ésta es aquélla?)

¿Comprendes?

Burgos

A ***El cantar del mío Cid*** Contesten.

1. ¿Quién escribió el poema épico *El cantar del mío Cid?*
2. ¿Quién es el Cid en realidad?
3. ¿Dónde nació?
4. ¿Por qué tuvo que salir de Burgos?
5. Al salir de Burgos, ¿qué hizo?
6. ¿Dónde conquistó a los árabes?
7. ¿Cómo es la escena de la despedida del Cid?
8. ¿Qué hicieron el Cid y su mujer al despedirse el uno de la otra?
9. Según el Cid, ¿quién va a proteger a su mujer y a sus hijas?
10. ¿Cómo describe el autor la pena de la familia del Cid?

B ***El libro de buen amor*** ¿Sí o no?

1. Muy poca gente lee este poema.
2. Hay elementos autobiográficos en la obra del Arcipreste de Hita.
3. El Arcipreste, Juan Ruiz, fue clérigo y su obra es muy religiosa.
4. En su obra él pinta la sociedad de su tiempo.
5. Según el poeta, el dinero no hace nada. No tiene ninguna importancia.

C ***El libro de buen amor*** Contesten.

1. Según el autor, ¿cómo es el torpe que tiene dinero?
2. ¿Qué puede hacer el cojo?
3. ¿Qué puede hacer el mudo?
4. ¿En qué se convierte un hombre necio o rudo labrador?
5. ¿Qué significa «El que no ha dinero, no es de sí señor»?

D ***Canción del pirata*** ¿Cómo lo expresa Espronceda?

1. Anda, capitán, y no tengas miedo.
2. El barco de un enemigo
   Una tempestad o una mar calma
   nada te puede hacer cambiar de dirección
   y nada puede disminuir tu valor.
3. Hemos capturado (tomado posesión de) mucho a pesar de los ingleses.
4. Muchas naciones nos han tenido que entregar sus banderas.

Islas Canarias

E *Cosas del tiempo* Contesten.

1. ¿Quién vuelve?
2. ¿A quién ve?
3. ¿Cuánto tiempo hace que no se ven?
4. ¿Se reconocen?
5. ¿Han cambiado?
6. ¿Qué dice cada uno para indicar que el otro ha cambiado?

F *Coplas*

En tus propias palabras, comenta sobre la filosofía de Jorge Manrique. Compara lo que dice él y lo que dice el Arcipreste de Hita en su *Libro de buen amor.*

G Mi opinión

De las poesías que acabas de leer, decide cual es tu favorita—cual te gustó más. Explica por qué te gustó o por qué te gustó más que las otras. ¿Cuál es el mensaje que recibiste al leer tu poesía favorita? ¿Cómo relacionas esta poesía con tu propia vida?

H Analizando y haciendo comparaciones

¿Estás de acuerdo con la filosofía de Jorge Manrique sobre la vida y la muerte? ¿Crees que todos somos iguales en la muerte? ¿Somos iguales también en la vida? ¿Qué diría el Arcipreste de Hita sobre esta última pregunta?

I Visualizando y describiendo

Si tienes talento artístico, dibuja un retrato describiendo el tema de una de las poesías que acabas de leer. Luego, en forma oral o escrita, da una descripción de tu retrato.

J Describiendo

En un grupo, escriban un cuento breve en el que el personaje principal es un señor o una señora bastante mayor. La persona ve a alguien que cree reconocer pero ya hace muchos años que no se ven. En su cuento contesten (a) las siguientes preguntas. ¿Dónde se encuentran? ¿Se reconocen? ¿Cómo? ¿Qué dicen? ¿Cómo se habían conocido antes?

Prosa El niño al que se le murió el amigo

Vocabulario para la lectura

El niño estiró los brazos. Y puso los codos en las rodillas.

¿Qué palabra necesito?

1 **Historieta** **El niño en el jardín** Contesten.

1. ¿Qué hay alrededor del jardín?
2. ¿Hay un pozo en el jardín?
3. ¿Dónde está sentado el niño?
4. ¿Tiene juguetes?
5. ¿Juega (a las) canicas el niño?
6. ¿Dónde puso los codos?
7. ¿Piensa en algo cuando pone los codos en las rodillas?
8. Cuando se levantó, ¿qué estiró el niño?

El niño al que se le murió el amigo

Ana María Matute

Introducción Ana María Matute nació en la capital española en 1926. Hizo sus estudios en las dos principales ciudades de su país, Madrid y Barcelona. Su primera novela, *Los Abel,* se publicó en 1947. Diez años más tarde se publicó *Los niños tontos,* donde aparece *El niño al que se le murió el amigo.* En 1996 ella ingresó en la Real Academia Española.

A veces algo ocurre en la vida de un niño y de repente el niño pasa a ser algo más, casi una persona mayor. A ver lo que le pasó al niño en este cuento de Ana María Matute.

El niño al que se le murió el amigo

Una mañana se levantó y fue a buscar al amigo, al otro lado de la valla. Pero el amigo no estaba, y, cuando volvió, le dijo la madre: «El amigo se murió. Niño, no pienses más en él y busca otros para jugar». El niño se sentó en el quicio de la puerta, con la cara entre las manos y los codos en las rodillas.

«Él volverá», pensó. Porque no podía ser que allí estuviesen las canicas, el camión y la pistola de hojalata°, y el reloj aquel que ya no andaba, y el amigo no viniese a buscarlos. Vino la noche, con una estrella muy grande, y el niño no quería entrar a cenar. «Entra niño, que llega el frío», dijo la madre. Pero, en lugar de entrar, el niño se levantó del quicio y se fue en busca del amigo, con las canicas, el camión, la pistola de hojalata y el reloj que no andaba. Al llegar a la cerca, la voz del amigo no le llamó, ni le oyó en el árbol, ni en el pozo. Pasó buscándole toda la noche. Y fue una larga noche casi blanca, que le llenó de polvo el traje y los zapatos. Cuando llegó el sol, el niño, que tenía sueño° y sed, estiró los brazos y pensó: «Qué tontos y pequeños son esos juguetes. Y ese reloj que no anda, no sirve para nada». Lo tiró al pozo, y volvía a la casa, con mucha hambre. La madre le abrió la puerta, y dijo: «Cuánto ha crecido este niño, Dios mío, cuánto ha crecido». Y le compró un traje de hombre, porque el que llevaba le venía muy corto.

hojalata *tin*

tenía sueño *estaba cansado*

¿Comprendes?

A ¿Qué pasó? Buscando hechos Contesten.

1. Cuando se levantó el niño, ¿a quién fue a buscar?
2. ¿Adónde fue a buscarlo?
3. ¿Estaba el amigo?
4. ¿Qué le aconsejó la madre?
5. ¿Dónde se sentó el niño?

B Lo que hizo el niño Completen.

1. El niño creía que volvería su _____.
2. Creía que vendría a buscar sus _____.
3. El niño se quedó afuera y no entró a _____.
4. La madre dijo que entrara porque hacía _____.
5. En lugar de entrar, el niño se fue _____ del amigo.

Málaga, Andalucía

C Interpretando Comenten.

1. Hay un momento en que el fin de la inocencia parece ocurrir. ¿Cuál es?
2. Hay una frase casi poética, que no tiene sentido literal. ¿Qué querrá decir: «Y fue una larga noche casi blanca, que le llenó de polvo el traje y los zapatos»?
3. Interpreta la frase de la madre al final del cuento.
4. ¿Crees que el traje que llevaba el niño realmente le quedaba corto? Explica.

D Describiendo causas y efectos No es solamente la muerte de un(a) amigo(a) la que puede doler. La separación duele mucho también. Lo más común es que nos mudamos de un pueblo y perdemos a los amigos o que un buen amigo tiene que mudarse con la familia. ¿Esto te ha pasado a ti? Describe como te sentiste.

E Reflexionando Para muchos de nosotros ha habido un evento que nos ha marcado el final de la niñez. Piensa en el momento en que dejaste de ser niño(a) y descríbelo en español.

Literatura de los países andinos

Una ojeada a la poesía

Vocabulario para la lectura

El amo quiere que el joven trabaje.
El joven indio está labrando la tierra.
Tiene una mirada taciturna, melancólica.
Está sudando (transpirando).

Más vocabulario

el amo el jefe, el patrón, el dueño
el ave (f.) el pájaro
el leño la madera
ignorar no saber

¿Qué palabra necesito?

1 **La tierra** Contesten.

1. ¿Qué está haciendo el joven?
2. ¿Quién quiere que él trabaje así?
3. ¿Qué expresión tiene el indio en la cara?
4. ¿Está sudando?
5. ¿Dónde tiene el sudor?

2 **Una expresión equivalente** Expresen de otra manera.

1. El indio está *trabajando en el campo.*
2. Su *patrón* es bastante cruel.
3. El indio trabaja duro y está *transpirando.*
4. Tiene *una expresión* triste.
5. Él *no conoce* las grandezas pasadas de su gente.
6. Él está cargando *madera.*
7. Hay *un pájaro* encima del leño.

¡Quién sabe!

José Santos Chocano

Parque Nacional Huascarán, Perú

Introducción José Santos Chocano (1875–1934) nació en Perú. Su vida tumultuosa fue en realidad una novela dramática. Él viajó mucho por Latinoamérica y España. En sus poesías Chocano cantó las hazañas de su gente y describió la naturaleza americana: los volcanes, la cordillera andina y las selvas misteriosas.

Chocano se sentía inca. Él quería ser indio y español a la vez. Esa fusión de lo indígena y lo español la sentía en sus venas porque una de sus abuelas descendía de un capitán español y la otra era de una familia inca. La voz del poeta era la de un mestizo que conocía a su gente y su tierra. Se declaró a sí mismo cantor «autóctono[1] y salvaje» de la América hispanohablante. –Walt Whitman tiene el Norte, pero yo tengo el Sur–dijo Chocano.

En el primer poema, un fragmento de *Tres notas del alma indígena,* Chocano le habla al indio de hoy. Le pregunta si se ha olvidado de la grandeza de su pasado, cuando los indios eran dueños de las Américas. La respuesta del indio, «¡Quién sabe, señor!» significa que se niega a opinar. Es una contestación típica del habla del indio.

El segundo poema se llama *Nostalgia.* Tiene una tonalidad romántica y un tema autobiográfico. El poeta refleja sobre su vida tumultuosa.

[1] autóctono *indigenous*

Cuzco, Perú

¡Quién sabe!

—Indio que labras con fatiga
tierras que de otros dueños son:
¿Ignoras tú que deben tuyas
ser, por tu sangre y tu sudor?
¿Ignoras tú que audaz codicia°,
siglos atrás te las quitó?
¿Ignoras tú que eres el Amo?
—¡Quién sabe, señor!

—Indio de frente taciturna
y de pupilas sin fulgor°.
¿Qué pensamiento es el que escondes°
en tu enigmática° expresión?
¿Qué es lo que buscas en tu vida?
¿Qué es lo que imploras a tu Dios?
¿Qué es lo que sueña tu silencio?
—¡Quién sabe, señor!

audaz codicia *bold greed*

sin fulgor *without a spark*
escondes *hide*
enigmática *puzzling*

José Santos Chocano

Nostalgia

Hace ya dos años
que recorro el mundo.
¡He vivido poco!
¡Me he cansado mucho!

Quien vive de prisa no vive de veras:
quien no echa raíces no puede dar frutos.

Ser río que corre, ser nube que pasa,
sin dejar recuerdos ni rastro ninguno,
es triste, y más triste para quien se siente
nube en lo elevado, río en lo profundo.

Quisiera ser árbol mejor que ser ave,
quisiera ser leño mejor que ser humo;
y al viaje que cansa
prefiero el terruño°:
la ciudad nativa con sus campanarios°,
arcaicos balcones, portales vetustos°
y calles estrechas, como si las casas
tampoco quisieran separarse mucho...

terruño *native land*
campanarios *bell towers*
vetustos *old, dilapidated*

Rastros en la arena

La victoria de Junín: Canto a Bolívar

José Joaquín Olmedo

Introducción El poeta ecuatoriano José Joaquín Olmedo (1790–1847) nació en Guayaquil. Es uno de los más importantes poetas latinoamericanos de la época de la independencia. Admiró mucho el heroísmo de Simón Bolívar, el gran libertador, y después de la batalla de Junín en agosto de 1824 escribió los primeros trescientos versos de su poema *La victoria de Junín: Canto a Bolívar.* Después de la batalla de Ayacucho en diciembre del mismo año añadió unos seiscientos versos más. Estas dos batallas en las que lucharon Simón Bolívar y el mariscal Sucre fueron decisivas para la independencia de la América del Sur.

En su poema Olmedo hace aparecer a Huayna Capac al frente de las tropas victoriosas. En los versos que siguen, Huayna Capac habla de la crueldad de los españoles durante la conquista. Y refiere a varios personajes históricos. El insolente y vil aventurero es Francisco Pizarro. El iracundo sacerdote es el padre Valverde quien estaba con Pizarro cuando capturó a Atahualpa. Y el rey poderoso es el rey Fernando de España.

Guayaquil, Ecuador

Parque Bolívar, Guayaquil, Ecuador

La victoria de Junín: Canto a Bolívar

No hay punto en estos valles y estos cerros
que no mande tristísimas memorias.
Torrentes mil de sangre se cruzaron
aquí y allí; las tribus numerosas
al ruido del cañón se disiparon;
y los restos mortales de mi gente
aun a las mismas rocas fecundaron°.
Más allá un hijo° expira entre los hierros°
de su sagrada majestad indignos...
un insolente y vil aventurero
y un iracundo sacerdote fueron
de un poderoso rey los asesinos...
¡tantos horrores y maldades tantas
por el oro que hollaban° nuestras plantas!

fecundaron *fertilized*
un hijo *Atahualpa*
hierros *weapons*

hollaban *trampled on*

¿Comprendes?

Cuzco, Perú

A ***¡Quién sabe!*** Contesten.

1. ¿Qué hace el indio hasta estar rendido (muy cansado)?
2. ¿Cuáles son tres cosas que es posible que el indio no sepa?
3. ¿Cómo contesta el indio?
4. ¿Sabemos si el indio tiene las respuestas a las preguntas?

B ***¡Quién sabe!*** **Interpretando**

1. ¿Por qué le dice el autor al indio que las tierras deben ser suyas por su sangre y su sudor?
2. El autor le pregunta al indio si sabe que ya hace siglos una audaz codicia le quitó sus tierras. ¿A qué o a quiénes se refiere el autor?
3. ¿Por qué habrá escrito el autor «el amo» con letra mayúscula?

C ***¡Quién sabe!*** **Parafraseando** Contesten.

1. ¿Cómo describe José Santos Chocano a los indios?
2. ¿Cómo dice Chocano... ?
   El indio parece melancólico.
   Parece que no tiene alegría ni esperanza.
   Tiene una mirada vaga.
   Parece que está pensando en algo pero no se lo revela a nadie.

D ***Nostalgia*** **Buscando información** Contesten.

1. ¿Hace cuánto tiempo que el poeta recorre el mundo?
2. ¿Ha vivido poco o mucho?
3. ¿Se ha cansado mucho o poco?
4. ¿Parece que el poeta está triste o contento?
5. ¿Quién no vive de veras?
6. ¿Quién no puede dar frutos?
7. ¿Prefiere el poeta ser árbol o ave?
8. ¿Prefiere ser leño o humo?
9. ¿Qué prefiere a un viaje?

E ***Nostalgia*** **Describiendo** Describan la ciudad nativa que nos presenta el poeta.

F ***Nostalgia*** Hagan lo siguiente.

1. Preparen una lista de cosas que nos presenta el poeta que indican estabilidad.
2. Preparen una lista de cosas que nos presenta el poeta que indican inestabilidad.
3. En sus propias palabras expresen como a su parecer quisiera vivir el poeta para ser feliz.

G *La victoria de Junín* Parafraseando

Busquen como expresa el poeta las siguientes ideas.

1. Hay muy tristes memorias por todas partes de la región.
2. Muchos han derramado su sangre aquí.
3. Muchos grupos indígenas han tratado de huir al oír el cañón de los españoles.
4. Muchos cayeron muertos sin poder huir.
5. Perdió su vida un hijo inca en manos de unos indignos.
6. Los asesinos eran un aventurero y un sacerdote enviados por un rey que tenía mucho poder.
7. Los indígenas sufrieron mucho por el deseo de los españoles de obtener oro.

H *¡Quién sabe!* Haciendo conexiones

Ernest Lewald dice en su libro *Latinoamérica: Sus culturas y sociedades:* «Según los investigadores antropológicos, el indio latinoamericano añadió a su estoicismo y rutina de tiempos precolombinos el silencio y la introversión tan propia de pueblos subyugados. Ha sido muy fácil observar que el indio en la actualidad se muestra inaccesible y pasivo frente al hombre moderno, aunque es locuaz y cooperativo dentro de su grupo comunal». ¿Cómo coinciden las palabras del poeta José Santos Chocano con las observaciones de los investigadores antropológicos?

Cuzco, Perú

I *¡Quién sabe!* Buscando mensajes

Las obras de la mayoría de los intelectuales o de los escritores latinoamericanos tienen algún mensaje para el pueblo. En estos versos, ¿qué le está diciendo el poeta al indio? ¿Quiere Chocano que el indio acepte su situación con una resignación fatalista?

J *Nostalgia* Identificando emociones y sentimientos

En su poema *Nostalgia,* Santos Chocano nos dice mucho sobre su filosofía de vida. En tus propias palabras cuenta su filosofía. Luego haz algunos comentarios. ¿Qué opinas? El poeta, ¿ha sido feliz o no? ¿Está satisfecho de su vida?

K *Nostalgia* Dando opiniones

Refleja un poco sobre tu filosofía de vida. ¿Estás de acuerdo con Santos Chocano cuando dice «Quien vive de prisa no vive de veras», «quien no echa raíces no puede dar frutos»? Comenta.

Prosa Los comentarios reales

Vocabulario para la lectura

Los indígenas subían y bajaban las cuestas.
Arrastraban grandes piedras.
Los bueyes tiraban del carro.

Más vocabulario

los avisos noticias o consejos que se comunican a alguien
la cantera sitio de donde se sacan piedras
las nuevas las noticias
la peña roca o piedra enorme
el pósito lugar comunal donde todos depositaban y almacenaban sus cereales y granos
el recaudo palabra antigua por recado, mensaje
ligero que no pesa mucho, ágil, rápido
de palabra oral(mente)

¿Qué palabra necesito?

Chinchero, Perú

1 **Historieta Durante el imperio incaico**
Contesten según se indica.

1. ¿En qué vivían los indígenas más humildes? (chozas)
2. ¿Dónde guardaban sus cereales? (en un pósito)
3. ¿A quién pertenecía el pósito? (al ayllu, a la comunidad)
4. ¿Para qué necesitaban piedras del tamaño de una peña? (construir fortalezas)
5. ¿De dónde sacaban las piedras? (de una cantera)
6. ¿Subían y bajaban las cuestas los hombres? (Sí)
7. ¿Qué arrastraban? (grandes piedras)
8. ¿Por qué no tiraban los bueyes de un carro? (en aquel entonces no había ni bueyes ni carros)

2 **¿Cuál es la palabra?** Den la palabra cuya definición sigue.

1. una casa bastante humilde
2. una roca de gran tamaño
3. terreno en pendiente
4. un mensaje
5. noticias o consejos que se comunican a otro
6. tirar de una cosa para moverla
7. que no pesa mucho, que se mueve con rapidez

Los comentarios reales

Inca Garcilaso de la Vega

Introducción El primer escritor de importancia mundial nacido en las Américas fue el Inca Garcilaso de la Vega (1539–1616). Su padre era un capitán español y su madre una princesa incaica. Él escribió *Los comentarios reales* que apareció en 1609. Una segunda parte con el título *Historia general del Perú* salió después de su muerte en 1617. *Los comentarios reales* se consideran una fuente importantísima en el estudio de la civilización de los incas. Describe el Imperio de los incas, sus leyendas, costumbres y monumentos.

Aquí tenemos dos fragmentos de *Los comentarios reales.*

Machu Picchu, Perú

Los comentarios reales

Chasqui llamaban a los correos que había puestos por los caminos para llevar con brevedad los mandatos del rey y traer las nuevas y avisos que por sus reinos y provincias, lejos o cerca, hubiese de importancia. Para lo cual tenían a cada cuarto de legua° cuatro o seis indios mozos y ligeros, los cuales estaban en dos chozas para repararse° de las inclemencias del cielo. Llevaban los recaudos por su vez, ya los de una choza, ya los de la otra, los unos miraban a la una parte del camino, y los otros a la otra, para descubrir los mensajeros antes que llegasen a ellos, a apercibirse° para tomar el recaudo, porque no se perdiese tiempo alguno.

Llamáronlos chasqui, que quiere decir trocar°, o dar y tomar, que es lo mismo, porque trocaban, daban y tomaban de uno en otro, y de otro en otro, los recaudos que llevaban. No les llamaron «cacha», que quiere decir mensajeros, porque este nombre lo daban al embajador o mensajero propio que personalmente iba de un príncipe al otro, o del señor al súbdito°. El recaudo o mensaje que los chasquis llevaban era de palabra, porque los indios del Perú no supieron escribir. Las palabras eran pocas, y muy concertadas, porque no se trocasen, y por ser muchas no se olvidasen.

legua *three and a half miles*

repararse *protegerse*

apercibirse *become aware of*

trocar *to trade*

súbdito *subject*

❖ ❖ ❖

Maravillosos edificios hicieron los Incas, reyes del Perú, en fortalezas, en templos, en casas reales, en pósitos y en caminos como se muestran hoy por las ruinas que de ellas han quedado; aunque mal se puede ver por los cimientos lo que fue todo el edificio.

La obra mayor y más soberbia, que mandaron hacer para mostrar su poder y majestad, fue la fortaleza del Cuzco, cuyas grandezas son increíbles a quien no las ha visto, y al que las ha visto y mirado con atención, le hacen imaginar, y aun creer, que son hechas por vía de encantamiento°, y que las hicieron demonios° y no hombres, porque la multitud de las piedras, tantas y tan grandes, (que son más peñas que piedras) causa admiración imaginar, como las pudieron cortar de las canteras de donde se sacaron, porque los indios no tuvieron hierro ni acero° para cortar ni labrarlas; pues pensar como las trajeron al edificio, es dar en otra dificultad, porque no tuvieron bueyes, ni supieron hacer carros, ni hay carros que las puedan sufrir, ni bueyes que basten a tirarlas. Llevábanlas arrastrando a fuerza de brazos con gruesas maromas°; ni los caminos por donde las llevaban eran llanas, sino sierras muy ásperas, con grandes cuestas por do° las subían y bajaban a pura fuerza de hombres.

encantamiento *enchantment*
demonios *devils*
acero *steel*
maromas *thick ropes*
do *donde*

Cuzco, Perú

¿Comprendes?

A Los chasquis Contesten.

1. ¿Quiénes eran los chasquis?
2. ¿Qué llevaban?
3. ¿Cómo eran los chasquis?
4. ¿En qué se quedaban para protegerse de las inclemencias del tiempo?
5. ¿Por qué miraban siempre una parte del camino?
6. ¿Querían recibir el recado rápido para no perder tiempo?
7. ¿Qué era un cacha?
8. ¿Por qué eran orales los mensajes de los chasquis?
9. ¿Eran largos o cortos los mensajes?

B Haciendo comparaciones

Expliquen en sus propias palabras la diferencia entre un chasqui y un cacha.

C Fortaleza ¿Verdad o falso?

1. Los incas hicieron maravillosos edificios.
2. Aún las ruinas de los edificios muestran su grandeza.
3. Mirando las ruinas se puede ver lo que fue todo el edificio.
4. La obra mayor de los incas es la fortaleza del Cuzco.
5. Las grandezas de la fortaleza del Cuzco son increíbles sólo a los que no las han visto.
6. La fortaleza fue construida de piedras pequeñas.
7. Algunas de las piedras son tan grandes que se parecen más a peñas que piedras.
8. Sabemos como los incas pudieron sacar estas piedras gigantescas de la cantera.
9. Trajeron las piedras al edificio que construían en carros tirados de bueyes.
10. Los caminos en las sierras por donde tenían que llevar las piedras tenían grandes cuestas.

Machu Picchu, Perú

D Usando la imaginación

Imagínate que estabas en Ecuador o Perú durante la época de los incas. Escríbele una carta a un(a) amigo(a) diciéndole todo lo que viste, todo lo que te fascinó, y todo lo que encontraste increíble.

E Haciendo investigaciones

Si a ti te interesa el tema indígena y si te es posible, lee una o sólo una parte de las siguientes novelas, *Huasipungo,* del ecuatoriano Jorge Icaza y *Aves sin nido* de la peruana Clorinda Matto de Turner. Son novelas fantásticas pero te advertimos que no son muy fáciles.

Machu Picchu, Perú

Una ojeada a la poesía

Vocabulario para la lectura

Más vocabulario

la pena sentimiento de tristeza, dolor, lástima
la pulpería tipo de bodega o colmado
la víbora culebra venenosa
atrevido(a) intrépido, osado, audaz
hondo(a) profundo
pelear luchar, combatir, batallar
procurar tratar, hacer esfuerzos

¿Qué palabra necesito?

1 Historieta **Una quinta** Contesten.

1. ¿Es una quinta un tipo de finca o estancia?
2. ¿Tiene una quinta animales y árboles?
3. ¿Tiene un árbol ramas y gajos?
4. ¿Tienen algunos árboles raíces profundas?
5. ¿Qué fruta produce la higuera?
6. ¿Es bonita la copa de algunos árboles?
7. ¿Hacen las aves sus nidos en un árbol?
8. A veces, ¿hay que tener cuidado con las víboras?
9. ¿Son algunas víboras bastante atrevidas?
10. ¿Se arrastran las víboras por el suelo?

2 **¿Cuál es la palabra?** Completen.

1. El _____ nada en el mar.
2. El _____ sale de una rama.
3. La higuera da _____.
4. En Argentina es una _____; en otras partes es una bodega o un colmado.

Una pulpería, Patagonia, Argentina

La araucana

Alonso de Ercilla y Zúñiga

Introducción El primer poema de gran valor literario escrito en el continente americano es *La araucana* de Alonso de Ercilla y Zúñiga (1533–1594). Ercilla llegó a las Américas de España a los veintiún años y tomó parte en la conquista de Perú. Más tarde pasó a Chile donde luchó contra los belicosos araucanos. Mientras peleaba, escribía, y así surgió el primer poema épico americano. El autor dedicó el poema al rey de España, Felipe II. En la dedicatoria del poema le declaró al rey que los acontecimientos del poema representaban la verdad histórica. La obra *La araucana* fue la primera en la que apareció el autor como actor en la epopeya y la primera que cantó acontecimientos o eventos no del pasado sino todavía en curso.

En la estrofa que sigue, Ercilla describe a los indígenas que lo esperaban a su llegada a Chile—los araucanos.

La araucana

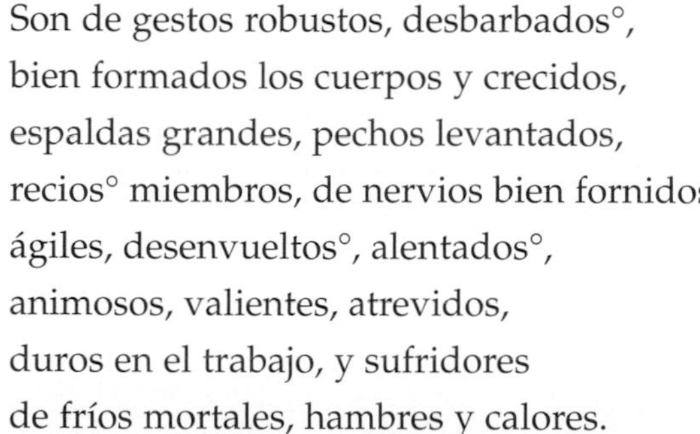

Son de gestos robustos, desbarbados°,
bien formados los cuerpos y crecidos,
espaldas grandes, pechos levantados,
recios° miembros, de nervios bien fornidos
ágiles, desenvueltos°, alentados°,
animosos, valientes, atrevidos,
duros en el trabajo, y sufridores
de fríos mortales, hambres y calores.

desbarbados *without body hair*

recios *fuertes*

desenvueltos *confident*

alentados *brave, gallant*

Chile

Martín Fierro

José Hernández

Introducción José Hernández nació el 10 de noviembre de 1834 no muy lejos de Buenos Aires. En sus venas corría sangre española, irlandesa y francesa. Cuando tenía dieciocho años su padre lo llevó consigo al sur de la provincia de Buenos Aires que en aquel entonces era una región primitiva poblada de caballos salvajes. Se dice que allí Hernández «se hizo gaucho y aprendió a jinetear». Él vivió en la campaña nueve años. En 1856 se reubicó en Buenos Aires y trabajó en el periodismo. Un poco más tarde ingresó en el ejército.

Con la acción de Ayacucho bajo el mando de Simón Bolívar y Sucre, se consumó la Independencia de América. Pero medio siglo después siguieron las batallas en los campos de la provincia de Buenos Aires y el ejército cumplía una función penal arreando gauchos arbitrariamente. Hernández escribió el *Martín Fierro* para denunciar el regimen del dictador Rosas y esta conscripción ilegal de los gauchos.

El protagonista, al principio, es impersonal—un gaucho cualquiera. Después como el autor iba imaginándolo con más precisión, su protagonista llegó a ser Martín Fierro —el individuo Martín Fierro.

La primera edición del poema salió en 1872 y enseguida fue un éxito tremendo. Se vendieron más de cien mil ejemplares. Se vendió aún en pulperías rurales donde nunca antes se había vendido libro alguno. Para el gaucho, Martín Fierro fue una descripción de su propia existencia en su propia lengua. Para el público más culto el *Martín Fierro* fue una obra literaria cuyo tema tiene raíces profundas en la vida de su nación. El *Martín Fierro* se considera el mejor y más elocuente de todos los poemas gauchescos.

En el trozo que sigue Martín nos habla y nos dice lo que es ser gaucho. ¡A ver!

Las pampas, Argentina

Martín Fierro

Un gaucho

Soy gaucho, y entiendaló
como mi lengua lo explica:
para mí la tierra es chica
y pudiera ser mayor°;
ni la víbora me pica
ni quema mi frente el sol.

y pudiera ser mayor *it would still be small to me*

Nací como nace peje°,
en el fondo de la mar;
naides° me puede quitar
aquello que Dios me dio:
lo que al mundo truje° yo
del mundo lo he de llevar.

peje *pez*
naides *nadie*
truje *traje*

Mi gloria es vivir tan libre
como el pájaro del cielo;
no hago nido en este suelo,
ande hay tanto que sufrir;
y naides me ha de seguir
cuando yo remuento° el vuelo.

remuento (remonto) *take off*

Yo no tengo en el amor
quien me venga con querellas;
como esas aves tan bellas
que saltan de rama en rama,
yo hago en el trébol° mi cama
y me cubren las estrellas.

trébol *clover*

Y sepan cuantos escuchan
de mis penas el relato,
que nunca peleo ni mato
Sino por necesidá,
y que a tanta alversidá°
sólo me arrojó el mal trato.

alversidá *adversidad*

Y atienda° la relación
que hace un gaucho perseguido°,
que padre y marido ha sido
empeñoso° y diligente,
y sin embargo la gente
lo tiene por un bandido.

atienda *keep in mind*
perseguido *persecuted*
empeñoso *persistent*

La higuera

Juana de Ibarbourou

Introducción Juana de Ibarbourou nació en 1895 en un pueblo pequeño de Uruguay donde pasó su adolescencia en pleno contacto con la naturaleza que siempre está presente en su poesía donde aparecen prados y bosques, árboles, frutas y flores. Ella lleva la naturaleza en sí de tal modo que una vez llegó a decir: «Estoy convencida de que en una vida ancestral, hace ya miles de años, yo tuve raíces y gajos, y di flores... »

El poema que sigue *La higuera* es de gran fuerza emotiva.

Una higuera

La higuera

Porque es áspera y fea;
Porque todas sus ramas son grises.
Yo le tengo piedad a la higuera.

En mi quinta hay cien árboles bellos:
Ciruelos redondos,
Limoneros rectos
Y naranjos de brotes° lustrosos.

En las primaveras,
Todos ellos se cubren de flores
En torno a la higuera.

Y la pobre parece tan triste
con sus gajos torcidos° que nunca
de apartados capullos° se visten...

Por eso
Cada vez que yo paso a su lado
Digo, procurando
Hacer dulce y alegre mi acento:
—Es la higuera el más bello
de los árboles todos del huerto.

Si ella escucha,
si comprende el idioma en que hablo,
¡Qué dulzura tan honda hará nido
en su alma sensible de árbol!

Y tal vez, a la noche,
cuando el viento abanique° su copa,
Embriagada° de gozo le cuente:
—Hoy a mí me dijeron hermosa.

brotes *buds*

torcidos *twisted, bent*

capullos *buds, blooms*

Higos

abanique *fans*

Embriagada *Drunk*

¿Comprendes?

A ***La araucana*** **Buscando información** Contesten.

1. ¿Qué es La *araucana?*
2. ¿Dónde luchó Ercilla?
3. ¿Qué hacía mientras peleaba?
4. ¿Qué le declaró al rey en la dedicatoria del poema?
5. ¿Qué tiene de único en su género el poema?

B ***La araucana*** **Categorizando**

Hagan una lista de las características físicas y de los atributos de los araucanos.

C **José Hernández Buscando información** Den la información.

1. donde nació
2. donde vivió y pasó su adolescencia
3. lo que poblaba esta región en aquel entonces
4. lo que se hizo Hernández
5. lo que hacía de ilegal el ejército
6. el motivo de Hernández en escribir el poema
7. como empezó y cambió el protagonista
8. lo que es el *Martín Fierro* para el gaucho
9. lo que es el *Martín Fierro* para el lector culto

D ***Martín Fierro*** **Parafraseando** Expliquen lo que nos dice el autor.

1. para mí la tierra es chica
   y pudiera ser mayor
2. ni la víbora me pica
   ni quema mi frente el sol
3. Nací como nace el peje
4. lo que al mundo truje yo
   del mundo lo he de llevar

E ***Martín Fierro*** **Analizando** Contesten.

1. ¿Cómo y por qué se compara Martín Fierro a sí mismo con un pájaro?
2. ¿Por qué pelea o mata el gaucho Martín Fierro?
3. ¿Qué ha sido el gaucho?
4. Sin embargo, ¿cómo lo considera la gente?

F **Juana de Ibarbourou**

Expliquen la importancia de la naturaleza en la vida y en la obra de Juana de Ibarbourou.

G ***La higuera*** Describan.

1. la higuera
2. los ciruelos
3. los limoneros
4. los naranjos

Una huerta en Chile

H ***La higuera* Buscando información** Contesten.

1. ¿Qué le dice la poeta al pasar por la higuera? ¿Cómo se lo dice?
2. ¿Cómo se sentirá la higuera si comprende el idioma de la poeta?
3. ¿Qué dirá la higuera embriagada de gozo? ¿Cuál es otro verbo que la poeta podría haber usado en vez de «dijeron»?

I ***Martín Fierro* Expresando tus sentimientos y emociones**

¿Cómo te sientes al leer este trozo de el *Martín Fierro?* ¿Puedes compadecerte de la pena de Martín Fierro? ¿Por qué? En tu opinión, ¿qué tipo de persona es? Para ti, ¿hay una injusticia grave? ¿Cuál es?

J ***Martín Fierro* Escribiendo una narración**

En forma de prosa, describe al gaucho Martín Fierro.

K ***La higuera* Visualizando y dibujando**

Si te gusta dibujar, dibuja lo que ves al leer *La higuera.* Luego describe tu dibujo.

L ***La higuera* Buscando emociones y sentimientos**

Indica en qué sentido es el tono del poema *La higuera* tierno, afectuoso, cariñoso, sensible y joven.

Prosa Historia de dos cachorros de coatí y dos cachorros de hombre

Vocabulario para la lectura

El señor llevaba el caballo de la soga.
El señor iba descalzo.

Más vocabulario

descalzo(a) sin zapatos
encaminarse a dirigirse a, marcharse hacia
soltar (ue) dejar ir, dar salida o libertad

¿Qué palabra necesito?

1 **Historieta** **El señor del taller** Contesten.

1. ¿Al señor le gustaba trabajar en su taller?
2. ¿Tenía muchas herramientas?
3. ¿Había una jaula en el taller?
4. ¿Era de alambre la jaula?
5. ¿Tenía el señor un gallo en la jaula?
6. ¿Cantaba el gallo?
7. De noche, ¿armaba el señor una trampa?
8. ¿Armaba la trampa para atrapar ratones?

2 **Animales** Completen.

1. Muchos animales, tales como un coatí, tiene cuatro ____ y una ____ larga. Muchas veces andan con la ____ levantada.
2. La parte del animal donde están la boca y la nariz es ____.
3. Un perrito que tiene sólo seis semanas es un ____.
4. Los ____ cantan y las ____ ponen huevos.
5. Muchos árboles pierden sus ____ en el otoño.
6. Él nunca anda ____ porque hay muchas víboras.
7. Él nunca ____ el caballo. Lo lleva de una ____.
8. El señor y su caballo ____ a la finca.

Historia de dos cachorros de coatí y dos cachorros de hombre

Horacio Quiroga

Introducción Horacio Quiroga (1878–1937) es considerado uno de los más importantes cuentistas de la literatura hispana. Él nació en Salto, Uruguay, de una familia bastante acomodada. Pero Quiroga pasó una gran parte de su vida en la provincia argentina de Misiones, una región de clima agobiante y densa vegetación tropical. Muchos de sus cuentos tratan de las realidades y peligros de la jungla. La tragedia y la muerte son temas que recurren en sus cuentos. Pero el cuento que sigue *La historia de dos cachorros de coatí y dos cachorros de hombre* es de su colección *Cuentos de la selva*—una serie de cuentos encantadores de tono más liviano[1] que como dice el autor mismo «son para los niños de todas las edades y de todas las tierras».

[1] liviano *light*

Provincia de Misiones, Argentina

Historia de dos cachorros de coatí y dos cachorros de hombre

Había una vez un coatí que tenía tres hijos. Vivían en el monte comiendo frutas, raíces y huevos de pajaritos. Cuando estaban arriba de los árboles y sentían un gran ruido, se tiraban al suelo de cabeza y salían corriendo con la cola levantada.

Una vez que los coaticitos fueron un poco más grandes, su madre los reunió un día arriba de un naranjo y les habló así:

—Coaticitos: ustedes son bastante grandes para buscarse la comida solos. Deben aprenderlo, porque cuando sean viejos andarán siempre solos, como todos los coatís. El mayor de ustedes, que es muy amigo de cazar cascarudos°, puede encontrarlos entre los palos podridos°, porque allí hay muchos cascarudos y cucarachas. El segundo, que es gran comedor de frutas, puede encontrarlas en este naranjal; hasta diciembre habrá naranjas. El tercero, que no quiere comer sino huevos de pájaros, puede ir a todas partes, porque en todas partes hay nidos de pájaros. Pero que no vaya nunca a buscar nidos al campo, porque es peligroso.

cascarudos *beetles*
podridos *rotten*

—Coaticitos: hay una sola cosa a la cual deben tener gran miedo. Son los perros. Yo peleé una vez con ellos. Y sé lo que les digo: por eso tengo un diente roto. Detrás de los perros vienen siempre los hombres con un gran ruido, que mata. Cuando oigan cerca este ruido, tírense de cabeza al suelo, por alto que sea el árbol. Si no lo hacen así los matarán con seguridad de un tiro°.

tiro *shot*

Así habló la madre. Todos se bajaron entonces y se separaron, caminando de derecha a izquierda, y de izquierda a derecha, como si hubieran perdido algo, porque así caminan los coatís.

El mayor quería comer cascarudos, buscó entre los palos podridos y las hojas de los yuyos, y encontró tantos, que comió hasta quedarse dormido. El segundo, que prefería las frutas a cualquier cosa, comió cuantas naranjas quiso, porque aquel naranjal estaba dentro del monte, como pasa en el Paraguay y Misiones, y ningún hombre vino a incomodarlo. El tercero que era loco por los huevos de pájaro, tuvo que andar todo el día para encontrar únicamente dos nidos; uno de tucán, que tenía tres huevos, y uno de tórtola, que tenía sólo dos. Total cinco huevos chiquitos, que eran muy poca comida; de modo que al caer la tarde el coaticito tenía tanta hambre como de mañana, y se sentó muy triste a la orilla del monte. Desde allí veía al campo, y pensó en la recomendación de su madre.

¿Por qué no querrá mamá —se dijo— que vaya a buscar nidos al campo?

Estaba pensando así cuando oyó, muy lejos, el canto de un pájaro.

—¡Qué canto tan fuerte! —dijo admirado—. ¡Qué huevos tan grandes debe tener ese pájaro!

El canto se repitió. Y entonces el coatí se puso a correr por entre el monte, cortando camino, porque el canto había sonado muy a su derecha. El sol caía ya, pero el coatí volaba con la cola levantada. Llegó a la orilla del monte, por fin, y moró el campo. Lejos vio la casa de los hombres, y vio un hombre con botas que llevaba un caballo de la soga. Vio también un pájaro muy grande que cantaba y entonces el coaticito se golpeó la frente y dijo:

—¡Qué zonzo° soy! Ahora ya sé qué pájaro es ése: es un gallo; mamá me lo mostró un día desde arriba de un árbol. Los gallos tienen un canto lindísimo, y tienen muchas gallinas que ponen huevos. ¡Si yo pudiera comer huevos de gallina!

zonzo *foolish*

Es sabido que nada gusta tanto a los bichos° chicos del monte como los huevos de gallina. Durante un rato el coaticito se acordó de las recomendaciones de su madre. Pero el deseo pudo más, y se sentó a la orilla del monte, esperando que cerrara bien la noche para ir al gallinero.

bichos *bugs*

La noche cerró por fin, y entonces, en punta de pie y paso a paso, se encaminó a la casa. Llegó allá y escuchó atentamente: no se sentía el menor ruido. El coaticito, loco de alegría porque iba a comer cien, mil, dos mil huevos de gallina, entró en el gallinero, y lo primero que vio bien en la entrada fue un huevo que estaba solo en el suelo. Pensó un instante en dejarlo para el final, como postre porque era un huevo muy grande; pero la boca se le hizo agua, y clavó los dientes en el huevo.

Apenas mordió, ¡TRAC!, un terrible golpe en la cara y un inmenso dolor en el hocico.

—¡Mamá, mamá! —gritó, loco de dolor, saltando a todos lados. Pero estaba sujeto, y en ese momento oyó el ronco ladrido° de un perro.

ronco ladrido *hoarse bark*

Mientras el coatí esperaba en la orilla del monte que cerrara bien la noche para ir al gallinero, el hombre de la casa jugaba sobre la gramilla° con sus hijos, dos criaturas rubias, de cinco y seis años, que corrían riendo, se caían, se levantaban riendo otra vez, y volvían a caerse. El padre se caía también, con gran alegría de los chicos. Dejaron por fin de jugar porque ya era de noche, y el hombre dijo entonces:

gramilla *grass lawn*

—Voy a poner la trampa para cazar a la comadreja° que viene a matar los pollos y robar los huevos.

comadreja *weasel*

Y fue y armó la trampa. Después comieron y se acostaron. Pero las criaturas no tenían sueño, y saltaban de la cama del uno a la del otro y se enredaban° en el camisón. El padre, que leía en el comedor, los dejaba hacer. Pero los chicos de repente se detuvieron en sus saltos y gritaron:

se enredaban *got tangled up with*

—¡Papá! ¡Ha caído la comadreja en la trampa! ¡Tuké está ladrando! ¡Nosotros también queremos ir papá!

Fueron. ¿Qué vieron allí? Vieron a su padre que se agachaba teniendo al perro con una mano, mientras con la otra levantaba por la cola a un coatí, un coaticito chico aún, que gritaba con un chillido° rapidísimo y estridente como un grillo°.

chillido *shriek*

grillo *cricket*

—¡Papá, no lo mates! —dijeron las criaturas—. ¡Es muy chiquito! ¡Dánoslo para nosotros!

—Bueno, se los voy a dar —respondió el padre—. Pero cuídenlo bien, y sobre todo no se olviden de que los coatís toman agua como ustedes. Esto lo decía porque los chicos habían tenido una vez un gatito montés al cual a cada rato le llevaban carne, que sacaban de la fiambrera°; pero nunca le dieron agua, y se murió.

fiambrera *food cabinet*

En consecuencia pusieron al coatí en la misma jaula del gato montés, que estaba cerca del gallinero, y se acostaron todos otra vez.

Y cuando era más de medianoche y había un gran silencio, el coaticito, que sufría mucho por los dientes de la trampa, vio, a la luz de la luna, tres sombras que se acercaban con gran sigilo. El corazón le dio un vuelco° al pobre coaticito al reconocer a su madre y sus dos hermanos que lo estaban buscando.

vuelco *tumble*

—¡Mamá, mamá! —murmuró el prisionero en voz muy baja para no hacer ruido—. ¡Estoy aquí! ¡Sáquenme de aquí! ¡No quiero quedarme, ma... má...! —y lloraba desconsolado.

Pero a pesar de todo estaban contentos porque se habían encontrado, y se hacían mil caricias en el hocico.

Se trató en seguida de hacer salir al prisionero. Probaron primero cortar el alambre tejido, y los cuatro se pusieron a trabajar con los dientes; mas no conseguían nada. Entonces a la madre se le ocurrió de repente una idea, y dijo:

—¡Vamos a buscar las herramientas del hombre! Los hombres tienen herramientas para cortar fierro. Se llaman limas°. Tienen tres lados como las víboras de cascabel. Se empuja y se retira. ¡Vamos a buscarla!

limas *files*

Fueron al taller del hombre y volvieron con la lima. Creyendo que uno solo no tendría fuerzas bastantes, sujetaron la lima entre los tres y empezaron el trabajo. Y se entusiasmaron tanto, que al rato la jaula entera temblaba con las sacudidas° y hacía un terrible ruido. Tal ruido hacía, que el perro se despertó, lanzando un ronco ladrido. Mas los coatís no esperaron a que el perro les pidiera cuenta de ese escándalo y dispararon al monte, dejando la lima tirada.

sacudidas *jolt, shake*

Al día siguiente, los chicos fueron temprano a ver a su nuevo huésped, que estaba muy triste.

—¿Qué nombre le pondremos? —preguntó la nena a su hermano.

¡Ya sé! —respondió el varoncito—. ¡Le pondremos *Diecisiete!*

¿Por qué *Diecisiete?* Nunca hubo bicho en el monte con nombre más raro. Pero el varoncito estaba aprendiendo a contar, y tal vez le había llamado la atención aquel número.

El caso es que se llamó *Diecisiete.* Le dieron, pan, uvas, chocolate, carne, langostas, huevos, riquísimos huevos de gallina. Lograron que en un solo día se dejara rascar° la cabeza; y tan grande es la sinceridad del cariño de las criaturas, que al llegar la noche, el coatí estaba casi resignado con su cautiverio°. Pensaba a cada momento en las cosas ricas que había para comer allí, y pensaba en aquellos rubios cachorros de hombre que tan alegres y buenos eran.

rascar *scratch*

cautiverio *captivity*

Durante dos noches seguidas, el perro durmió tan cerca de su jaula, que la familia del prisionero no se atrevió a acercarse, con gran sentimiento. Cuando la tercera noche llegaron de nuevo a buscar la lima para dar libertad al coaticito, éste les dijo:

—Mamá, yo no quiero irme más de aquí. Me dan huevos y son muy buenos conmigo. Hoy me dijeron que si me portaba bien me iban a dejar suelto° muy pronto. Son como nosotros. Son cachorritos también, y jugamos juntos.

Los coatís salvajes quedaron muy tristes, pero se resignaron, prometiendo al coaticito venir todas las noches a visitarlo.

Efectivamente, todas las noches, lloviera o no, su madre y sus hermanos iban a pasar un rato con él. El coaticito les daba pan por entre el tejido del alambre, y los coatís salvajes se sentaban a comer frente a la jaula.

Al cabo de quince días, el coaticito andaba suelto y él mismo se iba de noche a su jaula. Salvo algunos tirones de orejas que se llevaba por andar cerca del gallinero todo marchaba bien. Él y las criaturas se querían mucho y los mismos coatís salvajes, al ver lo buenos que eran aquellos cachorritos de hombre, habían concluido por tomar cariño a las dos criaturas.

Hasta que una noche muy oscura, en que hacía mucho calor y tronaba°, los coatís salvajes llamaron al coaticito y nadie les respondió. Se acercaron muy inquietos y vieron entonces, en el momento en que casi lo pisaban una enorme víbora que estaba enroscada° en la entrada de la jaula. Los coatís comprendieron en seguida que el coaticito había sido mordido° al entrar, y no había respondido a su llamado, porque acaso ya estaba muerto. Pero lo iban a vengar bien. En un segundo, entre los tres, enloquecieron a la serpiente de cascabel, saltando de aquí para allá, y en otro segundo cayeron sobre ella, deshaciéndole la cabeza a mordiscos.

Corrieron entonces adentro, y allí estaba en efecto el coaticito, tendido, hinchado°, con las patas temblando y muriéndose. En balde° los coatís salvajes lo movieron: lo lamieron° en balde por todo el cuerpo durante un cuarto de hora. El coaticito abrió por fin la boca y dejó de respirar, porque estaba muerto.

suelto *loose*

tronaba *thundered*

enroscada *entwined*

mordido *bitten*

hinchado *swollen*

En balde *In vain*

lamieron *they licked*

Los coatís son casi refractarios°, como se dice, al veneno de las víboras. No les hace casi nada el veneno, y hay otros animales como la mangosta°, que resisten muy bien el veneno de las víboras. Con toda seguridad el coaticito había sido mordido en una arteria o en una vena, porque entonces la sangre se envenena en seguida, y el animal muere. Esto le había pasado al coaticito.

refractarios *resistant*

mangosta *mongoose*

Al verlo así, su madre y sus hermanos lloraron un largo rato. Después, como nada más tenían que hacer allí, salieron de la jaula, se dieron vuelta para mirar por última vez la casa donde tan feliz había sido el coaticito, y se fueron otra vez al monte.

Pero los tres coatís, sin embargo, iban muy preocupados, y su preocupación era ésta: ¿qué iban a decir los chicos, cuando, al día siguiente, vieran muerto a su querido coaticito? Los chicos lo querían muchísimo, y ellos, los coatís, querían también a los cachorros rubios. Así es que los tres coatís tenían el mismo pensamiento, y era evitarles ese gran dolor a los chicos.

Hablaron un largo rato y al fin decidieron lo siguiente: el segundo de los coatís, que se parecía mucho al menor en cuerpo y en modo de ser, iba a quedarse en la jaula, en vez del difunto°. Como estaban enterados de muchos secretos de la casa, por los cuentos del coaticito, los chicos no conocerían nada; extrañarían un poco algunas cosas, pero nada más.

difunto *dead one*

Y así pasó en efecto. Volvieron a la casa, y un nuevo coaticito reemplazó al primero, mientras la madre y el otro hermano se llevaban sujeto a los dientes el cadáver del menor. Lo llevaron despacio al monte, y la cabeza colgaba, balanceándose, y la cola iba arrastrando por el suelo.

Al día siguiente los chicos extrañaron, efectivamente, algunas costumbres raras del coaticito. Pero como éste era tan bueno y cariñoso como el otro, las criaturas no tuvieron la menor sospecha. Formaron la misma familia de cachorritos de antes, y, como antes, los coatís salvajes venían noche a noche a visitar al coaticito civilizado, y se sentaban a su lado a comer pedacitos de huevo que él les guardaba, mientras ellos le contaban la vida de la selva.

¿Comprendes?

A La familia de coatís Den la siguiente información.

1. el número de hijos en la familia de coatís
2. donde vivían y lo que comían
3. como les enseñó su madre a buscar la comida solos
4. adonde no pueden ir nunca a buscar nidos
5. al que deben tener gran miedo y por qué
6. lo que le gustaba comer a cada uno de los cachorros
7. adonde fue el tercer cachorro atraído por el canto de un pájaro
8. lo que le pasó

B Buscando información Contesten.

1. ¿Cómo era la familia que vivía en la casa?
2. ¿Por qué pone la trampa el padre?
3. ¿Cómo saben los niños que la comadreja ha caído en la trampa?
4. ¿Por qué no les permite el padre andar descalzos de noche?
5. ¿Qué ven en la trampa?
6. ¿Qué le ruegan a su padre los niños?
7. ¿Dónde pusieron al coaticito?
8. ¿Qué hicieron su mamá y sus hermanos para tratar de liberar al coaticito de su jaula?
9. ¿Qué nombre le dieron los niños al coaticito y qué le dieron de comer?

C ¿Qué pasó? Contesten.

1. ¿Por qué no pudo la familia del «prisionero» visitarlo?
2. ¿Por qué dijo el coaticito, «Mamá, yo no quiero irme más de aquí»?
3. Los coatís salvajes quedaron muy tristes, ¿pero qué se resignaron a hacer? Y, ¿qué hicieron?
4. Al cabo de quince días, ¿qué hacía el coaticito?
5. Pero durante una noche muy oscura, ¿qué pasó?
6. ¿Cómo encontraron los coatís salvajes al coaticito «civilizado»? ¿Qué le había pasado?
7. Los tres coatís estaban muy tristes. Pero estaban muy preocupados también. ¿Por quiénes estaban preocupados? ¿Por qué razón?
8. ¿Qué decidieron hacer? ¿Cómo y adónde llevaron el cadáver?
9. ¿Cómo era la vida después para el coatí «civilizado»?
10. ¿Cómo era la vida después para los coatís «salvajes»?

D Buscando la idea principal

Explica el significado del título de este cuento.

E Analizando

Analiza como Quiroga emplea las palabras «civilizado» y «salvaje». ¿Quiénes son civilizados y quiénes son salvajes? ¿Por qué? En el cuento, ¿hay mucha diferencia entre el comportamiento civilizado y salvaje? Busca ejemplos de comportamiento muy civilizado o humano de parte de los «salvajes». ¿Es posible que Quiroga nos dé un mensaje? ¿Cuál es?

Una ojeada a la poesía

Vocabulario para la lectura

La señora se sentó a la sombra del árbol.
Miró el ramo de flores y empezó a llorar.

Más vocabulario

el rumbo la dirección, el sentido
dichoso(a) afortunado, que tiene suerte

¿Qué palabra necesito?

1 ¿Cuál es la palabra? Contesten.

1. ¿Da sombra el árbol?
2. ¿Es bonito el ramo de flores?
3. ¿Anda la señora sin rumbo?
4. ¿Llora ella?
5. ¿Mira su ramo de flores?
6. ¿Qué opinas? ¿Es dichosa la señora?
7. ¿Es dichosa la persona que encuentra la felicidad?

Lo fatal • Canción de otoño en primavera

Rubén Darío

Monumento a Rubén Darío

Introducción Rubén Darío (1867–1916) tiene fama de ser el príncipe de los poetas de las Américas. Su verdadero nombre es Félix Rubén García Sarmiento. Nació en una aldea pequeña de Nicaragua y cuando tenía sólo ocho meses sus padres lo abandonaron y fue recogido por una tía. Aprendió a leer y escribir muy temprano. Un joven pobre y angustiado, anduvo por muchos países de América y Europa sin echar raíces en ninguno. Trabajó en varias revistas y periódicos importantes. Vivió intensamente y volvió a su patria donde murió a los cuarenta y nueve años.

Rubén Darío pudo resumir muchas corrientes literarias—antiguas, modernas, clásicas, románticas, simbolistas y decadentes. Se dice que vivió de la poesía y para la poesía.

Los dos poemas que siguen reflejan la tristeza y pena que sintió el poeta durante toda su vida.

Lo fatal

Dichoso el árbol que es apenas° sensitivo,
y más piedra dura, porque ésa ya no siente,
pues no hay dolor más grande que el dolor de ser vivo,
ni mayor pesadumbre° que la vida consciente.
Ser, y no saber nada, y ser sin rumbo cierto,
y el temor de haber sido y un futuro terror...
y el espanto° seguro de estar mañana muerto,
y sufrir por la vida y por la sombra y por
lo que no conocemos y apenas sospechamos,
y la carne que tienta con sus frescos racimos,
y la tumba que aguarda con sus fúnebres ramos,
y no saber adónde vamos,
¡ni de dónde venimos... !

apenas *scarcely*

pesadumbre *grief, pain*

espanto *fright, terror*

Canción de otoño en primavera

Juventud, divino tesoro
¡ya te vas para no volver!
Cuando quiero llorar, no lloro,
y a veces lloro sin querer...

¿Comprendes?

A ***Lo fatal*** Contesten según el poeta.

1. ¿Por qué es dichoso el árbol?
2. ¿Por qué es aún más dichosa una piedra dura?
3. ¿Cuál es el dolor más grande?
4. ¿Qué es la vida consciente?

B ***Lo fatal***

Al leer este poema, ¿cuáles son las emociones y los sentimientos que les evoca? ¿Alguna vez te has sentido como el poeta?

C ***Canción de otoño en primavera***

Expliquen.

1. lo que simboliza el otoño
2. lo que simboliza la primavera
3. lo que es la juventud
4. lo que le pasa a la juventud

D **Comparando y analizando**

En el poema *Lo fatal*, ¿a quién está comparando Rubén Darío un árbol y una piedra? ¿Por qué?

E **Interpretando emociones y sentimientos**

Leer el poema *Lo fatal* no es ni fácil ni alegre. El poeta nos habla no sólo de su tristeza sino de su verdadero sufrimiento interior—de sus pesadumbres. En tus propias palabras, por sencillas que sean, expresa lo que el poeta te está diciendo. ¿Cómo te está hablando?

Nicaragua

F Conectando la literatura con la vida

De lo que has aprendido sobre la vida de Rubén Darío, ¿puedes comprender el tono triste y deprimente de su poema *Lo fatal?* ¿Por qué es así?

G Buscando la idea principal

Explica por qué el poeta le daría el título *Lo fatal* a este poema.

H Dando opiniones personales

Todavía eres muy joven, pero, ¿qué te parece? ¿Se va la juventud muy de prisa o no? ¿Quisieras más tiempo para disfrutar de la juventud? ¿Esperas que no pase muy rápido? ¿Por qué?

I Debatiendo

Trabajen en grupos de cuatro. Dos de ustedes van a decir que la juventud es un tesoro divino. Otros dos van a hablar en contra—que la juventud no es un tesoro. Preparen su debate.

Managua, Nicaragua

Prosa me llamo Rigoberta Menchú y así me nació la conciencia

Vocabulario para la lectura

Más vocabulario

el antepasado abuelo, ancestro
el/la ladino(a) mestizo(a) o indio(a) que habla español y que se ha adaptado a costumbres urbanas
compuesto(a) hecho(a), producido(a)
sagrado(a) venerable, santo(a), con valor religioso
desperdiciar perder, malgastar
herir (i, i) causar daño, lastimar

¿Qué palabra necesito?

Una milpa, Guatemala

1 **La naturaleza** Completen.

1. Los recursos naturales son limitados, no se deben ____.
2. Los indígenas respetan el agua y la tierra porque creen que son cosas ____.
3. Los indígenas también respetan a sus abuelos y otros ____.
4. Ellos prefieren los productos naturales, no los productos ____ por máquinas.
5. No puedo ver sin la luz que nos da ____.
6. Nunca debemos ____ o lastimar a nadie.
7. Los campesinos tienen que ____ bien los campos si quieren una cosecha buena.
8. El ____ del maíz es importante para los indígenas.
9. La tierra destinada al cultivo del maíz es la ____.
10. De vez en cuando una ____ pequeña puede causar un incendio que tiene grandes ____.

me llamo Rigoberta Menchú y así me nació la conciencia

Rigoberta Menchu

Introducción En muchas partes de Latinoamérica la población indígena es significativa, y en algunos países, mayoritaria. A pesar de lo numerosa que es la población indígena, su participación en la vida económica y social nacional es frecuentemente muy limitada. Las poblaciones indígenas se ven marginadas. Muchas veces son víctimas de pobreza y discriminación. Siempre ha habido defensores de los indígenas, como Fray Bartolomé de las Casas en el México del siglo XVI. Pero hoy, desde México hasta Tierra del Fuego, son los mismos indígenas los que luchan por la justicia y por sus derechos.

Rigoberta Menchú pertenece a los quichés, grupo indígena de Guatemala, descendientes de los mayas. Ella nació en 1959 en la pequeña aldea de Chimel en el estado guatemalteco de El Quiché en el norte del país.

A los veintitrés años de edad Rigoberta Menchú contó la historia de su vida a Elizabeth Burgos quien la redactó tal como se la contó Rigoberta. Dice Burgos:

> *«La historia de su vida es más un testimonio sobre la de Guatemala. Por ello es ejemplar, puesto que encarna la vida de todos los indios del continente americano. Lo que ella dice a propósito de su vida, de su relación con la naturaleza, de la vida, la muerte, la comunidad, lo encontramos igualmente entre los indios norteamericanos, los de América Central y los de Sudamérica.»*

Rigoberta Menchú ha luchado por los derechos de los indígenas, no sólo de Guatemala, sino de toda la América. En 1992 ella recibió el Premio Nóbel de la Paz.

En la selección de su libro *me llamo Rigoberta Menchú y así me nació la conciencia* ella nos habla de la importancia de la naturaleza en la vida de los quichés.

La selección comienza con unas frases del *Popul Vuh,* el libro sagrado de los quichés de Guatemala que data del sigo XVI.

Guatemala

me llamo Rigoberta Menchú y así me nació la conciencia

Tojil, en la oscuridad que le era propicia, con una piedra golpeó el cuero de su sandalia, y de ella, al instante, brotó una chispa, luego un brillo y en seguida una llama y el nuevo fuego lució esplendoroso. (Popol Vuh)

Entonces también desde niños recibimos una educación diferente de la que tienen los blancos, los ladinos. Nosotros, los indígenas, tenemos más contacto con la naturaleza.

... respetamos una serie de cosas de la naturaleza. Las cosas más importantes para nosotros. Por ejemplo, el agua es algo sagrado. La explicación que nos dan nuestros padres desde niños es que no hay que desperdiciar el agua, aunque haya. El agua es algo puro, es algo limpio y es algo que da vida al hombre. Sin el agua no se puede vivir, tampoco hubieran podido vivir nuestros antepasados... Tenemos tierra. Nuestros padres nos dicen «Hijos, la tierra es la madre del hombre porque es la que da de comer al hombre.» Y más nosotros que nos basamos en el cultivo, porque nosotros los indígenas comemos maíz, frijol y yerbas del campo y no sabemos comer, por ejemplo, jamón o queso, cosas compuestas con aparatos, con máquinas. Entonces se considera que la tierra es la madre del hombre. Y de hecho nuestros padres nos enseñan a respetar esa tierra. Sólo se puede herir la tierra cuando hay necesidad. Esa concepción hace que antes de sembrar nuestra milpa, tenemos que pedirle permiso a la tierra.

Cuando se pide permiso a la tierra, antes de cultivarla, se hace una ceremonia... En primer lugar se le pone una candela al representante de la tierra, del agua, del maíz, que es la comida del hombre. Se considera, según los antepasados, que nosotros los indígenas estamos hechos de maíz. Estamos hechos del maíz blanco y del maíz amarillo, según nuestros antepasados. Entonces, eso se toma en cuenta. Y luego la candela, que representa al hombre como un hijo de la naturaleza, del universo. Entonces, se ponen esas candelas y se unen todos los miembros de la familia a rezar. Más que todo pidiéndole permiso a la tierra, que dé una buena cosecha. También se reza a nuestros antepasados, mencionándoles sus oraciones, que hace tiempo, hace mucho tiempo existen.

¿Comprendes?

A Costumbres quichés Contesten.

1. ¿Qué reciben los indígenas que es diferente de lo que reciben los blancos o los ladinos?
2. ¿Con qué tienen más contacto y qué respetan más?
3. ¿Por qué tiene el agua tanta importancia para ellos?
4. Para ellos, ¿qué es la tierra? ¿Por qué?
5. ¿Qué comen? Y, ¿qué no comen los indígenas?
6. ¿Qué se hace antes de cultivar la milpa?
7. ¿Cómo es la ceremonia?
8. Según los antepasados, ¿de qué están hechos los indígenas?
9. Cuando rezan, ¿qué le piden a la tierra?
10. ¿A quiénes más rezan?

B Haciendo una entrevista

Imagínate un voluntario del Cuerpo de Paz en Guatemala. Acabas de llegar y estás entrevistando a un miembro del grupo quiché; tu compañero(a). En la entrevista hazle preguntas sobre su vida diaria, sus costumbres y tradiciones basadas en lo que has aprendido en el libro de Rigoberta Menchú. Tu compañero(a) contestará tus preguntas.

Lago Atitlán, Guatemala

Literatura mexicana

Una ojeada a la poesía

Vocabulario para la lectura

Las abejas extraen néctar de las flores.
Del néctar hacen miel.

El cura va a bendecir a todos.
El cura acaricia al bebé.
Él lo bendice también.
Él tiene una cara (faz) angelical.

El día declina en alta mar.

Los labradores están cosechando los vegetales.

El ave remonta su vuelo.

Más vocabulario

la agonía los últimos momentos antes de morir
la hiel la amargura, los trabajos, las adversidades
las lozanías los tiempos de vigor, la robustez, la fuerza
el ocaso la puesta del sol, la decadencia, el final de la vida
la plegaria el rezo, la oración
aleve traidor, infiel
áureo(a) dorado
fallido(a) frustrado, no logrado, no conseguido
inmerecido(a) injusto, no merecido
rudo(a) duro, tosco, riguroso

¿Qué palabra necesito?

1 Historieta **El día se acaba.** Completen.

1. El día se acaba. Se pone el sol. Es el ____.
2. Y el camino a casa no es bueno. Es un camino ____.
3. Pero allí comeremos sabrosas tostadas con ____.
4. Esa miel que ____ las abejas de las flores es muy dulce.
5. ¡Mira! Los campesinos acaban de ____ las papas.
6. Ay, los últimos rayos del sol me ____ la cara.

2 **¡Se dice así!** Expresen de otra manera.

1. El religioso *consagra* la obra del filántropo.
2. Por poco se ve *frustrada* la obra.
3. Las quejas no son válidas; son *injustas.*
4. Si una ciudad tiene vida, estas son *épocas de vigor.*
5. Con estas renovaciones, la ciudad tiene una nueva *cara.*

3 **¿Cuál es la palabra?** Completen.

1. Salimos en el barco ayer y hoy estamos en ____.
2. Mientras tanto las aves ____ su vuelo.
3. Pero es un día triste porque presenciamos la ____ del abuelo que pronto morirá.

En paz

Amado Nervo

Introducción Amado Nervo (1870–1919) nació en México. Estudió para sacerdote en el Seminario de Jacona, pero en 1891 dejó la carrera religiosa. Entró en el servicio diplomático de su país a principios del siglo XX y pasó gran parte de su vida en Madrid, París, Buenos Aires y Montevideo, donde murió mientras servía de embajador de México en Uruguay. Aunque el autor escribió en varios géneros, se destacó como poeta. En las poesías de su madurez se le nota una preocupación por la muerte y el amor.

En paz

Muy cerca de mi ocaso, yo te bendigo, Vida,
porque nunca me diste ni esperanza fallida
ni trabajos injustos, ni pena inmerecida;

porque veo al final de mi rudo camino
que yo fui el arquitecto de mi propio destino;
que si extraje las mieles o la hiel de las cosas,
fue porque en ellas puse hiel o mieles sabrosas;
cuando planté rosales, coseché siempre rosas.

...Cierto, a mis lozanías va a seguir el invierno;
¡mas° tú no me dijiste que mayo fuese eterno!
Hallé sin duda largas las noches de mis penas;
mas no me prometiste tú sólo noches buenas;
y en cambio tuve algunas santamente serenas...

Amé, fui amado, el sol acarició mi faz.
¡Vida, nada me debes! ¡Vida, estamos en paz!

mas *pero*

En Durango comenzó

Autor anónimo

Introducción El corrido es una composición popular mexicana. El corrido tiene un carácter muy descriptivo. Hay muchos tipos de corridos. Algunos hablan de hechos y eventos locales. Otros de personajes legendarios y de momentos históricos. Los más famosos cuentan relatos de la Revolución mexicana. El corrido que sigue, *En Durango comenzó,* trata de Pancho Villa, una figura importante de la revolución.

En Durango comenzó

En Durango comenzó
su carrera de bandido
En cada golpe que daba
Se hacía el desaparecido°

Cuando llegó a La Laguna
Robó la estación de Horizonte
Del entonces lo seguían
Por los pueblos y los montes

Un día ya en el nordoeste
Entre Tirso y la Boquilla
Se encontraban acampanadas°
Las fuerzas de Pancho Villa

Gritaba Francisco Villa
El miedo no lo conozco
Que viva Pancho Madero
Y que muera Pascual Orozco

Gritaba Francisco Villa
En su caballo tordillo°
En la bolsa traigo plata
Y en la cintura casquillo°.

Se hacía el desaparecido *He played a disappearing act*

acampanadas *in great danger*

tordillo *dapple-gray*

casquillo *empty shells, cartridges*

Pancho Villa

Para entonces

Manuel Gutiérrez Nájera

Introducción Manuel Gutiérrez Nájera (1859–1895) nació y murió en la capital de México. Murió muy joven, a los treinta y seis años. Fue uno de los iniciadores del movimiento literario conocido como *El modernismo.* Aunque es más famoso como poeta, también escribió en prosa. El poema que sigue tiene especial significado cuando uno piensa en la edad que tenía el poeta cuando falleció.

Para entonces

Quiero morir cuando decline el día,
en alta mar y con la cara al cielo;
donde parezca un sueño la agonía,
y el alma, un ave que remonta el vuelo.

No escuchar en los últimos instantes,
ya con el cielo y con el mar a solas,
más voces ni plegarias sollozantes°
que el majestuoso tumbo de las olas.

Morir cuando la luz, triste, retira
sus áureas redes° de la onda verde,
y ser como ese sol que lento expira:
algo muy luminoso que se pierde.

Morir, y joven: antes que destruya
el tiempo aleve la gentil corona;
cuando la vida dice aún: «¡soy tuya!»,
¡aunque sepamos bien que nos traiciona!

sollozantes *sobbing*

redes *nets*

¿Comprendes?

A ***En paz*** Escojan.

1. ¿A quién se dirige el poeta en este poema?
   - **a.** A Dios.
   - **b.** A la muerte.
   - **c.** A la vida.
2. ¿Por qué dice el poeta «muy cerca de mi ocaso»?
   - **a.** Habla por la tarde y se va a poner el sol.
   - **b.** Se están acercando sus días finales.
   - **c.** Él vive muy cerca de allí.
3. ¿Qué quiere decir el autor cuando dice que es «arquitecto de su propio destino»?
   - **a.** Toma responsabilidad por lo bueno y lo malo de su vida.
   - **b.** Está contento con los edificios que ha construido.
   - **c.** Siempre ha sabido adonde dirigirse.

Ciudad de México

B ***En paz*** Contesten.

1. ¿Tenía el autor noches de pena?
2. ¿Cómo las encontró?
3. ¿Tuvo sólo noches de pena?
4. ¿Qué dice el poeta en cuanto al amor?

Pancho Villa, Emiliano Zapata y sus seguidores

C ***En Durango comenzó*** Contesten.

1. ¿Dónde comenzó Pancho Villa su carrera?
2. ¿Qué carrera comenzó?
3. ¿Qué robó al llegar a La Laguna?
4. ¿Quiénes lo seguían?
5. ¿Dónde lo seguían?
6. ¿Dónde se encontraban acampanadas las fuerzas de Pancho Villa?
7. ¿Qué gritó Pancho Villa?
8. ¿En qué estaba montado?
9. ¿Qué tenía en la bolsa?
10. ¿Y en la cintura?

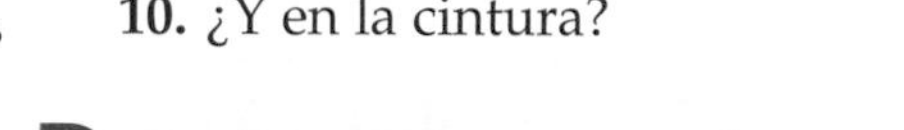
D ***En Durango comenzó*** ¿Cómo lo dice el corrido?

1. Pancho Villa les causaba daño a sus enemigos, las autoridades del gobierno.
2. Pero las autoridades no lo pudieron encontrar.
3. Yo no tengo miedo de nada ni temo a nadie.

E *En Durango comenzó*

Preparen una lista de todos los lugares mencionados en el corrido y búsquenlos en un mapa de México.

F *Para entonces* Escojan.

1. El autor prefiere morir…
   a. al amanecer. b. al anochecer. c. a la medianoche.
2. Él compara el momento de la muerte con…
   a. el sueño. b. una batalla. c. el mar.
3. Y hace una comparación del alma con…
   a. una ola. b. un ave. c. una red.
4. Él dice que el tiempo es…
   a. gentil. b. traidor. c. luminoso.
5. Las *áureas redes* son…
   a. las coronas. b. las plegarias. c. los rayos del sol.

G Buscando la idea principal

En tus propias palabras resume la idea principal de cada poema.

H Metáforas y símiles

Ya sabes lo que es una *metáfora* y un *símil.* Ahora busca en los versos que has leído por lo menos tres ejemplos de cada uno.

Emiliano Zapata
de Diego Rivera

I *En paz* Llegando a conclusiones

Amado Nervo dice que la vida no le debe nada y que «estamos en paz». Explica por qué el poeta ha llegado a esa feliz conclusión.

J *Para entonces* Haciendo observaciones

Manuel Gutiérrez Nájera escribe ***Para entonces*** cuando es bastante joven. ¿De qué trata el poema? ¿Qué quiere el poeta? ¿Es posible que el poeta esté prediciendo algo? ¿Qué?

K *En Durango comenzó* Escribiendo una biografía

En un párrafo escribe todo lo que aprendiste sobre Pancho Villa en el corrido ***En Durango comenzó.***

Prosa Como agua para chocolate

Vocabulario para la lectura

Más vocabulario

la clara parte blanca del huevo, contrario de yema
el carmín ingrediente para dar color rojo a la comida
ajeno(a) de otra persona
flojo(a) no muy sólido, no firme
azucarar cristalizarse
destrozar arruinar
empanizar tomar forma
de golpe de repente, sin anuncio ni preparación

¿Qué palabra necesito?

1 **La receta** Completen.

1. El pastel no está muy firme; al contrario, está muy ____.
2. Y es de color ____, un rojo muy brillante.
3. No usamos azúcar. Le echamos ____ para hacerlo dulce.
4. Y vamos a echar poquísimo jugo de limón, sólo dos o tres ____.
5. Es necesario ____ el caldo para que no quede mucha grasa.
6. Para hacer merengue el cocinero tiene que ____ los huevos y para hacer nata es necesario ____ la crema.
7. Esta receta lleva sólo ____ de los huevos, no las yemas.
8. No debemos arruinar o ____ la propiedad ____, es decir, la propiedad de otros.

2 **Palabras relacionadas** Den una palabra relacionada.

1. el azúcar
2. golpear
3. vacío
4. el colador
5. el destrozo

El cultivo del maíz
de Diego Rivera

Como agua para chocolate

Laura Esquivel

Introducción *Como agua para chocolate* es la primera novela de esta autora mexicana. La novela se publicó en 1989 y enseguida llegó a ser número uno en ventas en México. Se ha traducido al inglés y a muchos otros idiomas. Se hizo de la novela una popularísima película del mismo nombre.

La protagonista de la novela es Tita, la hija menor de Mamá Elena, matriarca de la familia. Tita se enamora de un joven, Pedro Muzquiz, pero Mamá Elena se opone y le obliga a Tita a seguir la vieja tradición de quedarse la hija menor en casa y no casarse nunca, quedarse, como decía la gente, «para vestir santos». Mamá Elena le propone al padre de Pedro que su hijo se case con Rosaura, la hermana mayor de Tita.

En el fragmento que sigue, Tita está en la cocina con Nacha, de ochenta y cinco años, vieja sirvienta de la familia. Mamá Elena le ha ordenado a Tita a ayudarle a Nacha a preparar el pastel de boda de Pedro y Rosaura. La vieja Nacha también se ha quedado para «vestir santos».

Como agua para chocolate

Para el fondant:

800 gramos de azúcar granulado

60 gotas de jugo de limón más bastante agua para disolver

Se ponen en una cacerola, el azúcar y el agua al fuego sin dejar de moverla hasta que empieza a hervir. Se cuela en otra cacerola y se vuelve a poner al fuego agregándole el limón hasta que toma punto de bola floja, limpiando de vez en cuando los bordes de la cacerola con un lienzo° húmedo para que la miel no se azucare; cuando ha tomado el punto anteriormente indicado se vacía en otra cacerola húmeda, se rocía por encima y se deja enfriar un poco.

Después, con una espátula de madera, se bate hasta que se empaniza.

Para aplicarlo, se le pone una cucharada de leche y se vuelve a poner al fuego para que se deslíe, se pone después una gota de carmín y se cubre con él únicamente la parte superior del pastel.

lienzo *cloth*

Nacha se dio cuenta de que Tita estaba mal, cuando ésta le preguntó si no le iba a poner el carmín.

—Mi niña, se lo acabo de poner, ¿no ves el color rosado que tiene?

—No...

—Vete a dormir, niña, yo termino el turrón. Sólo las ollas saben los hervores° de su caldo, pero yo adivino los tuyos, y ya deja de llorar, que me estás mojando° el fondant y no va a servir, anda, ya vete.

Nachita cubrió de besos a Tita y la empujó fuera de la cocina. No se explicaba de dónde había sacado nuevas lágrimas°, pero las había sacado y alterado con ellas la textura del turrón. Ahora le costaría doble esfuerzo dejarlo en su punto. Ya sola se dio a la tarea de terminar con el turrón lo más pronto posible, para irse a dormir. El turrón se hace con 10 claras de huevo y 500 gramos de azúcar batidos a punto de hebra° fuerte.

Cuando terminó se le ocurrió darle un dedazo° al fondant para ver si las lágrimas de Tita no habían alterado el sabor, pero, sin saber por qué, a Nacha le entró de golpe una gran nostalgia. Recordó uno a uno todos los banquetes de boda que había preparado para la familia de la Garza con la ilusión de que el próximo fuera el suyo. A sus 85 años no valía la pena llorar, ni lamentarse de que nunca hubieran llegado ni el esperado banquete ni la esperada boda, a pesar de que el novio sí llegó, ¡vaya que había llegado! Sólo que la mamá de Mamá Elena se había encargado de ahuyentarlo°. Desde entonces se había conformado con gozar de las bodas ajenas y así lo hizo por muchos años sin repelar. No sabía por qué lo hacía ahora. Sentía que era una reverenda tontería, pero no podía dejar de hacerlo. Cubrió con el turrón° lo mejor que pudo el pastel y se fue a su cuarto, con un fuerte dolor de pecho. Lloró toda la noche y a la mañana siguiente no tuvo ánimos para asistir a la boda.

Tita hubiera dado cualquier cosa por estar en el lugar de Nacha, pues ella no sólo tenía que estar presente en la iglesia, se sintiera como se sintiera, sino que tenía que estar muy pendiente° de que su rostro no revelara la menor emoción. Creía poder lograrlo siempre y cuando su mirada no se cruzara con la de Pedro. Ese incidente podría destrozar toda la paz y tranquilidad que aparentaba°.

Sabía que ella, más que su hermana Rosaura, era el centro de atención. Los invitados, más que cumplir con un acto social, querían regodearse° con la idea de su sufrimiento, pero no los complacería, no. Podía sentir claramente cómo penetraban por sus espaldas los cuchicheos° de los presentes a su paso.

—¿Ya viste a Tita? ¡Pobrecita, su hermana se va a casar con su novio! Yo los vi un día en la plaza del pueblo, tomados de la mano. ¡Tan felices que se veían!

hervores *boiling; figuratively, heartaches*

mojando *wetting*

lágrimas *tears*

hebra *thread*

darle un dedazo *stick a finger*

ahuyentarlo *driving him away*

turrón *icing (in this context)*

pendiente *aware*

aparentaba *it feigned*

regodearse *to take delight in*

cuchicheos *whisperings*

¿Comprendes?

Una pastelería, Baja California, México

A **Historieta** **El fondant de Nacha** Contesten.

1. ¿Qué es lo que le dio el color rosado al fondant?
2. ¿Qué le indicó a Nacha que Tita no estaba bien?
3. Algo alteró la textura del turrón. ¿Qué?
4. ¿Qué le metió Nacha al fondant para probar el sabor?
5. ¿Cuál es la «reverenda tontería» a la que se refiere Nacha?

B **Nachita** Completen.

1. La receta con que comienza este fragmento es para _____.
2. Nachita le dio muchos _____ a Tita y la echó de la cocina.
3. Nacha quería terminar pronto con el turrón, porque tenía ganas de _____.

C **En otras palabras** ¿Qué quiere decir… ?

1. Sólo las ollas saben los hervores de su caldo, pero yo adivino los tuyos…
2. … la mamá de Mamá Elena se había encargado de ahuyentarlo.
3. Tita hubiera dado cualquier cosa por estar en el lugar de Nacha…
4. Los invitados… querían regodearse con la idea de sus sufrimientos…

D **Interpretando**

Explica el significado de la siguiente frase: «Tita sabía que ella, más que su hermana Rosaura, era el centro de atención».

E **Dando opiniones personales**

¿Qué te parece la tradición de mantener a la hija menor soltera para que se quedara en casa a cuidar de su madre? Comenta.

F **Describiendo**

Explica en tus propias palabras lo que le hizo la mamá de Mamá Elena a Nacha hace muchos años.

Una ojeada a la poesía

Vocabulario para la lectura

el dinero, la plata

las galletas

La joven corrió.
El joven dio un paso atrás.

Allí en la playa vimos las palmas, las yerbas y las flores.

Más vocabulario

el alma el espíritu, la esencia
el engaño la mentira, la falsedad, la ilusión
la hazaña acción o gesto heroico
la valentía calidad de valiente
arrojar lanzar, tirar, echar
echar tirar, expulsar, lanzar

¿Qué palabra necesito?

1 **Historieta** **La compra** Expresen de otra manera.

1. El muchacho quería comer y fue a comprar *un tipo de pan duro.*
2. No tenía *mucho dinero,* pero las galletas eran baratas.
3. Tenía mucha prisa, así es que *anduvo muy rápidamente.*
4. Él no *retrocedió.* Siguió adelante.

2 **La flora** Contesten.

1. ¿Viste muchas palmas en la playa? (sí)
2. ¿También había flores? (no)
3. ¿Crecen muchas yerbas allí? (pocas)

3 **El malo** Completen.

1. No quiero verlo. Si lo veo en mi casa lo voy a _____ enseguida.
2. Lo que él dijo no es verdad, es un _____, una mentira.
3. Porque él es una bestia, no tiene _____.

Búcate plata

Nicolás Guillén

Introducción El poeta Nicolás Guillén (1902–1989) nació en Camagüey, Cuba. Muy temprano introdujo en sus versos el folklore afrocubano. Es el mejor cultivador de este género. Su poesía a la vez nos ofrece magníficas escenas costumbristas y un fervoroso ataque contra la explotación del negro antillano.

En *Búcate plata* Guillén emplea el habla de los negros cubanos. En el poema la mujer lamenta no poder gozar de las comodidades que tienen otros. Ella siente pena por el hombre, pero «hay que comer». Ella le llama «mi negro». En las Antillas, decirle a una persona querida «mi negro» o «mi negra» es expresarle cariño.

Camagüey, Cuba

Búcate plata

Búcate plata,
búcate plata,
porque no doy un paso má;
etoy a arró con galleta,
na má

Yo bien sé como etá tó,
pero viejo, hay que comer:
búcate plata,
búcate plata,
porque me voy a correr.

Depué dirán que soy mala,
y no me querrán tratar°,
pero amor con hambre, viejo,
¡qué va!
Con tanto zapato nuevo,
¡qué va!
Con tanto reló, compadre,
¡qué va!
Con tanto lujo°, mi negro,
¡qué va!

tratar *tener alguna relación con una persona*

lujo *opulencia, riqueza*

Versos sencillos

José Martí

Introducción Ensayista, poeta y sobre todo patriota cubano, José Martí (1853–1895) luchó y dio su vida por la independencia de su país. Estudió en España, en Zaragoza. Amigo de la «madre patria» pero enemigo de su política colonialista, comenzó su lucha a los dieciséis años cuando fue arrestado y exiliado. Mantuvo la lucha desde varios países hispanoamericanos y Estados Unidos. Martí fue una rara combinación de poeta y hombre de acción. Se le considera una de las preeminentes figuras literarias de las Américas. Murió en la batalla de Dos Ríos en mayo de 1895.

Martí escribió cuarenta y seis *Versos sencillos.* He aquí un fragmento del verso I.

Versos sencillos

I

Yo soy un hombre sincero
De donde crece la palma.
Y antes de morirme quiero
Echar mis versos del alma.

Yo vengo de todas partes,
Y hacia todas partes voy:
Arte soy entre las artes,
En los montes, monte soy.

Yo sé los nombres extraños
De las yerbas y las flores,
Y de mortales engaños,
Y de sublimes dolores.

Pinar del Río, Cuba

A Bolívar

Luis Lloréns Torres

Introducción El poeta y periodista puertorriqueño Luis Lloréns Torres (1876–1944) hizo sus estudios primarios y secundarios en Puerto Rico. Después estudió en las universidades de Barcelona y Granada en España.

Regresó a Puerto Rico en 1901 donde comenzó su actividad como autor. En gran parte de la poesía de Luis Lloréns Torres se encuentran el costumbrismo y el folklore del campo puertorriqueño. Pero en el poema que sigue canta de las hazañas del gran héroe latinoamericano Simón Bolívar.

A Bolívar

Político, militar, héroe, orador y poeta
y en todo grande. Como las tierras libertadas por él,
que no nació hijo de patria alguna
sino que muchas patrias nacieron hijas dél.

Tenía la valentía del que lleva una espada,
tenía la cortesía del que lleva una flor,
y entrando en los salones arrojaba la espada,
y entrando en los combates arrojaba la flor.

Los picos del Ande no eran más a sus ojos,
que signos admirativos de sus arrojos.
Fue un soldado poeta. Fue un poeta soldado.

Y cada pueblo libertado, era una hazaña del poeta
y era un poema del soldado.
Y fue crucificado.

Estatua de Simón Bolívar

¿Comprendes?

A ***Búcate plata*** Pareen.

1. arroz
2. nada más
3. búscate
4. está
5. después
6. todo
7. reloj

a. búcate
b. arró
c. tó
d. na má
e. etá
f. depué
g. reló

B ***Búcate plata*** Contesten.

1. ¿Qué es lo que le pide la mujer al hombre?
2. ¿Qué es lo único que ella come ahora?
3. ¿Qué va a hacer ella si las cosas no cambian?
4. ¿Qué ve ella que la hace sentir mal?

C ***Búcate plata*** Expliquen el significado.

1. … no doy un paso má;
2. Depué dirán que soy mala, y no me querrán tratar,
3. pero amor con hambre, viejo, ¡qué va!
4. Yo bien sé como etá tó.

Camagüey, Cuba

D ***Búcate plata*** Busquen donde indica…

1. que ella comprende que las cosas son difíciles
2. que ella va a abandonar a «su viejo»
3. que la gente hablará mal de ella
4. que otros tienen mucho

E ***Versos sencillos*** Contesten.

1. Dice el poeta que es de «donde crece la palma». ¿Dónde será?
2. ¿Qué quiere hacer él antes de morir?
3. ¿Dónde se encuentran sus versos?
4. ¿Qué sabe el poeta?

F ***A Bolívar*** Completen.

1. Además de militar, Bolívar fue _____, _____, _____ y _____.
2. Bolívar era tan grande como las _____ que él libertó.
3. Bolívar tiraba la _____ cuando entraba en un salón.
4. Y tiraba una _____ al entrar en un combate.

G Interpretando Expliquen.

1. La mujer en *Búcate plata* le dice al hombre:

    Depué dirán que soy mala,
    y no me querrán tratar,
    pero amor con hambre, viejo,
    ¡qué va!

    ¿Cómo interpretas tú las palabras de la mujer?

2. En el *Verso I* de los *Versos sencillos,* Martí dice lo siguiente:

    Yo vengo de todas partes y hacia todas partes voy:
    Arte soy entre las artes,
    En los montes, monte soy.

    ¿Cómo interpretas tú estas frases?

3. En *A Bolívar,* Lloréns Torres dice:

    … que no nació hijo de patria alguna
    sino que muchas patrias nacieron hijas dél.

    ¿Qué crees tú que quiere decir el poeta?

H Dando opiniones

De los tres poemas que leíste, ¿cuál te gustó más y por qué? Explica con algún detalle.

I Dialogando

En el poema *Búcate plata,* la señora le habla al hombre. Con un(a) compañero(a), entablen la conversación que tiene lugar entre los dos.

J Interpretando y analizando

¿Qué emociones sientes al leer *Búcate plata?* ¿Puedes compadecer *(sympathize)* con la señora? ¿Y con el hombre? ¿Cuál será la causa de los problemas que le traen tanta pena a la señora?

K Narrando

Escribe en forma de prosa todo lo que leíste en *Versos sencillos* de José Martí.

L Analizando

En *A Bolívar* aprendiste algunas características de la personalidad de Bolívar. Descríbelas.

Prosa Mi padre

Vocabulario para la lectura

Los hombres tallaban con una baraja.

El joven tragó algo.

Más vocabulario

el aliento la respiración
el/la cobarde una persona sin valentía
el escalofrío una sensación de frío, a veces debido al terror
la hazaña una acción importante o heroica
el temor el miedo
la virtud una cualidad moral
aturdido(a) lento por el efecto del alcohol o similar
envidiar querer algo que tiene otra persona
a hurtadillas furtivamente, a escondidas, sin que nadie se dé cuenta

¿Qué palabra necesito?

1 Historieta León tiene miedo. Completen.

1. León tiene miedo de todo, es un ____.
2. Se le ve el ____ en los ojos.
3. Y le dan ____ como si hiciera mucho frío.
4. Ni puede respirar, le falta el ____.
5. Le gusta escuchar los cuentos de las ____ de los héroes.
6. Pobre León, les ____ a los héroes porque no puede ser como ellos.

2 ¿Cuál es la palabra? Den la palabra cuya definición sigue.

1. un conjunto de pedazos de cartón que se usa para el póker y otros juegos
2. un objeto grande, de madera, que se usa para guardar vinos, pescado, etc.
3. la marca que queda después de curarse una herida
4. en estado confuso, sin todas sus facultades
5. la fuerza o el valor moral, la integridad
6. de manera furtiva, sin dejar que se note
7. hacer que una cosa pase por la boca

Mi padre

Manuel del Toro

Universidad de Puerto Rico

Introducción Este cuento es del autor puertorriqueño, Manuel del Toro. Apareció por primera vez en *Asomante,* la revista literaria de la facultad de graduados de la Universidad de Puerto Rico.

La obra literaria de Manuel del Toro no es abundante. Como tantos otros intelectuales hispanos, el señor del Toro se ha dedicado a otros intereses profesionales sin perder su vocación de escritor.

En el cuento que sigue veremos a un «guapo», un bravucón que trata de impresionar a los demás con su fanfarronería. Y veremos a un valiente de verdad.

El niño del cuento aprende una importante lección sobre la verdad y las apariencias.

Mi padre

De niño siempre tuve el temor de que mi padre fuera un cobarde. No porque le viera correr seguida de cerca por un machete como vi tantas veces a Paco el Gallina y a Quino Pascual. ¡Pero era tan diferente a los papás de mis compañeros de clase! En aquella escuela de barrio donde el valor era la virtud suprema, yo bebía el acíbar° de ser el hijo de un hombre que ni siquiera usaba cuchillo. ¡Cómo envidiaba a mis compañeros que relataban una y otra vez sin cansarse nunca de las hazañas de sus progenitores°! A Perico Lugo le dejaron por muerto en un zanjón° con veintitrés tajos de perrillo°. Felipe Chaveta lucía una hermosa herida desde la sien hasta el mentón.

Mi padre, mi pobre padre, no tenía ni una sola cicatriz en el cuerpo. Acababa de comprobarlo con gran pena mientras nos bañábamos en el río aquella tarde sabatina° en que como de costumbre veníamos de voltear las talas de tabaco°. Ahora seguía yo sus pasos hundiendo mis pies descalzos en el tibio polvo del camino y haciendo sonar mi trompeta. Era ésta un tallo de amapola° al que mi padre con aquella mansa habilidad para todas las cosas pequeñas había convertido en trompeta con sólo hacerle una incisión longitudinal.

Al pasar frente a La Aurora me dijo:

—Entremos aquí. No tengo cigarros para la noche.

acíbar *amargura, disgusto*

progenitores *padres*

zanjón *zanja o abertura larga en la tierra*

tajos de perrillo *el corte con un cuchillo*

sabatina *del sábado*

talas de tabaco *tobacco stalks*

tallo de amapola *poppy stem*

Del asombro por poco me trago la trompeta. Porque papá nunca entraba a La Aurora, punto de reunión de todos los guapos del barrio. Allí se jugaba baraja, se bebía ron y casi siempre se daban tajos. Unos tajos de machete que convertían brazos nervudos en cortos muñones°. Unos tajos largos de navaja que echaban afuera intestinos y se entraba la muerte.

Después de dar las buenas tardes, papá pidió cigarros. Los iba escogiendo uno a uno con fruición° de fumador, palpándolos° entre los dedos y llevándolos a la nariz para percibir su aroma. Yo, pegado al mostrador forrado de zinc, trataba de esconderme entre los pantalones de papá. Sin atreverme a tocar mi trompeta, pareciéndome que ofendía a los guapetones hasta con mi aliento, miraba a hurtadillas de una a otra esquina del ventorrillo°. Acostado sobre la estiba de arroz° veía a José el Tuerto comer pan y salchichón echándole los pellejos al perro sarnoso° que los atrapaba en el aire con un ruido seco de dientes. En la mesita del lado tallaban con una baraja sucia Nolasco Rivera, Perico Lugo, Chus Maurosa y un colorado que yo no conocía. En un tablero colocado sobre un barril se jugaba dominó. Un grupo de curiosos seguía de cerca las jugadas. Todos bebían ron.

Fue el colorado el de la provocación. Se acercó a donde estaba papá alargándole la botella de la que ya todos habían bebido.

—Dése un palo°, don.

—Muchas gracias, pero yo no puedo tomar.

—Ah, ¿conque me desprecia porque soy un pelao°?

—No es eso, amigo. Es que no puedo tomar. Déselo usted en mi nombre.

—Este palo se lo da usted… se lo echo por la cabeza.

Lo intentó pero no pudo. El empellón° de papá lo arrojó contra el barril de macarelas. Se levantó aturdido por el ron y por el golpe y palpándose el cinturón con ambas manos dijo:

—Está usted de suerte, viejito, porque ando desarmao.

—A ver, préstenle un cuchillo. —Yo no lo podía creer pero era papá el que hablaba.

muñones *lo que queda de un brazo o pierna amputada*

fruición *placer, anticipación de un placer*

palpándolos *tocando algo con las manos para saber como es*

ventorrillo *bodega*

estiba de arroz *montón de sacos de arroz*

sarnoso *mangy*

Dése un palo *Toma*

pelao *nadie*

empellón *empujón, golpe para mover a una persona*

Todavía al recordarlo un escalofrío me corre por el cuerpo. Veinte manos se hundieron en las camisetas sucias, en los pantalones raídos, en las botas enlodadas°, en todos los sitios en que un hombre sabe guardar su arma. Veinte manos surgieron ofreciendo en silencio de jíbaro encastado° el cuchillo casero, el puñal de tres filos, la sevillana corva... °

—Amigo, escoja el que más le guste.

—Mire, don, yo soy un hombre guapo pero usté es más que yo. Así dijo el colorado y salió de la tienda con pasito lento.

Pagó papá sus cigarros, dio las buenas tardes y salimos. Al bajar el escaloncito escuché al Tuerto decir con admiración:

—Ahí va un macho completo.

Mi trompeta de amapola tocaba a triunfo. ¡Dios mío que llegue el lunes para contárselo a los muchachos!

enlodadas *muddy*

jíbaro encastado *un puro y legítimo campesino puertorriqueño*

cuchillo casero, puñal de tres filos, sevillana corva *tres tipos de cuchillo*

¿Comprendes?

A No era cobarde. Completen.

1. El niño creía que posiblemente su padre era un _____.
2. A Paco el Gallina y a Quino Pascual muchas veces les corrían detrás con un _____.
3. El padre del niño era muy _____ a los padres de sus amigos.
4. La virtud más importante para los niños de la escuela era el _____.
5. Y el padre del niño no usaba _____.

San Juan, Puerto Rico

B Las cicatrices Contesten.

1. ¿Qué les había quitado Nolasco Rivera a unos guardias insulares?
2. ¿Qué le dejaron en el cuerpo de Perico Lugo?
3. ¿Qué tenía Felipe Chaveta entre la sien y el mentón?
4. ¿Cuántas cicatrices llevaba el padre del niño?
5. ¿En qué día de la semana ocurrió este incidente?
6. ¿Qué acababan de hacer padre e hijo antes de bañarse?

C Lo que ocurrió en La Aurora Escojan.

Amapolas

1. ¿De qué era la trompeta del niño?
   - **a.** De parte de una planta.
   - **b.** De madera y metal.
   - **c.** De papel.
2. ¿Dónde consiguió el niño la trompeta?
   - **a.** La compró en La Aurora.
   - **b.** Su padre se la hizo.
   - **c.** El niño la encontró en la escuela.
3. ¿Por qué entró el padre en La Aurora?
   - **a.** Para jugar baraja.
   - **b.** Para tomar ron.
   - **c.** Para comprar cigarros.
4. ¿Quiénes se reunían en La Aurora?
   - **a.** Los bravucones del barrio.
   - **b.** Los alumnos de la escuela.
   - **c.** Los músicos del pueblo.
5. ¿Qué es lo que palpaba y olía el padre?
   - **a.** Las talas de tabaco.
   - **b.** Los cigarros.
   - **c.** Las macarelas.
6. ¿Con qué frecuencia entraba el padre a La Aurora?
   - **a.** Nunca entraba.
   - **b.** De vez en cuando.
   - **c.** Todas las noches.
7. ¿Qué hacía José el Tuerto?
   a. Jugaba baraja. **b.** Dormía. **c.** Comía.
8. ¿Cuántas personas jugaban baraja?
   a. Tres. **b.** Cuatro. **c.** Cinco.
9. ¿Qué le ofrece uno de los hombres al padre?
   a. Un trago de ron. **b.** Un cigarro. **c.** Un árbol.
10. ¿Por qué no acepta el padre?
    a. Porque no fuma. **b.** Porque no bebe. **c.** Porque no tiene hambre.

D Analizando ¿Qué querrá decir… ?

1. ¡Dése un palo!
2. … ando desarmao.
3. … usted es más guapo que yo.
4. Ahí va un macho completo.
5. Mi trompeta de amapola tocaba a triunfo.

E Describiendo Describan.

En tus propias palabras, describe La Aurora en detalle.

F Identificando con un protagonista

Imagínate que eres el niño del cuento. ¿Qué les vas a decir a tus amiguitos cuando vuelvas a la escuela?

Remedios, Villa Clara, Cuba

G Discutiendo un problema serio

Hoy en día la «bravuconería» es un problema serio. En un grupo, discutan el problema de la «bravuconería» en su escuela o en la ciudad o pueblo donde viven. Piensen en ejemplos, en el efecto que tiene sobre otros y lo que se puede hacer para combatirla.

Literatura de Venezuela y Colombia

Una ojeada a la poesía

Vocabulario para la lectura

Los maderos con la sierra asierran la madera y el aserrín cae al suelo.

La abuela balancea al niño en las rodillas.
Su cara lleva hondas arrugas y sus manos son trémulas.

Más vocabulario

el alfeñique, alfandoque pastas dulces
el desengaño la desilusión, la decepción
la llaneza la sencillez, la modestia, la franqueza
la senda el camino, la forma o manera
fragoso(a) duro, difícil, áspero
mudo(a) silencioso, que no tiene voz
mustio(a) triste, melancólico
turbio(a) confuso, oscuro, opaco
yerto(a) rígido, muerto
alzar levantar
animarse entusiasmarse, darse vigor o energía
empañar oscurecer, hacer difícil de ver
morar residir, vivir, habitar
pregonar anunciar en voz alta

¿Qué palabra necesito?

1 **Historieta** **Los maderos** Contesten.

1. ¿Quiénes asierran la madera? ¿Los maderos?
2. ¿En el suelo hay mucho aserrín?
3. ¿Piden alfeñique para comer?
4. ¿También piden alfandoque?

2 **Historieta** **La abuela** Completen.

1. Vemos en la cara de la abuela muchas _____.
2. Las arrugas son _____.
3. Y las manos están _____. No están quietas.
4. Ella _____ a su nieto en las rodillas.
5. El niño está _____. No dice nada, mantiene el silencio.

3 **¿Cómo se dice?** Expresen de otra manera.

1. *La desilusión* le causó mucha pena.
2. Tenía la cara *triste.*
3. Se miró en el espejo pero su imagen parecía *oscurecida.*
4. No pudo moverse la mano que se quedó *inmóvil.*

4 **Historieta** **El pregonero** Completen.

1. El pregonero era un hombre sencillo. Su _____ le hacía querido del pueblo.
2. Él iba por el pueblo para _____ en voz alta las noticias del gobierno.
3. Tenía que _____ la voz para que la gente le oyera.
4. No _____ en el pueblo más de cien personas.
5. Él subía y bajaba las calles anchas y las _____ angostas.
6. Algunos caminos eran muy _____, difíciles para caminar.
7. Pero podía _____ con la idea de que su trabajo era importante para el pueblo.

Venezuela

Los maderos de San Juan

José Asunción Silva

Introducción El escritor colombiano José Asunción Silva nació en Bogotá en 1865. Murió muy joven, a los treinta y un años. Era de una familia acomodada. Estudió para diplomático, profesión que pronto abandonó a favor de los negocios. Pero tampoco tuvo éxito en ese campo. Su obra literaria se sitúa entre el romanticismo y el modernismo. En 1896 se suicidó. El poema de Asunción Silva toma como punto de partida una canción tradicional para niños. He aquí la canción tradicional.

Los maderos de San Juan
piden pan, no les dan.
Piden queso, les dan hueso,
se le atora en el pescuezo°
Y se sientan a llorar
en la puerta del zaguán°
Riqui, riqui, riqui trán.
Aserrín, aserrán,
Los maderos de San Juan
piden pan y no les dan,
piden queso y les dan hueso.
Les asierran el pescuezo.
Riqui, riqui, riqui trán.

se le atora en el pescuezo *gets stuck in their throats*

zaguán *entry hall*

Los maderos de San Juan

… Y aserrín
aserrán,
los maderos
de San Juan
piden queso,
piden pan;
los de Roque,
Alfandoque;
los de Rique,
Alfeñique;
los de Trique,
Triquitrán.
¡Triqui, triqui, triqui, tran!
¡Triqui, triqui, triqui, tran!…

Y en las rodillas duras y firmes de la abuela
con movimiento rítmico se balancea el niño,
y entrambos agitados y trémulos están…
La abuela se sonríe con maternal cariño,
mas cruza por su espíritu como un temor extraño
por lo que en el futuro, de angustia y desengaño,
los días ignorados del nieto guardarán…

Los maderos
de San Juan
piden queso,
piden pan;
¡Triqui, triqui, triqui, tran!

¡Esas arrugas hondas recuerdan una historia
de largos sufrimientos y silenciosa angustia!,
y sus cabellos blancos como la nieve están;
… de un gran dolor el sello marcó la frente mustia,
y son sus ojos turbios espejos que empañaron
los años, y que a tiempo las formas reflejaron
de seres y de cosas que nunca volverán…

… Los de Roque,
Alfandoque…
¡Triqui, triqui, triqui, tran!

Mañana, cuando duerma la abuela, yerta y muda,
lejos del mundo vivo, bajo la oscura tierra,
donde otros, en la sombra, desde hace tiempo están,
del nieto a la memoria, con grave voz que encierra
todo el poema triste de la remota infancia,
pasando por las sombras del tiempo y la distancia,
de aquella voz querida las notas volverán…

… Los de Rique,
Alfeñique…
¡Triqui, triqui, triqui, tran!…

En tanto, en las rodillas cansadas de la abuela
con movimiento rítmico se balancea el niño,
y entrambos agitados y trémulos están…
La abuela se sonríe con maternal cariño,
mas cruza por su espíritu como un temor extraño
por lo que en el futuro, de angustia y desengaño,
los días ignorados del nieto guardarán…

… Los maderos
de San Juan
piden queso,
piden pan;
los de Roque,
Alfandoque;
los de Rique,
Alfeñique;
los de Trique,
Triquitrán,
¡Triqui, triqui, triqui, tran!

Silva a la agricultura de la zona tórrida

Andrés Bello

Introducción Andrés Bello nació en Caracas, Venezuela en 1781. Murió en Santiago de Chile en 1865. Simón Bolívar fue su discípulo. Fue diplomático, jurista y gran educador. Fue el primer rector de la Universidad Nacional de Chile y tuvo gran influencia en el desarrollo cultural del país.

Quizás su mayor fama es la de filólogo. Su *Principios de Ortología* y sobre todo su *Gramática Castellana* son obras importantísimas y perdurables. La Real Academia Española de la Lengua lo nombró miembro honorario. En Hispanoamérica se le considera un líder intelectual de la independencia y el maestro de las generaciones modernas hispanoamericanas.

Como poeta, sus dos poemas fundamentales son *Alocución a la Poesía* y *Silva a la agricultura de la zona tórrida.* En este poema Bello dice que ya que la guerra se ha ganado, hay que construir la paz en una dedicación constante al cultivo del espíritu y del campo de América.

Silva a la agricultura de la zona tórrida (fragmento)

ceñida *crowned*

¡Oh, jóvenes naciones, que ceñida°
alzáis sobre el atónito occidente
de tempranos laureles la cabeza!
honrad el campo, honrad la simple vida
del labrador, y su frugal llaneza.
Así tendrán en vos perpetuamente
la libertad morada,
y freno la ambición, y la ley templo.
Las gentes a la senda
de la inmortalidad, ardua y fragosa,
se animarán, citando vuestro ejemplo.
La emulará celosa
vuestra posteridad; y nuevos nombres
añadiendo la fama
a los que ahora aclama,
¡hijos son éstos, hijos,
(pregonará a los hombres)
de los que vencedores superaron
de los Andes la cima;
de los que en Boyacá, los que en la arena
de Maipó, y en Junín, y en la campaña
gloriosa de Apurima,
postrar supieron al león de España!

Parque Nacional Canaima, Venezuela

¿Comprendes?

A ***Los maderos de San Juan*** Contesten.

1. En la canción tradicional, ¿qué piden los maderos?
2. ¿Cuándo les dan hueso?
3. ¿Qué ocurre cuando tragan el hueso?
4. ¿Qué hacen en la puerta del zaguán?
5. ¿Qué hacen para quitarse el hueso?

B ***Los maderos de San Juan*** Completen.

1. Los maderos de esta versión, además de pan y queso piden ____ y ____.
2. Las dos personas que aparecen en el poema son el niño y la ____.
3. La abuela lleva al niño sobre las ____.
4. En la cara tiene la abuela ____.
5. Y el pelo de la abuela es ____.

C ***Los maderos de San Juan*** **Interpretando**

Interpreten en sus propias palabras.

1. La abuela se sonríe con maternal cariño,
   mas cruza por su espíritu como un temor extraño
   por lo que en el futuro, de angustia y desengaño,
   los días ignorados del nieto guardarán…
2. Y son sus ojos turbios espejos que empañaron
   los años, y que a tiempo las formas reflejaron
   de seres y de cosas que nunca volverán…
3. Mañana, cuando duerma la abuela, yerta y muda,
   lejos del mundo vivo, bajo la oscura tierra,
   donde otros, en la sombra, desde hace tiempo están,
   del nieto a la memoria, con grave voz que encierra
   todo el poema triste de la remota infancia,
   pasando por las sombras del tiempo y la distancia
   de aquella voz querida las notas volverán…

D ***Silva a la agricultura de la zona tórrida***

Contesten.

1. ¿Cuáles serán las «jóvenes naciones» a las que refiere el poeta?
2. ¿De qué tienen ceñida la cabeza?
3. ¿Qué representa el laurel?
4. ¿Qué deben honrar las jóvenes naciones, según el poeta?
5. Según el poeta, si las naciones los honran, entonces ¿qué ocurrirá con la libertad?
6. ¿Y con la ambición?
7. ¿Y con la ley?
8. ¿Cómo es el camino que lleva a la inmortalidad?
9. Cuando dice el autor, «hijos son éstos, hijos… » ¿a quiénes se refiere como padres?

E *Los maderos de San Juan* Símiles y metáforas

Te acuerdas que el símil es la comparación de una cosa con otra, «tu cabello es como el oro». La metáfora es una figura retórica que consiste en una comparación tácita, «la primavera de la vida». Busca todos los ejemplos de símil y metáfora que puedas en *Los maderos de San Juan.*

F *Silva a la agricultura de la zona tórrida* Interpretando

Boyacá, Maipó, Junín y Apurima fueron escenarios de famosas batallas. Sabiendo eso, interpreta el siguiente verso:

¡... de los que vencedores superaron
de los Andes la cima;
de los que en Boyacá, los que en la arena
de Maipó, y en Junín, en la campaña
gloriosa de Apurima,
postrar supieron al león de España!

G *Silva a la agricultura de la zona tórrida* El mensaje

Acabas de leer sólo un fragmento del poema muy largo, *Silva a la agricultura de la zona tórrida.* No obstante, en este fragmento se nota el mensaje del autor. Con un(a) compañero(a), revisen el fragmento y digan, en su opinión, cual es el mensaje.

H *Los maderos de San Juan* Dando opiniones personales

Los maderos de San Juan se basa en una canción infantil. ¿Tiene un tema feliz? ¿Cuál es el tono del poema? ¿Te sorprende que se base en algo infantil? ¿Por qué?

I *Silva a la agricultura de la zona tórrida* Contando un mensaje en forma de carta

Andrés Bello les está hablando a las nuevas naciones latinoamericanas que recientemente recibieron su independencia. En forma de una carta, diles a estas naciones lo que Bello les sugiere hacer.

Caracas, Venezuela

Prosa Un día de éstos

Vocabulario para la lectura

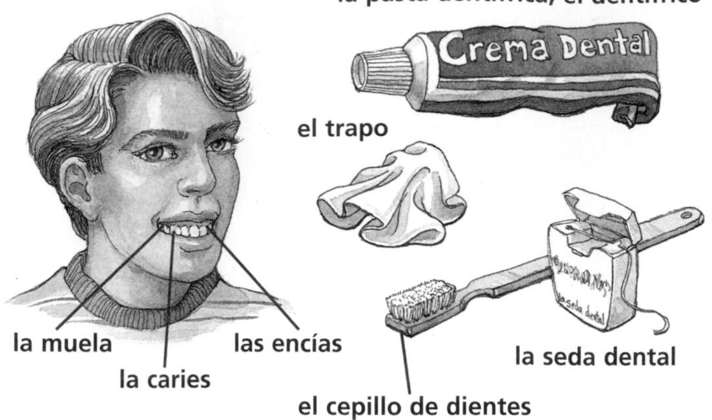

Más vocabulario

la gaveta cajón de un escritorio o armario
el trapo pedazo de tela viejo o roto
enjuto(a) flaco, muy delgado
tibio(a) ni muy caliente ni muy frío
amanecer empezar el día
apresurarse acelerar, ir rápido, darse prisa
enjuagar limpiar la boca con agua
girar dar vueltas
pulir dar brillo a una cosa

¿Qué palabra necesito?

1 El gabinete del dentista Describan lo que ven en el gabinete del dentista.

2 Historieta El diente de oro Sustituyan otra palabra.

1. El dentista era un hombre *flaco.*
2. Él *daba brillo* a un diente de oro.
3. Usaba un *pedazo de tela* para pulir el diente.
4. *Daba vueltas* al diente para mirarlo.
5. Cuando terminó, lo metió en *un cajón* del escritorio.

Un día de éstos

Gabriel García Márquez

Introducción Gabriel García Márquez nació en Aracataca, Colombia, en 1928. Ha sido periodista en Bogotá y Cartagena y ha trabajado también en Italia, España y México. García Márquez escribió cuentos cortos para los periódicos antes de escribir novelas. Se le considera uno de los más importantes novelistas de nuestros tiempos. *Cien años de soledad* y *El amor en los tiempos del cólera* son dos de sus novelas más importantes. García Márquez recibió el Premio Nóbel de Literatura en 1982.

En el cuento *Un día de éstos* el autor evoca la época de «la violencia» en Colombia. En los diez años después de 1948 murieron más de 300.000 personas, víctimas de una lucha fratricida. En este cuento, el dentista tiene la oportunidad de hacer sufrir al alcalde, hombre a quien él odia.

Un día de éstos

El lunes amaneció tibio y sin lluvia. Don Aurelio Escovar, dentista sin título y buen madrugador°, abrió su gabinete a las seis. Sacó de la vidriera una dentadura postiza° montada aún en el molde de yeso° y puso sobre la mesa un puñado de instrumentos que ordenó de mayor a menor, como en una exposición. Llevaba una camisa a rayas, sin cuello, cerrada arriba con un botón dorado, y los pantalones sostenidos con cargadores° elásticos. Era rígido, enjuto° con una mirada que raras veces correspondía a la situación, como la mirada de los sordos.

Cuando tuvo las cosas dispuestas sobre la mesa rodó la fresa hacia el sillón de resortes y se sentó a pulir la dentadura postiza. Parecía no pensar en lo que hacía, pero trabajaba con obstinación, pedaleando en la fresa incluso cuando no se servía de ella.

madrugador *early riser*
dentadura postiza *set of false teeth*
yeso *plaster*
cargadores *suspenders*
enjuto *lean*

Después de las ocho hizo una pausa para mirar el cielo por la ventana y vio dos gallinazos° pensativos que se secaban al sol en el caballete° de la casa vecina. Siguió trabajando con la idea de que antes del almuerzo volvería a llover. La voz destemplada de su hijo de once años lo sacó de su abstracción.

gallinazos *buzzards*
caballete *chimney cowl*

—Papá.

—¿Qué?

—Dice el alcalde que si le sacas una muela.

—Dile que no estoy aquí.

Estaba puliendo un diente de oro. Lo retiró a la distancia del brazo y lo examinó con los ojos a medio cerrar. En la salita de espera volvió a gritar su hijo.

—Dice que sí estás porque te está oyendo.

El dentista siguió examinando el diente. Sólo cuando lo puso en la mesa con los trabajos terminados, dijo:

—Mejor.

Volvió a operar la fresa. De una cajita de cartón donde guardaba las cosas por hacer, sacó un puente° de varias piezas y empezó a pulir el oro.

puente *dental bridge*

—Papá.

—¿Qué?

Aún no había cambiado de expresión.

—Dice que si no le sacas la muela te pega un tiro°.

te pega un tiro *he'll shoot you*

Sin apresurarse, con un movimiento extremadamente tranquilo, dejó de pedalear en la fresa, la retiró del sillón y abrió por completo la gaveta inferior de la mesa. Allí estaba el revólver.

—Bueno. —dijo. —Dile que venga a pegármelo.

Hizo girar el sillón hasta quedar de frente a la puerta, la mano apoyada en el borde de la gaveta. El Alcalde apareció en el umbral°. Se había afeitado la mejilla izquierda, pero en la otra, hinchada y dolorida, tenía una barba de cinco días. El dentista vio en sus ojos marchitos muchas noches de desesperación. Cerró la gaveta con la punta de los dedos y dijo suavemente:

umbral *doorway*

—Siéntese.

—Buenos días —dijo el Alcalde.

—Buenos —dijo el dentista.

Mientras hervían los instrumentos, el Alcalde apoyó el cráneo en el cabezal de la silla y se sintió mejor. Respiraba un olor glacial. Era un gabinete pobre: una vieja silla de madera, la fresa de pedal y una vidriera con pomos de loza°. Frente a la silla, una ventana con un cancel de tela° hasta la altura de un hombre. Cuando sintió que el dentista se acercaba el Alcalde afirmó los talones y abrió la boca.

pomos de loza *small porcelain bottles*
cancel de tela *cloth screen*

Don Aurelio Escovar le movió la cara hacia la luz. Después de observar la muela dañada, ajustó la mandíbula con una cautelosa presión de los dedos.

—Tiene que ser sin anestesia —dijo.

—¿Por qué?

—Porque tiene un absceso.

El Alcalde lo miró a los ojos. —Está bien —dijo, y trató de sonreír. El dentista no lo correspondió. Llevó a la mesa de trabajo la cacerola con los instrumentos hervidos y los sacó del agua con unas pinzas frías, todavía sin apresurarse. Después rodó la escupidera con la punta del zapato y fue a lavarse las manos en el aguamanil°. Hizo todo sin mirar al Alcalde. Pero el Alcalde no lo perdió de vista.

aguamanil *washstand*

Era un cordal inferior°. El dentista abrió las piernas y apretó la muela con el gatillo° caliente. El Alcalde se aferró° a las barras de la silla, descargó toda su fuerza en los pies y sintió un vacío helado en los riñones°, pero no soltó un suspiro. El dentista sólo movió la muñeca. Sin rencor, más bien con una amarga ternura, dijo:

cordal inferior *bottom wisdom tooth*
gatillo *forceps*
se aferró *clung to, grasped*
riñones *kidneys*

—Aquí nos paga veinte muertos°, teniente.

muertos *deaths (you have caused)*

El Alcalde sintió un crujido° de huesos en la mandíbula y sus ojos se llenaron de lágrimas. Pero no suspiró hasta que no sintió salir la muela. Entonces la vio a través de las lágrimas. Le pareció tan extraña a su dolor, que no pudo entender la tortura de sus cinco noches anteriores.

crujido *crackle, creak*

Inclinado sobre la escupidera, sudoroso°, jadeante°, se desabotonó la guerrera° y buscó a tientas° el pañuelo en el bolsillo del pantalón. El dentista le dio un trapo limpio.

sudoroso *sweaty*
jadeante *panting*
guerrera *military jacket*
a tientas *groping*

—Séquese las lágrimas —dijo.

El Alcalde lo hizo. Estaba temblando. Mientras el dentista se lavaba las manos, vio el cielo raso desfondado° y una telaraña° polvorienta con huevos de araña° e insectos muertos. El dentista regresó secándose las manos. —Acuéstese —dijo— y haga buches de agua de sal.

cielo raso desfondado *broken ceiling*
telaraña *spider web*
araña *spider*

El Alcalde se puso de pie, se despidió con un displicente saludo militar, y se dirigió a la puerta estirando las piernas, sin abotonarse la guerrera.

—Me pasa la cuenta —dijo.

—¿A usted o al municipio?

El Alcalde no lo miró. Cerró la puerta, y dijo, a través de la red° metálica:

red *screen*

—Es la misma vaina°.

misma vaina *misma molestia*

¿Comprendes?

A El dentista Contesten.

1. ¿Qué le dice al dentista su hijo?
2. ¿Qué quiere el dentista que su hijo le diga al alcalde?
3. ¿Qué le va a hacer el alcalde si no le saca la muela?
4. ¿Qué tomó el dentista de la gaveta inferior de su mesa?
5. Según el dentista, ¿cómo tenía que sacarle la muela?
6. ¿Qué le dijo el dentista al alcalde que hiciera?

B Describiendo Describan.

1. al dentista
2. el gabinete del dentista
3. al alcalde mientras el dentista le sacaba la muela

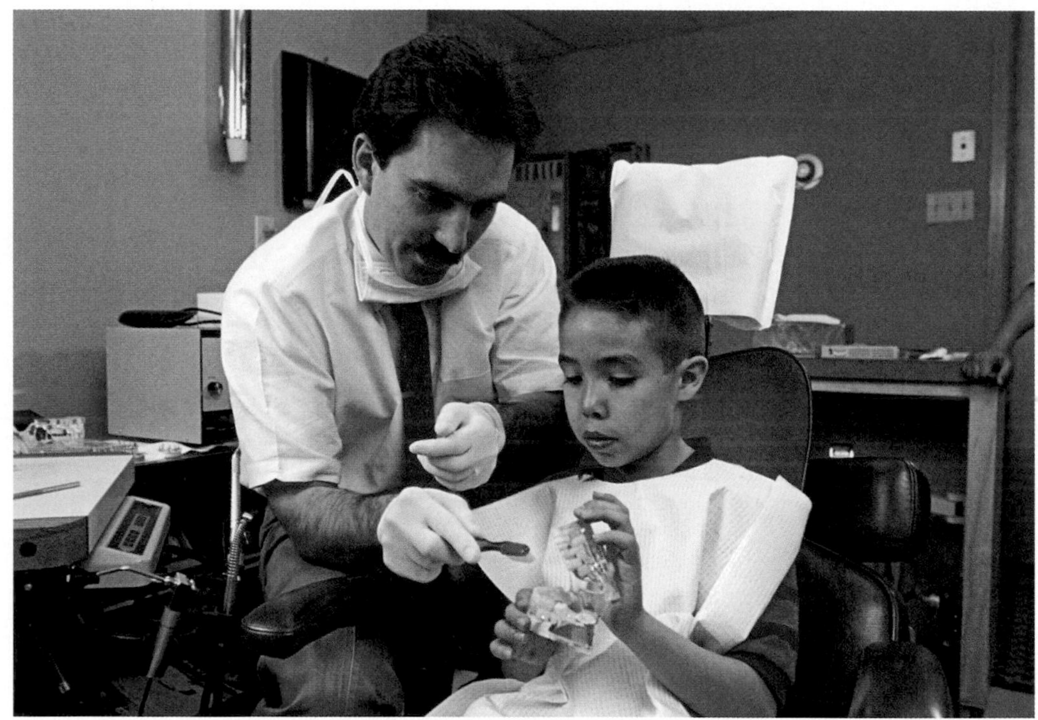

¿Comprendes?

C Interpretando Interpreten estas frases de la conversación entre el dentista y el alcalde.

1. Aquí nos paga veinte muertos, teniente.
2. Séquese las lágrimas.
3. —Me pasa la cuenta.
   —¿A usted o al municipio?
   —Es la misma vaina.

D Analizando La tensión

Entre el dentista y el alcalde existe mucha tensión. Prepara una lista de las acciones que introduce el autor para indicar esta tensión.

E Conectando la literatura con la realidad histórica

En un párrafo corto, explica como García Márquez critica la corrupción que existe en el gobierno.

F Debatiendo

En un grupo de cuatro, preparen un debate sobre este tema: ¿Son justos o aceptables los deseos de venganza y el comportamiento del dentista o no? Dos de ustedes tomarán la parte afirmativa y los otros dos la negativa.

Una ojeada a la poesía

Vocabulario para la lectura

la misa

Se celebró la misa ante un altar de mármol rodeado de cirios.

la grúa

✝

FERNANDO BUSTAMANTE FERNÁNDEZ

FALLECIÓ EN MADRID

EL DÍA 17 DE DICIEMBRE DE 2003

a los sesenta y tres años de edad

D. E. P.

Esposa, María del Carmen: madre, Concepción; madre política, Avelina; hijos, Elena, Cristina y Fernando; hermanos, hermanos políticos, sobrinos, primos y demás familia

RUEGAN una oración por su alma.

El entierro tendrá lugar hoy día 19, a las once cuarenta y cinco horas, desde el tanatorio de la M-30 (sala 3) al cementerio de Nuestra Señora de la Almudena.

* (1)

la esquela

En la cumbre del monte el águila metió sus garras en el papagayo.

Más vocabulario

el camarote lugar en un barco donde se pone la cama
la cordura buen juicio, prudencia, circunspección
el penacho grupo de plumas que tienen algunas aves en la parte superior de la cabeza
el rostro la cara
el romero una hierba fragante
arrancar quitar, sacar con violencia una cosa de su lugar
fallecer morir
velar pasar la noche al cuidado de un muerto

¿Qué palabra necesito?

1 **Historieta** **En el monte** Expresen de otra manera.

1. El águila subía hasta *el pico* de la montaña.
2. Allí sacó sus *uñas curvas* para atacar.
3. Abajo había *un ave de colores brillantes* que iba a ser su víctima.

2 **Historieta** **El muerto** Completen.

1. El moribundo había _____ a causa de un accidente.
2. Él era el operador de una enorme _____ que levantaba grandes cargas.
3. Los amigos lo _____ toda la noche.
4. No había luz eléctrica, la única luz era de unos _____.
5. Mañana saldrá una _____ en el periódico para anunciar su muerte.
6. Y habrá una _____ en su memoria en la iglesia.

3 **¿Cuál es la palabra?** Identifiquen.

1. donde uno duerme en un barco
2. el buen sentido, lo contrario de «locura»
3. una hierba aromática
4. quitar con fuerza
5. una piedra muy bella que se usa para monumentos

4 **¿Cuál es la palabra?** Contesten.

1. ¿Qué llevaba el rey en la cabeza?
2. ¿De qué ave eran las plumas del penacho?
3. ¿Qué tipo de chile usaban los cocineros?
4. ¿Qué usaban para mezclar los ingredientes?

5 **La cocina** Identifiquen.

1.

2.

3.

4.

Requiem

José Hierro

José Hierro con Juan Carlos, rey de España

Introducción José Hierro nació en Madrid en 1922. Aunque madrileño por nacimiento, vivió muchos años en Santander en el norte del país. Su obra poética se divide en dos grupos: de reportaje o narrativa y alucinaciones. Durante su vida literaria de más de medio siglo recibió varios premios, incluso el *Príncipe de Asturias* en 1981. José Hierro murió en 2002. Cuando Hierro escribió *Requiem,* España, pobre y devastada, todavía no se había recuperado de su guerra civil. Miles de españoles salieron del país para encontrar trabajo en el extranjero. En *Requiem* el poeta reflexiona ante la esquela de un inmigrante español muerto a consecuencia de un accidente laboral en Estados Unidos.

Requiem

Manuel del Río, natural°
de España, ha fallecido el sábado
11 de mayo, a consecuencia
de un accidente. Su cadáver
está tendido° en D´Agostino
Funeral Home, Haskell, New Jersey.
Se dirá una misa cantada
A las 9:30, en St. Francis.

Es una historia que comienza
con sol y piedra, y que termina
sobre una mesa, en D´Agostino,
con flores y cirios eléctricos.
Es una historia que comienza
en una orilla del Atlántico.
Continúa en un camarote
De tercera, sobre las olas
—sobre las nubes—de las tierras
sumergidas ante Platón.
Halla en América su término
con una grúa y una clínica,
con una esquela y una misa
cantada, en la iglesia St. Francis.

natural *nativo*

tendido *stretched out*

La costa de Nueva Jersey

Al fin y al cabo°, cualquier sitio
da lo mismo para morir:
el que se aroma de romero,
el tallado° en piedra o en nieve,
el empapado° de petróleo.
Da lo mismo que un cuerpo se haga
piedra, petróleo, nieve, aroma.
Lo doloroso no es morir
acá o allá...

Requiem aeternam,
Manuel del Río. Sobre el mármol
en D´Agostino, pastan toros
de España, Manuel, y las flores
(funeral de segunda, caja
que huele a abetos° del invierno),
cuarenta dólares. Y han puesto
unas flores artificiales
entre las otras que arrancaron
al jardín...*Liberame Domine*
de morte aeterna...Cuando mueran
James o Jacob verán las flores
que pagaron Giulio o Manuel...

Ahora descienden a tus cumbres
garras de águila. *Dies irae.*
Lo doloroso no es morir
Dies illa acá o allá;
sino sin gloria...
Tus abuelos
fecundaron la tierra toda,
la empapaban de la aventura.
Cuando caía un español
se mutilaba el universo.
Los velaban no en D´Agostino
Funeral Home, sino entre hogueras,
entre caballos y armas. Héroes
para siempre. Estatuas de rostro
borrado°. Vestidos aun
sus colores de papagayo
de poder y de fantasía.

al fin y al cabo *when all is said and done*

tallado *engraving*

empapado *oils anointed to the dying, a Roman Catholic rite*

abetos *spruce*

Un águila

borrado *impreciso, desaparecido*

Él no ha caído así. No ha muerto
por ninguna locura hermosa.
(Hace mucho que el español
muere de anónimo y cordura,
o en locuras desgarradoras°
entre hermanos: cuando acuchilla
pellejos de vino° derrama
sangre fraterna.) Vino un día
porque su tierra es pobre. El mundo
—*Liberame Domine*—es patria.
Y ha muerto. No fundó ciudades.
No dio su nombre a un mar. No hizo
más que morir por diecisiete
dólares (él los pensaría
en pesetas) *Requiem aeternam.*
Y en D´Agostino lo visitan
los polacos, los irlandeses,
los españoles, los que mueren
en el week-end.

Requiem aeternam.
Definitivamente todo
ha terminado. Su cadáver
está tendido en D´Agostino
Funeral Home. Haskell, New Jersey.
Se dirá una misa cantada
por su alma.
Me he limitado
a reflejar aquí una esquela
de un periódico de New York.
Objetivamente. Sin vuelo
en el verso. Objetivamente.
Un español como millones
de españoles. No he dicho a nadie
que estuve a punto de llorar.

desgarradoras *heartbreaking*

pellejos de vino *wineskins*

Tamalada

Angela de Hoyos

Introducción Ángela de Hoyos nació en México, en el pueblo de Coahuila. Cuando ella era muy joven, su familia se mudó a San Antonio, Texas. Su poesía ha sido reconocida internacionalmente. Ha recibido premios en Alemania, Argentina, India e Italia tanto como en Estados Unidos. Ángela de Hoyos es una de las más famosas intérpretes de la poesía «chicana». La poeta con frecuencia emplea el inglés y el español en el mismo poema—lo que se ve en *Tamalada.* Una tamalada es una reunión de familiares o amigos para preparar tamales. Significa mucho más que la simple preparación de un plato.

Tamalada de Carmen Lomas Garza

Tamalada

(a literary bouquet
for Diamantina Sanchez-Hatch
to honor our Azteca-Mexica
ancestors responsible for this
delicacy)

… more than the know-how
it's the cariño-love
that goes
into the makings for this feast:

El nixtamal°. Las hojas. Carne de puerco.
Chile colorado. El ajo. Comino°…

It's the symphony in the kitchen:
la cuchara canta
el molcajete baila
to the concert of hands at work
mixing el guisado: it's the hum of life
unhurried; the ballet of
fingers, spreading
—with patience of the saints—
each tiny blanket,
colchitao de masa
upon the water-softened husk of corn;
then comes the filling, now the folding,
and into the pot of steaming broth…

nixtamal *masa de maíz muy especial*

Comino *Cumin (a spice)*

colchita *rolled-out dough*

¡Ay! los tamalitos de azúcar,
de puerco, de gallina, de frijoles
con queso...
these tamalli°
danzantes
full of grace
that go
mano a mano a mano
—from la bella Diamantina
to Teri to Carol to Sylvia to Stella to Sheila—
on a journey towards completion

these tamalli, that His Majesty
the Emperor—in his sandals of
gold and precious stones, his
quetzal-plumed penacho—
would come down
from His-Royal-Highness throne,
Moctezuma Xocoyotzin
would come down
expressly
these tamalli
to praise

tamalli *corn bread wrapped in leaves (In Aztec-Nahuatl)*

¿Comprendes?

A ***Requiem*** Contesten.

1. ¿Qué le motivó al poeta a escribir la poesía?
2. ¿Qué causó la muerte de Manuel del Río?
3. ¿Dónde nació Manuel?
4. ¿En qué país murió?
5. ¿Cuál era su religión?
6. ¿En qué orilla del Atlántico comienza la historia?
7. Y, ¿en qué orilla termina?

B ***Requiem*** Completen.

1. Manuel del Río vino a América en _____.
2. Viajó en un camarote de _____ clase.
3. Un _____ causó la muerte de Manuel.
4. El trabajo de Manuel le pagaba _____ dólares.
5. El pueblo donde está la funeraria se llama _____ en el estado de _____.

C ***Requiem*** Interpreten.

1. Halla en América su término con una grúa y una clínica, con una esquela y una misa cantada, en la iglesia St. Francis.
2. Cuando mueran James o Jacob verán las flores que pagaron Giulio o Manuel.
3. Él no ha caído así. No ha muerto por ninguna locura hermosa.

D ***Tamalada*** Contesten.

1 ¿A quién le dedica la poesía?
2. Para la poeta, ¿qué es más importante que la técnica?
3. ¿Qué carnes van a usar?
4. ¿Cuáles son tres tipos de tamal que preparan?
5. ¿Quién es Moctezuma Xocoyotzin?

E ***Tamalada*** Expliquen.

¿Qué es lo que va «mano a mano a mano» de Diamantina a Teri a Carol a Sylvia a Sheila? ¿Qué hace cada una de ellas?

F **Buscando hechos biográficos**

Describe todo lo que aprendiste de la vida de Manuel del Río al leer el poema *Requiem.*

G **Haciendo comparaciones**

Con un(a) compañero(a), relean *Requiem* y busquen ejemplos que contrastan los españoles que vinieron a las Américas en la antigüedad con los que vinieron en épocas modernas.

H **Haciendo conexiones**

En un grupo, piensen en *Tamalada* y discutan la importancia de actividades similares y ejemplos en otras culturas y en sus propias familias y comunidades.

Austin, Texas

I **Haciendo investigaciones en la comunidad**

Busca a una persona de ascendencia mexicana en tu comunidad y pide una receta para tamales. Después, con un(a) compañero(a) visita un mercado local para ver si allí tienen todos los ingredientes necesarios.

J **Dando opiniones**

¿Te gustó leer *Tamalada?* ¿Qué te parece el uso de los dos idiomas en la poesía?

Prosa La casa en Mango Street

Vocabulario para la prosa

Mamá cuece la avena y la menea con una cuchara de palo.

La señora dibuja un águila y luego con hilo y aguja la crea en la tela.

Más vocabulario

la comadre la vecina, la amiga
el pulmón el órgano de la respiración
disgustado(a) malhumorado, descontento, molesto
largarse escaparse, abandonar a alguien

¿Qué palabra necesito?

1 **Historieta** **En la cocina** Contesten.

1. ¿Qué cuece la señora?
2. ¿Con qué menea la avena?
3. ¿De qué es la cuchara?

2 **Los vecinos** Completen.

1. Esa señora vecina es una _____ de mi tía.
2. Ella necesita _____ y una _____ para poder coser la camisa.
3. Ese vecino es artista y quiere un lápiz porque va a _____ una figurita.
4. Él tiene una enfermedad del _____ y le es difícil respirar.
5. Él se _____ una noche y abandonó a su familia
6. Todo el mundo está muy _____ con el hombre y nadie le habla.

La casa en Mango Street

Sandra Cisneros

Introducción La novelista, cuentista y poeta Sandra Cisneros nació en Chicago en 1954, una de siete hijos de una familia mexicana de escasos recursos económicos. Durante su niñez su familia se mudó a México y regresó a Chicago varias veces. Esta experiencia hizo que la autora se sintiera sin raíces. Estos sentimientos se reflejan en su obra *The House on Mango Street* (1983) donde la autora rememora las experiencias y conflictos que enfrenta una mujer latina.

Estudió en la Loyola University y la Universidad de Iowa y ha enseñado en escuelas secundarias y en varias universidades en California, Michigan y Nuevo México.

La casa en Mango Street ha recibido elogios de críticos, académicos, mayores y adolescentes. En la obra, Cisneros nos presenta a Esperanza, una jovencita pobre que, más que nada, quiere su propio cuarto y una casa bonita.

Cisneros escribió *La casa en Mango Street* en inglés. Fue traducida al español por Elena Poniatowska, una importante autora mexicana.

El fragmento que sigue es el capítulo titulado «Bien águila». Esperanza está en la cocina con su madre.

La casa en Mango Street

Bien águila

—Yo pude haber sido alguien, ¿sabes?—dice mi madre y suspira. Toda su vida ha vivido en esta ciudad. Sabe dos idiomas. Puede cantar una ópera. Sabe reparar la tele. Pero no sabe qué metro tomar para ir al centro. La tomo muy fuerte de la mano mientras esperamos a que llegue el tren.

Cuando tenía tiempo dibujaba. Ahora dibuja con hilo y aguja pequeños botones de rosa, tulipanes de hilo de seda. Algún día le gustaría ir al ballet. Algún día también, ver una obra de teatro. Pide discos de ópera en la biblioteca pública y canta con pulmones aterciopelados° y poderosos como glorias azules.

aterciopelados *velvety*

Hoy, mientras cuece la avena, es Madame Butterfly hasta que suspira y me señala con la cuchara de palo. —Yo pude haber sido alguien, ¿sabes? Ve a la escuela, Esperanza. Estudia macizo°—. Esa Madame Butterfly era una tonta. Menea la avena. Fíjate en mis comadres. Se refiere a Izaura, cuyo marido se largó°, y a Yolanda, cuyo marido está muerto. —Tienes que cuidarte solita— dice moviendo la cabeza.

macizo *duro*

se largó *se fue, salió*

Y luego, nada más porque sí:

—La vergüenza es mala cosa, ¿sabes? No te deja levantarte. ¿Sabes por qué dejé la escuela? Porque no tenía ropa bonita. Ropa no, pero cerebro sí.

—¡Ufa!— dice disgustada, meneando de nuevo—. Yo entonces era bien águila.

¿Comprendes?

A La madre de Esperanza Contesten.

1. ¿Cuántas lenguas puede hablar la madre?
2. ¿Qué puede hacer ella con la televisión?
3. ¿Por qué la hija la toma de la mano?
4. ¿Qué puede cantar la señora?
5. ¿Cuáles son dos cosas que a la madre le gustaría hacer?
6. ¿Qué es lo que la madre pide en la biblioteca?
7. ¿Qué escucha la madre en la cocina mientras cuece la avena?
8. ¿Qué opinión tiene la madre de Madame Butterfly?
9. ¿Qué le pasó a Izaura?
10. Y, ¿qué le pasó a Yolanda?

B Interpretando ¿Por qué dice lo siguiente la madre de Esperanza?

1. Ve a la escuela, Esperanza. Estudia macizo.
2. Tienes que cuidarte solita.
3. La vergüenza es mala cosa, ¿sabes? No te deja levantarte. ¿Sabes por qué dejé la escuela? Porque no tenía ropa bonita. Ropa no, pero cerebro sí.

C Interpretando y analizando

El capítulo de *La casa en Mango Street* que leíste se titula *Bien águila.* Sabes que el águila es un ave, pero aquí se usa la palabra como adjetivo. ¿Qué querrá decir que una persona es muy *águila?*

D Dando opiniones

Para ti, ¿cuál es el mensaje más importante de lo que leíste de *La casa en Mango Street?*

Prosa Cuando era puertorriqueña

Vocabulario para la lectura

Alguien puso un recorte de periódico y un retrato en la pizarra de corcho.

la mata de berenjenas

las llamas

Los niños se recostaron contra la pared.
La profesora le estrechó la mano al alumno.

Más vocabulario

el becado la persona que recibe una beca (scholarship)
cálido(a) caluroso, afectuoso
alzar levantar

¿Qué palabra necesito?

1 Historieta En la clase Contesten.

1. ¿Quién le estrechó la mano al alumno?
2. ¿De qué era la pizarra?
3. ¿Dónde pusieron un retrato?
4. ¿Qué más había en la pizarra de corcho?
5. ¿Quiénes estaban recostados contra la pared?
6. Cuando llamaron su nombre, ¿qué alzó la niña?
7. ¿Por qué no tenía que pagar la matrícula su familia?

2 Historieta En el campo Completen.

1. En el jardín tenían una mata de _____.
2. Estaban quemando la hierba y se veían las _____.
3. La temperatura subía, era un día muy _____.

Cuando era puertorriqueña

Esmeralda Santiago

Vista de Puerto Rico

Introducción Esmeralda Santiago nació en un pueblecito de Puerto Rico, una de once hermanos. A los trece años se mudó a Nueva York con su madre y sus hermanos. Asistió a una escuela intermedia en Brooklyn y se ganó entrada a la prestigiosa Performing Arts High School en Manhattan. Más tarde se graduó de la Universidad de Harvard con altos honores. Notarán que el título de su libro autobiográfico es *Cuando era puertorriqueña.* Santiago, como tantos otros emigrantes, reconoce que cuando vuelve a su lugar de origen, ya no es lo que era. Ya no es puertorriqueña, pero tampoco es completamente americana.

En el fragmento que sigue la joven describe su entrevista para la Performing Arts High School y, en el epílogo, una visita a la escuela después de haberse graduado.

La autora escribió el libro originalmente en inglés. Más tarde ella misma lo tradujo al español.

Cuando era puertorriqueña

Nos recostamos contra la pared. Enfrente de nosotras había una pizarra de corcho con recortes de periódico acerca de graduados de la escuela. En las orillas, alguien había escrito en letras de bloque, «P.A.» y el año cuando el actor, bailarín o músico se había graduado. Cerré mis ojos y traté de imaginar un retrato de mí contra el corcho y la leyenda «P. A. 66» en la orilla.

La puerta al otro lado del pasillo se abrió, y la señora vestida de pardo sacó la cabeza.

—¿Esmeralda?

—¡Presente! Quiero decir, aquí—alcé la mano.

Me esperó hasta que entré al salón. Había otra muchacha adentro, a quien me presentó como Bonnie, una estudiante en la escuela.

—¿Sabes lo que es una pantomima?—preguntó la señora. Señalé con la cabeza que sí—. Bonnie y tú son hermanas decorando el árbol de Navidad.

Bonnie se parecía mucho a Juanita Marín, a quien yo había visto por última vez cuatro años antes. Decidimos donde poner el árbol invisible, y nos sentamos en el piso y actuamos como que estábamos sacando las decoraciones de una caja y colgándolas en las ramas.

Mi familia nunca había puesto un árbol de Navidad, pero yo me acordaba de como una vez yo ayudé a Papi a ponerle luces de colores alrededor de una mata de berenjenas que dividía nuestra parcela de la de doña Ana. Empezamos por abajo, y le envolvimos el cordón eléctrico con las lucecitas rojas alrededor de la mata hasta que no nos quedaba más. Entonces Papi enchufó° otro cordón eléctrico con

enchufó *plugged in*

más luces, y seguimos envolviéndolo hasta que las ramas se doblaban con el peso y la mata parecía estar prendida en llamas.

En un ratito se me olvidó dónde estaba, y que el árbol no existía, y que Bonnie no era mi hermana. Hizo como que me pasaba una decoración bien delicada y, al yo extender la mano para cogerla, hizo como que se me cayó y se rompió. Me asusté de que Mami entraría gritándonos que le habíamos roto una de sus figuras favoritas. Cuando empecé a recoger los fragmentos delicados de cristal invisible, una voz nos interrumpió y dijo:

—Gracias.

Bonnie se paró, sonrió y se fue.

La señora elegante estiró su mano para que se la estrechara.

—Notificaremos a tu escuela en unos días. Mucho gusto en conocerte.

Les estreché la mano a las tres señoras, y salí sin darles la espalda, en una neblina silenciosa, como si la pantomima me hubiera quitado la voz y el deseo de hablar.

De vuelta a casa, mami me preguntaba qué había pasado, y yo le contestaba, «Ná. No pasó ná,» avergonzada de que, después de tantas horas de práctica con Missis Johnson, Mister Barone y Mister Gatti, después del gasto de ropa y zapatos nuevos, después de que Mami tuvo que coger el día libre sin paga para llevarme hasta Manhattan, después de todo eso, no había pasado la prueba y nunca jamás saldría de Brooklyn.

Epílogo: un día de éstos

El mismo jíbaro° con diferente caballo. (refrán puertorriqueño)

jíbaro *campesino puertorriqueño*

Diez años después de mi graduación de Performing Arts High School, volví a visitar la escuela. Estaba viviendo en Boston, una estudiante becada en la universidad de Harvard. La señora alta y elegante de mi prueba se había convertido en mi mentora durante mis tres años en la escuela.

(Le habla la señora.)

—Déjame contarte otra historia, entonces. El primer día de tu primer año, no llegaste a la escuela. Llamamos a tu casa. Me dijiste que no podías venir a la escuela porque no tenías qué ponerte. Yo no estaba segura de si estabas bromeando°. Pedí hablar con tu mamá,

bromeando *joking*

y tú tradujiste lo que ella dijo. Necesitaba llevarte a un sitio para que le interpretaras. Primero no me querías decir a dónde, pero luego admitiste que iban para el departamento de asistencia pública. Estabas llorando, y te tuve que asegurar que tú no eras la única estudiante en la escuela que recibía asistencia pública. Al otro día, llegaste feliz y contenta. Y ahora, aquí estás, casi graduándote de Harvard.

—Gracias por hacer esa llamada.

—Y gracias a ti por venirme a visitar. Pero ahora, tengo una clase—se paró, elegante como siempre—. Cuídate.

Su abrazo cálido, fragante a perfume caro, me sorprendió.

—Gracias—le dije a su espalda.

Anduve los pasillos de la escuela, buscando el salón donde había cambiado mi vida. Quedaba al frente del laboratorio del maestro de ciencia, unas puertas más abajo del pizarrón encorchado donde alguien con letra bonita todavía escribía «P. A.» seguido por el año del graduado.

—Un día de éstos—me dije a mí misma—. Un día de éstos.

¿Comprendes?

A Esmeralda Contesten.

1. ¿Dónde se recostaron las estudiantes?
2. ¿Qué había enfrente de ellas?
3. ¿De qué eran los recortes en la pizarra de corcho?
4. Para Esmeralda, ¿qué significaría «66» en la pizarra?
5. ¿Cuándo alzó la mano Esmeralda?
6. ¿Quién era Bonnie?
7. ¿Qué le preguntó la señora a Esmeralda?
8. ¿Alrededor de qué ponían lucecitas Esmeralda y su papá?
9. ¿A quiénes les estrechó la mano Esmeralda?
10. ¿Qué separaba las parcelas de doña Ana y los Santiago?

B Buscando hechos Completen.

1. La pantomima consistía en decorar un _____ de _____.
2. En la pantomima, Esmeralda y Bonnie pretendían ser _____.
3. Las ramas de la mata de berenjena se doblaban con el peso de las _____.
4. Con tantas luces la mata parecía estar en _____.
5. La señora dijo que en unos días ellos notificarían a la _____ de Esmeralda.
6. Cuando su madre le preguntó lo que había pasado, Esmeralda contestó que _____.

C Interpretando

1. ¿Por qué se sentía avergonzada la niña cuando la madre le preguntó qué había pasado?
2. ¿Qué significa el refrán *El mismo jíbaro con diferente caballo?*
3. En el epílogo la señora le dice a Esmeralda que no estaba segura de si estaba bromeando. ¿Bromeando de qué?
4. ¿Por qué le dice Esmeralda a la señora *Gracias por hacer esa llamada?*
5. Las últimas palabras del libro son «Un día de éstos». ¿Qué querrá decir ella?

D Interpretando

En el epílogo a *Cuando era puertorriqueña* Esmeralda Santiago vuelve a su escuela y dice que busca «el salón donde había cambiado mi vida». Explica lo que ella quiere decir.

E Debatiendo

En un grupo, piensen en las selecciones que leyeron. Todas tratan de la experiencia del inmigrante en Estados Unidos. ¿Cuáles son las diferencias y las semejanzas que notan ustedes? ¿Hay algo que todos tienen en común, o no? ¿Cuál de las selecciones le afectó más a cada uno(a) de ustedes? ¿Cuál le gustó más y por qué?

Nueva York

Handbook

Verb Charts

REGULAR VERBS			
INFINITIVO	**hablar** *to speak*	**comer** *to eat*	**vivir** *to live*
PRESENT PARTICIPLE	hablando	comiendo	viviendo
PAST PARTICIPLE	hablado	comido	vivido

SIMPLE TENSES			
INDICATIVE	**hablar** *to speak*	**comer** *to eat*	**vivir** *to live*
PRESENT	hablo hablas habla hablamos habláis hablan	como comes come comemos coméis comen	vivo vives vive vivimos vivís viven
IMPERFECT	hablaba hablabas hablaba hablábamos hablabais hablaban	comía comías comía comíamos comíais comían	vivía vivías vivía vivíamos vivíais vivían
PRETERITE	hablé hablaste habló hablamos hablasteis hablaron	comí comiste comió comimos comisteis comieron	viví viviste vivió vivimos vivisteis vivieron
FUTURE	hablaré hablarás hablará hablaremos hablaréis hablarán	comeré comerás comerá comeremos comeréis comerán	viviré vivirás vivirá viviremos viviréis vivirán
CONDITIONAL	hablaría hablarías hablaría hablaríamos hablaríais hablarían	comería comerías comería comeríamos comeríais comerían	viviría vivirías viviría viviríamos viviríais vivirían

SUBJUNCTIVE	hablar *to speak*	comer *to eat*	vivir *to live*
PRESENT	hable hables hable hablemos habléis hablen	coma comas coma comamos comáis coman	viva vivas viva vivamos viváis vivan
PAST	hablara hablaras hablara habláramos hablarais hablaran	comiera comieras comiera comiéramos comierais comieran	viviera vivieras viviera viviéramos vivierais vivieran

COMPOUND TENSES

INDICATIVE				
PRESENT PERFECT	he has ha hemos habéis han	hablado	comido	vivido
PLUPERFECT	había habías había habíamos habíais habían	hablado	comido	vivido
FUTURE PERFECT	habré habrás habrá habremos habréis habrán	hablado	comido	vivido
CONDITIONAL PERFECT	habría habrías habría habríamos habríais habrían	hablado	comido	vivido

SUBJUNCTIVE				
PRESENT PERFECT	haya hayas haya hayamos hayáis hayan	hablado	comido	vivido
PLUPERFECT	hubiera hubieras hubiera hubiéramos hubierais hubieran	hablado	comido	vivido

DIRECT COMMANDS			
INFORMAL *(TÚ AND VOSOTROS FORMS)*			
AFFIRMATIVE	habla (tú) hablad	come (tú) comed	vive (tú) vivid
NEGATIVE	no hables no habléis	no comas no comáis	no vivas no viváis
FORMAL			
	(no) hable Ud. (no) hablen Uds.	(no) coma Ud. (no) coman Uds.	(no) viva Ud. (no) vivan Uds.

STEM-CHANGING VERBS				
FIRST CLASS	**-ar verbs**		**-er verbs**	
	e → ie	o → ue	e → ie	o → ue
INFINITIVE	**sentar**[1] *to seat*	**contar**[2] *to sell*	**perder**[3] *to loose*	**poder**[4] *to be able*
PRESENT PARTICIPLE	sentando	contando	perdiendo	pudiendo
PAST PARTICIPLE	sentado	contado	perdido	podido
INDICATIVE				
PRESENT	siento sientas sienta sentamos sentáis sientan	cuento cuentas cuenta contamos contáis cuentan	pierdo pierdes pierde perdemos perdéis pierden	puedo puedes puede podemos podéis pueden
SUBJUNCTIVE				
PRESENT	siente sientes siente sentemos sentéis sienten	cuente cuentes cuente contemos contéis cuenten	pierda pierdas pierda perdamos perdáis pierdan	pueda puedas pueda podamos podáis puedan

[1] *Cerrar, comenzar, despertar, empezar,* and *pensar* are similar.

[2] *Acordar, acostar, almorzar, apostar, colgar, costar, encontrar, jugar, mostrar, probar, recordar, rogar,* and *volar* are similar.

[3] *Defender* and *entender* are similar.

[4] *Disolver, doler, envolver, llover,* and *volver* are similar; however their present participles are regular—*disolviendo, doliendo, envolviendo, lloviendo, volviendo.*

SECOND AND THIRD CLASSES			
	second class		third class
	e → ie, i	o → ue, u	e → i, i
INFINITIVE	**sentir**[5] *to regret*	**dormir**[6] *to sleep*	**pedir**[7] *to ask for, request*
PRESENT PARTICIPLE	sintiendo	durmiendo	pidiendo
PAST PARTICIPLE	sentido	dormido	pedido
INDICATIVE			
PRESENT	siento sientes siente sentimos sentís sienten	duermo duermes duerme dormimos dormís duermen	pido pides pide pedimos pedís piden
PRETERITE	sentí sentiste sintió sentimos sentisteis sintieron	dormí dormiste durmió dormimos dormisteis durmieron	pedí pediste pidió pedimos pedisteis pidieron
SUBJUNCTIVE			
PRESENTE	sienta sientas sienta sintamos sintáis sientan	duerma duermas duerma durmamos durmáis duerman	pida pidas pida pidamos pidáis pidan
IMPERFECT	sintiera sintieras sintiera sintiéramos sintierais sintieran	durmiera durmieras durmiera durmiéramos durmierais durmieran	pidiera pidieras pidiera pidiéramos pidierais pidieran

[5] *Mentir, preferir,* and *sugerir* are similar.

[6] *Morir* is similar; however, the past participle is irregular—*muerto.*

[7] *Conseguir, despedir, elegir, freír, perseguir, reír, sonreír, repetir,* and *seguir* are similar. Past participle of *freír* is *frito.*

IRREGULAR VERBS	
	andar *to walk, to go*
PRETERITE	anduve, anduviste, anduvo, anduvimos, anduvisteis, anduvieron
	caber *to fit*
PRESENT	quepo, cabes, cabe, cabemos, cabéis, caben
PRETERITE	cupe, cupiste, cupo, cupimos, cupisteis, cupieron
FUTURE	cabré, cabrás, cabrá, cabremos, cabréis, cabrán
CONDITIONAL	cabría, cabrías, cabría, cabríamos, cabríais, cabrían
	caer[8] *to fall*
PRESENT	caigo, caes, cae, caemos, caéis, caen
	conocer *to know, to be acquanted with*
PRESENT	conozco, conoces, conoce, conocemos, conocéis, conocen
	dar *to give*
PRESENT	doy, das, da, damos, dais, dan
PRESENT SUBJUNCTIVE	dé, des, dé, demos, deis, den
PRETERITE	di, diste, dio, dimos, disteis, dieron
	decir *to say, to tell*
PRESENT PARTICIPLE	diciendo
PAST PARTICIPLE	dicho
PRESENT	digo, dices, dice, decimos, decís, dicen
PRETERITE	dije, dijiste, dijo, dijimos, dijisteis, dijeron
FUTURE	diré, dirás, dirá, diremos, diréis, dirán
CONDITIONAL	diría, dirías, diría, diríamos, diríais, dirían
DIRECT COMMAND (TÚ)	di

[8] Spelling changes are found in the present participle—*cayendo;* past participle—*caído;* and preterite—*caí, caíste, cayó, caímos, caísteis, cayeron.*

Verb Charts

	estar *to be*
PRESENT	estoy, estás, está, estamos, estáis, están
PRESENT SUBJUNCTIVE	esté, estés, esté, estemos, estéis, estén
PRETERITE	estuve, estuviste, estuvo, estuvimos, estuvisteis, estuvieron

	haber *to have*
PRESENT	he, has, ha, hemos, habéis, han
PRESENT SUBJUNCTIVE	haya, hayas, haya, hayamos, hayáis, hayan
PRETERITE	hube, hubiste, hubo, hubimos, hubisteis, hubieron
FUTURE	habré, habrás, habrá, habremos, habréis, habrán
CONDITIONAL	habría, habrías, habría, habríamos, habríais, habrían

	hacer *to do, to make*
PAST PARTICIPLE	hecho
PRESENT	hago, haces, hace, hacemos, hacéis, hacen
PRETERITE	hice, hiciste, hizo, hicimos, hicisteis, hicieron
FUTURE	haré, harás, hará, haremos, haréis, harán
CONDITIONAL	haría, harías, haría, haríamos, haríais, harían
DIRECT COMMAND (TÚ)	haz

	incluir[9] *to include*
PRESENT	incluyo, incluyes, incluye, incluimos, incluís, incluyen

	ir[10] *to go*
PRESENT	voy, vas, va, vamos, vais, van
PRESENT SUBJUNCTIVE	vaya, vayas, vaya, vayamos, vayáis, vayan
IMPERFECT	iba, ibas, iba, íbamos, ibais, iban
PRETERITE	fui, fuiste, fue, fuimos, fuisteis, fueron
DIRECT COMMAND (TÚ)	ve

[9] Spelling changes are found in the present participle—*incluyendo;* and preterite—*incluyó, incluyeron.* Similar are *atribuir, constituir, contribuir, distribuir, fluir, huir, influir,* and *sustituir.*

[10] A spelling change is found in the present participle—*yendo.*

	oír[11] *to hear*
PRESENT	**oigo, oyes, oye, oímos, oís, oyen**

	poder *to be able*
PRESENT PARTICIPLE	**pudiendo**
PRETERITE	**pude, pudiste, pudo, pudimos, pudisteis, pudieron**
FUTURE	**podré, podrás, podrá, podremos, podréis, podrán**
CONDITIONAL	**podría, podrías, podría, podríamos, podríais, podrían**

	poner *to put, to place*
PAST PARTICIPLE	**puesto**
PRESENT	**pongo, pones, pone, ponemos, ponéis, ponen**
PRETERITE	**puse, pusiste, puso, pusimos, pusisteis, pusieron**
FUTURE	**pondré, pondrás, pondrá, pondremos, pondréis, pondrán**
CONDITIONAL	**pondría, pondrías, pondría, pondríamos, pondríais, pondrían**
DIRECT COMMAND (TÚ)	**pon**

	producir *to produce*
PRESENT	**produzco, produces, produce, producimos, producís, producen**
PRETERITE	**produje, produjiste, produjo, produjimos, produjisteis, produjeron**

	querer *to wish, to want*
PRETERITE	**quise, quisiste, quiso, quisimos, quisisteis, quisieron**
FUTURE	**querré, querrás, querrá, querremos, querréis, querrán**
CONDITIONAL	**querría, querrías, querría, querríamos, querríais, querrían**

	saber *to know*
PRESENT	**sé, sabes, sabe, sabemos, sabéis, saben**
PRESENT SUBJUNCTIVE	**sepa, sepas, sepa, sepamos, sepáis, sepan**
PRETERITE	**supe, supiste, supo, supimos, supisteis, supieron**
FUTURE	**sabré, sabrás, sabrá, sabremos, sabréis, sabrán**
CONDITIONAL	**sabría, sabrías, sabría, sabríamos, sabríais, sabrían**

[11] Spelling changes are found in the present participle—*oyendo;* past participle—*oído;* and preterite—*oí, oíste, oyó, oímos, oísteis, oyeron.*

	salir *to leave, to go out*
PRESENT	salgo, sales, sale, salimos, salís, salen
FUTURE	saldré, saldrás, saldrá, saldremos, saldréis, saldrán
CONDITIONAL	saldría, saldrías, saldría, saldríamos, saldríais, saldrían
DIRECT COMMAND (TÚ)	sal

	ser *to be*
PRESENT	soy, eres, es, somos, sois, son
PRESENT SUBJUNCTIVE	sea, seas, sea, seamos, seáis, sean
IMPERFECT	era, eras, era, éramos, erais, eran
DIRECT COMMAND (TÚ)	sé

	tener *to have*
PRESENT	tengo, tienes, tiene, tenemos, tenéis, tienen
PRETERITE	tuve, tuviste, tuvo, tuvimos, tuvisteis, tuvieron
FUTURE	tendré, tendrás, tendrá, tendremos, tendréis, tendrán
CONDITIONAL	tendría, tendrías, tendría, tendríamos, tendríais, tendrían
DIRECT COMMAND (TÚ)	ten

	traer[12] *to bring*
PRESENT	traigo, traes, trae, traemos, traéis, traen
PRETERITE	traje, trajiste, trajo, trajimos, trajisteis, trajeron

	valer *to be worth*
PRESENT	valgo, vales, vale, valemos, valéis, valen
FUTURE	valdré, valdrás, valdrá, valdremos, valdréis, valdrán
CONDITIONAL	valdría, valdrías, valdría, valdríamos, valdríais, valdrían

[12] Spelling changes are found in the present participle—*trayendo;* and the past participle—*traído.*

	venir *to come*
PRESENT PARTICIPLE	viniendo
PRESENT	vengo, vienes, viene, venimos, venís, vienen
PRETERITE	vine, viniste, vino, vinimos, vinisteis, vinieron
FUTURE	vendré, vendrás, vendrá, vendremos, vendréis, vendrán
CONDITIONAL	vendría, vendrías, vendría, vendríamos, vendríais, vendrían
DIRECT COMMAND (TÚ)	ven

	ver *to see*
PAST PARTICIPLE	visto
PRESENT	veo, ves, ve, vemos, veis, ven
IMPERFECT	veía, veías, veía, veíamos, veíais, veían

Spanish-English Dictionary

*The Spanish-English Dictionary contains all productive and receptive vocabulary from Levels 1, 2, and 3. The numbers following each productive entry indicate the chapter and lesson in which the word is introduced. For example, **3.2** in dark print means that the word was taught in this textbook **Capítulo 3, Lección 2.** A reference to LC means the word was taught in this textbook in the Literary Companion section. A light print number preceded by I means that the word was introduced in **¡Buen viaje!,** Level 1. A light print number preceded by II means that the word was introduced in **¡Buen viaje!,** Level 2. BV refers to the introductory **Bienvenidos** lessons in Level 1. If there is no number following an entry, this means that the word or expression is there for receptive purposes only.*

a at; to
a bordo de aboard, on board, II: 7.1
a eso de at about (time), I: 4.1
a fines de at the end of
a la española Spanish style
a lo menos at least
a menudo often, II: 3.2
a pie on foot, I: 4.1
a plazos in installments
a propósito by the way
a solas alone
a tiempo on time, I: 11.1
a veces sometimes, I: 7.1
a ver let's see
abandonar el cuarto to check out, II: 6.1
abarrotes: la tienda de abarrotes grocery store, II: 4.2
la **abdicación** abdication
el **abdomen** abdomen, **5.3**
la **abeja** bee, II: 8.1; LC5
el/la **abogado(a)** lawyer, II: 14.1
abordar to get on, board
abrazar to hug, LC1
el **abrigo** overcoat, II: 4.1
abril April, BV
abrir to open, I: 8.2
abrochado(a) fastened, **3.3**
abrochar to buckle, **5.2**
abrocharse to fasten, II: 7.1
abrocharse el cinturón de seguridad to fasten one's seatbelt, II: 7.1
la **abuela** grandmother, I: 6.1
el **abuelo** grandfather, I: 6.1
los **abuelos** grandparents, I: 6.1
abundante plentiful
abundar to abound, **5.3**
aburrido(a) boring, I: 2.1
aburrir to bore
el **abuso** abuse
acabar de to have just (done something), II: 8.1
la **academia** academy, school
acariciar to caress
el **acceso** access
el **accidente** accident, II: 8.1
la **acción** action
el **aceite** oil, I: 14.2; II: 2.2
acelerar to accelerate
aceptar to accept
la **acera** sidewalk, II: 9.1
acerca de about, concerning
acercarse(a) to approach
acertar (ie) to guess right
acogedor welcoming (personality), **2.3**
acomodado(a) well-off, rich, **2.1**
acomodar to accommodate
el **acompañamiento** accompaniment
acompañar to accompany, **6.2**
aconsejar to advise
acostarse (ue) to go to bed, I: 12.1
el **acrílico** acrylic
la **actividad** activity
activo(a) active
el **acto** act (of a play)
el **actor** actor, I: 10.2
la **actriz** actress, I: 10.2
la **actuación** behavior
actualmente at the present time
la **acuarela** watercolor
acuático(a): el esquí acuático water-skiing, I: 9.1
el **acueducto** aqueduct
el **acuerdo** agreement, **5.3**
de acuerdo OK, all right; in agreement
acuñar to coin, mint
adaptar to adapt
adecuado(a) adequate, **3.3**
adelantado(a) advanced, **5.1**
adelantar to overtake, pass (car), II: 11.2
adelante ahead
además moreover; besides
además de in addition to
la **adicción** addiction
adiós good-bye, BV
adivinar to guess
admirar to admire
admitir to admit, II: 8.2
la **adolescencia** adolescence
el/la **adolescente** adolescent, teenager
¿adónde? where?, I: 1.1
el **adoquín** paving stone
la callejuela de adoquines paved stone alley, **4.1**
la **adoración** adoration
adorar to adore
adornar to adorn
el **adorno** ornament
la **aduana** customs, I: 11.2
la **adversidad** adversity
advertir (ie) to warn; to notice, **8.3**
aérea: la línea aérea airline
aérobico(a) aerobic
el **aerodeslizador** hydrofoil
el **aeropuerto** airport, I: 11.1; **1.2**
afeitarse to shave, I: 12.1
la crema de afeitar shaving cream, I: 12.1
el **afiche** poster, **7.3**
aficionado(a) fond of, I: 10.1
el/la **aficionado(a)** fan (sports)
aflojar to loosen, **8.3**
afortunado(a) fortunate
africano(a) African
afroamericano(a) African American
las **afueras** outskirts, II: 9.1
la **agencia** agency
la agencia de empleos employment agency
el/la **agente** agent, I: 11.1
el/la agente de aduana customs agent, I: 11.2
el/la agente de policía police officer
agigantado(a) huge, **8.3**
la **agonía** throes of death, agony, LC5
agosto August, BV

agotado(a) sold out, **7.2**
agradable pleasant, **2.3**
agradecer to appreciate to thank, **7.3**
agregar to add, II: 10.2
agrícola agricultural
el/la **agricultor(a)** farmer, II: 9.2
agrio(a) sour, **2.1**
el **agua** (*f.*) water, I: 9.1
el agua corriente running water
el agua mineral mineral water, I: 12.2
esquiar en el agua to water-ski, I: 9.1
el **aguacate** avocado, II: 10.2
el **águila** (*f.*) eagle, **5.1**
la **aguja** needle, LC8
el **agujero** hole
ahora now, I: 4.2
ahorrar to save
el **aire** air, II: 11.1
al aire libre outdoor (*adj.*)
el **aire acondicionado** air conditioning, II: 6.2
el **ajedrez** chess, II: 5.1
ajeno(a) another's, LC5
el **ají** chili pepper
el **ajo** garlic, I: 14.2; II: 2.2; **1.1;** LC8
el **ajuar de novia** trousseau
ajustar to adjust
el **ajuste** adjustment, **5.1**
al to the
al aire libre outdoor (*adj.*)
al bordo de alongside, on the banks of (river)
al contrario on the contrary
al lado de beside, II: 5.2
al máximo at the most
al principio at the beginning
el **alambre** wire, LC3
alarmarse to be alarmed
el/la **albañil** bricklayer, II: 14.1
la **alberca** swimming pool, I: 9.1; **1.1**
el **albergue para jóvenes (juvenil)** youth hostel, I: 12.2
el **álbum** album
la **alcachofa** artichoke, I: 14.2; II: 2.2
el **alcalde** mayor, II: 14.1
la **alcaldesa** mayor
la **alcaldía** city hall, II: 14.1
alcanzar to reach, attain, **2.3**
el **alcázar** fortress
el **alcohol** alcohol
el **alcoholismo** alcoholism
la **alegoría** allegory
alegrarse de to be glad about, II: 13.1
alegre happy
la **alegría** happiness
alejado(a) remote
el **alemán** German (language), I: 2.2
la **alergia** allergy, I: 8.2
aleve treacherous, LC5
el **alfandoque** almond-flavored sugar paste, LC7
el **alfeñique** almond-flavored sugar paste, LC7
la **alfombra** rug, **1.1**
el **álgebra** algebra, I: 2.2
algo something, I: 5.2
¿Algo más? Anything else?, I: 5.2
el **algodón** cotton, II: 12.1; **3.2**
alguien someone
algunos(as) some, I: 4.1
el/la **aliado(a)** ally, **5.1**
la **alianza** alliance
el **aliento** breath, LC6
el **alimento** food, I: 14.2; II: 2.2
allá there
allí there
el **alma** soul, LC6
almacenar to store
la **almeja** clam, I: 14.2; II: 2.2
la **almendra** almond, **1.1**
la **almohada** pillow, II: 6.2; **1.1**
almorzar (ue) to eat lunch
el **almuerzo** lunch, I: 5.2
tomar el almuerzo to have, eat lunch
alojarse to stay, lodge
la **alpargata** sandal
alquilar to rent, II: 5.2
alrededor de around, I: 6.2
los **alrededores** outskirts
el **altar** altar, LC8
alternar to alternate
el **altiplano** high plateau, II: 7.2
la **altitud** altitude, II: 7.2
altivo arrogant, haughty
alto(a) tall, I: 1.1; high, II: 4.2; **3.1**
en voz alta aloud
la nota alta high grade, I: 4.2
la **altura** height; altitude, II: 7.2
el **alumbrado** lighting, **7.2**
el/la **alumno(a)** student, I: 1.1
alzar to raise, LC7; LC8
el **amanecer** dawn, daybreak
amanecer to start the day, LC7
amar to love
la **amargura** bitterness
amarillo(a) yellow, I: 3.2
amazónico(a) Amazonian
ambicioso(a) hardworking, I: 1.1
el **ambiente** environment; atmosphere
la **ambulancia** ambulance, II: 8.1
ambulante itinerant
la **América Central** Central America
la **América del Norte** North America
la **América del Sur** South America
americano(a) American, I: 1.1
el/la **amigo(a)** friend, I: 1.1
el **amo** landlord, LC2
el **amor** love
amplio(a) ample, wide, **1.2**
amurallado(a) walled, **7.1**
una ciudad amurallada walled city, **7.1**
el/la **analfabeto(a)** illiterate person, **6.3**
el **análisis** analysis
analítico(a) analytical
analizar to analyze
anaranjado(a) orange, I: 3.2
el/la **anarquista** anarchist
ancho(a) wide, II: 4.1
la **anchoa** anchovy
anciano(a) old, I: 6.1
el/la **anciano(a)** old person
el/la **ancla** news anchor, **8.2**
la mujer ancla female news anchor, **8.2**
andaluz(a) Andalusian
andante: el caballero andante knight errant
el **andén** railway platform, I: 13.1; II: 1.1
andino(a) Andean
la **anécdota** anecdote
angelical angelical, LC5
angosto(a) narrow, II: 9.1
el **anillo** ring, II: 4.1
el **animal** animal
el animal doméstico farm animal, II: 9.2
el animal tallado carved animal, **4.1**
animarse to take heart, LC7
el **aniversario** anniversary
anoche last night, I: 9.2
el **anochecer** dusk, nightfall
el **anorak** parka, I: 9.2
la **Antártida** Antarctic
el **ante** suede, **3.2**
tela de ante (gamuza) fabric made of suede
anteayer the day before yesterday
antemano beforehand
la **antena: la antena parabólica** satellite dish, **8.2**
antenupcial prenuptial

los **anteojos de sol** sunglasses, I: 9.1
el **antepasado** ancestor, LC4
antes de before, I: 5.1
el **antibiótico** antibiotic, I: 8.2
anticipación: de anticipación ahead of time
anticuado(a) antiquated
la **antigüedad** antiquity
antiguo(a) old, ancient, II: 5.1
la **antipatía** dislike
anular to cancel (a flight)
anulado(a) cancelled, annulled *(adj.)*, **1.2**
anunciar to announce
el **anuncio** announcement; II: 7.1; advertisement, II: 14.2
el anuncio televiso television commercial
dar anuncios to make announcements, II: 7.1
añadir to add, II: 10.2
el **año** year, BV
el año pasado last year, I: 9.2
cumplir... años to be . . . years old
este año this year, I: 9.2
tener... años to be . . . years old, I: 6.1
el **Año Nuevo** New Year, II: 13.2
¡Próspero Año Nuevo! Happy New Year!, II: 13.2
apagar to turn off, 3.1
el **aparato** appliance, device, II: 3.2
el **aparcamiento** parking lot
aparcar to park, II: 11.2
aparecer to appear
la **apariencia** appearance
apartado(a) distant, **6.1**
el **apartamento** apartment, I: 6.2
la casa de apartamentos apartment house, I: 6.2
apasionado(a) passionate
el **apellido** last name
la **apendicitis** appendicitis
la **apertura** opening
la apertura de clases beginning of the school year
apetecer to hunger for
¿Qué te apetece? What are you hungry for?
aplaudir to applaud, I: 10.2
el **aplauso** applause, I: 10.2
dar aplausos to applaud, II: 10.2
recibir aplausos to receive applause, I: 10.2
aplicar to apply
aportar to contribute, **8.3**
el **apóstol** apostle
apoyar to support, **2.1**

aprender to learn, I: 5.1
apresurarse to hurry, LC7
apretar (ie) to squeeze, to tighten, **3.2**
apropiado(a) appropriate
la **aptitud** aptitude
el **apunte: tomar apuntes** to take notes, I: 4.2
aquel, aquella that
en aquel entonces at that time
aquí here
Aquí tiene (tienes, tienen)... Here is (are) . . .
por aquí right this way
el/la **árabe** Arab
aragonés(esa) from Aragon (Spain)
el **árbol** tree
el árbol de Navidad Christmas tree, II: 13.2
el **arcén** shoulder (of a road), **5.2**
el **archipiélago** archipelago
el **arcipreste** archpriest
el **arco** arc
el **área** *(f.)* area
la **arena** sand, I: 9.1
el **arete** earring, II: 4.1; **5.3**
argentino(a) Argentine, I: 2.1
el **argumento** plot
árido(a) arid, **5.1**
el desierto árido arid desert
la **aritmética** arithmetic, I: 2.2
el **arma** *(f.)* weapon
el **armario** closet, II: 6.2
la **arqueología** archeology
arqueológico(a) archaeological
el/la **arqueólogo(a)** archaeologist
el/la **arquitecto(a)** architect, II: 14.1
arrancar to pull out (up), LC8
arrastrar to drag, LC2
el **arreglo** adjustment
arrogante arrogant
arrojar to throw, to hurl, LC1; LC6
el **arroyo** stream, brook
el **arroz** rice, I: 5.2
el arroz con frijoles (habichuelas) rice with beans, **6.1**
la **arruga** wrinkle
arrugar to wrinkle
arrugarse to wrinkle, **3.2**
arruinar to ruin, LC5
el **arsenal** arsenal
el **arte** *(f.)* art, I: 2.2
las bellas artes fine arts
el **artefacto** artifact
artesano(a) artisan *(adj.)*
el/la **artista** artist, I: 10.2

artístico(a) artistic
el **arzobispo** archbishop
asado(a) roasted
asar to roast, I: 10.1
la **ascendencia** background
de ascendencia mexicana (peruana, etc.) of Mexican (Peruvian, etc.) ancestry
ascender to rise
el **ascensor** elevator, I: 6.2
asegurar to assure
asemejarse a to be similar to, **7.1**
el **aseo** restroom, II: 7.1
aserrar to saw, LC7
el **aserrín** sawdust, LC7
así so; thus
el **asiento** seat, I: 11.1
el número del asiento seat number, I: 11.1
la **asignatura** subject, discipline, I: 2.1
el/la **asistente de vuelo** flight attendant, I: 11.2
asistir to attend
el **asno** donkey
el **aspa** sail (of a windmill)
el **aspecto** aspect
áspero(a) rough
el/la **aspirante** candidate, II: 14.2
la **aspirina** aspirin, I: 8.2
astuto(a) astute
asustar to scare, **8.3**
asustarse to be frightened
atacar to attack
el **ataque** attack
la **atención: prestar atención** to pay attention, I: 4.2
atender (ie) to assist, wait on (customer), II: 4.1
atento(a) polite, courteous
aterrador(a) terrifying, **5.1**
el **aterrizaje** landing, II: 7.2
aterrizar to land, I: 11.2
el/la **atleta** athlete
atlético(a) athletic
la **atmósfera** atmosphere
las **atracciones** amusement park rides, II: 5.2
el parque de atracciones amusement park, II: 5.2
atractivo(a) attractive
atrapar to catch, I: 7.2; to trap, **8.3**
atrás behind, in the rear
atravesar (ie) to cross
atrevido(a) bold, LC3
el **atún** tuna, I: 5.2
aturdido(a) reckless, LC6
audaz audacious
los **audífonos** earphones, II: 7.1
aumentar to increase
el **aumento** increase

aun even
aún yet
aunque although
áureo(a) golden, LC5
el **auricular** telephone receiver, II: 3.2; headphone, II: 7.1
austral former Argentine unit of currency; southern, **3.1**
auténtico(a) authentic
el **autobús** bus, I: 10.1
perder el autobús (la guagua, el camión) to miss the bus, I: 10.1
el **autocar** shuttle (airport), **1.2**
automáticamente automatically, II: 7.1
el **automóvil** automobile
la **autopista** highway, II: 11.2; **1.2**
el/la **autor(a)** author, I: 10.2
la **autoridad** authority
autorizado(a) authorized
el **autorretrato** self-portrait
la **autovía** highway, II: 11.2
los **auxilios: los primeros auxilios** first aid
el **avance** advance
el **ave** *(f.)* bird, LC2
la **avena** oats, LC8
la **avenida** avenue, II: 9.1
la **aventura** adventure
la **avería** breakdown
averiado(a) broken down
la **aversión** aversion
la **aviación** aviation
el **avión** airplane, I: 11.1
el **avión de reacción** jet, II: 7.2
la **avioneta** small airplane, II: 7.2
avisar to advise
el **aviso** advice, LC2
ayer yesterday, I: 9.2
ayer por la mañana yesterday morning, I: 9.2
ayer por la tarde yesterday afternoon, I: 9.2
la **ayuda** assistance, help
ayudar to help, I: 13.1; II: 1.1
el **azafrán** saffron
el **azúcar** sugar, II: 10.1
azucarar to sugar, LC5
azul blue, I: 3.2
azul oscuro dark blue

B

el **bache** pothole
el **bachillerato** bachelor's degree
la **bacteria** bacteria
la **bahía** bay
bailar to dance, I: 4.2
el **baile** dance
bajar to lower; to go down, I: 9.2; to get off, I: 13.2; II: 1.2
bajar(se) del tren to get off the train, I: 13.2; II: 1.2
bajar las maletas to take the luggage down, II: 6.1
bajo: bajo cero below zero, I: 9.2
bajo(a) short, I: 1.1; low, I: 4.2
la nota baja low grade, I: 4.2
la planta baja ground floor, I: 6.2
balancear to balance
el **balcón** balcony, **2.1**
la **ballena** whale, **3.1**
el **balneario** beach resort, I: 9.1
el **balón** ball, I: 7.1
tirar el balón to throw (kick) the ball, I: 7.2
el **baloncesto** basketball, I: 7.2
la **banana** banana, II: 10.2
la **banca** banking
bancario(a) banking, **4.2**
la tarjeta bancaria bankcard
el **banco** bank, II: 12.2
la **banda** music band
la **banda elástica** elastic band
la **bandeja** tray, II: 7.1
la **bandera** flag
la bandera mexicana Mexican flag, **5.1**
el **bandido** bandit
el **bando** team
el **bañador** bathing suit, I: 9.1
bañarse to take a bath, I: 12.1
la **bañera** bathtub, II: 6.2
el **baño** bathroom, I: 6.2; bath
el cuarto de baño bathroom, I: 6.2
el traje de baño bathing suit, I: 9.1
barato(a) cheap, inexpensive, I: 3.2
la **barba** beard
el/la **barbero(a)** barber, II: 12.1
la **barra** bar
la barra de jabón bar of soap, I: 12.2
la barra de sujeción handrail, **1.3**
el **barril de macarelas** barrel of mackerel, LC6
el **barrio** neighborhood, II: 9.1
basado(a) based (on)
basar to base
basarse to be based
la **báscula** scale, I: 11.1
la **base** base, I: 7.2; basis
básico(a) basic
el **básquetbol** basketball, I: 7.2
la cancha de básquetbol basketball court, I: 7.2
bastante enough, rather, quite, I: 1.1
bastar to suffice, to be enough, **5.3**
el **bastón** ski pole, I: 9.2
la **batalla** battle
el **bate** bat, I: 7.2
el/la **bateador(a)** batter, I: 7.2
batear to hit (baseball), I: 7.2
la **batería** battery
batir to beat, LC5
el **batú** Taíno Indian game
el **baúl** trunk, II: 11.1
el **bautizo** baptism
el/la **bebé** baby
beber to drink, I: 5.1
la **bebida** beverage, drink, II: 7.1
la **beca** scholarship
el **becado** person with a scholarship, LC8
el **béisbol** baseball, I: 7.2
el campo de béisbol baseball field, I: 7.2
el juego de béisbol baseball game, I: 7.2
el/la jugador(a) de béisbol baseball player, I: 7.2
el/la **beisbolista** baseball player
belicoso(a) aggressive, warlike, **3.1**
la **belleza** beauty
bello(a) beautiful, pretty, I: 1.1, **2.1**
las bellas artes fine arts
bendecir to bless, LC5
la **bendición** blessing
el **beneficio** benefit
la **berenjena** eggplant, I: 14.2; II: 2.2, **1.1**
la mata de berenjenas eggplant bush, LC8
besar to kiss, LC1
bíblico(a) biblical
la **bicicleta** bicycle
ir en bicicleta to go by bike, I: 12.2
bien fine, well, BV
muy bien very well, BV
los **bienes y servicios** goods and services
la **bienvenida: dar la bienvenida** to welcome, I: 11.2
el **bife** beef
el **biftec** steak, I: 14.2; II: 2.2
bilingüe bilingual
el **billete** ticket, : 11.1; bill (currency), II: 12.2; **4.2**
un billete grande (pequeño) large (small)

denomination bill
el billete de ida y vuelta round-trip ticket, I: 13.1; II: 1.1
el billete sencillo one-way ticket, I: 13.1; II: 1.1
la **biografía** biography
la **biología** biology, I: 2.2
biológico(a) biological
el/la **biólogo(a)** biologist
el **bizcocho** cake, II: 13.1
blanco(a) white, I: 3.2
el **blanqueador** bleach
el **bloc** notebook, writing pad, I: 3.1
bloquear to stop, block, I: 7.1
el **blue jean** jeans, I: 3.2
la **blusa** blouse, I: 3.2; **3.2**
una blusa rayada (de rayos) striped blouse
la **boca** mouth, I: 8.2
boca abajo face down, II: 3.1
boca arriba face up, II: 3.1
la **boca del metro** subway entrance, II: 9.1
la **bocacalle** intersection, II: 11.2
el **bocadillo** sandwich, I: 5.1
la **bocina** horn, II: 11.1
tocar la bocina to honk the horn
la **boda** wedding, II: 13.1; **4.3**
el **bohío** hut, shack, **4.1; 7.1**
un bohío lacustre hut on river (lake)
la **bola** ball
la **boletería** ticket window, I: 9.2; **7.2**
el **boleto** ticket, I: 9.2
el **bolígrafo** ballpoint pen, I: 3.1
la **bolsa** bag, I: 5.2
la bolsa de plástico plastic bag, II: 4.2
el **bolsillo** pocket, I: 4.1; **2.2; 3.2**
bonito(a) pretty, I: 1.1
boquiabierto(a) open-mouthed
el **borde** border, side, shoulder (road), LC7
bordear to border
borrascoso(a) stormy, **3.1**
la **bota** boot, I: 9.2; **3.2**
botas de cuero leather boots
botas de tacón alto high-heeled boots
botar to throw, **4.1**
botar la pelota to throw the ball, **4.1**
el **bote** can, I: 5.2; boat, II: 5.2
la **botella: la botella de agua mineral** bottle of mineral water, I: 12.2
el **botón** button (on a machine), II: 3.1; **4.2;** (on clothing), II: 4.1; **3.2; 3.3**
un botón abrochado buttoned button
un botón desabrochado unbuttoned button
el **botones** bellhop, II: 6.1
la **bragueta** zipper (on pants), **3.2**
el **brazo** arm, I: 7.1; **5.3;** branch (of candelabra, menorah, etc.), II: 13.2
breve brief
brillante bright
brillar to shine, I: 9.1
el **brillo** brightness, LC4
el **brinco** bounce, **5.3**
dar unos brincos to be bounced off
el **bronce** bronze, I: 10.2
bronceado(a) tan
bronceador(a): la loción bronceadora suntan lotion, I: 9.1
bucear to dive; to scuba, I: 9.1
el **buceo** diving, underwater swimming, I: 9.1
buen good
estar de buen humor to be in a good mood, I: 8.1
Hace buen tiempo. The weather is nice., I: 9.1
la **buenaventura** fortune
bueno(a) good, I: 1.2
Buenas noches. Good evening., BV
Buenas tardes. Good afternoon., BV
Buenos días. Hello, Good morning., BV
sacar una nota buena to get a good grade, I: 4.2
tener buena pinta to look good (food), II: 4.2
el **buey** ox, LC2
la **bufanda** scarf, II: 4.1; **3.2**
una bufanda de cuadros checkered scarf
el **bufete del abogado** law firm, II: 14.1
el **bulevar** boulevard, II: 9.1
el **bus** bus, I: 4.1
el bus escolar school bus, I: 4.1
busca: en busca de in search of
buscar to look for, I: 3.1
la **butaca** seat (theater), I: 10.1; **7.2**
el patio de butacas orchestra seat, **7.2**
el **buzón** mailbox, II: 12.2

C

el **caballero** knight; gentleman, man, II: 4.1
el caballero andante knight errant
la tienda de ropa para caballeros men's clothing shop, II: 4.1
el **caballete** easel
el **caballito** carousel horse, II: 5.2
el **caballo** horse, LC1
pasear a caballo to go horseback riding
el **cabello** hair, II: 12.1
caber to fit, II: 7.1
la **cabeza** head, I: 7.1
el **cabezal** cushion, pillow, LC7
la **cabina** cabin, II: 7.1
la cabina de mando (vuelo) cockpit, II: 7.1
el **cacahuete (cacahuate)** peanut
la **cacerola** saucepan, II: 10.2, LC5
el **cachorro** cub, LC3
el **cacique** chief, **6.1**
el **cacto** cactus, **5.1**
cada each, every, I: 1.2
el **cadáver** cadaver
la **cadena** chain (necklace), II: 4.1; shackles, **6.1**
la cadena de oro gold chain, II: 4.1
caerse to fall, drop, II: 7.1
el **café** coffee, BV; café, I: 5.1
el café al aire libre outdoor café
el café con leche coffee with milk, I: 5.1
el café solo black coffee, I: 5.1
la **cafetería** cafeteria
la **caída** fall, 7.1
la caída de agua waterfall
la **caja** cash register, I: 3.1; box, II: 4.2
el/la **cajero(a)** teller, II: 12.2; cashier, II: 14.1
el **cajero automático** automatic teller; **4.2**
los **calamares** squid, II: 10.2
los **calcetines** socks, I: 3.2
la **calculadora** calculator, I: 3.1
calcular to calculate
el **cálculo** calculus, I: 2.2
el **caldo** broth, sauce, LC5
el **calentamiento** warmup, **5.3**
calentarse (ie) to heat
la **caleta** cove, **7.1**
la **calidad** quality
cálido(a) warm, hot (weather), **7.1;** LC8

la **calificación** qualification
la **calle** street, I: 6.2
la calle de sentido único one-way street, II: 11.2
la calle peatonal pedestrian street
la **callecita** narrow street, alley, II: 9.1
la **callejuela** alley
la callejuela de adoquines paved stone alley, **4.1**
el **calor: Hace calor.** It's hot., I: 9.1
la **caloría** calorie
caluroso(a) hot (climate), **2.1**
el **calzado** footwear, **3.2**
una tienda de calzado footwear store
el **calzón** shorts, **5.2**
calzar to take, wear (shoe size), I: 3.2
la **cama** bed, I: 8.1
guardar cama to stay in bed, I: 8.1
hacer la cama to make the bed, II: 6.2
la **cámara** camera, **8.2**
la **camarera** maid, II: 6.2
el/la **camarero(a)** waiter, waitress, I: 5.1
los **camarones** shrimp, I: 14.2; II: 2.2
el **camarote** cabin (of a boat), LC8
cambiar to change; exchange, II: 12.2; **4.2**
cambiar de tren to change trains (transfer), I: 13.2; II: 1.2
cambiar las toallas to change the towels, II: 6.2
el **cambio** change, exchange, I: 12.2
la casa de cambio foreign exchange office, II: 12.2
el tipo (la tasa) de cambio exchange rate, II: 12.2; **4.2**
el/la **cambista** money changer, II: 12.2
el **camello** camel, II: 13.2
la **camilla** stretcher, II: 8.1
caminar to walk, II: 5.1
caminar por la senda to walk along the path, II: 5.2
la **caminata: dar una caminata** to take a hike, I: 12.2
el **camino** trail, path
el **camión** bus (Mexico), I: 10.1, truck, **5.2**
el/la **camionero(a)** truck driver, 5.**2; 8.3**
la **camisa** shirt, I: 3.2; **3.2**
la camisa de mangas cortas short-sleeved shirt, II: 4.1
la camisa de mangas largas long-sleeved shirt, II: 4.1
la **camiseta** T-shirt, undershirt, I: 3.2
la **campaña** campaign
el/la **campeón(ona)** champion, II: 5.1
el **campeonato** championship, **6.3**
el/la **campesino(a)** farmer, peasant, II: 9.2
el **campo** country; field, I: 9.2
el campo de béisbol baseball field, I: 7.2
el campo de fútbol soccer field, I: 7.1
la casa de campo country home
canadiense Canadian
el **canal** channel (TV); water channel
la **canasta** basket, I: 7.2
la **cancha** court, I: 7.2
la cancha cubierta enclosed court, I: 9.1
la cancha de básquetbol basketball court, I: 7.2
la cancha de tenis tennis court, I: 9.1
la **canción** song
la **candela** candle, LC4
el/la **candidato(a)** candidate, II: 14.2
la **canica** marble (toy), LC1
la **canoa** canoe
cansado(a) tired, I: 8.1
cantar to sing, I: 4.2
el **cante jondo** traditional flamenco singing
la **cantera** quarry, LC2
la **cantidad** amount
el **canto** singing
la **caña: la caña de azúcar** sugarcane, **6.1**
el **cañón** canyon
el **capacho** cloth shopping bag
la **capital** capital
el/la **capitán** captain
el **capítulo** chapter
el **capó** hood (automobile), II: 11.1
la **cara** face, I: 12.1; LC5
la **carabela** caravel, a fifteenth century Spanish or Portuguese sailing ship, **1.1**
el **carácter** character
la **característica** characteristic
el **carbohidrato** carbohydrate
la **cárcel** prison, **6.3**
cardinal: los puntos cardinales cardinal points
la **cardiología** cardiology
el/la **cardiólogo(a)** cardiologist
el **cardo** thistle
el **cargo** charge (money), **4.2; 5.2**
el **Caribe** Caribbean
el mar Caribe Caribbean Sea
el/la **caricaturista** caricaturist
la **caries** tooth decay, LC7
el **cariño** care, **5.3**
el **carmín** carmine, LC5
la **carne** meat, I: 5.2
la carne de res beef, I: 14.2; II: 2.2
la **carnicería** butcher shop, meat market, II: 4.2
caro(a) expensive, I: 3.2
la **carpeta** folder, I: 3.1
el/la **carpintero(a)** carpenter, II: 14.1
la **carrera** race, career
la **carretera** highway, II: 11.2; **5.2**
el **carril** lane (of highway), II: 11.2
el **carrito** cart (shopping), II: 4.2; (airplane), II: 7.1
empujar el carrito to push the cart, II: 4.2
el **carro** car, I: 4.1; wagon, LC2
el carro deportivo sports car, II: 11.1
en carro by car, I: 4.1
la **carta** letter, II: 12.2
la carta de recomendación letter of recommendation
la **cartera** wallet, **2.2**
el/la **carterista** pickpocket, **2.2**
la **casa** home, house, I: 6.2
en casa at home
la casa de apartamentos (departamentos) apartment house, I: 6.2
la casa de campo country home, II: 9.2
la casa privada (particular) private house, I: 6.2
la **casa de cambio** foreign exchange office, II: 12.2; **4.2**
casado(a): estar casado(a) to be married
casarse to get married, II: 13.1
el **casco** shell, peel
el casco de guayaba guava shell (peel), **6.2**
el **casete** cassette, I: 4.2
casi almost, practically
el **caso** case, II: 7.1
castellano(a) Castillian
castigar to punish, **6.1**
el **castigo** punishment
el **castillo** castle
el **catarro** cold (illness), I: 8.1
tener catarro to have a cold, I: 8.1

el/la **cátcher** catcher, I: 7.2
la **catedral** cathedral
la **categoría** category
católico(a) Catholic
catorce fourteen, BV
caudal(oso) abundant
un río caudal(oso) abundant river, LC1
la **causa** cause
causar to cause; **2.3; 4.1**
la **caza** hunt, **5.1**
la **cazuela** pot, II: 10.1
el **CD** compact disc
el **CD-ROM** CD-ROM, II: 3.1
la **cebolla** onion, II: 10.1
la **cédula** documentation, **4.3**
la **celebración** celebration
celebrar to celebrate, II: 13.1
célebre famous
la **célula** cell
celular: el teléfono celular cell phone, II: 3.2
la **cena** dinner, I: 5.2
cenar to have dinner
la **ceniza** ash, **2.3**
el **centauro** centaur, **5.1**
el **centavo** penny
central central
el **centro** downtown, II: 5.1; center
cepillarse to brush one's hair, I: 12.1
cepillarse los dientes to brush one's teeth, I: 12.1
el **cepillo** brush, I: 12.2
el cepillo de dientes toothbrush, I: 12.2; LC7
la **cerca** fence, LC1
cerca de near, I: 6.2
cercano(a) nearby, close
el **cerdo** pig (pork), I: 14.2; II: 2.2
el **cereal** cereal, I: 5.2; grain, II: 9.2
la **ceremonia** ceremony, II: 13
cero zero, BV
cerrar (ie) to close, II: 8.2
cerrar la herida to close the wound, II: 8.2
el **cerro** hill, **3.1**
el **cese** ceasing, stopping, **8.1**
el cese de fuego ceasefire
la **cesta** basket (jai alai)
el **cesto** basket, I: 7.2
la **chabola** shack
el **chaleco** vest
el **chaleco salvavidas** life jacket, II: 7.1; **5.3**
el **chalet** chalet
el **champú** shampoo, I: 12.2
¡Chao! Good-bye!, BV
el **chaparrón** downpour, **3.1**
la **chaqueta** jacket, I: 3.2; **3.2**

charlar to chat
el **chasqui** messenger
la **chaucha** string beans
el **cheque** check (money), **4.2**
el cheque de viajero traveler's check, II: 12.2
la **chequera** checkbook, **4.2**
el/la **chico(a)** boy (girl)
el **chile colorado** red chili, LC8
chileno(a) Chilean
la **chimenea** chimney
la **china** orange (fruit)
el **chisme** gossip
la **chispa** spark, LC4
¡chist! shh!
chocar, to crash, **1.3**
el **choclo** corn, **2.1**
el **chocolate: de chocolate** chocolate *(adj.)*, I: 5.1
el **chófer** chauffeur
el **chorizo** pork and garlic sausage, II: 10.1
la **choza** hut, LC2
la choza de paja straw hut, **4.1**
la **chuleta** chop, II: 10.1
la chuleta de cerdo pork chop, II: 10.1
el **churrasco** barbecue, **6.2**
el **churro** (type of) doughnut
la **cicatriz** scar, LC6
el **ciclismo** cycling
el **cielo** sky, I: 9.1; **2.3**
un cielo despejado clear sky
la **ciencia-ficción** science fiction
las **ciencias** science, I: 2.2
las ciencias naturales natural sciences
las ciencias políticas political science
las ciencias sociales social sciences, I: 2.2
el/la **científico(a)** scientist
científico(a) scientific
cien(to) one hundred, I: 3.2
el **cierre** clasp, fastener, **3.2**
cierto: Es cierto que… It is certain that . . .
cierto(a) certain
la **cifra** number, stat, **8.3**
cinco five, BV
cincuenta fifty, I: 2.2
el **cine** movie theater, I: 10.1
la **cinta** ribbon
el **cinturón** belt, II: 4.1; **3.2**
el cinturón de seguridad seat belt, II: 7.1; **5.2**
circular to circulate, travel, drive
el **círculo** circle
la **circunspección** circumspection, LC8

el **cirio** wax candle, LC8
el **ciruelo** plum, LC3
el/la **cirujano(a)** surgeon, II: 8.2
el/la cirujano(a) ortopédico(a) orthopedic surgeon, II: 8.2
cítrico(a) citric
la **ciudad** city, II: 9.1
el/la **ciudadano(a)** citizen, **6.1**
clandestinamente secretly
la **claridad** clarity
el **clarinete** clarinet
la **clara** egg white, LC5
claro(a) clear
¡Claro! Certainly!, Of course!
¡Claro que no! Of course not!
la **clase** class (school), I: 2.1; class (ticket), I: 13.1; II: 1.1; kind, type
la apertura de clases beginning of the school year
la sala de clase classroom, I: 4.1
el salón de clase classroom, I: 4.1
primera clase first class, I: 13.1; II: 1.1
segunda clase second class, I: 13.1; II: 1.1
clásico(a) classic
clasificar to classify
el **clavado** dive (water), **6.3**
la **clave de área** area code, II: 3.2
el **claxon** horn, II: 11.1
el **clero** clergy
el **clic** click
el/la **cliente** customer, I: 5.1; hotel guest, II: 6.1
el **clima** climate
climático(a) climatic
la **clínica** clinic
el **club** club, I: 4.2
el Club de español Spanish Club, I: 4.2
el **coatí** coati, a raccoonlike animal in Central and South America, LC3
el/la **cobarde** coward, LC6
el/la **cobrador(a)** collector (financial), **3.3**
cobrar to charge
cobrar el cheque to cash the check, II: 12.2; **4.2**
la **cocción** cooking
cocer (ue) to cook, LC8
el **coche** car, I: 4.1; train car, I: 13.2; II: 1.2
el coche deportivo sports car, II: 11.1
en coche by car, I: 4.1
el **coche-cafetería** cafeteria (dining) car, I: 13.2; II: 1.2

el **coche-cama** sleeping car, I: 13.2; II: 1.2
el **coche-comedor** dining car, I: 13.2; II: 1.2
el **coche deportivo** sports car, II: 11.1
el **cocido** stew
la **cocina** kitchen, I: 6.2
cocinar to cook, II: 10.1
el/la **cocinero(a)** cook, I: 14.1; II: 2.1; **1.1**
el **coco** coconut, II: 10.2; **6.1**
el **cóctel** cocktail party
el **código** code, password, **4.2**
el **codo** elbow, II: 8.1, LC1
la **coincidencia** coincidence
el/la **cojo(a)** crippled, lame, LC1
cojo(a) lame
el **cola** soda, soft drink, I: 5.1
la **cola** line (queue), I: 10.1; tail (animal), LC3
hacer cola to line up, to stand in line, I: 10.1
el/la **colaborador(a)** collaborator
colar to strain, LC5
la **colchita** dough, LC8
la **colección** collection
coleccionar to collect, II: 5.1
el/la **coleccionista** collector, II: 5.1
la **colecta: hacer una colecta** to take up a collection
el **colector** collector
el **colegio** school, I: 1.1
el **colesterol** cholesterol
el **colgador** clothes hanger, II: 6.2
colgar (ue) to hang, hang up, **4.1**
la **coliflor** cauliflower, II: 10.1
la **colina** hill, **1.1**
el **colmado** grocery store, II: 4.2
la **colocación** placement
colocar to put, place
colombiano(a) Colombian, I: 1.1
la **colonia** suburb, colony
colonial colonial, **2.1**
el **color** color, I: 3.2
de color colored
de color marrón brown, I: 3.2
¿De qué color es? What color is it?, I: 3.2
la **comadre** friend, neighbor, LC8
el/la **comandante** pilot, captain, I: 11.2
el **combustible** fuel, **7.3**
la **comedia** comedy
el **comedor** dining room, I: 6.2
comenzar (ie) to begin
comer to eat, 5.1
comercial: la zona comercial business district, II: 9.1
el/la **comerciante** businessperson, II: 14.1
el **comercio** business
el **comestible** food, I: 14.2; II: 2.2
cómico(a) funny, I: 1.1
la **comida** food, meal, I: 5.2
la **comisaría** police station, **2.2**
la **comisión** commission
el **comité** committee
como like; as; since, I: 1.2
¿cómo? how?, what?, I: 1.1
¿Cómo está... ? How is ...?, I: 8.1
¡Cómo no! Of course!
la **comodidad** comfort
compacto(a): el disco compacto compact disk, CD, I: 4.2
el/la **compañero(a)** friend, I: 1.2
la **compañía** company
la **comparación** comparison
comparar to compare
el **compartimiento** compartment, I: 13.2; II: 1.2
el compartimiento sobre la cabeza overhead compartment, II: 7.1
el compartimiento superior overhead compartment, II: 7.1
compartir to share, **3.3**
la **competencia** competition
la **competición** competition, contest
competir (i, i) to compete
completar to complete
completo(a) full (train), I: 13.2; II: 1.2
a tiempo completo full time *(adj.)*, II: 14.2
componer to compose
comportarse to behave
la **composición** composition
la **compra** buying, II: 4.1
comprar to buy, I: 3.1
las **compras** shopping; purchases, II: 4.2
hacer las compras to go shopping, II: 4.2
ir de compras to go shopping, to shop, I: 5.2
comprender to understand, I: 5.1
comprometerse to get engaged
el **compromiso** engagement
compuesto(a) compound, LC4
la **computadora** computer, II: 3.1
común common
la **comunicación** communication
comunicarse to communicate with each other, II: 3.1
la **comunidad** community
con with
con cuidado carefully, cautiously, II: 11.1
con frecuencia often, II: 3.2
con mucha plata rich
¿Con quién? with whom?
con retraso with a delay, I: 13.2; II: 1.2
con una demora with a delay, late, I: 11.1
el **concierto** concert
conciliar to reconcile
el/la **conde(sa)** count(ess)
la **condición** condition
el **condimento** seasoning
el **condominio** condominium, II: 9.1
conducir to drive, II: 11.1
la **conducta** conduct
el/la **conductor(a)** driver, II: 11.1; **1.1**
conductual with regard to conduct, **6.3**
conectar to connect
la **conexión** connection
la **conferencia** lecture
la **confianza** confidence, **5.3**
confirmar to confirm
la **confitería** café, tearoom
Conforme. Agreed., Fine., I: 14.2; II: 2.2
confrontar to confront
confuso(a) confusing
congelado(a): los productos congelados frozen food, I: 5.2
el **congelador** freezer, II: 10.1
el **conjunto** set, collection
conmovedoro(a) moving, touching
conocer to know, to be familiar with, I: 11.1
el/la **conocido(a)** acquaintance
el **conocimiento** knowledge, understanding, **6.3**
el **conjunto** set, group, **7.2**
la **conquista** conquest
el **conquistador** conquerer
conquistar to conquer
la **consecuencia** consequence
conseguir (i, i) to get, obtain
el/la **consejero(a) de orientación** guidance counselor
el **consejo** advice, **2.3**
consentir (ie, i) to allow, tolerate
conservar to save
considerar to consider
consiguiente: por consiguiente consequently

consistir (en) to consist of
constitucional constitutional
construir to construct
la **consulta del médico** doctor's office, I: 8.2
consultar to consult, I: 13.1; II: 1.1
el **consultorio** medical office, I: 8.2
el/la **consumidor(a)** consumer
el **consumo** consumption
consumir to consume
la **contabilidad** accounting
el/la **contable** accountant, II: 14.1
el **contacto** touch
contagioso(a) contagious
la **contaminación** pollution
contaminado(a) polluted
contaminar to pollute
contar (ue) to count, **2.1**
contemporáneo(a) contemporary
contener (ie) to contain
contento(a) happy, I: 8.1; **3.3**
la **contestación** answer, response
el **contestador automático** answering machine, II: 3.2
contestar to answer, II: 3.2
el **continente** continent
la **contingencia** contingency
continuar to continue, I: 7.2
contra against, I: 7.1
contrario(a) opposite
  contrario de opposite of
  lo contrario the opposite
contrastar to contrast
el **contrato** contract, **5.2**
contribuir to contribute
el **control** inspection, I: 11.1
  el control remoto remote control, **8.2**
  el control de pasaportes passport inspection, I: 11.1
  el control de seguridad security check, I: 11.1
el/la **controlador(a)** air traffic controller
controlar to control
convencer to convince
conveniente convenient
el **convenio** pact
el **convento** convent
la **conversación** conversation
conversar to talk, speak
el **convertible** convertible, II: 11.1
convertir (ie, i) to convert, transform
la **coordinación** coordination
la **copa** cup, goblet, LC3
  la Copa mundial World Cup
la **copia** copy
copiar to copy
el/la **co-piloto** copilot, I: 11.2
la **copla** couplet
el **corazón** heart
la **corbata** tie, I: 3.2; **3.2**
el **cordero** lamb, I: 14.2; II: 2.2
la **cordillera** mountain range, II: 7.2
el **cordón** lace, shoelace **3.2**
el **cordoncillo** piping (embroidery)
la **cordura** prudence, LC8
la **coreografía** choreography
coreográfico(a) choreographic
la **córnea** cornea
el **coro** choir, chorus
la **corona** crown, **1.1**
el **correo** mail; post office, II: 12.2
  el correo aéreo airmail, II: 12.2
  el correo electrónico e-mail, electronic mail, II: 3.1
  el correo ordinario regular mail, II: 12.2
correr to run, I: 7.2; LC6
la **correspondencia** correspondence
corriente: el agua corriente running water
cortar to cut, II: 8.1; **1.1**
  cortarse el pelo to get one's hair cut
la **corte** court, II: 14.1
el **corte de pelo** haircut, II: 12.1
el **cortejo** courtship, **4.3**
cortés courteous
la **cortesía** courtesy, BV
corto(a) short, I: 3.2
  el pantalón corto shorts, I: 3.2
  las mangas cortas (largas) short (long) sleeves, II: 4.1
la **cosa** thing
la **cosecha** crop, harvest, II: 9.2
  la cosecha del maíz corn harvest
cosechar to harvest, II: 9.2
coser to sew
la **costa** coast
costar (ue) to cost, I: 3.1
costarricense Costa Rican
la **costilla** rib, II: 10.1
la **costumbre** custom
la **costura** sewing
cotidiano(a) daily, LC1
el **cráter** crater
la **creación** creation
crear to create
crecer to grow, increase, **3.3**
el **crecimiento** growth
crédito: la tarjeta de crédito credit card, I: 14.1; II: 2.1
creer to believe, I: 8.2; to think so
la **crema: la crema de afeitar** shaving cream, I: 12.1
  la crema dentífrica toothpaste, I: 12.2
  la crema protectora sunblock, I: 9.1
la **cremallera** zipper, **3.2**
criar to raise, II: 9.2
la **criatura** creature
  una criatura mítica mythical creature
el **crimen** crime, **2.2**
criollo(a) Creole
el **criollo** a person of Spanish descent born in Latin America
cristalizarse to crystallize, LC5
cristiano(a) Christian
el **cruce** crossing, intersection, II: 11.2
  el cruce de peatones crosswalk, II: 9.1
el **crucigrama** crossword puzzle, II: 5.1
  llenar un crucigrama to do a crossword puzzle, II: 5.1
la **crueldad** cruelty
cruzar to cross, II: 9.1
el **cuaderno** notebook, I: 3.1
la **cuadra** (city) block, II: 11.2
el **cuadro** painting, I: 10.2
cuadros: a cuadros check, plaid
  de cuadros checkered, **3.2**
  una bufanda de cuadros checkered scarf
¿cuál? which?, what?, BV
  ¿Cuál es la fecha de hoy? What is today's date?, BV
¿cuáles? which ones?, what?
cualquier any
cuando when, I: 4.2
¿cuándo? when?, I: 4.1
cuanto: en cuanto a in regard to
¿cuánto? how much?, I: 3.1
  ¿A cuánto está(n)... ? How much is (are) ...?, I: 5.2
  ¿Cuánto es? How much does it cost?, I: 3.1
  ¿Cuánto cuesta(n)... ? How much do(es) . . . cost?, I: 3.1
¿cuántos(as)? how many?, I: 2.1
  ¿Cuántos años tienes? How old are you?
cuarenta forty, I: 2.2
el **cuarto** room, bedroom, I: 6.2; quarter, I: 2.2

el cuarto de baño bathroom, I: 6.2
el cuarto de dormir bedroom
el cuarto doble double room, II: 6.1
el cuarto sencillo single room, II: 6.1
menos cuarto a quarter to (the hour), I: 2.2
y cuarto a quarter past (the hour), I: 2.2
cuarto(a) fourth, I: 6.2
cuatro four, BV
cuatrocientos(as) four hundred, I: 3.2
cubano(a) Cuban
cubanoamericano(a) Cuban American
cubierto(a) covered, **2.3**
cubrir to cover
la **cuchara** tablespoon, I: 14.1; II: 2.1
la cuchara de palo wooden spoon, LC8
la **cucharada** spoonful, LC5
la **cucharita** teaspoon, I: 14.1; II: 2.1
el **cuchillo** knife, I: 14.1; II: 2.1
el **cuello** neck, II: 4.1
la **cuenca** basin
la **cuenta** bill, check, I: 5.1
la **cuenta corriente** checking account, II: 12.2; 4.2
la **cuenta de ahorros** savings account
el/la **cuentista** short-story writer
el **cuento** story
la **cuerda** string (instrument); cord, rope, **2.1**
el **cuero** leather, **3.2**
botas de cuero leather boots
tela de cuero leather fabric
el **cuerpo** body, II: 8.1
el **Cuerpo de Paz** Peace Corps
la **cuesta** hill, LC2
el **cuestionario** questionnaire
¡cuidado! careful!
con cuidado carefully
el cuidado intensivo intensive care
tener cuidado to be careful
cuidar to raise, look after, care for
culminar to culminate, **4.3**
cultivar to cultivate, to grow, II: 9.2; **2.1**
el **cultivo** cultivation, growing, II: 9.2; **6.1**
culto(a) cultured
cultural cultural

la **cumbre** top, LC8
el **cumpleaños** birthday, I: 6.1
¡Feliz cumpleaños! Happy birthday!, II: 13.1
cumplir: cumplir... años to be . . . years old, I: 6.1
el **cupé** coupe, II: 11.1
el **cura** priest, LC5
la **cura** cure, treatment
el/la **curandero(a)** folk healer
curar to heal, get well
cursi flashy (person), **3.3**
el **curso** course, class, I: 2.1
el curso obligatorio required course
el curso opcional elective course

D

la **dama** lady-in-waiting, woman
la dama de honor maid of honor, II: 13.1
las **damas** checkers, II: 5.1
la **danza** dance
dañar to hurt
daño: hacerse daño to hurt oneself, II: 8.1
dar to give, I: 4.2
dar a to open onto, look out on
dar a entender to imply
dar auxilio to help
dar énfasis to emphasize
dar la mano to shake hands
dar la vuelta to turn around
dar las doce to strike twelve, II: 13.2
dar un examen to give a test, I: 4.2
dar un paseo to take a walk, II: 5.2
dar un paso to take a walk, LC6
dar una fiesta to give (throw) a party, I: 4.2
dar una representación to put on a performance, I: 10.2
datar to date
los **datos** data, information, II: 3.1
entrar los datos to enter, keyboard information, II: 3.1
de of, from, for, BV
de... a... from (time) to (time), I: 2.2
de joven as a young person
De nada. You're welcome., BV
de ninguna manera by no means, I: 1.1

¿De parte de quién? Who's calling?, II: 3.2
de repente suddenly
de vez en cuando sometimes
debajo (de) under, below, II: 7.1
deber must; should; to owe
debilitar to debilitate
la **debutante** debutante, **4.3**
la **década** decade
la **decadencia** decadence
la **decepción** deception
el **deceso** death, **4.3**
decidir to decide
décimo(a) tenth, I: 6.2
decir to say, I: 13
¡Diga! Hello! (answering the telephone [Spain]), I: 14.2; II: 2.2
decisivo(a) decisive
declarar to declare
declinar to decline
la **decoración** decoration; scenery (of a play), set, **7.2**
el **decorado** scenery (of a play), set, **7.2**
decorado(a) decorated
decorar to decorate
dedicarse to devote oneself, II: 14.1; **6.1**
el **dedo** finger, II: 4.1
el **defecto** fault, flaw
defender (ie) to defend
la **definición** definition
definir to define
definitivamente once and for all
la **deforestación** deforestation, **5.1**
dejar to leave (something), I: 14.1; II: 2.1; to let, allow
dejar un mensaje to leave a message, II: 3.2
del of the, from the
delante de in front of, I: 10.1
delantero(a) front *(adj.)*
delgado(a) thin
delicado(a) delicate
delicioso(a) delicious
demás other, rest
demasiado too (much)
la **demografía** demography
el/la **demógrafo(a)** demographer
la **demora: con una demora** with a delay, I: 11.1; **1.2**
demostrar (ue) to demonstrate
el **dénim** denim, **3.2**
tela de dénim denim fabric
la **densidad** density
dentífrico(a): la pasta (crema) dentífrica toothpaste, I: 12.2; LC7

el/la **dentista** dentist
dentro de within
dentro de poco soon
la **denuncia** report (police), denunciation, **2.2**
deparar to supply
el **departamento** apartment, I: 6.2; department, II: 14.2
la casa de departamentos apartment house, I: 6.2
el departamento de recursos humanos human resources department, II: 14.2
depender (ie) (de) to depend (on)
el/la **dependiente(a)** salesperson, I: 3.1
el **deporte** sport, I: 7.1
el deporte de equipo team sport
el deporte individual individual sport
deportivo(a) (related to) sports, I: 6.2
la emisión deportiva sports program (TV), I: 6.2
el **depósito** deposit; tank (at a gas station), **7.3**
el **derecho** right
derecho(a) right, I: 7.1
a la derecha to the right, I: 5.2
derecho straight (ahead), II: 11.2
seguir derecho to go straight, II: 11.2
la **dermatología** dermatology
el/la **dermatólogo(a)** dermatologist
derramar to spill
derrotar to defeat
desabrochado(a) unbuttoned, **3.3**
desafecto(a) hostile, **6.1**
desagradable unpleasant
desamparado(a): los niños desamparados homeless children
desaparecer to disappear, **5.1**
desarrollado(a) developed, advanced
el **desarrollo** development
el **desastre** disaster
desastroso(a) disastrous
desayunarse to eat breakfast, I: 12.1
el **desayuno** breakfast, I: 5.2
tomar el desayuno to eat breakfast, I: 12.1
descalzo(a) shoeless, LC3
descansar to rest, **5.2**
el **descanso** intermission, **7.2**
el **descapotable** convertible, II: 11.1
el/la **descendiente** descendant
descolgar (ue) to pick up (the telephone), II: 3.2
descortés impolite, **6.2**
describir to describe
descubrir to discover
el **descuento** discount
desde since, from
desear to want, wish, I: 3.2; **4.3**
¿Qué desea Ud.? May I help you? (in a store), I: 3.2
los **desechos** waste
desembarcar to disembark, I: 11.2
la **desembocadura** mouth (of a river), **7.1**
desembocar to lead, go (one street into another), II: 9.1; to empty
el **desengaño** disappointment, LC7
el **desenlace** conclusion
el **deseo** desire
el **desierto** desert, **5.1**
el desierto árido arid desert
la **desilusión** disillusionment
desinflarse to deflate, **7.3**
desorientado(a) disoriented
despachar to sell, I: 8.2
despacio slowly
despegar to takeoff (airplane), I: 11.2
el **despegue** take-off (airplane), II: 7.2
despejado(a) clear (weather), **2.3**
desperdiciar to waste, to squander, LC4
despertarse (ie) to wake up, I: 12.1
despistado(a) off-track, lost, **7.3**
después (de) after, I: 5.1; later
destilado(a) distilled
el **destino** destination, I: 11.1
con destino a to
destrozar to shatter, LC5
la **destrucción** destruction, **2.3; 4.1**
desvanecer to dissipate, **2.3**
la **desventaja** disadvantage
el **desvío** detour, **8.3**
el **detalle** detail
detenidamente carefully, thoroughly, **7.3**
el **detergente** detergent, II: 4.2
determinar to determine
detrás de behind, II: 5.2
la **deuda** debt, **7.1**
devolver (ue) to return (something), I: 7.2; **4.3**
devorar to devour, **5.1**
el **día** day, BV
Buenos días. Good morning., BV
el Día de los Reyes Epiphany (January 6), II: 13.2
hoy (en) día nowadays, these days
¿Qué día es (hoy)? What day is it (today)?, BV
la **diagnosis** diagnosis, I: 8.2
el **diálogo** dialogue
el **diamante** diamond
diario(a) daily
dibujar to draw, LC8
el **dibujo** drawing
dichoso(a) lucky, LC4
diciembre December, BV
diecinueve nineteen, BV
dieciocho eighteen, BV
dieciséis sixteen, BV
diecisiete seventeen, BV
el **diente** tooth
cepillarse los dientes to brush one's teeth, I: 12.1
el cepillo de dientes toothbrush, I: 12.2
la **dieta** diet
diez ten
la **diferencia** difference
diferente different
difícil difficult, I: 2.1
la **dificultad** difficulty
el/la **difunto(a)** deceased, **4.3**
¡Diga! Hello! (telephone), I: 14.2; II: 2.2
diminuto(a) tiny, minute
la **dinamita** dynamite
el **dinero** money, I: 14.1; II: 2.1; **4.2;** LC6
el dinero en efectivo cash, II: 12.2
el giro de dinero money order, **8.3**
¡Dios mío! Gosh!
el/la **diplomado(a)** graduate
diplomático(a) diplomatic
el **diputado: congreso de diputados** house of representatives
la **dirección** direction; address
en dirección a toward
las **direccionales** turn signals, II: 11.1
directo(a) direct
el/la **director(a)** director, principal
dirigir to direct
dirigirse a to address
la **disciplina** subject area (school), I: 2.2
el **disco** dial (of telephone), II: 3.2

el **disco compacto** compact disk, CD, I: 14.2; II: 3.1
discutir to discuss
el/la **diseñador(a)** designer
el **diseño** design
disfrutar to enjoy
disgustado(a) tasteless, LC8
disponible available
la **disputa** quarrel, argument
el **disquete** disk, diskette, I: 3.1
la **distancia** distance
distinto(a) different, distinct
distraer to distract
la **distribución** distribution
la **distribuidora** parking meter that dispenses tickets
distribuir to pass out, distribute, II: 7.1
la **diversión** amusement
divertido(a) fun, amusing
divertirse (ie, i) to enjoy oneself, I: 12.2
dividir to divide
las **divisas** foreign currency, **8.3**
la **división** division
divorciarse to get divorced
doblado(a) dubbed, I: 10.1
doblar to turn, II: 11.2
doble: el cuarto doble double room, II: 6.1
dobles doubles, I: 9.1
doce twelve, BV
la **docena** dozen, II: 4.2
el/la **doctor(a)** doctor
la **documentación** documentation
el **documento** document, II: 3.1
el **dólar** dollar, **4.2**
doler (ue) to hurt, I: 8.2
Me duele(n)... My . . . hurt(s) me, I: 8.2
el **dolor** pain, ache, I: 8.1
el dolor de cabeza headache, I: 8.1
el dolor de estómago stomachache, I: 8.1
el dolor de garganta sore throat, I: 8.1
Tengo dolor de... I have a pain in my . . . , I: 8.2
doméstico(a): los animales domésticos farm animals, II: 9.2
la economía doméstica home economics, I: 2.2
dominar to dominate
el **domingo** Sunday, BV
dominicano(a) Dominican, I: 2.1
la República Dominicana Dominican Republic
el **dominio** control, authority
el **dominó** dominos, II: 5.1
don courteous way of addressing a man
donar to donate, **2.3**
donde where, I: 1.2
¿dónde? where?, I: 1.2
doña courteous way of addressing a woman
dorado(a) golden
dormido(a) asleep
el/la **dormilón(ona)** sleepyhead
dormir (ue, u) to sleep
el saco de dormir sleeping bag, I: 12.2
dormirse (ue, u) to fall asleep, I: 12.1
el **dormitorio** bedroom, I: 6.2
dos two, BV
doscientos(as) two hundred, I: 3.2
la **dosis** dose, I: 8.2
el/la **dramaturgo(a)** playwright
driblar to dribble, I: 7.2
la **droga** drug
la **drogadicción** drug addiction
la **ducha** shower, I: 12.1
tomar una ducha to take a shower, I: 12.1
la **duda** doubt
dudar to doubt
dudoso(a) doubtful
duele(n): Me duele(n) mucho. It (They) hurt(s) me a lot., II: 8.2
el/la **dueño(a)** owner, **4.3; 6.2**
dulce sweet, **3.1**
el pan dulce sweet roll, I: 5.1
la **duración** duration
durante during
durar to last, II: 13.2
duro(a) hard, difficult, I: 2.1
el **DVD** digital video disk (DVD)

E

la **ebullición** boiling
echar to throw, LC6
echar la carta (en el buzón) to mail the letter, II: 12.2
echar (tomar) una siesta to take a nap
echarle flores to pay someone a compliment
echar raíces to put down roots
la **ecología** ecology
ecológico(a) ecological
la **economía** economics; economy
la economía doméstica home economics, I: 2.2
económico(a) economical, I: 12.2
la **ecuación** equation
ecuatoriano(a) Ecuadorean, I: 2.1
la **edad** age
el **edificio** building, II: 9.1
la **educación** education
la educación física physical education, I: 2.2
educar to educate
efectivo: el dinero en efectivo cash
el **efecto** effect
efectuar to carry out
efectuarse to take place, **4.3**
el/la **egresado(a)** graduate, **3.3**
ejemplo: por ejemplo for example
el **ejercicio** exercise, **5.3**
hacer los ejercicios to exercise
ejercitar to exercise (a body part), **5.3**
el **ejército** army
el **ejote** string beans
el the *(m. sing.)*, I: 1.1
él he, I: 1.1
la **electricidad** electricity
el/la **electricista** electrician, II: 14.1
eléctrico(a) electric
electrónico(a): el correo electrónico e-mail, electronic mail
el **elefante** elephant
el **elefante marino** elephant seal, **3.1**
la **elegancia** elegance
elegante elegant, II: 13.1
el **elemento** element
el **elenco** cast (of a play), **7.2**
la **elevación** elevation
elevado(a) elevated, high
el **elevador** elevator, II: 6.1
elevar to elevate
eliminar to eliminate
ella she, I: 1.1
ellos(as) they, I: 2.1
el **elote** corn (Mex.)
eludir to elude
el/la **embajador(a)** ambassador
la **embarcación** boat, **1.3**
embarcar to board, I: 11.2
embarque: la tarjeta de embarque boarding pass, I: 11.1
la puerta de embarque departure gate
el **embotellamiento** traffic jam, **1.2**
la **emergencia** emergency, II: 7.1

la sala de emergencia emergency room, II: 8.1
la **emisión** program (TV), I: 6.2; **8.2;** emisión
la emisión deportiva sports program, I: 6.2
emitir to emit
la **emoción** emotion
emocional emotional
empalmar to connect
empanizar to rise (bread), LC5
empañar to blur, LC7
empatado(a) tied (score), I: 7.1
El tanto queda empatado. The score is tied., I: 7.1
empezar (ie) to begin, I: 7.1
el/la **empleado(a)** employee, clerk, I: 3.1
emplear to employ
el **empleo** employment, job
la solicitud de empleo job application, II: 14.2
emprender to undertake (a journey), **6.1**
la **empresa** business; undertaking, **7.1**
el/la **empresario(a)** entrepreneur, businessperson
empujar to push, II: 4.2; **2.2**
empujar el carrito to push the cart, II: 4.2
en in; on
en aquel entonces at that time
en caso de in case of
en efectivo: el dinero en efectivo cash, **4.2**
en punto on the dot, sharp, I: 4.1
en sí in itself
el/la **enamorado(a)** sweetheart, lover
en vivo live, **8.2**
encabezar to lead, to head up, **6.3**
encaminarse a to set out for, LC3
encantador(a) charming
encantar to delight
encargarse to take charge
encender (ie) to light, II: 13.2
encestar to put in (make) a basket, I: 7.2
la **enchilada** enchilada, BV
las **encías** gums (of the mouth), LC7
encima (de) above
por encima de above, I: 9.1
encogerse to shrink, **3.2**
encontrar (ue) to find; **4.3**
encontrarse (ue) to meet
la **encuesta** survey
endosar to endorse, II: 12.2
el/la **enemigo(a)** enemy
la **energía** energy
enero January, BV
enfadado(a) angry
el **énfasis: dar énfasis** to emphasize
enfatizar to emphasize
la **enfermedad** illness
la **enfermería** nursing
el/la **enfermero(a)** nurse, II: 8.2
enfermo(a) sick, I: 8.1
el/la **enfermo(a)** sick person, I: 8.1
enfrente de in front of
el **enganche** down payment
el **engaño** deception, LC6
¡Enhorabuena! Congratulations!, II: 13.1
enjuagar to rinse out, LC7
enjuto(a) lean, skinny, LC7
el **enlace** union
enlatado(a) canned
enlazar to join; connect, **1.2**
enorme enormous
enriquecerse to get rich, **7.1**
la **ensalada** salad, I: 5.1
enseguida right away, immediately, I: 5.1
enseñar to teach, I: 4.1; to show, II: 4.1
entablar to start, begin
el **entendimiento** understanding
entero(a) entire, whole
enterrar (ie) to bury
el **entierro** burial; **4.3**
entonces then
en aquel entonces at that time
la **entrada** inning, I: 7.2; admission ticket, I: 10.1; **7.2;** entrance, II: 5.2
entrar to enter, I: 4.1
entrar en escena to come (go) on stage, I: 10.2
entre between, I: 7.1
entregar to deliver
el **entrenamiento** training
entretenido(a) entertaining
la **entrevista** interview, II: 14.2; **8.2**
el/la **entrevistador(a)** interviewer, II: 14.2
entrevistar to interview
entusiasmado(a) enthusiastic
entusiasmarse to become enthusiastic
el **envase** gas can, **7.3**
el/la **envejeciente** aging person
enviar to send
envidiar to envy, LC6
envuelto(a) wrapped
el **episodio** episode
la **época** period of time, epoch, **2.1**
el **equilibrio** equilibrium
el **equipaje** baggage, luggage, I: 11.1
el equipaje de mano carry-on luggage, I: 11.1
el **equipo** team, I: 7.1; equipment
el deporte de equipo team sport, I: 7.2
el **equivalente** equivalent
erróneo(a) wrong, erroneous
la **erupción** eruption, **2.3**
la **escala** stopover, II: 7.2
hacer escala to stop over, make a stop, II: 7.2
la **escalera** stairway, I: 6.2
la **escalera mecánica** escalator, II: 9.1
los **escalofríos** chills, I: 8.1, LC6
escamotear to secretly take
escapar to escape
el **escaparate** shop window, II: 4.1
la **escasez** shortage, **7.3**
escaso(a) scarce, **2.1**
la **escena** stage
entrar en escena to come (go) on stage, I: 10.2
el **escenario** scenery, set (theater), I: 10.2; **7.2**
el **escenografía** scenery (of a play), set, **7.2**
escoger to choose
escolar (related to) school, I: 2.1
el bus escolar school bus, I: 4.1
el horario escolar school schedule
la vida escolar school life
los materiales escolares school supplies, I: 3.1
esconder to hide
escondido(a) hidden
a escondidas secretly, **8.1**
espeso(a) thick, dense, **7.1**
escribir to write, I: 5.1
escuchar to listen (to), I: 4.2
el **escudero** squire, knight's attendant
la **escuela** school, I: 1.1
la escuela intermedia middle school
la escuela primaria elementary school
la escuela secundaria high school, I: 1.1
la escuela superior high school
el/la **escultor(a)** sculptor, I: 10.2
la **escultura** sculpture
la **escupidera** spit cup, LC7
ese(a) that
esencial essential

la **esmeralda** emerald
eso that (one)
a eso de at about (time), I: 4.1
esos(as) those
el **espacio** space
el **espagueti** spaghetti
la **espalda** back (body), **3.3**
espantoso(a) frightful, frightening
la **España** Spain
el **español** Spanish (language), I: 2.2
español(a) Spanish *(adj.)*
la **espátula** palette knife, spatula
la **especia** spice
especial special
la **especialidad** specialty, specialization
el/la **especialista** specialist, II: 14.1
especializar to specialize
especialmente especially
el **espectáculo** show, I: 10.2
ver un espectáculo to see a show, I: 10.2
el/la **espectador(a)** spectator, I: 7.1
el **espejo** mirror, I: 12.1
espera: la sala de espera waiting room, I: 13.1; II: 1.1
esperar to wait (for), I: 11.1; to hope, **2.3**
espontáneo(a) spontaneous
la **esposa** wife, spouse, I: 6.1
el **esposo** husband, spouse, I: 6.1
el **espíritu** spirit
la **esquela** obituary, **4.3;** announcement, LC8
el **esquí** skiing, I: 9.2; ski
el esquí acuático water skiing, I: 9.1
el/la **esquiador(a)** skier, I: 9.2
esquiar to ski, I: 9.2
esquiar en el agua to water-ski, I: 9.1
la **esquina** corner, II: 9.1
establecer to establish, **1.1**
establecerse to settle
el **establecimiento** establishment
la **estación** season, BV; station, I: 10.1
la estación de esquí ski resort, I: 9.2
la estación de ferrocarril train station, I: 13.1; II: 1.1
la estación del metro subway station, I: 10.1
la estación de servicio service station, II: 11.1
el **estacionamiento** parking
estacionar to park
la **estadía** stay
el **estadio** stadium, I: 7.1
la **estadística** statistic
el **estado** state
el **estado del banco** bank statement
Estados Unidos United States
estadounidense from the United States
estampado(a) printed, **3.3**
la **estancia** ranch (Argentina)
estar to be, I: 4.1
¿Está... ? Is . . . there?, II: 3.2
estar cansado(a) to be tired, II: 8.1
estar contento(a) (triste, etc.) to be happy (sad, etc.), II: 8.1
estar de buen (mal) humor to be in a good (bad) mood, II: 8.1
estar enfermo(a) to be sick
estar nervioso(a) (tranquilo[a]) to be nervous (calm), II: 8.1
estar resfriado(a) to have a cold, I: 8.1
estatal pertaining to state *(adj.)*
la **estatua** statue, I: 10.2
este(a) this
el **este** east
la **estela** stone monument, **4.1**
estereofónico(a) stereo
el **estilo** style
estimado(a) esteemed
los **estiramientos** stretches, **5.3**
estirar to stretch, LC1
esto this (one)
el **estoicismo** stoicism
el **estómago** stomach, I: 8.1
estornudar to sneeze, I: 8.1
estos(as) these
la **estrategia** strategy
estrechar la mano to shake hands, LC8
estrecho(a) narrow, II: 4.1
la **estrella** star
la **estrofa** stanza
la **estructura** structure
el/la **estudiante** student
el/la estudiante de intercambio exchange student
la residencia para estudiantes student housing, dormitory, II: 3.2
estudiantil (relating to) student
estudiar to study, I: 4.1
el **estudio** study, II: 14
la **estufa** stove, II: 10.1
estupendo(a) stupendous
eterno(a) eternal
étnico(a) ethnic
el **euro** euro (currency)
la **Europa** Europe
europeo(a) European
evadir to evade
evitar to avoid, **6.2**
exactamente exactly
exacto(a) exact
exagerado(a) exaggerated
exagerar to exaggerate
el **examen** test, exam, I: 4.2
examinar to examine, I: 8.2
la **excavación** excavation
excavar to dig, excavate
exceder to exceed
excelente excellent
la **excepción** exception
exclamar to exclaim
exclusivamente exclusively
la **exhibición** exhibition
exigir to demand
la **existencia** existence
existir to exist
el **éxito** success
la **expedición** expedition
la **experiencia** experience
experimentar to experiment
el/la **experto(a)** expert, I: 9.2
explicar to explain, I: 4.2
el/la **explorador(a)** explorer
la **explosión** explosion
exportar to export
la **exposición (de arte)** (art) exhibition, I: 10.2
la **expresión** expression
el modo de expresión means of expression
la **extensión** extension
extraer to extract, LC5
extranjero(a) foreign
el país extranjero foreign country, I: 11.2
el/la **extranjero(a)** foreigner
en el extranjero abroad
extraordinario(a) extraordinary
extravagante strange
extraviarse to get lost, to go astray, **4.3**
el **extravío** going astray, **4.3**
extremo(a) extreme
exuberante exuberant

la **fábrica** factory, II: 9.1
fabricado(a) manufactured

fabuloso(a) fabulous
fácil easy, I: 2.1
facilitar to facilitate
el **facsímil** fax, II: 3.1
la **factura** bill, II: 6.1; **4.2;** invoice
facturar el equipaje to check luggage, I: 11.1
la **facultad** school (of a university)
la **faja** sash
la **falda** skirt, II: 3.2
fallecer to die, **4.3;** LC8
el **fallecimiento** death, **4.3**
fallido(a) failed, LC5
falso(a) false
la **falta** lack
la **fama: tener fama de** to have the reputation of
la **familia** family, I: 6.1
familiar (related to the) family
el **familiar** relative, **4.3**
famoso(a) famous, I: 1.2
fantástico(a) fantastic, I: 1.2
el/la **farmacéutico(a)** druggist, pharmacist, I: 8.2
la **farmacia** drugstore, I: 8.2
fascinar to fascinate
la **fatiga** fatigue
la **fauna** fauna, **5.1**
Favor de (+ infinitive) Please (+ verb), II: 11.1
favorito(a) favorite, II: 11
el **fax** fax, II: 3.1
mandar (transmitir) un fax to send a fax, to fax, II: 3.1
la **faz** face, LC5
febrero February, BV
la **fecha** date, BV
¿Cuál es la fecha de hoy? What is today's date?, BV
la **felicidad** happiness
¡Felicitaciones! Congratulations!, II: 13.1
felicitar to congratulate, **4.3**
feliz happy
¡Feliz cumpleaños! Happy birthday!, II: 13.1
¡Feliz Hanuka! Happy Chanukah!, II: 13.2
¡Feliz Navidad! Merry Christmas!, II: 13.2
feo(a) ugly, I: 1.1
el **ferrocarril** railroad, I: 13.1, II: 1.1
la estación de ferrocarril train station, I: 13.1, II: 1.1
festejar to celebrate; **4.3**
la **ficción** fiction
la **ficha** piece (game), II: 5.1; registration card, II: 6.1
ficticio(a) fictitious

la **fiebre** fever, I: 8.1
tener fiebre to have a fever, I: 8.1
fiel faithful
la **fiesta** party, II: 13.1
dar una fiesta to give (throw) a party, I: 4.2
la **fiesta de las luces** The Festival of Lights, II: 13.2
la **figura** figure
figurativo(a) figurative
fijar to fix
fijo(a) fixed
la **fila** row (of seats); line (queue), I: 10.1
el **filete** fillet
filial childlike, filial, LC1
el **film** film, I: 10.1
filmar to film
el **fin** end
a fines de at the end of
el fin de semana weekend, BV
el **final: al final (de)** at the end (of)
financiero(a) financial
las **finanzas** finances
la **finca** farm, II: 9.2
fino(a) fine
firmar to sign, II: 12.2; **5.2**
la **firmeza** firmness
la **física** physics, I: 2.1
físico(a): la educación física physical education, I: 2.2
flaco(a) skinny, I: 1.2
flamenco(a) flamenco
la **flauta** flute
flechar to become enamored of (to fall for)
flojo(a) loose. LC5
la **flor** flower, **5.1**
la flor silvestre wildflower, **5.1**
fluvial fluvial, riverlike, **7.1**
el **folleto** pamphlet
el **fondo** fund
el/la **fontanero(a)** plumber, II: 14.1
la **forma** shape
formar to make up, form
el **formulario** form, II: 8.2
llenar un formulario to fill out a form, II: 8.2
fornido(a) husky
el **forro** covering (clothing), **3.2**
la **fortaleza** strength
la **fortificación** fortification
la **foto** photo
la **fotografía** photograph
el/la **fotógrafo(a)** photographer
fracasar to fail, **3.3**
la **fractura** fracture, II: 8.1
el **fragmento** fragment
fragoso(a) rough, LC7

el **francés** French, I: 2.2
franco(a) frank, candid, sincere
la **franqueza** frankness
el **frasco** jar, II: 4.2
la **frase** phrase, sentence
la **frazada** blanket, II: 6.2
frecuentemente frequently
freír (i, i) to fry, I: 14.1; II: 2.1
los **frenos** brakes, II: 11.1
la **frente** forehead, II: 8.1; LC2
la **fresa** cutter, LC7; strawberry
fresco(a) fresh, II: 4.2
el **frijol** bean, I: 5.2
los frijoles negros black beans, II: 10.2
arroz con frijoles (habichuelas) rice with beans, **6.1**
el **frío: Hace frío.** It's cold., I: 9.2
frito(a) fried, I: 5.1
las papas fritas French fries, I: 5.1
la **frontera** border
fronterizo(a) frontier, border *(adj.)*, **8.1**
el **frontón** wall (of a jai alai court)
la **fruta** fruit, I: 5.2
la **frutería** fruit store, II: 4.2
el **fuego** fire, II: 10.2
a fuego lento on a low flame, heat
quitar (retirar) del fuego to take (something) off the heat, II: 10.2
la **fuente** source
fuerte strong, **4.1**
la **fuerza** strength; force
fumar: la sección de (no) fumar (no) smoking area, I: 11.1
la señal de no fumar no smoking sign, II: 7.1
la **función** performance, I: 10.2; function
el **funcionamiento** functioning
el/la **funcionario(a)** city hall employee, II: 14.1
la **fundación** foundation
fundado(a) founded, established
fundar to found, establish, **8.1**
la **furia** fury
furioso(a) furious
furtivamente furtively
la **fusión** fusion
el **fútbol** soccer, I: 7.1
el campo de fútbol soccer field, I: 7.1
el **futbolín** table soccer, II: 5.1
el **futuro** future

la **gabardina** raincoat, II: 4.1
el **gabinete** cabinet
el gabinete del dentista dentist's cabinet, LC7
las **gafas de sol** sunglasses, I: 9.1
el **gajo** broken branch, LC3
el **galán** beau, heartthrob
la **galaxia** galaxy
el **galeón** galleon, **6.1**
la **galería comercial** shopping mall
el **galón** gallon
gallardo(a) gallant, fine-looking
la **galleta** cracker, cookie LC6
la **gallina** hen, II: 9.2; LC3
el **gallinero** top gallery (of a theater), **7.2;** hen house, LC3
el **gallo** rooster, LC3
las **gambas** shrimp, II: 10.2
la **gamuza** antelope, chamois, **3.2**
la **ganadería** cattle, **3.1**
el **ganado** cattle, II: 9.2; **3.1**
ganar to win, I: 7.1; to earn
ganar la vida to earn one's living
la **ganga** bargain
el **garaje** garage, I: 6.2
la **garantía** guarantee
garantizar to guarantee, to ensure
la **garganta** throat, I: 8.1
la **garita de peaje** toll booth, II: 11.2
la **garra** claw
la garra de águila eagle claw, LC8
el **gasoil** diesel fuel
la **gasolina** gasoline, II: 11.1
la **gasolinera** service station, 11.1
gastar to spend
el/la **gato(a)** cat, I: 6.1
el **gaucho** gaucho, Argentine cattle handler, **3.1**
la **gaveta** drawer, LC7
el/la **gemelo(a)** twin
la **generación** generation
general: en general generally
por lo general in general, usually
generalmente usually, generally
el **género** genre
generoso(a) generous, I: 1.2
la **gente** people
la **geografía** geography, I: 2.2
la **geometría** geometry, I: 2.2
geométrico(a) geometric
gerencial managerial
el/la **gerente** manager, II: 14.1
el **gesto** gesture
el **gigante** giant
el **gimnasio** gymnasium
la **ginecología** gynecology
el/la **ginecólogo(a)** gynecologist
la **gira** tour, I: 12.2
girar to turn, LC7
el **glaciar** glacier, **3.1**
el **globo** balloon, II: 5.2
el/la **gobernadora** governor
el **gobierno** government, II: 14.1
el gobierno estatal state government
el gobierno federal federal government
el gobierno municipal municipal government
el **gol: meter un gol** to score a goal, I: 7.1
el **golfo** gulf
el **golpe** coup (overthrow of a government); blow
de golpe suddenly, LC5
golpear to hit, I: 9.2
la **goma** tire, II: 11.1; rubber, **3.2**
la suela de goma rubber sole
la **goma de borrar** eraser, I: 3.1
gordo(a) fat, I: 1.2
la **gorra** cap, hat, I: 3.2
la **gota** drop, LC5
la gota de agua drop of water
gozar to enjoy
la **grabadora DVD** DVD player, **8.2**
grabar to record, **8.2**
Gracias. Thank you., BV
gracioso(a) funny, I: 1.1
el **grado** degree (temperature), I: 9.2; grade
graduarse to graduate
la **gramática** grammar
el **gramo** gram
gran, grande big, large, great
las Grandes Ligas Major Leagues
el **grano** grain
la **grasa** fat
grave serious, grave
el/la **griego(a)** Greek
la **gripe** flu, I: 8.1
gris gray, I: 3.2
grosero(a) rude
la **grúa** crane (construction), LC8
el **grupo** group
el **guacamayo** macaw, **5.1**
la **guagua** bus (Puerto Rico, Cuba), I: 10.1
el **guante** glove, I: 7.2
guapo(a) handsome, I: 1.1
guardar to guard, I: 7.1; to keep, save, II: 3.1
guardar cama to stay in bed, I: 8.1
el/la **guardia** police officer
guatemalteco(a) Guatemalan
la **guayaba** guava
el casco de guayaba guava (peel), **6.2**
la **guerra** war, **1.1**
la **guerrilla** band of guerrillas
el/la **guía** tour guide; guide
la **guía telefónica** telephone book, II: 3.2
el **guisado** stew, LC8
el **guisante** pea, I: 5.2
la **guitarra** guitar
gustar to like, to be pleasing
el **gusto** pleasure; taste
Mucho gusto. Nice to meet you.

haber to have (in compound tenses)
la **habichuela** bean, I: 5.2
la habichuela tierna string bean
las habichuelas negras black beans, II: 10.2
arroz con habichuelas (frijoles) rice with beans, **6.1**
la **habitación** bedroom, room, II: 6.1
el/la **habitante** inhabitant, **2.3**
habla: los países de habla española Spanish-speaking countries
hablar to speak, talk, I: 3.1
hace: Hace… años . . . years ago
Hace buen tiempo. The weather is nice., I: 9.1
Hace calor. It's hot., I: 9.1
Hace frío. It's cold., I: 9.2
Hace mal tiempo. The weather is bad., II: 9.1
Hace sol. It's sunny., I: 9.1
hacer to do, make
hacer caso to pay attention
hacer cola to line up, I: 10.1
hacer la cama to make the bed, II: 6.2
hacer falta to need, **3.2**
Te hace falta un número mayor You need a bigger size.

hacer juego to match (clothes), **3.2**
La chaqueta y la blusa hacen juego. The jacket and the blouse match.
hacer la maleta to pack one's suitcase
hacer las compras to shop, II: 4.2
hacer las tareas to do homework, II: 3.1
hacer preguntas to ask questions, II: 14.2
hacer un viaje to take a trip, I: 11.1
hacer una llamada telefónica to make a telephone call, II: 3.2
hacerse daño to hurt oneself, II: 8.1
hacia toward
la **hacienda** ranch
hallar to find
la **hamaca** hammock, **4.1**
hambre: tener hambre to be hungry, I: 14.1; II: 2.1
la **hamburguesa** hamburger, I: 5.1
Hanuka Chanukah, II: 13.2
¡Feliz Hanuka! Happy Chanukah!, II: 13.2
harmonioso(a) harmonious
hasta until, BV
¡Hasta luego! See you later!, BV
¡Hasta mañana! See you tomorrow!, BV
¡Hasta pronto! See you soon!, BV
hay there is, there are, BV
hay que one must
Hay sol. It's sunny., I: 9.1
No hay de qué. You're welcome., BV
la **hazaña** feat, deed, LC1; LC6
hebreo(a) Hebrew, II: 13.2
hecho(a) made
bien hecho(a) well-done, **6.2**
la carne bien hecha (quemada) well-done meat
helado(a): el té helado iced tea, I: 5.1
el **helado** ice cream, I: 5.1
el helado de chocolate chocolate ice cream, I: 5.1
el helado de vainilla vanilla ice cream, I: 5.1
el **helicóptero** helicopter, II: 7.2
el **hemisferio norte** northern hemisphere
el **hemisferio sur** southern hemisphere
la **herencia** inheritance
la **herida** wound, II: 8.1
el/la **herido(a)** injured person
herir (i, i) to injure, to wound, **5.3,** LC4
la **hermana** sister, I: 6.1
el **hermano** brother, I: 6.1
hermoso(a) beautiful, pretty, I: 1.1
el/la **héroe** hero
heróico(a) heroic
la **herramienta** tool, LC3
hervir (ie, i) to boil, II: 10.1
el **hidrofoil** hydrofoil
el **hiel** sorrow, LC5
la **hierba** grass, **3.1**
la **higiene** hygiene
higiénico(a): el papel higiénico toilet paper, I: 12.2
el **higo** fig, LC3
la **higuera** fig tree, LC3
la **hija** daughter, I: 6.1
el **hijo** son, I: 6.1
los hijos children, I: 6.1
el **hilo** thread, LC8
hinchado(a) swollen, II: 8.1; LC7
el **hipermercado** hypermarket, II: 4.2
la **hipoteca** mortgage, **4.2**
hispano(a) Hispanic
hispanoamericano(a) Spanish-American
hispanohablante Spanish-speaking
el/la **hispanohablante** Spanish speaker
la **historia** history, I: 2.2; story
el/la **historiador(a)** historian
histórico(a) historical
la **historieta** short story
el **hobby** hobby, II: 5.1
el **hocico** snout, LC3
el **hogar** home, **3.3**
la **hoja** leaf, LC3; LC8
la hoja de papel sheet of paper, I: 3.1
¡Hola! Hello!, BV
el **hombre** man
¡hombre! good heavens!, you bet!
el **hombro** shoulder, II: 8.1; **5.3**
hondo(a) deep, LC3
la **honestidad** honesty
honesto(a) honest, I: 1.2
el **hongo** mushroom, **2.3**
el **honor** honor
la **hora** hour; time
¿A qué hora? At what time?, I: 2.2
la hora de la cena dinner hour
la hora de salida departure hour
el **horario** schedule, I: 13.1; II: 1.1
el horario escolar school schedule
la **horchata** cold drink made from milk, sugar, cinnamon, and rice
la **hornilla** stove burner, II: 10.1
el **hornillo** portable stove, II: 10.1
el **horno** oven, II: 10.1
el **horno de microondas** microwave oven, II: 10.1
horrible horrible
hospedarse to lodge, stay
el **hospital** hospital, II: 8.1
la **Hostia** Host (religious)
el **hostal** inexpensive hotel, I: 12.2
el **hotel** hotel, II: 6.1
hoy today, BV
hoy (en) día nowadays, these days
el **huarache** sandal
la **huelga** strike
en huelga on strike, **1.2**
el/la **huerto(a)** vegetable garden, orchard, II: 9.2; **3.1**
el **hueso** bone, II: 8.2
el/la **huésped** guest, II: 6.1
el **huevo** egg, I: 5.2
huir to flee, **1.1**
humano(a): el ser humano human being
húmedo(a) humid
humilde humble
el **humo** smoke
el **humor** mood, I: 8.1
estar de buen humor to be in a good mood, I: 8.1
estar de mal humor to be in a bad mood, I: 8.1
hundirse to sink, **6.1**
el **huracán** hurricane, **6.1**
a hurtadillas by stealth, LC6
el **huso horario** time zone

el **icono** icon
ida: de ida y vuelta round-trip (ticket), I: 13.1; II: 1.1
la **idea** idea
ideal ideal, I: 1.2
el/la **idealista** idealist
identificar to identify
idílico(a) idyllic
el **idioma** language
la **iglesia** church, **4.3**
ignorar to ignore, LC2
igual equal, alike

igual que like, as
la **iluminación** lighting, **7.2**
la **ilusión** illusion
ilustre distinguished, illustrious
la **imagen** image
la **imaginación** imagination
imaginado(a) imagined, dreamed of
imaginar to imagine
imaginario(a) imaginary
impar: el número impar odd number
imperante imperial, commanding **7.1**
el **imperativo** imperative
el **impermeable** raincoat, II: 4.1
la **implementación** implementation
importante important
importar to be important
imposible impossible
imprescindible indispensable, **6.3**
impresionar to affect, influence
la **impresora** printer, II: 3.1
inaugurar to inaugurate
el/la **inca** Inca
la **inclinación** inclination
incluido(a): ¿Está incluido el servicio? Is the tip included?, I: 5.1
incluir to include, I: 5.1
increíble incredible
la **independencia** independence
la **indicación** indication
el **indicador: el tablero indicador** scoreboard, I: 7.1
indicar to indicate, I: 11.1
el **indicio** sign, token, **5.3**
indígena indigenous
el/la **indígena** indigenous person, **2.1**
indio(a) Indian
indispensable indispensable
individual individual
el deporte individual individual sport
el **individuo** individual
la **indumentaria** clothing, outfit, **3.1**
industrial: la zona industrial industrial area, II: 9.1
ineducado(a) rude
la **inferencia** inference
infiel unfaithful
la **influencia** influence
la **información** information
informar to inform, I: 13.2; II: 1.2
la **informática** computer science, I: 2.2
el **informe** report

la **ingeniería** engineering
el/la **ingeniero(a)** engineer, II: 14.1
el **inglés** English, I: 2.2
el **ingrediente** ingredient
ingresar to make a deposit (bank)
inhospital inhospitable
inhóspito(a) desolate, inhospitable
iniciar to initiate
injusto(a) unjust
inmediatamente immediately
inmediato(a) immediate
inmenso(a) immense
inmerecido(a) undeserved, LC5
la **innovación** innovation
inocente innocent
el **inodoro** toilet, II: 6.2
inolvidable unforgettable, **7.1**
la **Inquisición** the Spanish Inquisition, **8.1**
la **inundación** flood, **8.3**
insistir to insist
insolente insolent
inspeccionar to inspect, I: 11.1
la **instalación** installation
instantáneo(a) instantaneous
el **instante** instant
la **instrucción** instruction, **4.2**
el **instrumento** instrument
el instrumento musical musical instrument
la **insuficiencia** insufficiency
insuficiente insufficient
integrar to integrate, **6.3**
íntegro(a) integral
inteligente intelligent, I: 2.1
la **intención** intention
el **intercambio** exchange
el/la estudiante (alumno[a]) de intercambio exchange student
el **interés** interest; (bank) interest
la taza de interés interest rate, **4.2**
interesante interesting, I: 2.1
interesar to interest
intergaláctico(a) intergalactic
el **intermedio** intermission, **7.2**
intermedio(a): la escuela intermedia middle school
el **intermitente** turn signal (of a car), **5.2**
internacional international
el **Internet** Internet, II: 3.1
la **interpretación** interpretation
el/la **intérprete** interpreter
interrumpir to interrupt
la **interrupción** interruption
intervenir to intervene
íntimo(a) intimate, close

intrépido(a) intrepid
la **introducción** introduction
introducir to insert, II: 3.2; **4.2**
introducir la tarjeta telefónica to insert the phone card, II: 3.2
invadir to invade, **1.1**
el/la **invasor(a)** invader, **1.1.**
el **invento** invention
inverso(a) reverse
la **investigación** investigation
el/la **investigador(a)** researcher
el **invierno** winter, BV
la **invitación** invitation
el/la **invitado(a)** guest
invitar to invite, I: 6.1
involucrado(a) involved in, caught up in, **5.3**
involucrar to include, **8.3**
la **inyección** injection, shot, I: 8.2
poner una inyección to give a shot
ir to go, I: 4.1
ir a (+ infinitive) to be going to (do something)
ir a pie to go on foot, to walk, I: 4.1
ir de compras to go shopping, I: 5.2
ir en bicicleta to go by bicycle, I: 12.2
ir en carro (coche) to go by car, I: 4.1
ir en tren to go by train
iracundo(a) angry
la **irrigación** irrigation
la **isla** island
italiano(a) Italian
izquierdo(a) left, I: 7.1
a la izquierda to the left, II: 5.2

el **jabón** soap, I: 12.2
la barra (pastilla) de jabón bar of soap, I: 12.2
el **jaguar** jaguar, **5.1**
jamás never
el **jamón** ham, I: 5.1
el **jardín** garden, I: 6.2
el jamón serrano smoked ham, **1.1**
el/la **jardinero(a)** outfielder, I: 7.2
la **jaula** cage, II: 5.2, LC3
el/la **jefe(a)** boss
el **jet** jet
jinetear to break in (horses)
el **jonrón** home run, I: 7.2

joven young, I: 6.1
de joven as a young person
el/la **joven** youth, young person, I: 10.1
la **joya** jewel, II: 4.1; **1.1**
la **joyería** jewelry store, II: 4.1
la **judía verde** green bean, I: 5.2
los **judios** Jewish people
el **juego** game
el juego de béisbol baseball game, I: 7.2
el juego de tenis tennis game, I: 9.1
el juego de video video game, II: 5.1
los Juegos Olímpicos Olympic Games
la sala de juegos game arcade, II: 5.1
el **jueves** Thursday, BV
el/la **juez** judge, II: 14.1
el/la **jugador(a)** player, I: 7.1
el/la jugador(a) de béisbol baseball player, I: 7.2
jugar (ue) to play, I: 7.1
jugar (al) béisbol (fútbol, baloncesto, etc.) to play baseball (soccer, basketball, etc.), I: 7.1
el **jugo** juice
el jugo de naranja orange juice, I: 12.1
el **juguete** toy, LC1
el **juicio** judgment
a juicio de in the judgment of, **3.3**
julio July, BV
la **jungla** jungle
junio June, BV
juntarse to join, **5.1**
juntos(as) together
juvenil: el albergue juvenil youth hostel, I: 12.2
la **juventud** youth

K

el **kilo** kilogram, I: 5.2
el **kilometraje** distance in kilometers
el kilometraje ilimitado unlimited kilometers, **5.2**
el **kilómetro** kilometer

L

la the *(f. sing.)*, **I: 1.1; it, her** *(pron.)*

el **labio** lip, II: 8.1
el **laboratorio** laboratory
labrar to plow, LC2
lacustre on the shore of a river or lake, **7.1**
un bohío lacustre hut on a river
la **ladera** slope (of a hill or mountain)
la ladera de la montaña mountain side, **7.1**
el/la **ladino(a)** indigenous person who speaks Spanish and has adopted urban customs, LC4
el **lado** side
al lado de beside, next to, II: 5.2
el **lago** lake, II: 5.2
la **lágrima** tear, LC7
el **lamento** lament
la **lana** wool, II: 12.1; **3.2**
la tela de lana wool fabric
la **langosta** lobster, I: 14.2; II: 2.2
la **lanza** lance
el/la **lanzador(a)** pitcher, I: 7.2
lanzar to throw, I: 7.1; to launch
la **lapicera** pencil holder, **3.3**
el **lápiz** pencil, I: 3.1
largarse to move away, LC8
largo(a) long, I: 3.2
a lo largo along, lenthwise, **1.1**
de largo recorrido long distance (trip)
las the, them
la **lástima: ser una lástima** to be a pity (a shame)
lastimar to injure, **5.3**
lastimarse to get hurt, II: 8.1
la **lata** can, I: 5.2
lateral side *(adj.)*, I: 13.2; II: 1.2
el **latín** Latin, I: 2.2
latino(a) Latin *(adj.)*
Latinoamérica Latin America, I: 1.1
latinoamericano(a) Latin American
el **lavabo** washbasin, II: 6.2; restroom, II: 7.1
el **lavado** laundry, II: 12.1
la **lavandería** laundromat
lavar: la máquina de lavar washing machine, II: 12.1
lavarse to wash oneself, I: 12.1
lavarse los dientes to brush one's teeth, I: 12.1
el **lazo** tie
le to him, to her; to you
la **lección** lesson, I: 4.2
la **leche** milk
el café con leche coffee with milk, I: 5.1

el **lechón** suckling pig
el lechón asado roast suckling pig, **6.1**
la **lechuga** lettuce, I: 5.2
la **lectura** reading
leer to read, I: 5.1
la **legumbre** vegetable
lejos far, II: 12.2
la **lengua** language, I: 2.2
el **lenguaje** language
la **lenteja** lentil
lentamente slowly
lento(a) slow, II: 10.2; **6.2**
el **leño** wood, LC2
el **león** lion
les to them; to you *(formal pl.) (pron.)*
el/la **lesionado(a)** injured person
la **letra** letter (of alphabet)
levantar to lift, to raise
levantarse to get up, I: 12.1; to rise up (against)
levantarse el sol to rise (sun)
el/la **libertador(a)** liberator
la **libra** pound
libre free, I: 5.1
al aire libre outdoor *(adj.)*
el **libro** book, I: 3.1
la **licencia** driver's license, II:11.1
la licencia de conductor driver's license, **5.2**
el **liceo** high school
el **lienzo** canvas (painting)
la **liga** league
las Grandes Ligas Major Leagues
ligero(a) light (cheerful); light (weight), LC2
los **ligeros** hand weights, **5.3**
la **lima** lime, II: 10.1
limeño(a) from Lima (Peru)
el **límite de velocidad** speed limit, **5.2**
el **limón** lemon, II: 10.1
la **limonada** lemonade, BV
el **limonero** lemon tree
limpiar to clean, I: 6.2
limpiar el cuarto to clean the room, II: 6.2
limpiar en seco to dry clean, II: 12.1
limpio(a) clean
la **limusina** limousine
lindo(a) pretty, I: 1.1
la **línea** line
la línea aérea airline
la línea ecuatorial equator
la línea paralela parallel line
la línea telefónica telephone line

el **lípido** lipid, fat
líquido(a) liquid
lírico(a) lyric
la **lista** list
listo(a) ready; clever, II: 5.1; intelligent, **6.1**
la **litera** berth, I: 13.2; II: 1.2
literal literal
literario(a) literary
la **literatura** literature, I: 2.1
el **litro** liter
la **llama** flame, LC4; LC8
la **llamada larga** long-distance call, II: 3.2
la **llamada telefónica** telephone call, II: 3.2
hacer una llamada telefónica to make a (telephone) call, I: 3.2
poner la llamada to put the call through
llamado(a) called
llamar to call; to telephone, II: 3.2
llamarse to be named, to call oneself, I: 12.1
llamativo(a) loud, flashy (related to colors), **3.3**
el **llanero** plainsman
la **llaneza** simplicity, LC7
la **llanta** tire, II: 11.1
la llanta de recambio (repuesto) spare tire, II: 11.1
la **llanura** plain, II: 7.2; **1.1; 3.1**
la llanura de color pardo brown plain
la **llave** key, II: 6.1
la **llegada** arrival, arriving, I: 11.1
llegar to arrive, I: 4.1
llenar to fill, fill out
llenar un crucigrama to do a crossword puzzle, II: 5.1
llenar el formulario to fill out the form, II: 8.2
lleno(a) full
llevar to carry, I: 3.1; to wear, I: 3.2; to bring, I: 6.1; to bear; to have (subtitles, ingredients, etc.); to take, I: 8.1
llevar a cabo to carry out, 5.3
llorar to cry, LC1; LC4
llover (ue) to rain
Llueve. It's raining., I: 9.1
la **lluvia** rain
lluvioso(a) rainy, **2.1**
lo it; him *(m. sing.) (pron.)*
lo que what, that which
el **lobo** wolf
el **lobo marino** sea lion, **3.1**
local local, I: 13.2; II: 1.2
la **localidad** seat (in a theater), **7.2**
la **loción: la loción bronceadora** suntan lotion, I: 9.1
loco(a) insane
el **lodo** mud
la ola de lodo mudslide, **8.3**
lógico(a) logical
lograr to achieve, to attain, **7.3**
el **lomo** back (of an animal), **4.3**
los them
el **loto** lotto
la **lozanía** luxuriance, LC5
las **luces** headlights, II: 11.1
luchar to fight, **1.1**
luego later; then, BV
¡Hasta luego! See you later!, BV
el **lugar** place
tener lugar to take place, I: 8.1
lujo: de lujo deluxe
lujoso(a) luxurious
la **luna** moon
la **luna de miel** honeymoon
lunares: con lunares with polka dots
el **lunes** Monday, BV
lustroso(a) shining, bright
la **luz** light
la luz roja red light, II: 11.2

M

la **madera** wood, **2.1; LC7**
el **madero** log, beam, LC7
la **madre** mother, I: 6.1
madrileño(a) native of Madrid
la **madrina** godmother
el/la **maestro(a)** teacher
magnífico(a) magnificent
magrebí related to three North African countries: Morocco, Algeria, and Tunisia, **1.3**
el **maíz** corn, I: 14.2; II: 2.2; **2.1**
majestuoso(a) majestic
mal bad, I: 14.2; II: 2.2
estar de mal humor to be in a bad mood, I: 8.1
Hace mal tiempo. The weather's bad., I: 9.1
la **maldad** evil
la **maleta** suitcase, I: 11.1
el/la **maletero(a)** trunk (of a car), I: 11.1; porter, I: 13.1; II: 1.1
malgastar to waste
malhumorado(a) bad-tempered
malo(a) bad, I: 2.1
sacar una nota mala to get a bad grade, I: 4.2
la **mamá** mom
el **mambo** mambo
mandar to send, II: 3.1; to order
manear to wield, LC8
manejar to drive, I: 11.1; to handle, **6.3**
la **manera** way, manner, I: 1.1
de ninguna manera by no means, I: 1.1
la **manga** sleeve, II: 4.1; **3.2**
de manga corta (larga) short- (long-) sleeved, II: 4.1
el **mango** mango, **6.1**
la **manguera** hose, **7.3**
el **maní** peanut
la **mano** hand, I: 7.1; 5.3
dar la mano to shake hands
la **mano de obra** workforce, **8.1**
la **manta** blanket, II: 6.2
el **mantel** tablecloth, I: 14.1; II: 2.1
mantener to maintain
mantenerse en forma to keep in shape
la **mantequilla** butter, II: 10.2
la **manzana** apple, I: 5.2
el **manzano** apple tree, II: 9.2
mañana tomorrow, BV
¡Hasta mañana! See you tomorrow!, BV
la **mañana** morning
de la mañana A.M. (time), I: 2.2
por la mañana in the morning
el **mapa** map, **1.2**
el **maquillaje** makeup, I: 12.1
ponerse el maquillaje to put one's makeup on, I: 12.1
maquillarse to put one's makeup on, I: 12.1
la **máquina** machine, device
la máquina de lavar washing machine, II: 12.1
prender la máquina to turn (a device) on, II: 3.1
el **mar** sea, I: 9.1
el mar Caribe Caribbean Sea
maravilloso(a) marvelous
el **marcador** marker, I: 3.1
marcar to dial, II: 3.2
marcar el número to dial the number, II: 3.2
marcar un tanto to score a point, I: 7.1
marchar to march
el **marfil** ivory
la **marginalidad** marginality, **6.3**
el **marido** husband, I: 6.1

el/la **marino(a)** sailor
marino(a) marine, sea *(adj.)*, **3.1**
el **mariscal** blacksmith
los **mariscos** shellfish, I: 5.2
el **mármol** marble (stone), LC8
marrón: de color marrón brown, I: 3.2
el **martes** Tuesday, BV
marzo March, BV
más more, I: 2.2
más tarde later
más o menos more or less
la **masa** mass; dough, LC8
la **máscara de oxígeno** oxygen mask, II: 7.1
la **mascota** pet, **4.3**
la **mata: mata de berenjenas** eggplant bush, LC8
matar to kill
las **matemáticas** mathematics, I: 2.1
la **materia** matter, subject; material
la materia prima raw material
el **material** supply, I: 3.1; material
la material prima raw material, **2.1**
los **materiales escolares** school supplies, I: 3.1
el **matrimonio** marriage, **4.3**
máximo(a) maximum, II: 11.2
la velocidad máxima speed limit, II: 11.2
el/la **maya** Maya
mayo May, BV
la **mayonesa** mayonnaise, II: 4.2
mayor greater, greatest, **3.2;** elderly, older, **2.3**
la mayor parte the greater part, the most
la **mayoría** majority
la **mazorca de maíz** ear of corn, **7.1**
me me
el/la **mecánico(a)** mechanic
la **medalla** medal
media average
y media half-past (time)
mediano(a) medium, II: 4.1
la **medianoche** midnight
mediante by means of, **6.3**
las **medias** stockings, pantyhose
el **medicamento** medicine (drugs), I: 8.2
la **medicina** medicine (discipline), I: 8.2; medicine
el/la **médico(a)** doctor, I: 8.2
la **medida** measurement
el **medio** medium, means
el medio de transporte means of transportation
el **medio oeste** midwest (region), **8.1**
medio(a) half, II: 5.2; average
media hora half an hour
el **medio ambiente** environment
el **mediodía** noon
medir (i, i) to measure
la **meditación** meditation
la **mejilla** cheek, II: 8.1
los **mejillones** mussels, II: 10.2
mejor better
el/la mejor the best
melancólico(a) melancholic
el **melocotón** peach, II: 10.1
la **memoria** memory
mencionar to mention
menor lesser, least
la **menora** menorah, II: 13.2
menos less, fewer
a menos que unless
menos cuarto a quarter to (the hour)
el **mensaje** message, II: 3.2
dejar un mensaje to leave a message, II: 3.2
la **mensualidad** monthly installment
mentiroso(a) lying
el **mentón** chin, LC6
el **menú** menu, I: 5.1
el **mercadeo** marketing
el **mercado** market, I: 5.2
la **mercancía** merchandise, II: 14.1
el **merengue** merengue
la **merienda** snack, I: 4.2
tomar una merienda to have a snack, I: 4.2
la **mermelada** jam, marmalade
el **mes** month, BV
la **mesa** table, I: 5.1; LC7; plateau
la **mesera** waitress, I: 5.1
el **mesero** waiter, I: 5.1
la **meseta** plateau, II: 7.2
la **mesita** tray table, II: 7.1
Mesoamérica Mesoamerica, **5.1**
la **mesquita** mosque (Islam)
el/la **mestizo(a)** mestizo
la **meta** goal, 3.3
el **metabolismo** metabolism
el **metal: instrumentos de metal** brass (instruments in orchestra)
meter to put, place, I: 7.1; to put in, insert, II: 3.1
meter un gol to score a goal, I: 7.1
el/la **meteorólogo(a)** meteorologist, **8.2**
el **método** method
la **métrica** metrics
el **metro** subway, I: 10.1; **1.2;** meter, II: 7.2
mexicano(a) Mexican, I: 1.1
mexicanoamericano(a) Mexican American
la **mezcla** mixture
mi my
mí me
el **microbio** microbe
el **micrófono** microphone, **8.2**
microscópico(a) microscopic
el **microscopio** microscope
el **miedo** fear
tener miedo to be afraid
la **miel** honey, LC5
el **miembro** member, I: 4.2
mientras while, **2.2**
el **miércoles** Wednesday, BV
la **migración** migration
mil (one) thousand, I: 3.2
el **militar** soldier
la **milla** mile
el **millón** million
el/la **millonario(a)** millionaire
la **milpa** cornfield, LC4
el/la **mimo** mime, II: 5.2
la **miniatura** miniature
la **miniaturización** miniaturization
el **ministerio** ministry
el **minusválidos** disabled, handicapped
el **minuto** minute
la **mira** purpose, **6.3**
mirar to look at, watch, I: 3.1
mirarse to look at oneself, I: 12.1
¡Mira! Look!
el/la **mirón(ona)** spectator
la **misa** mass (Catholic), LC8
la **miseria** poverty
mismo(a) same, I: 2.1; myself, yourself, him/her/itself, ourselves, yourselves, themselves
el **misterio** mystery
misterioso(a) mysterious
la **mitad** half
mítico(a) mythical
la **mitología** mythology
mixto(a) co-ed (school)
la **mochila** backpack, I: 3.1; **1.2;** knapsack, I: 12.2
la **moción** motion
la **moda** style
de moda in style
la **modalidad** mode, type
el/la **modelo** model
el **modem** modem
la **moderación** moderation

modernizado(a) modernized
moderno(a) modern
la **modestia** modesty
la **modificación** modification
el **modo** manner, way
el modo de expresión means of expression
la **mola** type of blouse, **4.1**
el **molcajete** grindstone, LC8
el **molino de viento** windmill
el **momento** moment
el **monarca** monarch
la **monarquía** monarchy, **1.1**
el **monasterio** monastery
la **moneda** coin, currency, II: 3.2; **4.2**
el **monitor** monitor, computer screen, II: 3.1
el **mono** monkey, II: 5.2
monocelular single-celled
el **monstruo** monster
la **montaña** mountain, I: 9.2
la montaña submarina underwater mountain
la **montaña rusa** roller coaster, II: 5.2
montañoso(a) mountainous
montar (caballo) horseback ride
el **monte** mountain, **3.**
el **monto** sum, fare (taxi), **1.2; 4.2**
el **monumento** monument
morar to reside, to live, LC7
mortal mortal
moreno(a) dark, brunette, I: 1.1
morir (ue, u) to die
el/la **moro(a)** Moor
morrón: el pimiento morrón sweet pepper
la **mortalidad** mortality
el **mostrador** counter, I: 11.1
mostrar (ue) to show, **5.3**
el **motivo** reason, motive; theme
el **motor** motor
mover (ue) to move
el **movimiento** movement
el/la **mozo(a)** porter (train station) I: 13.1; II: 1.1; bellhop (hotel), II: 6.1
mozo(a) young
la **muchacha** girl, I: 1.1
el **muchacho** boy, I: 1.1
mucho(a) a lot; many, I: 2.1
Mucho gusto. Nice to meet you.
mudarse to move
el **mudo** mute, LC1; LC7
los **muebles** furniture
la **muela** back tooth, LC7
la **muerte** death
la **muestra** sign, sample **5.3**
la **mujer** wife, I: 6.1
la **muleta** crutch, II: 8.2
la **multa** fine
multinacional multinational
la **multiplicación** multiplication
multiplicar to multiply
mundial worldwide, (related to the) world, **6.3**
la Copa mundial World Cup
la Serie mundial World Series
el **mundo** world
todo el mundo everyone
la **muñeca** wrist, II: 4.1
el **mural** mural, I: 10.2
el/la **muralista** muralist
la **muralla** wall
muscular muscular
el **músculo** muscle, **5.3**
el **museo** museum, I: 10.2
la **música** music, I: 2.2
el/la **músico(a)** musician
mustio(a) gloomy, sad, LC7
mutuo(a) mutual
muy very, BV
muy bien very well, BV

nacer to be born, II: 13.1
nacido(a) born
nacional national
la **nacionalidad** nationality, I: 1.2
¿de qué nacionalidad? what nationality?
nada nothing, I: 5.2
De nada. You're welcome., BV
Nada más. Nothing else., I: 5.2
Por nada. You're welcome., BV
el/la **nadador(a)** swimmer, **6.3**
nadar to swim, I: 9.1
nadie no one
el **nado** swimming, **6.3**
el torneo de nado (natación) swim meet
la **naranja** orange, II: 5.2
el **naranjo** orange tree
el **narcótico** narcotic
la **nariz** nose, II: 8.1
la **narración** narration
narrar to narrate
la **natación** swimming, I: 9.1; **6.3**
el torneo de natación (nado) swim meet
natural: los recursos naturales natural resources, I: 2.1
las ciencias naturales natural sciences
la **naturaleza** nature
naufragar to be shipwrecked, **1.3**
la **navaja** razor, I: 12.1
navegar to navigate
navegar por la red to surf the Net
la **Navidad** **Christmas, II: 13.2**
el árbol de Navidad Christmas tree, II: 13.2
¡Feliz Navidad! Merry Christmas!, II: 13.2
el **navío** ship, LC1
la **neblina** fog, mist, **1.1**
necesario(a) necessary
la **necesidad** necessity
necesitar to need, I: 3.1
necio(a) foolish, LC1
el **nectar** nectar, LC5
negativo(a) negative
negro(a) black, I: 3.2
nervioso(a) nervous, I: 8.1
el **neumático** tire, II: 11.1
nevado(a) snow-covered, **2.1**
nevar (ie) to snow, I: 9.2
la **nevera** refrigerator, II: 10.1
el **nido** nest, LC3
la **nieta** granddaughter, I: 6.1
el **nieto** grandson, I: 6.1
la **nieve** snow, I: 9.2
el **nilón** nylon, **3.2**
ninguno(a) not any, none
de ninguna manera by no means, I: 1.1
el/la **niño(a)** child
los niños desamparados homeless children
el **nivel** level
el nivel del mar sea level
no no, BV
No hay de qué. You're welcome., BV
no hay más remedio there's no other alternative
noble noble
la **noche** night, evening
Buenas noches. Good night., BV
de la noche P.M. (time), I: 2.2
esta noche tonight, I: 9.2
por la noche in the evening, at night
la **Nochebuena** Christmas Eve, II: 13.2
la **Nochevieja** New Year's Eve, II: 13.2
nocturno(a) nocturnal, night-time
nombrar to mention
el **nombre** name
¿A nombre de quién? In whose name?, I: 14.2; II: 2.2
la **noria** Ferris wheel, II: 5.2
normal regular (gas), II: 11.1

el **nordeste** northeast (region), **8.1**
el **noroeste** northwest (region), **8.1**
el **norte** north
norteamericano(a) North American
el/la **norteño(a)** person from the north, northerner, **8.1**
nos (to) us
nosotros(as) we, I: 2.2
la **nostalgia** nostalgia
la **nota** grade, I: 4.2
la nota buena (alta) good (high) grade, I: 4.2
la nota mala (baja) bad (low) grade, I: 4.2
sacar una nota buena (mala) to get a good (bad) grade, I: 4.2
notable notable
notar to note
las **noticias** news, I: 6.2; **8.2**
el **noticiero** news report, **8.2**
los **novatos** novices, **5.3**
novecientos(as) nine hundred, I: 3.2
la **novela** novel
el/la **novelista** novelist
noveno(a) ninth, I: 6.2
noventa ninety, I: 2.2
la **novia** bride, II: 13.1; fiancée, girlfriend
noviembre November, BV
el **novio** groom, II: 13.1; fiancé, boyfriend
los **novios** bride and groom, newlyweds, II: 13.1
la **nube** cloud, I: 9.1
Hay nubes. It's cloudy., I: 9.1
nublado(a) cloudy, I: 9.1
el **nudo** knot, **2.1**
nuestro(a) our
las **nuevas** news, LC2
nueve nine, BV
nuevo(a) new
de nuevo again
el **número** number, I: 1.2; size (shoes), I: 3.2
el número de teléfono telephone number, II: 3.2
el número del asiento seat number, I: 11.1
el número del vuelo flight number, II: 11.1
el número equivocado wrong number
numeroso(a) numerous
nunca never
nupcial nuptial, wedding
la **nutrición** nutrition

o or
o sea in other words
el **objetivo** objective
el **objeto** object
la **obligación** obligation
obligatorio(a): el curso obligatorio required course
la **obra** work
la obra de arte work of art
la obra dramática play
la obra teatral play, I: 10.2
el/la **obrero(a)** worker, II: 9.1
la **observación** observation
el/la **observador(a)** observer
observar to observe
el **obstáculo** obstacle
obtener to obtain
obvio(a) obvious
la **ocasión** occasion
el **ocaso** end, death, setting, LC5
occidental western
el **océano** ocean
ochenta eighty, I: 2.2
ocho eight, BV
ochocientos(as) eight hundred, I: 3.2
octavo(a) eighth, I: 6.2
octubre October, BV
ocupado(a) taken, I: 5.1; busy (phone); occupied, II: 7.1
ocurrir to happen
el **odio** hate, **3.1**
el **oeste** west
oficial official
la **oficina** office, II: 9.1
el **oficio** trade, profession II: 14.1
ofrecer to offer, II: 14.2
la **oftalmología** ophthalmology
el/la **oftalmólogo(a)** ophthalmologist
el **oído** ear, II: 4.1
oír to hear
oír el tono to hear the dial tone, II: 3.2
ojalá I hope, II: 14.1; **6.3**
la **ojeada** glimpse
el **ojo** eye, I: 8.2
la **ola** wave, I: 9.1; **5.3**
el **óleo** oil (religious)
la **oliva: el aceite de oliva** olive oil
el **olivar** olive grove, **1.1**
la **olla** pot, II: 10.1
once eleven, BV
la **oncología** oncology
el/la **oncólogo(a)** oncologist
la **onda** wave (water), **5.3**
la **onza** ounce
opaco(a) opaque
opcional: el curso opcional elective course
la **ópera** opera
el/la **operador(a)** operator
operar to operate
la **opereta** operetta
opinar to think, to express an opinion, II: 10.2
la **opinión** opinion
la **oportunidad** opportunity
oprimir to push; to press, **4.2;** to oppress, **7.1**
opuesto(a) opposite
oralmente orally
la **orden** order (restaurant), I: 5.1
el **ordenador** computer, II: 3.1
la **oreja** ear, II: 4.1
el **orfanato** orphanage
el **organillo** organ
el **organismo** organism
organizar to organize
el **órgano** organ
oriental eastern
el **origen** origin
original: en versión original in its original (language) version, I: 10.1
la **orilla** bank (of a river, lake, etc.), **1.1**
a orillas de on the shores of
el **oro** gold, **2.1**
de oro (made of) gold, II: 4.1
la **orquesta** orchestra, II: 13.1
la orquesta sinfónica symphony orchestra
la **ortiga** nettle
la **ortopedia** orthopedics
osado(a) daring
oscurecer to darken
oscuro(a) dark
la **ostra** oyster, II: 10.2
otavaleño(a) of or from Otavalo (Ecuador)
el **otoño** autumn, BV
otro(a) other, another
la **oveja** sheep, **3.1**
el **oxígeno** oxygen
¡Oye! Listen!

pacer to graze, **3.1**
la **paciencia** patience
el/la **paciente** patient
pacífico(a) calm, peaceful, **3.1**
el **padre** father, I: 6.1
el padre (religioso) father

(religious)
los padres parents, I: 6.1
el **padrino** godfather; best man, II: 13.1
los padrinos godparents
pagar to pay, I: 3.1; **1.2**
pagar en la caja to pay at the cashier, I: 3.1
pagar al contado to pay in full, **4.2**
pagar a cuotas (a plazos) to pay in installments, **4.2**
pagar la factura to pay the bill, II: 6.1
la **página** page
la página Web Web page
el **pago** payment
el pago mensual monthly payment
el **país** country, I: 11.2; countryside, **1.1**
el país extranjero foreign country
el **paisaje** landscape
la **paja** straw, II: 13.2
la choza de paja straw hut, **4.1**
el **pájaro** bird
el **paje** page (wedding)
la **palabra** word
de palabra spoken, LC2
el **palacio** palace
la **palma** palm tree
el **palo** pole, LC3
el **pan** bread, II: 4.2
el pan dulce sweet roll, I: 5.1
el pan tostado toast, I: 5.2
la **panadería** bakery, II: 4.2
panameño(a) Panamanian, I: 2.1
panamericano(a) Pan American
el **panqueque** pancake
la **pantalla** screen (movies), I: 10.1; computer monitor, II: 3.1; **4.2; 8.2**
la pantalla de salidas y llegadas arrival and departure screen, I: 11.1
el **pantalón** pants, trousers, I: 3.2; **3.2**
el pantalón corto shorts, I: 3.2
el **pañuelo** handkerchief, II: 4.1
la **papa** potato, I: 5.1; **2.1**
las papas fritas French fries, I: 5.1
el **papá** dad
el **papagayo** parrot, LC8
la **papaya** papaya, II: 10.2; **6.1**
el **papel** paper, I: 3.1; role, part, II: 5.1
el papel higiénico toilet paper, I: 12.2
la hoja de papel sheet of paper, I: 3.1
la **papelería** stationery store, I: 3.1
el **papelógrafo** flipchart, **7.3**
el **paquete** package, I: 5.2
par: número par even number
el **par** pair, II: 4.1
el par de tenis pair of tennis shoes, I: 3.2
para for
¿Para cuándo? For when?, I: 14.2; II: 2.2
el **parabrisas** windshield, II: 11.1
la **parada** stop, I: 13.2; II: 1.2
la parada de bus bus stop, II: 9.1
el **parador** inn
el parador (del gobierno) hotel (government-run), **1.1**
el **paraíso** paradise; top gallery (of a theater), **7.2**
parar to stop, to block, I: 7.1
parcial: a tiempo parcial part-time *(adj.)*, II: 14.2
pardo(a) brown
de color pardo brown, **1.1**
parear to pair, match
parecer to look like; to seem, II: 8.1
parecerse a to look like, **1.1**
parecido(a) similar
la **pared** wall
la **pareja** couple; **4.3**
el/la **pariente** relative, I: 6.1
el **parque** park, II: 5.2
el parque de atracciones amusement park, II: 5.2
el **parquímetro** parking meter, II: 11.2
el **párrafo** paragraph
la **parrilla** grill, II: 10.1
parroquial parochial, **4.3**
la **parte** part, II: 8.1
¿De parte de quién? Who's calling?, II: 3.2
la mayor parte the greatest part, the most
la parte superior upper part
por todas partes everywhere
particular private, I: 6.2
la casa particular private house, I: 6.2
particularmente especially
la **partida** departure
el **partido** game, match, I: 7.1
el **pasado** the past
pasado(a) past; last
el (año) pasado last (year)
el/la **pasajero(a)** passenger, I: 11.1; **1.2**
el **pasaporte** passport, I: 11.1
el **pasador** lace, shoelace, **3.2**
pasar to pass, I: 7.2; to spend; to happen
Lo están pasando muy bien. They're having a good time., I: 12.2
pasar por to go through by, I: 11.1
pasar el tiempo to spend time, I: 5.1
¿Qué te pasa? What's the matter (with you)?, I: 8.1
el **pasatiempo** hobby, II: 5.1
el **pase** pass (permission)
pasear a caballo to go horseback riding
el **pasillo** aisle, I: 13.2; II: 1.2; **1.3**
un pasillo amplio (estrecho) wide (narrow) corridor
el **paso** step
la **pasta (crema) dentífrica** toothpaste, I: 12.2
el **pastel** pastry, II: 4.2; cake, II: 13.1
la **pastelería** bakery, II: 4.2
la **pastilla** pill, I: 8.2
la pastilla de jabón bar of soap, I: 12.2
la **pata** paw, LC3
la **patata** potato, II: 10.1
la **patera** small boat, raft, **1.3**
el **patinaje lineal** roller blading
el **patio de butacas** orchestra seat, **7.2**
el **patrón** pattern
el/la **patrón(ona)** patron saint; patron (of the arts)
la **patrulla** patrol**, 1.3**
pavimentado(a) paved
el **pavimento** pavement
el **payaso** clown, II: 5.2; **8.2**
el **peaje** toll, II: 11.2; **1.2**
la garita de peaje tollbooth, II: 11.2
el **peatón** pedestrian, II: 9.1
el **pecado** sin
el **pecho** chest, II: 8.1; **5.3**
el **pedacito** little piece, II: 10.2
el **pedazo** piece
el/la **pediatra** pediatrician
la **pediatría** pediatrics
el **pedido** order, request, **1.3**
pedir (i, i) to ask for, I: 14.1; II: 2.1
pedir la cuenta to ask for the bill, II: 6.1
pedir prestado to borrow
el **peinado** hairdo
peinarse to comb one's hair, I: 12.1

el **peine** comb, I: 12.1
pelar to peel, II: 10.2; **1.1**
la **pelea** fight, argument, **5.3**
pelear to fight, LC3
la **película** film, movie, I: 6.2
ver una película to see a film, I: 10.1
el **peligro** danger
peligroso(a) dangerous
el **pelo** hair, I: 12.1
la **pelota** ball (tennis, baseball, etc.), I: 7.2; **4.1**
botar la pelota to throw the ball, **4.1**
la pelota vasca jai alai
el/la **pelotari** jai alai player
la **peluca** wig
la **peluquería** hair salon, II: 12.1
el/la **peluquero(a)** hair stylist, II: 12.1
la **pena** grief; LC1; LC3
el **penacho** plume, LC8
el **pendiente** earring, II: 4.1
el **pendón** banner
la **península** peninsula
el **pensamiento** thought
pensar (ie) to think
la **pensión** boarding house, I: 12.2
la **peña** boulder, LC2
peor worse, worst
el/la peor the worst
el **pepino** cucumber, II: 10.1
pequeño(a) small, I: 2.1
la **pera** pear, II: 9.2
el **peral** pear tree, II: 9.2
la **percha** clothes hanger, II: 6.2
la **percusión** percussion
perder (ie) to lose, I: 7.1; to miss, I: 10.2
perder el autobús (la guagua, el camión) to miss the bus, I: 10.2
perdón excuse me
el/la **peregrino(a)** pilgrim
perezoso(a) lazy, I: 1.1
perfeccionar to perfect
el **periódico** newspaper, I: 6.2
el **período** period
el **permiso de conducir** driver's license, II: 11.1
permitir to permit, I: 11.1
pero but
el **perrito** puppy
el **perro** dog, I: 6.1
la **persona** person, I: 1.2
el **personaje** character
el **personal** personnel, II: 14.2
la **personalidad** personality
personalmente personally
pertenecer to belong
peruano(a) Peruvian
la **pesa** weight
pesado(a) heavy
los pesados heavy weights, **5.3**
pesar to weigh, II: 12.2
la **pescadería** fish market, II: 4.2
el **pescado** fish, I: 5.2
la **peseta** former Spanish unit of currency
el **peso** peso (monetary unit of several Latin American countries), BV; weight
la **petición** petition
el **petróleo** petroleum, oil
petrolero(a) oil (relating to)
el **pez** fish (live), LC3
el **piano** piano
la **picadura** sting, II: 8.1
picante spicy, **4.1**
picar to sting, II: 8.1; to dice, II: 10.2; **1.1**
ajo picado chopped garlic
el **pico** peak, II: 7.2
y pico just after (time)
el **pie** foot, I: 7.1; down payment
a pie on foot, I: 4.1
al pie de at the foot of
de pie standing
la **piedra** stone
la **pierna** leg, I: 7.1; **5.3**
la **pieza** room; piece
la **píldora** pill, I: 8.2
los **pilotes** stilts, **7.1**
el/la **piloto** pilot, I: 11.2
la **pimienta** pepper, I: 14.1; II: 2.1
el **pimiento** bell pepper, II: 10.2
el **pimiento morrón** sweet pepper
el **pin** pin number (automatic teller), **4.2**
pinchado(a) flat
el **pincel** **brush,** paintbrush
el **pingüino** penguin, **3.1**
la **pinta** pint
pinta: tener buena pinta to look good (food), II: 4.2
pintar to paint, II: 14.1
el/la **pintor(a)** painter
pintoresco(a) picturesque, II: 9.1
la **pintura** painting
la **pinza** clothespin, LC7
la **piña** pineapple, **6.1**
la **piragua** crushed ice with syrup over it, II: 5.2
los **pirineos** Pyrenees
la **pirueta** pirouette
la **piscina** swimming pool, I: 9.1
el **piso** floor, I: 6.2; **2.1;** apartment
la **pista** (ski) slope, I: 9.2; runway, II: 7.2
el/la **pítcher** pitcher, I: 7.2
la **pizarra** chalkboard, I: 4.2; **6.3**
la pizarra de corcho corkboard, LC8
el **pizarrón** chalkboard, I: 4.2
la **pizca** pinch
la **pizza** pizza, BV
la **placa** license plate
la **plaga** plague, menace
la **plancha de vela** sailboard, I: 9.1
practicar la plancha de vela to go windsurfing, I: 9.1
planchar to iron, II: 12.1; **3.2**
planear to plan
el **plano** plan, map, II: 9.1
la **planta** floor, I: 6.2; plant
la planta baja ground floor, I: 6.2
plástico(a) plastic, II: 4.2
la bolsa de plástico plastic bag, II: 4.2
la **plata** money (income), LC6; silver, **2.1**
el **plátano** banana, plantain, I: 5.2
la **platea** orchestra
el palco de platea orchestra pit, **7.2**
platicar to chat; talk, **5.3**
el **platillo** home plate, I: 7.2; saucer, I: 14.1; II: 2.1
el **plato** plate, dish, I: 14.1; II: 2.1; (satellite), **8.2**
la **playa** beach, I: 9.1
playera: la toalla playera beach towel, I: 9.1
la **plaza** seat, I: 13.2; II: 1.2; town square, II: 9.1; **2.1**
la plaza central town square
plazo: a corto (largo) plazo short- (long-)term, **4.2**
un préstamo de largo (corto) plazo long- (short-) term loan
la **plegaria** prayer, LC5
pleno: en pleno + (noun) in the middle of (noun)
el **pliegue** pleat, crease, **3.3**
el/la **plomero(a)** plumber, II: 14.1
plomo: con plomo leaded (gasoline), II: 11.1
sin plomo unleaded, II: 11.1
la **pluma** pen, I: 3.1
la **población** population, people
poblar (ue) to populate, **8.1**
pobre poor
el/la **pobre** the poor boy (girl)
el/la **pobretón(ona)** poor man (woman)
poco(a) little, few, I: 2.1
un poco (de) a little
el **poder** power
poder (ue) to be able, I: 7.1
poderoso(a) powerful

el **poema** poem
la **poesía** poetry
el/la **poeta** poet
el/la **policía** police officer, **2.2**
policíaco: novela policíaca detective fiction, mystery
el **poliéster** polyester, **3.2**
político(a) political
el **pollo** chicken, I: 5.2
el **polvo** dust, LC1
el **poncho** poncho, shawl, wrap
poner to put, I: 11.1
poner en un yeso to put a cast on, II: 8.2
poner la mesa to set the table, I: 14.1; II: 2.1
ponerse to put on, I: 12.1
ponerse el maquillaje to put one's makeup on, I: 12.1
ponerse la ropa to dress oneself, to put on clothes, I: 12.1
popular popular, I: 2.1
la **popularidad** popularity
por for
por aquí over here
por ciento percent
por colmo to make matters worse, **6.2**
por ejemplo for example
por eso therefore, for this reason, that's why
por favor please, BV
por fin finally
por hora per hour
por la noche in the evening
por lo general in general
Por nada. You're welcome., BV
por poco almost, **6.1**
por tierra overland
¿por qué? Why?
el **porche** porch
el **pordiosero** beggar
el **poroto** string bean
porque because
portátil portable
el/la **porteño(a)** inhabitant of Buenos Aires
la **portería** goal line, I: 7.1
el/la **portero(a)** goalkeeper, goalie, I: 7.1
poseer to possess
la **posesión** possession
la **posibilidad** possibility
posible possible
la **posición** position
el **pósito** grain bin, LC2
la **postal** postcard, II: 12.2
el **poste:** el poste de teléfono telephone pole, **8.3**
el **postre** dessert, I: 5.1
el **pozo** well, LC1
el/la **practicante** nurse practitioner
practicar to practice
practicar el surfing (la plancha de vela, etc.) to go surfing (windsurfing, etc.), I: 9.1
el **precio** price
precioso(a) precious, beautiful
la **precipitación** precipitation, **2.1**
preciso(a) precise
precolombino(a) pre-Columbian
la **predicción** prediction
predominar to predominate
el **predominio** predominance
preferir (ie, i) to prefer
el **prefijo de país** country code, II: 3.2
pregonar to proclaim, LC7
la **pregunta** question
preguntar to ask (a question)
el **premio: el Premio Nóbel** Nobel Prize
prender to turn on, II: 3.1
prender la máquina to turn (a device) on, II: 3.1
la **preparación** preparation
preparar to prepare
la **presencia** presence
la **presentación** presentation
presentar to show (movie); to present
presente present *(adj.)*
el/la **presidente** president
la **presión** pressure, II: 11.1
la presión arterial blood pressure, II: 8.2
prestado: pedir prestado to borrow
el **préstamo** loan, **4.2**
un préstamo de largo (corto) plazo long- (short-) term loan
prestar: prestar atención to pay attention, I: 4.2
el **prestigio** prestige
prevalecer to prevail
primario(a): la escuela primaria elementary school
la **primavera** spring, BV
primero(a) first, BV
en primera (clase) first-class, I: 13.1; II: 1.1
los primeros auxilios first aid
el/la **primo(a)** cousin, I: 6.1
primordial fundamental
la **princesa** princess
principal main, principal
principalmente mainly
el/la **principiante** beginner, I: 9.2
prisa: a toda prisa as fast as possible
privado(a) private
la casa privada private house, I: 6.2
probable probable
probarse (ue) to try on, II: 4.1
el **problema** problem
procesar to process
la **procesión** procession
el **proceso** process
proclamar to proclaim
proclive inclined, **6.3**
procurar to strive for, LC3
pródigo prodigal
la **producción** production
producido(a) produced
producir to produce
el **producto** product, I: 5.2
los productos congelados frozen food, I: 5.2
la **profesión** profession, II: 14.1
el/la **profesor(a)** teacher, professor, I: 2.1
profundo(a) deep
el **prognóstico** prediction
el prognóstico del tiempo weather forecast, **8.2**
el **programa** program
el/la **programador(a) de informática** computer programmer, II: 14.1
progresivo(a) progressive
el **progreso** progress
prohibido(a) forbidden, II: 11.2
la **promesa** promise
la **promoción** promotion
promover (ue) to promote
el **pronombre** pronoun
el **pronóstico** forecast
el **pronto** down payment
pronto: ¡Hasta pronto! See you soon!, BV
la **propaganda** publicity, advertising
la **propina** tip, I: 14.1; II: 2.1
el/la **propietario(a)** owner
propio(a) (one's) own
el **propósito** intention, aim
la **prosa** prose
prosperar to prosper
próspero(a): ¡Próspero Año Nuevo! Happy New Year, II: 13.2
el/la **protagonista** protagonist
la **protección** protection
protector(a): la crema protectora sunblock, I: 9.1
la **proteína** protein
protestar to protest
el **protoplasma** protoplasm

el/la **proveedor(a)** provider
proveer to provide, **8.3**
la **provisión** provision
próximo(a) next, I: 13.2; II: 1.2; close
en la próxima parada at the next stop, I: 13.2; II: 1.2
proyectar to project, I: 10.1
el **proyecto** project
la **prudencia** prudence
el/la **psiquíatra** psychiatrist
la **psiquiatría** psychiatry
publicar to publish
el **público** audience, I: 10.2
el **pueblo** town, II: 9.2; 2.3
los pueblos jóvenes shantytowns (Peru)
el **puente** bridge
el puente aéreo direct flight between two cities, **1.2**
el **puerco** pork
la **puerta** gate, I: 11.1; door, II: 6.1
la puerta de salida departure gate, I: 11.1
el **puerto** harbor, port, 1.1
puertorriqueño(a) Puerto Rican
pues well
la **puesta: la puesta del sol** sunset
el **puesto** market stall, II: 4.2; position, II: 14.2
la **pulgada** inch
pulir to polish, LC7
el **pulmón** lung, LC8
la **pulpería** grocery store, LC3
pulsar: pulsar el botón to push the button, II: 3.1; **4.2**
la **pulsera** bracelet, II: 4.1
el **pulso: tomar el pulso** to take one's pulse, II: 8.2
el **punto** stitch, II: 8.1; 3.2; dot, point
en punto on the dot, sharp, I: 4.1
los puntos cardinales cardinal points
poner puntos to give (someone) stitches
tela de punto stitch (knit) fabric, **3.2**
puntual punctual
puntualizar to give a detailed account of
el **puré de papas** mashed potatoes
puro(a) pure

que who, that
¿qué? what? how?
qué what; how, BV
¡Qué absurdo! How absurd!
¡Qué enfermo(a) estoy! I'm so sick!
¿Qué tal? How are you?, BV
¿Qué te pasa? What's the matter (with you)?, I: 8.2
quechua Quechuan
quedar to remain, I: 7.1
quedar: No me queda(n) bien. It (They) doesn't (don't) look good on (fit) me., II: 4.1
los **quehaceres** chores
quemado(a) well-done, **6.2**
la carne quemada (bien hecha) well-done meat
querer (ie) to want, wish; to love
el **queso** cheese, I: 5.1
el queso blanco white cheese, **6.2**
el queso manchego Spanish-style cheese
el **quetzal** quetzal (currency of Guatemala); type of bird, LC8
el **quicio de la puerta** door hinge , LC1
¿quién? who?, I: 1.1
¿De parte de quién? Who is calling?, II: 3.2
¿quiénes? who? *(pl.)*, I: 2.1
la **química** chemistry, I: 2.2
químico(a) chemical
quince fifteen, BV
la **quinceañera** fifteen-year-old (girl)
quinientos(as) five hundred, I: 3.2
la **quinta** villa, LC3
quinto(a) fifth, I: 6.2
el **quiosco** newsstand, I: 13.1; II: 1.1
el **quipu** a system of cords and knots used by indigenous people of Perú to count, **2.1**
el **quirófano** operating room
Quisiera... I would like . . . , I: 14.2; II: 2.2
quitar to take off, remove, II: 10.2; **2.2**
quizá(s) perhaps, II: 14.2

el **radiador** radiator, II: 11.1
radicarse to settle, **8.1**
la **radiografía** X-ray, II: 8.2
la **ráfaga** gust (of wind), **3.1**
la **raíz** root, LC3
rallar to grate, II: 10.2
la **rama** branch, LC3
el **ramo** bouquet, LC4
la **ranura** disk drive, II: 3.1; slot, II: 3.2
rápidamente quickly
rápido quickly
la **raqueta** racket (sports), I: 9.1
raro(a) rare
el **rascacielos** skyscraper, II: 9.1; **9.1**
el **rastro** rake, LC2
el **rato** while
el **ratón** mouse (computer), I: 3.1
la **raya** part (in hair), II: 12.1; stripe
rayado(a) (de rayas) striped, **3.2**
una blusa rayada (de rayas) striped blouse
los **rayos equis** X-rays
la **razón** reason
razonable reasonable
la **reacción** reaction
real royal
realista realistic
el/la **realista** realist
realizar to fulfill, carry out, **6.3**
realmente really
reanudar to resume, **8.3**
la **rebanada** slice, II: 4.2; **1.1**
rebanar to slice, II: 10.2; **1.1**
el **rebaño** flock, **3.1**
un rebaño de ovejas flock of sheep
rebasar to overtake, to pass (traffic), **5.2**
la **rebeldía** rebelliousness
rebosar to overflow, **6.1**
rebotar to rebound
la **recámara** bedroom, I: 6.2
el **recaudo** message, LC2
la **recepción** front desk (hotel), II: 6.1; admissions (hospital), I: 8.2; reception (party)
el/la **recepcionista** hotel clerk, II: 6.1
el/la **receptor(a)** catcher, I: 7.2
la **receta** prescription, I: 8.2; recipe, II: 10.2
recetar to prescribe, I: 8.2
rechazar to reject, to resist, **4.3**
recibir to receive, I: 5.1
el **reciclaje** recycling
recién recently
reciente recent
recitar to recite
reclamar to claim (luggage), I: 11.2
el **reclamo de equipaje** baggage claim, I: 11.2
el **recluso** inmate, **6.3**
reclutar to recruit

recoger to pick up
recoger el equipaje to claim one's luggage, I: 11.2
la **recomendación** recommendation
recomendar (ie) to recommend
reconocer to recognize
recordar (ue) to remember
recorrer to travel through, **1.2**
el **recorrido** trip, distance traveled
de largo recorrido long distance
el **recorte: recorte de periódico** newspaper clipping, LC8
recostar (ue) to lean (against), LC8
el **recreo** recreation
el **rectángulo** rectangle
el **recuerdo** memory, recollection
la **recuperación: la sala de recuperación** recovery room
el **recurso: los recursos naturales** natural resources
el departamento de recursos humanos human resources department, II: 14.2
la **red** net, network I: 9.1
navegar por la red to surf the Net
reducido(a) reduced (price)
reducir to set (bone), II: 8.2
reemplazar to replace
referir (ie, i) to refer
reflejar to reflect
el **reflejo** reflection
reflexionar to reflect
la **reforestación** reforestation
el **refresco** drink, beverage, I: 5.1
el **refrigerador** refrigerator, II: 10.1
el **refugio** refuge
regalar to give
el **regalo** gift, I: 6.1
la **región** region
regional regional
el **regionalismo** regionalism
registrar to register
la **regla** rule
regresar to return
el **regreso** return
el viaje de regreso return trip, trip back
regular regular, average, I: 2.2
la **reina** queen, **1.1**
reinar to reign, **1.1**
reír to laugh
la **relación** relation
relacionado(a) related
el **relámpago** lightning, **8.3**
relativamente relatively
religioso(a) religious
rellenar to fill
el **reloj** watch, II: 4.1; clock, II: 13.2
remar to row, II: 5.2
el **remedio** solution
remoto(a) remote
remozado(a) rejuvenated, **6.3**
el **rencor** rancor
rendir (i, i) to subdue, LC1
renegar (ie) to deny, **2.3**
renombrado(a) well-known
renovado(a) renewed, renovated
rentar to rent
renunciar to renounce, give up
reparar to repair
de repente suddenly
repentinamente suddenly
repetir (i, i) to repeat; to take seconds (meal)
el **reportaje** report
reposar to rest on, **6.1**
la **representación** performance (theater), I: 10.2
dar una representación to put on a performance, I: 10.2
el/la **representante** representative
representar to represent
representativo(a) representative
la **república** republic
la **República Dominicana** Dominican Republic
la **repulsión** repulsion, **3.1**
requerible required, **6.3**
requerir (ie, i) to require, II: 14.1
el **requisito** requirement
resbalarse to slide, **5.3**
rescatar to rescue, **1.3; 8.3**
la **reservación** reservation, II: 6.1
reservado(a) reserved, I: 13.2; II: 1.2
reservar to reserve, I: 14.2; II: 2.2
resfriado(a): estar resfriado(a) to have a cold, I: 8.1
la **residencia: la residencia para estudiantes** student housing, dormitory, II: 3.2
el/la **residente** resident
residir to reside
el **residuo** residue
resistir to resist
la **resolución** resolution
resolver (ue) to solve
el **respaldo** back (of seat), II: 7.1
respetar to respect, **2.3**
la **respiración** breathing
respirar to breathe
responder to respond
la **responsabilidad** responsibility
responsabilizarse to make oneself responsible
la **respuesta** answer
restar to subtract
el **restaurante** restaurant, I: 14.1; II: 2.1
restaurar to restore
restituir to return, to give back
el **resto** rest, remainder, residue, **5.1**
los **restos** remains
el **resultado** result
la **retina** retina
el **retintín** jingle
retirar del fuego to remove from the heat (stove), II: 10.1
el **retraso: con retraso** with a delay, late, I: 13.2; II: 1.2; **1.2**
el **retrato** portrait; photograph, LC8
retroceder backup (in a car), **5.2**
reubicarse to relocate, **2.3; 4.1**
la **reunión** gathering
reunirse to get together
revelar to reveal
revisar to inspect, I: 11.1; to check
revisar el boleto to check the ticket, I: 11.1
revisar el aceite to check the oil (car), II: 11.1
el/la **revisor(a)** (train) conductor, I: 13.2; II: 1.2
la **revista** magazine, I: 6.2
la **revolución** revolution
revolver (ue) to turn around; to stir, II: 10.1
el **rey** king, **1.1**
los **Reyes Magos** Three Wise Men, II: 13.2
el Día de los Reyes Epiphany (January 6), II: 13.2
el **rezo** prayer
rico(a) rich; delicious, I: 14.2; II: 2.2; **6.2**
el/la **rico(a)** rich person
el **riesgo** risk, **5.2; 7.3**
riguroso(a) rigorous
el **río** river, II: 7.2
el **ritmo** rhythm
el **rito** ritual, **8.1**
el **ritual** ritual
el **rival** rival
robar to rob, **2.2**
el **robo** robbery, **2.2**
la **robustez** robustness

la **roca** rock, **1.3**
rociar to sprinkle, LC5
rodar (ue) to roll
rodear to surround
la **rodilla** knee, I: 7.1; LC1
rogar (ue) to beg, to plead; **4.3**
rojo(a) red, I: 3.2
el **rol** role
el **rollo de papel higiénico** roll of toilet paper, I: 12.2
el/la **romano(a)** Roman
romántico(a) romantic
el **romero** rosemary, LC8
romperse to break, II: 8.1
la **ropa** clothing, I: 3.2
la ropa interior underwear, II: 4.1
la ropa para caballeros (señoras) men's (women's) clothing, II: 4.1
la ropa sucia dirty laundry, II: 12.1
la tienda de ropa clothing store, I: 3.2
la **rosa** rose
rosado(a) pink, I: 3.2
el **rostro** face, LC8
el **rótulo** sign, II: 11.2
el **rubí** ruby
rubio(a) blond(e), I: 1.1
rudo(a) severe, course, LC5
las **ruedas: la silla de ruedas** wheelchair, II: 8.2
la **ruina** ruin
el **rumbo** bearing, direction, LC1; LC4
el **rumor** rumor
la **ruta** route
la **rutina** routine, I: 12.1
la rutina libre freestyle, **6.3**
rutinario(a) routine *(adj.)*

el **sábado** Saturday, BV
la **sabana** savanna, **3.1**
la **sábana** sheet, II: 6.2
el/la **sabelotodo** know-it-all
saber to know (how), I: 11.2
sabio(a) wise
sabroso(a) delicious
el **sacapuntas** pencil sharpener, **6.3**
sacar to get, I: 4.2; to take out, II: 3.1
sacar un billete to buy a ticket
sacar una nota buena (mala) to get a good (bad) grade, I: 4.2
el **sacerdote** priest
el **saco** jacket, II: 4.1; **3.2**
el saco cruzado twill jacket, **3.2**
el saco de dormir sleeping bag, I: 12.2
sacrificar to sacrifice
el **sacrificio** sacrifice
sagrado(a) sacred, LC4
la **sal** salt, I: 14.1; II: 2.1
la **sala** room; living room, I: 6.2
la sala de clase classroom, I: 4.1
la sala de consulta doctor's office
la sala de emergencia emergency room, II: 8.1
la sala de espera waiting room, I: 13.1; II: 1.1
la sala de juegos game arcade, II: 5.1
la sala de recuperación recovery room
la sala de salida departure area, I: 11.1
la sala de urgencias emergency room
el **salario** salary
la **salchicha** sausage, II: 10.1
el **saldo** balance (bank), **4.2**
la **salida** departure, leaving, I: 11.1; exit, II: 11.2
la hora de salida departure hour, I: 13.1; II: 1.1
la pantalla de llegadas y salidas arrival and departure screen, I: 11.1
la sala de salida departure area, I: 11.1
la salida de emergencia emergency exit, II: 7.1
salir to leave, I: 10.1; to go out; to turn out
salir a tiempo to leave on time, I: 11.1
salir bien (en un examen) to do well (on an exam), I: 10.1
salir tarde to leave late, I: 11.1
el **salón** hall, II: 13.1; room
el salón de clase classroom, I: 4.1
saltar to jump
el **salto** jump, leap, **5.3;** waterfall, **7.1**
la **salud** health
saludar to greet
el **saludo** greeting, BV
salvaje wild
salvar to save
salvo(a) safe
la **sandalia** sandal, II: 4.1
la **sandía** watermelon, II: 10.2; **3.1**
el **sándwich** sandwich, BV
la **sangre** blood
sano(a) healthy
el **santo** saint
el **santuario** sanctuary
el/la **sartén** frying pan, II: 10.1
satisfacer to satisfy
satisfecho(a) satisfied, II: 14.1
el **saxofono** saxophone
sazonar to season
el **secador** hair dryer, II: 12.1
secar to dry, II: 12.2
la **sección de (no) fumar** (no) smoking section, I: 11.1
seco(a) dry
el/la **secretario(a)** secretary, II: 14.1
el **secreto** secret
la **secuela** result, **7.3**
secundario(a) secondary
la escuela secundaria high school, I: 1.1
sed: tener sed to be thirsty, I: 14.1; II: 2.1
la **seda: seda dental** dental floss, LC7
el **sedán** sedan, II: 11.1
la **sede** seat (of government)
el/la **sefardí** Sephardi, Jewish person expelled from Spain during the Spanish Inquisition
seguir (i, i) to follow, to continue, II: 11.2
Sigue derecho. Go straight.
según according to
segundo(a) second, I: 6.2
el segundo tiempo second half (soccer), I: 7.1
en segunda (clase) second-class, I: 13.1; II: 1.1
la **seguridad** security, II: 7.1
el control de seguridad security (airport), I: 11.1
el **seguro** insurance, **5.2**
seguro(a): estar seguro(a) to be sure
seis six, BV
seiscientos(as) six hundred, I: 3.2
la **selección** selection
seleccionar to select
sellar to seal, to stamp, **7.1**
el **sello** stamp, II: 5.1
la **selva** jungle, **5.1**
la selva tropical (lluviosa) rainforest
el **semáforo** traffic light, II: 9.1; **5.2**
la **semana** week, BV

el fin de semana weekend, BV
el fin de semana pasado last weekend
la semana pasada last week, I: 9.2
sembrar to sow, plant, II: 9.2
semejante similar
el **semestre** semester
el/la **senador(a)** senator
la **sencillez** simplicity
sencillo(a) easy, simple
el billete sencillo one-way ticket, I: 13.1; II: 1.1
el cuarto sencillo single room, II: 6.1
la **senda** path, II: 5.2; LC7
caminar por la senda to walk along the path, II: 5.2
las **sentadillas** sit-ups, **5.3**
sentar (ie) to fit, **3.2**
La camisa te sienta bien. The shirt fits you well.
sentarse (ie) to sit down, I: 12.1
el **sentido** meaning, significance; direction, II: 11.2
en cada sentido in either direction, II: 11.2
una calle de sentido único one-way street, II: 11.2
el sentido contrario opposite way, II: 11.2
sentir (ie, i) to be sorry
sentirse (ie, i) bien (mal) to feel well (ill), II: 8.1
la **señal de no fumar** no smoking sign, II: 7.1
la **señal de tráfico (tránsito)** traffic sign, **5.2**
el **señor** sir, Mr., gentleman, BV
la **señora** Ms., Mrs., madam, BV
la **señorita** Miss, Ms., BV
la **separación** separation
separado(a) separated
el **sepelio** burial, **4.3**
septiembre September, BV
séptimo(a) seventh, I: 6.2
la **sequía** drought, **7.1**
ser to be
ser una lástima to be a pity
el **ser: el ser humano** human being
el ser viviente living creature, being
la **serie** series
la Serie mundial World Series
serio(a) serious, I: 1.1
en serio seriously
la **serpiente** snake, serpent, **5.1**
el **servicio** service, tip, I: 5.1
¿Está incluido el servicio? Is the tip included?, I: 5.1
el **servicio de primeros auxilios** first aid service, paramedics, II: 8.1
la **servilleta** napkin, I: 14.1; II: 2.1
servir (i, i) to serve, I: 14.1; II: 2.1
¿En qué puedo servirle? How may I help you?, II: 4.1
sesenta sixty, I: 2.2
la **sesión** show (movies), I: 10.1
setecientos(as) seven hundred, I: 3.2
setenta seventy, I: 2.2
severo(a) severe
el **sexo** sex
sexto(a) sixth, I: 6.2
el **show** show
si if
sí yes
el **SIDA** AIDS
la **siembra** sowing
siempre always, I: 7.1
de siempre y para siempre eternally, forever
la **sien** temple (of head), LC6
la **sierra** sierra, mountain range, LC7
siete seven, BV
el **sigilo** seal
la **sigla** acronym (AAA, NATO), abbreviation, **4.3**
el **siglo** century, **1.1**
el **significado** meaning
significante meaningful
significar to mean
significativo(a) significant
siguiente following
la **silla** chair
la **silla de ruedas** wheelchair, II: 8.2
el **sillón** armchair, II: 6.2; dentist's chair, LC7
silvestre wild
similar similar
simpático(a) nice, I: 1.2
simple simple
sin without
sin escala nonstop
sincero(a) sincere, I: 1.2
singles singles, I: 9.1
el **síntoma** symptom, I: 8.2
el **sirope** syrup
el/la **sirviente(a)** servant
el **sistema** system
el sistema métrico metric system
el **sitio** place
la **situación** situation
situar to situate
situarse to be situated, **2.1**
soberbio(a) arrogant, proud
sobre on top of; over; on, about
sobre todo especially
el **sobre** envelope, II: 12.2
sobrepasar to surpass
sobresaltar to jump up
sobrevolar to fly over, II: 7.2
la **sobrina** niece, I: 6.1
el **sobrino** nephew, I: 6.1
social: las ciencias sociales social sciences
la **sociedad** society
la **sociología** sociology
socorrer to help
el/la **socorrista** paramedic, II: 8.1; rescue worker, **8.3**
el **socorro** help
el **sofá** sofa, II: 6.2
la **soga** rope, cord, LC3
el **sol** Peruvian coin; sun, I: 9.1
Hace (Hay) sol. It's sunny., I: 9.1
tomar el sol to sunbathe, I: 9.1
solamente only
la **solapa** lapel, **3.2**
el/la **soldado** soldier, **1.1**
solemne solemn
soler (ue) to be accustomed to, tend to, **2.1; 4.1**
solicitar to apply for, **1.3**
la **solicitud de empleo** job application, II: 14.2
solitario(a) solitary, lone
sólo only
solo(a) alone
a solas alone
el café solo black coffee, I: 5.1
soltar (ue) to let go, to set free, LC3
soltero(a) single, bachelor
la **solución** solution
la **sombra** shade, LC4
el **sombrero** hat
someter subdue
someterse to surrender, **6.1**
sonar (ue) to ring, II: 3.2
el **sonido** sound
la **sonrisa** smile, **2.3**
la **sonrisita** little smile
la **sopa** soup, I: 5.1
el **soporte** support, **8.3**
el **sorbete** sherbet, sorbet
el/la **sordo(a)** deaf person
sorprender to surprise
sostener to support
su his, her, their, your
súbito sudden, **8.3**
subir to go up, I: 6.2; to board, to get on; to take up
subir al tren to get on, to board the train, I: 13.1; II: 1.1

subterráneo(a) underground
el **subtítulo** subtitle, I: 10.1
con subtítulos with subtitles, I: 10.1
el **suburbio** suburb
subyugar to subjugate, **2.1**
suceder to happen, to occur, **5.3**
suceso: el buen suceso great event, **1.3**
sucio(a) dirty
la ropa sucia dirty laundry, II: 12.1
la **sucursal** branch (office)
sudamericano(a) South American
sudar to sweat, LC2
el **sudeste** southeast (region), **8.1**
el **sudoeste** southwest (region), **8.1**
el **sudor** sweat, LC2
el **suegro** father-in-law
la **suela** sole (shoes), **3.2; 5.3**
la suela de goma rubber sole
el **suelo** ground, LC3; floor
el **suelto** change, II: 12.2; **4.2**
el **sueño** dream
la **suerte** luck
¡Buena suerte! Good luck!
el **suéter** sweater, II: 4.1; **3.2**
un suéter de lana wool sweater
suficiente enough
sufrir to suffer
la **sugerencia** suggestion
sugerir (ie, i) to suggest
la **Suiza** Switzerland
sujetar subject, LC1
sumar to add
suministrar to provide, **8.3**
súper super (gas), II: 11.1
superar to surpass, **8.1**
la **superficie** surface
superior: la escuela superior high school
el **supermercado** supermarket, I: 5.2
la **superstición** superstition
supuesto: por supuesto of course
el **sur** south
sureste southeast (region), **8.1**
el **surf de nieve** snowboarding
surfear (los canales) to channel surf, **8.2**
el **surfing** surfing, I: 9.1
practicar el surfing to surf, I: 9.1
surgir to arise, **7.1**
el **suroeste** southwest (region), **8.1**
el **surtido** assortment
sus their, your *(pl.)*, I: 6.1
suspirar to sigh
la **sustancia: la sustancia controlada** controlled substance
la **sutura** stitch

T

el **T-shirt** T-shirt, I: 3.2
la **tabla** board (surfboard), **5.3**
la tabla hawaiana surfboard, I: 9.1
el **tablero** board, I: 7.1; gameboard, II: 5.1
el tablero de llegadas arrival board, I: 13.1; II: 1.1
el tablero de salidas departure board, I: 13.1; II: 1.1
el tablero indicador scoreboard, I: 7.1
la **tableta** pill, I: 8.2
taciturno(a) taciturn, LC2
el **taco** taco, BV
el **tacón** heel, II: 4.1; **3.2**
de tacón alto high-heeled
botas de tacón alto high-heeled boots
zapatos de tacón alto high-heeled shoes
taíno(a) Taino
la **tajada** slice, II: 4.2
tal: ¿Qué tal? How are you?, BV
el **talento** talent, II: 14.1
la **talla** size (clothing), I: 3.2
tallado(a) carved
el **taller** workshop, LC3
el **talón** luggage claim ticket, I: 11.1
el **talonario** checkbook, **4.2**
el **tamal** tamale, BV
el **tamaño** size, I: 3.2
también also
tampoco either
tan so
tan… como as . . . as, II: 8.2
el **tango** tango
el **tanque** gas tank, II: 11.1
llenar el tanque de gasolina to fill the tank with gas, II: 11.1
el tanque de gasolina diesel truck, **7.3**
el **tanto** point, I: 7.1
marcar un tanto to score a point
tanto(a) so much
tanto(a)… como as much . . . as
tantos(as)… como as many . . . as, II: 8.2
tapar to cover, II: 10.2
el **tapón** traffic jam, **1.2**
la **taquilla** box office, I: 10.1
tardar to take time
tarda el viaje the trip takes (+ time)
tarde late
la **tarde** afternoon
Buenas tardes. Good afternoon., BV
esta tarde this afternoon, I: 9.2
por la tarde in the afternoon
la **tarea** task
hacer las tareas to do one's homework, II: 3.1
la **tarifa** fare, rate
la **tarjeta** card, I: 11.1; **4.2;** registration card (hotel), II: 6.1
la tarjeta bancaria bankcard
la tarjeta de crédito credit card, I: 14.1; II: 2.1; **5.2**
la tarjeta de embarque boarding pass, I: 11.1
la tarjeta de identidad estudiantil student I.D. card
la tarjeta postal postcard, II: 12.2
la tarjeta telefónica telephone card, II: 3.2
el **tarro: el tarro de agua** water bottle, 7.3
la **tasa** rate
la tasa de cambio exchange rate, II: 12.2
la tasa de desempleo unemployment rate
el **taxi** taxi, I: 11.1; **1.2**
el **taxímetro** taxi meter, **1.2**
la **taza** cup, I: 14.1; II: 2.1
te you
el **té** tea, I: 5.1
el té helado iced tea, I: 5.1
teatral theatrical, I: 10.2
el **teatro** theater, I: 10.2
salir del teatro to leave the theater, I: 10.2
el **techo** roof, **4.1**
la **tecla** key (on keyboard), II: 3.2
el **teclado** keyboard, II: 3.1; telephone keypad, II: 3.2
el/la **técnico(a)** technician, II: 8.2
la **tecnología** technology
el/la **tejedor(a)** weaver, **2.1**
tejer to weave, **2.1**
el **tejido** weave, **2.1**
la **tela** fabric, **3.2**
tela de algodón cotton fabric
tela de ante (gamuza) fabric made of suede
tela de cuero leather fabric

tela de dénim denim fabric
tela de lana wool fabric
tela de punto knit fabric
la **telecomunicación** telecommunication, II: 3.1
telefonear to telephone
telefónico(a) (related to the) telephone
la línea telefónica telephone line
la llamada telefónica telephone call, II: 3.2
el **teléfono** telephone
el teléfono de botones push-button telephone, II: 3.2
el teléfono celular cellular telephone, II: 3.2
el teléfono público public (pay) telephone, II: 3.2
hablar por teléfono to talk on the phone
el poste de teléfono telephone pole, **8.3**
la **telenovela** soap opera, **8.2**
el **telesilla** chairlift, I: 9.2
el **telesquí** ski lift, I: 9.2
el/la **televidente** television viewer, **8.2**
la **televisión** television, I: 6.2
el **televisor** television set, II: 6.2; **8.2**
el **telón** curtain (stage), I: 10.2; **7.2**
el **tema** theme, subject
temer to fear
temible fearful, terrible, **5.1**
el **temor** fear, LC6
la **temperatura** temperature, I: 9.2
la **tempestad** storm
templado(a) temperate
temprano early, I: 12.1
la **tendencia** tendency
el tenedor fork, I: 14.1; II: 2.1
tener (ie) to have, I: 6.1
tener un accidente to have an accident, II: 8.1
tener... años to be . . . years old, I: 6.1
tener buena pinta to look good, II: 4.2
tener cuidado to be careful
tener hambre to be hungry, I: 14.1; II: 2.1
tener lugar to take place, occur, II: 8.1
tener miedo to be afraid
tener que to have to
tener sed to be thirsty, I: 14.1; II: 2.1
el **tenis** tennis, I: 9.1
los **tenis** tennis shoes, I: 3.2; **5.3**
el par de tenis pair of tennis shoes, I: 3.2
el/la **tenista** tennis player
la **tensión arterial** blood pressure, II: 8.2
tercer(o)(a) third, I: 6.2
la **terminal: la terminal de pasajeros** passenger terminal, II: 7.2
terminar to end, finish, II: 3.1
el **término** term
el **termo** thermos, **7.3**
la **ternera** veal, I: 14.2; II: 2.2
la **terraza** terrace (sidewalk café)
el **terremoto** earthquake, **4.1**
terrible terrible
el **territorio** territory
el **terror** terror, fear
el **tesoro** treasure
el **tétano** tetanus
la **tía** aunt, I: 6.1
tibio(a) luke warm, LC7
el **ticket** ticket, I: 9.2
el **tiempo** time; weather, I: 9.1; half (game**)**
a tiempo on time, I: 11.1
a tiempo completo (parcial) full- (part-) time *(adj.),* II: 14.2
el segundo tiempo second half (game), I: 7.1
pasar el tiempo to spend (pass) time, II: 5.1
la **tienda** store, I: 3.2
la tienda de abarrotes grocery store, II: 4.2
la tienda de departamentos department store
la tienda de ropa clothing store, I: 3.2
la tienda de ropa para caballeros men's clothing store, II: 4.1
la tienda de ropa para señoras women's clothing store, II: 4.1
la tienda de ultramarinos grocery store, II: 4.2
la tienda de videos video store
tierno(a) tender
la **tierra** land
por tierra by land, overland
el **tigre** tiger
las **tijeras** scissors, II: 12.1
el **tilde** accent
tímido(a) timid, shy, I: 1.2
la **tintorería** dry cleaner, II: 12.1
el/la **tintorero(a)** dry cleaner, II: 12.1
el **tío** uncle, I: 6.1
los tíos aunt and uncle, I: 6.1
el **tiovivo** merry-go-round, II: 5.2
típicamente typically
típico(a) typical
el **tipo** type
el **tipo de cambio** exchange rate, II: 12.2; **4.2**
el **tique** ticket, II: 9.1
tirar to kick, I: 7.1; to throw
tirar el balón to kick (throw) the ball, I: 7.2
el **título universitario** university degree, II: 14.1
la **toalla** towel, II: 6.2
la toalla playera beach towel, I: 9.1
el **tobillo** ankle, II: 8.1
tocar to touch; to play (music)
tocar la bocina to honk the horn
todavía yet, still
todo: todo el mundo everyone
todos(as) everybody, I: 2.2; everything, all
por todas partes everywhere
el **todoterreno** SUV, **5.2**
la **toma** capture, **6.1**
tomar to take, I: 4.1
tomar agua (leche, café) to drink water (milk, coffee)
tomar apuntes to take notes, I: 4.2
tomar el bus (escolar) to take the (school) bus, I: 4.1
tomar el desayuno to eat breakfast, I: 12.1
tomar una ducha to take a shower, I: 12.1
tomar fotos to take photos
tomar una merienda to have a snack, I: 4.2
tomar el pulso to take one's pulse, II: 8.2
tomar una radiografía to take an X-ray
tomar un refresco to have (drink) a beverage
tomar el sol to sunbathe, I: 9.1
tomar la tensión (presión) arterial to take one's blood pressure, II: 8.2
tomar un vuelo to take a flight, I: 11.1
el **tomate** tomato
el **tomo** volume
la **tonalidad** tonality
la **tonelada** ton
el **tono** dial tone, II: 3.2; hue
tonto(a) foolish
el **tórax** thorax, **5.3**
torcerse (ue) to twist, II: 8.1
la **tormenta** storm, **8.3**
el **torneo** tournament

el torneo de nado (natación) swim meet
el **torniquete** turnstile, II: 9.1
la **toronja** grapefruit, II: 10.1
el **torpe** stupid person, LC1
torpe stupid
la **torre: la torre de control** control tower, II: 7.2
la **torta** cake, sandwich, II: 13.1
la **tortilla** tortilla, I: 5.1
la **tórtola** turtle dove
la **tos: tener tos** to have a cough, I: 8.1
tosco(a) course, rough
toser to cough, I: 8.1
la **tostada** toast
tostadito(a) sunburned, tanned
tostado(a): el pan tostado toast, I: 5.2
tostar to toast
el **tostón** fried, plantain slice
totalmente totally, completely
tóxico(a) toxic
el/la **trabajador(a)** worker
trabajar to work, I: 3.2
trabajar a tiempo completo to work full-time, II: 14.2
trabajar a tiempo parcial to work part-time, II: 14.2
el **trabajo** work; job, II: 14.2
el trabajo a tiempo completo (parcial) full-time (part-time) job, II: 14.2
la **tradición** tradition
tradicional traditional
traducir to translate
traer to bring, I: 14.1; II: 2.1
el **tráfico** traffic
tragar swallow, LC6
la **tragedia** tragedy
el **traidor** traitor
el **traje** suit, I: 3.2; **3.3**
el traje de baño bathing suit, I: 9.1
el traje de gala evening gown, dress
el **tramo** stretch
la **trampa** trap, LC3
tranquilo(a) peaceful; calm; quiet
transbordar to transfer, I: 13.2; II: 1.2
transformar to transform
transmitir to send, to transmit, II: 3.1; **8.2**
transpirar to transpire, LC2
el **transporte** transportation
el **trapo** rag, LC7
tras after
trasladar to transfer, move, **4.1**
el **tratamiento** treatment
tratar to treat; to try
el **trayecto** stretch (of road)
trece thirteen, BV
la **tregua** truce, **2.3**
treinta thirty, BV
treinta y uno thirty-one, I: 2.2
el **tren** train, I: 13.2; II: 1.2
el tren directo nonstop train, I: 13.2; II: 1.2
el tren local local train, I: 13.2; II: 1.2
el tren subterráneo underground train
la **trenza** braid
tres three, BV
trescientos(as) three hundred, I: 3.2
la **tribu** tribe
el **tribunal** court, II: 14.1
el **tributario** tributary (of a river)
el **trigo** wheat, II: 9.2
la **tripulación** crew, I: 11.2
triste sad, I: 8.1
triunfante triumphant
trocarse to change
el **trocito** piece, II: 10.2
el **trombón** trombone
la **trompeta** trumpet
tropical tropical
el **trozo: trocito** small piece, **1.1**
el **trono** throne
la **tropa** troop, 1.1
tu your
tú you
el **tubo de escape** exhaust pipe
el **tubo de pasta (crema) dentífrica** tube of toothpaste, I: 12.2
tumultuoso(a) tumultuous, LC2
turbio(a) confused, obscure, LC7
la **turbulencia** turbulence, II: 7.2
el/la **turista** tourist, I: 10.2

u or (used instead of **o** before words beginning with **o** or **ho**)
ubicarse to be located, **2.3; 6.3**
Ud., usted you, I: 3.2
Uds., ustedes you, I: 2.2
último(a) last
ultramarinos: la tienda de ultramarinos grocery store, II: 4.2
un(a) a, an, I: 1.1
la **una** one o'clock, I: 2.2
único(a) only; unique
la **unidad: la unidad de cuidado intensivo** intensive care unit
el **uniforme** uniform
unirse to join
la **universidad** university
universitario(a) (related to) university
uno one, BV
unos(as) some
urbano(a) urban
urgencias: la sala de urgencias emergency room
la **urología** urology
el/la **urólogo(a)** urologist
usado(a) used
usar to wear (size), I: 3.2; to use
el **usuario** user, **1.3**
utilizar to use
las **uvas** grapes, II: 10.1

la **vaca** cow, II: 9.2
la **vacación** vacation, II: 6.2
vacio(a) empty
el/la **vago(a)** loafer, idler, wanderer
el **vagón** train car, I: 13.1; II: 1.1
la **vainilla: de vainilla** vanilla *(adj.)*, I: 5.1
la **vainita** string bean
¡Vale! OK!
la **valentía** valor, bravery, LC6
valer to be worth
valeroso(a) brave
valiente brave
valientemente valiantly
la **valla** fence, LC1
el **valle** valley, II: 7.2
el **valor** value, worth
el valor real true value
vamos let's go
la **variación** variation
variado(a) varied
variar to vary, change
la **variedad** variety
vario(a) various
el **varón** male
vasco(a) Basque
la pelota vasca jai alai
el **vaso** (drinking) glass, I: 12.1
vasto(a) vast
el **váter** toilet, II: 6.2
el/la **vecino(a)** neighbor
la **vegetación** vegetation
el **vegetal** vegetable, I: 5.2
el/la **vegetariano(a)** vegetarian
veinte twenty, BV
veinticinco twenty-five, BV

veinticuatro twenty-four, BV
veintidós twenty-two, BV
veintinueve twenty-nine, BV
veintiocho twenty-eight, BV
veintiséis twenty-six, BV
veintisiete twenty-seven, BV
veintitrés twenty-three, BV
veintiuno twenty-one, BV
la **vela** candle, II: 13.1; sail, **5.3**
velar to hold a wake, LC8
el **velatorio** wake (of a funeral)
la **velocidad** speed, II: 11.2
  la velocidad máxima speed limit, II: 11.2
el **velorio** wake (of a funeral), **4.3**
la **vena** vein
vencer to conquer, to defeat, LC1
el **vendaje** bandage, II: 8.2
  poner un vendaje to put a bandage on, II: 8.2
el/la **vendedor(a)** salesperson, II: 11.1
vender to sell, I: 5.2
el **veneno** poison
venenoso(a) poisonous
venezolano(a) Venezuelan
venir to come, I: 11.1
  el viernes (sábado, etc.) que viene next Friday (Saturday, etc.)
la **venta** sale, II: 14.1; inn, **1.2**
la **ventaja** advantage
la **ventanilla** ticket window, I: 9.2; window (airplane), II: 7.1; teller's window, II: 12.2
ver to see; to watch, I: 5.1
veraniego(a) summer *(adj.)*, **1.1**
  una casa veraniega summer house
el **verano** summer, BV
el **verbo** verb
la **verdad** truth
  ¡Verdad! That's right (true)!
verdadero(a) true, real
verde green, I: 3.2
  la judía verde green bean, I: 5.2
la **verdulería** greengrocer store, II: 4.2
la **verdura** vegetable
verificar to check, I: 13.1; II: 1.1
la **versión: en versión original** in (its) original version, I: 10.1
el **verso** verse
vertical vertical
vestido(a) dressed
el **vestido** dress, II: 4.1
  los vestidos clothes *(pl.)*
el **vestigio** vestige
vestirse (i, i) to get dressed
el **vesturario** costumes (in a play), **7.2**
el/la **veterinario(a)** veterinarian
la **vez** time
  a veces at times, sometimes, I: 7.1
  de vez en cuando now and then
  en vez de instead of
  una vez más one more time, again
la **vía** track, I: 13.1; II: 1.1
viajar to travel
  viajar en avión to travel by plane, I: 11.1
el **viaje** trip
  el viaje de novios honeymoon
  el viaje de regreso return trip
  hacer un viaje to take a trip, I: 11.1
el/la **viajero(a)** traveler
la **víbora** viper, LC3
viceversa vice versa
el **vicio** vice
víctima victim, II: 8.1; **2.2**
victorioso(a) victorious
la **vida** life
  la vida escolar school life
el **video** video
viejo(a) old, I: 6.1
el/la **viejo(a)** old person
el **viento** wind
el **viernes** Friday, BV
el **vigor** vigor
vil vile
villa: villa miseria shantytown (Arg.)
el **vinagre** vinegar
el **vínculo** bond, **8.1**
el **viñedo** vineyard, **3.1**
la **viola** viola
la **violencia** violence
violento(a) violent, **2.3**
el **violín** violin
la **virtud** virtue, LC6
visible visible
visitar to visit
la **víspera de Año Nuevo** New Year's Eve, II: 13.2
la **vista** view
vital vital
la **vitamina** vitamin
la **vitrina** shop window, II: 4.1
la **viuda** widow, **2.3**
la **vivienda** housing
viviente: el ser viviente living creature, being
vivir to live, I: 5.2
vivo(a) living, alive
la **vocal** vowel
volar (ue) to fly, II: 7.2
el **volcán** volcano, **2.3**
volcánico(a) volcanic, **2.3**
el **voleibol** volleyball
voltearse to roll over, **5.3**
el/la **voluntario(a)** volunteer
volver (ue) to return, I: 7.1
  volver a casa to return home, I: 10.2
la **voz** voice
  en voz alta aloud
el **vuelo** flight, I: 11.1; 1.1
  el número del vuelo flight number, I: 11.1
  tomar un vuelo to take a flight, I: 11.1
  el vuelo directo direct flight, II: 7.2
  el vuelo nacional domestic flight
la **vuelta: dar la vuelta** to turn around

Y

y and, BV
  y cuarto a quarter past (the hour)
  y media half past (the hour)
  y pico just after (the hour)
ya now, already
la **yarda** yard
la **yema** yolk
la **yerba** herb, LC6
yerto(a) stiff, LC7
el **yeso** cast, II: 8.2
yo I, I: 1.1
el **yogur** yogurt

Z

la **zanahoria** carrot, I: 5.2
la **zapatería** shoe store, II: 4.1; **3.2**
el **zapato** shoe, I: 3.2; **3.2**
  zapatos de tacón alto high-heeled shoes
la **zona** zone, area, neighborhood
  la zona comercial business zone, II: 9.1
  la zona industrial industrial area, II: 9.1
  la zona residencial residential area, II: 9.1
el **zumo de naranja** orange juice (Spain)
zurdo(a) left-handed, **6.3**

English-Spanish Dictionary

The English-Spanish Dictionary contains all productive and receptive vocabulary from Levels 1, 2 and 3. The numbers following each productive entry indicate the chapter and lesson in which the word is introduced. For example, **3.2** *in dark print means that the word was taught in this textbook* **Capítulo 3, Lección 2.** *A reference to LC means the word was taught in this textbook in the Literary Companion section. A light print number preceded by I means that the word was introduced in* **¡Buen viaje!,** *Level 1. A light print number preceded by II means that the word was introduced in* **¡Buen viaje!,** *Level 2. BV refers to the introductory* **Bienvenidos** *lessons in Level 1. If there is no number following an entry, this means that the word or expression is there for receptive purposes only.*

a, an un(a), I: 1.1
abdication la abdicación
abdomen el abdomen, **5.3**
aboard, on board a bordo de
  to abound abundar, **5.3**
about sobre; acerca de; (time) a eso de, II: 4.1
above encima; por encima de, I: 9.1
abroad en el extranjero
abstract abstracto(a)
abundant caudal(oso)
  abundant river un río caudal(oso)
abuse el abuso
academic académico(a)
academy la academia
to **accelerate** acelerar
accent el tilde
to **accept** aceptar
access el acceso
accident el accidente, II: 8.1
to **accommodate** acomodar
accompaniment el acompañamiento
to **accompany** acompañar, **6.2**
according to según
account (bank) la cuenta
  checking account la cuenta corriente, II: 12.2
  savings account la cuenta de ahorros
accountant el/la contable, II: 14.1
to **be accustomed to** soler (ue), **2.1; 4.1**
ache el dolor, I: 8.1
to **ache: My . . . ache(s).** Me duele(n)… , II: 8.2
to **achieve** lograr, **7.3**
acronym la sigla, **4.3**
acrylic el acrílico
action la acción
active activo(a)
activity la actividad
act el acto
actor el actor, I: 10.2
actress la actriz, I: 10.2
to **adapt** adaptar
to **add** sumar; agregar, añadir, II: 10.2
addiction la adicción
addition: in addition to además de
address la dirección
to **address** dirigirse a
adequate adecuado(a), **3.3**
to **adjust** ajustar
adjustment el ajuste, el arreglo, **5.1**
to **admire** admirar
admission ticket la entrada, I: 10.1; **7.2**
to **admit** admitir, II: 8.2
adolescence la adolescencia
adolescent el/la adolescente
adorable adorable
adoration la adoración
to **adore** adorar
to **adorn** adornar
advance el avance
advanced adelantado(a), **5.1**
advantage la ventaja
adventure la aventura
adversity la adversidad
advertisement el anuncio, II: 14.2
advertising la propaganda
advice el consejo, **2.3;** el aviso, LC2
to **advise** aconsejar; avisar
aerobic aeróbico(a)
to **affect** impresionar
African africano(a)
African American afroamericano(a)
after después (de), I: 5.1; tras
afternoon la tarde
  Good afternoon. Buenas tardes., BV
  in the afternoon por la tarde
  this afternoon esta tarde, I: 9.2
again de nuevo
against contra, I: 7.1
age la edad
  How old are you? ¿Cuántos años tienes?
agency la agencia
  employment agency la agencia de empleos
agent el/la agente, I: 11.1
  customs agent el/la agente de aduana, I: 11.2
aggressive belicoso(a), **3.1**
aging person el/la envejeciente
agony la agonía, LC5
agreed, fine conforme, I: 14.2
agreement el acuerdo, **5.3**
agricultural agrícola
ahead adelante
AIDS el SIDA
air el aire, II: 11.1
air conditioning el aire acondicionado, II: 6.2
air traffic controller el/la controlador(a), II: 7.2
airline la línea aérea
airmail el correo aéreo, II: 12.2
airplane el avión, I: 11.1
  small airplane la avioneta, II: 7.2
airport el aeropuerto, I: 11.1; **1.2**
aisle el pasillo, I: 13.2; II: 1.2
album el álbum
alcohol el alcohol
alcoholism el alcoholismo
algebra el álgebra, I: 2.2
alive vivo(a)
all todos(as)
allegory la alegoría
allergy la alergia, I: 8.2
alley la callejuela

paving stone alley la callejuela de adoquines, **4.1**
alliance la alianza
to **allow** consentir (ie, i); dejar
ally el/la aliado(a), **5.1**
almond la almendra, **1.1**
almost casi; por poco, **6.1**
alone solo(a); a solas
along a lo largo
aloud en voz alta
already ya
also también
altar el altar, LC8
to **alternate** alternar
although aunque
altitude la altitud, la altura, II: 7.2
always siempre, I: 7.1
ambassador el/la embajador(a)
ambulance la ambulancia, II: 8.1
American americano(a), I: 1.1
amount la cantidad
ample amplio(a), **1.3**
amusement la diversión
amusement park el parque de atracciones, II: 5.2
amusement park ride la atracción, II: 5.2
amusing divertido(a)
analysis el análisis
analytical analítico(a)
to **analyze** analizar
ancestor el antepasado, LC4
anchor (boat) la ancla, **8.2**
news anchor el/la ancla, **8.2**
woman news anchor la mujer ancla, **8.1**
anchovy la anchoa
ancient antiguo(a), II: 5.1
and y, BV
Andalusian andaluz(a)
Andean andino(a)
anecdote la anécdota
angelical angelical, LC5
angry enfadado(a); iracundo(a)
animal el animal
farm animal el animal doméstico, II: 9.2
ankle el tobillo, II: 8.1
anniversary el aniversario
to **announce** anunciar
announcement el anuncio, II: 7.1; la esquela, LC8
another otro(a)
another's ajeno(a), LC5
to **answer** contestar, II: 3.2
answer la respuesta
answering machine el contestador automático, II: 3.2
Antarctic la Antártida
antibiotic el antibiótico, I: 8.2
antiquated anticuado(a)
antiquity la antigüedad
any cualquier
apartment el apartamento, el departamento, I: 6.2; el piso
apartment house la casa de apartamentos (departamentos), I: 6.2
apostle el apóstol
to **appear** aparecer
appearance la apariencia
appendicitis la apendicitis
to **applaud** aplaudir, I: 10.2
applause el aplauso, I: 10.2
to receive applause recibir aplausos, I: 10.2
apple la manzana, I: 5.2
apple tree el manzano, II: 9.2
application (job) la solicitud (de empleo)
to **apply (for a job)** solicitar trabajo, **1.3**
to **appreciate** agradecer, **7.3**
to **approach** acercarse (a)
appropriate apropiado(a)
April abril, BV
aptitude la aptitud
aqueduct el acueducto
Arab el/la árabe
archaeological arqueológico(a)
archaeologist el/la arqueólogo(a)
archbishop el arzobispo
archeology la arqueología
archipelago el archipiélago
architect el/la arquitecto(a), II: 14.1
archpriest el arcipreste
area el área *(f.)*; la zona
area code la clave de área, II: 3.2
Argentine argentino(a), I: 2.1
argument la disputa
arid arido(a), **5.1**
arid desert el desierto árido
to **arise** surgir, **7.1**
arithmetic la aritmética, I: 2.2
arm el brazo, I: 7.1; **5.3**
armchair el sillón, II: 6.2; (dentist's chair), LC7
army el ejército
around alrededor de, I: 6.2
arrival la llegada, I: 11.1
arrival and departure screen la pantalla de llegadas y salidas, I: 11.1
to **arrive** llegar, I: 4.1
arrogant altivo(a), arrogante; soberbio(a)
art el arte *(f.)*, I: 2.2
fine arts las bellas artes
artichoke la alcachofa, I: 14.2; II: 2.2
artifact el artefacto
artisan *(adj.)* artesano(a)
artist el/la artista, I: 10.2
artistic artístico(a)
as como, I: 1.2
as . . . as tan... como, II: 8.2
as many . . . as tantos(as)... como, II: 8.2
as much . . . as tanto(a)... como
ash la ceniza, **2.3**
to **ask (a question)** preguntar; **(questions)** hacer preguntas, II: 14.2
to **ask for** pedir (i, i), I: 14.1
to ask for the bill pedir la cuenta, II: 6.1
to **ask questions** hacer preguntas, II: 14.2
asleep dormido(a)
aspect el aspecto
aspirin la aspirina, I: 8.2
to **assist** atender (ie), II: 4.1
assortment el surtido
to **assure** asegurar
astray el extravío, **4.3**
to go astray extraviarse, **4.3**
astute astuto(a)
at a
at that time en aquel entonces
athlete el/la atleta
athletic atlético(a)
atmosphere el ambiente; la atmósfera
to **attack** atacar
attack el ataque
to **attend** asistir
attention: to pay attention prestar atención, I: 4.2
attractive atractivo(a)
audacious audaz
audience el público, I: 10.2
August agosto, BV
aunt la tía, I: 6.1
aunt and uncle los tíos, I: 6.1
authentic auténtico(a)
author el/la autor(a), I: 10.2
authority la autoridad
automatic teller el cajero automático, **4.2**
automatically automáticamente
automobile el automóvil
autumn el otoño, BV
available disponible
avenue la avenida, II: 9.1
average medio(a); regular, I: 2.2
aversion la aversión, **3.1**
aviation la aviación

avocado el aguacate, II: 10.2
to **avoid** evitar, **6.2**

baby el/la bebé
bachelor's degree el bachillerato
back (body) la espalda, **3.3; (of an animal)** el lomo, **4.3**
back (of seat) el respaldo, II: 7.1
background (ancestry) la ascendencia
backpack la mochila, I: 3.1; **1.2**
to **back up (in a car)** retroceder, **5.2**
bacteria la bacteria
bad malo(a), I: 2.1; mal, I: 14.2; II: 2.2
to be in a good (bad) mood estar de buen (mal) humor, II: 8.1
bad-tempered malhumorado(a)
bag la bolsa, I: 5.2
cloth shopping bag el capacho
plastic bag la bolsa de plástico, II: 4.2
baggage el equipaje, I: 11.1
baggage claim el reclamo de equipaje, I: 11.2
carry-on baggage el equipaje de mano
bakery la panadería, la pastelería, II: 4.2
balance (bank) el saldo, **4.2**
to **balance** balancear
balcony el balcón, **2.1**
ball (soccer, basketball) el balón I: 7.1;
(baseball, tennis) la pelota, I: 7.2; **4.1**
to throw the ball botar la pelota
balloon el globo, II: 5.2
ballpoint pen el bolígrafo, I: 3.1
banana el plátano, I: 5.2; la banana, II: 10.2
band (music) la banda
bandage el vendaje, II: 8.2
to put a bandage on poner un vendaje, II: 8.2
bandit el bandido
bank (of a river) la orilla
bank el banco, II: 12.2
bank statement el estado del banco
banking *(adj)* bancario(a), **4.2**
bankcard la tarjeta bancaria
banner el pendón
baptism el bautizo
bar: bar of soap la barra (pastilla) de jabón, I: 12.2
barbecue el churrasco, **6.2**
barber el barbero, II: 12.1
bargain la ganga
to **base** basar
base la base, I: 7.2
baseball el béisbol, I: 7.2
baseball field el campo de béisbol, I: 7.2
baseball game el juego de béisbol, I: 7.2
baseball player el/la beisbolista; el/la jugador(a) de béisbol, I: 7.2
based (on) basado(a)
basic básico(a)
basket (basketball) el canasto la canasta, el cesto, I: 7.2;
(jai alai) la cesta
basketball el baloncesto, el básquetbol, I: 7.2
basketball court la cancha de básquetbol, I: 7.2
to put in (make) a basket encestar, I: 7.2
Basque vasco(a)
bat el bate, I: 7.2
bath el baño
to take a bath bañarse, I: 12.1
bathing suit el bañador, el traje de baño, I: 9.1
bathroom el baño, el cuarto de baño, I: 6.2
bathtub la bañera, II: 6.2
batter el/la bateador(a), I: 7.2
battery la batería
battle la batalla
bay la bahía
to **be** ser, I: 1.1; estar, I: 4.1
to be afraid tener miedo
to be in a good (bad) mood estar de buen (mal) humor
to be happy (sad) estar contento(a) (triste)
to be hungry tener hambre, I: 14.1; II: 2.1
to be married estar casado(a)
to be sick estar enfermo(a)
to be thirsty tener sed, I: 14.1; II: 2.1
to be tired esta cansado(a)
to be . . . years old tener... años, I: 6.1
to be able poder (ue), I: 7.1
to **be accustomed to, tend to** soler (ue), **2.1; 4.1**
to **be alarmed** alarmarse
to **be based** basarse
to **be born** nacer, II: 13.1
to **be called** llamarse, I: 12.1
to **be familiar with** conocer, I: 11.1
to **be frightened** asustarse
to **be glad about** alegrarse de, II: 13.1
to **be going to (do something)** ir a + infinitive
to **be important** importar
to **be named** llamarse, I: 12.1
to **be sorry** sentir (i, i)
to **be worth** valer
beach la playa, I: 9.1
beach resort el balneario, I: 9.1
beach towel la toalla playera, I: 9.1
bean el frijol, la habichuela, I: 5.2
black bean la habichuela negra, el frijol negro, II: 10.2
rice with beans el arroz con frijoles (habichuelas), **6.1**
string (green) bean la habichuela tierna
to **bear** llevar
beard la barba
bearing el rumbo, LC1; LC4
to **beat** batir, LC5
beau, heartthrob el galán
beautiful bello(a), hermoso(a), I: 1.1; precioso(a)
beauty la belleza
because porque
to **become enamored of** (to fall for) flechar
bed la cama, II: 8.1
to go to bed acostarse (ue), I: 12.1
to make the bed hacer la cama, II: 6.2
to stay in bed guardar cama, I: 8.1
bedroom el cuarto de dormir; el cuarto, el dormitorio, la recámara, I: 6.2; la habitación, II: 6.1
bee la abeja, II: 8.1; LC5
beef la carne de res, I: 14.2; II: 2.2
before antes de, I: 5.1
beforehand antemano
to **beg** rogar (ue)
to **begin** comenzar (ie); empezar (ie), I: 7.1
beginner el/la principiante, I: 9.2
beginning: at the beginning al principio
beginning of the school year la apertura de clases
to **behave** comportarse
behavior la actuación
behind atrás; detrás de, II: 5.2

to **believe** creer, I: 8.2
bell pepper el pimiento, II: 10.2
bellhop el botones, II: 6.1
to **belong** pertenecer
below debajo (de), II: 7.1
below zero bajo cero, I: 9.2
belt el cinturón, II: 4.1; **3.2**
seat belt el cinturón de seguridad, II: 7.1
benefit el beneficio
berth la litera, I: 13.2; II: 1.2
beside al lado de, II: 5.2
besides además
best man el padrino, II: 13.1
better, best mejor
between entre, I: 7.1
beverage el refresco, I: 5.1; la bebida, II: 7.1
biblical bíblico(a)
to **bicycle** ir en bicicleta, I: 12.2
bicycle la bicicleta
big gran, grande
bilingual bilingüe
bill la factura, II: 6.1; **4.2; (money)** el billete, II: 12.2; **4.2; (check)** la cuenta, I: 5.1
large (small) denomination bill un billete grande (pequeño)
biography la biografía
biological biológico(a)
biologist el/la biólogo(a)
biology la biología, I: 2.2
bird el ave *(f.)*, LC2; el pájaro
birthday el cumpleaños, I: 6.1
bitterness la amargura
black negro(a), I: 3.2
blacksmith el mariscal
blanket la frazada, la manta, II: 6.2
bleach el blanqueador
to **bless** bendecir, LC5
blessing la bendición
block (city) la cuadra, II: 11.2
to **block** bloquear, parar, I: 7.1
blond(e) rubio(a), I: 1.1
blood la sangre
blood pressure la presión arterial, la tension arterial, II: 8.2
blouse la blusa, I: 3.2; **3.2**
blue azul , I: 3.2
dark blue azul oscuro
blue jeans el blue jean, I: 3.2
to **blur** empañar, LC7
to **board** embarcar, I: 11.2; subir, I: 13.1; II: 1.1; abordar
to **board the train** subir al tren, I: 13.1; II: 1.1
board el tablero, I: 7.1; **(surfboard)** la tabla, **5.3**
arrival board el tablero de llegadas, I: 13.1; II: 1.1
boarding house la pensión, I: 12.2
boarding pass la tarjeta de embarque, I: 11.1
departure board el tablero de salidas, I: 13.1; II: 1.1
scoreboard el tablero indicador, I: 7.1
boat el bote, II: 5.2; **(small boat, raft)** la patera, **1.3**
body el cuerpo, II: 8.1
to **boil** hervir (ie, i), II: 10.1
boiling la ebullición
bold atrevido(a), LC3
bond el vínculo, **8.1**
bone el hueso, II: 8.2
to set the bone reducir el hueso, II: 8.2
book el libro, I: 3.1
boot la bota, I: 9.2; **3.2**
high-heeled boots botas de tacón alto
to **border** bordear
border el borde, LC7; la frontera
border *(adj.)* fronterizo(a), **8.1**
to **bore** aburrir
boring aburrido(a), I: 2.1
born nacido(a)
to **borrow** pedir prestado
boss el/la jefe(a)
bottle la botella, II: 4.2
bottle of mineral water la botella de agua mineral, I: 12.2
boulder la peña, LC2
boulevard el bulevar, II: 9.1
bounce el brinco, **5.3**
to be bounced off dar unos brincos
bouquet el ramo, LC4
box office la taquilla, I: 10.1
boy el muchacho, I: 1.1; el chico
boyfriend el novio
bracelet la pulsera, II: 4.1
braid la trenza
to **brake** poner los frenos
brakes los frenos, II: 11.1
branch (of menora) el brazo, II: 13.2
branch (office) la sucursal; la filial
branch (tree) la rama, LC3
brass (instruments in orchestra) instrumentos de metal
brave valeroso(a); valiente
bread el pan, II: 4.2
to **break** romperse, II: 8.1
to **break in (horses)** jinetear
breakdown la avería
breakfast el desayuno, I: 5.2
breath el aliento, LC6
to **breathe** respirar
breathing la respiración
bricklayer el/la albañil, II: 14.1
bride la novia, II: 13.1
bridge el puente
brief breve
bright brillante
brightness el brillo, LC4
to **bring** llevar, I: 6.1; traer, I: 14.1; II: 2.1
broken branch el gajo, LC3
broken down averiado(a)
bronze el bronce, I: 10.2
brooch el pasador, **3.2**
brook el arroyo
broth el caldo, LC5
brother el hermano, I: 6.1
brown de color marrón, I: 3.2; pardo(a); de color pardo, **1.1**
brunette moreno(a), I: 1.1
brush el cepillo, I: 12.2; **(paint)** el pincel
to **brush one's hair** cepillarse, I: 12.1
to **brush one's teeth** cepillarse los dientes, lavarse los dientes, I: 12.1
to **buckle** abrochar, **5.2**
building el edificio, II: 9.1
burial el entierro, el sepelio, **4.3**
burner (stove) la hornilla, II: 10.1
to **bury** enterrar (ie)
bus el bus, I: 4.1; el autobús, I: 10.1; **(Mexico)** el camión, I: 10.1; **(Puerto Rico, Cuba)** la guagua, I: 10.1
bus stop la parada de bus, II: 9.1
school bus el bus escolar, I: 4.1
business el comercio; la empresa, II: 14.1
business district la zona comercial, II: 9.1
businessperson el/la comerciante, II: 14.1; el/la empresario(a)
busy (phone) ocupado
but pero
butcher shop la carnicería, II: 4.2
butter la mantequilla, II: 10.2
button el botón, II: 3.1; **(clothing) 3.2; (on a machine), 4.2**
buttoned abrochado(a), **3.3**
to **buy** comprar, I: 3.1
buying la compra, II: 14.1

by no means de ninguna manera, I: 1.1
by the way a propósito

cabin la cabina, II: 7.1; la choza, LC2; **(of a boat)** la camarote, LC8
cabinet el gabinete
dentist's cabinet el gabinete del dentista, LC7
cactus el cacto, **5.1**
cadaver el cadáver
café el café, I: 5.1; la confitería
outdoor café el café al aire libre
cafeteria la cafetería
cage la jaula, II: 5.2; LC3
cake el bizcocho, la torta, el pastel, II: 13.1
to **calculate** calcular
calculator la calculadora, I: 3.1
calculus el cálculo, I: 2.2
to **call oneself, be named** llamarse, I: 12.1
to **call; to telephone** llamar, II: 3.2
Who is calling? ¿De parte de quién?, II: 3.2
call la llamada (telefónica), II: 3.2
long-distance call la llamada larga, II: 3.2
called llamado(a)
calm tranquilo(a); pacífico(a), **3.1**
calorie la caloría
camel el camello, II: 13.2
camera la cámara, **8.2**
campaign la campaña
can el bote, la lata, I: 5.2
Canadian canadiense
cancelled anulado(a), **1.2**
candid franco(a)
candidate el/la aspirante, el/la candidato(a), II: 14.2
candle la vela, II: 13.1; la candela, LC4
wax candle el cirio, LC8
canned enlatado(a)
canoe la canoa
canvas (painting) el lienzo
canyon el cañón
cap la gorra, I: 3.2
capital la capital
captain (airplane) el/la comandante, I: 11.2
capture la toma, **6.1**
car el carro, el coche, I: 4.1
by car en carro, I: 4.1
dining car el coche-comedor, el coche-cafetería, I: 13.2
sleeping car el coche-cama, I: 13.2
sports car el carro deportivo, II: 11.1
train car el coche, I: 13.2
carbohydrate el carbohidrato
card la tarjeta, I: 11.1; **4.2**
bankcard la tarjeta bancaria
credit card la tarjeta de crédito, I: 14.1; II: 2.1
registration card (hotel) la tarjeta, la ficha, II: 6.1
student I.D. card la tarjeta de identidad estudiantil
telephone card la tarjeta telefónica, II: 3.2
cardinal points los puntos cardinales
cardiologist el/la cardiólogo(a)
cardiology la cardiología
care el cariño, **5.3**
intensive care el cuidado intensivo
career la carrera
careful! ¡cuidado!
to be careful tener cuidado
carefully con cuidado
carefully detenidamente, **7.3**
to **caress** acariciar
Caribbean el Caribe
Caribbean Sea el mar Caribe
caricaturist el/la caricaturista
carmine el carmín, LC5
carousel horse el caballito, I: 5.2
carpenter el/la carpintero(a), II: 14.1
carrot la zanahoria, I: 5.2
to **carry** llevar, I: 3.1
to **carry out** efectuar; llevar a cabo, **5.3**
cart el carrito, II: 4.2
carved tallado(a)
carved animal el animal tallado, **4.1**
case el caso, II: 7.1
cash el dinero en efectivo, II: 12.2; **4.2**
cash register la caja, I: 3.1
to **cash the check** cobrar el cheque, II: 12.2; **4.2**
cashier el/la cajero(a), II: 14.1
casserole la cacerola, LC7
cassette el casete, I: 4.2
cast el yeso, II: 8.2
cast (of a play) el elenco, **7.2**
Castillian castellano(a)
castle el castillo
cat el/la gato(a), I: 6.1
to **catch** atrapar, I: 7.2
catcher el/la cátcher, el/la receptor(a), I: 7.2
category la categoría
cathedral la catedral
catholic católico(a)
cattle el ganado, la ganadería, II: 9.2; **3.1**
cauliflower la coliflor, II: 10.1
to **cause** causar, **2.3; 4.1**
cause la causa
ceasing el cese, **8.1**
ceasefire el cese de fuego
CD-ROM el CD-ROM, II: II: 3.1
to **celebrate** celebrar, II: 13.1; festejar, **4.3**
celebration la celebración
cell phone el teléfono celular, II: 3.2
cellular celular
centaur el centauro, **5.1**
center el centro
central central
Central America la América Central
century el siglo, **1.1**
cereal el cereal, I: 5.2
ceremony la ceremonia
certain cierto(a)
Certainly!, Of course! ¡Claro!
chain (necklace) la cadena, II: 4.1; **(shackles), 6.1**
gold chain la cadena de oro, II: 4.1
chair la silla
armchair el sillón, II: 6.2
chairlift el telesilla, I: 9.2
chalkboard la pizarra, **6.3;** el pizarrón, I: 4.2
champion el/la campeón(ona), II: 5.1
championship el campeonato, **6.3**
change el cambio, II: 12.2; **(money)** el suelto, **4.2**
to **change** variar; cambiar, II: 12.2; **(money), 4.2; (seats)** trocarse
to change the towels cambiar las toallas, II: 6.2
to change trains (transfer) transbordar, I: 13.2; II: 1.2
channel (TV) el canal
to channel surf surfear las canales, **8.2**
Chanukah Hanuka, II: 13.2
Happy Chanukah! ¡Feliz Hanuka!, II: 13.2
chapter el capítulo
character el carácter; el personaje
characteristic la característica

to **charge** cobrar
charge (money) el cargo, **4.2; 5.2**
charming encantador(a)
to **chat** charlar
chauffeur el chófer
cheap barato(a), I: 3.2
check (money) el cheque, **4.2**
check (plaid) a cuadros
to **check luggage** facturar el equipaje, I: 11.1
to **check out** abandonar el cuarto, II: 6.1
to **check the oil** revisar el aceite, II: 11.2
to **check the ticket** revisar el boleto, I: 11.1
checkbook la chequera; el talonario, **4.2**
checkered de cuadros, **3.2**
checkered scarf una bufanda de cuadros
checkers las damas, II: 5.1
checking account la cuenta corriente, II: 12.2; **4.2**
cheek la mejilla, II: 8.1
cheese el queso, I: 5.1
white cheese el queso blanco, **6.2**
chemical químico(a)
chemistry la química, I: 2.2
chess el ajedrez, II: 5.1
chest el pecho, II: 8.1; **5.3**
chicken el pollo, I: 5.2
chief el cacique, **6.1**
child el/la niño(a)
childlike filial, LC1
children los hijos, I: 6.1
chilean chileno(a)
chili pepper el ají
chills los escalofríos, I: 8.1; LC6
chimney la chimenea
chin el mentón, LC6
chocolate *(adj.)* de chocolate, I: 5.1
choir el coro
cholesterol el colesterol
to **choose** escoger
chop la chuleta, II: 10.1
chores los quehaceres
chorus el coro
Christian cristiano(a)
Christmas la Navidad, II: 13.2
Merry Christmas! ¡Feliz Navidad!, II: 13.2
Christmas Eve la Nochebuena, II: 13.2
Christmas tree el árbol de Navidad, II: 13.2
church la iglesia, **4.3**
circle el círculo
to **circulate** circular
circumspection la circunspección, LC8
citizen el/la ciudadano, **6.1**
citric cítrico(a)
city la ciudad, II: 9.1
walled city una ciudad amurallado(a)
city hall la alcaldía, II: 14.1
city hall employee el/la funcionario(a), II: 14.1
to **claim (luggage)** reclamar, I: 11.2
to claim one's luggage recoger el equipaje, I: 11.2
clam la almeja, I: 14.2; II: 2.2
clarinet el clarinete
clarity la claridad
clasp el cierre, **3.2**
class la clase, el curso, I: 2.1
first class primera clase, I: 13.1; II: 1.1
second class segunda clase, I: 13.1
classic clásico(a)
to **classify** clasificar
classroom la sala de clase, el salón de clase, I: 4.1
claw la garra
eagle claw la garra de águila, LC8
clean limpio(a)
to **clean** limpiar, II: 6.2
to clean the room limpiar el cuarto, II: 6.2
clear claro(a); **(weather)** despejado(a), **2.3**
clergy el clero
clerk el/la dependiente(a); el/la empleado(a), I: 3.1
clever listo(a), II: 5.1
click el clic
climate el clima
clinic la clínica
close cercano(a); próximo(a), **7.1**
to **close** cerrar (ie)
to close the wound cerrar la herida, II: 8.2
closet el armario, II: 6.2
clothes *(pl.)* la ropa, los vestidos
to put on (one's) clothes ponerse la ropa, II: 12.1; vestirse (i, i)
clothes hanger el colgador, la percha, II: 6.2
clothespin la pinza, LC7
clothing la ropa, I: 3.2; la indumentaría, **3.1**
clothing store la tienda de ropa, I: 3.2
men's clothing store la tienda de ropa para caballeros, II: 4.1
women's clothing store la tienda de ropa para señoras, II: 4.1
cloud la nube, I: 9.1
cloudy nublado(a), I: 9.1
It's cloudy. Hay nubes., I: 9.1
clove (of garlic) el diente (de ajo)
clown el payaso, II: 5.2; **8.2**
club el club, I: 4.2
Spanish Club el Club de español, I: 4.2
co-ed (school) mixto(a)
coast la costa
coat el abrigo, II: 4.1
coati el cuatí, LC3
cockpit la cabina de mando (vuelo), II: 7.1
coconut el coco, II: 10.2; **6.1**
code el código, **4.2**
area code la clave de área, II: 3.2
country code el prefijo de país, II: 3.2
coffee el café, BV
black coffee el café solo, I: 5.1
coffee with milk el café con leche, I: 5.1
coin, currency la moneda, II: 3.2; **4.2**
coincidence la coincidencia
cold (illness) el catarro, I: 8.1
It's cold. Hace frío., I: 9.2
to have a cold tener catarro, estar resfriado(a), I: 8.1
collaborator el/la colaborador(a)
to **collect** coleccionar, II: 5.1
collection el conjunto; la colección; la colecta
collector el/la coleccionista, II: 5.1; **(financial)** el/la cobrador(a) **3.2**
Colombian colombiano(a), I: 1.1
colonial colonial, **2.1**
colony la colonia
color el color, I: 3.2
What color is it? ¿De qué color es?, I: 3.2
colored de color
comb el peine, I: 12.1
to **comb one's hair** peinarse, II: 12.1
to **come** venir, I: 11.1
to come (go) on stage entrar en escena, I: 10.2
comedy la comedia

comfort la comodidad
television commercial el anuncio televiso
commission la comisión
committee el comité
common común
to **communicate with each other** comunicarse, II: 3.1
communication la comunicación
community la comunidad
compact disc CD el disco compacto, I: 4.2
company la compañía
to **compare** comparar
comparison la comparación
compartment el compartimento, I: 13.2; II: 1.2
overhead compartment el compartimiento superior, el compartimiento sobre la cabeza, I: 7.1
to **compete** competir (i, i)
competition la competencia; la competición
to **complete** completar
completely totalmente
compliment: to pay someone a compliment echarle flores
to **compose** componer
composition la composición
computer el ordenador, la computadora, II: 3.1
computer programmer el/la programador(a) de informática, II: 14.1
computer science la informática, I: 2.2
concert el concierto, I: 2.1
conclusion el desenlace
condition la condición
condominium el condominio, II: 9.1
conduct la conducta
with regard to conduct conductual, **6.3**
conductor (train) el/la revisor(a), I: 13.2; II: 1.2
confidence la confianza, **5.3**
to **confirm** confirmar
to **confront** confrontar
confused turbio(a), LC7
confusing confuso(a)
to **congratulate** felicitar, **4.3**
Congratulations! ¡Enhorabuena!, ¡Felicitaciones!, II: 13.1
to **connect** conectar; enlazar, **1.2**
connection la conexión
to **conquer** conquistar; vencer
conqueror el conquistador
conquest la conquista
consequence la consecuencia
consequently por consiguiente
to **consider** considerar
to **consist of** consistir (en)
constitutional constitucional
to **construct** construir
to **consult** consultar, I: 13.1; II: 1.1
to **consume** consumir
consumer el/la consumidor(a)
consumption el consumo
contagious contagioso(a)
to **contain** contener (ie)
contemporary contemporáneo(a)
content contento(a), **3.3**
contest la competición
continent el continente
contingency la contingencia
to **continue** continuar, I: 7.2; seguir (i, i), II: 11.2
contract el contrato, **5.2**
contrary: on the contrary al contrario
to **contrast** contrastar
to **contribute** aportar, contribuir, **8.3**
to **control** controlar
control tower la torre de control, II: 7.2
convenient conveniente
convent el convento
conversation la conversación
to **convert** convertir (ie, i)
convertible el convertible, el descapotable, II: 11.1
to **convince** convencer
to **cook** cocinar, II: 10.1; cocer (ue), LC8
cook el/la cocinero(a), I: 14.1; II: 2.1; **1.1**
cooking la cocción
coordination la coordinación
copilot el/la co-piloto, I: 11.2
to **copy** copiar
copy la copia
cord la cuerda, **2.1**
corkboard la pizarra de corcho, LC8
corn (Mex.) el elote; el choclo; el maíz, I: 14.2; II: 2.2; **2.1**
cornea la córnea
corner la esquina, II: 9.1
cornfield la milpa, LC4
correspondence la correspondencia
corridor el pasillo, I: 13.2; II: 1.2; **1.3**
to **cost** costar (ue), I: 3.1
how much do(es) it (they) cost? ¿Cuánto cuesta(n)?
Costa Rican costarricense
costumes (in a play) el vestuario, **7.2**
cotton el algodón, II: 12.1
cough la tos, I: 8.1
to have a cough tener tos, I: 8.1
to **cough** toser, I: 8.1
to **count** contar (ue), **2.1**
counter el mostrador, I: 11.1
country el país, I: 11.2; el campo, II: 9.2
foreign country el país extranjero
countryside el país, **1.1** el paisaje
coup (overthrow of a government) el golpe
coupe el cupé, I: 11.1
couple la pareja, **4.3**
couplet la copla
course el curso, I: 2.1
elective course el curso opcional
required course el curso obligatorio
course tosco(a)
court la corte, el tribunal, II: 14.1
court la cancha, I: 7.2
basketball court la cancha de básquetbol, I: 7.2
enclosed court la cancha cubierta, I: 9.1
outdoor court la cancha al aire libre, I: 9.1
tennis court la cancha de tenis, I: 9.1
courteous atento(a); cortés
courtesy la cortesía, BV
courtship el cortejo, **4.3**
cousin el/la primo(a), I: 6.1
cove la caleta, **7.1**
to **cover** cubrir; tapar, II: 10.2
covered cubierto(a), **2.3**
covering (clothing) el foro, **3.2**
cow la vaca, II: 9.2
coward el/la cobarde, LC6
cracker la galleta, LC6
crane (construction) la grúa, LC8
to **crash** chocar, **1.3**
crease el pliegue, **3.3**
to **create** crear
creature la criatura
mythical creature una criatura mítica
credit card la tarjeta de crédito, I: 14.1; II: 2.1; **5.2**
Creole criollo(a)

crew la tripulación, I: 11.2
crime el crimen, **2.2**
crop la cosecha, II: 9.2
to **cross** atravesar (ie); cruzar, II: 9.1
crossing el cruce, II: 11.2
crosswalk el cruce de peatones, II: 9.1
crossword puzzle el crucigrama, II: 5.1
  to do a crossword puzzle llenar un crucigrama, II: 5.1
crown la corona, **1.1**
cruelty la crueldad
crutch la muleta, II: 8.2
to **cry** llorar, LC1; LC4
to **crystallize** cristalizarse, LC5
cub el cachorro, LC3
Cuban cubano(a)
Cuban American cubanoamericano(a)
cucumber el pepino, II: 10.1
to **culminate** culminar, **4.3**
to **cultivate** cultivar, II: 9.2; **2.3**
cultivation el cultivo, **6.1**
cultural cultural
cultured culto(a)
cup la taza, I: 14.1; II: 2.1; la copa, LC3
cure la cura
curtain (stage) el telón, I: 10.2; **7.2**
cushion la cabezal, LC7
custom la costumbre
customer el/la cliente, I: 5.1
customs la aduana, I: 11.2
customs agent el/la agente de aduana, II: 11.2
to **cut** cortar, II: 8.1; **1.1**
cutter la fresa, LC7
cycling el ciclismo

dad el papá
daily diario(a); cotidiano(a), LC1
to **dance** bailar, I: 4.2
dance el baile
dance la danza
danger el peligro
dangerous peligroso(a)
daring osado(a)
dark oscuro(a)
to **darken** oscurecer
dark-haired moreno(a), I: 1.1
data los datos, II: 3.1
to **date** datar
date la fecha, BV
  What is today's date? ¿Cuál es la fecha de hoy?, BV
daughter la hija, I: 6.1
dawn el amanecer
day el día, BV
  What day is it (today)? ¿Qué día es (hoy)?, BV
death la muerte; el deceso, el fallecimiento, **4.3**
to **debilitate** debilitar
debt la deuda, **7.1**
to **debut** debutar, **4.3**
debutante la debutante, **4.3**
decade la década
decadence la decadencia
deceased el/la difunto(a), **4.3**
December diciembre, BV
deception el engaño, LC6; la decepción
to **decide** decidir
decisive decisivo(a)
to **declare** declarar
to **decline** declinar
to **decorate** decorar
decorated decorado(a)
decoration la decoración
to **dedicate** dedicar, II: 14.1
deep profundo(a); hondo(a), LC3
to **defeat** derrotar; vencer, LC1
to **defend** defender (ie)
to **define** definir
definition la definición
to **deflate** desinflarse, **7.3**
deforestation la deforestación, **5.1**
degree (temperature) el grado, I: 9.2
delay la demora; el retraso, **1.2**
  with a delay con una demora, I: 11.1; con retraso, I: 13.2; II: 1.2
delicate delicado(a)
delicious rico(a), I: 14.2; II: 2.2; **6.2;** delicioso(a), sabroso(a)
to **delight** encantar
to **deliver** entregar
deluxe de lujo
to **demand** exigir
demography la demografía
to **demonstrate** demostrar (ue)
denim el dénim, **3.2**
  denim fabric tela de dénim
density la densidad
dental floss la seda dental, LC7
dentist el/la dentista
to **deny** renegar (ie), **2.3**
department el departamento, II: 14.2
  department of human resources el departamento de recursos humanos, II: 14.2
  department store la tienda de departamentos
departure la salida, I: 11.1; la partida
  departure area la sala de salida, I: 11.1
  departure gate la puerta de salida, I: 11.1; la puerta de embarque
departure hour la hora de salida, I: 13.1; II: 1.1
to **depend (on)** depender (ie) (de)
deposit el depósito
  to make a deposit ingresar
dermatologist el/la dermatólogo(a)
dermatology la dermatología
descendant el/la descendiente
to **describe** describir
desert el desierto, **5.1**
  arid desert el desierto árido
design el diseño
designer el/la diseñador(a)
dessert el postre, I: 5.1
destination el destino, I: 11.1
destruction la destrucción, **2.3; 4.1**
detail el detalle
detective policíaco(a)
detergent el detergente, II: 4.2
to **determine** determinar
detour el desvío, **8.3**
developed desarrollado(a)
development el desarrollo
device el aparato, II: 3.1
to **devote oneself to** dedicarse, II: 14.1; **6.1**
to **devour** devorar, **5.1**
diagnosis la diagnosis, I: 8.2
dial (of telephone) el disco, II: 3.2
to **dial** marcar (el número), II: 3.2
dial tone el tono, II: 3.2
dialogue el diálogo
diamond el diamante
to **dice** picar, II: 10.2; **1.1**
to **die** morir (ue, u); fallecer, 4.3; LC8
diesel fuel gasoil
diesel truck el tanque de gasolina, **7.3**
diet la dieta
difference la diferencia
different diferente
difficult difícil, duro(a), I: 2.1
difficulty la dificultad
to **dig** excavar
to **dine, have dinner** cenar
  dining car el coche-comedor,

el coche-cafetería, I: 13.2
dining room el comedor, I: 6.2
dinner la cena, I: 5.2
diplomatic diplomático(a)
direct directo(a)
to **direct** dirigir
direction la dirección; el sentido, II: 11.2
in each direction en cada sentido, II: 11.2
in the opposite direction en el sentido contrario, II: 11.2
director el/la director(a)
dirty sucio(a), II: 11.1
dirty laundry la ropa sucia, II: 12.1
disabled minusválido(a)
disadvantage la desventaja
to **disappear** desaparecer, **5.1**
disappointment el desengaño, LC7
disaster el desastre
disastrous desastroso(a)
discount el descuento
to **discover** descubrir
to **discuss** discutir; platicar, **5.3**
to **disembark** desembarcar, I: 11.2
dish el plato, I: 14.1; II: 2.1; **(satellite), 8.2**
disillusionment la desilusión
disk, diskette el disquete, I: 3.1
disk drive la ranura, II: 3.1
dislike la antipatía
disoriented disorientado(a)
dispute la disputa
to **dissipate** desvanecer, **2.3**
distance la distancia
distant apartado(a), **6.1**
distilled destilado(a)
distinct distinto(a)
distinguished ilustre
to **distract** distraer
to **distribute** distribuir, II: 7.1
distribution la distribución
dive (water) el clavado, **6.3**
to **dive** bucear, I: 9.1
to **divide** dividir
diving el buceo, I: 9.1
division la división
divorce: to get divorced divorciarse
to **do** hacer
to do homework hacer las tareas, II: 3.1
to do well (on an exam) salir bien (en un examen)
doctor el/la doctor(a); el/la médico(a), I: 8.2
doctor's office la consulta (el consultorio) del médico, I: 8.2; la sala de consulta
document el documento, II: 3.1
documentation la documentación; la cédula, **4.3**
dog el perro, I: 6.1
dollar el dólar, II: 11; **4.2**
to **dominate** dominar
domination el dominio
Dominican dominicano(a), I: 2.1
Dominican Republic la República Dominicana
dominos el dominó, II: 5.1
to **donate** donar, **2.3**
donkey el asno
door la puerta, II: 6.1
dose la dosis, I: 8.2
dot el punto
on the dot, sharp en punto, I: 4.1
doubles dobles, I: 9.1
to **doubt** dudar
doubt la duda
doubtful dudoso(a)
dough la masa, la colchita, LC8
down payment el enganche; el pronto, el pie
downpour el chaparrón, **3.1**
downtown el centro; en el centro (de la ciudad)
dozen la docena, II: 4.2
to **drag** arrastrar, LC2
to **draw** dibujar, LC8
drawer la gaveta, LC7
drawing el dibujo
dream el sueño
dress el vestido, II: 4.1
to **dress oneself, to put on clothes** ponerse la ropa, I: 12.1
to get dressed vestirse (i, i)
dressed (in) vestido(a) (de)
to **dribble** driblar, I: 7.2
to **drink** beber, I: 5.1
to drink a beverage tomar un refresco
to drink water (milk, coffee) tomar agua (leche, café)
drink el refresco, I: 5.1; la bebida, II: 7.1
to **drive** conducir, manejar
driver el/la conductor(a), II: 11.1
driver's license la licencia, el permiso de conducir, II: 11.1; la licencia de conductor, **5.2**
drop la gota, LC5
drought la sequía, **7.1**
drug la droga
drug addiction la drogadicción
druggist el/la farmacéutico(a), I: 8.2
drugstore la farmacia, I: 8.2
to **dry** secar, II: 12.2
dry seco(a)
to **dry clean** limpiar en seco, II: 12.1
dry cleaner el/la tintorero(a), II: 12.1
dry cleaners la tintorería, II: 12.1
dubbed doblado(a), I: 10.1
during durante
dusk anochecer
dust el polvo, LC1
DVD player la grabadora DVD, **8.2**

e-mail, electronic mail el correo electrónico, II: 3.1
each cada, I: 1.2
in each direction en cada sentido, II: 11.2
eagle el águila *(f.)*, **5.1**
ear la oreja, II: 4.1; el oído, II: 8.1
ear of corn la mazorca de maíz, **7.1**
early temprano, I: 12.1
to **earn** ganar
to earn one's living ganar la vida
earphones los audífonos, los auriculares, II: 7.1
earring el arete, **5.3;** el pendiente, II: 4.1
earthquake el terremoto, **4.1**
easel el caballete
east el este
eastern oriental
easy fácil, I: 2.1; sencillo(a)
to **eat** comer, I: 5.1
to eat breakfast desayunarse, tomar el desayuno, I: 12.1
to eat dinner cenar
ecological ecológico(a)
ecology la ecología
economical económico(a), I: 12.2
economics la economía
home economics la economía doméstica, I: 2.2
economy la economía
Ecuadorean ecuatoriano(a), I: 2.1
to **educate** educar

education la educación
physical education la educación física, I: 2.2
effect el efecto
egg el huevo, I: 5.2
egg white la clara, LC5
eggplant la berenjena, I: 14.2; II: 2.2; **1.1**
eggplant bush la mata de berenjenas, LC8
eight ocho, BV
eight hundred ochocientos(as), I: 3.2
eighteen dieciocho, BV
eighth octavo(a), I: 6.2
eighty ochenta, I: 2.2
either tampoco
elbow el codo, II: 8.1; LC1
elderly mayor, **2.3**
elective course el curso opcional
electric eléctrico(a)
electrician el/la electricista, II: 14.1
electricity la electricidad
electronic electrónico(a)
electronic mail el correo electrónico, II: 3.1
elegance la elegancia
elegant elegante, II: 13.1
element el elemento
elementary school la escuela primaria
to **elevate** elevar
elevated elevado(a)
elevation la elevación
elevator el ascensor, I: 6.2; el elevador, II: 6.1
eleven once, BV
to **eliminate** eliminar
to **elude** eludir
emerald la esmeralda
emergency la emergencia, II: 7.1
emergency exit la salida de emergencia, II: 7.1
emergency room la sala de emergencia, la sala de urgencias, II: 8.1
emission la emisión, **8.2**
to **emit** emitir
emotion la emoción
emotional emocional
to **emphasize** dar énfasis; enfatizar
to **employ** emplear
employee el/la dependiente(a), el/la empleado(a), I: 3.1
empty vacio(a)
enchilada la enchilada, BV
end el fin; el ocaso, LC5
at the end (of) al final (de); a fines de
to **end** terminar, II: 3.1
to **endorse** endosar, II: 12.2
enemy el/la enemigo(a)
energy la energía
engagement el compromiso
engine el motor
engineer el/la ingeniero(a), II: 14.1
engineering la ingeniería
English el inglés, I: 2.2
to **enjoy** disfrutar; gozar
to **enjoy oneself** divertirse (ie, i), I: 12.2
enormous enorme
enough bastante, I: 1.1; suficiente
to **enter** entrar, I: 4.1
entertaining entretenido(a)
enthusiastic entusiasmado(a)
to become enthusiastic entusiasmarse
entire entero(a)
entrance la entrada, II: 5.2
entrepreneur el/la empresario(a)
envelope el sobre, II: 12.2
environment el ambiente; el medio ambiente
to **envy** envidiar, LC6
episode el episodio
epoch la época, **2.1**
equal igual; par
equation la ecuación
equator la línea ecuatorial
equilibrium el equilibrio
equipment el equipo
equivalent el equivalente
eraser la goma de borrar, I: 3.1
erroneous erróneo(a)
escalator la escalera mecánica, II: 9.1
to **escape** escapar
especially especialmente; particularmente; sobre todo
essential esencial
to **establish** establecer, **1.1;** fundar
establishment el establecimiento
eternal eterno(a)
eternally de siempre y para siempre
ethnic étnico(a)
euro euro (currency)
Europe la Europa
European europeo(a)
to **evade** evadir
even aun
evening la noche
evening gown el traje de gala
in the evening por la noche
event el suceso, **1.3**
great event el buen suceso
every cada, I: 1.2
everybody todos(as), I: 2.2
everyone todo el mundo
everything todos(as)
everywhere por todas partes
evil la maldad
exact exacto(a)
exactly exactamente
to **exaggerate** exagerar
exaggerated exagerado(a)
exam el examen, I: 4.2
to **examine** examinar, I: 8.2
example: for example por ejemplo
to **excavate** excavar
excavation la excavación
to **exceed** exceder
excellent excelente
exception la excepción
to **exchange** cambiar, II: 12.2; **4.2**
exchange: exchange rate el tipo (la tasa) de cambio, II: 12.2; **4.2**
exchange student el/la estudiante de intercambio
to **exclaim** exclamar
exclusively exclusivamente
excuse me perdón
exercise el ejercicio, **5.3**
to **exercise** hacer los ejercicios
to **exercise (a body part)** ejercitar, **5.3**
exhaust pipe el tubo de escape
exhibition (art) la exposición (de arte), I: 10.2; la exhibición
to **exist** existir
existence la existencia
exit la salida, II: 11.2
expedition la expedición
expensive caro(a), I: 3.2
experience la experiencia
to **experiment** experimentar
expert el/la experto(a), I: 9.2
to **explain** explicar, I: 4.2
explorer el/la explorador(a)
explosion la explosión
to **export** exportar
to **express an opinion** opinar, II: 10.2
expression la expresión
means of expression el modo de expresión
expressway la autopista, II: 11.2
extension la extensión

to **extract** extraer, LC5
extraordinary extraordinario(a)
extreme extremo(a)
exuberant exuberante
eye el ojo, I: 8.2

fabric la tela, **3.2**
fabulous fabuloso(a)
face la cara, la faz, I: 12.1; LC5; el rostro, LC8
face down boca abajo, II: 3.1
face up boca arriba, II: 3.1
to **facilitate** facilitar
factory la fábrica, II: 9.1
factory worker el/la obrero(a), II: 9.1
to **fail** fracasar, **3.3**
failed fallado(a), LC5
faithful fiel
fall la caída, **7.1**
to **fall** caerse
to **fall asleep** dormirse, I: 12.1
false falso(a)
fame la fama
family la familia, I: 6.1
family (related to the) familiar
famous famoso(a), I: 1.2; célebre
fan (sports) el/la aficionado(a)
fantastic fantástico(a), I: 1.2
far lejos, II: 12.2
far away a lo largo, **1.1**
fare la tarifa; **(taxi)** el monto, **1.2**
farm la finca, II: 9.2
farm animals los animales domésticos, II: 9.2
farmer el/la agricultor(a)
to **fascinate** fascinar
fast: as fast as possible a toda prisa
to **fasten** abrocharse, II: 7.1
fastener el cierre, **3.2**
fat gordo(a), I: 1.2
fat la grasa
father el padre, I: 6.1
father-in-law el suegro
fatigue la fatiga
fault el defecto
fauna la fauna, **5.1**
favorite favorito(a)
fax el facsímil, el fax, II: 3.1
fear el miedo; el terror; el temor, LC6
to **fear** temer
fearful temible, **5.1**
feat la hazaña, LC1; LC6
February febrero, BV
to **feel** sentirse (ie, i), II: 8.1
fence la valla, la cerca, LC1
Ferris wheel la noria, II: 5.2
to **fete** festejar
fever la fiebre, I: 8.1
to have a fever tener fiebre, I: 8.1
few poco(a), I: 2.1
fewer menos
fiancé(e) el/la novio(a)
fiction la ficción
fictitious ficticio(a)
field el campo, II: 9.2
baseball field el campo de béisbol, I: 7.2
soccer field el campo de fútbol, I: 7.1
fifteen quince, BV
fifteen-year-old (girl) la quinceañera
fifth quinto(a), I: 6.2
fifty cincuenta, I: 2.2
fig el higo, LC3
fig tree la higuera, LC3
fight la pelea, **5.3**
to **fight** luchar, **1.1;** pelear, LC3
figurative figurativo(a)
figure la figura
to **fill** rellenar
to **fill out** llenar, II: 5.1
to **fill out the form** llenar el formulario, II: 8.2
fillet el filete
film la película, I: 6.2; el film, I: 10.1
to see a film ver una película, I: 10.1
to **film** filmar
finally por fin
finances las finanzas
financial financiero(a)
to **find** encontrar (ue), **4.3;** hallar
fine bien, BV
fine la multa
finger el dedo, II: 4.1
to **finish** terminar, II: 3.1
fire el fuego, II: 10.2
firmness la firmeza
first primero(a), BV
first aid service el servicio de primeros auxilios, II: 8.1
first class en primera (clase), I: 13.1
fish (food) el pescado, I: 5.2
fish (live) el pez, LC3
fish market la pescadería, II: 4.2
to **fit** caber; sentar (ie), **3.2**
It (They) do(es)n't fit me. No me queda(n) (sienta) bien., II: 4.1
five cinco, BV
five hundred quinientos(as), I: 3.2
to **fix** fijar
fixed fijo(a)
flag la bandera
Mexican flag la bandera mexicana, **5.1**
flame la llama, LC4; LC8
flamenco flamenco(a)
traditional flamenco singing el cante jondo
flashy (person) cursi, **3.3**
flat (tire) pinchado(a)
flaw el defecto
to **flee** huir, **1.1**
flight el vuelo, I: 11.1; **1.2**
direct flight el vuelo directo
direct flight service el puente aéreo, **1.2**
domestic flight el vuelo nacional
flight number el número del vuelo, I: 11.1
to take a flight tomar un vuelo, I: 11.1
flight attendant el/la asistente de vuelo, I: 11.2
flipchart el papelógrafo, **7.3**
flock el rebaño, **3.1**
flood la inundación, **8.3**
floor el piso, **2.1;** la planta, I: 6.2; **(ground)** el suelo, LC3
ground floor la planta baja, I: 6.2
flower la flor
wildflower la flor silvestre, **5.1**
flu la gripe, I: 8.1
flute la flauta
fluvial, from a river fluvial, **7.1**
to **fly** volar (ue), II: 7.2
to **fly over** sobrevolar, II: 7.2
fog la neblina, **1.1**
folder la carpeta, I: 3.1
folk healer el/la curandero(a)
to **follow** seguir (i, i)
following siguiente
fond of aficionado(a) a, I: 10.1
food la comida, I: 5.2; el alimento, el comestible, I: 14.2; II: 2.2
foolish tonto(a); necio(a), LC1
foot el pie, I: 7.1
on foot a pie, I: 4.1
footwear el calzado, **3.2**
footwear store una tienda de calzado
for de, BV; para; por
for example por ejemplo

for when? ¿para cuándo?, I: 14.2; II: 2.2
forbidden prohibido(a), II: 11.2
forecast el pronóstico
forehead la frente, II: 8.1; LC2
foreign extranjero(a)
foreign country el país extranjero, I: 11.2
foreign currency las divisas, **8.3**
foreign exchange office la casa de cambio, II: 12.2; **4.2**
foreigner el/la extranjero(a)
forever de siempre y para siempre
fork el tenedor, I: 14.1; II: 2.1
form el formulario, II: 8.2
to **form** formar
fortification la fortificación
fortress el alcazar
fortunate afortunado(a)
fortune la buenaventura
forty cuarenta, I: 2.2
to **found** fundar, **8.1**
foundation la fundación
four cuatro, BV
four hundred cuatrocientos(as), I: 3.2
fourteen catorce, BV
fourth cuarto(a), I: 6.2
fracture la fractura, II: 8.1
fragment el fragmento
frank franco(a)
frankness la franqueza
free libre, I: 5.1
freestyle (swimming) la rutina libre, **6.3**
freezer el congelador, II: 10.1
French el francés, I: 2.2
French fries las papas fritas, I: 5.1
frequently frecuentemente, con frecuencia, II: 3.2
fresh fresco(a), II: 4.2
Friday el viernes, BV
fried frito(a), I: 5.1
friend el/la amigo(a), I: 1.1; el/la compañero(a), I: 1.2; la comadre, LC8
frightful espantoso(a)
from de, BV; desde
  from (time) to (time) de… a…, I: 2.2
front delantero(a)
  in front of delante de, I: 10.1
frontier *(adj.)* fronterizo(a), **8.1**
frozen congelado(a), II: 4.2
frozen food los productos congelados, I: 5.2
fruit la fruta, I: 5.2
fruit store la frutería, II: 4.2
to **fry** freír (i, i), I: 14.1; II: 2.1
frying pan el/la sartén, II: 10.1
fuel el combustible, **7.3**
full lleno(a)
  full (train) completo(a), I: 13.2
  full-time job un trabajo a tiempo completo, II: 14.2
to **fulfill** realizar, **6.3**
fun divertido(a)
function la función, I: 10.2
functioning el funcionamiento
fund el fondo
fundamental primordial
funny cómico(a), gracioso(a), I: 1.1
furious furioso(a)
furniture los muebles
furtively furtivamente
fury la furia
fusion la fusión
future el futuro

galaxy la galaxia
gallant gallardo(a)
galleon el galeón, **6.1**
top gallery (of a theater) el gallinero, el paraíso, **7.2**
gallon el galón
game el juego; (match) el partido, I: 7.1; (of dominos, etc.) la partida
  baseball game el juego de béisbol, I: 7.2
  Olympic Games los Juegos Olímpicos
  tennis game el juego de tenis, I: 9.1
  video game el juego de video, II: 5.1
game arcade la sala de juegos, II: 5.1
game board el tablero, II: 5.1
game piece la ficha, II: 5.1
garage el garaje, I: 6.2
garden el jardín, I: 6.2
garden (small) la huerta, **3.1**
garlic el ajo, I: 14.2; II: 2.2; **1.1;** LC8
gas can el envase, **7.3**
gas station la gasolinera, I: 11.1
gas tank el tanque, II: 11.1
gasoline la gasolina, II: 11.1
  regular (super) gasoline normal (súper), II: 11.2
  (un)leaded con (sin) plomo, II: 11.1
gate la puerta, I: 11.1
gathering la reunión
gaucho el gaucho, **3.1**
generally en general; generalmente
in general, usually por lo general
generation la generación
generous generoso(a), I: 1.2
genre el género
gentleman el caballero, II: 4.1
geography la geografía, I: 2.2
geometric geométrico(a)
geometry la geometría, I: 2.2
German (language) el alemán, I: 2.2
gesture el gesto
to **get** sacar, I: 4.2; conseguir (i, i)
to **get a good (bad) grade** sacar una nota buena (mala), I: 4.2
to **get, buy a ticket** sacar un billete
to **get engaged** comprometerse
to **get off** bajar, I: 13.2; II: 1.2
to **get off the train** bajar(se) del tren, I: 13.2; II: 1.2
to **get on** subir, I: 13.2; abordar
to **get on the train** subir al tren, I: 13.1; II: 1.1
to **get together** reunirse
to **get up** levantarse, I: 12.1
giant el gigante
gift el regalo, I: 6.1
girl la muchacha, I: 1.1; la chica
girlfriend la novia
to **give** dar, I: 4.2
  to give back devolver (ue)
  to give a detailed account of puntualizar
  to give (throw) a party dar una fiesta, I: 4.2
  to give (someone) a present regalar
  to give (someone) a shot (an injection) poner una inyección
  to give a test dar un examen, I: 4.2
to **give up** renunciar
glacier el glaciar, **3.1**
glass (drinking) el vaso, I: 12.1
glimpse la ojeada
gloomy mustio(a), LC7
glove el guante, I: 7.2
to **go** ir, I: 4.1
  let's go vamos
  to go back volver (ue), I: 7.1
  to go back home volver (ue) a casa, I: 10.2

to go by bicycle ir en bicicleta, I: 12.2
to go by car ir en carro (coche), I: 4.1
to go by train ir en tren
to go on a trip viajar, I: 11.1
to go on foot ir a pie, I: 4.1
to go shopping ir de compras, I: 5.2
to go through pasar por, I: 11.1
to **go down** bajar, I: 9.2
to **go surfing (windsurfing, etc.)** practicar el surfing (la plancha de vela, etc.), I: 9.1
to **go swimming** nadar, I: 9.1
to **go to bed** acostarse (ue), I: 12.1
to **go over/through** recorrer, **1.2**
to **go up** subir, I: 6.2
goal la meta, **3.3**
goal line la portería, I: 7.1
goalkeeper, goalie el/la portero(a), I: 7.1
godfather el padrino, II: 13.1
godmother la madrina
godparents los padrinos
gold el oro, **2.1**
gold chain una cadena de oro, II: 4.1
golden dorado(a); áureo(a), LC5
good buen; bueno(a), I: 1.2
Good afternoon. Buenas tardes., BV
Good evening. Buenas noches., BV
Good heavens!, You bet! ¡hombre!
Good morning. Hello. Buenos días., BV
to be in a good mood estar de buen humor, I: 8.1
good-bye adiós, ¡Chao!, BV
goods and services los bienes y servicios
Gosh! ¡Dios mío!
gossip item el chisme
government el gobierno, II: 14.1
federal government el gobierno federal
municipal government el gobierno municipal, II: 14.1
state government el gobierno estatal
governor el/la gobernador(a)
grade el grado; la nota, **I: 4.2**
high grade la nota alta, I: 4.2
low grade la nota baja, I: 4.2
to get a good (bad) grade sacar una nota buena (mala), I: 4.2
graduate el/la diplomado(a); el/la egresado(a), **3.3**
to **graduate** graduarse
grain el cereal, II: 9.2
grain el grano
grain bin el pósito, LC2
gram el gramo
grammar la gramática
granddaughter la nieta, I: 6.1
grandfather el abuelo, I: 6.1
grandmother la abuela, I: 6.1
grandparents los abuelos, I: 6.1
grandson el nieto, I: 6.1
grapefruit la toronja, II: 10.1
grapes las uvas, II: 10.1
grass la hierba, **3.1**
to **grate** rallar, II: 10.2
grave (serious) grave
gray gris, I: 3.2
to **graze** pacer, **3.1**
great gran, grande
greater, greatest mayor
greater part, the most la mayor parte
Greek el/la griego(a)
green verde, I: 3.2
green bean la judía verde, I: 5.2
greengrocer store la verdulería, II: 4.2
to **greet** saludar
greeting el saludo, BV
grief la pena, LC1; LC3
grill la parrilla, II: 10.1
grindstone el molcajete, LC8
grocery store el colmado, la tienda de abarrotes, la tienda de ultramarinos, II: 4.2; la pulpería, LC3
groom el novio, II: 13.1
ground el suelo
group el grupo
to **grow** cultivar, II: 9.2; **2.1**
to **grow up** crecer, **3.1**
growth el crecimiento
guarantee la garantía
to **guarantee** garantizar
to **guard** guardar, II: 7.1
Guatemalan guatemalteco(a)
guava la guayaba
guava shell (peel) el casco de guayaba, **6.2**
guerrilla band la guerrilla
to **guess** adivinar
to **guess right** acertar (ie)
guest el/la invitado(a); el/la huésped, II: 6.1
guidance counselor el/la consejero(a) de orientación
guide el/la guía
guitar la guitarra
gulf el golfo
gums (of the mouth) las encías, LC7
gust (of wind) la ráfaga, **3.1**
gymnasium el gimnasio
gynecologist el/la ginecólogo(a)
gynecology la ginecología

hair el pelo, II: 12.1; el cabello, II: 12.1
hair dryer el secador, II: 12.1
hair salon la peluquería, II: 12.1
hair stylist el/la peluquero(a), II: 12.1
haircut el corte de pelo, II: 12.1
hairdo el peinado
half la mitad
half medio(a), I: 5.2
half an hour media hora
half-past (time) y media
half (game) el tiempo
second half (game) el segundo tiempo, I: 7.1
hall el salón, II: 13.1
ham el jamón, I: 5.1
smoked ham el jamón serrano, **1.1**
hamburger la hamburguesa, I: 5.1
hammock la hamaca, **4.1**
hand la mano, I: 7.1; **5.3**
to hand out distribuir, II: 7.1
to shake hands dar la mano
hand weights los ligeros, **5.2**
handkerchief el pañuelo, II: 4.1
to **handle** manejar, **6.3**
handrail la barra de sujeción, **1.3**
handsome guapo(a), I: 1.1
to **hang, hang up** colgar (ue), **4.1**
to **happen** ocurrir, suceder; pasar
happiness la alegría; la felicidad
happy contento(a), I: 8.1; alegre
Happy birthday! ¡Feliz cumpleaños!, II: 13.1
harbor el puerto, **1.1**
hard duro(a), I: 2.1
hardworking ambicioso(a), I: 1.1
harmonious armonioso(a)
to **harvest** cosechar, II: 9.2
harvest la cosecha, II: 9.2
corn harvest la cosecha del maíz, LC4
hat el sombrero; la gorra, I: 3.2
hate el odio, **3.1**

to **have** tener (ie), I: 6.1
to have (subtitles, ingredients, etc.) llevar
to have a cold tener catarro, estar resfriado(a), I: 8.1
to have a cough tener tos, I: 8.1
to have a headache tener dolor de cabeza, I: 8.1
to have a snack tomar una merienda, II: 4.2
to have a sore throat tener dolor de garganta, I: 8.1
to have to tener que
to **have just (done something)** acabar de, II: 8.1
he él, I: 1.1
head la cabeza, I: 7.1
headache el dolor de cabeza, I: 8.1
health la salud
healthy sano(a)
to **hear** oír
to hear the dial tone oír el tono, II: 3.2
heart el corazón
heat: on low heat a fuego lento
heavy pesado(a)
heel el tacón, II: 4.1; **3.2**
high-heeled de tacón alto
high-heeled boots botas de tacón alto
high-heeled shoes zapatos de tacón alto
height la altura, II: 7.2
helicopter el helicóptero, II: 7.2
Hello! ¡Hola!, BV
Hello! (answering the telephone–Spain) ¡Diga!, I: 14.2; II: 2.2
to **help** ayudar, I: 13.1; dar auxilio; socorrer
help el socorro, la ayuda
hemisphere: northern hemisphere el hemisferio norte
southern hemisphere el hemisferio sur
hen la gallina, II: 9.2; LC3
hen house el gallinero, LC3
her la
her su
herb la yerba, LC6
here aquí
Here is (are) . . . Aquí tiene (tienes, tienen)
hero el/la héroe
heroic heróico(a)
hidden escondido(a)
to **hide** esconder

high alto(a), I: 4.2; elevado
high school el liceo; la escuela secundaria, I: 1.1; la escuela superior
highway la carretera, **1.2; 5.2;** la autovía, la autopista, II: 11.2
hike: to take a hike dar una caminata, I: 12.2
hill la colina, **1.1;** el cerro, **3.1;** la cuesta, LC2
him lo
to him, to her; to you le
hinge (of a door) el quicio de la puerta, LC1
his su
Hispanic hispano(a), hispánico(a)
historian el/la historiador(a)
historical histórico(a)
history la historia, I: 2.2
to **hit** golpear, I: 9.2
to **hit (baseball)** batear, I: 7.2
hobby el pasatiempo, el hobby, I: 5.1
hole el agujero
home la casa, I: 6.2; el hogar, **3.3**
at home en casa
country home la casa de campo, II: 9.2
home economics la economía doméstica, I: 2.2
home plate el platillo, I: 7.2
home run el jonrón, I: 7.2
honest honesto(a), I: 1.2
honesty la honestidad
honey la miel, LC5
honeymoon la luna de miel
to **honk the horn** tocar la bocina
honor el honor
maid of honor la dama de honor, II: 13.1
hood (automobile) el capó, II: 11.1
to **hope** esperar, **2.3**
I hope ojalá, II: 14.1; **6.3**
horn el claxon, la bocina, II: 11.1
horse el caballo, LC1
horseback: to go horseback riding pasear a caballo; montar a caballo
hose la manguera, **7.3**
hospital el hospital, II: 8.1
hostile desafecto, **6.1**
hot (climate) caluroso(a), **2.1**
It's hot. Hace calor., I: 9.1
hotel el hotel, II: 6.1
hotel (government-run) el parador (del gobierno), **1.1**
inexpensive hotel el hostal, I: 12.2

hour la hora
departure hour la hora de salida
house la casa, I: 6.2
apartment house la casa de apartamentos (departamentos), I: 6.2
private house la casa privada (particular), I: 6.2
house of representatives el congreso de diputados
housing la vivienda
how? ¿qué?, BV; ¿cómo?, I: 1.1
How absurd! ¡Qué absurdo!
How are you? ¿Qué tal?, BV
How is . . . ? ¿Cómo está...?, I: 8.1
How may I help you? ¿En qué puedo servirle?, II: 4.1
How much do(es) . . . cost? ¿Cuánto cuesta(n)... ?, I: 3.1
How much is (are) . . . ? ¿A cuánto está(n)... ?, I: 5.2
how many? ¿cuántos(as)?, I: 2.1
how much? ¿cuánto?, I: 3.1
to **hug** abrazar, LC1
huge agigantado(a), **8.3**
human being el ser humano
humble humilde
humid húmedo(a)
to **hunger for** apetecer
hungry: to be hungry tener hambre, I: 14.1; II: 2.1
hunt la caza, **5.1**
hurricane el huracán, **6.1**
to **hurry** apresurarse, LC7
to **hurt** doler (ue), I: 8.2
My . . . hurt(s) me Me duele(n)..., I: 8.2
to **hurt oneself** hacerse daño, lastimarse, II: 8.1
husband el marido, el esposo, I: 6.1
husky fornido(a)
hut el bohío, **4.1; 7.1;** la choza
straw hut una choza de paja, **4.1**
hydrofoil el aerodeslizador; el hidrofoil
hygiene la higiene
hypermarket el hipermercado, II: 4.2

I

I yo, I: 1.1
ice cream el helado, I: 5.1
chocolate ice cream el

helado de chocolate, I: 5.1
vanilla ice cream el helado de vainilla, I: 5.1
icon el icono
idea la idea
ideal ideal, I: 1.2
idealist el/la idealista
to **identify** identificar
if si
to **ignore** ignorar, LC2
illiterate person el/la analfabeto(a), **6.3**
illness la enfermedad
illusion la ilusión
illustrious ilustre
image la imagen
imaginary imaginario(a)
imagination la imaginación
to **imagine** imaginar
imagined, dreamed of imaginado(a) immediate inmediato(a)
immediately enseguida, I: 5.1; inmediatamente
immense inmenso(a)
imperative el imperativo
imperial imperante, **7.1**
implementation la implementación
to **imply that** dar a entender
impolite descortés, **6.2**
important importante
impossible imposible
in en
in case of en caso de, II: 7.1
in general por lo general
in itself en sí
in regard to en cuanto a
to **inaugurate** inaugurar
Inca el/la inca
inch la pulgada
inclination la inclinación
inclined proclive, **6.3**
to **include** incluir, I: 5.1; **8.3**
to **increase** aumentar
incredible increíble
independence la independencia
indispensable indispensable, imprescindible, **6.3**
Indian indio(a)
to **indicate** indicar, I: 11.1
indication la indicación
indigenous indígena
indigenous (person) el/la indígena, **2.1**
indispensable indispensable
individual el individuo
individual: individual sport el deporte individual
industrial industrial
inexpensive barato(a), I: 3.2
to **influence** impresionar
influence la influencia
to **inform** informar, I: 13.2; II: 1.2
information la información; los datos, I: 3.1
ingredient el ingrediente
inhabitant el/la habitante, **2.3**
inheritance la herencia
inhospitable inhospitable
to **initiate** iniciar
injection la inyección, I: 8.2
to give (someone) an injection poner una inyección
to **injure** lastimar, herir (i, i), **5.3;** LC4
inmate el recluso, **6.3**
inn el parador; el albergue; la venta, **1.2**
inning la entrada, I: 7.2
innocent inocente
innovation la innovación
inquisition: the Spanish Inquisition la Inquisición, **8.1**
insane loco(a)
to **insert** meter, II: 3.1; introducir, II: 3.2; **4.2**
insolent insolente
to **inspect** inspeccionar, I: 11.1
inspection el control, I: 11.1
installation la instalación
installments: in installments a plazos
instant el instante
instantaneous instantáneo(a)
instead of en vez de
instruction la instrucción, **4.2**
instrument el instrumento
insufficiency la insuficiencia
insufficient insuficiente
insurance el seguro, **5.2**
integral íntegro(a)
to **integrate** integrar, **6.3**
intelligent inteligente, I: 2.1; listo(a), **6.2**
intention la intención, el propósito
interest el interés
interest rate la taza de interés, **4.2**
to **interest** interesar
interesting interesante, I: 2.1
intermission el descanso, el intermedio, **7.2**
international internacional
Internet Internet, II: 3.1
interpretation la interpretación
interpreter el/la intérprete
to **interrupt** interrumpir
interruption la interrupción
intersection el cruce, la bocacalle, II: 11.2
to **intervene** intervenir
to **interview** entrevistar
interview la entrevista, II: 14.2; **8.2**
interviewer el/la entrevistador(a), II: 14.2
intrepid intrépido(a)
introduction la introducción
to **invade** invadir, **1.1**
invader el/la invasor(a), **1.1**
invention el invento
investigation la investigación
invitation la invitación
to **invite** invitar, I: 6.1
invoice la factura, II: 6.1
involved in involucrado(a), **5.3**
to **iron** planchar, II: 12.1; **3.2**
irrigation la irrigación
island la isla
it la, lo
Italian italiano(a)
itinerant ambulante
ivory el marfil

jacket la chaqueta, I: 3.2; **3.2;** el saco, II: 4.1
jaguar el jaguar, **5.1**
jai alai la pelota vasca
jai alai player el/la pelotari
jam la mermelada
January enero, BV
jar el frasco, II: 4.2
jeans el blue jean, II: 3.2
jet el avión de reacción, el jet, II: 7.2
jewel la joya, II: 4.1; **1.1**
jewelry store la joyería, II: 4.1
Jewish hebreo(a), II: 13.2
Jewish people los judios
job el trabajo
job application la solicitud de empleo, II: 14.2
full- (part-) time job el trabajo a tiemp completo (parcial), II: 14.2
to **join** enlazar; juntarse, unirse, **5.1**
judge el/la juez, II: 14.1
judgement el juicio
in the judgement of a juicio de, **3.3**
juice el jugo
orange juice el jugo de naranja, I: 12.1

July julio, BV
jump el salto, **5.3**
to **jump** saltar
June junio, BV
jungle la jungla; la selva, **5.1**
  rainforest la selva tropical (lluviosa)
just: just after (time) y pico
  to have just (done something) acabar de (+ infinitivo), II: 8.1

K

to **keep** guardar, II: 3.1
to **keep in shape** mantenerse en forma
key la tecla, II: 3.2; la llave, II: 6.1
keyboard el teclado, II: 3.1
to **keyboard** entrar los datos, II: 3.1
to **kick** tirar, I: 7.1
  to kick (throw) the ball tirar el balón, I: 7.2
to **kill** matar
kilogram el kilo, I: 5.2
kilometer el kilómetro
kilometers (distance in) el kilometraje
  unlimited kilometers el kilometraje ilimitado, **5.2**
kind la clase
king el rey, **1.1**
  The Three Kings (Wise Men) Los Reyes Magos, II: 13.2
to **kiss** besar, LC1
kitchen la cocina, I: 6.2
knapsack la mochila, I: 12.2
knee la rodilla, I: 7.1; LC1
knife el cuchillo, I: 14.1; II: 2.1
knight: knight errant el caballero andante
knot el nudo, **2.1**
to **know** conocer, I: 11.1
to **know (how)** saber, I: 11.2
knowledge el conocimiento, **6.3**

laboratory el laboratorio
lack la falta
lady-in-waiting la dama
lake el lago, II: 5.2
  lake (river) house un bohío lacustre
  on the shore of a river or lake lacustre, **7.1**
lamb el cordero, I: 14.2; II: 2.2
lame cojo(a)
lame person el/la cojo(a), LC1
lament el lamento
lance la lanza
to **land** aterrizar, I: 11.2
land la tierra
  by land por tierra
landing el aterrizaje, II: 7.2
landlord el amo, LC2
landscape el paisaje
lane (of highway) el carril, II: 11.2
language la lengua, I: 2.2; el lenguaje; el idioma
lapel la solapa, **3.2**
large gran, grande
  larger mayor, **3.2**
to **last** durar, II: 13.2
last pasado(a); último(a)
last (year) el (año) pasado
late tarde; con una demora, I: 11.1; con retraso, I: 13.2; II: 1.2
later luego, BV; después; más tarde
  See you later! ¡Hasta luego!, BV
Latin el latín, I: 2.2
Latin *(adj.)* latino(a)
Latin America Latinoamérica, I: 1.1
Latin American Latinoamericano(a)
to **laugh** reír
to **launch** lanzar
laundromat la lavandería
laundry el lavado, II: 12.1
  dirty laundry la ropa sucia, II: 12.1
lavatory el aseo, el lavabo, II: 7.1
lawyer el/la abogado(a), II: 14.1
lawyer's office el bufete del abogado, II: 14.1
lazy perezoso(a), I: 1.1
to **lead, go (one street into another)** desembocar, II: 9.1; ecabezar, **6.3**
leaded (gasoline) con plomo, II: 11.1
leaf la hoja, LC3; LC8
league la liga
Major Leagues las Grandes Ligas
lean (weight) enjuto(a), LC7
to **lean (against)** recostar (ue), LC8
to **learn** aprender, I: 5.1
leather el cuero, **3.2**
  leather fabric tela de cuero
to **leave (something)** dejar, I: 14.1; II: 2.1
  to leave a tip dejar una propina, I: 14.1; II: 2.1
to **leave** salir, I: 10.1
  to leave late salir tarde, I: 11.1
  to leave on time salir a tiempo, I: 11.1
  to leave the theater salir del teatro, I: 10.2
lecture la conferencia
left izquierdo(a), I: 7.1
  to the left a la izquierda, II: 5.2
left-handed zurdo(a), **6.3**
leg la pierna, I: 7.1; **5.3**
lemon el limón, II: 10.1
lemon tree el limonero
lentil la lenteja
less menos
lesser, least menor
lesson la lección, I: 4.2
to **let** dejar
to **let go (set free)** soltar (ue), LC3
letter (of alphabet) la letra
letter la carta, II: 12.2
letter of recommendation la carta de recomendación
lettuce la lechuga, I: 5.2
level el nivel
liberator el/la libertador(a)
license plate la placa
life la vida
  school life la vida escolar
life jacket el chaleco salvavidas, II: 7.1; **5.3**
to **lift** levantar; alzar, LC7; LC8
light la luz, II: 11.1
  red light la luz roja, II: 11.2
light (cheerful) ligero(a)
light (weight) ligero(a), LC2
to **light** encender (ie), II: 13.2
lighting el alumbrado, la iluminación, **7.1**
lightning el relámpago, **8.3**
like como, I: 1.2
to **like, to be pleasing** gustar
lime la lima, II: 10.1
line (queue) la cola, I: 10.1; la fila, II: 5.2
  to stand (wait) in line hacer cola, I: 10.1
line la línea
  parallel line la línea paralela
  telephone line la línea telefónica

to **line up** hacer cola, I: 10.1
lion el león
lip el labio, II: 8.1
liquid líquido(a)
list la lista
to **listen (to)** escuchar, I: 4.2
Listen! ¡Oye!
liter el litro
literal literal
literary literario(a)
literature la literatura, I: 2.1
little poco(a), I: 2.1
a little un poco (de)
live en vivo, **8.2**
to **live** vivir, I: 5.2
living: to earn one's living ganar la vida
living room la sala, I: 6.2
loan el préstamo, **4.2**
long- (term-) loan un préstamo de largo (corto) plazo
lobster la langosta, I: 14.2; II: 2.2
local local, I: 13.2; II: 1.2
to **locate** ubicar
to be located ubicarse, **2.3; 6.3**
to **lodge** alojarse; hospedarse
log el madero, LC7
logical lógico(a)
long largo(a), I: 3.2
long-term a largo plazo, **4.2**
un préstamo de largo plazo long-term loan
to **look at** mirar, I: 3.1
Look! ¡Mira!
to **look at oneself** mirarse, I: 12.1
to **look for** buscar, I: 3.1
to **look good (food)** tener buena pinta, II: 4.2
to **look like** parecer (a), II: 8.1; **1.1**
loose flojo(a)
to **loosen** aflojar, **8.3**
to **lose** perder (ie), I: 7.1
to get lost extraviarse, **4.3**
lotto el loto
loud (colors) llamativo(a), **3.3**
love el amor
to **love** querer; amar; encantar
low bajo(a), I: 4.2
to **lower** bajar, I: 9.2
luck la suerte
Good luck! ¡Buena suerte!
lucky dichoso(a), LC4
luggage el equipaje, I: 11.1
carry-on luggage el equipaje de mano, I: 11.1
to check luggage facturar el equipaje, I: 11.1
to claim luggage reclamar
luke warm tibio(a), LC7
lunch el almuerzo, I: 5.2
to have, eat lunch tomar el almuerzo, almorzar (ue)
lung el pulmón, LC8
luxuriance la lozanía, LC5
luxurious lujoso(a)
lying mentiroso(a)
lyric lírico(a)

M

macaw el guacamayo, **5.1**
made hecho(a)
magazine la revista, I: 6.2
magnificent magnífico(a)
maid la camarera, II: 6.2
maid of honor la dama de honor, II: 13.1
mail el correo, II: 12.2
air mail el correo aéreo, II: 12.2
e-mail el correo electrónico, II: 3.1
regular mail el correo ordinario, II: 12.2
to **mail the letter** echar la carta (en el buzón), II: 12.2
mailbox el buzón, II: 12.2
main principal
mainly principalmente
to **maintain** mantener
majestic majestuoso(a)
majority la mayoría
to **make** hacer
to make a telephone call hacer una llamada telefónica, II: 3.2
to make the bed hacer la cama, II: 6.2
make matters worse por colmo, **6.2**
to **make up** formar
makeup el maquillaje, I: 12.1
to put one's makeup on maquillarse, poner el maquillaje, I: 12.1
male el varón
man el hombre; el caballero, II: 4.1
manager el/la gerente, II: 14.1
mango el mango, **6.1**
manner el modo; la manera, I: 1.1
manufactured fabricado(a)
many; a lot muchos(as), I: 2.1
map el mapa; el plano, II: 9.1; **1.2**
marble (stone) el mármol, LC8
marble (toy) la canica, LC1
March marzo, BV
to **march** marchar
marginality la marginalidad, **6.3**
marine *(adj.)* marino(a), **3.1**
marker el marcador, I: 3.1
market el mercado, I: 5.2
meat market la carnicería, II: 4.2
to **match (clothes)** hacer juego, **3.2**
marketing el mercadeo
marmalade la mermelada
marriage el matrimonio, **4.3**
to get married casarse, II: 13.1
marvelous maravilloso(a)
mass la masa
mass (Catholic) la misa, LC8
to **match** parear
material el material
raw material la material prima, **2.1**
mathematics las matemáticas, I: 2.1
matter la materia
maximum máximo(a), II: 11.2
May mayo, BV
Maya el/la maya
mayonnaise la mayonesa
mayor el alcalde, II: 14.1; la alcaldesa
me *(pron.)* me
to me a mí
meal la comida, I: 5.2
to prepare the meal preparar la comida
to **mean** significar
meaning el significado; el sentido
meaningful significante
means el medio
by means of mediante, **6.3**
means of expression el modo de expresión
means of transportation el medio de transporte
to **measure** medir (i, i)
measurement la medida
meat la carne, I: 5.2
mechanic el/la mecánico(a)
medal la medalla
medical office el consultorio, I: 8.2
medicine (discipline) la medicina, I: 8.2
medicine (drugs) el medicamento, I: 8.2
meditation la meditación
medium mediano(a), II: 4.1
medium el medio
to **meet** encontrarse (ue)
melancholic melancólico(a)

member el miembro, I: 4.2
memory la memoria; el recuerdo
men: men's clothing store a tienda de ropa para caballeros, II: 4.1
menace la plaga
menorah la menora, II: 13.2
to **mention** mencionar
menu el menú, I: 5.1
merchandise la mercancía, I: 14.1
merengue el merengue
merry-go-round el tiovivo, II: 5.2
Mesoamerica Mesoamérica, **5.1**
message el mensaje, II: 3.2; el recaudo, LC2
messenger el chasqui
mestizo el/la mestizo(a)
metabolism el metabolismo
meteorologist el/la meteorólogo(a), **8.2**
meter el metro
meter (taxi) el taxímetro, **1.2**
method el método
metrics la métrica
metro entrance la boca del metro, II: 9.1
Mexican mexicano(a), I: 1.1
Mexican American mexicanoamericano(a)
microbe el microbio
microphone el micrófono, **8.2**
microscope el microscopio
microscopic microscópico(a)
microwave oven el horno de microondas, II: 10.1
middle: in the middle of (noun) en pleno + *noun*
middle school la escuela intermedia
midnight la medianoche
midwest (region) el medio oeste, **8.1**
migration la migración
mile la milla
milk la leche
million el millón
millionaire el/la millonario(a)
mime el/la mimo, II: 5.2
miniature la miniatura
miniaturization la miniaturización
ministry el ministerio
to **mint** acuñar
minute diminuto(a)
minute el minuto
mirror el espejo, I: 12.1
to **miss** perder (ie), I: 10.2
to miss the bus perder el autobús (la guagua, el camión), I: 10.1
Miss, Ms. la señorita, BV
mist la neblina, **1.1**
mixture la mezcla
mode la modalidad
model el/la modelo
modem el módem
moderation la moderación
modern moderno(a)
modernized modernizado(a)
modesty la modestia
modification la modificación
mom la mamá
moment el momento
monarch el monarca
monarchy la monarquía, **1.1**
monastery el monasterio
Monday el lunes, BV
money el dinero, I: 14.1; II: 2.1; **4.2;** LC6
money (income) la plata, LC6
money changer el/la cambista, II: 12.2
money order el giro de dinero, **8.3**
monitor el monitor, II: 3.1
monkey el mono, II: 5.2
monster el monstruo
month el mes, BV
monthly installment la mensualidad
monument el monumento
mood el humor, I: 8.1
to be in a bad (good) mood estar de mal (buen) humor, I: 8.1
moon la luna
Moor el/la moro(a)
more más, I: 2.2
more or less más o menos
moreover además
morning la mañana
A.M. (time) de la mañana
in the morning por la mañana
mortal mortal
mortality la mortalidad
mortgage la hipoteca, **4.2**
mosque la mesquita (Islam)
mother la madre, I: 6.1
motion la moción
motive el motivo
motor el motor
mountain la montaña, I: 9.2; el monte, **3.1**
underwater mountain la montaña submarina
mountain range la sierra; la cordillera, II: 7.2; LC7
mountainous montañoso(a)
mouse el ratón, II: 3.1
mouth la boca, I: 8.2
mouth (of a river) la desembocadura, **7.1**
to **move** mover (ue), mudarse; **(residence)** trasladar, **4.1**
to **move away** largarse, LC8
movement el movimiento
movie la película, I: 6.2
movie theater el cine, I: 10.1
moving conmovedoro(a)
Ms., Mrs., madam la señora, BV
much; a lot mucho(a), I: 2.1
mud el lodo
mudslide la ola de lodo, **8.3**
multinational multinacional
multiplication la multiplicación
to **multiply** multiplicar
mural el mural, I: 10.2
muralist el/la muralista
muscle el músculo, **5.3**
muscular muscular
museum el museo, I: 10.2
mushroom el hongo, **2.3**
music la música, I: 2.2
musical instrument el instrumento musical
musician el/la músico(a)
mussels los mejillones, II: 10.2
must deber
mute el mudo, LC1; LC7
mutual mutuo(a)
my mi
mysterious misterioso(a)
mystery el misterio
mythical mítico(a)
mythology la mitología

name el nombre
in whose name? ¿a nombre de quién?, I: 14.2; II: 2.2
last name el apellido
nap: to take a nap echar (tomar) una siesta
napkin la servilleta, I: 14.1; II: 2.1
narcotic el narcótico
to **narrate** narrar
narration la narración
narrow estrecho(a), II: 4.1; angosto(a), II: 9.1
narrow street la callecita, II: 9.1
national nacional
nationality la nacionalidad, I: 1.2

what nationality? ¿de qué nacionalidad?
native indígena
native person el/la indígena
natural resources los recursos naturales, I: 2.1
natural sciences las ciencias naturales
nature la naturaleza
navegable navegable
to **navigate** navegar
near cerca de, I: 6.2
nearby cercano(a)
necessary necesario(a)
necessity la necesidad
neck el cuello, II: 4.1
nectar el néctar, LC5
to **need** necesitar, I: 3.1; hacer falta, **3.2**
needle la aguja, LC8
negative negativo(a)
neighbor el/la vecino(a)
neighborhood el barrio, II: 9.1; la zona
nephew el sobrino, I: 6.1
nervous nervioso(a), I: 8.1
nest el nido, LC3
net la red, I: 9.1
Net (Internet) net
nettle la ortiga
never jamás; nunca
new nuevo(a)
newlyweds los novios, II: 13.**1**
New Year el Año Nuevo, II: 13.2
Happy New Year! ¡Próspero Año Nuevo!, II: 13.2
New Year's Eve la Nochevieja, la víspera de Año Nuevo, II: 13.2
news las noticias, I: 6.2; **8.2;** las nuevas, LC2
news report el noticiero, **8.2**
newspaper el periódico, I: 6.2
newspaper clipping el recorte de periódico, LC8
newsstand el quiosco, I: 13.1; II: 1.1
next próximo(a), I: 13.2; I: 1.2
at the next stop en la próxima parada, I: 13.2; I: 1.2
nice simpático(a), I: 1.2
niece la sobrina, I: 6.1
night la noche
Good night. Buenas noches., BV
in the evening, at night por la noche
last night anoche, I: 9.2
P.M. (time) de la noche
nine nueve, BV
nine hundred novecientos(as), I: 3.2
nineteen diecinueve, BV
ninety noventa, I: 2.2
ninth noveno(a), I: 6.2
no no, BV
no one nadie
no smoking sign la señal de no fumar, II: 7.1
Nobel Prize el Premio Nóbel
noble noble
nocturnal nocturno(a)
none, not any ninguno(a)
by no means de ninguna manera, I: 1.1
nonstop sin escala
noon el mediodía
north el norte
North America la América del Norte
North American norteamericano(a)
northeast (region) el nordeste, **8.1**
northerner el/la norteño(a), **8.1**
northwest (region) el noroeste, **8.1**
nose la nariz, II: 8.1
nostalgia la nostalgia
notable notable
to **note** notar
notebook el cuaderno, I: 3.1
notes: to take notes tomar apuntes, I: 4.2
nothing nada, I: 5.2
Nothing else. Nada más., I: 5.2
to **notice** advertir (ie, i), **8.3**
novel la novela
novelist el/la novelista
November noviembre, BV
novices los novatos, **5.3**
now ahora, I: 4.2; ya
now and then de vez en cuando
nowadays, these days hoy (en) día
number el número, I: 1.2; la cifra, **8.3**
flight number el número del vuelo, I: 11.1
local number el número local
seat number el número del asiento, I: 11.1
telephone number el número de teléfono
wrong number el número equivocado
numerous numeroso(a)
nuptial, wedding nupcial
nurse el/la enfermero(a), II: 8.2; el/la practicante
nutrition la nutrición
nylon el nilón, 3.2

O

oats la avena, LC8
obituary la esquela, **4.3**
object el objeto
objective el objetivo, **3.3**
obligation la obligación
observation la observación
to **observe** observar
observer el/la observador(a)
obstacle el obstáculo
to **obtain** obtener
obvious obvio(a)
occasion la ocasión
occupied, taken ocupado(a), I: 5.1
to **occur** suceder, **5.3**
ocean el océano
October octubre, BV
odd: odd number el número impar
of de, BV
Of course! ¡Cómo no!; por supuesto
of the, from the del
off-track despistado(a), **7.3**
to **offer** ofrecer, II: 14.2
office la oficina, II: 9.1
official oficial
often con frecuencia, a menudo, II: 3.2
oil el aceite, I: 14.2; el óleo
oil (relating to) petrolero(a)
OK, all right; in agreement de acuerdo; ¡vale!
old viejo(a), anciano(a), I: 6.1; antiguo(a), II: 5.1
older mayor, **2.3**
old person el/la anciano(a); el/la viejo(a)
olive oil el aceite de oliva
olive grove el olivar, **1.1**
on en; sobre
on foot a pie, I: 4.1
on the dot, sharp en punto, I: 4.1
once and for all definitivamente
oncologist el/la oncólogo(a)
oncology la oncología
one uno, BV
one o'clock la una

one-way street la calle de sentido único, II: 11.2
one-way ticket el billete sencillo, I: 13.1; II: 1.1
one hundred cien(to), I: 3.2
onion la cebolla, II: 10.1
only único(a); sólo; solamente
opaque opaco(a)
to **open** abrir, I: 8.2
open-mouthed boquiabierto(a)
opening la apertura
opera la ópera
to **operate** operar
operating room el quirófano
operator el/la operador(a)
operetta la opereta
ophthalmologist el/la oftalmólogo(a)
ophthalmology la oftalmología
opinion la opinión
opportunity la oportunidad
opposite opuesto(a); contrario(a)
the opposite lo contrario
the opposite direction el sentido contrario, II: 11.2
the opposite of contrario de
to **oppress** oprimir, **7.1**
or o; u (used instead of **o** before words beginning with **o** or **ho**)
orally oralmente
orange (fruit) la china; la naranja, I: 5.2
orange anaranjado(a), I: 3.2
orange juice el jugo de naranja, I: 12.1; el zumo de naranja
orange tree el naranjo
orchard el/la huerto(a), II: 9.2
orchestra la platea
el palco de platea orchestra pit, **7.2**
symphony orchestra la orquesta sinfónica
orchestra seat la butaca, el patio de butacas, **7.2**
order (restaurant) la orden, I: 5.1; el pedido, **1.3**
to **order** mandar; **(restaurant)** pedir (i, i)
organ el órgano
organism el organismo
to **organize** organizar
origin el origen
ornament el adorno
orthopedic surgeon el/la cirujano(a) ortopédico(a), II: 8.2
orthopedics la ortopedia
other otro(a)
ounce la onza
our nuestro(a)
outdoor *(adj.)* al aire libre
outdoor café (market, etc.) el café (mercado, etc.) al aire libre
outfielder el/la jardinero(a), I: 7.2
outfit la indumentaría, **3.1**
outskirts los alrededores; las afueras, II: 9.1
oven el horno, II: 10.1
over sobre
overcoat el abrigo, II: 4.1
to **overflow** rebosar, **6.1**
overland por tierra
to **overtake** adelantar, II: 11.2; **(traffic)** rebasar, **5.2**
to **owe** deber
own: one's own propio(a)
owner el/la dueño(a), **4.3; 6.1**
ox el buey, LC2
oxygen el oxígeno
oxygen mask la máscara de oxígeno, II: 7.1
oyster la ostra, II: 10.2

to **pack one's suitcase** hacer la maleta
package el paquete, I: 5.2
pact el convenio, **5.3**
page la página
pain el dolor, I: 8.1
I have a pain in my . . . Tengo dolor de..., I: 8.2
to **paint** pintar, II: 14.1
paintbrush el pincel
painter el/la pintor(a)
painting el cuadro, I: 10.2; la pintura
pair el par, II: 4.1
pair of tennis shoes el par de tenis, I: 3.2
palace el palacio
palette knife la espátula
palm tree la palma
pamphlet el folleto
Panamanian panameño(a), I: 2.1
Pan American panamericano(a)
pancake el panqueque
pants el pantalón, I: 3.2; **3.2**
papaya la papaya, II: 10.2; **6.1**
paper el papel, I: 3.1
sheet of paper la hoja de papel, I: 3.1
toilet paper el papel higiénico, I: 12.2
paradise el paraíso
paramedics el servicio de primeros auxilios, los socorristas, II: 8.1
paragraph el párrafo
parents los padres, I: 6.1
to **park** aparcar, estacionar
park el parque, II: 5.2
parka el anorak, I: 9.2
parking el estacionamiento
parking lot el aparcamiento
parking meter el parquímetro
parochial parroquial, **4.3**
parrot el papagayo, LC8
part (in hair) la raya, I: 12.1
part la parte
the greatest part, the most la mayor parte
upper part la parte superior
party la fiesta, II: 13.1
to give (throw) a party dar una fiesta, I: 4.2
pass (permission) el pase
to **pass** pasar, I: 7.2; **(car)** adelantar, II: 11.2; **(traffic)** rebasar, **5.2**
passenger el/la pasajero(a), I: 11.1; **1.2**
passionate apasionado(a)
passport el pasaporte, I: 11.1
passport inspection el control de pasaportes, I: 11.1
past pasado(a)
pastry el pastel, II: 4.2
path el camino; la senda, II: 5.2; LC7
to walk along the path caminar por la senda, II: 5.2
patience la paciencia
patient el/la paciente
patrol la patrulla, **1.3**
patron el/la patrón(na)
patron saint el patrón; la patrona
pattern el patrón
paved pavimentado(a)
pavement el pavimento
paving stone el adoquín
paving stone alley la callejuela de adoquines, **4.1**
paw la pata, LC3
to **pay** pagar, I: 3.1; **1.2**
to pay at the cashier pagar en la caja, I: 3.1

to pay attention hacer caso; prestar atención, II: 4.2
to pay the bill pagar la factura, II: 6.1
to pay in full pagar al contado, **4.2**
to pay in installments pagar a cuotas (a plazos), **4.2**
payment el pago
monthly payment el pago mensual
pea el guisante, I: 5.2
Peace Corps el Cuerpo de Paz
peaceful tranquilo(a)
peak el pico, II: 7.2
peanut el cacahuete (cacahuate); el maní
pear la pera, II: 9.2
pear tree el peral, II: 9.2
pedestrian el peatón, II: 9.1
pedestrian street la calle peatonal, II: 9.1
pediatrician el/la pediatra
pediatrics la pediatría
to **peel** pelar, II: 10.2; **1.1**
pen la pluma, I: 3.1
pencil el lápiz, I: 3.1
pencil holder la lapicera, **3.3**
pencil sharpener el sacapuntas, **6.3**
penguin el pingüino, **3.1**
peninsula la península
penny el centavo
people la gente
pepper la pimienta, I: 14.1; II: 2.1
bell pepper el pimiento, II: 10.2
percent por ciento
percussion la percusión
to **perfect** perfeccionar
performance la función, **(theater)** la representación, I: 10.2
perhaps quizás, II: 14.2
period el período
period of time la época
to **permit** permitir, I: 11.1
person la persona, I: 1.2
personality la personalidad
personally personalmente
Peruvian peruano(a)
pet la mascota, **4.3**
petition la petición
petroleum el petróleo
pharmacist el/la farmacéutico(a), I: 8.2
phone el teléfono
cell phone el teléfono celular, II: 3.2
pay phone el teléfono público, II: 3.2
phone book la guía telefónica, II: 3.2
phone call la llamada telefónica, II: 3.2
push-button phone el teléfono de botones, II: 3.2
photo la foto
photograph la fotografía; el retrato, LC8
photographer el/la fotógrafo(a)
phrase la frase
physics la física, I: 2.2
piano el piano
to **pick up** recoger
to **pick up (the telephone)** descolgar (ue), II: 3.2
pickpocket el/la carterista, **2.2**
picturesque pintoresco(a), I: 9.1
piece el pedazo, I: 12.1; el trocito, I: 10.2; **1.1**
little piece el pedacito, II: 10.2
pig (pork) el cerdo, I: 14.2; II: 2.2
roast suckling pig el lechón asado, **6.1**
pilgrim el/la peregrino(a)
pill la pastilla, la píldora, la tableta, I: 8.2
pillow la almohada, II: 6.2; **1.1**
pilot el/la piloto, I: 11.2
pin number (automatic teller) el pin, **4.2**
pinch la pizca
pineapple la piña, **6.1**
pink rosado(a), I: 3.2
pint la pinta
piping (embroidery) el cordoncillo
pirouette la pirueta
pitcher el/la lanzador(a), el/la pítcher, I: 7.2
pity la lástima
pizza la pizza, BV
to **place** colocar; meter, I: 7.1
place el lugar; el sitio
placement la colocación
plague la plaga
plaid a cuadros
plain la llanura, II: 7.2; **1.1; 3.1**
plainsman el llanero
plan el plano, II: 9.1
to **plan** planear
plant la planta
to **plant** sembrar, II: 9.2
plantain el plátano, I: 5.2
fried plantain slice el tostón
plastic plástico(a), II: 4.2
plate el plato, I: 14.1; II: 2.1
plateau la mesa; la meseta, II: 7.2
high plateau el altiplano, II: 7.2
to **play (music)** tocar
play la obra teatral, I: 10.2; la obra dramática
to **play** jugar (ue), I: 7.1
to play baseball (soccer, basketball, etc.) jugar (al) béisbol (fútbol, baloncesto, etc.), I: 7.1
player el/la jugador(a), I: 7.1
playwright el/la dramaturgo(a)
plaza la plaza, **2.1**
to **plead** rogar (ue)
pleasant agradable, **2.3**
please por favor, BV; favor de, I: 11.2
pleasure el gusto
pleat el pliegue, **3.3**
plentiful abundante
plot el argumento
to **plow** labrar, LC2
plum el ciruelo, LC3
plumber el/la fontanero(a), el/la plomero(a), II: 14.1
plume el penacho, LC8
pocket el bolsillo, II: 4.1; **2.2; 3.2**
poem el poema
poet el poeta
poetry la poesía
point el tanto, I: 7.1; el punto
poisonous venenoso(a)
pole el palo, LC3
police el policía, **2.2**
police officer el/la guardia; el/la agente de policía; el/la policía, **2.2**
police station la comisaría, **2.2**
to **polish** pulir, LC7
polite atento(a)
political político(a)
political science las ciencias políticas
polka dots: with polka dots con lunares
to **pollute** contaminar
polluted contaminado(a)
pollution la contaminación
polyester el poliéster, **3.2**
poncho el poncho
pool la alberca, **1.1**
poor pobre
poor boy (girl) el/la pobre
poor man (woman) el/la pobretón(ona)

popular popular, I: 2.1
popularity la popularidad
to **populate** poblar (ue), **8.1**
population, people la población
porch el porche
pork el puerco
port el puerto, **1.1**
portable portátil
porter el/la maletero(a), el/la mozo(a), I: 13.1; II: 1.1
portrait el retrato
position la posición; el puesto, II: 14.2
to **possess** poseer
possession la posesión
possibility la posibilidad
possible posible
post office el correo, II: 12.2
postcard la postal, la tarjeta postal, II: 12.2
poster el afiche, **7.3**
pot la cazuela, la olla, II: 10.1
potato la papa, I: 5.1; **2.1;** la patata
  mashed potatoes el pure de papas
pothole el bache
pound la libra
power el poder
powerful poderoso(a)
practically casi
to **practice** practicar
to **pray** rogar (ue), **4.3**
prayer la plegaria, LC5; el rezo
pre-Columbian precolombino(a)
precious precioso(a)
precipitation la precipitación, **1.2**
precise preciso(a)
prediction la predicción; el prognóstico
  weather forecast el prognóstico del tiempo, **8.2**
predominance el predominio
to **predominate** predominar
to **prefer** preferir (ie, i)
prenuptial antenupcial
preparation la preparación
to **prepare** preparar
to **prescribe** recetar, I: 8.2
prescription la receta, I: 8.2
presence la presencia
to **present** presentar
present *(adj.)* presente
  at the present time actualmente
presentation la presentación
president el/la presidente
to **press** oprimir, pulsar, **4.2**
pressure la presión, II: 11.1
prestige el prestigio
pretty bello(a), bonito(a), hermoso(a), lindo(a), I: 1.1; **2.1**
to **prevail** prevalecer
price el precio
to **prick** picar, I: 8.1
priest el sacerdote; el cura, LC5
princess la princesa
principal el/la director(a)
principal principal
printed estampado(a), **3.3**
printer la impresora, II: 3.1
prison la cárcel, **6.3**
private particular, I: 6.2; privado(a)
  private house la casa particular, la casa privada, I: 6.2
probable probable
problem el problema
process el proceso
to **process** procesar
procession la procesión
to **proclaim** proclamar; pregonar
produced producido(a)
product el producto, I: 5.2
production la producción
profession la profesión, II: 14.1
professor el/la profesor(a), I: 2.1
program (TV) la emisión, I: 6.2; el programa
  sports program la emisión deportiva, I: 6.2
progress el progreso
progressive progresivo(a)
project el proyecto
to **project** proyectar, I: 10.1
promiscuity la promiscuidad
promise la promesa
to **promote** promover (ue)
promotion la promoción
pronoun el pronombre
prose la prosa
to **prosper** prosperar
prosperous próspero(a)
protagonist el/la protagonista
protection la protección
protein la proteína
to **protest** protestar
protoplasm el protoplasma
to **provide** proveer; suministrar, **8.3**
provider el/la proveedor(a)
provision la provisión
prudence la cordura, LC8; la prudencia
psychiatrist el/la psiquíatra
psychiatry la psiquiatría
public público(a)
publicity la propaganda
to **publish** publicar
Puerto Rican puertorriqueño(a)
to **pull out (up)** arrancar, LC8
pulse el pulso, II: 8.2
punctual puntual
to **punish** castigar, **6.1**
punishment el castigo
puppy el perrito
pure puro(a)
purpose la mira, **6.3**
to **push** oprimir; pulsar, II: 3.1; empujar, II: 4.2; **2.2**
to **put** poner, I: 11.1; colocar
to **put a cast on** poner en un yeso, II: 8.2
to **put in** meter, II: 3.1
to **put on** ponerse, I: 12.1
  to put on a performance dar una representación, I: 10.2
  to put on makeup ponerse el maquillaje, I: 12.1
Pyrenees los pirineos

qualification la calificación
quality la calidad
quarrel la disputa
quarry la cantera, LC2
quarter el cuarto, I: 2.2
  quarter after (the hour) y cuarto
  quarter to (the hour) menos cuarto
queen la reina, **1.1**
question la pregunta
questionnaire el cuestionario
quickly rápidamente; rápido
quiet tranquilo(a)
quipu el quipu, **2.1**
quite bastante, I: 1.1

race la carrera
racket (sports) la raqueta, I: 9.1
radiator el radiador, II: 11.1
rag el trapo, LC7
railroad el ferrocarril, I: 13.1, II: 1.1
railway platform el andén, I: 13.1; II: 1.1

rain la lluvia
to **rain** llover (ue)
It's raining. Llueve., I: 9.1
raincoat el impermeable, la gabardina, II: 4.1
rainforest la selva tropical
rainy lluvioso(a), **2.1**
to **raise** criar, II: 9.2;
rake el rastro, LC2
ranch la hacienda; **(Argentina)** la estancia
rancor el rancor
rare raro(a)
rate la tarifa; la tasa
exchange rate el tipo de cambio, la tasa de cambio, II: 12.2
unemployment rate la tasa de desempleo
rather bastante, I: 1.1
razor la navaja, I: 12.1
to **reach** alcanzar, **2.3**
reaction la reacción
to **read** leer, I: 5.1
reading la lectura
ready listo(a)
realist el/la realista
realistic realista
really realmente
reason el motivo; la razón
reasonable razonable
rebelliousness la rebeldía
to **rebound** rebotar
to **receive** recibir, I: 5.1
recent reciente
recently recién
reception la recepción, II: 6.1
receptionist el/la recepcionista, II: 6.1
recipe la receta
to **recite** recitar
reckless aturdido(a), LC6
to **recognize** reconocer
recollection el recuerdo
to **recommend** recomendar (ie)
recommendation la recomendación
to **reconcile** conciliar
to **record** grabar, **8.2**
recreation el recreo
to **recruit** reclutar
rectangle el rectángulo
recycling el reciclaje
red rojo(a), I: 3.2
to **reduce (dislocated bone)** reducir, II: 8.2
reduced (price) reducido(a)
to **refer** referir (ie, i)
to **reflect** reflejar; reflexionar
reflection; reflex el reflejo
reforestation la reforestación
refrigerator el refrigerador, la nevera, II: 10.1
refuge el refugio
region la región
regional regional
regionalism el regionalismo
to **register** registrar
registration card la ficha, II: 6.1
regular (gasoline) normal, II: 11.1
to **reign** reinar, **1.1**
to **reject** rechazar, resistir, **4.3**
rejuvenated remozado(a), **6.3**
related relacionado(a)
relation la relación
relative el/la pariente, I: 6.1; el familiar, **4.3**
relatively relativamente
religious religioso(a)
to **relocate** reubicar; reubicarse, **2.3**
to **remain** quedar, I: 7.1
remainder el resto
remains los restos
to **remember** recordar (ue)
remote alejado(a); remoto(a)
remote control el control remoto, **8.2**
to **remove** quitar, **2.2**
renewed renovado(a)
to **renounce** renunciar
to **rent** alquilar, II: 5.2; rentar
to **repair** reparar
to **repeat; to take seconds (meal)** repetir (i, i)
to **replace** reemplazar
report el informe; el reportaje; **(police)** la denuncia, **2.2**
to **represent** representar
representative el/la representante
representative representativo(a)
republic la república
repulsion la repulsión, **3.1**
request el pedido, **1.3**
to **require** requerir (ie, i)
required requerible, **6.3**
requirement el requisito
to **rescue** rescatar, **1.3; 8.3**
rescue worker el socorrista, **8.3**
researcher el/la investigador(a)
reservation la reservación, II: 6.1
to **reserve** reservar, I: 14.2; II: 2.2
reserved reservado(a), I: 13.2; II: 1.2
to **reside** morar, LC7; residir
residence la residencia
resident el/la residente
residue el residuo
to **resist** resistir
resolution resolución
resort la estación, I: 10.1
to **respect** respetar, **2.3**
respiration la respiración
to **respond** responder
responsibility la responsabilidad
to make oneself responsible responsabilizarse
rest demás; el resto, **5.1**
to **rest** descansar, **5.2**
to **rest on** reposar, **6.1**
restaurant el restaurante, I: 14.1; II: 2.1
to **restore** restaurar
result el resultado; la secuela, **7.3**
to **resume** reanudar, **8.3**
retina la retina
to **return** regresar; volver (ue), I: 7.1; **4.3**
to return home volver a casa, I: 10.2
to **return (something)** devolver (ue), I: 7.2
return el regreso
return trip, trip back el viaje de regreso
to **reveal** revelar
reverse inverso(a)
revolution la revolución
rhythm el ritmo
rib la costilla, II: 10.1
ribbon la cinta
rice el arroz, I: 5.2
rice with beans el arroz con frijoles (habichuelas), **6.1**
rich rico(a), I: 14.2; II: 2.2; con mucha plata
to get rich enriquecerse, **7.1**
rich person el/la rico(a)
ride la atracción, II: 5.2
right el derecho
right derecho(a), I: 7.1
to the right a la derecha, II: 5.2
right: that's right (true)! ¡verdad!
right away enseguida, I: 5.1
rigorous riguroso(a)
ring el anillo, II: 4.1
to **ring** sonar (ue), II: 3.2
to **rinse out** enjuagar, LC7
to **rise** ascender
to **rise (bread)** empanizar, LC5

risk riesgo, **5.2; 7.3**
rite el rito, **8.1**
ritual el rito, el ritual
rival el rival
river el río, II: 7.2
riverlike fluvial, **7.1**
to **roast** asar, II: 10.1
roasted asado(a)
to **rob** robar, **2.2**
robbery el robo, **2.2**
robustness la robustez
rock la roca, **1.3**
role el rol; el papel
roll of toilet paper el rollo de papel higiénico, I: 12.2
to **roll** rodar (ue)
to **roll over** voltearse, **5.3**
roller blading el patinaje lineal
roller coaster la montaña rusa, II: 5.2
Roman el/la romano(a)
romantic romántico(a)
roof el techo, **4.1**
room el cuarto, la sala, I: 6.2; la pieza
  double room el cuarto doble, II: 6.1
  recovery room la sala de recuperación
  single room el cuarto sencillo, II: 6.1
  waiting room la sala de espera, I: 13.1; II: 1.1
rooster el gallo, LC3
root la raíz, LC3
  to put down roots echar raíces
rope la soga, LC3
rose la rosa
rosemary el romero, LC8
rough áspero(a); fragoso(a), LC7
round-trip (ticket) de ida y vuelta, I: 13.1; II: 1.1
route la ruta
routine la rutina, I: 12.1
routine *(adj.)* rutinario(a)
row (of seats) la fila, I: 10.1
to **row** remar, II: 5.2
royal real
rubber (shoe soles) la goma, **3.2**
  rubber soles la suela de goma
ruby el rubí
rude grosero(a), ineducado(a)
rug la alfombra, **1.1**
ruin la ruina
to **ruin** arruinar, LC5
rule la regla
rumor el rumor
to **run** correr, I: 7.2; LC6
runway la pista
rural rural

sacred sagrado(a), LC4
sacrifice el sacrificio
to **sacrifice** sacrificar
sad triste, I: 8.1
safe salvo(a)
saffron el azafrán
sail la vela, **5.3**
sail (of a windmill) el aspa
sailboard la plancha de vela, I: 9.1
sailor el/la marino(a)
saint el santo
salad la ensalada, I: 5.1
salary el salario
sale la venta, II: 14.1
salesperson el/la dependiente(a), II: 4.1; el/la vendedor(a), II: 11.1
salt la sal, I: 14.1; II: 2.1
same mismo(a), I: 2.1
sanctuary el santuario
sand la arena, I: 9.1
sandal el huarache; la alpargata; la sandalia, II: 4.1
sandwich el sándwich, BV; el bocadillo, I: 5.1
sash la faja
satellite dish la antena parabólica, **8.2**
satisfied satisfecho(a), II: 14.1
to **satisfy** satisfacer
Saturday el sábado, BV
saucepan la cacerola, II: 10.2
saucer el platillo, I: 14.1; II: 2.1
sausage (pork and garlic) el chorizo, la salchicha, II: 10.1
savanna la sabana, **3.1**
to **save** ahorrar; conservar; salvar; guardar, II: 3.1
savings account la cuenta de ahorros
to **saw** aserrar, LC7
sawdust el aserrín, LC7
saxophone el saxofono
to **say** decir
scales la báscula, I: 11.1
scar la cicatriz, LC6
scarce escaso(a), **2.1**
to **scare** asustar, **8.3**
scarf la bufanda, II: 4.1; **3.2**
scene la escena
scenery, set (theater) el escenario, I: 10.2; la decoración, el decorado, el escenografía, **7.2**
schedule el horario, I: 13.1; II: 1.1
  school schedule el horario escolar
scholarship la beca
school el colegio, la escuela, I: 1.1; la academia
  elementary school la escuela primaria
  high school la escuela secundaria, I: 1.1; la escuela superior
  middle school la escuela intermedia
school (of a university) la Facultad
school (related to) escolar, I: 2.1
school bus el bus escolar, I: 4.1
school life la vida escolar
school schedule el horario escolar
school supplies los materiales escolares, I: 3.1
science las ciencias, I: 2.2
science fiction la ciencia ficción
scientific científico(a)
scientist el/la científico(a)
scissors las tijeras, II: 12.1
to **score a goal** meter un gol, I: 7.1
to **score a point** marcar un tanto, I: 7.1
scoreboard el tablero indicador, I: 7.1
screen la pantalla, I: 10.1; **4.2; 8.2**
  arrival and departure screen la pantalla de salidas y llegadas, I: 11.1
sculptor el/la escultor(a), I: 10.2
sculpture la escultura
sea el mar, I: 9.1
sea level el nivel del mar
sea lion el lobo marino, **3.1**
seal (animal) el elefante marino, **3.1**
seal el sigilo
to **seal** sellar, **7.1**
search: in search of en busca de
season la estación, BV
to **season** sazonar
seasoning el condimento
seat el asiento, I: 11.1; la plaza, I: 13.2; II: 1.2; (theater) la localidad, **7.2**

seat (of government) la sede
seat (theater) la butaca, I: 10.1
seat belt el cinturón de seguridad, II: 7.1; **5.2**
seat number el número del asiento, I: 11.1
second segundo(a), I: 6.2
second class en segunda (clase), I: 13.1; II: 1.1
second half (soccer) el segundo tiempo, I: 7.1
secondary secundario(a)
secret el secreto
secretary el/la secretario(a), II: 14.1
secretly a escondidas, **8.1;** clandestinamente
to **secretly take** escamotear
security la seguridad, II: 7.1
security check el control de seguridad, I: 11.1
sedan el sedán, II: 11.1
see: See you later! ¡Hasta luego!, BV
See you soon! ¡Hasta pronto!, BV
See you tomorrow! ¡Hasta mañana!, BV
to **see** ver, I: 5.1
to see a show ver un espectáculo, I: 10.2
to **seem** parecer, II: 8.1
to **select** seleccionar
selection la selección
self-portrait el autorretrato
to **sell** vender, I: 5.2; despachar, II: 8.2
semester el semestre
senator el/la senador(a)
to **send** enviar; mandar, transmitir, II: 3.1
sentence la frase
separated separado(a)
separation la separación
Sephardi el/la sefardí, **8.1**
September septiembre, BV
series la serie
World Series la Serie mundial
serious serio(a), I: 1.1; grave
servant el/la sirviente
to **serve** servir (i, i), I: 14.1; II: 2.1
How may I help you? ¿En qué puedo servirle?, II: 4.1
service el servicio, I: 5.1
service station la estación de servicio, la gasolinera, II: 11.1
set el conjunto, **7.2; (of a play)** la decoración, el decorado, la escenografía, **7.2**
to **set out for** encaminarse a, LC3
to **set the bone** reducir el hueso, II: 8.2
to **set the table** poner la mesa, I: 14.1; II: 2.1
to **settle** radicarse, **8.1**
seven siete, BV
seven hundred setecientos(as), I: 3.2
seventeen diecisiete, BV
seventh séptimo(a), I: 6.2
seventy setenta, I: 2.2
severe severo(a); rudo(a), LC5
to **sew** coser
sewing la costura
sex el sexo
shack la chabola; el bohío, **4.1**
shade la sombra, LC4
to **shake hands** dar la mano; estrechar la mano, LC8
shampoo el champú, I: 12.2
shantytown la villa miseria (Arg.); el pueblo jóven (Peru)
shape la forma
to **share** compartir, **3.3**
to **shatter** destrozar, LC5
to **shave** afeitarse, I: 12.1
shaving cream la crema de afeitar, I: 12.1
shawl el poncho
she ella, I: 1.1
sheep la oveja, **3.1**
sheet la sábana, II: 6.2
sheet of paper la hoja de papel, I: 3.1
shell el casco
guava shell (peel) el casco de guava, **6.2**
shellfish los mariscos, I: 5.2
sherbet, sorbet el sorbete
shh! ¡chist!
to **shine** brillar, I: 9.1
shining lustroso(a)
ship el navío, LC1
to **be shipwrecked** naufragar, **1.3**
shirt la camisa, I: 3.2; **3.2**
long-sleeved shirt la camisa de mangas largas, II: 4.1
short-sleeved shirt la camisa de mangas cortas, II: 4.1
shoe el zapato, I: 3.2; **3.2**
high-heeled shoes zapatos de tacón alto
tennis shoes los tenis, **5.3**
shoelace el cordón, el pasador **3.2**
shoeless descalzo(a), LC3
shoe store la zapatería, II: 4.1; **3.2**
to **shop** ir de compras, II: 5.2; hacer las compras, II: 4.2
shop window el escaparate, la vitrina, II: 4.1
shopping: to go shopping hacer las compras, II: 4.2; ir de compras, II: 5.2
shopping mall la galería comercial
shore la orilla, **1.1**
short bajo(a), I: 1.1; corto(a), I: 3.2
short- (long-) term a corto (largo) plazo, **4.2**
short- (long)- term loan un préstamo de corto (largo) plazo
shortage la escasez, **7.3**
shorts el pantalón corto, I: 3.2
shot: to give (someone) a shot poner una inyección
should deber
shoulder (body) el hombro, II: 8.1; **5.3**
shoulder (road) el arcén, **5.2**
to **show (movie)** presentar; mostrar (ue), **5.3**
show (movies) la sesión, I: 10.1
show el espectáculo, I: 10.2; el show
shower la ducha, I: 12.1
to take a shower tomar una ducha, I: 12.1
shrimp los camarones, I: 14.2; II: 2.2; las gambas, II: 10.2
to **shrink** encogerse, **3.2**
shuttle (airport) el autocar, **1.2**
shy tímido(a), I: 1.2
sick enfermo(a), I: 8.1
sick person el/la enfermo(a), I: 8.1
side *(adj.)* lateral, I: 13.2; II: 1.2
side el borde; el lado
sidewalk la acera, II: 9.1
to **sigh** suspirar
sign el rótulo, II: 11.2; la muestra, el indicio, **5.3**
traffic sign la señal de tránsito
to **sign** firmar, II: 12.2; **5.2**
significance el sentido, II: 11.2
significant significativo(a)
silver la plata, **2.1**
similar parecido(a); similar; semejante
to **be similar to** asemejarse a, **7.1**
simple sencillo(a); simple
simplicity la llaneza, LC7;

la sencillez
sin el pecado, **3.3**
to **sin** pecar, **3.3**
since como; desde
sincere franco(a); sincero(a), I: 1.2
to **sing** cantar, I: 4.2
singing el canto
single soltero(a)
singles singles, I: 9.1
to **sink** hundirse, **6.1**
sir, Mr., gentleman el señor, BV
sister la hermana, I: 6.1
to **sit down** sentarse (ie), I: 12.1
sit-ups las sentadillas, **5.3**
to **situate** situar
to be situated situarse, **2.1**
situation la situación
six seis, BV
six hundred seiscientos(as), I: 3.2
sixteen dieciséis, BV
sixth sexto(a), I: 6.2
sixty sesenta, I: 2.2
size (shoes) número, I: 3.2
size el tamaño, la talla, I: 3.2
What size (shoe) do you wear (take)? ¿Qué número calza Ud.?, II: 3.2
What size (clothing) do you wear (take)? ¿Qué tamaño (talla) usa Ud.?, II: 3.2
ski el esquí
to **ski** esquiar, I: 9.2
ski lift el telesquí, I: 9.2
ski pole el bastón, I: 9.2
ski resort la estación de esquí, I: 9.2
ski slope la pista, I: 9.2
skier el/la esquiador(a), I: 9.2
skiing el esquí, I: 9.2
skirt la falda, I: 3.2
sky el cielo, I: 9.1, **2.3**
clear sky un cielo despejado
skyscraper el rascacielos, II: 9.1; **4.1**
to **sleep** dormir (ue, u)
to fall asleep dormirse (ue, u), I: 12.1
sleeping bag el saco de dormir, I: 12.2
sleeve la manga, II: 4.1; **3.2**
long- (short-) sleeved de mangas largas (cortas), II: 4.1
slice la rebanada, **1.1;** la tajada, II: 4.2
to **slice** rebanar, II: 10.2; **1.1**
to **slide** resbalarse, **5.3**
slope la ladera
mountain side la ladera de la montaña, **7.1**
slot la ranura, II: 3.1
slow lento(a), II: 10.2; **6.2**
slowly despacio; lentamente
small pequeño(a), I: 2.1
smile la sonrisa, **2.3**
little smile la sonrisita
smoke el humo
smoking: (no) smoking area la sección de (no) fumar, I: 11.1
snack la merienda, I: 4.2
to have a snack tomar una merienda, I: 4.2
snake la serpiente, **5.1**
to **sneeze** estornudar, I: 8.1
snout el hocico, LC3
snow la nieve, I: 9.2
snow-covered nevado(a), **2.1**
to **snow** nevar (ie), I: 9.2
snowboarding el surf de nieve
so así
so, so much tan, tanto(a)
soap el jabón, I: 12.2
bar of soap la barra (pastilla) de jabón, I: 12.2
soap opera la telenovela, **8.2**
soccer el fútbol, I: 7.1
soccer field el campo de fútbol, I: 7.1
social sciences las ciencias sociales, I: 2.2
society la sociedad
sociology la sociología
socks los calcetines, I: 3.2
soda el cola, I: 5.1
sofa el sofá, II: 6.2
sold out agotado(a), **7.2**
soldier el militar; el/la soldado, **1.1**
sole (shoes) la suela, **3.2; 5.3**
rubber sole la suela de goma
solemn solemne
solitary, lone solitario(a)
solution el remedio; la solución
to **solve** resolver (ue)
some algunos(as), I: 4.1; unos(as)
someone alguien
something algo, I: 5.2
sometimes de vez en cuando; a veces, I: 7.1
son el hijo, I: 6.1
song la canción
soon dentro de poco
sore throat el dolor de garganta, I: 8.1
sorrow el hiel, LC5
sorry: to be sorry sentir (ie, i)
soul el alma, LC6
sound el sonido
soup la sopa, I: 5.1
sour agrio(a), **2.1**
source la fuente
south el sur
South America la América del Sur
South American sudamericano(a)
southeast (region) el sureste, **8.1**
southern austral, **3.1**
southwest (region) el sudoeste; el suroeste, **8.1**
to **sow** sembrar, II: 9.2
sowing la siembra
space el espacio
spaghetti el espagueti
Spain la España, I: 1.2
Spanish *(adj.)* español(a)
Spanish American hispanoamericano(a)
Spanish (language) el español, I: 2.2
Spanish speaker el/la hispanohablante
Spanish-speaking hispanohablante
Spanish-speaking countries los países de habla española
Spanish-style a la española
spare tire la llanta de recambio (repuesto), II: 11.1
spark la chispa, LC4
to **speak** hablar, I: 3.1; conversar
special especial
specialist el/la especialista, II: 14.1
to **specialize** especializar
specialty la especialidad
spectator el/la espectador(a), I: 7.1; el/la mirón(ona)
speed la velocidad, II: 11.2
speed limit el límite de velocidad, **5.2**
to **spend** pasar; gastar
to **spend time** pasar el tiempo, II: 5.1
spice la especia
spicy picante, **4.1**
to **spill** derramar
spirit el espíritu
spit cup la escupidera, LC7
spoken de palabra, LC2
spontaneous espontáneo(a)
spoon la cuchara
wooden spoon la cuchara de palo, LC8
spoonful la cucharada, LC5

sport el deporte, I: 7.1
individual sport el deporte individual
(related to) sports deportivo(a), I: 6.2
sports program (TV) la emisión deportiva, I: 6.2
team sport el deporte de equipo
spring la primavera, BV
to **sprinkle** rociar, LC5
to **squeeze** apretar (ie), **3.2**
squid los calamares, II: 10.2
squire, knight's attendant el escudero
stadium el estadio, I: 7.1
stage el escenario, **7.2**
stage: to come (go) on stage entrar en escena, I: 10.2
stairway la escalera, I: 6.2
stall el puesto, II: 4.2
stamp el sello, la estampilla, II: 5.1
to **stand on line** hacer cola
standing de pie
stanza la estrofa
star la estrella
to **start** entablar
to start the day amanecer, LC7
state el estado
station la estación, I: 10.1
stitch el punto, **3.2**
stitch (knit) fabric tela de punto
subway station la estación del metro, II: 10.1, la estación de ferrocarril, I: 13.1; II: 1.1
stationery store la papelería, I: 3.1
statistic la estadística
statue la estatua, I: 10.2
stay la estadía
to **stay** alojarse
to **stay in bed** guardar cama, I: 8.1
steak el biftec, I: 14.2; II: 2.2
by stealth a hurtadillas, LC6
step el paso
stereo estereofónico(a)
stew el guisado, LC8
stiff yerto(a), LC7
still todavía
stilts los pilotes, **7.1**
sting la picadura, II: 8.1
to **stir** revolver (ue), II: 10.1
stitch el punto, la sutura, II: 8.1
stoicism el estoicismo
stomach el estómago, I: 8.1
stomachache el dolor de estómago, I: 8.1
stone la piedra
stop la parada, I: 13.2; II: 1.2
to **stop** bloquear, parar, I: 7.1
stopover la escala, II: 7.2
store la tienda, I: 3.2
to **store** almacenar
storm la tormenta, **8.3,** LC1; la tempestad
stormy borrascoso(a), **3.1**
story el cuento; la historia
short story la historieta
stove la estufa, II: 10.1
stove burner la hornilla, II: 10.1
straight derecho, II: 11.2
to go straight seguir derecho, II: 11.2
to **strain** colar, LC5
strange extravagante
strategy la estrategia
straw la paja, II: 13.2
stream el arroyo
street la calle, I: 6.2
one-way street la calle de sentido único, II: 11.2
pedestrian street la calle peatonal
strength la fortaleza
stretch (of road) el trayecto; el tramo
to **stretch** estirar, LC1
stretcher la camilla, II: 8.1
stretches los estiramientos, **5.3**
strike (work) la huelga
on strike en huelga, **1.2**
to **strike twelve** dar las doce, II: 13.2
string (instrument) la cuerda
string bean la judía verde; el poroto; la vainita; el ejote; la chaucha
striped a rayas; rayado(a) (de rayos), **3.2**
striped blouse una blusa rayada (de rayas)
to **strive for** procurar, LC3
strong fuerte, **4.1**
structure la estructura
student (relating to) estudiantil
student el/la alumno(a), I: 1.1; el/la estudiante
student housing la residencia para estudiantes, II: 3.2
study el estudio
to **study** estudiar, I: 4.1
stupendous estupendo(a)
stupid torpe
stupid person el torpe, LC1
style el estilo; la moda
in style de moda
to **subdue** someter; rendir (i, i), LC1
subject la asignatura, I: 2.1; la materia; el tema
subject area (school) la disciplina, I: 2.2
to **subject** sujetar, LC1
to **subjugate** subyugar, **2.1**
substance: controlled substance la sustancia controlada
subterranean subterráneo(a)
subtitle el subtítulo, I: 10.1
with subtitles con subtítulos, I: 10.1
to **subtract** restar
suburb el suburbio; la colonia
subway el metro, I: 10.1; **1.3**
subway station la estación de metro, I: 10.1
success el éxito
suckling pig el lechón; el cochinillo
sudden súbito, **8.3**
suddenly repentinamente; de repente; de golpe, LC5
suede ante, gamuza, **3.2**
to **suffer** sufrir
to **suffice** bastar, **5.3**
sugar el azúcar, II: 10.1
to **sugar** azucarar, LC5
sugarcane la caña de azúcar, **6.1**
to **suggest** sugerir (ie, i)
suggestion la sugerencia
suit el traje, I: 3.2; **3.2**
suitcase la maleta, I: 11.1
sum el monto, **1.1; 4.2**
summer el verano, BV
summer *(adj.)* veraniego(a), **1.1**
summer house la casa veraniega
to **sunbathe** tomar el sol, I: 9.1
sunblock la crema protectora, I: 9.1
sunburned, tanned tostadito(a)
Sunday el domingo, BV
sunglasses las gafas de sol, los anteojos de sol, I: 9.1
suntan lotion la loción bronceadora, I: 9.1
sunny: It's sunny. Hace (Hay) sol., I: 9.1
sunset la puesta del sol
supermarket el supermercado, I: 5.2

supermarket cart el carrito, II: 4.2
superstition la superstición
support el soporte, **8.3**
to **support** sostener; apoyar, **2.1**
sure seguro(a)
to **surf** practicar el surfing (la tabla hawaiana), I: 9.1
to surf the Net navegar por la red
surface la superficie
surfboard la tabla hawaiana, I: 9.1
surfing el surfing, I: 9.1
surgeon el/la cirujano(a), II: 8.2
to **surpass** superar, **8.1;** sobrepasar
to **surprise** sorprender
to **surrender** someterse, **6.1**
to **surround** rodear
survey la encuesta
SUV el todoterreno, **5.2**
to **swallow** tragar, LC6
sweat el sudor, LC2
to **sweat** sudar, LC2
sweater el suéter, II: 4.1; **3.2**
wool sweater un suéter de lana
sweet dulce, **3.1**
sweet roll el pan dulce, I: 5.1
sweetheart, lover el/la enamorado(a)
to **swim** nadar, I: 9.1
swim meet el torneo de nado (natación)
to **swim underwater** bucear, I: 9.1
swimmer el/la nadador(a), **6.3**
swimming la natación, el nado, I: 9.1; **6.3**
swimming pool la alberca, la piscina, I: 9.1
swollen hinchado(a), II: 8.1; LC7
symptom el síntoma, I: 8.2
syrup el sirope
system el sistema
metric system el sistema métrico

T-shirt la camiseta, el T-shirt, I: 3.2
table la mesa, I: 5.1; LC7
table soccer el futbolín, II: 5.1
tablecloth el mantel, I: 14.1; II: 2.1
tablespoon la cuchara, I: 14.1; II: 2.1
taciturn taciturno(a), LC2
taco el taco, BV
tail la cola, LC3
to **take** tomar, I: 4.1
to take notes tomar apuntes, I: 4.2
to take one's blood pressure tomar la tensión (presión) arterial, II: 8.2
to take one's pulse tomar el pulso, II: 8.2
to take out sacar, II: 3.1
to take photos tomar fotos
to take place tener lugar, II: 8.1; efectuarse, **4.3**
to take the luggage down bajar las maletas, II: 6.1
to take the (school) bus tomar el bus (escolar), I: 4.1
to take a walk dar un paso, LC6
to **take charge** encargarse
to **take off** quitar, II: 10.2
to take off (airplane) despegar, II: 11.2
to take off the fire retirar del fuego, II: 10.1
to **take time** tardar
takeoff (of an airplane) el despegue, I: 7.2
talent el talento
to **talk** hablar, I: 3.1; conversar
tall alto(a), I: 1.1; high, **3.1**
tamale el tamal, BV
tan bronceado(a)
tank el tanque, II: 11.1; (gas station) el depósito, **7.3**
task la tarea
tasteless disgustado(a), LC8
taxi el taxi, I: 11.1; **1.2**
tea el té, I: 5.1
iced tea el té helado, II: 5.1
to **teach** enseñar, I: 4.1
teacher el/la maestro(a); el/la profesor(a), I: 2.1
team el bando; el equipo, I: 7.1
team sport el deporte de equipo, I: 7.2
tear la lágrima, LC7
tearoom la confitería
teaspoon la cucharita, I: 14.1; II: 2.1
technician el/la técnico(a), II: 8.2
technology la tecnología
teenager el/la adolescente
telecommunication la telecomunicación
to **telephone** telefonear
to talk on the phone hablar por teléfono
telephone el teléfono
cell phone el teléfono celular, II: 3.2
public (pay) telephone el teléfono público, II: 3.2
push-button telephone el teléfono de botones, II: 3.2
(related to the) telephone telefónico(a)
telephone book la guía telefónica, II: 3.2
telephone call la llamada telefónica, II: 3.2
telephone keypad el teclado, II: 3.2
telephone line la línea telefónica
telephone pole el poste de teléfono, **8.3**
telephone receiver el auricular, II: 3.2
television la televisión, I: 6.2
television set el televisor, II: 6.2; **8.2**
television viewer el/la televidente, **8.2**
teller el/la cajero(a), II: 12.2
teller's window la ventanilla, II: 12.2
temperate templado(a)
temperature la temperatura, I: 9.2
temple (head) la sien, LC6
ten diez
tendency la tendencia
tender tierno(a)
tennis el tenis, I: 9.1
pair of tennis shoes el par de tenis, I: 3.2
tennis player el/la tenista
tennis shoes los tenis, I: 3.2
tenth décimo(a), I: 6.2
term el término
terminal el terminal
passenger terminal el terminal de pasajeros, II: 7.2
terrace (sidewalk café) la terraza
terrible terrible
terrifying aterrador(a)
territory el territorio
terror el terror
test el examen, I: 4.2
tetanus el tétano
Thank you. Gracias., BV
that aquel, aquella; ese(a)

that (one) eso
the la, el, I: 1.1
theater el teatro, I: 10.2
theatrical teatral, I: 10.2
their su, sus, I: 6.1
them las, los
to them; to you *(formal pl.) (pron.)* les
theme el motivo; el tema
then luego, BV; entonces
there allí, allá
there is, there are hay, BV
therefore, for this reason, that's why por eso
thermos el termo, **7.3**
these estos(as)
they ellos(as), I: 2.1
thick espeso(a), **7.1**
thin delgado(a); flaco(a), I: 1.2
thing la cosa
to **think** pensar (ie); opinar, II: 10.2
third tercer(o)(a), I: 6.2
thirsty: to be thirsty tener sed, I: 14.1; II: 2.1
thirteen trece, BV
thirty treinta, BV
thirty-one treinta y uno, I: 2.2
this este(a)
this (one) esto
thistle el cardo
thorax el tórax, **5.3**
those aquellos(as), esos(as)
thought el pensamiento
thousand mil, I: 3.2
thread el hilo, LC8
three tres, BV
three hundred trescientos(as), I: 3.2
Three Wise Men los Reyes Magos, II: 13.2
throat la garganta, I: 8.1
throne el trono
to **throw** echar, LC6; lanzar, I: 7.1; tirar; botar, **4.1;** arrojar, LC1
to throw (kick) the ball tirar el balón, I: 7.2
Thursday el jueves, BV
thus así
ticket el boleto, el ticket, I: 9.2; el billete, I: 11.1; el tique, II: 9.1
luggage claim ticket el talón, I: 11.1
one-way ticket el billete sencillo, I: 13.1; II: 1.1
round-trip ticket el billete de ida y vuelta, I: 13.1; II: 1.1
ticket window la boletería, **7.2;** la ventanilla, I: 9.2
tie (clothing) la corbata, I: 3.2; **3.2**
tie el lazo
tied (score) empatado(a), I: 7.1
The score is tied. El tanto queda empatado., I: 7.1
tiger el tigre
time la hora; el tiempo, II: 9.1
At what time? ¿A qué hora?
on time a tiempo, I: 11.1
What time is it? ¿Qué hora es?
time la vez
at times, sometimes a veces, I: 7.1
at that time en aquel entonces
one more time, again una vez más
time zone el huso horario
timid tímido(a), I: 1.2
tiny diminuto(a)
tip el servicio, I: 5.1; la propina, I: 14.1; II: 2.1
Is the tip included? ¿Está incluido el servicio?, I: 5.1
tire el neumático, la goma, la llanta, II: 11.1
flat tire la llanta pinchada
spare tire la llanta de recambio (repuesto), II: 11.1
tired cansado(a), I: 8.1
to a
toast la tostada; el pan tostado, I: 5.2
to **toast** tostar
today hoy, BV
together juntos(as)
toilet el inodoro, el váter, II: 6.2
toilet paper el papel higiénico, I: 12.2
to **tolerate** consentir (ie, i)
toll el peaje, II: 11.2; **1.2**
toll booth la garita de peaje, II: 11.2
tomato el tomate
tomorrow mañana, BV
ton la tonelada
tonality la tonalidad
tonight esta noche, I: 9.2
too much demasiado
tool la herramienta, LC3
tooth el diente
back tooth la muela, LC7
tooth decay la caries, LC7
toothbrush el cepillo de dientes, I: 12.2; LC7
toothpaste la pasta (crema) dentífrica, I: 12.2; LC7
top la cumbre, LC8
tortilla la tortilla, I: 5.1
totally totalmente
touch el contacto
to **touch** tocar
tour la gira, I: 12.2
tour guide el/la guía
tourist el/la turista, I: 10.2
tournament el torneo
toward en dirección a; hacia
towel la toalla, I: 9.1; II: 6.2
beach towel la toalla playera, I: 9.1
tower la torre
control tower la torre de control, II: 7.2
town el pueblo, II: 9.2; **2.3**
town square la plaza, II: 9.1
toxic tóxico(a)
toy el juguete, LC8
track la vía, I: 13.1; II: 1.1
trade el oficio, II: 14.1
tradition la tradición
traditional tradicional
traffic el tráfico
traffic jam el embotellamiento, el tapón, **1.2**
traffic light el semáforo, II: 9.1; **5.2**
traffic sign la señal de tráfico (tránsito), **5.2**
tragedy la tragedia
trail el camino
train el tren, I: 13.2; II: 1.2
local train el tren local, I: 13.2
nonstop train el tren directo, I: 13.2; II: 1.2
underground train el tren subterráneo
train car el coche, el vagón, I: 13.1; II: 1.1
cafeteria (dining) car el coche-cafetería, el coche-comedor, I: 13.2; II: 1.2
sleeping car el coche-cama, I: 13.2
train conductor el/la revisor(a), I: 13.2; II: 1.2
train station la estación de ferrocarril, I: 13.1; II: 1.1
training el entrenamiento
traitor el traidor
to **transfer** transbordar, I: 13.2; II: 1.2; trasladar
to **transform** convertir (ie, i); transformar

to **translate** traducir
to **transmit** transmitir, II: 3.1; **8.2**
to **transpire** transpirar, LC2
transportation el transporte
trap la trampa, LC3
to **trap** atrapar, **8.3**
to **travel** circular; recorrer; viajar
to **travel by air** viajar en avión, I: 11.1
traveler el/la viajero(a)
traveler's check el cheque de viajero, II: 12.2
tray la bandeja, II: 7.1
tray table la mesita, II: 7.1
treacherous aleve, LC5
treasure el tesoro
treat tratar
treatment el tratamiento; la cura
tree el árbol
triangle el triángulo
tribe la tribu
tributary (of a river) el tributario
trip el viaje
return trip el viaje de regreso
to take a trip hacer un viaje, I: 11.1
trip (distance traveled) el recorrido
triumphant triunfante
trombone el trombón
troop la tropa, **1.1**
tropical tropical
trousers el pantalón, I: 3.2
trousseau el ajuar de novia
truce la tregua, **2.3**
true verdadero(a)
truck el camión, **5.2**
truck driver el/la camionero(a), **5.2; 8.3**
trumpet la trompeta
trunk (of a car) el/la maletero(a), I: 11.1; la maletera, I: 13.1; II: **1.1;** el baúl, II: 11.1
to **try** tratar
to **try on** probarse (ue), II: 4.1
tube of toothpaste el tubo de pasta (crema) dentífrica, I: 12.2
Tuesday el martes, BV
tumultuous tumultuoso(a), LC2
tuna el atún, I: 5.2
turbulance la turbulencia, II: 7.2
to **turn** doblar, II: 11.2; girar, LC7
to **turn around** revolver (ue), II: 10.1
to **turn off** apagar, II: 3.1
to **turn on** prender, II: 3.1
turning signal la direccional, II: 11.1; el intermitente, **5.2**
turnstile el torniquete, II: 9.1
turtle dove la tórtola
twelve doce, BV
twenty veinte, BV
twenty-eight veintiocho, BV
twenty-five veinticinco, BV
twenty-four veinticuatro, BV
twenty-nine veintinueve, BV
twenty-one veintiuno, BV
twenty-seven veintisiete, BV
twenty-six veintiséis, BV
twenty-three veintitrés, BV
twenty-two veintidós, BV
twin el/la gemelo(a)
twist torcer (ue), II: 8.1
two dos, BV
two hundred doscientos(as), I: 3.2
type el tipo; la modalidad
typical típico(a)

ugly feo(a), I: 1.1
unbuttoned desabrochado(a), **3.3**
uncle el tío, I: 6.1
under debajo (de)
undershirt la camiseta, I: 3.2
to **understand** comprender, I: 5.1
understanding el entendimiento
to **undertake (a journey)** emprender, **6.1**
undertaking la empresa, **7.1**
underwater swimming el buceo, I: 9.1
underwear la ropa interior, II: 4.1
undeserved inmerecido(a), LC5
unfaithful infiel
unforgettable inolvidable, **7.1**
uniform el uniforme
union el enlace
unique único(a)
unit la unidad
United States los Estados Unidos
from the United States estadounidense
university la universidad
related to university universitario(a)
university degree el título universitario, II: 14.1
unjust injusto(a)
unleaded sin plomo, II: 11.1
unless a menos que
unpleasant desagradable
until hasta, BV
urban urbano(a)
urologist el/la urólogo(a)
urology la urología
us nos
to **use** utilizar
used usado(a)
user el usuario, **1.3**
usually generalmente

vacation la vacación, II: 6.2
valiantly valientemente
valley el valle, II: 7.2
valor la valentía, LC6
value el valor
vanilla *(adj.)* de vainilla, I: 5.1
variation la variación
varied variado(a)
variety la variedad
various varios(as)
to **vary** variar
vast vasto(a)
veal la ternera, I: 14.2; II: 2.2
vegetable el vegetal, I: 5.2; la legumbre
vegetable garden el/la huerto(a), II: 9.2
vegetation la vegetación
vegetarian el/la vegetariano(a)
vein la vena
Venezuelan venezolano(a)
verse el verso
version: in its original (language) version en versión original, I: 10.1
very muy, BV
vest el chaleco
vestige el vestigio
veterinarian el/la veterinario(a)
vice el vicio
vice versa viceversa
victim la víctima, II: 8.1; **2.2**
victorious victorioso(a)
video el video
video store la tienda de videos
view la vista
vigor el vigor
vile vil
villa la quinta, LC3
village el pueblo, **2.3**
vinegar el vinagre
vineyard el viñedo, **3.1**

violence la violencia
violent violento(a), **2.3**
violin el violín, I: 2.1
viper la víbora, LC3
virtue la virtud, LC6
to **visit** visitar
vitamin la vitamina
voice la voz
volcanic volcánico(a), **2.3**
volcano el volcán, **2.3**
volleyball el voleibol
volume el tomo
volunteer el/la voluntario(a)
vowel la vocal

wagon el carro, LC2
to **wait (for)** esperar, I: 11.1
waiter, waitress el/la camarero(a), el/la mesero(a), I: 5.1
waiting room la sala de espera, I: 13.1; II: 1.1
wake (of a funeral) el velorio, el velatorio, **4.3**
wake (of a storm) la estela, **4.1**
to hold a wake velar, LC8
to **wake up** despertarse (ie), I: 12.1
to **walk** ir a pie, I: 4.1; andar; caminar, II: 9.1
to take a walk dar un paseo, II: 5.2
wall la muralla; la pared
walled amurallado(a), **7.1**
walled city una ciudad amurallado(a)
wallet la cartera, **2.2**
to **want** desear, I: 3.2; **4.3;** querer (ie)
I would like . . . Quisiera..., I: 14.2; II: 2.2
war la guerra, **1.1**
warlike belicoso(a), **3.1**
warm (weather) cálido(a), **7.1;** LC8
warmup el calentamiento, **5.3**
to **warn** advertir (ie, i)
to **wash oneself** lavarse, I: 12.1
washbasin el lavabo, II: 6.2
washing machine la máquina de lavar
waste los desechos
to **waste** desperdiciar, LC4; malgastar
watch el reloj, II: 4.1
to **watch** mirar, I: 3.1
water el agua *(f.)*, I: 9.1
mineral water el agua mineral, I: 12.2
running water el agua corriente
water bottle el tarro de agua, **7.3**
to **water-ski** esquiar en el agua, I: 9.1
water-skiing el esquí acuático, I: 9.1
watercolor la acuarela
watermelon la sandía, II: 10.2; **3.1**
wave la ola, la onda, I: 9.1; **5.3**
way el modo; la manera, I: 1.1
we nosotros(as), I: 2.2
weak flojo(a), LC5
weapon el arma *(f.)*
to **wear** llevar, I: 3.2
to **wear (size)** usar, I: 3.2; **(shoe size)** calzar, I: 3.2
weather el tiempo, I: 9.1
It's cold. Hace frío., I: 9.2
It's hot. Hace calor., I: 9.1
It's sunny. Hace sol., I: 9.1
The weather is bad. Hace mal tiempo., I: 9.1
The weather is nice. Hace buen tiempo., I: 9.1
weather forecast el prognóstico del tiempo, **8.2**
weave el tejido, **2.1**
to **weave** tejer, **2.1**
weaver el/la tejedora, **2.1**
Web page la página Web
wedding la boda, II: 13.1; **4.3**
Wednesday el miércoles, BV
week la semana, BV
last week la semana pasada, I: 9.2
weekend el fin de semana, BV
last weekend el fin de semana pasado
to **weigh** pesar
weight la pesa; el peso
heavy weights los pesados, **5.3**
welcome dar la bienvenida, I: 11.2
You're welcome. De nada., Por nada., No hay de qué., BV
welcoming (personality) acogedor, **2.3**
well (water) el pozo, LC1
well bien, BV; pues
very well muy bien, BV
well-done bien hecho(a), quemado(a), **6.2**
well-done meat la carne bien hecha (quemada)
well-known renombrado(a)
well-off acomodado(a), **2.1**
west el oeste
western occidental
whale la ballena, **3.1**
what, that which lo que
what? ¿qué?, BV
What's the matter (with you)? ¿Qué te pasa?, I: 8.2
wheat el trigo, II: 9.2
wheelchair la silla de ruedas, II: 8.2
when cuando, I: 4.2
when? ¿cuándo?, I: 4.1
where donde, I: 1.2
where? ¿adónde?, I: 1.1; ¿dónde?, I: 1.2
which?, what? ¿cuál?, BV
while el rato; mientras, **2.2**
white blanco(a), I: 3.2
who? ¿quién?, I: 1.1; *(pl.)* ¿quiénes?, I: 2.1
Who is calling? ¿De parte de quién?, II: 3.2
whole entero(a)
why? ¿por qué?
wide ancho(a); amplio(a), **1.3**
widow la viuda, **2.3**
to **wield** manear, LC8
wife la mujer, la esposa, I: 6.1
wig la peluca
wild salvaje, silvestre
to **win** ganar, I: 7.1
wind el viento
windmill el molino de viento
window (post office, etc.) la ventanilla; **(shop)** el escaparate, la vitrina, II: 4.1
windshield el parabrisas, II: 11.1
winter el invierno, BV
wire el alambre, LC3
wise sabio(a)
The Three Wise Men Los Reyes Magos, II: 13.2
to **wish** desear, I: 3.2
with con
within dentro de
without sin
woman la dama
wood la madera, **2.1;** LC7
wool la lana, II: 12.1; **3.2**
wool fabric tela de lana
word la palabra
work el trabajo
to **work** trabajar, I: 3.2
to work full time trabajar a tiempo completo, II: 14.2
to work part time trabajar a tiempo parcial, II: 14.2

work la obra
work of art la obra de arte
worker el/la trabajador(a); el/la obrero(a), II: 9.1
workforce la mano de obra, **8.1**
workshop el taller, LC3
world el mundo
World Cup la Copa mundial
World Series la Serie mundial
worldwide, (related to the world) mundial, **6.3**
worse, worst peor, el/la peor
wound la herida, II: 8.1
wounded person el/la herido(a)
wrapped envuelto(a)
wrinkle la arruga
to **wrinkle** arrugar; arrugarse, **3.2**
wrist la muñeca, II: 4.1
to **write** escribir, I: 5.1
writing pad el bloc, I: 3.1
wrong erróneo(a)

X-ray la radiografía, los rayos equis, II: 8.2

yard la yarda
year el año, BV
to be . . . years old tener...años, I: 6.1; cumplir... años
last year el año pasado, I: 9.2
this year este año, I: 9.2
yellow amarillo(a), I: 3.2
yes sí
yesterday ayer, I: 9.2
day before yesterday anteayer
yesterday afternoon ayer por la tarde, I: 9.2
yesterday morning ayer por la mañana, I: 9.2
yet aún; todavía
yogurt el yogur
yolk la yema
you tú; Ud., usted, I: 3.2; Uds., ustedes, I: 2.2
You're welcome. De nada., No hay de qué., BV
young joven, I: 6.1; mozo(a)
as a young person de joven
your tu; su, sus, I: 6.1
youth la juventud
youth, young person el/la joven, I: 10.1
youth hostel el albergue juvenil, el albergue para jóvenes (juvenil), I: 12.2

zero cero, BV
zipper la cremallera, **3.2; on pants** la bragueta, **3.2**
zone la zona
commercial zone la zona comercial, II: 9.1
industrial zone la zona industrial, II: 9.1
residential zone la zona residencial, II: 9.1
zoo el parque zoológico, II: 5.2

Index

Index

Credits

Cover i (t)Tom Bean/CORBIS, (tc)Darrell Jones/CORBIS, (bc)Randy Faris/CORBIS, (b)Enzo & Paola Ragazzini/CORBIS, (students)Ed McDonald; **iv** (l)Ken Karp, (r)Andrew Payti; **v** (t)Getty Images, (b)Nik Wheeler/CORBIS; **vi** Robert Frerck/Odyssey Productions; **vii** (t)Wolfgang Kaehler/CORBIS, (b)Andrew Payti; **viii** Andrew Wenzel/Masterfile; **ix** Andrew Payti; **x** (l)Gianni Gagli Orti/CORBIS, (r)Jose Raga/CORBIS; **xi** (l)Danny Lehman/CORBIS, r)J. Raga/Masterfile; **xii** Danny Lehman/CORBIS; **xiii** (t)Rick Doyle/CORBIS, (b)Nik Wheeler/CORBIS; **xiv** Bruce Fleming/Masterfile; **xv** (t)Elsie Amendola/AP/Wide World Photos, (c)Index Stock Imagery, (b)Laura Sifferlin; **xvi** (l)James Marshall/CORBIS, (r)Omar Bechara Baruque/Eye Ubiquitous/CORBIS; **xvii** (t)Gianni Dagli Orti/CORBIS, (b)Jeremy Horner/CORBIS; **xviii** Ric Vasquez/AP World Wide; **xix** (l)Scott Gilchrist/Masterfile, (r)Franz-Marc Frei/CORBIS; **xxiii** (t)Randy Faris/CORBIS, (bl br)Andrew Payti, (bc)Getty Images; **xxxvii** Timothy Fuller; **xliv** Getty Images; **0–1** Premium Stock/CORBIS; **2** (tl)Carlos Alvarez/Getty Images, (tr b)Andrew Payti; **3** (tl tcl tcr)Getty Images, (tr)Dave G. Houser/CORBIS, (b)John Evans; **4 5** Andrew Payti; **6** (t b) Andrew Payti, (c)Tom Bean/CORBIS; **7** Andrew Payti; **8** (l)Nik Wheeler/CORBIS, (r)SuperStock; **9** Getty Images; **10** (t)Toledo Museum of Art/Erich Lessing/Art Resource, NY, (b)Andrew Payti; **11** (t)Adam Woolfitt/CORBIS, (b)Bettmann/CORBIS; **12** (t)Dave G. Houser/CORBIS, (c b)Andrew Payti; **13** (t)CORBIS, (cl)Robert Frerck/Odyssey Productions, (cr)Laura Sifferlin, (b)Michelle Chaplow/Andalucia Slide Library; **14** Andrew Payti; **15** (t)Robert Frerck/Odyssey Productions, (b)Centro de Arte Reina Sofia, Madrid, Spain/Giraudon, Paris/SuperStock; **16** (t)Andrew Payti, (b)Reuters NewMedia Inc./CORBIS; **17 18** Andrew Payti; **20** (t)Owen Franken/CORBIS, (bl)Reunion des Musees Nationaux/Art Resource, NY, (bcl)Archivo Iconografico, S.A./CORBIS, (bcr)Hulton-Deutsch Collections/CORBIS, (br)Bettmann/CORBIS; **22** Andrew Payti; **23** David Ball/CORBIS; **25** (t)Andrew Payti, (b)Robert Frerck/Odyssey Productions; **26** Andrew Payti; **27** (t)Getty Images, (b)Tim Fuller; **28** Hidekazu Nishibata/SuperStock; **29** (t)Michelle Chaplow, (b)Robert Frerck/Odyssey Productions; **31** (t)Robert Frerck/Odyssey Productions, (b)Andrew Payti; **32** (t)Michelle Chaplow, (b)Andrew Payti; **33** Andrew Payti; **34** (l)Massimo Borchi/Atlantide/Bruce Coleman, Inc., (r)Michelle Chaplow; **35** Reuters NewMedia Inc./CORBIS; **37** Andrew Payti; **38** Courtesy ALSTOM; **39** Vittoriano Rastelli/CORBIS; **40** AFP/CORBIS; **41** J.B. Russell/CORBIS SYGMA; **42** Michelle Chaplow/CORBIS; **43 44** Aaron Haupt; **46 47 48** Andrew Payti; **49** Stuart Franklin/Magnum Photos; **50** CORBIS; **51** Vittoriano Rastelli/CORBIS; **52** Getty Images; **53** Bettmann/CORBIS; **55** One Nation Films, LLC; **56–57** Gisela Damm/eStock Photo; **58** (tl)Rick Weber, (tcl)Getty Images, (tc)CORBIS, (tcr)Bill Allen, (tr)Glencoe photo, (bl)Andrea Pistolesi/Getty Images, (br)Richard Lord/The Image Works; **59** Robert Frerck/Odyssey Productions; **60** Andrew Payti; **61** (l)Andrew Payti, (r)Getty Images; **62** (l)Andrew Payti, (r)Werner Forman/CORBIS; **63** (l)Andrew Payti, (r)Pablo Corral V/CORBIS; **64** (t)Hulton-Deutsch Collections/CORBIS, (bl)Bettmann/CORBIS, (br)Andrew Payti; **65 66 67** Andrew Payti; **68** (t)Hubert Stadler/CORBIS, (cl b)Andrew Payti, (cr)Wolfgang Kaehler/CORBIS; **69** Andrew Payti; **70** (t)CORBIS, (b)Andrew Payti; **71 72** Andrew Payti; **73** (l)Eric L Wheater/Lonely Planet Images, (r)Andrew Payti; **74** (t)Andrew Payti, (b)Getty Images; **75 76** Andrew Payti; **79** (l)Andrew Payti, (r)Bob Daemmrich/The Image Works; **80** through **85** Andrew Payti; **87** Michael & Patricia Fogden/CORBIS; **90** Andrew Payti; **91** Ronnie Kaufman/CORBIS; **93** (l)Bettmann/CORBIS, (r)Craig Lovell/CORBIS; **94** Jose Luis Pelaez/CORBIS; **95** Brian A. Vikander/CORBIS; **96** (t)John Slater/CORBIS, (b)Woods Wheatcroft/Lonely Planet Images; **97** Andrew Payti; **98** (t)Andrew Payti, (b)Getty Images; **99 100** Andrew Payti; **101** (l)Robert Frerck/Odyssey Productions, (r)Andrew Payti; **102** (t)Martin Bernetti/AFP/CORBIS, (b)Carl & Ann Purcell/CORBIS; **104** Andrew Payti; **107** Getty Images; **109** One Nation Films, LLC; **110–111** Vladpans/eStock Photo; **112** (tl)Charles O'Rear/CORBIS, (tr)Ernst Haas/Getty Images, (cl)Kelly-Mooney Photography/CORBIS, (cr)Craig Lovell/CORBIS, (bl)Morton Beebe/CORBIS, (br)Kit Houghton/CORBIS; **113** (tl)Yann Arthus-Bertrand/CORBIS, (tr)Reuters NewMedia Inc./CORBIS, (cl)Amos Nachoum/Getty Images, (cr)Tu De Roy/Minden Pictures, (bl)CORBIS, (br)Galen Rowell/CORBIS; **114** (tl)Reuters NewMedia Inc./CORBIS, (tr)Yann Arthus-Bertrand/CORBIS, (b)Andrew Payti; **115** (tl)Andrew Payti, (tr)Bamabas Bosshart/CORBIS, (b)Yann Arthus-Bertrand/CORBIS; **116** (t)Hubert Stadler/CORBIS, (cl)Andrew Wenzel/Masterfile, (cr)Kit Houghton/CORBIS, (b)Andrew Payti; **117** (t)Terry Whitaker, Frank Lane Picture Agency/CORBIS, (b)Andrew Payti; **118** (l)Peter Guttman/CORBIS, (r)Bojan Brecelj/CORBIS; **119** (t)Langevin Jacques/CORBIS SYGMA, (c)Yan Arthus-Bertrand/CORBIS, (b)Cory Sorensen/CORBIS; **120** (t)Bettmann/CORBIS, (c)Russell Gordon/Odyssey Productions, (b)Andrew Payti; **121** (t)Marcello Calandrini/CORBIS, (c b)Andrew Payti; **122 123 124** Andrew Payti; **125** (l)Diego Lezama Orezzoli/CORBIS, (r)Andrew Payti; 126 Wayne Walton/Lonely Planet Images; **127** Andrew Payti; **128** (t)Andrew Payti, (b)Kit Houghton/CORBIS; **129** Andrew Payti; **130** (l)Hulton-Deutsch Collection/CORBIS, (r)Pablo Corral Vega/CORBIS; **131** Andrew Payti; **132** (tl)John Evans, (tcl)Que-Net Media, (bcl)Getty Images, (bl)Tim Courlas, (r)Que-Net Media; **133** (tl)Mullenix/KS Studios, (tc bc)Getty Images, (tr)Aaron Haupt, (bl)StudiOhio, (br)Tim Courlas; **134** (t)Beryl Goldberg, (c)Que-Net media, (b)Andrew Payti; **135** (t)Robert Frerck/Odyssey Productions, (c b)Tim Fuller; **136** Andrew Payti; **137** Robert Frerck/Odyssey Productions; **138 139** Andrew Payti; **141** (t b)Andrew Payti, (c)Ric Ergenbright/CORBIS; **143** Chad Ehlers/Getty Images; **144** Que-Net Media; **147 150 151** Andrew Payti; **152** CORBIS; **153** Huber Stadler/CORBIS; **154** Dave G. Houser/CORBIS; **155** Richard T. Nowitz/CORBIS; **157** Andrew Payti; **158** Getty Images; **161** One Nation Films, LLC; **162–163** Massimo Listri/CORBIS; **164** (tl)Bettmann/CORBIS, (tr)Carl & Ann Purcell/CORBIS, (cl)Macduff Everton/CORBIS, (cr)Jeffrey N. Becom/Lonely Planet Images, (b)Andrew Payti; **165** (tl)Carl & Ann Purcell/CORBIS, (tr b)Danny Lehman/CORBIS; **166** (l)Alain Le Garsmeur/CORBIS, (r)Ryan Fox/Lonely Planet Images; **167** (t)J. Raga/Masterfile, (bl)Tim Brown/Index Stock Imagery, (br)Alfredo Maiquez/Lonely Planet Images; **168** (t)Darrell Gulin/CORBIS, (b)Gary Braasch/CORBIS; **169** (t)Russell Gordon/Odyssey Productions, (c)Andrew Payti, (b)Enzo & Paolo Ragazzini/CORBIS; **170** (t)Lynsey Addario/CORBIS, (c)Carmen Redondo/CORBIS, (bl)Owen Franken/CORBIS, (br)Stuart Cohen/The Image Works; **171** (t)Nik Wheeler/CORBIS, (c)Jose Raga/CORBIS, (b)Martin Rogers/CORBIS; **172** (t b)Andrew Payti, (cl)Macduff Everton/CORBIS, (cr)Dave G.Houser/CORBIS; **173** (t)Wolfgang Kaehler/CORBIS, (c)Danny Lehman/CORBIS, (b)Tony Arruza/CORBIS; **174** (t)Cynthia Brown Studio/StockFood, (b)Adrien Duey/Getty Images; **175** Andrew Payti; **176** Ted Wilcox/Index Stock Imagery; **177** Tibor Bognar/CORBIS; **178** (t)Dave G. Houser/CORBIS, (bl)Werner Forman/CORBIS, (br)Gianni Gagli Orti/CORBIS; **179** Bettmann/CORBIS; **181** J. Raga/Masterfile; **182** (t)HIRB/Index Stock Imagery, (b)Michelle Chaplow; **183** Dominic Oldershaw; **184** (t)Beryl Goldberg, (b)Andrew Payti; **185** (l)Bill Aron/PhotoEdit, (r)Andrew Payti; **186** (t)Andrew Payti, (b)Aaron Haupt; **187** Jose Fuste Raga/CORBIS; **188 189** Andrew Payti; **190** Dave G. Houser/CORBIS; **191** Robert Frerck/Odyssey Productions; **193** Jose Fuste Raga/CORBIS; **194** (t)Andrew Payti, (b)Beryl Goldberg; **195** Andrew Payti; **196** (tl)Spencer Grant/PhotoEdit, (tr)Andrew Payti, (bl)Rob Lewine/CORBIS, (br)Getty Images; **197** Buddy Mays/CORBIS; **198** Rene Burri/Magnum Photos; **202** (t)Andrew Payti, (b)David Young-Wolff/PhotoEdit; **203** (l)Andrew Payti, (r)Michael Newman/PhotoEdit; **204 205** Robert Frerck/Odyssey Productions; **206** Andrew Payti; **209** Getty Images; **211** One Nation Films, LLC; **212–213** CORBIS; **14** (tl)Annie Griffiths Belt/Getty Images, (tr)Mark Burnett, (bl)Getty Images, (br)CORBIS; **215** (t)Freeman Patterson/Masterfile, (b)Andrew Payti; **216** (l)Carolyn Brown/Getty Images, (r)Getty Images; **217** (l)Cliff Hollenbeck/International Stock, (r)Danny Lehman/CORBIS; **218** (l)Werner Forman/CORBIS, (r)Danny Lehman/CORBIS; **219** (l)SuperStock, (r)CORBIS; **220** (l)Archivo Iconografico, S.A./CORBIS, (r)Dave G. Houser/CORBIS; **221** (t)CORBIS, (c)Danny Lehman/CORBIS, (b)Bridgeman Art Library, London/SuperStock; **222** (tl)Ann Summa, (tr)Randy Faris/CORBIS, (bl)Rich Brommer, (br)Yann Arthus-Bertrand/CORBIS; **223** Danny Lehman/CORBIS; **224** Pascale Beroujon/Lonely Planet Images; **225** (t)Vladimir Pcholkin/Getty Images, (b)Rich Brommer; **227** (t)R. Faris/Westlight/CORBIS, (b)Charles & Josette

Lenars/CORBIS; **228** (t)Tim Fuller, (b)Lindsay Hebberd/CORBIS; **229** (t)Danny Lehman/CORBIS, (b)Dave G. Houser/CORBIS; **230** Tim Thompson/CORBIS; **231** (t)Uripos/eStock Photo, (b)The Museum of Modern Art, NY; **233** Robert Fried; **234** (l)Doug Bryant/DDB Stock Photo, (c)Curt Fischer, (r)Getty Images; **235** (l)Joel W. Rogers/CORBIS, (r)Walter Bibikow/Age FotoStock; **236** (l)Macduff Everton/CORBIS, (r)Jeff Greenberg/PhotoEdit; **237** Stewart Cohen/Getty Images; **238** MAPS.com/CORBIS; **239** Dan Herrick/Lonely Planet Images; **240** (tl)Great American Stock/Index Stock Imagery, (tr)FoodPix/Getty Images, (b)FOTO Powers/StockFood; **241** Danny Lehman/CORBIS; **242** (t)Nik Wheeler/CORBIS, (b)Getty Images; **243** (t)Veronica Garbutt/Lonely Planet Images, (b)John Neubauer/Lonely Planet Images; **244** Getty Images; **246** (t)Aaron Haupt, (c)Ann Summa, (b)Jeff Greenberg/PhotoEdit; **248** (l)V.C.L./Getty Images, (r)Neil Rabinowitz/CORBIS; **249** (l)Peter Sterling/Getty Images, (r)Warren Bolster/Getty Images; **250** Rick Doyle/CORBIS; **251** (t)Timothy Fuller, (b)Bob Daemmrich/The Image Works; **254** Ronnie Kaufman/CORBIS; **255** (t)Danny Lehman/CORBIS, (b)Jan Butchofsky-Houser/CORBIS; **256** (l)Buddy Mays/CORBIS, (r)John Neubauer/PhotoEdit; **258** (l)A. Ramey/PhotoEdit, (r)CORBIS; **259** Danny Lehman/CORBIS; **260** Macduff Everton/CORBIS; **261** (t)CORBIS, (b)Steve Vidler/SuperStock; **262** Richard l'Anson/Lonely Planet Images; **263** Neil Setchfield/Lonely Planet Images; **265** Neil Rabinowitz/CORBIS; **266** Getty Images; **269** One Nation Films, LLC; **270–271** Timothy O'Keefe/Index Stock Imagery; **272** (tl)Tony Arruza/CORBIS, (tr)Robert Frerck/Odyssey Productions, (bl bcr br)Getty Images, (bcl)Matt Meadows; **273** (t)Tim Page/CORBIS, (r)Art Wolfe/Getty Images; **274** (t)Larry Hamill, (c)Lori Shetler, (b)Art Wolfe/Getty Images; **275** (t)Louis Grandadam/Getty Images, (c)Tony Arruza/CORBIS, (b)Andrew Payti; **276** (t)Andrew Marshall & Leanne Walker/Lonely Planet Images, (b)Stephanie Maze/CORBIS; **277** (l)Larry Hamill, (r)Index Stock Imagery; **278** (tl)Lori Shetler, (tr)Jeremy Horner/CORBIS, (c bl)Bob Krist/CORBIS, (br)Tom Bean/CORBIS; **279** (t)Neil Rabinowitz/CORBIS, (c)Greg Stott/Masterfile, (b)David R. Frazier; **280** (t)Bettmann/CORBIS, (c)Burand Patrick/CORBIS SYGMA, (b)Kohlhas/Zefa/Masterfile; **281** (tl)Puzant Apkarian/Masterfile, (tr)Bruce Fleming/Masterfile, (b)Robert Frerck/Odyssey Productions; **282** Franz-Marc Frei/CORBIS; **283** (tl)Laura Sifferlin, (tr)John Neubauer/PhotoEdit, (b)Reuters NewMedia Inc./CORBIS; **285** Jeff Greenberg/PhotoEdit; **286** Michelle Chaplow; **287** Lori Shetler; **288** (t)Bruce Fleming/Masterfile, (b)Lori Shetler; **289** (t)Larry Hamill, (b)Andrew Payti; **290** Siegfried Tauqueuer/eStock Photo; **292** (tl)Barb Stimpert, (tr)Michael Newman/PhotoEdit, (b)Robert Holmes/CORBIS; **293** (t)Que-Net Media, (b)Carl & Ann Purcell/CORBIS; **294** Zefa/Masterfile; **295** AFP/CORBIS; **296** Puzant Apkarian/Masterfile; **297** (t)Larry Hamill, (b)Wally McNamee/CORBIS; **298** Caroline Von Trumpling-Manning/Getty Images; **301** Robert Holmes/CORBIS; **302** (l)Joe McBride/CORBIS, (c)Bill Ross/CORBIS, (r)Mark Gamba/CORBIS; **303** (l)Joe Cavaretta/AP/Wide World Photos, (r)Elsie Amendola/AP/Wide World Photos; **306** Lori Shetler; **307** (t)Zefa/Masterfile, (b)Lori Shetler; **308** (t)David R. Frazier/Photo Researchers, (b)Jeremy Horner/CORBIS; **309** Johnathan Smith/Cordaiy Photo Library/CORBIS; **310** Robert Frerck and Odyssey Productions; **311** Robert Fried; **312** (t)Larry Hamill, (b)Jeremy Horner/CORBIS; **313** Ulrike Welsch/PhotoEdit; **314** Lori Shetler; **315** Larry Hamill; **319** One Nation Films, LLC; **320–321** SuperStock; **322** (tl)Jane Sweeney/Lonely Planet Images, (tc)Yann Arthus-Bertrand/CORBIS, (tr)Krzysztof Dydynski/Lonely Planet Images, (cl)James Marshall/CORBIS, (c)Getty Images, (cr)Jeremy Horner/CORBIS, (b)Bo Zaunders/CORBIS; **323** (t)Neil Rabinowitz/CORBIS, (b)Omar Bechara Baruque/Eye Ubiquitous/CORBIS; **324** (l)Richard List/CORBIS, (c)Arnal Kike/CORBIS SYGMA, (r)David Mendelsohn/CORBIS; **325** (t b)Jeremy Horner/CORBIS, (c)Timothy Ross/The Image Works; **326** (t)Reunion des Musees Nationaux/Art Resource, NY, (c)Bettmann/CORBIS, (b)Krzysztof Dydynski/Lonely Planet Images; **327** James Marshall/CORBIS; **328** (t)Norman Tomalin/Bruce Coleman, Inc., (b)Reuters NewMedia, Inc./CORBIS; **329** Juan Herrera/AP/Wide World Photos; **330** (t)Timothy Ross/The Image Works, (c)Andrew Payti, (bl)SuperStock, (br)Jay Dickman/CORBIS; **331** (t)Beryl Goldberg, (c)Pablo Corral V/CORBIS, (b)Adrien Duey/Getty Images; **332** Alfredo Maiquez/Lonely Planet Images; **333** Curt Fischer; **334** Index Stock Imagery; **335** Andrew Payti; **336** Luis Delgado; **338** Pablo Corral V/CORBIS; **339** Andrew Payti; **341** David Mendelsohn/CORBIS; **342** (l)Ann Summa, (r)Getty Images; **343** Jeremy Horner/CORBIS; **344** (l)Que-Net Media, (r)David Uribe Photography/eStock Photo; **345** (l)Jeremy Horner/CORBIS, (r)Gianni Dagli Orti/CORBIS; **346** James Goodman Gallery, New York/Bridgeman Art Library; **347** (t)Franklin McMahon/CORBIS, (b)Index Stock Imagery; **349** CORBIS; **353** Gabe Palmer/CORBIS; **354** Reuters NewMedia, Inc./CORBIS; **356** Kevin Fletcher/CORBIS; **357** CORBIS; **358** (t)Pablo Corral V/CORBIS, (b)Krzysztof Dydynski/Lonely Planet Images; **359** Robert Frerck/Odyssey Productions; **360** (t)Pablo Corral V/CORBIS, (b)Jeremy Horner/CORBIS; **361** Jeremy Horner/CORBIS; **362** Krzysztof Dydynski/Lonely Planet Images; **363** Owen Franken/CORBIS; **364** (t)Carl & Ann Purcell/CORBIS, (b)Pablo Corral V/CORBIS; **365** Index Stock Imagery; **367 369** Getty Images; **371** One Nation Films, LLC; **372–373** Sandy Felsenthal/CORBIS; **374** Bettmann/CORBIS; **375** Bob Daemmrich/CORBIS; **376** (l)Franz-Marc Frei/CORBIS, (r)Richard Cummins/Lonely Planet Images; **377** (t)Karl Lehmann/Lonely Planet Images, (b)Robert Holmes/CORBIS; **378** (tl)Rob Crandall/Alamy, (tr)Richard Cummins/Lonely Planet Images, (bl)Ric Vasquez/AP/World Wide, (br)CORBIS; **379** (l)Richard Cummins/Lonely Planet Images, (c)Sandy Felsenthal/CORBIS, (r)Scott Gilchrist/Masterfile; **380** (t)Larry Hamill, (b)Beryl Goldberg; **381** (t)John Springer/CORBIS, (bl)Tony Arruza/CORBIS, (br)Bettmann/CORBIS; **382** (t c)Beryl Goldberg, (b)Steven Rubin/The Image Works; **383** (t)Greg Elms/Lonely Planet Images, (cl)Susan C. Bourgoin/CORBIS, (cr)Beryl Goldberg, (b)Richard Cummins/Lonely Planet Images; **384** Jim Wark/Lonely Planet Images; **385** (l)Bettmann/CORBIS, (r)Bob Daemmrich/PhotoEdit; **386** (t)Tina Gerson/AP/World Wide, (b)Richard Cummins/CORBIS; **387** (t)Stewart Cook/CORBIS, (c)Jean-Yves Ruszniewski/CORBIS, (b)Bettmann/CORBIS; **388** Jeff Geissler/AP/World Wide; **389** Steve Skjold/Alamy; **390** (tl b)David Young-Wolff/PhotoEdit, (tr)Tim Fuller, (cl)Bob Daemmrich/The Image Works, (cr)Robert Daly/Getty Images; **391** (t)Michael Pole/CORBIS, (b)Ann Johansson/CORBIS; 392 (t)Tim Street-Porter/Alamy, (b)Tim Fuller; **393** Getty Images; **394** Morton Beebe/CORBIS; **395** Robert Ginn/PhotoEdit; **396** Beryl Goldberg; **397** Bob Daemmrich/The Image Works; **398** ImageState; **399** Dave G. Houser/CORBIS; **400** (t)Marc Asnin/CORBIS SABA, (bl)Beryl Goldberg, (br)Charles Gupton/CORBIS; **401 402** Beryl Goldberg; **404** SuperStock; **405** CORBIS; **406** George Hall/CORBIS; **407** Andrew Payti; **408** (t)Andrew Payti, (c)Owen Franken/CORBIS, (b)Beryl Goldberg; **409** (t)Beryl Goldberg, (c)Susan Stocker/CORBIS SYGMA, (b)Alison Wright/Lonely Planet Images; **410** CORBIS; **411** Patrick Ward/CORBIS; **412 413** Getty Images; **415** One Nation Films, LLC; **416** Getty Images; **417** CORBIS; **419** Andrew Payti; **420** (t)Martin Jones/Ecoscene/CORBIS, (b)Jose Fuste Raga/CORBIS; **421** The Art Archive/Dagli Orti; **422** Voz Noticias/CORBIS; **423** (tl)Mike Southern/Eye Ubiquitous/CORBIS, (tr)Michael Busselle/CORBIS, (b)Pepe Diaz/The Image Works; **424** (t)O. Alamany & E. Vicens/CORBIS, (b)Getty Images; **425** (t)Jon Hicks/CORBIS, (b)Siqui Sanchez/Getty Images; **426** Getty Images; **428** (l)Colita/CORBIS, (r)Getty Images; **429** David Tomlinson/Lonely Planet Images; **431** (l)Richard List/CORBIS, (r)Richard I'Anson/Lonely Planet Images; **432** Getty Images; **433** (l)Richard I'Anson/Lonely Planet Images, (r)Pablo Corral V/CORBIS; **434** Mark A. Johnson/CORBIS; **435** John Borthwick/Lonely Planet Images; **436** Enzo & Paolo Ragazzini/CORBIS; **437** Brian A. Vikander/CORBIS; **438** Robert Frerck/Odyssey Productions; **439** (t)Robert Frerck/Odyssey Productions, (b)Woods Wheatcroft/Lonely Planet Images; **440** Hubert Stadler/CORBIS; **441** (t)The State Hermitage Museum, (b)AFP/CORBIS; **442** (t)Barb Stimpert, (b)Robert Van Der Hilst/Getty Images; **443** Pablo Corral Vega/CORBIS; **444** (t)Widener Library/Harvard College, (c)Getty Images, (b)SuperStock; **446** Pablo Corral Vega/CORBIS; **447** (l)Gerald Cubitt, (r)Peter Weimann/Animals Animals; **448** (t)Cindy Charles/PhotoEdit, (c)Karen Whyie/Masterfile, (b)Getty Images; **449** Yann Arthus-Bertrand/CORBIS; **453** Joe McDonald/CORBIS; **457** Nik Wheeler/CORBIS; **458** (t)Getty Images, (b)Buddy Mays/CORBIS; **459** Charles & Josette Lenars/CORBIS; **460** (t)Nogues Ala/CORBIS SYGMA, (b)Richard I'Anson/Lonely

Credits

Planet Images; **461** Barb Stimpert; **463** (t)Getty Images, (b)Jan Butchofsky–Houser/ CORBIS; **464 466** CORBIS; **467** Bettmann/CORBIS; **468** CORBIS; **469** (t)AFP/CORBIS, (b)Culver Pictures Inc.; **470** Schalkwijk/Art Resource, NY; **472** National Palace, Mexico City; **473** James Leynse/CORBIS; **475** (t)David Peevers/CORBIS, (b)Robert Brenner/PhotoEdit; **476** (tl)Aaron Haupt, (tr)CORBIS, (b)Mike Zens/CORBIS; **477** Rick Gerharter/Lonely Planet Images; **478** (t)Bettmann/CORBIS, (b)Simon Foale/Lonely Planet Images; **479** (t)Colección Ateneo Puertorriqueño/Grolier, (b)Richard I'Anson/Lonely Planet Images; **480** Rick Gerharter/Lonely Planet Images; **483** David R. Frazier; **484** Donna Day/CORBIS; **485** Greg Johnston/Lonely Planet Images; **486** CORBIS; **487** Richard I'Anson/Lonely Planet Images; **489** Peter Guttman/CORBIS; **490** CORBIS; **491** Getty Images; **493** (t)courtesy Ruth Wallach, USC, (b)David Frazier/The Image Works; **494** Maurice Nimmo, Frank Lane Picture Agency/CORBIS; **495** Index Stock Imagery; **497** (t)David Cantor/AP/Wide World Photos, (b)Curt Fischer; **500** Bob Daemmrich/The Image Works; **501** HIRB/Index Stock Imagery; **502** Ralph Lee Hopkins/Lonely Planet Images; **503** (tl)Philip Gould/CORBIS, (tr br)Getty Images, (bl)Danny Lehman/CORBIS; **504** (t)AFP/CORBIS, (b)Bob Krist/CORBIS; **505** CORBIS; **507** (t)Arte Público Press, (b)M. Lee Fatherree, Collection of Paula Maciel–Benecke and Norbert Benecke Aptos, California; **509** (l)Park Street/PhotoEdit, (r)Great American Stock/Index Stock Imagery; **511** (l)Eric Gay/AP/Wide World Photos, (r)Barb Stimpert; **512** David Young–Wolff/PhotoEdit; **514** (t)Lori Shetler, (b)Barb Stimpert; **515** Wally Eberhart/Getty Images; **517** Beryl Goldberg; **558–H1** Hideo Kurihara/Getty Images.

Glencoe would like to acknowledge the artists and agencies who participated in illustrating this program: Matthew Pippin represented by Beranbaum Artist's Representative; Meg Aubrey and Antonio Castro represented by Cornell & McCarthy; Four Lakes Colorgraphics Inc.; Glencoe; Higgins Bond represented by Anita Grien Representing Artists; Viviana Diaz represented by Irmeli Holmberg; Karen Maizel; Tom McNeely; David Broad and Jane McCreary represented by Remen-Willis Design Group; Karen Rhine; Don Stewart; Studio InkLink; Ann Barrow, Kathleen O'Malley and Meryl Treatner represented by Christina A. Tugeau; Barbara Kiwak, Peter Thornton and Gary Torrisi represented by Gwen Walters.